DATE DUE FOR RETURN

NEW ACCESSIONS

CANCELLED

THE BUILDWAS BOOKS

BOOK PRODUCTION, ACQUISITION AND USE AT AN ENGLISH
CISTERCIAN MONASTERY, 1165–*c*.1400

Jennifer M. Sheppard

Oxford Bibliographical Society
Bodleian Library
Oxford
1997

Published by the Oxford Bibliographical Society,
care of the Bodleian Library, Oxford, OX1 3BG

© Oxford Bibliographical Society 1997

ISBN 0 901420 53 0

Inquiries about the Society and its publications should be addressed to the
Honorary Secretary at the Bodleian Library. Proposals for publications
should be sent to the Honorary Editors at the same address.

OXFORD BIBLIOGRAPHICAL SOCIETY
PUBLICATIONS

THIRD SERIES VOLUME II

CONTENTS

ACKNOWLEDGMENTS

Many people have provided invaluable assistance during the long course of preparation of this study, and I acknowledge this with warmest appreciation. First and foremost among these are the Librarians and Curators of the collections which I repeatedly visited, and their staff, for their never-failing courtesy, patience and help. Particular appreciation is due to the staff at the Wren Library, Trinity College, Cambridge, whose doors I darkened more than most. Alan Piper kindly read early drafts of some of the descriptions and provided wise comment and advice. Jayne Ringrose thoughtfully brought to my attention a fragmentary Missal in Cambridge University Library which I would otherwise have missed. James Lawson enthusiastically provided much information about the post seventeenth-century history of the Buildwas manuscript in his care at Shrewsbury School, and Jeremy Griffiths generously allowed me to see his description of Oxford, Christ Church MS 88 which is to be published in his forthcoming catalogue of the Christ Church Manuscripts. I have benefited extensively from Christopher Clarkson's and Nicholas Hadgraft's expertise and experience of medieval binding structures. Countless members of the Seminar in the History of the Book to 1500 have listened patiently to papers and responded to material presented to them, always to my profit. Catherine Byfield miraculously created the computer-generated page layout diagrams I would otherwise have had to produce by hand with far less clarity, and also provided much-needed computing help. Special thanks are also due to many careful and eagle-eyed proof-readers, in particular the editor of this volume, James McLaverty, who has patiently provided advice at every turn. Responsibility for all that appears in this book, however, rests entirely with me.

My work was supported at the outset by a two-year research grant from the Leverhulme Trust. I have also been the recipient of several research grants from Lucy Cavendish College, Cambridge (from the Wood-Legh and Ernest Cassel Funds). A travel grant from the British Academy allowed me to examine the surviving manuscripts from Savigny (the mother house of Buildwas) in the Bibliothèque Nationale, Paris, and a further grant, from the Neil Ker Memorial Fund, has assisted the final stages of the work. The Marc Fitch Fund generously awarded a grant towards the cost of illustrating the book. Such assistance is the *sine qua non* of research, and the financial help I have received from these bodies is also most gratefully acknowledged.

Finally, my thanks are due to the Council of the Oxford Bibliographical Society, whose patience over the years while waiting for the completion of this study, has been both admirable and a source of constant encouragement.

PHOTOGRAPHIC ACKNOWLEDGMENTS

Permission to reproduce photographs of manuscripts has been kindly granted by the bodies and institutions listed below. Particular thanks are extended to those who generously waived the usual reproduction fees.

The Master and Fellows of Pembroke College, Cambridge (fig. 22).

The Master and Fellows of St. John's College, Cambridge (fig. 18).

The Master and Fellows of Trinity College, Cambridge (figs. 5, 7, 8, 9, 20, 28, 30, 31, 32,).

The Syndics of the University Library, Cambridge (figs. 10, 13, 14).

The Trustees of the National Library of Scotland (figs. 16, 33).

The British Library, London (fig. 4).

His Grace the Archbishop of Canterbury and the Trustees of Lambeth Palace Library (figs. 2, 12, 29).

The Master and Fellows of Balliol College, Oxford (figs. 11, 15, 23, 24, 25, 26, 27, 36).

The Bodleian Library, Oxford (figs. 17, 19, 21, 34, 35).

The Governing Body, Christ Church, Oxford (figs. 1, 3, 6).

ABBREVIATIONS

1. Frequently cited works

CCSL	*Corpus Christianorum, Series Latina* (Turnhout, 1953–).
CCCM	*Corpus Christianorum Continuatio Mediaevalis* (Turnhout, 1970–).
Cheney 1953	C.R. Cheney, 'Les bibiothèques cisterciennes en Angleterre au XIIe siècle,' *Mélanges Saint Bernard*, (Dijon, 1953), 375–382.
Cheney 1973	C.R. Cheney, 'English Cistercian Libraries: the First Century' in *Medieval Texts and Studies* (Oxford, 1973), 328–345.
Chibnall, *VCH*	M.M. Chibnall, 'The Abbey of Buildwas', in *The Victoria History of the Counties of England, A History of Shropshire* (London, 1973), II, 50–59.
Cod. Boethiani	M.T. Gibson and L. Smith with J. Ziegler, eds., *Codices Boethiani: a Conspectus of Manuscripts of the Works of Boethius* (London, 1995), I.
de Hamel, *Glossed Books*	C.F.R. de Hamel, *Glossed Books of the Bible and the Origins of the Paris Booktrade* (Woodbridge, 1984).
James, *Lambeth MSS*	M.R. James, *A Descriptive Catalogue of the Manuscripts in the Library of Lambeth Palace*, 3 vols (Cambridge, 1930–1932).
James, *Pembroke MSS*	M. R. James, *A Descriptive Catalogue of the Manuscripts in the Library of Pembroke College, Cambridge* (Cambridge, 1905).
James, *Trinity MSS*	M.R. James, *A Descriptive Catalogue of the Manuscripts in the Library of Trinity College, Cambridge,* 4 vols (Cambridge, 1900–1904).
Ker, *MLGB*	N.R. Ker, ed., *Medieval Libraries of Great Britain. A List of Surviving Books*, 2nd edn. (London, 1964).
Ker, *MMBL*	N.R. Ker, *Medieval Manuscripts in British Libraries*, 4 vols (Oxford, 1969–1983; vol. IV 1992, see below).
Ker and Piper, *MMBL*	N.R. Ker and A.J. Piper, *Medieval Manuscripts in British Libraries*, vol. IV (Oxford, 1992).
Madan *et al.* *Summary Catalogue*	F. Madan and H.H.E. Craster, *A Summary Catalogue of Western Manuscripts in the Bodleian Library at Oxford,* 7 vols (Oxford 1895–1953).

Mynors, *Balliol MSS* R.A.B. Mynors, *Catalogue of the Manuscripts of Balliol College, Oxford* (Oxford, 1963).

PL J.-P. Migne, *Patrologiae Latinae Cursus Completus,* (Paris, 1844–)

PL Suppl. A. Hamman, *Patrologiae Latinae Supplementum*, 5 vols (Paris, 1958–1974).

Registrum *Registrum Anglie de Libris Doctorum et Auctorum Veterum* (See Rouse & Rouse for printed edition).

Rouse & Rouse R.H. Rouse and M.A. Rouse, eds. intro. and notes, *Registrum Anglie de Libris Doctorum et Auctorum Veterum* (London, 1991).

Sheppard 1988 J.M. Sheppard, 'Magister Robertus Amiclas: a Buildwas Benefactor?', *Transactions of the Cambridge Bibliographical Society*, IX (1988), 281–288.

Sheppard 1990 J.M. Sheppard, 'The Twelfth Century Library and Scriptorium at Buildwas: Assessing the Evidence' in D. Williams, ed., *England in the Twelfth Century* (Woodbridge, 1990), 193–204.

Sheppard 1995 J.M. Sheppard, 'Some Twelfth-Century Monastic Bindings and the Question of Localization', in L.L. Brownrigg, ed., *Making the Medieval Book: Techniques of Production* (Los Altos Hills, 1995), 181–198.

Thomson 1995 R.M. Thomson,' Robert Amiclas: a Twelfth-Century Parisian Master and his Books', *Scriptorium, XLIX* (1995), 238–243.

Watson, *MLGB* Supplement A.G. Watson, ed., *Medieval Libraries of Great Britain* (ed. N.R. Ker), Supplement to the Second Edition (London, 1987).

Wittekind, *Kommentar* S. Wittekind, *Kommentar mit Bildern (Bamberg, Staatsbibliothek, Ms Bibl. 59)* (Frankfurt, 1994).

2. Manuscripts

Cross-references to Buildwas manuscripts are by abbreviated location (or collection name) and shelfmark only, as follows:

Balliol 35A (etc.) Oxford, Balliol College MS 35A

Bodley 371 (etc.) Oxford, Bodleian Library MS Bodley 371

BL Add. 11881 London, British Library, Additional MS 11881

Christ Church 88	Oxford, Christ Church MS Latin 88
CUL 4079 (etc.)	Cambridge, University Library MS Add. 4079
Edinburgh 6121	Edinburgh, National Library of Scotland MS 6121
Harley 3038	London, British Library MS Harley 3038
Lambeth 107 (etc.)	London, Lambeth Palace Library MS 107
Pembroke 154	Cambridge, Pembroke College MS 154
St. John's D.2	Cambridge, St. John's College MS D.2
Shrewsbury XII	Shrewsbury School MS XII
Trinity B.1.1 (etc.)	Cambridge, Trinity College MS B.1.1

EXPLANATION OF TERMS

1. Terms used in describing medieval binding structures or their remains.

Note that many of these elements are illustrated in figs. 33 and 34.

Sewing station Any point at which the sewing needle is taken through the spinefold of a quire.

S- or Z-twist thread Like all thread, the thread used for sewing medieval books was made by twisting thinner strands together. Sometimes each component thread was also formed of yet thinner twisted threads. The letters S and Z denote, by the direction of their central stroke (S: \ Z: /), the direction of the outermost twist of the thread used.

All-along sewing The most common type of sewing. It is executed with a single needle by means of which the sewing thread is taken from one sewing support to the next along the centre spinefold of each quire.

Kettle stitch A chain stitch executed as part of the primary sewing of a book, between the head or tail of the spine and the nearest primary sewing support, by means of which the sewing thread is taken through the spinefold of the quire just sewn and into the spinefold of the next quire to be sewn. Before the thread is taken into the next quire, it is usually also taken through the kettle stitch of the *previous* quire, thus contributing to the linking of all the quires into one book.

Sewing support The material, usually skin or cord, on which (i.e. to which) the quires of a book are sewn. A split sewing support is one, usually of skin, which has been split where it crosses the back of the spine, to facilitate the sewing. These supports, disposed between the head and tail of the spine, are usually called primary sewing supports (cf. *Endband* below).

Endband A sewing support at the extreme head or tail of the spine. Endbands are usually, but not always, sewn in a separate operation, after the sewing on the primary supports has been completed. They are sometimes also provided with extra decorative sewing with coloured threads. See Tab below.

Tab An extra piece of thick skin at the head and tail which projects from the spine, having a semicircular, square or oblong shape. It is usually sewn with the endband, and at its edges to a matching extension of the primary covering.

Lacing path The ends or 'slips' of the sewing supports (including the endbands) were threaded, or laced, into a combination of holes, tunnels and channels in the boards and finally wedged in place, in order to attach the boards to the sewn book. The path taken by the sewing supports is called the lacing path.

Primary covering The first covering to be applied to the book, regardless of the presence or absence of a chemise. The primary covering is often of thin skin, but can also be made of a textile. The primary covering is turned-in onto the inner surface of the boards and either sewn or pasted to secure it. The corners are usually cut at an angle of 45° ('mitred'), so that they lie neatly together. Sometimes a strip of covering is left between the mitred turn-ins, to strengthen the covering of the vulnerable corners of the boards. This is called a 'tongue'.

Tawed skin A white, soft skin which was widely used during the middle ages in book-binding. It looks like leather, but is not leather in the strict sense since it is the product of a different manufacturing process.

Chemise An extra, outermost covering of skin or a textile, attached to the book over the primary covering usually by means of folded and sewn flaps or by 'pockets' which are also sewn to the chemise and which fit tightly over the boards. Chemises once extended beyond the edges of the book to protect them. Most have been removed since the medieval period. Evidence of lost chemises can sometimes be detected on surviving medieval bindings. These include impressions of sewing on the primary covering, usually along board edges, traces of a chemise pocket once pasted to the inner face of the boards but since ripped away, or surviving fragments of the chemise under extant bosses.

2. Terms adopted in describing decoration

Arrow fin

Bird's-head flourishes

Comb or Jawbone

Curled leaf

Curled leaf and horn

Curled petal

Folded leaf

Hairpin flourish

Ladder motif

Lion's-paw terminal

Sunburst

Snakes-head

Tadpole motif

Trefoil terminal

Channel style A term used to describe a manner of decorating painted initials practised on both sides of the channel from about 1165 to the end of the twelfth century. Among its principal characteristics are rather bare coiled vine-scrolls, sometimes with elaborate stylised flower terminals, which are often inhabited by a variety of stylised creatures, especially buff or white lions.

LIST OF ILLUSTRATIONS
WITH NOTES

N.B. The percentage reductions given are linear.

1. Oxford, Christ Church MS 88 fol. 2v (cat. 1): title page. Note: pricking in outer and lower margins for written lines and vertical bounding lines. 38% of actual size.
2. London, Lambeth Palace Library MS 109 fol. 12 (cat. 2): hand of 'flyleaf scribe' and initial Q. Compare fig. 3 (initial design) and figs. 4 and 5 (scribal hand). Note: punctus flexus punctuation mark used twice in second line (col. a) and elsewhere; use of double vertical lines to position small initial letters – a useful means of marking off sections of text for easier reading; ruled lines clearly visible. 54% of actual size.
3. Oxford, Christ Church MS 88 fol. 65v (cat. 1): hand of 'master scribe' and initial Q. Compare fig. 2 (initial design). Note ruling pattern, especially edge-to-edge lines. 51% of actual size.
4. London, British Library MS Harley 3038 (cat. 9): front flyleaf verso: a reused discarded leaf. Compare figs. 2 and 5 (hand of 'flyleaf scribe'). This leaf is from the same discarded quire as that shown in fig. 5. Note 3 dark indentations, now on fore-edge (bottom of photograph), made at 3 former sewing stations by sewing supports, and between them the impression of a former sewing thread. 52% of actual size.
5. Cambridge, Trinity College MS B.1.3 (cat. 4): front flyleaf verso, a reused discarded leaf. Compare figs. 2 and 4 (hand of 'flyleaf scribe'). Note: the ex libris inscription has an undulating aspect. It appears in 5 Buildwas books. 60% of actual size.
6. Oxford, Christ Church MS 88 fol. 77 (cat. 1): hand and elegant page layout of 'master scribe', and his initial V. Note: upper margin, '*capitulum* vi' (s.xv) indicates relevant chapter of John's gospel; partially trimmed medieval Arabic 27 (top right corner) added by indexer (s.xiii) to mark beginning of sermon 27 (see the incipit just above initial, written in red and appearing pale in the photograph); scribal sloping S-shaped marks indicate quotation from John 6. 77 is a modern folio number. 37% of actual size.
7. Cambridge, Trinity College MS B.1.3 fol. 46v (cat. 4): two corrections (col. a line 3, col. b lines 11–15) by the 'flyleaf scribe' or text scribe 13 over erasures of work by scribe 5. 74% of actual size.
8. Cambridge, Trinity College MS B.14.5 (cat. 3): first leaf of thirteenth-century index. Note: references are to sermon numbers, then to the page within the sermon; so Abstinencia, sermon 44 page 1; sermon 47 page 1. Note that alphabetical arrangement is according to first letter only. Note also grainy texture of hair side of parchment. 91% of actual size.
9. Cambridge, Trinity College MS B.14.5 fol. 89v (cat. 3): the Buildwas indexer's stylus notes (words and Arabic numbers). These are most clearly visible in the lower half of the photograph. Three letters d in ink are probably pen trials by the indexer (compare fig. 8). Note also the text scribe's quire number xi in lower margin of fol 8v of this final quire, and worm damage (showing as white marks in the photograph). 70% of actual size.
10. Cambridge, University Library MS Ii.2.3 fol. 29v (cat. 8): marginal note in the indexer's hand. Compare figs. 8, 11. 73% of actual size.

11. Oxford, Balliol College MS 35A (cat. 30), front flyleaf: dated ex libris inscription (1277) written by the Buildwas indexer, mentioning Walter the Palmer of Bridgnorth and Abbot William Tyrry. Compare figs. 8, 10. Note: 4 rust-stained holes at each upper corner, made by former boss nails, and stub of excised leaf, once conjoint with the surviving leaf. 62% of actual size.
12. London, Lambeth Palace Library MS 488 fol. 89v (cat. 26): former flyleaf: ex libris inscription (s.xv) which also records an indenture between Henry of Valle, a Savigniac monk and Abbot John Gnossal (his name is at the very end of the first line). The leaf was once part of a much larger leaf which carried text (some visible in the photograph) and several four-line staves. It is now badly damaged. 105% of actual size.
13. Cambridge, University Library MS Ii.2.3 fol. 3v (cat. 8). Note the beautifully flowing initial A, set into a more rigidly shaped space left by the scribe, and the shadow of an initial R by the same scribe/artist on the previous page which now shows through in col. b. Note also the change in scribe in mid-word (col. b line 10: 'o/mnem), and part of the running book number ('liber primus') recorded across the opening on a ruled line. 49% of actual size.
14. Cambridge, University Library MS Add. 4079 fol. 28v (cat. 10). Note the rudimentary flourishing of the minor initials, a crude parchment repair across the lower right corner, and a page marker (of pink skin) sewn to the lower left corner of the page. Stub of an excised leaf also visible at right edge of page. 53% of actual size.
15. Oxford, Balliol College MS 229 fol 45 (cat. 11). Compare the initial in fig. 16. Note the double pricking in both margins for lines ruled edge-to-edge. 54% of actual size.
16. Edinburgh, National Library of Scotland MS 6121 fol. 45v (cat. 12). Compare initials in fig. 15. Two of the marking-up pricks (arrowed), for the middle and lower primary sewing stations, are just visible in the photograph. See also fig. 22. 50% of actual size.
17. Oxford, Bodleian Library MS Bodley 730 fol. 130v (cat. 16). Col. a written by scribe 2, col. b by scribe 3 (compare fig. 18) who corrected his own mistake ('etiam'changed to punctus flexus, line 11). The sub-headings were written by the 'round hand' scribe; compare figs. 19–21. Note the number of lines ruled edge-to-edge. 55% of actual size.
18. Cambridge, St. John's College MS D.2 fol. 33 (cat. 15). The scribe also wrote in Bodley 730 fol. 130v col. b (compare fig. 17), and he made and corrected the same mistake several times on this page ('etiam' changed to punctus flexus). Note the very evident grainy appearance of the hair side of the parchment. 67% of actual size.
19. Oxford, Bodleian Library MS Bodley 730 fol. 65 (cat. 16): text scribe 2 and the 'round hand' scribe's rubrication (compare figs. 17, 20, 21). Note the tear in the parchment (lower margin) edged with sewing holes where the parchment maker roughly pulled the tear together before stretching the skin during manufacture. Note also trimmed tip of initial ascender. 54% of actual size.
20. Cambridge, Trinity College MS B.2.30 fol. 61 (cat. 17). The text scribe is the same as scribe 2 of Bodley 730 (compare fig. 19). Here he also omitted to allow space for rubricated headings, which are added in the margins by the 'round hand' scribe, with signes de renvoi to link them to the right section of text (compare figs. 17, 19, 21). 61% of actual size.
21. Oxford, Bodleian Library MS Bodley 395 fol. 29 (cat. 14): the 'round hand' scribe as text scribe (compare figs. 17, 19, 20). Note: the scribe made a note of

the sub-headings which he later wrote in red: the heading for chapter 4 is noted vertically at the outer edge of the page and the heading for chapter 3 is noted at the bottom of the page. Note also running book number in upper margin. 52% of actual size.

22. Cambridge, Pembroke College MS 154 fol. 21 (cat. 13). Note: correction over an erasure col. b lines 21–28, though the corrector over-estimated the space needed and filled in the last line after 'cum' with minim strokes. The letter (epistle) number was added (s.xiii) in the centre of the lower margin (4) and the number of the page within the letter in the lower left corner (3). Another hand added the folio number (21) to the top right corner. Two of the marking-up pricks (arrowed), for the middle sewing station and the lower kettle stitch, are just visible in the photograph. See also fig. 16. 43% of actual size.

23. Oxford, Balliol College MS 150 fol. 81v (cat. 22): text scribe (compare figs. 25, 28) and initial E (compare figs. 24, 25). Note elaborate running sermon number in upper margin, the extended 'nota' marks in the margins and additional, decorative ruled lines at the top of the page. 62% of actual size.

24. Oxford, Balliol College MS 39 fol. 66v (cat. 20): text scribe and initial O (compare figs. 23, 25). Note the additional vertical ruled line at the outer edge of the page. 63% of actual size.

25. Oxford, Balliol College MS 40 fol. 79 (cat. 21): text scribe (compare fig. 23, 28) and initial Q (compare figs. 23, 24). Note the marginal sub-heading enclosed in a (coloured) frame. 60% of actual size.

26. Oxford, Balliol College MS 150 fol. 32v (cat. 22). Note the unusual 'floor-tile' motifs within the letter, and the profiles incorporated into the elaborate flourishing. Note also the extra double ruled lines in the outer margins and holes in the parchment at the fore-edge (possibly flaymarks) and lower margins. 38% of actual size.

27. Oxford, Balliol College MS 150 fol. 2v (cat. 22): historiated initial H with portrait of St. Bernard; compare fig. 29. Note also the erased Buildwas ex libris (col. a, at end of capitula list); only part of L(iber) remains. 37% of actual size.

28. Cambridge, Trinity College MS B.1.29, front flyleaf (cat. 24): ex libris and list of contents written by the scribe of Balliol 40 and 150 (compare figs. 23, 25, 27). Note the ruling specially done for these items. The apparently random prick marks near the spinefold are unexplained. 78% of actual size

29. London, Lambeth Palace Library MS 107 fol. 84v (cat. 18): the monastic 'wheel of fortune' of the virtuous religious life. Compare the good Abbot at the top of the page with the later illustration of St. Bernard in Balliol 150 (fig. 27). Note the double pricking for the penultimate line in the outer margin which is ruled edge-to-edge on the written leaves. The leaf has at some time been torn and mended. 50% of actual size.

30. Cambridge, Trinity College MS B.1.11 flyleaf stub (cat. 45): Master Robert's ownership inscription: 'Iste liber est magistri Roberti amiclas', now covered by laid paper and visible only with back-lighting. 146% of actual size.

31. Cambridge, Trinity College MS B.1.13 fol. 67 (cat. 38): text and gloss in Master Robert's hand. Another hand added the interlinear gloss between the top two lines in this photograph, using an angular paraph mark. 69% of actual size.

32. Cambridge, Trinity College MS B.1.6 fol. 30v (cat. 50): decorated initial P. The decoration was perhaps executed at Buildwas (note the crude flourishing along the left side of the vertical stroke of the letter which breaks off around a

reader's annotations). Master Robert was responsible for the notes in a tiny hand in the extreme outer margins. 62% of actual size.

33. Edinburgh, National Library of Scotland MS 6121, back cover with detached chemise (cat. 12). Note: bevelled edges of exposed board; tawed skin sewing supports and endbands laced through channels in the board (also just visible across spine); tabs at head and tail of the spine now distorted (tail tab clearest in photograph); torn tawed skin primary covering; half of chemise, made of dark leather with partially-detached tawed skin pocket, and extant sewing near upper and lower edges that once attached the chemise to the pocket; the surviving chemise flap at upper edge with fragment of tawed skin edging; holes in square formation on chemise and primary covering – the marks left by a former label; and holes in chemise and primary covering near lower spine corner, left by lost chain attachment. 32% of actual size.

34. Oxford, Bodleian Library MS Bodley 395, inside front board, and detached pastedown (cat. 14). Note: tawed skin sewing supports broken at the spine edge (joint) and the ends (slips) laced into boards and wedged; projecting but distorted tabs at head and tail of spine; spine lining strips pasted to inner surface of board, bearing impressions (across the spine) of the sewing around the sewing supports; primary covering turn-ins pasted to inner surface of board, the corners mitred; the white remains (on the outer half of the cover and on the outer half of the detached pastedown) of a former chemise pocket once pasted in place and now ripped away; a vertical, rectangular corroded (rust) mark and hole in centre of lower edges of cover and detached pastedown, left by an iron chain attachment; nail holes in each corner of board and detached pastedown (most easily visible at upper, outer corners of each) left by former bosses on outer surface of cover; worm damage on pastedown matched by damage on inner face of cover (e.g. the reversed-E-shaped mark in the upper margin of the flyleaf and its reflection on the upper turn-in, etc.). 31% of actual size.

35. Oxford, Bodleian Library MS Bodley MS 371, spinefold at fols. 52v–53 (cat. 19). Note four double stitches disposed along the spinefold, an unusual type of sewing ('helical sewing'). Just visible in the photograph is the text laid out in continuous format: the biblical text is underlined and the commentary follows on at once. 51% of actual size.

36. Oxford, Balliol College MS 39, spinefold at fols. 46v–47 (cat. 20). The book has been resewn all-along, but thread impressions left by former helical sewing survive and are most clearly visible in the photograph at the top of the spinefold, where the more recent sewing has broken down. Compare fig. 30. Note also tiny guide letters 'q' and 'a' in the margin, prompts for the initials scribe. 45% of actual size.

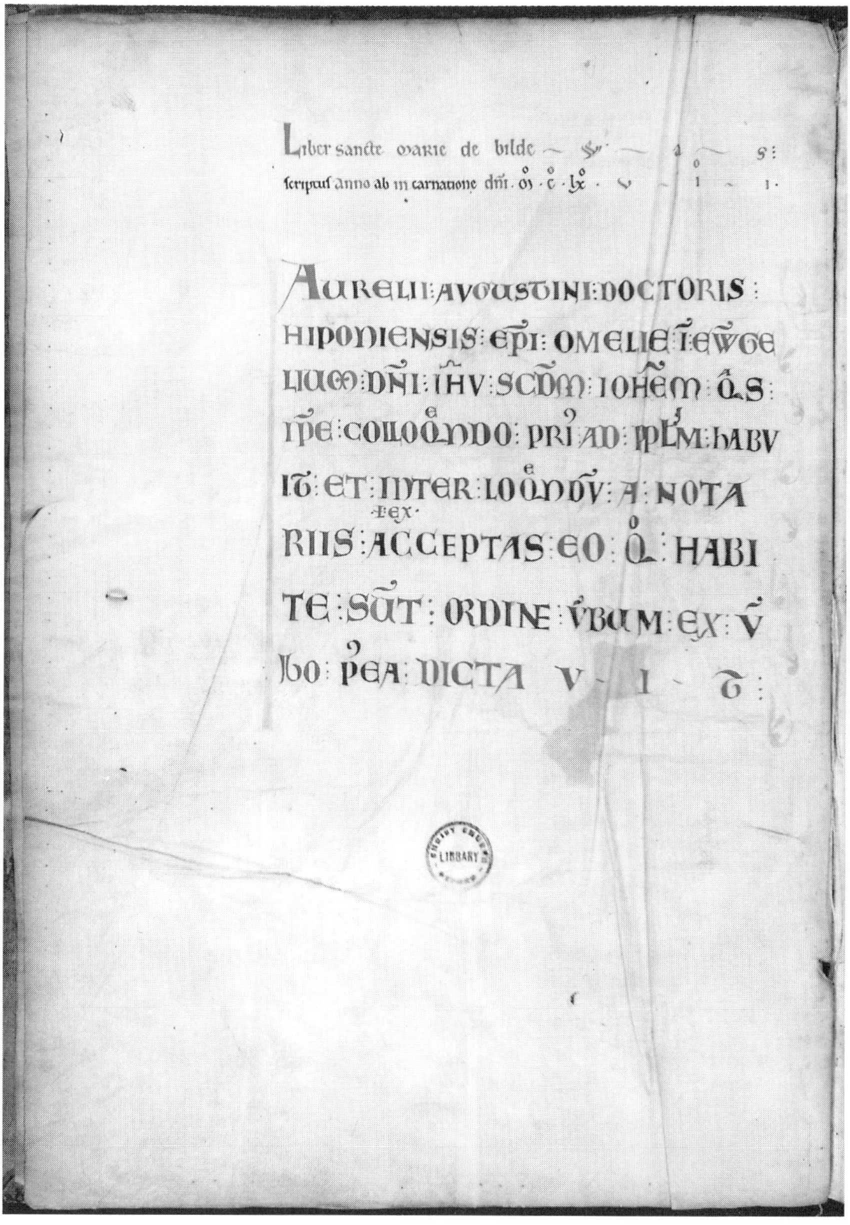

Fig. 1. Oxford, Christ Church MS 88 fol. 2v (cat. 1): 38%.

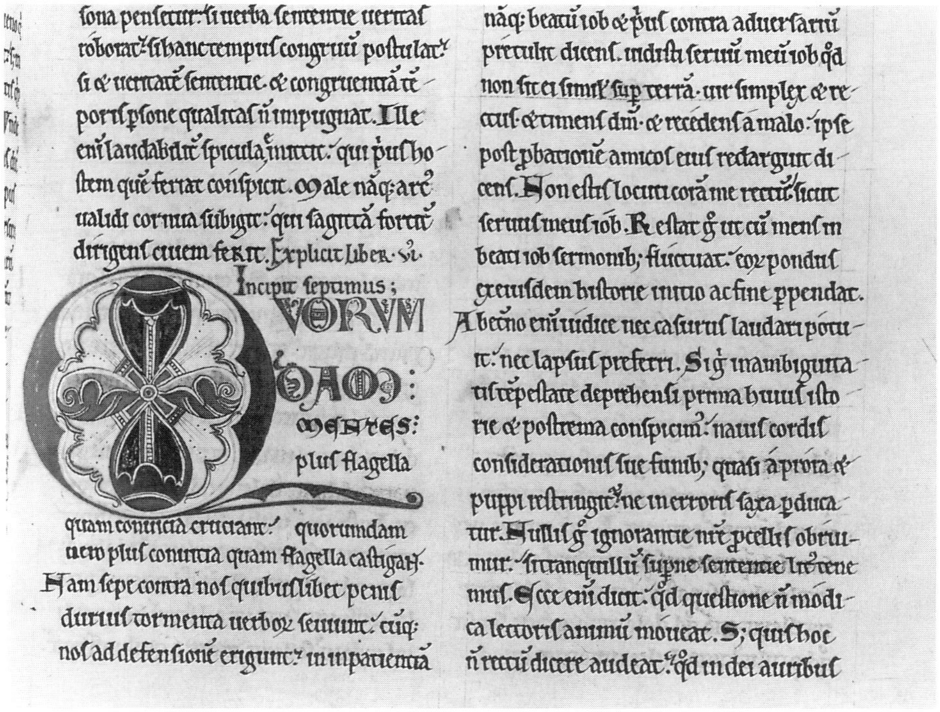

Fig. 2. London, Lambeth Palace Library MS 109 fol. 12 (cat. 2): 54%.

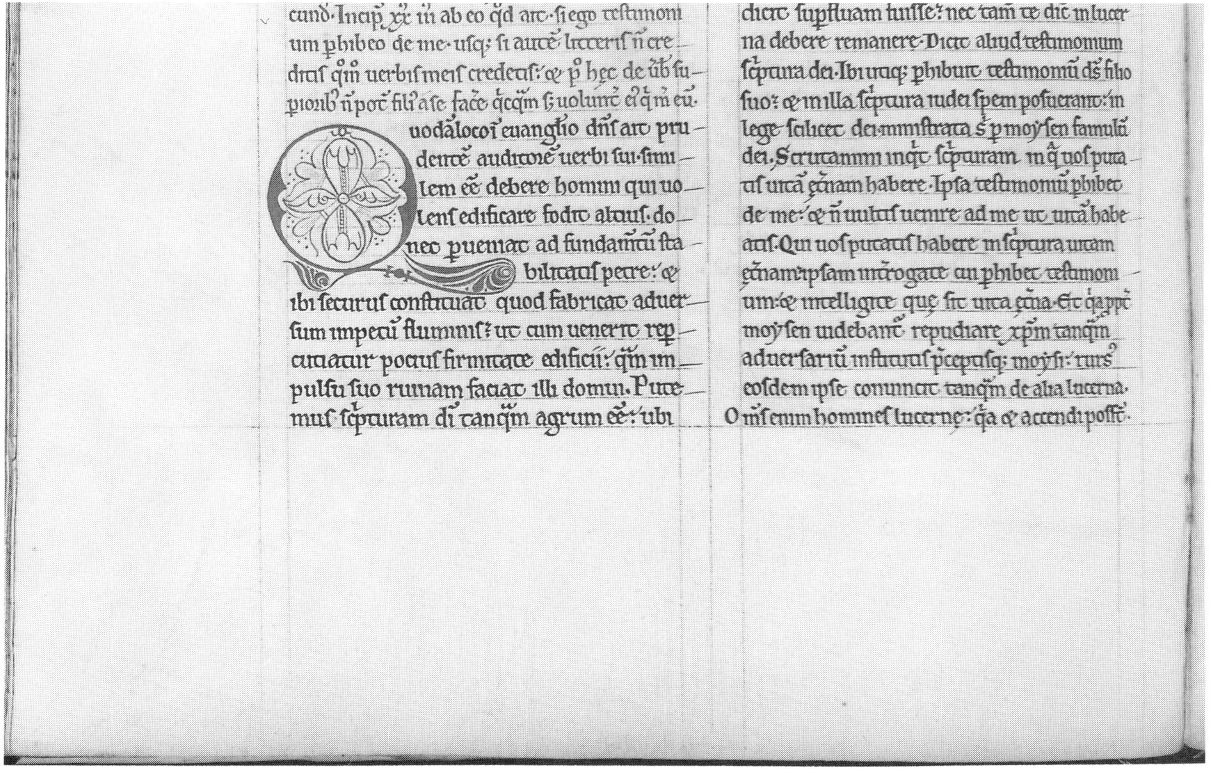

Fig. 3. Oxford, Christ Church MS 88 fol. 65v (cat. 1): 51%.

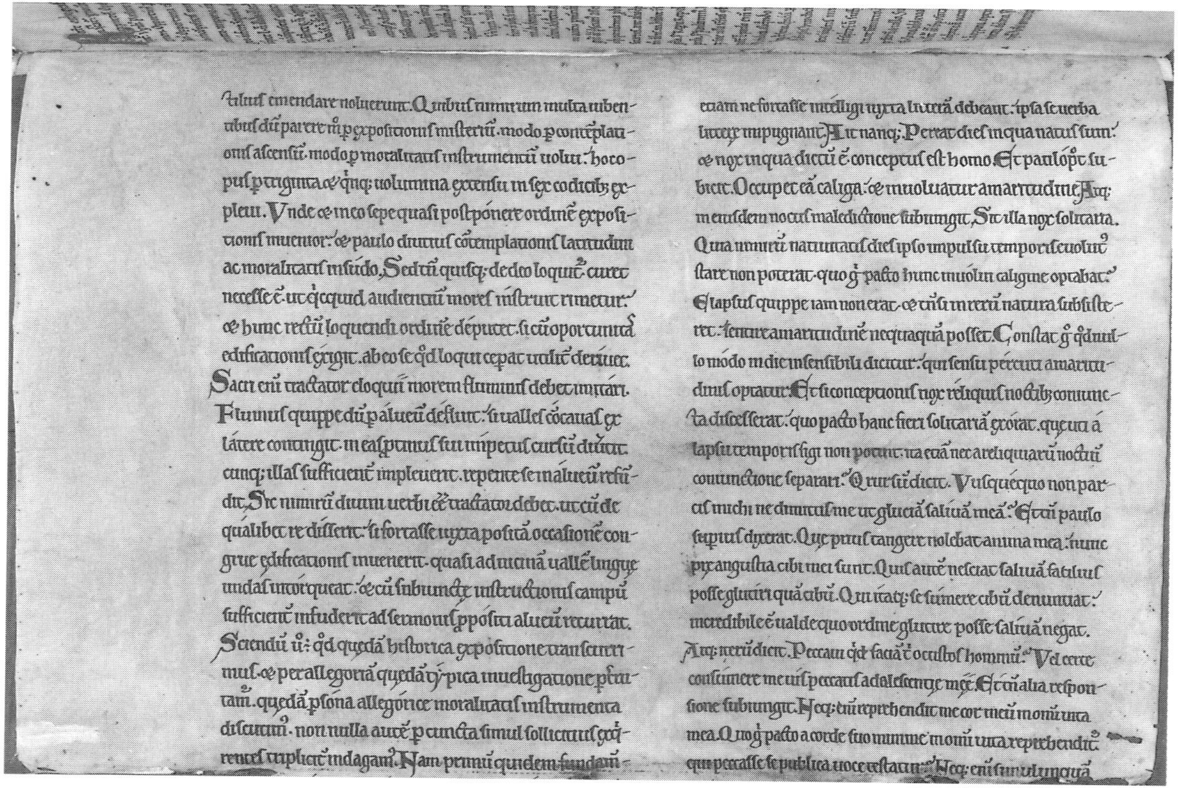

Fig. 4. London, British Library MS Harley 3038, front flyleaf verso (cat. 9): 52%.

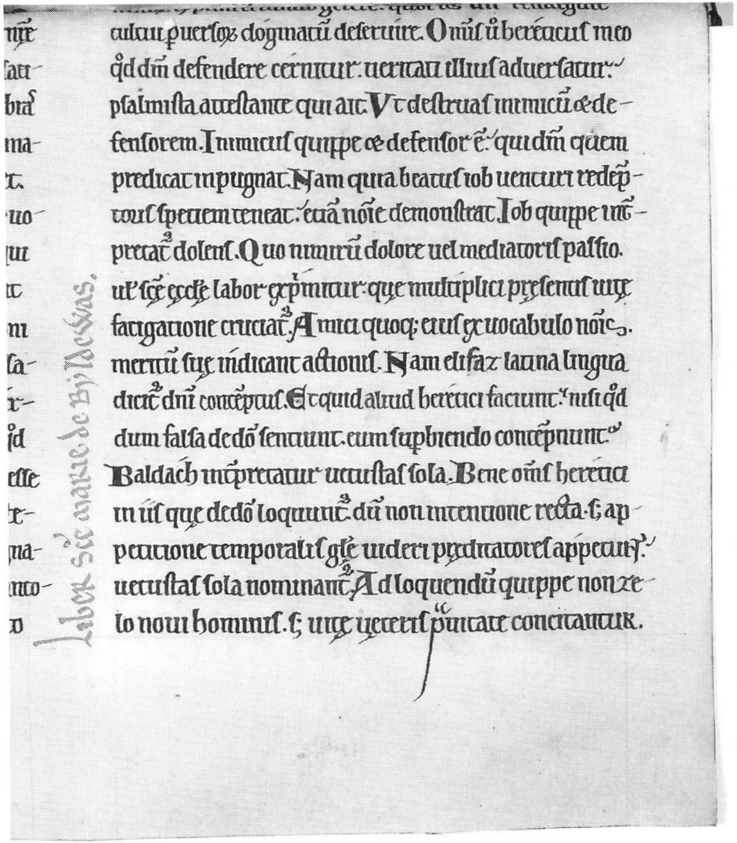

Fig. 5. Cambridge, Trinity College
MS B.1.3, front flyleaf verso (cat. 4):
60%.

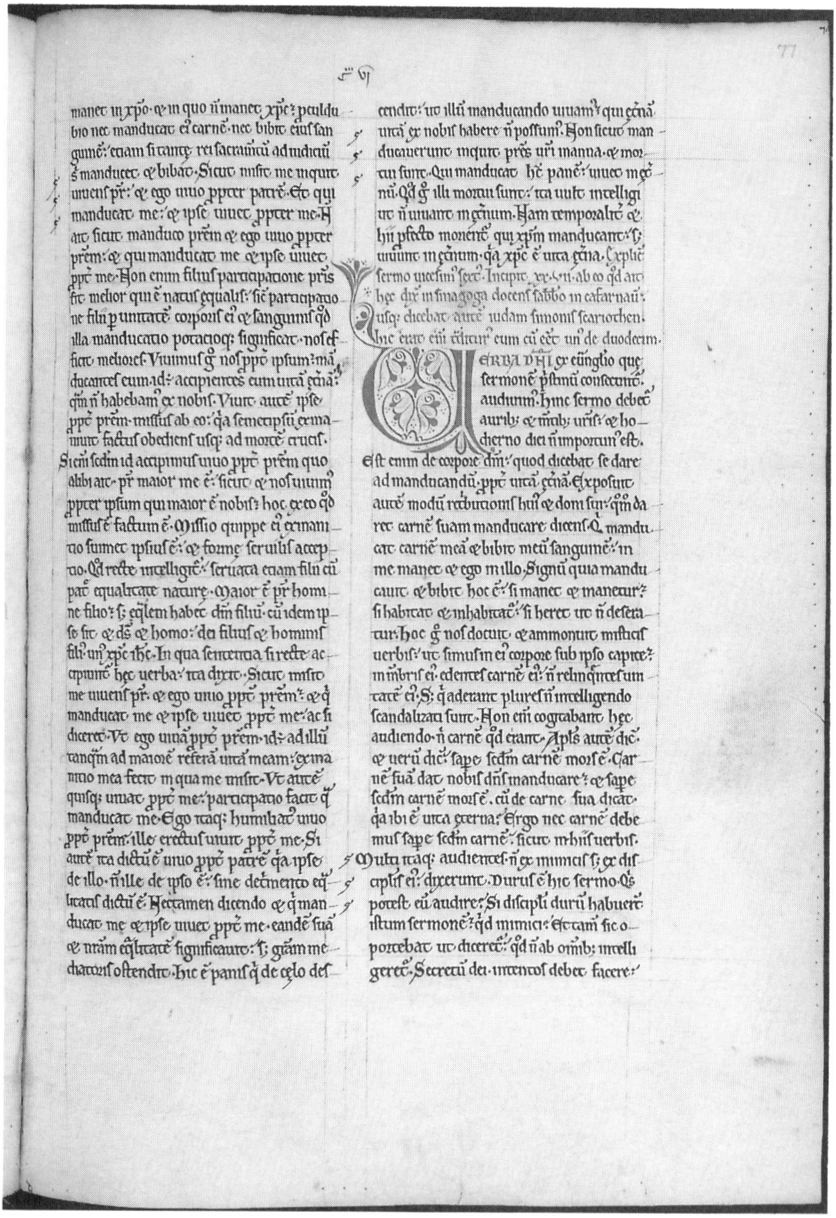

Fig. 6. Oxford, Christ Church MS 88 fol. 77 (cat. 1): 37%.

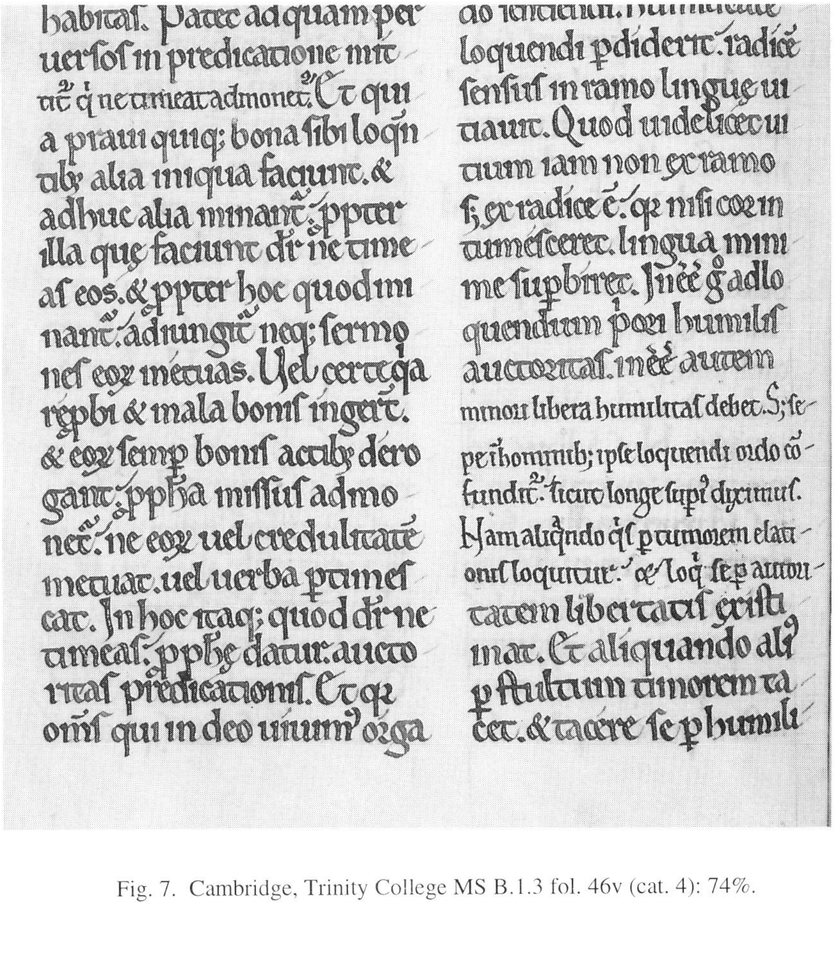

habitas. Patet ad quam per-
uersos in predicatione mit-
titur qui ne timeat admonetur. Et qui
a prauis quique bona sibi loquen-
tibus alia iniqua faciunt. &
adhuc alia minantur. propter
illa que faciunt dicitur ne timeas eos. & propter hoc quod minantur adiungitur neque sermones eorum metuas. Uel certe qua
reprobi & mala bonis ingerunt.
& eorum semper bonis actibus dero-
gant. propheta missus admonetur ne eorum uel credulitatem
metuat. uel uerba pertimes-
cat. In hoc itaque quod dicitur ne
timeas. prophete datur auctoritas predicationis. Et quia
omnis qui in deo uiuunt orga

... humilitate
loquendi perdiderit. radicem
sensus in ramo lingue ui-
tiauit. Quod uidelicet ui-
tium iam non ex ramo
sed ex radice est. quia nisi cor in-
tumesceret. lingua mini-
me superbiret. Inest ergo ad lo-
quendum [illegible] humilis
auctoritas. inesse autem
minori libera humilitas debet. Sed sepe in hominibus ipse loquendi ordo con-
funditur. sicut longe superius diximus.
Nam aliquando quisquis per tumorem elationis loquitur. & loqui se per aucto-
ritatem libertatis existi-
mat. Et aliquando aliquis
per stultum timorem ta-
cet. & tacere se per humili-

Fig. 7. Cambridge, Trinity College MS B.1.3 fol. 46v (cat. 4): 74%.

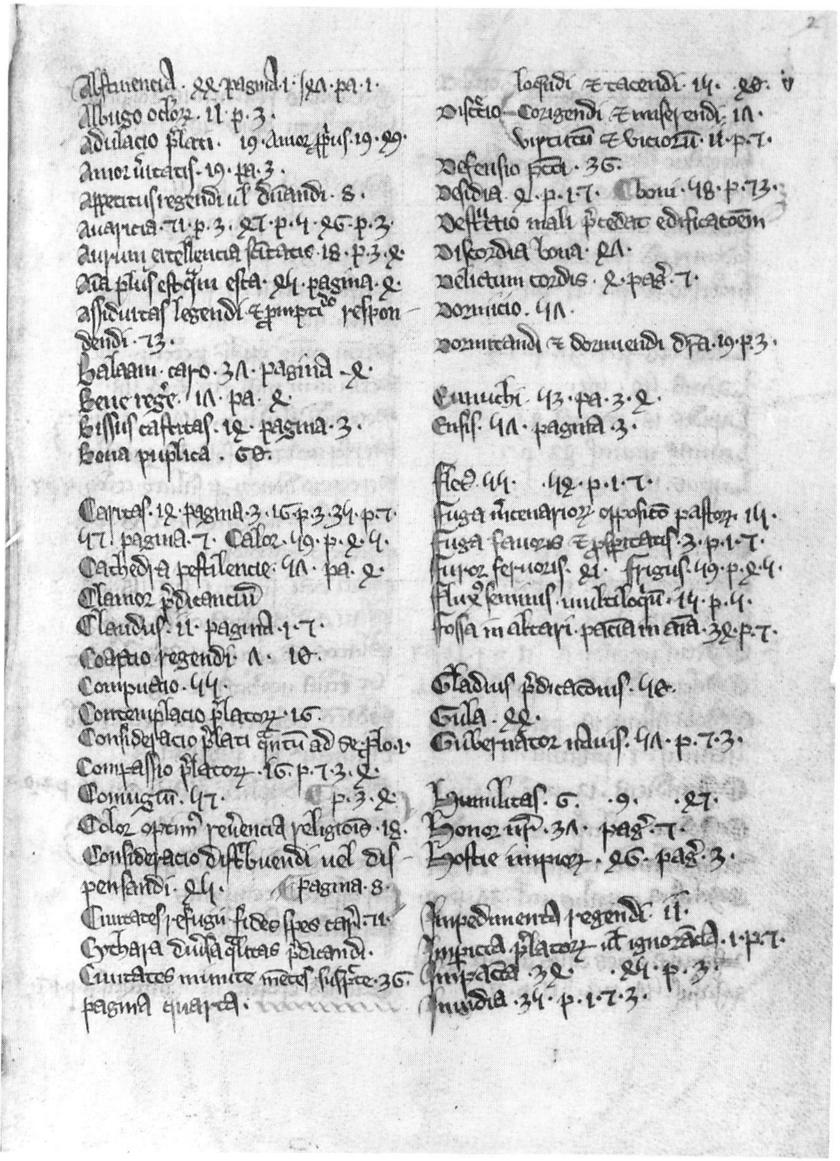

Fig. 8. Cambridge, Trinity College MS B.14.5, first leaf of index (cat. 3): 91%.

Fig. 9. Cambridge, Trinity College MS B.14.5 fol. 89v (cat. 3): 70%.

Fig. 10. Cambridge, University Library MS Ii.2.3 fol. 29v (cat. 8): 73%.

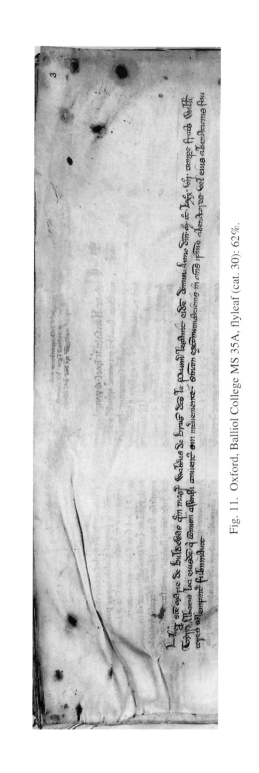

Fig. 11. Oxford, Balliol College MS 35A, flyleaf (cat. 30): 62%.

Fig. 12. London, Lambeth Palace Library MS 488, fol. 89v (cat. 26): 105%.

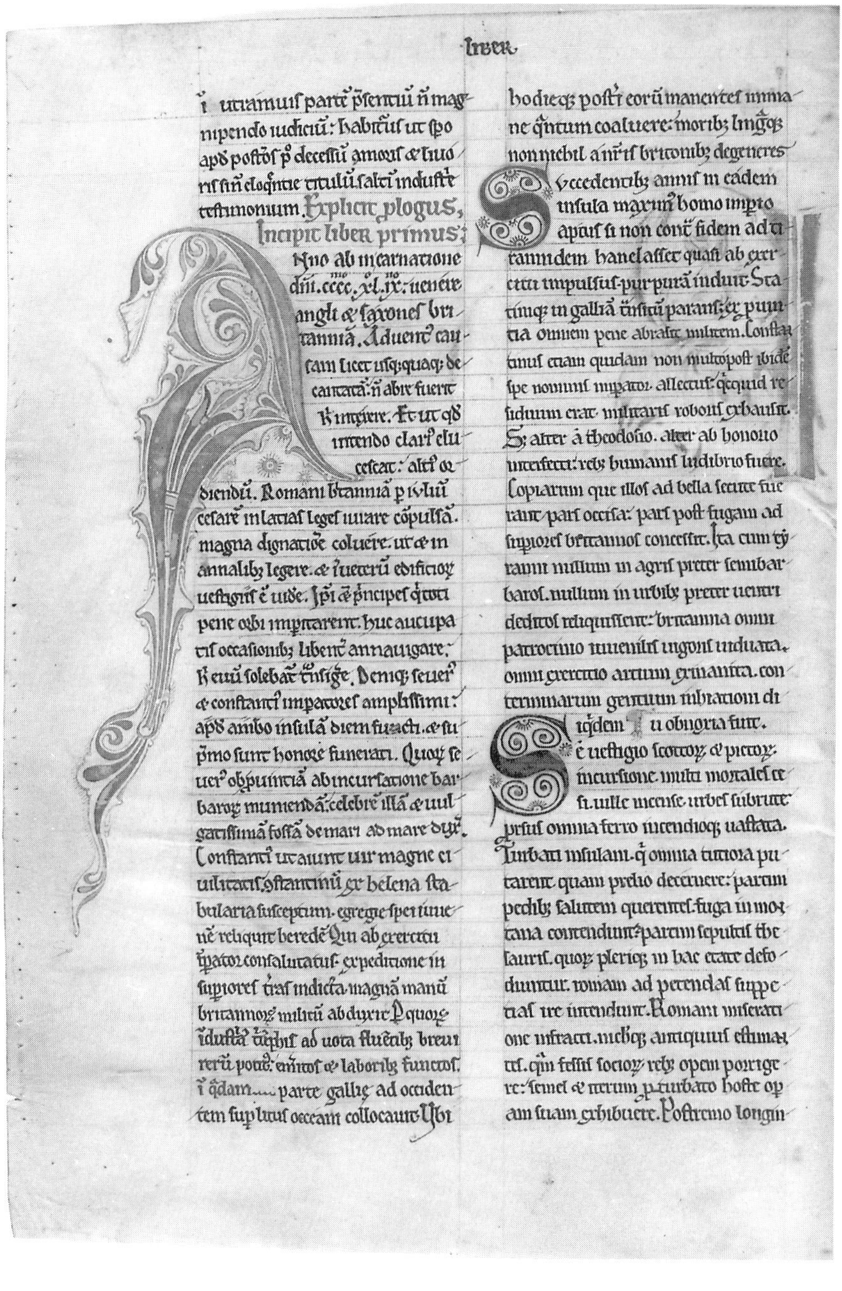

Fig. 13. Cambridge, University Library MS Ii.2.3 fol. 3v (cat. 8): 49%.

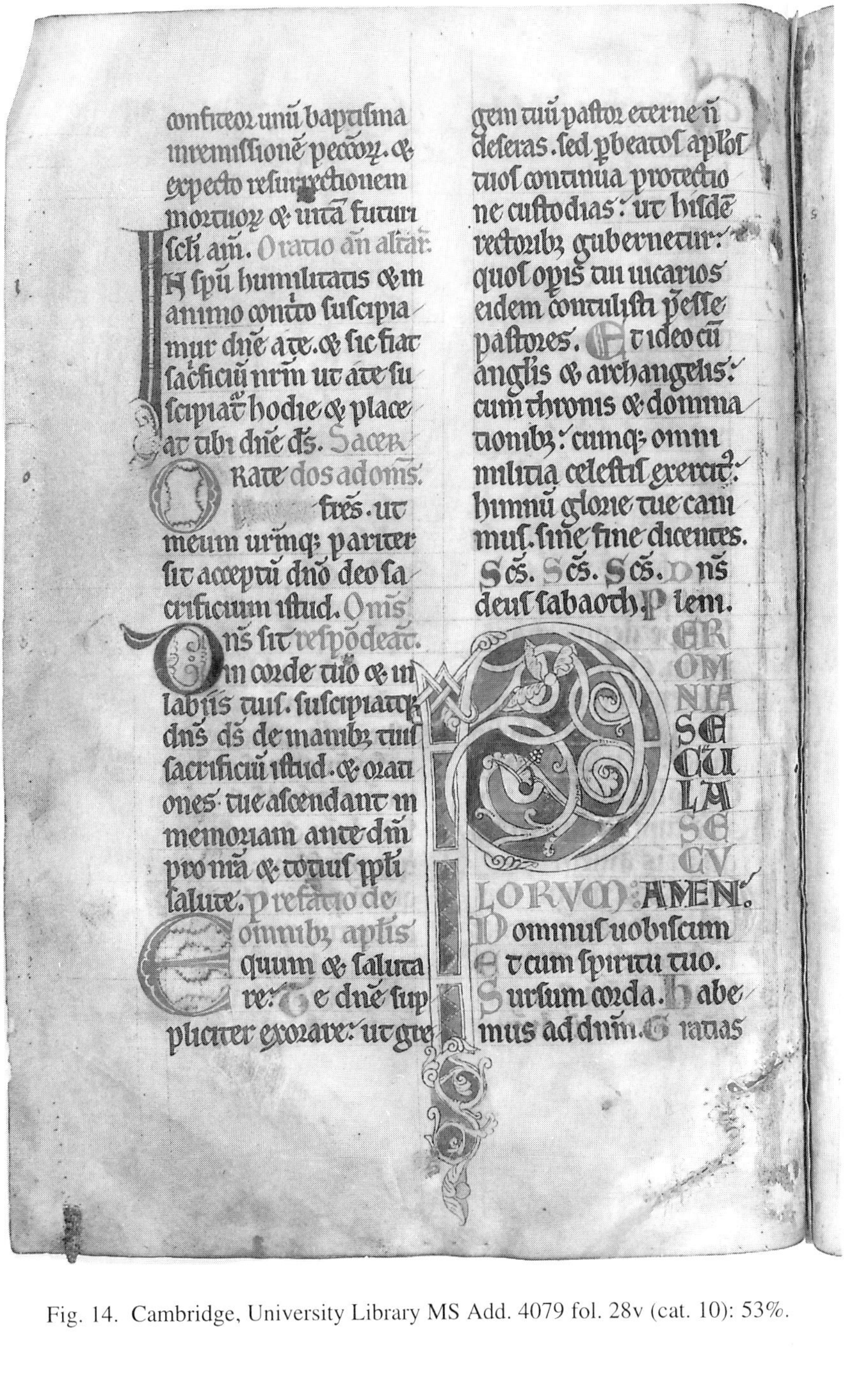

confiteor unū baptisma
inremissione peccoꝝ. e
expecto resurrectionem
mortuoꝝ et uita futuri
seli am. Oratio an altar.
spu humilitatis et in
animo contrito suscipia
mur dñe aꝗ. et sic fiat
sacficiu nrm ut ate su
scipiat hodie et place
at tibi dñe dś. Sacer
Rate dos adoms.
fres. ut
meum urmq; pariter
sit acceptū dño deo sa
crificium istud. O nꝭ
nꝭ sit respondeat.
in corde tuo et in
labiis tuis. suscipiat
dñs dś de manib; tuis
sacrificiu istud. et orati
ones tue ascendant in
memoriam ante dñm
pro nra et totius ipli
salute. prefatio de
omnib; aplis
quum et saluta
re: e dñe sup
pliciter exorare: ut gre

gem tuū pastor eterne ñ
deseras. sed pbeatos aplos
tuos continua protectio
ne custodias: ut hisdē
rectorib; gubernetur:
quos opis tui uicarios
eidem contulisti pesse
pastores. Et ideo cū
anglis et archangelis:
cum thronis et domina
tionib; cumq; omni
militia celestis exercit;
hymnū glorie tue cani
mus. sine fine dicentes.
Sctś. Sctś. Sctś. Dñs
deus sabaoth. Plem.
GR
OM
NIA
SE
CU
LA
SE
CU
LORVM AMEN.
Dominus uobiscum
et cum spiritu tuo.
Sursum corda. hȝ abe
mus ad dñm. Gratias

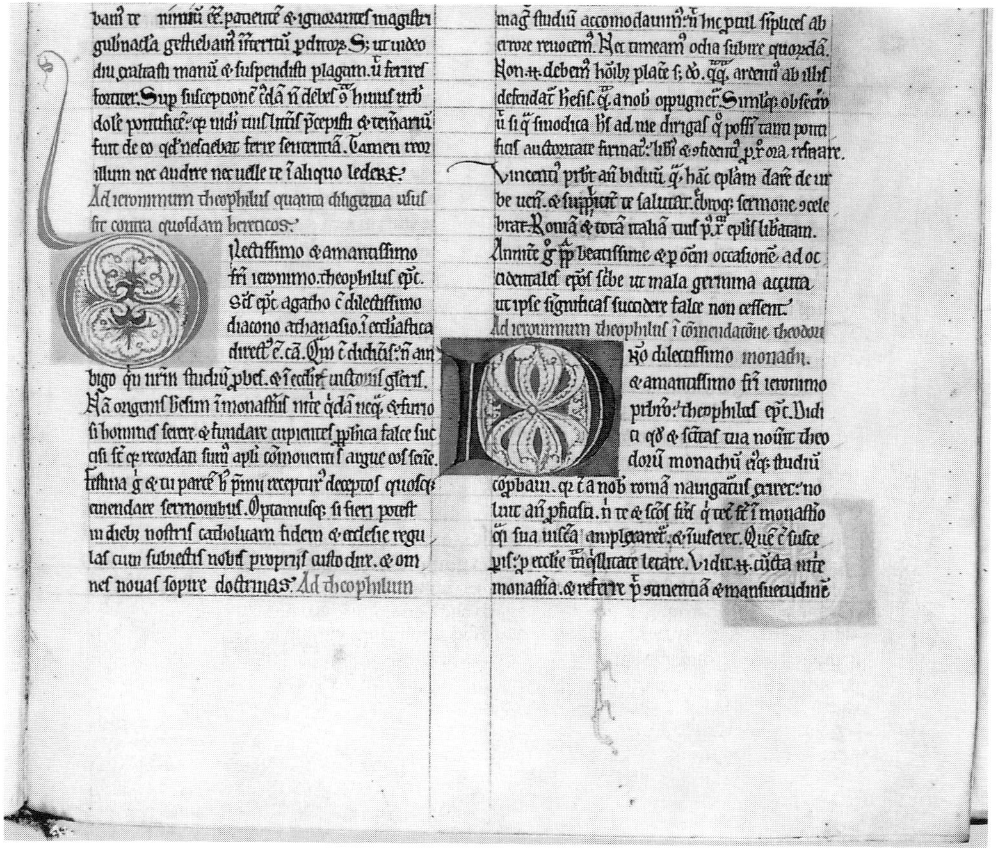

Fig. 15. Oxford, Balliol College MS 229 fol. 45 (cat. 11): 54%.

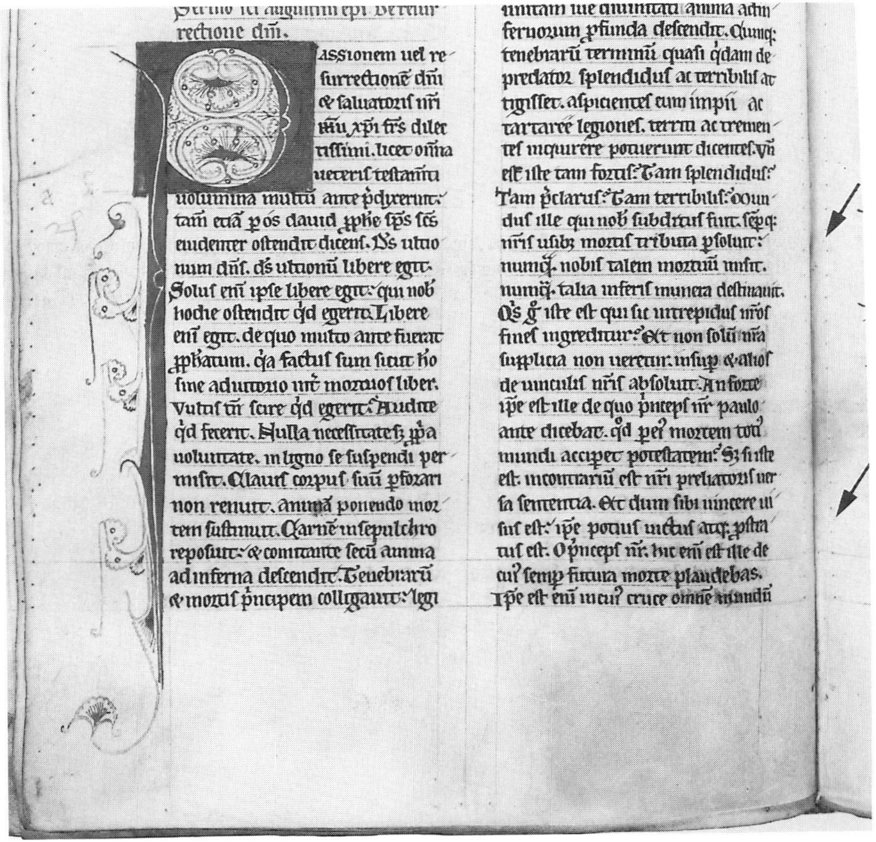

Fig. 16. Edinburgh, National Library of Scotland MS 6121 fol. 45v (cat. 12): 50%.

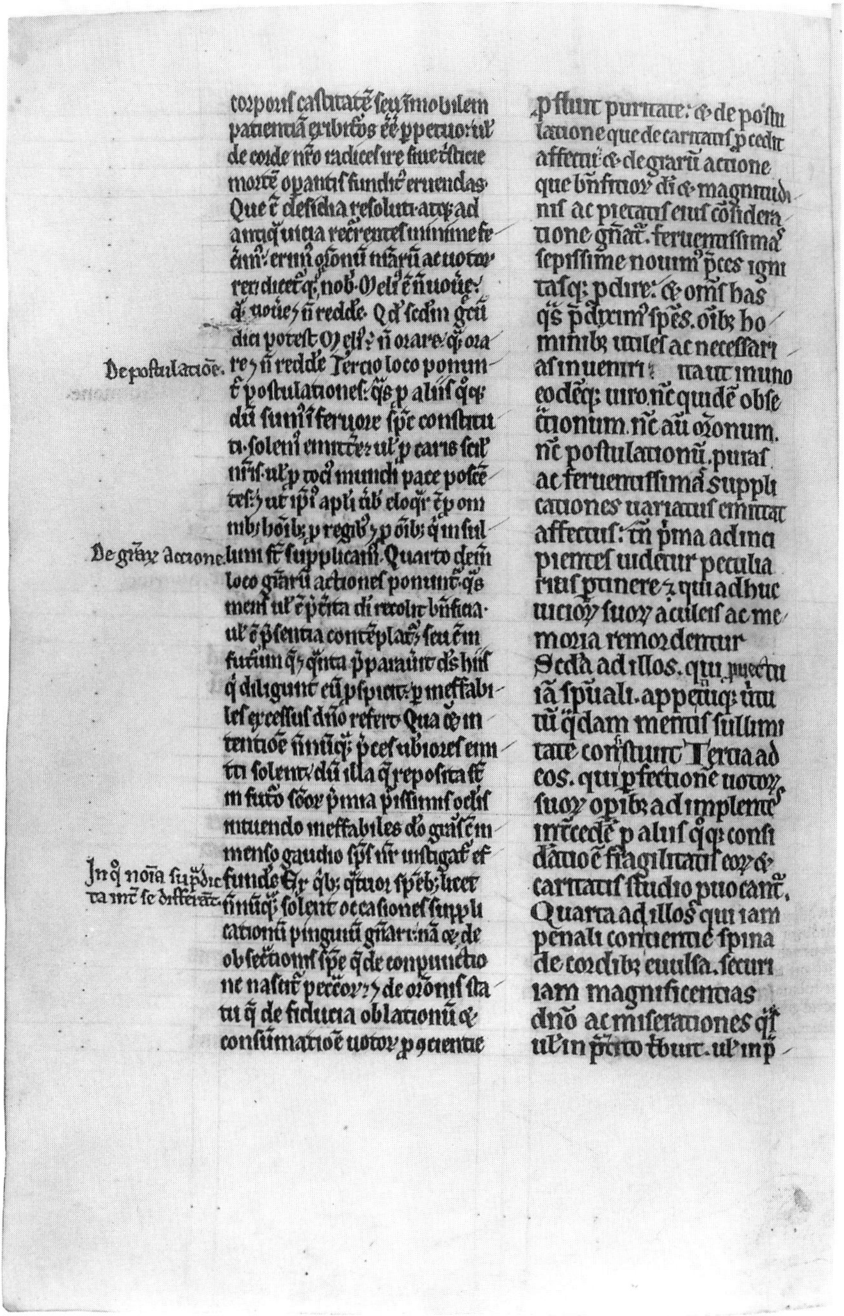

Fig. 17. Oxford, Bodleian Library Ms Bodley 730 fol. 130v (cat. 16): 55%.

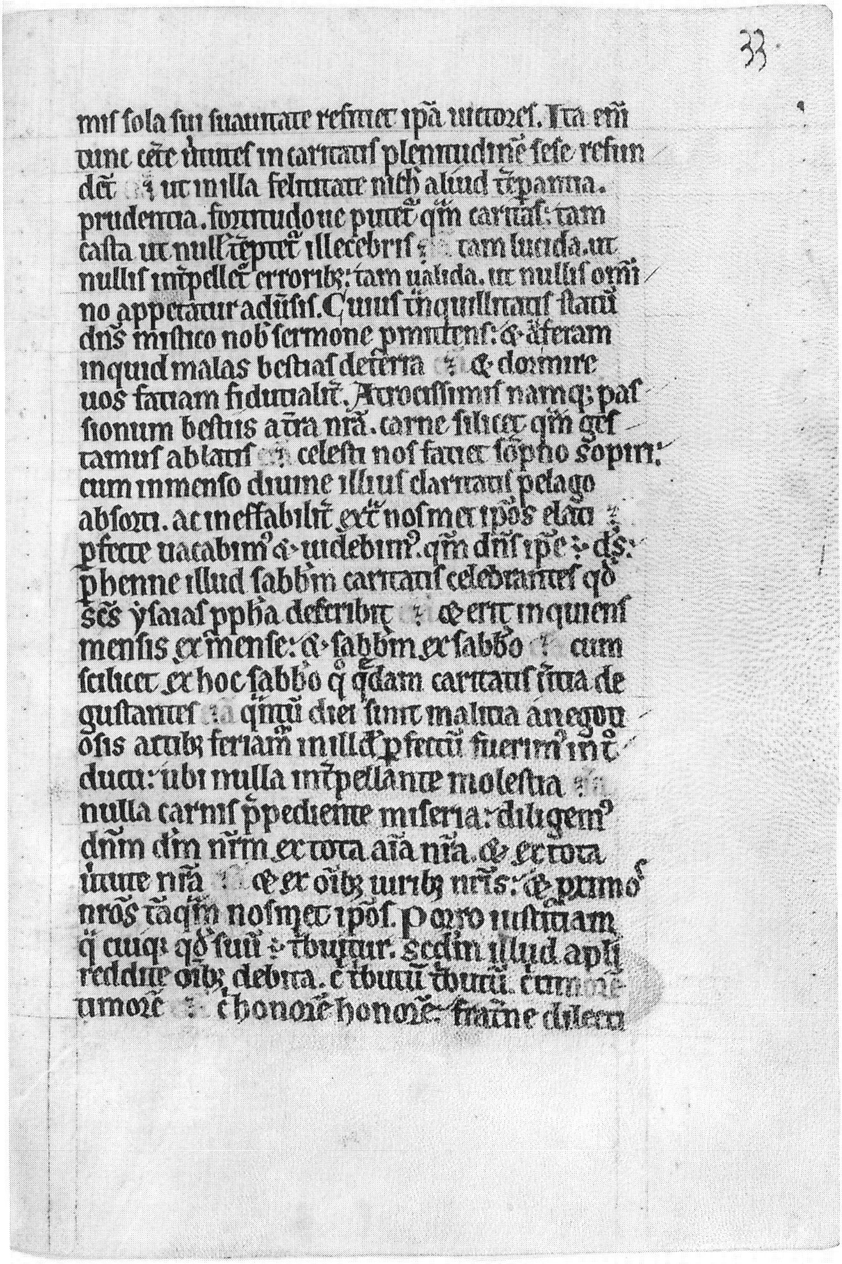

mis sola sui suauitate resinet ipam uictores. Ita enim
oune cete uirtutes in caritatis plenitudine sese resun
det ut in illa felicitate nich aliud temptanna.
prudentia. fortitudone putet qm caritas: tam
casta ut nullis temptet illecebris tam lucida. ut
nullis impellet erroribz: tam ualida. ut nullis omi
no appetatur aduis. Cuius tranquillitatis statum
dns mistico nob sermone pmittens: & aferam
inquid malas bestias de terra & dormire
uos faciam fiducialit. Atrocissimis namq pas
sionum bestiis a tra nra. carne silicet qm ges
tamus ablatis celesti nos facet sopho sopiri.
cum inmenso diuine illius claritatis pelago
absorti. ac ineffabilit ext nosmet ipos elati
pfecte uacabim & uidebim. qm dns ipe ds.
phenne illud sabbm caritatis celebrantes qd
ses ysaias ppha describit & erit inquiens
mensis ex mense: & sabbm ex sabbo cum
scilicet ex hoc sabbo q qdam caritatis itinera de
gustantes qngui diei sunt malitia an egou
osis acubz feriam in illa pfectu fuerim in t
ducti: ubi nulla impellante molesta
nulla carnis ppediente miseria: diligem
dnm dm nrm ex tota aia nra. & ex tota
itute nra & ex oibz uiribz nris: & primo
nros taqm nosmet ipos. p qro iustitiam
q cuiq qd suu tbuitur. sedm illud apli
reddite oibz debita. c tbutu tbutu cum
timore c honore honore: fratre dilecti

Fig. 18. Cambridge, St. John's College MS D.2 fol. 33 (cat. 15): 67%.

Incipit prefacio Iohannis heremite in decem collationibus missa ad papam leonciu̅ ⁊ helladiu̅ fr̅em karissimu̅.

BReuuo[...]
quod beatis-
simo pape
castorio in
eorum uolu-
minum prefa-
tione p̅misen̅ que de instru-
[...]cenobioru̅ · ⁊ de octo p̅n-
cipaliu̅ uicioru̅ remedus-
[...] libellis d̅no adiuuante
digesta sunt · in q̅ tenuitas
n̅ri sufficit ingenii · uirtuiq̅:
[...]aritatum est · [...]iderim sane
q̅d sup hoc ut illi ut̅ uri fuerit eramini[...] eq̅tate ppensu̅:
umo̅ in rob̅ tam p fundis tam
q̅ sullimib̅ · q̅ que in usu stili
uitarbitro̅ alia n̅ uenu̅t̅ · dign
um aliq̅d cognitione uita om
n̅iuq̅ s̅c̅o̅ si̅m desiderio p̅m
seru̅ · Hunc autcqq̅ c̅l̅elunq̅s̅
nos ponit fex supdict̅ m̅igu̅t
addu̅ · has m̅u̅ · x· collati
one summoru̅ patru̅ id̅ ana
choitaru̅ q̅ in heremo seit̅bi
entioabant̅ · q̅s̅ ille meo̅ paxa
bj̅u flag̅us studio serta̅uit su̅m
ti sufficit̅ sermone cone̅bu:
ig̅ pendens p̅ multitudine
caritatis q̅ut̅o infirmas e̅tu̅
cesponde p̅g̅uarer · ti obis
potissimu̅ o beatissime pa
pa leonu̅ · ⁊ s̅c̅e̅ fr̅ helladu̅ cre-
dici consecrandas · At̅ siq̅
d̅ut̅ si̅m memorato uiro q̅
germanitatis affectu q̅ sae̅do-

ru̅ dignitate q̅ q̅d hui mai e sei stu-
dii seruore continner? Be dit̅ar̅io fra
u̅tu̅ debitu̅ iure deposcit · At̅ ana
ehontaru̅ institu̅ta sullimia · siut
q̅da̅ p̅pa aggressus e p̅ suptione sec-
tart̅ e legi̅untu̅ dot̅ne t̅u̅t̅e s̅c̅o̅ spi
ritu suggerente pene an̅q̅in disce-
ret app̅ hendens̅ · n̅ ta̅ sui̅ s̅ adiuuen-
tionib̅ q̅m illoru̅ eruditioib̅ · ma
luit erudiri · In q̅b̅ m̅ nunc in po̅
tu si̅l̅iutu̅ constituto · minimu̅ pela-
gus apie̅ · ut silicet de institruto
atq̅ doctrina tantoru̅ uiro̅ q̅dam
et̅tere audea memo̅ne lit̅aru̅ · Tan
to enim p fundio̅ r̅ si̅ nauigationis p̅-
ciliffrag̅ il ingenii ei̅ ba iactanda e̅ ·
q̅u̅tu̅ ac̅enobiis anachoresis q̅ ab
actuali uita que in cong̅gationib̅:
q̅ ex cet contemplatio di̅ · cui illi mesh
mabiles uiri semp intena siu̅t · ma
io̅ · atq̅ sullimio̅ e̅ · U̅ r̅ m̅ g̅ e̅ conat̅
n̅r̅os p̅s̅i o̅r̅oib̅ · adiuuare · ne aut
ta̅ s̅c̅a̅ materia impito q̅de̅ s̅ fideli ser
mone p̅ i̅ nda pidurct in nob̅ · aut rursu eide materie abissis · obruat̅ nostra
rusticitas · P̅ si̅ ab extio̅ e ac uisibili mo
nachoru̅ cultu que̅ p̅ ou̅b̅ · digessim̅
libs · ad inuisibile i̅ntious hominis
habitu̅ t̅n̅ seam̅ · q̅ de canonicart̅u̅ o̅r̅o̅
n̅u̅ modo · ad illi q̅in apl̅s p̅ce̅pit̅ o̅r̅o̅
ms p̅ petue iugitate ascendat elo q̅u̅
U̅ r̅ q̅ si̅ ta̅ supio̅ s̅ opis̅ leone · iacob
illis intelligibilis non̅ carnalium
uiciou̅ supplantatione p̅ m̅ u̅ t̅ · t̅n̅ c̅
etia̅ non ta̅ mea q̅a̅ patru̅ si̅ tu̅
ta suscipiens̅ diuine ta̅ puritatis

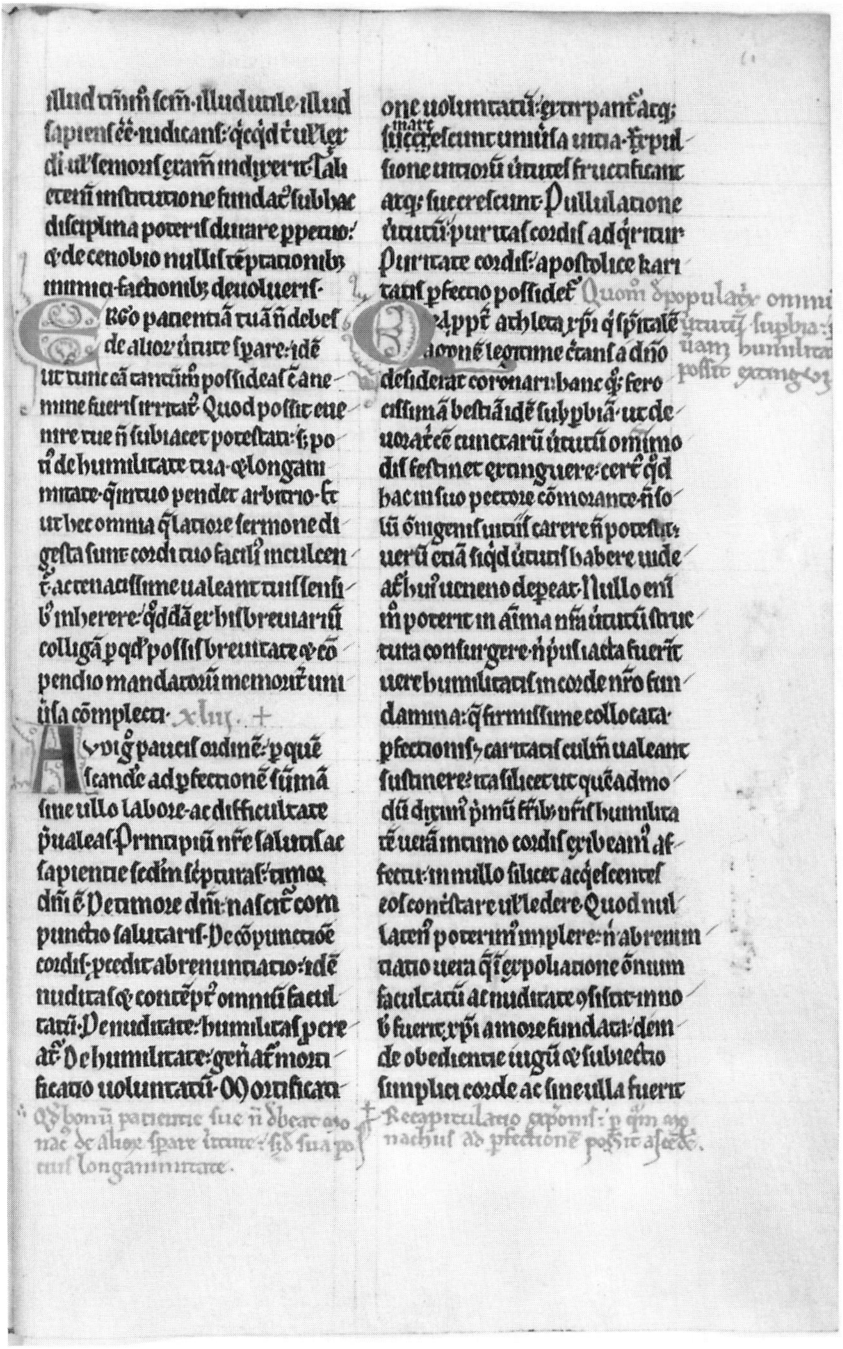

Fig. 20. Cambridge, Trinity College MS B.2.30 fol. 61 (cat. 17): 61%.

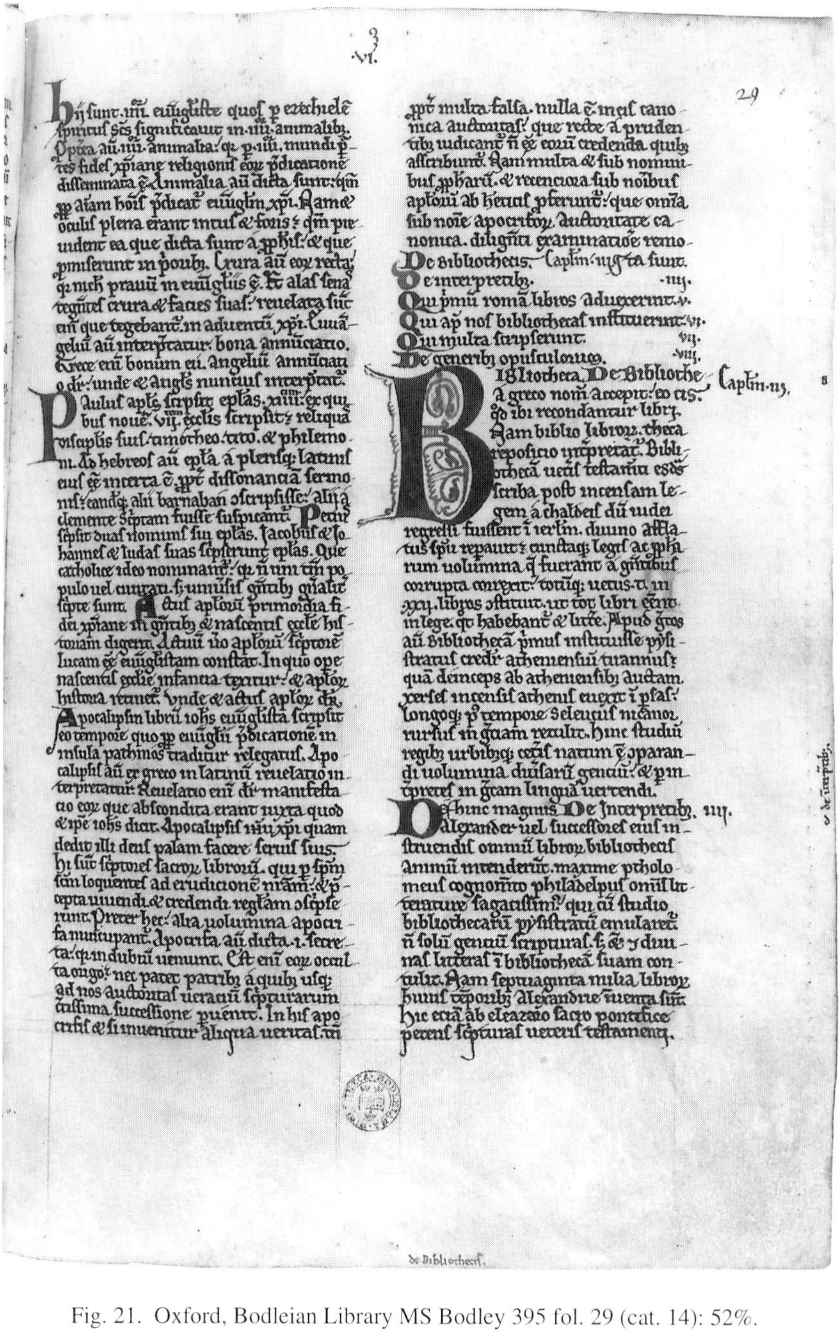

Fig. 21. Oxford, Bodleian Library MS Bodley 395 fol. 29 (cat. 14): 52%.

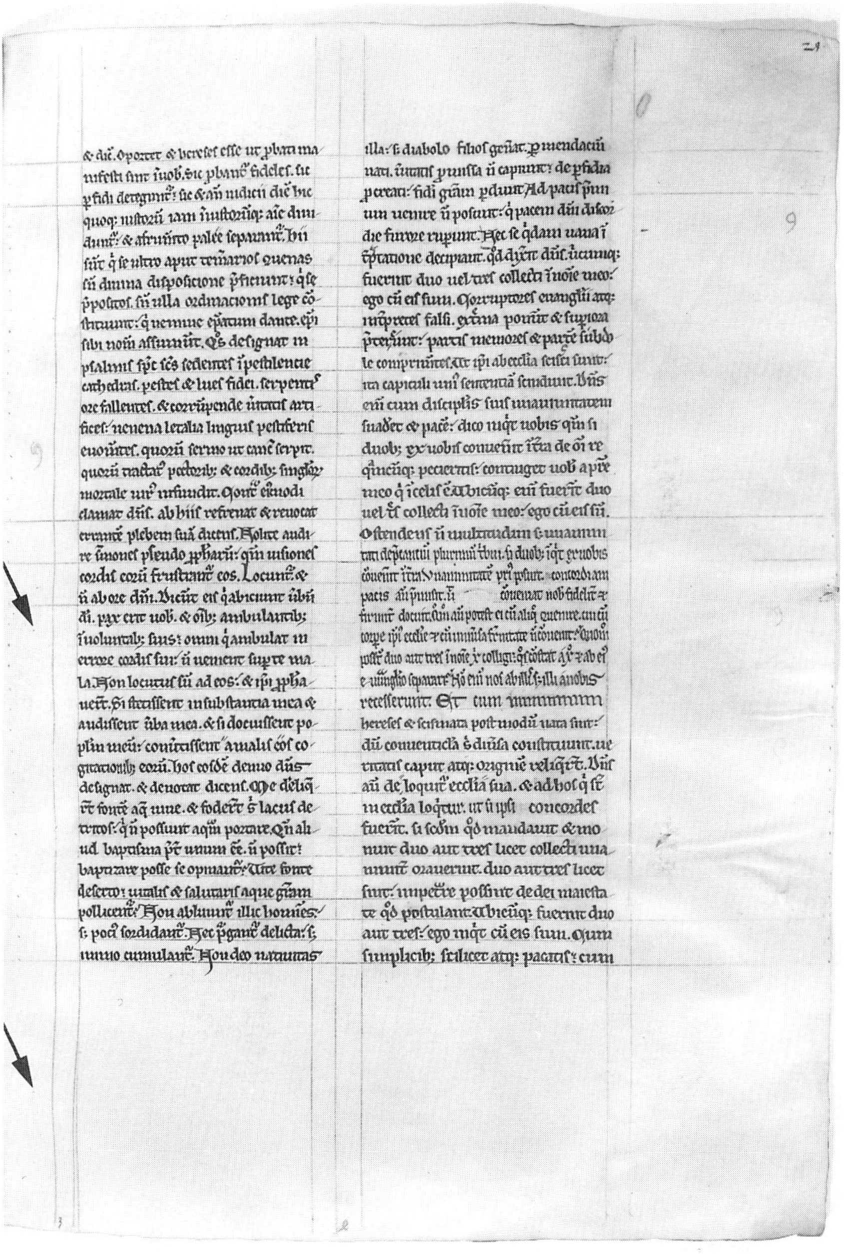

Fig. 22. Cambridge, Pembroke College MS 154 fol. 21 (cat. 13): 43%.

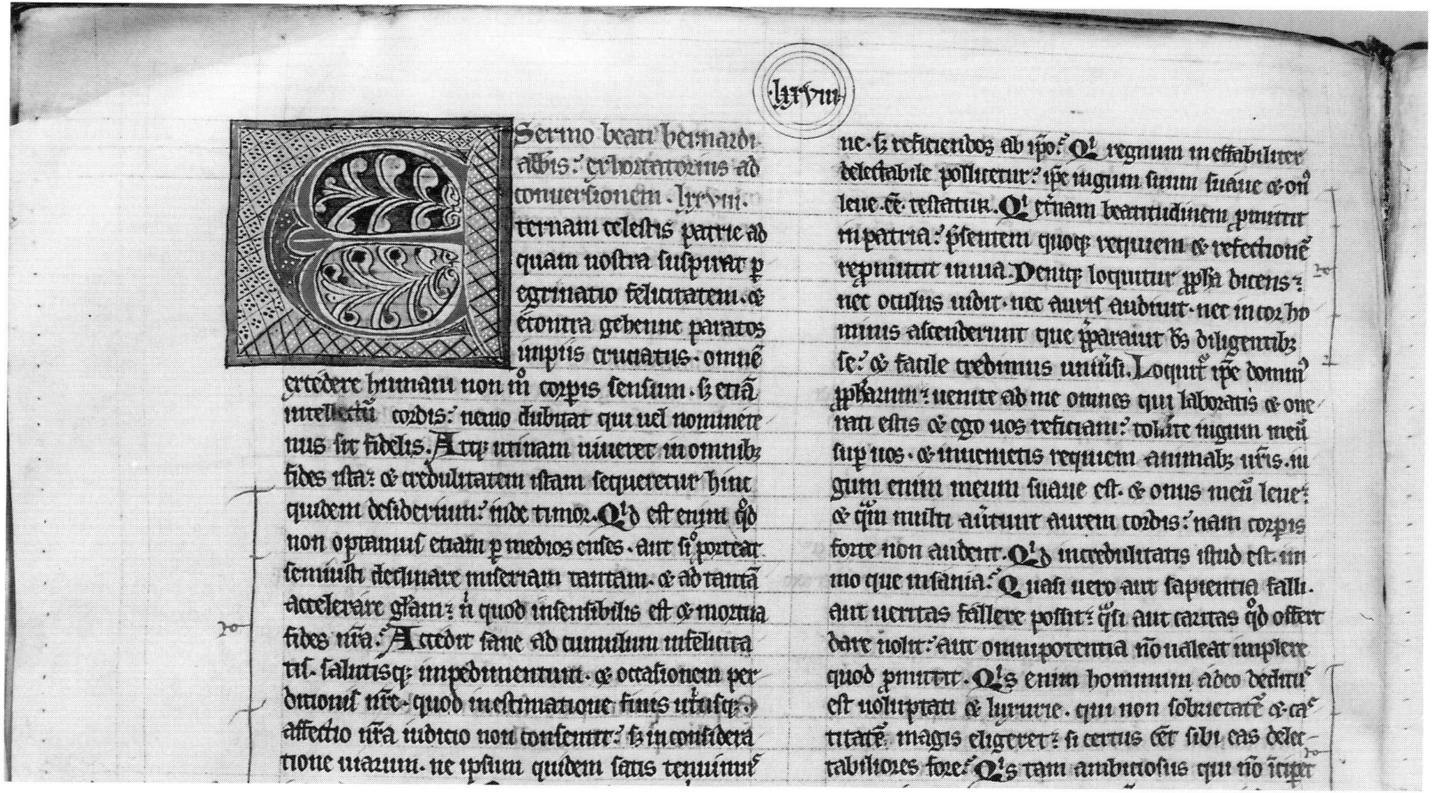

Sermo beati bernardi abbatis. Exhortatorius ad conuersionem. lxxviii.

Fig. 23. Oxford, Balliol College MS 150 fol. 81v (cat. 22): 62%.

meliora sunt ubera tua uino fragrantia
unguentis optimis. XI

Laut maï comendat et tanta ratione multi-
plicat benefici qd' mudo conialit. XII

Onque tho pie maï fraint suyra crute & ad
filuum tiba dolors diruigetur. XIII

Ozalt expostio et qd' scriptum ã; oleu effusu
noïn tuũ idō adolescentule dilxeir te nimis. XIIII

De adiuuabit asensione diũ que uaï dul-
cis. dulcibz tibus psequitur. XV

Tropologia expostio et qd' scriptum ã; trahe
me p te curreï in odore unguentor tuos. XVI

De assumptione glose di generaï que ado-
lescentula suas ad intarï currendu ut
pmisceat inuitat. XVII

Partum allegorica. partum moralis expostio
et qd' scriptum ã; introduxit me rex in cubi-
culum suu, gruitabui & letabinur in te.
memores ubce tuoz sup uinum, recti
diligunt te. XVIII

CANTICVM
me osculo oris
sui. Audire

....ech que loquor
....ndiar tia tiba
....eus mei. Terraiï
....ech & seuilat
....in: conuenunt
celum & terra; lugna mus locamur.
Conloquiaur terrena celestibz; numo
eua celi freta: ut trigine celebret ef-
taimur. Audce celi. edos inclinat & ster-
nedit. & tia que manuf ee undebaï &
uacua: illustraï sup ue luci ga. & ozna-
tu suo decozata fructu pfar sublimi.
Concitaï g in plurimam doctrina mea.
hoc: in modum plune, qz ope dinna.
scribendo usq; adeo pfict. ut ad mistui
incar nationi f que eta rui: in qua pña
signeam humectaï & feundaï disaï

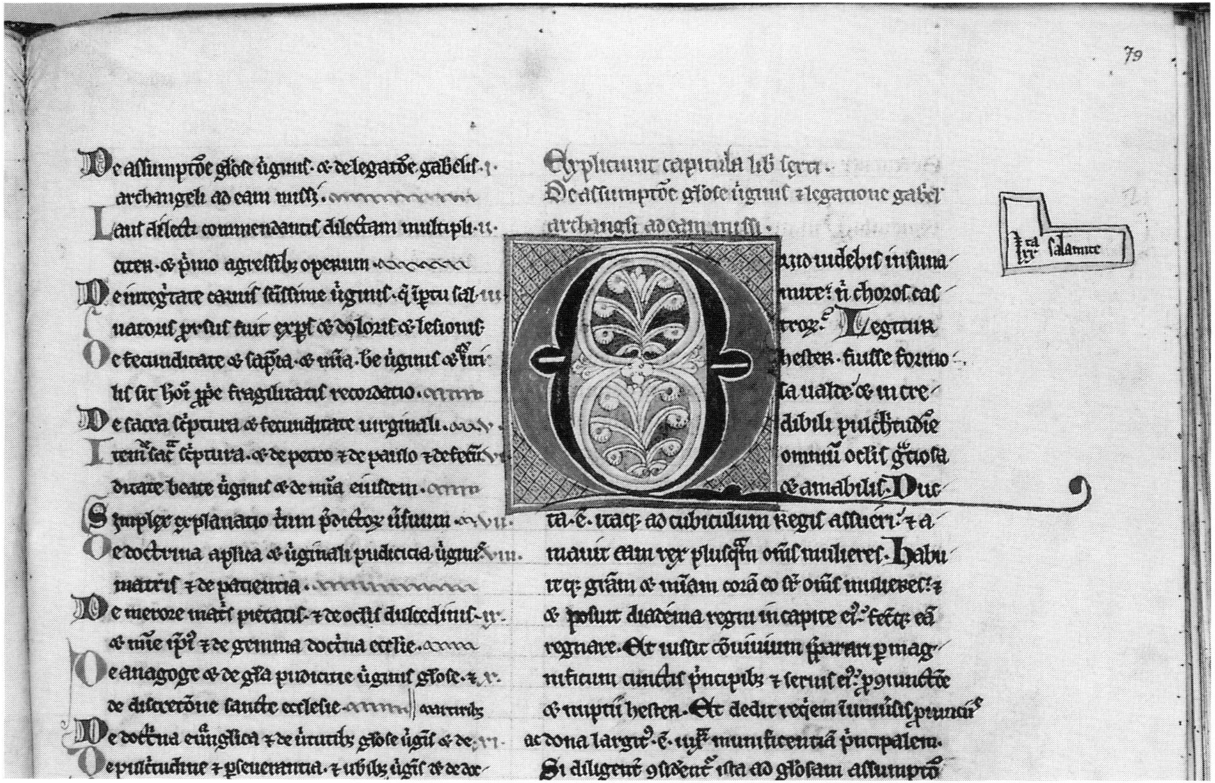

Fig. 25. Oxford, Balliol College MS 40 fol. 79 (cat. 21): 60%.

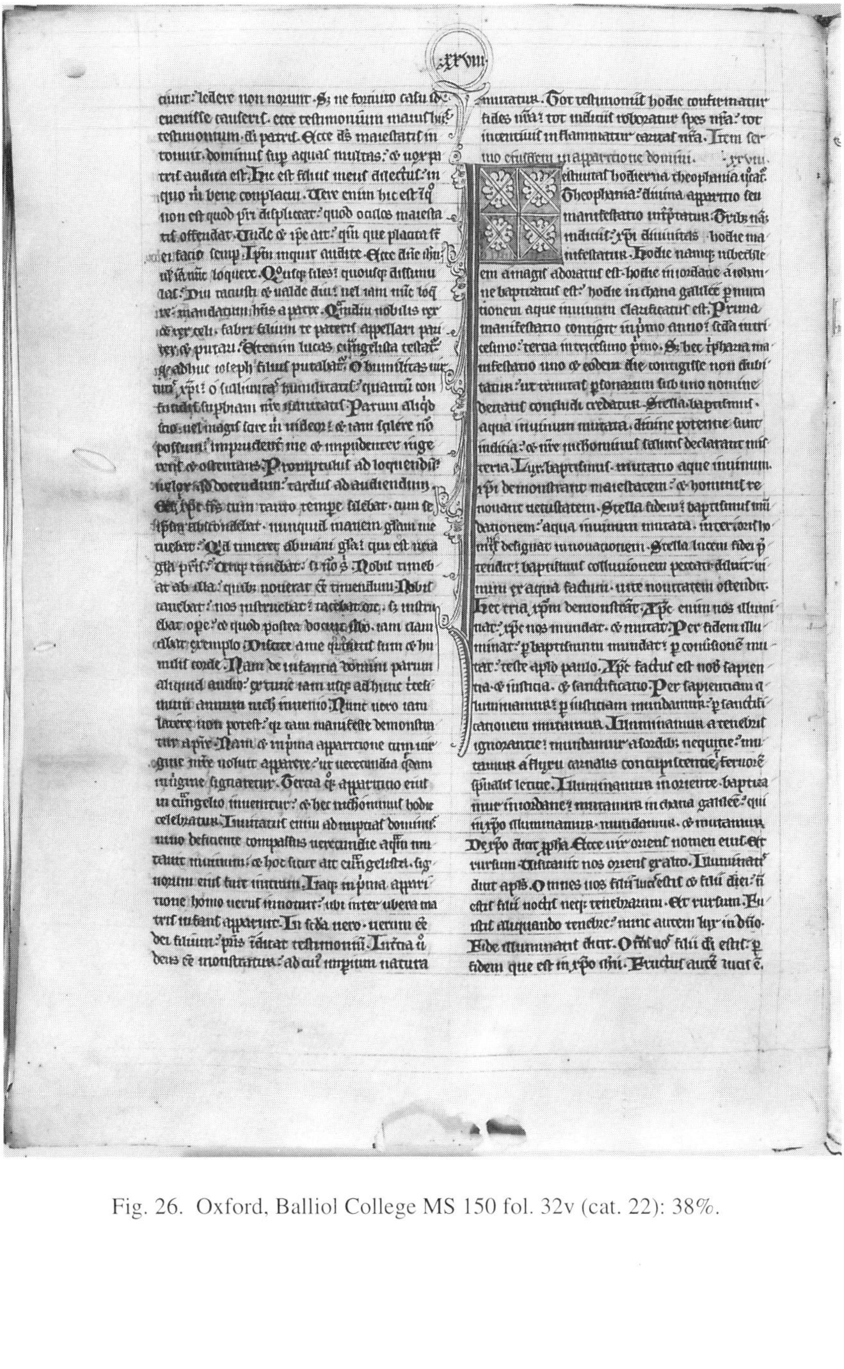

Fig. 26. Oxford, Balliol College MS 150 fol. 32v (cat. 22): 38%.

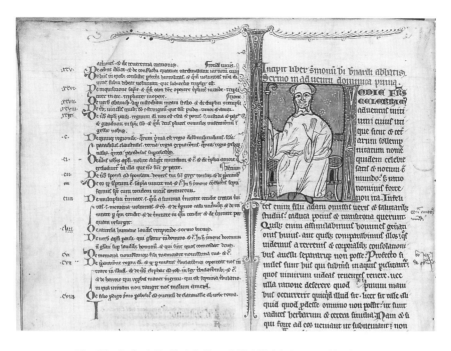

Fig. 27. Oxford, Balliol College MS 150 fol. 2v (cat. 22): 37%.

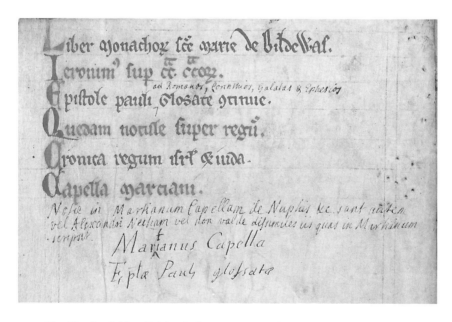

Fig. 28. Cambridge, Trinity College MS B.1.29, front flyleaf (cat. 24): 78%.

Fig. 29. London, Lambeth Palace Library MS 107 fol. 84v (cat. 18): 50%.

Fig. 30. Cambridge, Trinity College MS B.1.11, flyleaf stub (cat. 45): 146%.

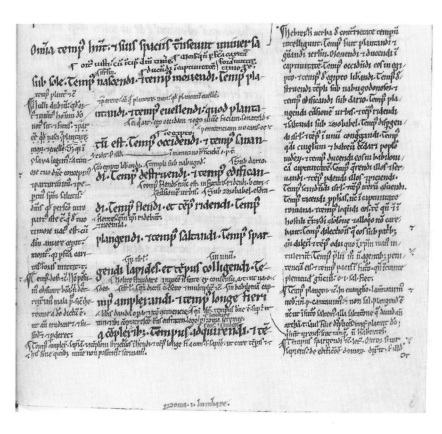

Fig. 31. Cambridge, Trinity College MS B.1.13 fol. 67 (cat. 38): 69%.

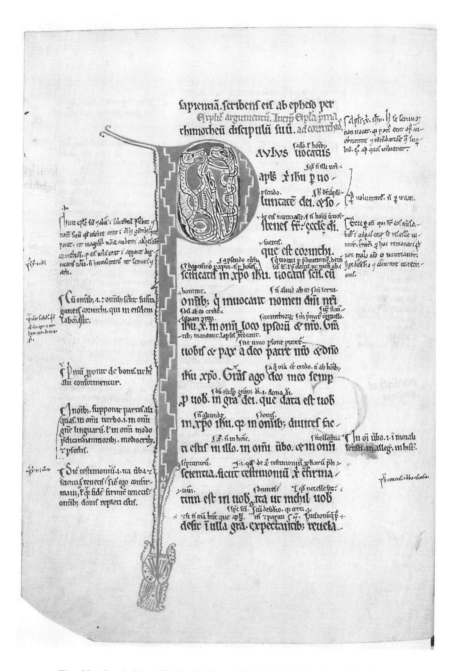

Fig. 32. Cambridge, Trinity College MS B.1.6 fol. 30v (cat. 50): 62%.

Fig. 33. Edinburgh. National Library of Scotland MS 6121, back cover and chemise (cat. 12): 32%.

Fig. 34. Oxford, Bodleian Library MS Bodley 395, inside front board and detached pastedown (cat. 14): 31%.

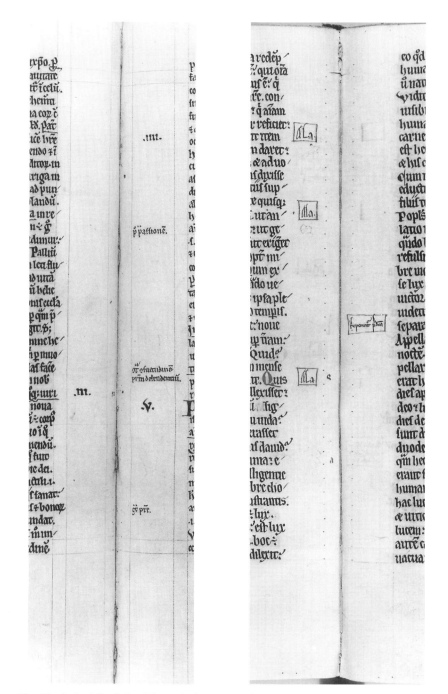

Fig. 35. Oxford, Bodleian Library MS
Bodley 371 fols. 52v–53 (cat. 19): 51%.

Fig. 36. Oxford, Balliol College MS 39
fols. 46v–47 (cat. 20): 45%.

INTRODUCTION

The Abbey of St. Mary and St. Chad was founded at Buildwas, Shropshire, in 1135 by Roger de Clinton, Bishop of Chester. It was at first a Savigniac house, but became Cistercian when the Savigniac and Cistercian orders merged in 1147.[1] It was not well endowed, and the history of its early years is obscure. It was under Ranulf, Abbot of Buildwas from 1155 to 1187 that the Abbey prospered. The surviving buildings, which are considerable,[2] mainly date from Ranulf's Abbacy, and the evidence presented by the surviving books also suggests that it was he who instituted the acquisition of books for the monastery. The Buildwas books have not previously been studied,[3] though Dr. Neil Ker identified 36 books from the Abbey[4] to which Prof. Andrew Watson added a further three.[5] This then comprised the second largest group of books to survive from an English Cistercian house, second only to Fountains, from which Ker identified 39 books,[6] and to which Watson also added three.[7] During the course of the present study, six books rejected by Ker have been re-established as books once at Buildwas,[8] and four more have been newly identified as such.[9] This brings the current total to 49 books;[10] and it is to be hoped that the publication of this study may lead to the identification of more.

No medieval lists of the books at Buildwas have so far been discovered. The only evidence of this sort is contained in the early fourteenth-century *Registrum Anglie de Libris Doctorum et Auctorum Veterum*.[11] Of 111 texts listed in the *Registrum* as having been found at Buildwas, only 18 can now be identified among the extant books.[12] But the surviving books contain over 150 texts (excluding service books and glossed books of the Bible) that were not among those for which the *Registrum* compilers were searching, and a few texts survive that were on the list but overlooked by the compilers. It is tempting to infer from this evidence that Buildwas must have contained a notable collection of books, of sufficient size and reputation to have made it worth while for the Friars to have

---

[1] D. Knowles and R.N. Hadcock, *Medieval Religious Houses, England and Wales*, 2nd edn. (London, 1971), 116; Chibnall, *VCH*, 50–59; L. Butler and C. Given-Wilson, *Medieval Monasteries of Great Britain* (London, 1979), 160–161.
[2] See Chibnall, *VCH*, 58, and two photographs, one an aerial view of the site and another of the interior of the church; also Butler and Given-Wilson, 160–161, and one photograph of the church from the cloister foundations.
[3] But see Chibnall, *VCH*, 51, 55–56, and Cheney 1953, 377 (1973, 332-3 and passim). Each gives a brief account of the surviving books as far as they were then known.
[4] Ker, *MLGB*, 14–15.
[5] Watson, *MLGB supplement*, 5.
[6] Ker, *MLGB*, 14–15.
[7] Watson, *MLGB supplement*, 5.
[8] Trinity B.1.12, B.1.13, B.1.14, B.1.32, B.1.33, B.3.16, all having once belonged to Master Robert Amiclas.
[9] Trinity B.1.6, B.1.10, B.2.30; CUL Add. 4079.
[10] One book, which was bound at Buildwas as one volume, is now dispersed among three books which were rebound in the seventeenth century: Lambeth 488, 457 and 456. They are described separately in the catalogue, bringing the total to 51.
[11] See Rouse & Rouse for the published text and an exhaustive commentary on it.
[12] See below, 262–265.

included it in their survey. But this must remain speculative.[13] The inconsistency with which the texts were recorded, however, may reflect with greater truth the fact that the books were dispersed throughout the monastery when the compilers visited it, and not all were located during their inspection. Physical evidence of use (for example, bosses on bindings, stress marks added to texts and readers' marginal notes) confirms the researcher's expectation that the books were kept in a variety of places during their medieval lives.

Of the 49 books described here as once having been at Buildwas, considerably fewer than half (15) were certainly made there, though up to ten further books may have had a Buildwas origin. And while these home-produced books are characteristically Cistercian, and certain books can be shown to have been produced by recognisable groups of scribes, there are no features that can be described as distinctive and peculiar to Buildwas in their design and execution. Many books are identifiable as from Buildwas solely by means of surviving ex libris inscriptions, while others can be linked with these by means of common scribes and/or annotators. A total of 22 volumes containing glossed books of the bible were certainly gifts to the monks, as was Bodley 371, and many other texts, often copied into small booklets which were later bound into single volumes at Buildwas, could not have been copied there by reason of date alone. An unusual set of four rusted marks in trapezoid formation found on the back boards of all extant early bindings and on back endleaves, which were almost certainly left by one (or by two successive) chain attachments, may prove to be a useful piece of supporting evidence of a Buildwas provenance for books for which other evidence is suggestive rather than conclusive.[14] The practice evident in a few books, especially those bound in the later twelfth century, of marking-up the sewing stations in each quire by pricking from the back of the quire to the front, sometimes omitting a mark for the upper kettle stitch because it was exactly level with the top ruled line, may similarly prove to be a useful piece of corroborative evidence.[15]

The Buildwas books are distinguished by having among their number two which are inscribed with the date of copying. The earlier of the two is also the earliest English book to be precisely dated: Christ Church 88, Augustine's Homilies on the Gospel of John, copied in 1167 (cat. 1). The second is Harley 3038, a glossed copy of Leviticus and John with extensive prefatory passages on good and evil and on the virtues (cat. 9). It is dated 1176. Both dates fall well within the Abbacy of Ranulf, and it is quite possible that they were commissioned by him. Research has confirmed that both were written at Buildwas rather than simply for the monastery, and that books were being made there from the 1160s onwards.[16] The surviving books reflect a more or less continuous campaign of book production and acquisition from this period until the early to mid-thirteenth century, after which a different though equally interesting involvement with books is evident. But inscriptions in some Buildwas books, for example those now at Balliol College, Oxford, demonstrate that some were already on the market, probably in Oxford, by the early fifteenth century.[17] Another group consisting largely of an almost complete set of glossed books were, on the

---

[13] For a complete list of surviving texts see below, 266–272.
[14] Sheppard 1995, 196 and fig. 8.
[15] Sheppard 1995, 190–192.
[16] Sheppard 1990, 193–204.
[17] Balliol 35A, 39, 40, 150, 173B, 229.

1

evidence of late medieval inscriptions, at Buildwas until at least the mid-fifteenth century, and remained together to be given to Trinity College, Cambridge by Archbishop Whitgift.[18]

The earliest books c.1160–1170 (cat. 1–8)

Insufficient evidence survives to allow us to identify any distinctive pattern of book manufacture during this first phase. Some books are copied by one scribe, some by many, but when one scribe copied the entire text, he also executed his own rubrics and initials. Trinity B.1.3 (cat. 4), copied by multiple scribes, is witness to organised rubricating and correction, and Trinity B.14.5 (cat. 3) demonstrates quite clearly that scribes were being trained during this period. The hands of only two scribes, however, the 'master scribe' and the 'flyleaf scribe', seem to reflect an attempt to achieve a common or 'house' style of writing. There are no surviving bindings from this period, and the evidence of lost bindings has been considerably obscured by later rebinding. However the endleaves of Trinity B.1.3 (cat. 4) and the slightly later Harley 3038 (cat. 9) show beyond doubt that binding was being carried out at Buildwas from the outset.

It is not surprising that five of the eight surviving early texts are patristic: the Christ Church Augustine (which provides a distinctive and dated anchor to which the others in the group can be linked), and four by Gregory (the *Cura Pastoralis, Dialogues, Moralia in Job* and sermons on Ezechiel).[19] Four of these five books are all satisfactorily linked both to each other and securely to a 'scriptorium' at Buildwas.[20] Cats. 6 and 7 contain *Lives of Saints* and an Epistle by Jerome on the Assumption of the Virgin, the second of these (BL Add. 11881) written in a hand not unlike that of the Christ Church volume. Cat. 8 (William of Malmesbury, *De Gestis Regum Anglorum*) is the first surviving witness of what was to become a growing interest in contemporary writers. It is possible that this reflects the guiding influence of Abbot Ranulf but in general, historical texts do not figure to any marked extent in the surviving books. On the evidence of the *Registrum*, however, the monastery's stock of patristic texts was far stronger than the few surviving texts alone would suggest.

The single quire now bound at the end of Trinity O.7.9 (cat. 25, booklet 5), if copied at Buildwas as the scribal hands suggest, is witness to another activity during this period, namely the compilation of compendia of letters, dicta and excerpts from patristic and other authorities.

The later twelfth century c.1170–1200 (cat. 9–19)

Books made at Buildwas during the remainder of the twelfth century now present themselves as three sub-groups, each linked among themselves by scribes and, to a certain extent, by the texts they contain. The first, slightly earlier group

---

[18] Trinity B.1.1, B.1.6, B.1.10, B.1.11, B.1.12, B.1.13. B.1.14, B.1.31. B.1.32, B.1.33, B.1.34, B.1.35, B.1.36, B.1.39, B.2.6, B.2.15, B.3.15, B.3.16, B.4.3. See Sheppard, 1988, 281–288.
[19] See Appendix, however, for the list of patristic texts found at Buildwas by the compilers of the *Registrum*. Even this list was not exhaustive. We know, for example, that Buildwas owned a copy of Gregory's *Moralia in Job* (Lambeth 109; cat. 2) but it was not recorded in the *Registrum*.
[20] Sheppard 1990.

(cat. 9–10) comprises the dated glossed Leviticus and John (Harley 3038, 1176; cat. 9), the only glossed book so far known to have been copied at Buildwas, and the datable fragmentary Missal (CUL 4079, cat. 10). Liturgical evidence indicates a date for the latter of 1174–1202, but the scribal hands and the decoration suggest a fairly early date within this period. It is the only liturgical book from Buildwas that survives, though leaves from an apparently unfinished Missal were used in the binding of Bodley 395, of which only one leaf survives as the (detached) pastedown. The origin of CUL 4079 at Buildwas is not beyond doubt, but on the evidence of additions and emendations it was certainly used there.

Balliol 229 (cat. 11), Edinburgh 6121 (cat. 12) and Pembroke 154 (cat. 13) share scribes and initial makers among them. They are all miscellanies, the kind of content that Prof. Christopher Cheney described as characteristically Cistercian.[21] Here the texts are mainly patristic: Jerome, Augustine, Cyprian, and Anselm, but in Pembroke 154, the evidence clearly indicates a last-minute decision to add at the beginning and end of the book, several texts by contemporary writers: Peter of Blois's *De Transfiguratione Domini* and *De Conversione Sancti Pauli*, Peter of Celles's D*e Claustrali Disciplina*, together with Roger of Byland's *Lac Parvulorum*, written to Gilbert of Hoyland, and a prayer to a guardian angel: *Oratio ad Sanctum Angelum Dei*. The presence of these texts and the nature of their last-minute addition would seem to indicate an active search for new and relevant texts both at home and in France and is, perhaps, indicative of a more active intellectual environment than the lack of any known Buildwas authors or preachers might suggest.[22]

These interests and activities are all reflected in texts in the surviving books made at Buildwas towards the end of the twelfth century. This third sub-group, consisting of Bodley 395 (cat. 14), St. John's D.2 (cat. 15), Bodley 730 (cat. 16) and Trinity B.2.30 (cat. 17), shares a different group of scribes who were less careful than their predecessors, and produced books which, in appearance, would certainly not have pleased the 'master scribe' of Christ Church 88. The texts copied by these scribes include Isidore's *Ethymologiae* and Aelred of Rievaulx's *Speculum Caritatis*, but also two works on early Greek monasticism: Cassian's *Regula* and *Decem Collationes*, and Palladius's *Vitae Sanctorum Patrum*, known as the *Lausiac History*. The book containing this last text (Trinity B.2.30; cat. 17) is attributed to Buildwas for the first time on the evidence of its scribes and rubricators. Also part of this group are two books which may have been copied at Buildwas, but if so, not by any scribes so far identified in other books. They may have been acquired by gift or even purchase. One contains a text which complements those of Cassian and Palladius: it is Hugh of Fouilly's *De Claustro* (Lambeth 107; cat. 18). The other is an early copy of Peter Cantor's Sermons (Bodley 371, cat. 19) which seems possibly to have been made in France. Both books are known to have been at Buildwas at the end of the twelfth century because of the ex libris inscriptions of that period which they still contain.

Of the eleven books in this later twelfth-century group, seven retain an early, if not an original, binding and four bear evidence of systematic pricking near the

---

[21] Cheney 1953, 379–380 (1973, 336–7).
[22] See, however, Lambeth 488 for William of Lafford, who just might have been a Buildwas author.

spinefolds to indicate the position of sewing stations (i.e. 'marking-up').[23] The group also contains the only two Buildwas books in which there are surviving colour notes for the initials: Pembroke 154 (cat. 13) and St. John's D.2 (cat. 15).

The early thirteenth century c.1200–1230 (cat. 20–23)

Books copied at Buildwas during the early thirteenth century are by no means as handsome as those made in the first years of the monastery's output, though there was manifestly a continuing effort to expand its book holdings. The four books in this group seem, however, to represent the last major book-copying campaign. The effort, enthusiasm even, that was put into the decoration of the books, especially Balliol 150 (cat. 22) is evident, though quality seems to have fallen well short of that aspired to; compare, for example, the early thirteenth-century version in Balliol 150 (fol. 2v; fig. 27) of a seated Abbot (St. Bernard) and its source, a drawing in the late twelfth-century Lambeth 107 (fol. 84v; fig. 29). Two of the four books surviving from the early thirteenth century share scribes and initial makers: Balliol 40 and 150, whose scribe also seems to have acted as a librarian, writing the monastery's ex libris and a list of contents on an endleaf of a composite volume (Trinity B.1.29; see below). Balliol 39 was not certainly made at Buildwas but there appears to have been Buildwas input into its decoration. These three books contain exclusively contemporary texts: Alexander Nequam's commentary on the Song of Songs (Balliol 39 and 40; cat. 20, 21), and the Sermons of Bernard of Clairvaux (Balliol 150; cat. 22). The fourth in this group is Lambeth 73 (cat. 23) which contains principally William of Newburgh's *Historia Rerum Anglicarum* and *Sermons*, and, at the end, *Pastor Hermae*. As in the case of Bodley 371, it cannot be said with certainty that this last book was made at Buildwas and it may have been an import.

These survivors constitute only a tiny proportion of recent or contemporary texts found at Buildwas by the compilers of the *Registrum* (see Appendix), and our picture of book acquisition and intellectual life of the Buildwas monks in the late twelfth and early thirteenth centuries must take the evidence of this vital witness into account. The monks were, for example, the owners of several texts by Hugh and Richard of St. Victor[24] and, not surprisingly, of many more of Bernard of Clairvaux's writings than have survived or have to date been identified.

At about the time of the copying of the four books just considered, there seems also to have been the beginning of a re-direction of effort in the sphere of scholarly activity at Buildwas. Shorter texts, some of which may have been a part of the monastery's collection for some time and others perhaps newly copied or acquired, were collected and bound together as compilations (cat. 24–28). Trinity B.1.29 (cat. 24) is one such book and the earliest, containing principally a mixture of patristic and contemporary scholarly texts copied during the twelfth century. The main scribe of Balliol 40 and 150, evidently acting as a librarian, wrote the monastery's ex libris and a list of contents in this book, and this fact usefully indicates the date of the beginning of this new activity. Many of the texts in Trinity B.1.29 were copied by scribes with continental, scholarly hands, originally,

---

[23] One of these is Balliol 229 which has lost its early binding. The marking-up therefore provides vital evidence about the earlier binding.

[24] Andrew of St. Victor's *Commentary on Kings and Chronicles* survives in Trinity B.1.29 (cat. 24 booklet 3).

perhaps, for their own use. The schools origin of some of these texts raises the possibility that they came to Buildwas as part of the gift of Master Robert Amiclas, the donor of Buildwas's still largely complete set of glossed books of the Bible, though even if this were the case, none is written in his hand or annotated by him.

Trinity O.7.9. (cat. 25) is a more wide-ranging compilation than B.1.29, containing one fragmentary text, perhaps copied at Buildwas during the early stages of book production, together with (among other unattributed texts and sermons and epistolary formulae) other schools texts: Peter Comestor's sermons, a short work by Alexander Nequam, *De Utensilibus* and Boethius's *De Sophisticis Elenchis*. The interest in sermons, those of others and resources for writing one's own, over-rides all other interests in many of these later books. The slightly later Lambeth 477 (cat. 29; see below) is the *ne plus ultra* of such books. They are all small (none larger than *c*.230 x 150mm and some considerably smaller), and those copied in the thirteenth century are written in a multitude of small, rapid and untidy hands. Little or no attention is paid to presentation or clarity; the importance clearly lay in the texts themselves.

One further compilation survives, now itself dispersed among three books in Lambeth Palace Library as MSS 488, 457, 456 (cat. 26–28). Among the varied texts once in this volume are almost the only classical texts known to survive from Buildwas (extracts from Seneca's letters, Priscian Minor and Aristotle, *Praedicamenta*)[25], Boethius's *De Divisione* and *De Topicis*,[26] the *De Sex Principiis* (wrongly attributed to Gilbert Porretanus), as well as selected letters of Jerome, Aelred's *De Onere Babilonis* and so on. Buried amidst these closely-packed texts is a newly discovered name, that of William of Lafford. He appears to be the author of a sermon entitled *De Muliere Chananaea* (Lambeth 488 fols. 101–106). The explicit expresses the joy of the author on his having completed his work, and its presence in the Buildwas copy suggests that William of Lafford may have been a Buildwas monk, and even that this copy is in his own hand.[27] If this were the case, he was also the scribe of all the preceding items in this booklet, and he both annotated other items in this booklet, thereby indicating an interest in Seneca, and added a paragraph to Lambeth 457 (cat. 27), originally a part of the thirteenth-century compilation. But regardless of identity of this particular scribe, the evidence provided by his contributions to the composite volume and by the varied contributions on the part of other scribes suggests on balance that the components of this book were mainly, if not all, copied at Buildwas, by monks who were both copying and using the texts for study. If James was right in thinking that the virtually indecipherable notes in Lambeth 456 are indeed lecture notes, it may be that some Buildwas monks were studying formally, perhaps at Oxford where, by the early fifteenth century, it is clear that former Buildwas books were already appearing on the market.[28]

Trinity B.1.39 (cat. 39) is a similar compilation with a later thirteenth-century list of contents, but its texts (mainly glossed books of the Bible) belong with

---

[25] A commentary on Martianus Capella's *De Nuptiis* survives in Trinity B.1.29 (cat. 24 booklet 4).

[26] Boethius's *De Sophisticis Elenchis* survives in Trinity O.7.9 (cat. 25 booklet 4).

[27] Chibnall, *VCH*, 58 notes that there are records of an Abbot of Buildwas named William between *c*.1204 and *c*.1206 and another *c*.1263.

[28] Note that several of the texts in Lambeth 456 and the Boethius in Trinity O.7.9 were among those studied in the Trivium.

another group described below. It is entirely possible that the addition of a copy of the *De Interpretatione Nominum Hebraicorum*, copied by a thirteenth-century scribe, to Trinity B.3.15 (another glossed book, cat. 37), took place at Buildwas, making it into a sort of compilation. However there is now no recoverable evidence about the earlier binding of the book and it is uncertain exactly when the later text was bound with it.

The later thirteenth century c.1230–80 (cat. 29–31)

The transition to the later thirteenth century as manifest in the surviving books is seamless, since Lambeth 477 (cat. 29) contains, among texts copied during the earlier thirteenth century, a version of a Concordance not composed until the second half of the century. It is a curious but fascinating book, quite plainly put together as a handbook or encyclopaedia for preachers. Its first item is, most interestingly, *Pictor in Carmine*, a text described by M.R. James as 'containing the largest known collection of types and antitypes intended to be used for artists'.[29] Here, however, it is clear from the context that it also was found useful as a thematic source by those writing sermons. The book also contains other lists of themes for sermons including separate notes on virtues and vices, biblical texts for sermons, examples of sermons, Richard of Thetford's *Ars Praedicandi* and two biblical concordances each derived from the work of Hugh of St. Cher and later Dominicans.

If Lambeth 477 was copied or at least compiled at Buildwas, it is the latest and the last surviving Buildwas-made book. At about this time, the monks received, clearly with considerable pleasure, two luxurious, illuminated glossed books which probably came together to the monastery in 1277, though the evidence is indisputable only for one of them.[30] They are Balliol 35A and Balliol 173B (cat. 30 and 31), Peter Lombard's Glosses on the Psalms and the Pauline Epistles. These books, or at least Balliol 35A for which the evidence is plain, were clearly highly prized, since MS 35A, alone among the Buildwas books, still bears an elaborate, dated ex libris and ex dono inscription which includes the name of the donor (Walter the Palmer of Bridgnorth) and the name of the Abbot (William Tyrry), and which threatens anyone daring to remove it from Buildwas with excommunication. It is likely that MS 173B, a companion text made in the same milieu as MS 35A, was also given to the monks by Walter the Palmer, and that it, too, once bore the same inscription. The original endleaves, however, are now incomplete, though Langbaine seems to have seen, or knew of, a former Buildwas ex libris inscription. Even so, these two books were among six, all now at Balliol College, in which later ex libris and ex dono inscriptions written by Balliol librarians indicate that they were no longer at Buildwas in the early fifteenth century.

A further manifestation of the change in the use to which books were put at Buildwas during the later thirteenth century is the personal, alphabetical index created by a Buildwas monk during the last half, perhaps the last quarter, of the century. The index survives, pasted to the first leaf of Trinity B.14.5 (cat. 3; fig. 8), Gregory's *Cura Pastoralis*. His stylus working notes are still just legible on the last endleaf of the same book (fig. 9) and his distinctive notae are found in the

---

[29] 'Pictor in Carmine', *Archaeologia*, 94 (1951), 141.
[30] One other illuminated book from Buildwas has survived, also part of a gift: Trinity B.4.3 (cat. 43), one of Master Robert's glossed books.

margins in this and in other Buildwas books. An essential part of the process of constructing an index is numbering, both the leaves and/or pages and the chapters or other sub-sections of a larger work. While there is no other surviving index among the Buildwas books, there is ample evidence in the form of numbering in many of the surviving books of a widespread change in the way the books were used. Patristic texts such as Augustine's Sermons on St. John's Gospel (Christ Church 88, cat. 1), Gregory's *Moralia in Job* (Lambeth 109; cat. 2), the miscellanies of patristic writings in Balliol 229, Pembroke 154 and Edinburgh 6121 (cat. 11–13), works on monasticism such as Cassian's *Regula* and *Decem Collationes* (Bodley 730; cat. 16) and Hugh of Fouilloy's *De Claustro* (Lambeth 107: cat. 18), and more modern works such as Aelred's *Speculum Caritatis* (St. John's D. 2; cat. 15) and William of Newburgh's *Historia Rerum Anglicarum* (Lambeth 73; cat. 23) are among those works in which thirteenth-century Buildwas readers expressed their interest by inserting various types of numbering. From the viewpoint of the late twentieth century it is surprising to see in these books the struggle which attended the effort both to come to terms with Arabic numbers as against Roman numerals which are cumbersome (frequently we see a numerator mixing Arabic and Roman), and to devise a workable system of several numbers: leaf or page numbers, sub-section numbers (i.e. for chapter or epistle), and page-within-sub-section number (e.g. leaf 3 of chapter 5), by placing such numbers on different parts of the page. It is instructive about the way a medieval reader thought about his text, even a reader who needed to look things up and for whom reading from the beginning to the end as prescribed by St. Benedict was no longer the only way of using a book, that the idea of numbering pages, or even leaves, from the first to the last in a continuous sequence, simply did not occur to him. Among the Buildwas books, it is only in the long *Concordanciae Anglicanae*, composed in the later thirteenth-century and copied into Lambeth 477 (cat. 29), that the leaves, nearly 200 of them, are numbered consecutively. Even here, the numbering is not accurate, but a reader was able to use these leaf numbers to insert cross-references to additional passages which he himself wished to add but for which there was no space on the proper leaf.

Book production may have declined in the late thirteenth century at Buildwas, but scholarly reading was most certainly taking place, in the interests of preaching (it is worth reiterating that the text for which an index survives is the *Cura Pastoralis*), or of university study, but perhaps also for personal interest. The indexer, for example, annotated parts of William of Malmesbury's *De Gestis Regum Anglorum* (CUL Ii.2.3; see fig. 10). And it was he who, evidently acting as a librarian, wrote the lengthy and informative ex libris and ex dono inscription in Balliol 35A (fig. 11). Perhaps he, too, like William of Lafford, was a hitherto unsung Buildwas scholar.

Master Robert's glossed books (Cat. 32–51)

The set of glossed books from Buildwas is set apart from similar collections once held by other monastic houses both because of the number of books that have survived and because the original owner not only wrote his name on the flyleaf of Trinity B.1.11: 'Iste liber est magistri Roberti amiclas' (fig. 30), but annotated many of them copiously.[31] Master Robert's books range in date from

---

[31] See Sheppard 1988, 281–288, and Thomson 1995, 238–243.

*c.*1130–40 (Trinity B.1.10; cat. 44) which manifests the earliest form of the glossed text page layout identified by Dr. Christopher de Hamel, in which the text lines were pricked, ruled and written before the gloss lines were added ad hoc,[32] to *c.*1165, the date of a glossed copy of the Minor Prophets (Trinity B.4.3; cat. 43). Most of the others exemplify the more flexible form of the early layout, dating to around the middle of the twelfth century. But a few (Trinity B.1.35; cat. 34, B.1.32; cat 40, B.1.1; cat. 42, B.1.33; cat. 46, and B.1.36; cat. 48) exemplify the 'alternate line layout', in which the gloss lines are pricked and ruled and the text is written on alternate lines, a development which de Hamel dates to the years shortly after 1160.[33] Especially interesting is the evidence of one scribe who copied two glossed gospel texts, one using the old layout and one the new (Trinity B.1.11, cat. 45, and B.1.36, cat. 48), evidently equally at home with both. The evidence of the scribe of Trinity B.1.32 (cat. 40), however, presents a different picture. He began using the alternate line layout, but abandoned it part way through the copying, reverting to the old layout with gloss lines ruled independently from the text lines and only as needed.

Many of Robert's books seem to have originated in Northern France, but a few, including the latest, Trinity B.4.3 (cat. 43), were made in England. Master Robert was evidently collecting and using these books for a considerable period, perhaps beginning in Paris and, as Dr. Rodney Thomson has recently surmised, retiring to Buildwas where he continued to collect and use glossed books. He copiously annotated almost every volume and he wrote a list of titles, perhaps of texts he owned, at the end of Trinity B.1.6 (cat. 50). As Thomson observes, 'these books provide the only example presently known of a collection of teaching-texts belonging to a Parisian master of the twelfth century.'[34] Who Robert Amiclas was has yet to be established; his annotations, which include extensive additional glosses and excerpts, as well as corrections to text, gloss and punctuation, merit study by historians.

The evidence of these books, however, also provides much useful information about the production and circulation of common-or-garden glossed books during the twelfth century. Mention has already been made of the glimpse they provide of scribes who had to come to terms, some more successfully than others, with changing styles in page layout. Some glossed books include a miscellany of short passages and extracts, written by the main scribe and so intentionally a part of these particular copies. This suggests that glossed texts may sometimes have been copied to order with specified inclusions, or perhaps that masters copied and arranged their own additional texts (see Shrewsbury XII; cat. 51, and Trinity B.1.39 item 5; cat. 39). Others seemed to have been obtainable even though incomplete: Trinity B.1.33 (cat. 46) and Trinity B.1.13 (cat. 38) are examples, and in the latter case, Master Robert copied the missing text and most of the gloss himself, giving further weight to the possibility raised above that masters could and did sometimes make their own books. Less surprising is the evidence that glossed books were available without rubrics and/or initials (e.g. Trinity B.1.6; cat. 50 (see fig. 32) and B.3.16; cat. 36), or without glosses (e.g. Trinity B.1.39; cat. 39 item 4). Conversely, in Trinity B.4.3 (cat. 43), the English

---

[32] See de Hamel, *Glossed Books*, 14–27, for an authoritative account of the development of the page layouts of glossed texts.

[33] de Hamel, *Glossed Books*, 24.

[34] Thomson 1995, 241.

copy of the glossed Minor Prophets, the text was copied and the illuminated initials provided, before the prefaces and glosses.

It is to be expected that these glossed texts circulated and were first used in temporary, limp bindings, the quires perhaps simply tacketed and then looped together for ease of carrying about.[35] There is very little clear evidence about such matters in Robert's books, largely because they have all, with one exception, been rigidly rebound in recent centuries, and evidence is seldom visible. In the case of the glossed book still in a late twelfth-century binding (Shrewsbury XII; cat. 51), repairs made a century ago have had the same result. Possible tacket evidence has been noted here and there. A few of the glossed books have clear marking-up pricks, all including pricks for both kettle stitches, a practice observed in a number of Buildwas-made books in the later twelfth century. It is likely that all Master Robert's books were presented in temporary bindings, and that they were bound at the monastery at various times between the date of their donation and the end of the century, when most of the ex libris inscriptions that survive in these books were written.

It is not clear when the glossed books arrived at Buildwas. It is tempting to surmise that they had not arrived by 1176, when a glossed copy of Leviticus and John was copied at the monastery, as far as is known the only glossed book to have been made there. Master Robert's set contained both texts, though the glosses are not quite identical and the combined text also carries a selection of short prefatory texts. But they may have arrived very soon after this. What is much clearer is that although certain books from Buildwas, as we have seen, were already on the market in Oxford by the early fifteenth century, Master Robert's glossed books remained at Buildwas, virtually intact, until at least the end of the fifteenth century. The evidence for this is a deed copied into Trinity B.2.6 (cat. 32) in a late fifteenth-century hand and the doodled name 'Gnossal' in Trinity B.3.15 (cat. 37). John Gnossal was the Abbot of Buildwas in the second quarter of the fifteenth century. Since the books have remained together, what is true for B.2.6 and B.3.15 must be true for all. The exception is Shrewsbury XII. This was purchased by Shrewsbury School on the London book market in the early seventeenth century. There is nothing to indicate when or why this book became separated from the set, but it is encouraging to think that since it has survived separately from its original companions, others, recognisable by Master Robert's annotations, might yet surface.[36]

---

[35] For tackets, see Michael Gullick, 'From Scribe to Binder: Quire Tackets in Twelfth Century European Manuscripts', in J.L. Sharpe, ed., *The Compleat Binder – Studies in Book-making and Conservation, in Honour of Roger Powell* (Turnhout, 1996), 240–259. Evidence, or possible evidence, of tackets among the Buildwas books can be found in Trinity B.1.6, B.1.39, B.2.15, B.3.8, B.14.5 and Bodley 730.

[36] Missing from Robert's set are: Genesis, Chronicles, Esdras, Nehemiah, Job, Psalms, Baruch, Ezechiel, Daniel, Maccabees. It seems unlikely that he would have been without Genesis, Psalms and the other two major prophets. The New Testament is complete.

THE CATALOGUE

NOTES TO THE CATALOGUE

The books are described in the probable order of their acquisition by the monastery, with the exception of Master Robert's glossed books. These probably arrived during the last quarter of the twelfth century, but, as far as the catalogue is concerned, to have included them at this point would have interrupted the account of what seems to have been a continuous campaign of book production. They are therefore included after the two Lombard glosses (the last books known to have been acquired by the monks), and are described in the order of the books in the Vulgate, regardless of their estimated date of copying. Thirteenth-century compilations are described as thirteenth-century books.

1. Existing bindings have been briefly described, but greater emphasis has been given to the medieval bindings, existing or vanished.
2. The disposition of sewing stations and/or marking-up pricks is denoted between short vertical lines which indicate the head and tail of the spine, with distances given in mm. K denotes kettle stitch, and * the point of sewing to a sewing support, e.g.: (tail) I 29 K 50*78*81*45 K 28 I mm (head).
3. In measurements, height is always given first. 'Space ruled for writing' denotes the distance between the uppermost and the last lines, and between the innermost of the outer vertical bounding lines. Individual column widths are not given.
4. Under Pricking, the device 1→8 denotes the direction in which the pricking was done, in this case from front to back of the quire, regardless of the number of leaves in the quire. 8→1 denotes pricking in the reverse direction.
5. Page design diagrams are not to scale and are intended simply to convey characteristic page layouts at a glance. Dotted lines in these diagrams denote lines that are inconsistently ruled.
6. Some of the terms adopted or devised to facilitate the description of bindings and decorated initials are explained above. See Explanation of terms.
7. Square brackets [ ] in the headings denote post-medieval elements of a book. Elsewhere in the catalogue they denote missing text or a hypothetical restoration of missing text.

1. OXFORD, CHRIST CHURCH MS 88

Augustine, Sermons on St. John's Gospel　　　　　　　　**Date** 1167
Leaves i, 172
Foliation i, 1–172
Origin Buildwas　　　　　　　　　　　　　　　　　　　**Figs.** 1, 3, 6

This is the earliest dated English book. It has the appearance of a presentation
volume. The evidence of the greasy corners of leaves and marginal annotations
throughout in two distinctive fourteenth- or fifteenth-century hands (see fols. 2,
2v, 24) and the fact that it was rebound in the fourteenth or fifteenth century,
suggest that the book was much used. For added running sermon numbers, see
section VI below.

I PHYSICAL DESCRIPTION

Binding Rebound s.xiv/xv; spine rounded; possible repairs to front pastedown
and flyleaf; primary covering cracking along spine; opens well.

Endleaves

Front *Pastedown* Fol. 1 of separate bifolium in place, original, retained in the
rebinding; impressions of original binding eradicated by later pasting; a second
leaf (now partly torn away) pasted over the pastedown and part of the conjoint
flyleaf, a repair, after which an inscription in English written on it s.xvi med.,
much of this lost: '[Anno] *millessimo* quingentesi[mo] / T[W]illiams John Er[ ] /
warden [o]ur lady of Red[ ] / ther vestry [i]n the [ ] / gret & smalle [ ]st *with* st
chey[ ]et sa[ ]' (see below, Provenance). Other inscriptions: shelfmark E.3 (ink),
LXXXVIII (pencil) and 'G.Salteren J.C. Bristow*ensis*' (s.xvii); Christ Church
bookplate.

　　　Flyleaves Fol. 2 of separate bifolium (original, retained in the rebinding);
recto: 'Ex dono Georgii Salteren J.C. Bristowensis quondam huius Aedis
Commensalis' s.xvi/xvii; *verso*: list of initia s.xii (see below, Contents).

Back *Flyleaves* Probably fols. 1–3 of a separate quaternion, now excised to
stubs, probably blank.

　　　Pastedown Fol. 4 of a quaternion in place, not necessarily the original,
blank.

Sewing stations Now 5, not marked-up: (tail) I 26 K 32*76*76*75*26 K 26 I mm
(head); formerly 3, not marked-up: (tail) approx. I 58 K 47*105*105*41 K 54 I
mm (head), evidence of sewing thread impressions fol. 116.

Sewing All-along with thin white S-twist thread; earlier all-along, with S-twist
thread.

Sewing supports 5 split tawed skin supports, approx. 11mm wide. Earlier, 3.

Lacing path Laced into the boards from channels in the outer faces, then
channels on the inner faces *c.*75mm long, the channels of the outer two pairs
converging (V I V pattern). Secured by wedges.

Endbands Tawed skin cores, rolled where sewn but laced in flat, *c.*7mm wide.
Laced into the boards at *c.*30° through channels in the outer faces then on the
inner faces, ends secured with wedges. Sewn first with thick buff S-twist thread
and tied down in the centre of each quire; then sewn to primary covering with
fine red and blue S-twist thread over 2 cores of thread, one along the top and
another along the base of the endbands. Both sewings have broken down, but
the endbands are intact.

Tabs None.

Spine lining 6 strips of parchment, mostly blank but with some fragments of writing (s.xiii) visible between each sewing support and between top and bottom supports and head and tail of book, with remains of crusted, opaque paste bearing impressions of spine folds (visible where quires missing). These are pasted to the outer face of each board under the primary covering.

Boards Wood, 416 x 294 x 15mm; boards slightly cushion-shaped, with edges sharply bevelled; leaves probably once flush, the boards now projecting *c.*3mm at the upper edge, 1mm at the lower edge.

Primary covering Rectangular pieces of discoloured skin, white and faded pinkish-brown (probably once red), of various sizes sewn together with white S-twist thread, pasted to boards; sections of covering lost in area of former chain staples and pins; corners tongued and mitred. Tie marks across spine and fore-edges, front and back.

Fastenings 2 tawed skin straps 23mm wide, 3mm and 4.5mm thick, dyed deep pink, each held in place in recesses in fore-edge by triangular-headed nails; 2 corresponding pin holes in outer surface back board, 130mm from fore-edge and 100mm and 110mm from upper and lower edges respectively.

Chemise None present. Clear traces remain (fragments of flesh side of skin) of chemise pocket, 160mm wide, on pastedown and covering turn–ins of back board; sewing impressions along outer edge of pastedown and primary cover are also evidence of a former chemise. No similar marks on front board, but clear, clean line of pocket 130–140mm wide visible on leaf pasted over the front pastedown (see above, Front pastedown). Shelfmark E3 (s.xvii) on this clean space shows the chemise was removed at or before that date.

Bosses Large square holes with green traces at each corner of both boards, all set between 65 and 75mm from the nearest edges of the boards, indicate the earlier position of brass bosses.

Chain attachments **1**) A rectangular slot 20mm long surrounded by a rust-corroded area of exposed board at lower edge of front board 105mm from spine edge and a corresponding rusted patch and groove in the inner surface of the board (on the pastedown) indicate the position of a lost chain attachment. Above the marks on the inner surface are 3 small nail holes in a row (with one remaining nail; see below 3); **2**) 2 projecting brass nails without heads at lower fore-edge of back board, 12 and 42mm from fore–edge, and corresponding holes with greenish edges on inner surface indicate the position of a lost chain attachment; **3**) lower edge of back board 95mm from spine edge, clear impression of a lost stirrup-type chain attachment, rusted, once held in place by two nails disposed vertically, the upper nail extant. Leaves protected by a roughly cut piece of white skin held in place by three brass, round-headed nails.

Labels 14 small nail holes in rectangular formation, *c.*40 x 68mm, to the right of centre on the back board indicate the former position of a label. There are no impressions and the area is not cleaner than the surrounding covering, so the label was probably on the chemise. Remains of a small paper label at top of spine with shelfmark 88 and extant, newer printed label with shelfmark.

Structure of Book

Parchment Evenly coloured, well prepared, hair layer entirely removed, leaves pliable to handle, a nap on both sides (except at lower corners where handling has worn it away); some careful repairs at the beginning of the book, e.g. fols. 7v–8.

2

Collation 1 (outer bifolium only extant), 2–18^8, 19^8 (8 excised), 20^8 (1 excised), 21–22^8, 23^4, (2 bifolia, fols. 1–3 excised, 4 is pastedown). Quires missing between qq. 16 and 17.

Quire nos. None. Leaves of each quire lettered, though many letters trimmed especially in the first and last quires; fols. 1v–8: a–o in lower margin very near spinefold (very clear in q. 17). Letters probably made when the original binding replaced in s. xiv/xv.

Catchwords Q. 18 only; others possibly lost in trimming.

Page Layout
Dimensions
Page 412 x 302mm.
Space ruled for writing 290–293 x 206mm.
Columns 2.
Pricking Leaves folded, 1→8 (except q. 13 lower margin 8→1), outer margin only, template used.
Ruling In brown and in grey, very regular and neat, following the pricking.
Lines per page 41; fols. 171v–172: 44; fol. 172v: 43 (the extra lines of text added on lines ruled ad hoc).
Page design

fols. 1–11

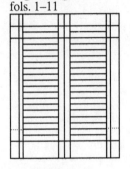

fols 11v–172v

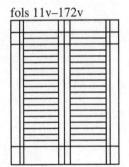

II SCRIBES
One scribe wrote the text throughout in a very fine upright and regular hand, round and with a large loop to g, and using the punctus flexus punctuation mark throughout.
A second scribe probably wrote the ex libris inscription on fol. 1 and a third added the table of initia on verso of first endleaf in a less regular hand s.xii ex.

III DECORATION, RUBRICS AND ARTICULATION OF TEXT
Text initials Capitula fol. 1v have 1-line capitals alternately red and green. Elsewhere, brown ink capitals written by the text scribe.
Minor initials None.
Major decorated initials Rubbed red offset on title page at spine margin indicates that a full page initial **I**(ntuens) opened sermon 1, leaf now missing; subsequently about 90 (originally about 124) very fine penwork initials, 5–6 lines high (letters with stems often very much taller). Some are quite plain and of one colour (e.g. fols. 31v, 126), some of one colour with simple self-coloured flourishes (e.g fol. 10v), some of one colour but flourished with brown ink and sometimes also with ochre (e.g. fols. 19v, 45), and others of one colour but

3

elaborately flourished and decorated with self-colour, with symmetrical designs of folded leaves and interlocking petal motifs. The sequence of colours is mostly consistent: blue with ochre, red, green, ochre.

Historiated initials None.

Display script Fol. 22v (sermon 9): (A)**ssit** in small red mixed 1–line capitals; fol. 81v (sermon 29): (Q)**uod sequit*ur* de** in small mixed 1–line capitals, the words alternately red and black, as are the words in minuscule on the next 5 lines. Elsewhere opening word or words are sometimes written in small rustic capitals, but are hardly distinguishable from the text minuscule.

Titles etc. No running titles; incipits and explicits in red by text scribe.

Title page Fol. 1v: 'Aurelii Augustini Doctoris Hiponiensis ep*iscop*i omelie i*n* ew*a*ngelium d*omi*ni ie*h*su *se*cu*n*du*m* iohann*em* q*u*as ip*s*e colleq*u*endo pri*mus* ad p*opulu*m habuit et inter loq*u*endu*m* a notariis acceptas (*v*el ex) eo q*u*o habite sunt ordine v*er*bum ex v*er*bo p*o*st*e*a dictavit' in 2-line mixed display capitals, the first 6 words with letters alternately red, blue and green, and subsequently with words alternately green, red and blue. An ochre line marks the left margin, and a very simple scroll design, also in ochre, marks the right margin; ex libris and date written in minuscule above.

IV CONTENTS

Table of contents Fol. i verso: 'Hic notant*ur* initia evang*eli*or*um* *se*cu*n*dum ioh*a*nn*em* q*ua*e legunt*ur* in eccle*s*ia p*er* annu*m* ut expositiones eor*um* facile inveniri possint in hoc volumine' followed by a list of 63 initia of readings used in the church through the year, with the number of the relevant sermon in red beside each.

Main texts Augustine, *Sermons on St. John's Gospel.*

1. Fol. 2: *Omelie in Evangelium Domini Iehsu Secundum Iohannem.* Begins imperfectly in sermon 3: '/lite e*ss*e tenebre, nolite e*ss*e infideles iniqui rapaces, avari amatores *se*c*u*li.' The end of sermon 48 (fol. 122v) to the middle of sermon 77 (fol. 123) is missing: 'unde participant n*on* e*ss*e de*u*s. Si lumina...illis invisibilis loquebatur. Paraclit*us* aute*m*'. The end of sermon 102 and the beginning of 103 (fols. 145v–146) are also missing: 'hec inq*u*it in p*r*overbiis locutus su*m* vob*is* ve/...enim ut sidera non cogerent.'

Text ends fol. 172: 'etia*m* ipse compellerer meu*m* te*r*minare sermonem. Expliciunt omelie *s*ancti augustini yponiensis ep*iscop*i in e*v*angeliu*m* *iehsu christi* *se*cu*n*du*m* iohann*em* evang*e*listam'. *CCSL* XXXVI.

2. Fol. 172, a sermon of Pseudo Augustine: 'Aug*ustinus*. Cotidie eucaristie comunione*m* accipere nec laudo nec vitup*er*o...magis gravari dico sacre co*m*munionis p*er*ceptione q*u*am purificari. Sermo *s*ancti augustini ep*iscop*i de lazaro q*ua*rtiduano *s*ancti iohann*em* [sic]. Licet o*mn*es v*i*rtutes q*ua*s in te*rr*is'. Ends fol. 172v: 'Et ne quid quisqu*am* deesse diceret resurgenti presentibus cunctis agit gratias redemptori.' *PL* XXXIX, 1929–31.

V ORIGIN AND PROVENANCE

Ex Libris Fol. 2v: 'Liber sancte marie de bildewas, scriptus anno ab incarnatione d*omi*ni m° c° lx° vi° i.'

Secundo folio Original fol. 2 lost; present fol. 2 is opening of text [no]lite esse; fol. 3: nati sunt.

The book was written at Buildwas by a scribe who also wrote part of Trinity B.1.3. This scribe almost certainly made the fine initials throughout the book;

the quality of these initials is commensurate with that of the scribal hand, and in several initials some of the flourishing is executed in what appears to be exactly the same colour of ink (e.g. fol. 124). One initial by the same scribe survives in Lambeth 109, where the text is written by a different scribe whose hand is related and whose work at Buildwas is certain. This text is recorded in the *Registrum* as being held at Buildwas.

In view of the later history of the book, Jeremy Griffiths infers that the inscription on the front pastedown refers to the church of St. Mary Redcliffe in Bristol where the book may have been chained. George Salterne of Bristol matriculated and entered Christ Church on 23 March 1581–2, aged 14, was admitted barrister at Law, Middle Temple 1590 as son and heir to William of Bristol (*Alumniae Oxoniensis*, ed. by Joseph Foster (Oxford, 1892), IV, 1303). The gift of this book and a two-volume printed bible in French to Christ Church is recorded in the library benefactions book for 1621.

VI NOTES
Medieval sermon numbers The indexer of Trinity B.14.5 (q.v.) made one of his characteristic nota signs in the outer margin on fol. 147, and it is possible that it was he who also entered running sermon numbers on the upper right corners of each recto to fol. 122 (sermon 48). Another hand, s.xv?, added running chapter numbers of John's Gospel over the central margin of rectos and versos and in the margin where the change occurs, indicating the text on which the current sermon is a commentary. This numerator includes the Pseudo Augustine sermon. Occasional large stylus notes (e.g. fols. 1v, 76) may also have been made by the indexer.

VII BIBLIOGRAPHY AND PLATES
G.W. Kitchin, *Catalogus Codicum MSS qui in Bibliotheca Aedis Christi apud Oxoniensis Adservantur* (Oxford, 1867), cat. Latin 88; Ker, *MLGB*, 15; N.R. Ker, *English Manuscripts in the Century after the Norman Conquest* (Oxford, 1960), 38–9; A.G. Watson, *Dated and Datable Manuscripts c.435–1600 in Oxford Libraries* (Oxford, 1984), II, pl.75; C. de Hamel, *A History of Illuminated Manuscripts* (London, 1986), pl. 85; Sheppard 1990, 198.

The author is most grateful to Jeremy Griffiths for sight of the description of this manuscript to be published in his forthcoming catalogue of Christ Church Manuscripts.

2. LONDON, LAMBETH PALACE LIBRARY MS 109
Gregory, Moralia in Job books 6–10, fragment   Date *c.*1160–70
Leaves [i paper], 52, [i paper]
Foliation Not foliated in present state; medieval foliation 1–104, once beginning on fol. 1 of text (now missing, as are many other leaves). This foliation used in the description below.
Origin Buildwas   Fig. 2

I PHYSICAL DESCRIPTION
Binding Rebound s.xvii–xviii, since rebacked, refurbished 1958 (note on back pastedown).
Endleaves
  Front *Pastedown* **1)** Single leaf of laid paper in place, once fol. 1 of a bifolium,

now damaged at joint and repaired, blank; **2**) original pastedown now detached, see below.

Flyleaves **1**) Single leaf of laid paper, once conjoint with pastedown (see above); watermark: fleur-de-lis in a crest surmounted by a crown, WR monogram below; blank except for stamped number (recto); **2**) fols. 1–2 of q. 1; fol. 1 was original pastedown, now detached; recto: remains of grainy paste, impressions of earlier primary covering turn–ins with mitred, possibly tongued, corners and irregular edges, marks of 2 sewing support channels (see below), and green-rimmed marks at fore-edge indicating former presence of fastening; also pencil shelfmark; verso: ink inscription s.xvii: '#J.ii.8 fol. vol. 57'; stylus inscription now erased and virtually illegible, beginning 'liber monac[horum]'; fol. 2: blank except for title in late hand; fol. 2v: a preface (s.xii ex) and ex libris inscription.

Back *Flyleaves* **1**) Last 3 leaves of the last quire were probably intended as pastedown and two flyleaves, but a short text was added to the free leaves; final quarter of fol. 7 of last quire blank, inscription in lower margin s.xv: 'Nunc finem feci da mihi quod merui'; **2**) Fol. 8 of last quire was the original pastedown, now detached; *recto*: outer half very white where once probably covered by chemise pocket, smudged inscription s.xiii, 'A*utem* dico vobis super'; square central hole just beyond edge of chemise pocket mark, probably made by a former pin; *verso*: grainy paste remains, impressions of earlier primary covering turn-ins and sewing support channels, as on front detached pastedown; **3**) Laid paper leaf, once conjoint with pastedown (see below) with watermark as for front flyleaves, blank.

Pastedown **1**) Original pastedown is now detached (see above). **2**) Single leaf of laid paper in place, probably once conjoint with flyleaf, now repaired at joint, blank except for refurbishment note.

Sewing stations Now 6; impressions on detached pastedowns indicate that earlier, probably originally, there were 2: (tail) | 117*109*100 | mm (head) approx. No evidence about kettle stitch; pastedowns now trimmed at upper and lower margins.

Sewing Resewn; no evidence of earlier sewing visible.

Sewing supports Now 6 cords; impressions on detached parchment pastedowns indicate that the book was earlier, probably originally, sewn on 2 supports,

Lacing path Over outer edges of boards, through to inner face, fixed under pastedowns. Earlier supports laced parallel through long tunnels, the total length of the lacing paths *c*.110mm (close to half the width of the surviving pastedowns).

Endbands Present at head and tail, replacements, sewn with discoloured thread; no clear evidence about former endbands.

Tabs None present; no other evidence.

Spine lining None present; no other evidence.

Boards Pasteboard, 335 x 230 x 5mm.

Primary covering Now brown calf, with pairs of deeply impressed, narrow blind fillets parallel with and close to edges and 45mm from spine, a stamped gilt crest (mitre and pallium) front and back, and a gold fillet along all edges of covers front and back. The title and library shelfmark, also in gold, are on rebacked spine. Impressions on both detached pastedowns indicate an earlier, probably the original, cover probably of white tawed skin, with irregular, wide turn-ins and mitred and tongued corners.

Fastenings 2 pairs of greenish holes in centre of fore-edge of front detached pastedown indicate that there was earlier, almost certainly originally, a central strap fastening *c.*22mm wide; a mark on the detached back pastedown was probably left by a square pin, *c.*100mm from fore-edge.

Chemise None present; clean outer half of original back pastedown (see above) indicates former presence of a chemise.

Bosses None present; no other evidence.

Chain attachments None present; no other evidence.

Labels None.

Structure of Book

Parchment Thick, uniformly coloured though yellowish, good nap on both hair and flesh sides; many holes (e.g. fols. 8, 9, 71, 92), most leaves in last quire (fols. 98–102) with holes, probably flaymarks (see also fols. 20–22), and some parchment maker's repairs (fol. 20), contemporary patches (e.g. fol. 68), a contemporary sewn repair (fol. 92), though probably resewn later, and a contemporary, unrepaired cut (fol. 60).

Collation 1^8 (3–6 missing), 2–3^8, (4 qq. missing), 4–5^8, (1 q. missing), 6–7^8; hair side outside in all quires.

Quire nos. Several partly trimmed; qq. 1 and 2 numbered I and II, qq. 4 and 5 numbered VIII (shaded in yellow) and IX, q. 6 numbered XI, in brown ink, lower margin of verso of last leaf.

Catchwords In lower margin, verso of last leaf of q. 4 (VIII) only; others possibly trimmed off.

Page Layout
Dimensions
Page 325 x 225mm (unevenly trimmed at all margins).
Space ruled for writing Very variable; 226–239 x 155–159mm.

Columns 2.

Pricking Leaves folded, outer margins only (except q. 4, inner and outer margins), 1→8; template used throughout; where fewer lines are ruled, the last hole on the template was not pricked.

Ruling Neatly ruled in grey sometimes appearing brown, with narrow vertical margins.

Lines per page 35 except qq. 4–5 (VIII–IX), 34. Written above top line.

Page design
fols. 5–102v, 103v–104   fol. 103

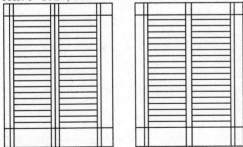

II SCRIBES
One scribe wrote the text throughout, the incipit on the flyleaf and the incipit and

explicit on fol. 12 in a clear, fairly compressed, upright hand. The aspect of the hand changes as the writing progresses, becoming less taut and compressed and the minims less tall. The hand is slightly more angular than that of the 'flyleaf scribe' (see Harley 3038, Trinity B.1.3) where the text concerned is also Gregory's *Moralia in Job*, the text of this volume, but in other respects is so similar that it is almost certainly a later version of the same hand. The scribe used the punctus flexus punctuation mark, and the text is stressed for reading aloud. See also below, Notes. Corrections over erasure by scribe (e.g. fols. 8, 22, 68v) and by another hand over an erasure fol. 71v. A second hand wrote an added text fols. 103–104. A third hand, large, rather uneven and slightly later than the text hand, added a preface on the flyleaf.

III DECORATION, RUBRICS AND ARTICULATION OF TEXT

Text initials Half-line initials written by the scribe in brown ink, touched with ochre. Scribal marginal notae signifying a quotation from patristic authority are shaded in yellow.

Minor initials Fol. 103: **1-line red D**(ilectissimo), oxidised.

Major initials Fol. 16: **8-line red Q**(uorumdam), with a reserved section in the tail, the centre of the letter filled with a symmetrical foliate-floral design with 4 multicoloured petals (red, green, blue, ochre and brown inks) joined at the centre with a diamond–shaped motif. The design is almost identical to that of the monochromatic initials C and P on fols. 143v and 65v of Christ Church 88 (q.v.), and this initial is certainly designed by the scribe who wrote and decorated that book (though he may not have coloured it).

Historiated Initials None.

Title page None.

Display script Fol. 16: (Q)**uorumdam mentes**: (q)uorum/ in 1-line blue mixed square and uncial capital letters delicately filled with small flourishes in red; /dam/ in red capitals flourished with blue; /mentes in half-line brown mixed capital letters shaded with ochre.

Titles etc. No running titles or chapter headings. Incipits and explicits and heading for text on fol. ii in red ink (oxidised) by the text scribe.

IV CONTENTS

Table of contents None.

Main texts Gregory, *Moralia in Job* books 6–10 fragmentary and incomplete (See James, *Lambeth MSS*, 184–5).

1. Fol. ii v: 'Prosper in libro de contemplativa vita. Caritas est ut mihi videtur recta voluntas ab omnibus terrenis ac presentibus prorsus anulfa'. Ends fol. ii v: 'que semel habita nunquam amittitur.' Fol. 5 begins imperfectly (VI.16): 'redire posse desperent'. Ends (fol. 102v): 'quanto ex lectionis quoque incisione respirat. Explicit liber decimus'. *CCSL* CXLIII, 284–577.
2. Fol. 103: 'Dilectissimo amico *et* plurimus diligendo vitellio dei gratia sancte Romani ecclesie cardinale diacono atque legato domini pape Johannes lateralensis ecclesie sancti johannis omnium fratrum servus eternam in domino cum oratione salve. Nova que in urbe sunt novas revelationes que divinitus facte sunt'. Ends incomplete fol. 104: 'Quid plura? ad eius signaculum quaedam ceca mulier est illuminat', an account of a vision of the destruction of the city of Rome.

Fol. 104v blank except for inscription (see above, Back flyleaves 1).

V ORIGIN AND PROVENANCE
Ex libris Fol. ii v: 'Liber sancte Marie de Bildewas', the words alternately green and red.
Secundo folio (now) stabimini
The book was made at Buildwas during the first campaign (c.1160–70) which also produced other books copied or corrected by the 'flyleaf scribe' and/or the Christ Church 88 'master scribe'. It was acquired for the Lambeth Palace Library in the seventeenth century by Archbishop Sancroft, whose arms are impressed on the covers.

VI NOTES
1. Two flyleaves in other books (Trinity B.1.3, Harley 3038, q.v.) written by a scribe who is almost certainly the scribe of this book, carry the opening texts of Gregory's *Moralia in Job*. The format of those leaves is much larger than those of the present book, and it would seem, from the fact that the larger leaves were used as flyleaves not long after they were written, that this first quire at least was abandoned, probably to be re-written on a smaller scale. The space left for decorative initials on the discarded leaf was never filled and there is no evidence that this quire was sewn into a book before being reused by the binder. The *Registrum* does not record a copy of this work at Buildwas. So far it appears that the other volumes have not survived, but see note 2 below.
2. Cambridge, Pembroke College MSS 177, 178 and 179 carry a complete copy of Gregory's *Moralia in Job*. On the basis of partially erased ex libris inscriptions, James (*Pembroke MSS*, 169–170) suggested that these books were probably from Buildwas. However, Ker (*MLGB*, 15) rejected them as Buildwas books, on the grounds of the lack of any positive evidence. In favour of the possibility of a Buildwas provenance, if not origin, is that they are without any doubt Cistercian books, and an integral set; the punctuation, the penwork initials, and the surviving elements of the ex libris (Liber sancte Marie de) all support such an attribution. The scribes write in hands similar to those found in late twelfth-century Buildwas books. In addition to this, the Pembroke books, like certain Buildwas books, acquired detailed contents lists and foliation during the thirteenth century. However, all Cistercian monasteries were dedicated to the Virgin and so the partially erased ex libris inscriptions are not really helpful. None of the scribes or artists is identical to any known Buildwas scribe, and the added foliation was carried out in the Pembroke MSS exclusively in Roman numerals, and not in Arabic (see note 4 below). Added to this is the fact that the surviving Lambeth fragments of this text, which are certainly attributable to Buildwas, date from no more than 15 years earlier than the Pembroke books and possibly rather less than this. On the basis of currently available evidence, therefore, it is unlikely that the Pembroke MSS were made or kept at Buildwas.
3. *Chapter numbers* have been added to the top right-hand corner of the rectos of all leaves in Arabic numbers s.xiii. Numbers at the bottom of the rectos of leaves in the inner margin indicate the leaf number within each chapter, beginning in each case with 2 on leaf 2. Similar numbering is found in other Buildwas books.
4. *Leaf numbers* were added in very neat Arabic numerals, probably in the thirteenth century, in the upper margin of the rectos, always in the left margin of the double central margin. Gaps in the number sequence (e.g. between 22 and 46) confirm that the numbering was done before the book was shattered. The numbers begin in q. 1 (now only 4 leaves) with 6, showing that the first quire

was originally a quire of 8 (the flyleaf not numbered) and that it has lost its two central bifolia. This evidence confirms that provided by the detached pastedowns and other evidence, that this book was completed, bound and used.

5. *Other numbers* A series of small Roman numerals in the outer margins, added probably at the same time as the other numbers, refers the reader to the relevant chapter in the text of Job. The chapter numbers on the top right recto and leaf numbers on the bottom left recto are almost certainly by the same hand, though one set of numbers is large and the other small. The central running leaf numbers are by a different hand. It is not possible to say whether either hand was responsible for the Roman numerals or if any hand is that of the Buildwas indexer, though one Buildwas reader, possibly the indexer, annotated the large Concordance (Lambeth 477) with cross-references to the *Moralia* books 1–5.

VII BIBLIOGRAPHY AND PLATES
James, *Lambeth MSS*, 184–185; Ker *MLBG*, 15; Sheppard 1990, 199–200, pls. 15, 19; see also pl. 18; N.R. Ker, 'The English Manuscripts of the Moralia of Gregory the Great', in *Kunsthistorische Forschungen Otto Pächt zu Ehren*, ed. by A. Rosenauer and G. Weber, (Salzburg, 1973), 77–89.

3. CAMBRIDGE, TRINITY COLLEGE MS B.14.5
Gregory, Cura Pastoralis   **Date** *c.*1160–70
Leaves [i paper], i, 88, [i paper]
Foliation 1–89
Origin Buildwas   **Figs**. 8, 9

This book contains a late-thirteenth-century alphabetical index, together with notes and marks which demonstrate how it was constructed.

I PHYSICAL DESCRIPTION
Binding Rebound s. xvii, since rebacked; covering repaired at front edges and corners; opens fairly well.

Endleaves

    Front *Pastedown* Modern wove paper leaf in place, fol. 1 of bifolium, blank except for old and new shelfmarks written in ink on rectangle of laid paper pasted on.

        Flyleaves 1) Modern wove paper leaf, fol. 2 of bifolium, stained at edges by dark brown primary covering, blank; 2) single parchment leaf, now sewn in behind q. 1 (stub visible after fol. 9), conjoint pastedown probably excised; recto: pen drawing (upside down) of Christ blessing, full length but incomplete, stylised hair, beard and drapery suggest a date *c.*1160; verso: Trinity College bookplate, capitula. Since the drawing (recto) is now upside down but the capitula on the reverse are the right way up, it is possible this was a discarded leaf reused as an endleaf. It is clear it was never used as a pastedown.

    Back *Flyleaves* Modern wove paper leaf, fol. 1 of a bifolium, blank.

        Pastedown Modern wove paper leaf in place, fol. 2 of a bifolium, blank.

Sewing stations Now 5. Evidence at spinefolds (e.g. fol. 56) suggests formerly, probably originally, 2: (tail) I 47 K 35*66*40 K 37 I mm (head).

Sewing Now all-along with brownish S-twist thread. Impressions in spinefolds indicate an earlier, probably original sewing all-along with Z-twist thread. There is widespread evidence of tacketing in inner margins in the form of 2 holes, 5mm from the spinefold and 20 and 33 mm from the lower edge on first 4 leaves of each quire; fols. 56–60 provide a good example, with a fragment of tawed skin tacket in place at fol. 59.

Sewing supports Now sewn on 5 thin white tawed skin supports. Very faint marks on the last leaf of impressions made by wedges coincide with the evidence of sewing holes in spinefolds (see above), indicating that there were formerly, probably originally, 2 sewing supports *c*.8mm wide.

Lacing path Now over outer edges of boards to inner face, very close to spine edge, and fixed in place at an angle to direction of lacing, under pastedowns. Faint impressions of former wedges suggest earlier supports were laced parallel through the boards for about 60mm.

Endbands Present at head and tail, rolled white tawed skin core sewn with pink and blue ?silk Z-twist threads, tied down in 3 or 4 spinefolds. Not now and probably never laced into boards. Impressions of thread at head and tail indicate that earlier endbands were tied down in every spinefold.

Tabs None present; no other evidence.

Spine lining None present; no other evidence.

Boards Pasteboard, 230 x 161 x 5mm, edges projecting very slightly from edges of leaves.

Primary covering Dark tanned leather, corners on back board overlapped; triple fillets parallel and very close to edges of each board, the centre fillet gilt; small impressed gilt Whitgift arms front and back; gilt fillet along thin edges of boards front and back; much repaired at spine, and at corners and edges of front board.

Bosses Greenish indentations on first and last leaves suggest the presence in an earlier binding of 4 corner bosses and a central one on each board.

Chain attachments None present; no other evidence.

Labels Printed paper labels on spine with elements of present shelfmark.

Notes Page marker (cut from the edges of leaves and threaded through slits so as to project from the book) at lower margin of fol. 31 marking the beginning of the series of chapters headed 'De diversitate admonendor*um*'.

Structure of Book

Parchment Thick, even quality with a good nap on both sides, well prepared with little colour variation; follicle marks on some leaves. Some holes, and several outer corners missing, showing natural shape of skins.

Collation i, 1–6⁸, 7⁶, 8¹⁰, 9–11⁸, hair side outermost.

Quire nos. QQ. 1–11 numbered I–III iiii–xi lower margin verso of last leaf in brown ink.

Catchwords None.

Page Layout
Dimensions
Page 227 x 159mm, trimmed at upper and fore-edges (evidence of sewing thread impressions, trimmed chapter numbers and marginal chapter headings).
Space ruled for writing Height variable, width constant: 163–170 x 105mm.
Columns Long lines.
Pricking Leaves folded, outer margin only, 1→8; last leaf of q. 11 re-pricked 8→1, probably because first pricking did not penetrate this leaf.

Ruling Slightly variable: q. 1 in brown, outer bounding lines erratically crossed by text lines; qq. 2–3: blind ruled on hair side, neatly executed with first and second or first and third lines ruled edge-to-edge and similarly at the bottom of the ruled page; qq. 4–11: brown lines, neatly executed, mainly with first 2 and last 2 lines ruled edge-to-edge.

Lines per page Slightly variable, 25 or 26.

Page design

fols.2–89.

II SCRIBES

Nine scribes contributed to the copying of the text in hands c.1160–70, seven of whom wrote only short passages. They seem to have been attempting to achieve uniformity of letter forms, but the hands are too irregular for the result to be a handsome book. All are clearly legible, however; none used punctus flexus. Changes of scribe often occurred in mid-line and mid-sentence, the copying evidently constituting an opportunity for several scribes to practise. Scribes 2 and 3 did most of the work. On fols. 3v–7v, scribe 2 ignored chapter divisions; this had subsequently to be corrected by the rubricator. The hands of most of the scribes are uneven and variable, only scribes 1 and 5 producing a pleasing, even hand. The distribution of work is as follows: **Scribe 1**: fol. 2, opening $5^{1}/_{4}$ lines only, including the display script, as if to provide a pattern of letter size for others. **Scribe 2**: fols. 2 (line 6)–5 (last line); fols. 5v (line 12)–9 (line 20); fols. 34v (line 1)–45 (line 20); fols. 45v (line 1)–55v (last line). **Scribe 3**: fol. 5v (lines 1–12); fols. 9 (line 20)– 9v (last line); fols. 19 (line 5)–34v (line 1); fols. 76 (line 2)–89 (end of text). **Scribe 4**: fols. 10 (line 1)–13v (line 19, end of chapter). **Scribe 5**: fols. 13v (line 20)–16 (line 13). **Scribe 6**: fols. 16 (line 13)–18 (last line). **Scribe 7**: fol. 19 (lines 1–5). **Scribe 8**: fol. 45 (lines 20–25). **Scribe 9**: fols. 56 (line 1)–76 (line 2). The succession of scribal stints is: 1, 2, 3, 2, 3, 4, 5, 6, 7, 3, 2, 8, 2, 9, 3. The capitula on fol. 1 were added by another contemporary hand, and an extraneous paragraph at the end of the text (fol. 89) appears to have been another practice passage, the first two lines written by the 'flyleaf scribe' (see Trinity B.1.3) or by a scribe with a hand very like his, the remainder copied by yet another scribe.

Corrections were written in the margins by a variety of hands, often in pale ink. One correcting hand added several marginal corrections in a distinctive hand with a sharply angled serif to the top stroke of long s (e.g. fols. 2, 80v, 81v, 83v etc.), and also a sentence at the end of the text (fol. 89): 'Benedic*tus* es d*omi*ne d*eu*s q*ui* adiuuiste *et* consola*tus* es me'. A single scribe added both tick and flex punctuation marks to points throughout the text and also stress marks (e.g. fol. 3), indicating that this book was used for reading aloud. This is supported by the evidence of former bosses on front and back covers of an earlier binding. The rubrication was mainly executed by a single but variable hand, like but not identical to any of the text hands. The rubrication on fol. 2 was done by the scribe who made the coloured initial (see below). A different hand wrote the explicit and incipit on fol. 30v.

III DECORATION, RUBRICS AND ARTICULATION OF TEXT

Text initials Small brown ink capitals by the text scribes.

Minor initials 1- or 2-line red initials throughout to mark beginning of new chapters, sometimes with reserved line or dotted line decoration, or very simple foliate tails. Two initials once missing were supplied: that on fol. 65 by a contemporary hand in a pale brown ink, possibly one of the correctors; that on fol. 77 by a slightly later hand in grey.

Major initials Fol. 2: **10-line red and ochre P**(astoralis), the colours separated in the main stem by a stepped reserved line, with very simple ochre flourishes inside letter.

Historiated initials None.

Display script Fol. 2: (P)**astoralis cure** [sic] **pondera fugere**, the first word in 1-line square capitals, the rest in smaller 1-line rustic capitals, all in brown ink by the first text scribe. Subsequently there is no display script.

Titles etc. No running titles; an elegant incipit fol. 2, explicit and incipit fol. 30v; no final explicit; chapter headings throughout added in the margins in red as far as chapter 28 (fol. 33) on lines ruled ad hoc in grey; after this no further headings added.

Title page None.

IV CONTENTS

Table of contents Fol. 1: 'Incipiunt capitula libri pastoralis i. De venire imperiti ad magisterium audeant – xxiiii'; then a note: 'decem et octo scilicet capitula de diversitate admonendorum', but numbered capitula resume at lxi. Ends fol. 1: 'lxvi. Per actas rite omnibus qualiter praedicator ad semet ipsum redeat ne hunc vel vita vel praedicatio extollat. Expliciunt capitula.'

An alphabetical index added on pasted-in bifolium by a reader s.xiii (see below, Notes).

Main texts Gregory, *Cura Pastoralis.*

1. Fol. 2: 'Incipit liber pastoralis cure beati gregorii pape urbis rome ad iohanem ravenatensem. Pastoralis cure pondera fugere delitescendo voluisse.' Ends fol. 89: 'ut quem pondus proprium deprimit tui meriti manus levet.' (Another hand added to this: 'Benedictus es domine deus qui adiuuisti me et consolatus es me'.) *PL* LXXVII, 13.

2. Fol. 89: An added passage: 'Ebrietas tota est inbecillis. Primum abolet memoriam. Dissipat sensum.... Sobrietas autem formosa est tota, utilis tota.' Ends fol. 89: 'Sine istis ministeriis omnis homo contemptibilis est.'

Fol. 89v: originally blank, now covered with indexer's notes in stylus (see below, Notes).

V ORIGIN AND PROVENANCE

Ex Libris Fol. 1, below capitula, in red ink, in the undulating hand (s.xii ex)

found in Trinity B.1.3, B.1.4, B.1.31, B.1.34: 'Liber s*ancte* marie de Byldewas'.
Secundo folio regnaverunt

The book was made at Buildwas during the first campaign of book production. Both the text itself and the evidence of the participation of many scribes together with lack of careful control of elements like chapter headings are perhaps indications that it was among the earliest (compare Christ Church 88, dated 1167). The scribe who wrote the first two lines of the added passage on drunkenness and sobriety (fol. 89) is almost certainly the 'flyleaf scribe' known from Trinity B.1.3 and Harley 3038 (q.v.). The book was acquired by Archbishop Whitgift s.xvi ex and given to Trinity College.

VI NOTES

1. An alphabetical index, written on a small bifolium in a hand dating to the third quarter of the thirteenth century, is pasted onto fol. 2. Each leaf measures 168 x 125mm and is ruled in grey. A series of Arabic numbers (coinciding with the current chapter numbers), mainly in the top right or left corners though now largely trimmed, and a page of notes in stylus on fol. 89v provide a clear picture of the indexer's system. He jotted the points he wished to index on the unused page at the back (fol. 89v), with the chapter number in which the point occurs and the number of the page within the chapter on which the point can be found. Neither pages nor leaves are now numbered except fols. 50–55 on which 2 is written in the centre of the lower margin, indicating the second leaf of a chapter (not accurate in the case of fol. 52). These numbers may have been added by the reader who added running chapter numbers on fols. 3v–6, sometimes in the upper, sometimes in the lower margins of each page.

The indexer then arranged the points alphabetically, though not alphabetically within each letter group, and copied his list onto the bifolium now pasted to fol. 2. e.g. 'Abstinencia 44 pagina 1; 47 pagina 1'. Chapter numbers added by the indexer survive intact on some pages (e.g. in the margins of fols. 17, 21, 24, 31v, where the rubricator had omitted them), and on others in the upper right corner (e.g. on fol. 26, where chapter number 21 survives untrimmed). Fragmentary numbers (trimmed) survive on fols. 32, 33, 33v, 41v, 50v etc. Other numbers in stylus survive, e.g. on fols. 36v, 47v etc., suggesting that the indexer put his numbering system in place first with a stylus before inking it in. Very large, distinctive nota signs are found throughout the text in the margins in stylus, which seem to have been made by this reader-indexer, though the points indexed are not necessarily those marked with a nota sign. The same nota marks are found in Christ Church 88, together with a similar numbering of chapters in the top corners, and in Trinity B.1.3 (fol. 87). In Trinity B.1.3 he also added a detailed list of contents on fol. 140v. In Lambeth 109 the chapters are numbered, the leaf numbers within each chapter are written in the lower margin and continuous foliation is also added.

The 13th-century indexer's hand is also found in CUL Add Ii.2.3, where he annotated William of Malmesbury's text, and he wrote the ex libris inscription in Balliol 35A. The inscription is dated 1277.

This text is listed in the *Registrum* but no copy is recorded for Buildwas.

VII BIBLIOGRAPHY AND PLATES

James, *Trinity MSS*, I, 407–8; Ker, *MLGB*, 14; Chibnall, *VCH*, 56; Sheppard 1990, 199–202 and pl. 22.

4. CAMBRIDGE, TRINITY COLLEGE MS B.1.3
Gregory, Sermons on Ezechiel Date *c.*1160–70
Leaves [i paper], i, 140, [i paper]
Foliation 1–140
Origin Buildwas Figs. 5, 7

I PHYSICAL DESCRIPTION
Binding Rebound s.xvi, recently rebacked, very tightly resewn with guards in centre of each quire; spine stiff.
Endleaves
Front *Pastedown* Laid paper leaf in place, probably once conjoint with flyleaf, paper cracked at joint; Trinity College bookplate and shelfmark, otherwise blank.
    Flyleaves **1**) Laid paper leaf, probably once conjoint with pastedown, no watermark, blank except for title in ink, s.xvii; **2**) a bifolium, the first leaf excised to stub, itself once a single leaf from a discarded book, fully written on both recto and verso. The text is the opening of Gregory, *Moralia in Job*, and the leaf was once part of the same quire as the flyleaf in Harley 3038 (q.v.). This scribe is referred to elsewhere as the 'flyleaf scribe'. Verso: Buildwas ex libris.
Back *Flyleaves* **1**) Original structure unclear; 1 or possibly 2 leaves (fols. 3–4 of last quire) now excised to stubs, probably blank; **2**) laid paper leaf, probably once conjoint with pastedown, watermark: unclear motif, surmounted by crown, initials ?LA underneath; blank.
    Pastedown **1**) Originally probably fol. 4 of last quire, now excised to stub; **2**) laid paper leaf in place, probably once conjoint with paper flyleaf, blank.
Sewing stations Now 5; no other evidence.
Sewing Spinefolds inaccessible.
Sewing supports Now cords; no other evidence.
Lacing path Present supports laced over the outer spine edges of the boards, fixed at an angle to the spine edge under pastedown.
Endbands None present; no other available evidence.
Tabs None present; no other evidence.
Spine lining None present; no other evidence.
Boards Pasteboard, 273 x 191 x 6mm.
Primary covering Dark tanned leather with overlapped corners; Whitgift's coat of arms (small version) impressed front and back, gilt; triple fillets parallel with and adjacent to all edges of both covers, the central fillet gilt; a single fillet also along inner edges of covering.
Fastenings Ends of 2 rolled textile ties near fore-edge front and back.
Chemise None present; no other evidence.
Bosses None present; no other evidence.
Chain attachments None present; no other evidence.
Labels Modern printed paper labels on spine, each with an element of the present shelfmark.
Notes Remains of a page marker made of thread, lower edge fol. 38 (there is no text break at this point, but 'vox carnis', 'vox super firmamentum', and 'vox de firmamento' written in the margin with a stylus; remains of threaded parchment page marker lower edge fol. 116, made from a written fragment possibly in the hand of the indexer; close to this a stylus note, not legible. Edges of leaves now stained yellowish-green.

15

Structure of Book

Parchment Good quality, even colour, some holes but very few repairs; some leaves are shiny and smooth, others have a nap.

Collation $1-6^8, 7^4, 8-10^8, 11^8$ (7 and 8 excised to stubs, probably blank – end of book 1), $12-18^8, 19^4$ (3 and 4 excised, probably blank – end of book 2); hair side outermost in each quire except q. 7.

Quire nos. Q. 1 only, numbered I in Roman numeral in brown ink, lower margin of fol. 8v under inner column of text.

Catchwords None.

Page Layout

Dimensions

Page 268 x 190mm, trimmed at outer margin and probably also at upper and lower margins (evidence of trimmed marginal notes).

Space ruled for writing Varies according to scribe: fols.1–82 (book 1): 201 x 135mm; fols. 83–140 (book 2): 215–225 x 135–140mm.

Columns Fols.1–82 (book 1): 2; fols.83–140 (book 2): long lines.

Pricking Leaves folded, but patterns and methods variable: qq. 1–3: none visible; q. 4: both margins 1→8; q. 5: both margins 8→1, clear triangular marks; q. 6: both margins, 1→8, (double pricks for inner vertical lines but only one ruled until fol. 46); q. 7: both margins 8→1; qq. 8–11: both margins, 1→8; qq. 12–17: most evidence trimmed, remains suggest outer margin only, 1→8; q. 18: both margins 1→8; q. 19: none visible.

Ruling QQ. 1–5: mainly in brown; qq. 6–19: grey sometimes appearing brown. Single vertical lines until fol. 45v when inner vertical lines only become double; fols. 83–140 (qq. 12–19): vertical lines are sometimes single, sometimes double. Edge-to-edge ruling similarly erratic: first and last, or first 2 and last line or first and third and last lines on each page ruled edge-to-edge. q.1 only: an extra line ruled as a minim height guide.

Lines per page Very variable, 30–34; fol. 85 (q. 11): 39; fol. 106 (q. 14): 38.

Page design

fols. 1–45, 71–82v   fols.45v–70v   fols. 83–140

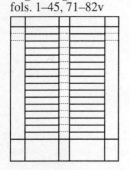 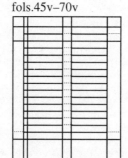 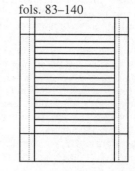

II SCRIBES

At least 10 scribes collaborated in the writing of the text and a further hand added a passage in a blank space at the end, datable by the activity of some of them in other books to *c*.1165. The scribe whose discarded work forms the flyleaf of this book and that of Harley 3038 (q.v.) wrote in a distinctive, upright and compressed hand, the letter forms having a rectangular aspect; he used thickened capitals, more Roman than rustic. He wrote none of the text in this book, but he wrote the two explicits in red on fols. 82v and 140, and his may possibly have been the hand which corrected many of the other scribes (but see below, scribe 13).

Scribe 1 wrote fols.1–22 (col. a) in a backward-sloping, square-looking hand; he used the punctus flexus punctuation mark. **Scribe 2** wrote fols. 22 (col. b)–23v (col. a line 9), taking over in mid-line using dark ink; this hand is characterised by prolific use of long thin serifs and hyphens, e.g. at the lower stroke of ampersand and the final closing stroke of the loop to g; this scribe used punctus flexus. **Scribe 3** wrote fol. 23v from col. a mid-line 9 in a very regular, upright hand, the pen held at a very sharp angle; this scribe also used punctus flexus. Scribes 2 and 3 alternated on fol. 24, changing at col. a (line 22), col. b (line 3) and col. b (line 28), scribe 2 then continuing to fol. 40v, the end of q. 5. **Scribe 4** wrote fols. 41–45, beginning at a new quire, in a firm upright hand which becomes smaller and less firm on fol. 44; this scribe wrote the incipits and explicits on fol. 1 and throughout book 1, showing both the firmer and the less firm variations of his hand. **Scribe 5** wrote fol. 45v (col. b), beginning on a new page in mid-quire, in a large round hand; this hand deteriorates in the following pages and loses its stature, perhaps due to a different pen or to instructions to write smaller, until fol. 52 after which it remains consistent until fol. 70v; this could even be the work of a different scribe. The scribe or scribes did not use punctus flexus, but the flex mark has been added here and there in this stint, by another hand. **Scribe 6** wrote fols. 70v (col. b line 23)–82v (end q. 9) in a very compressed upright hand, not unlike that of scribe 4, and used punctus flexus; he corrected his own work (on fol. 77) and that of scribe 5 (on fol. 53). **Scribe 7** wrote fols. 83–86 (to line 32) in a small, round slightly backward-sloping hand, above the line; he did not use punctus flexus. **Scribe 8** wrote fols. 86 (line 33)–87 in an upright hand, scribe 7 interpolating 4 words on fol. 86v (line 28). **Scribe 9** wrote fols. 87–98v in a hand rather like that of scribe 7, but larger and much less even at first, then settling down to become tall and compressed, like several other hands in this book; the hand could possibly be a version of the hand of scribe 7. **Scribe 10** wrote fols. 99–102, but another scribe interpolated groups of lines (2–3 or 8, e.g. at the top of fols. 99, 99v, 101, 102) and sometimes within the page (e.g. fol. 101v); scribe 10's hand is upright and compressed; the interpolating hand is larger. **Scribe 11** wrote fols. 102–106v (line 22) in a very uneven hand using black ink. **Scribe 12** wrote fol. 106v (lines 22–36) in a hand very similar to that of scribe 9. **Scribe 13** wrote fol. 106v (line 37)–140 (end of text) in a very fine, even and upright hand, beginning well spaced but becoming quite compressed. The hand is very similar in details to that of the 'flyleaf scribe' (see above) but with a more rounded and fluid aspect. He used written rustic capitals and punctus flexus. It is probably this scribe who corrected throughout (eg. fols. 53, 72v, 90v) and who wrote the incipits and explicits throughout book 2, but the restrictions placed on the hand by the need to condense many words into a small, erased space (corrections) and the different consistency of the red ink (headings) make it very difficult to be certain whether this scribe or the 'flyleaf scribe' was the overseer of this book. It is perhaps more likely to have been scribe 13.

A fourteenth scribe added a short passage to the blank space at the end of the text fol. 140 in a small neat hand, contemporary with or very slightly later than

17

those of the other scribes.

III DECORATION, RUBRICS AND ARTICULATION OF TEXT

Text initials All scribes used written rustic capitals. The 'flyleaf scribe' used thickened capitals of Roman character.

Minor initials None.

Major initials Fol. 1: **6-line yellow D**(ilectissimo), made with compasses; horizontal curved ascender, otherwise plain. Fol. 1: **7-line D**(ei), made with compasses; horizontal ascender with serif and 2 enlarged dots at top and bottom, otherwise plain. Fol. 5v: **3-line red U**(sus), with a vertical reserved line in the right-hand ascender. Fol. 11v: **3-line red S**(*ancta*), plain with serifs. Fol. 16: **7-line red P**(er), the stem extending into the lower margin and with a reserved line. Fol. 19: **4-line red O** (quam) plain, a compass-drawn circle used to form the letter, though the final form is oval. Fol. 22v: **6-line red T**(enebrosa), vertical reserved line in the vertical stroke and long serifs. Fol. 28v: **5-line red S**(icut), plain; compass-drawn circles in grey only roughly used to form the letter. Fol. 35v: **4-line red Q**(uod) plain, compass-drawn guideline visible. Fol. 43v: **7-line blue and pale brown I**(nitium), the colours separated by scalloped reserved line. Fol. 54v: **3-line blue S**(ola) plain. Fol. 67: **10-line blue and red I**(nter), the colours separated by a scalloped reserved line (cf. fol. 43v). Fol. 75: **4-line brown S**(ervata) with 2 red dot-in-circle motifs in upper and lower sections of the letter. Fol. 83: **4-line red Q**(uoniam) with reserved scalloped lines and dots at top and bottom. Fol. 87v: **4-line red N**(e), ungainly, with reserved scalloped line in diagonal stroke and left descender extended with lines and dots. Fol. 91: **2-line red V**(ir), with irregular reserved scalloped lines, otherwise plain. Fol. 96: **6-line red V**(ir), with irregular reserved scalloped lines and tentative design for flourishes added in grey in the lower half of the letter. Fol. 100: **5-line red M**(emoratis) with a variety of scalloped and curved reserved lines in all but one of the strokes of the letter. Fol. 106: **12-line red P**(ostquam) with stem extended in the margin beyond the 9 lines left by the scribe and with a reserved line. Fol. 113v: **7-line red M**(agna), like that on fol. 100. Fol. 120v: **13-line red P**(rophete) with stem extended in the margin beyond the 6-line space left by the scribe, and scalloped reserved line decoration. Fol. 126v: **7-line red Q**(uid) drawn with compasses, with reserved scalloped lines, and very crudely executed green fringe-like flourishes inside the letter. Fol. 135v: **6-line red S**(acri) with a reserved line and long serifs. Fol. 139v: **3-line red E**(cce), plain, now with green stain at edges.

On fol. 120v, in the top left corner, is a 2-line green letter P unconnected to the text. There are further green marks on fols. 131, 132 and 133, mainly rectangular though the last few may comprise indistinct letters.

In addition, there is on fol. 136v a scribbled sketch of a symmetrical foliage design in lower margin, and on fol. 140 the explicit scribe has drawn a red dragon line filler.

Historiated initials None.

Display script Fol. 1: (D)**ilectissimo** *fratri* **mariano...dei** and (D)**ei omnipotentis ...ezechiele** in 1-line brown ink rustic capitals with red shading executed by text scribe. Elsewhere, the first word or two after a coloured initial is written in small rustic letters by the text scribe. Scribe 3 used rustic letters touched with red for the last words of the book in his stint (*per omnia secula seculorum* Amen).

18

Title page None.

Titles etc. No running titles; incipits and explicits in red in good hands: in Book 1 by scribe 4 in both the larger and smaller versions of his hand, and Book 3 by Scribe 13. An extra incipit fol. 82v in another, unknown hand in brown ink.

IV CONTENTS

Table of contents No original list survives; a later hand added a detailed list of contents on fol. 140v (see below).

Main texts Gregory, *Sermons on Ezechiel*, Books I and II.

1. Fol. 1: 'Incipit prologus in libro omeliarum beati gregorii pape in primam partem ezechielis propheta que sunt numero duodecim. Dilectissimo fratri mariano episcopo...Omelias quas in beatum ezechielem prophetam ita ut coram populo loquebar excepte sunt'. Ends fol. 1: 'ad subtiliores epulas avidius redeatur. Explicit prologus.' Fol. 1: 'Incipit omelia prima. Dei omnipotentis aspiratione de ezechiele propheta locuturus'. Ends fol. 82v: 'per omnia saecula saeculorum amen. Explicit liber primus beati Gregorii pape super ezechielem prophetam.' In slightly later hand: 'Incipit secundus de visione edificii constituti in monte.' Fol. 83: 'Incipit liber secundus Omelia prima. Quoniam multis curis prementibus'. Ends fol 140: 'ad hereditatem perpetuam erudit. Sit itaque gloria...per omnia secula seculorum amen. Explicit liber secundus beate Gregorii paper super ezechielem prophetam.' PL LXXVI, 785.

2. Fol. 140: a passage added in another hand: 'Quadratum quippe lapidem in quamcunque partem verteris rectus stabit et si quadratum lapidem aut aliud quicquid quadrati potest diligenter inspexeris perfectionem ecclesie in eo esse depictam deprehendere poteris.' Ends fol. 140: 'Hoc totum de quadrato lapido ideo diximus ut demonstraremus per quadraturam civitatis perfectionem ecclesie designatam.'

3. Fol. 140v: a detailed list of contents added in a hand s.xiii (the indexer): 'Omelia prima. De diverso tempore prophete. De diversis modis et qualitatibus prophetie. De utilitate psalmodie. De moderamine dei erga peccatores et de moderamina [sic] dei protegens peccatores'. Ends fol. 140v: 'Omelia x^a De duabus vitis etcetera. De tribus viis et gazofilia.'

V ORIGIN AND PROVENANCE

Ex libris Fol. i verso: 'Liber sancte marie de Byldewas' in red ink, in the undulating, hand known from other such inscriptions (B.1.4, B.1.31, B.1.34, B.14.5).

Secundo folio vocavit

The presence in this book of the 'flyleaf hand' in explicits and of the 'master hand' of Christ Church 88, the use throughout of the punctus flexus and the evidently cooperative nature of the scribal contributions make it certain that this was one of the early texts copied at Buildwas, and that it was also bound there, probably c.1160–70 (see also Harley 3038). A series of striking nota marks in stylus on fols. 87–90 and in ink on fols. 90, 93–95, indicates that the Buildwas indexer used this book (for the indexer, see Trinity B.14.5). On fol. 140v the indexer wrote out a detailed contents list for each homily in each of the two books. Buildwas is recorded as having a copy of this text in the *Registrum*. It was acquired by Archbishop Whitgift s.xvi ex and given by him to Trinity College.

VI NOTES
The book presents evidence of the workings of a new scriptorium, scribes being tried out, or given an opportunity to practise their hands while supervised (witness two occasions when scribes were apparently told to reduce the size of their letters, the interchange between 2 scribes in q. 9 and the insertion of the punctus flexus punctuation mark in the work of scribe 5).

VII BIBLIOGRAPHY AND PLATES
James, *Trinity MSS*, I, 3–4; Ker, *MLGB*, 14; Chibnall, *VCH*, 56; Sheppard 1988, 199–202 and pl. 13; Sheppard 1994, 183.

5. CAMBRIDGE, TRINITY COLLEGE MS B.1.4
Gregory, Dialogues   **Date** *c.*1160–70
Leaves [ii paper], 80, i, [i paper]
Foliation 1–81
Origin Probably Buildwas

I PHYSICAL DESCRIPTION
Binding Rebound s.xvi and recently rebacked, spine rigid and spinefolds inaccessible.
Endleaves
Front *Pastedown* 2 wove paper leaves in place, one pasted over the other, and both over an earlier laid paper pastedown s.?xvi; windows cut in the new leaves to reveal Trinity bookplate and shelfmark in ink; otherwise blank. Q. 1 is a regular quire of 8, so the original endleaf structure was probably a separate bifolium, lost in rebinding.
   Flyleaves 2 wove paper leaves, conjoint with those now pasted down; s.xvii list of contents in ink on laid paper pasted to second leaf, otherwise blank.
   Back *Flyleaves* 1) Single parchment leaf after last quire, once a pastedown: *recto*: chemise shadow, names, phrases and ex libris in various hands s.xv; *verso*: white paste remains and sewing support impressions. Possibly once the second leaf of a parchment bifolium; 2) wove paper leaf, blank.
   Pastedown 1) see Back Flyleaves 1) above; 2) wove paper leaf in place, conjoint with paper flyleaf, blank.
Sewing stations Now 3; formerly, perhaps originally, 3 (evidence of impressions on detached back pastedown): (tail) I 56*74*75*59 I mm (head); no evidence about kettle stitch.
Sewing Inaccessible.
Sewing supports Now 3 supports, probably double repair cords over existing earlier tawed skin supports, *c.*12mm wide, the broken ends of which are just visible at the front joint. These could be the supports which left impressions on the detached back pastedown (see below, Lacing path).
Lacing path Unclear evidence; present supports laced into short channels on the outer face of the boards and pulled through to the inner face and fixed under the pastedown; on the front board, a zigzag lacing path is visible, possibly part of a repair, in no clear relationship to the point of entry of the supports into the board. Earlier supports laced through parallel lacing paths of roughly equal length, 70–75mm long (evidence of impressions on back detached pastedown, see above).

Endbands Present at head and tail, sewn with blue white threads in an alternating pattern, tied down into alternate quires.

Tabs None present; no other evidence.

Spine lining None present; no other evidence.

Boards Pasteboard, 265 x 175 x 5mm.

Primary covering Dark tanned leather with small, impressed gilt Whitgift arms front and back; triple fillets parallel with and adjacent to all 4 edges of both covers, the centre fillet gilt, and a single fillet along edges (thickness) of each cover, also gilt. Spine re-covered. An impression on lower edge of back detached pastedown suggests that a former cover had a narrow turn-in and a mitred lower corner.

Fastenings 1) Greenish hole on back pastedown in centre, 71mm from fore-edge, suggests the earlier, probably original, presence of a single pin for a strap and pin fastening; **2)** ends of two rolled ties, material unclear, possibly a textile, remain on each cover, 12mm from fore-edge.

Chemise Outer half of recto of detached back pastedown is relatively clean and blank, once protected by a chemise pocket. The scribbles, including an ex libris inscription, in the inner half of the same leaf, date to s.xv and so it seems likely that the chemise was still in place at that date.

Bosses None present; no other evidence.

Chain attachments None present; no other evidence.

Labels Printed paper labels on spine with elements of present shelfmark.

Notes A page marker formed by a strip of parchment partially cut from the edge of the page and folded back through slits in the page on fol. 14 (beginning of the second dialogue); possibly the remains of a similar one fol. 53 (beginning of book 4). Edges of leaves now stained greenish-yellow.

Structure of Book

Parchment Mainly fairly good quality, a few holes and some follicle marking throughout; uniformly yellow. A nap on hair sides, less on flesh sides.

Collation $1-9^8$, 10^8 + 1 leaf after 8 (possibly once fol. 2 of an endleaf bifolium). Hair side outside in each quire.

Quire nos. None.

Catchwords None.

Page Layout

Dimensions

Page 265 x 172mm, trimmed at all edges (evidence of a folded lower corner, fol. 59).

Space ruled for writing 199 x 124mm.

Columns Long lines.

Pricking Leaves folded, 1→8, both margins. More than one template used. Fol. 9: a faint impressed line runs between the first 11 marks, as if the pricking tool was dragged from notch to notch of a template in the form of a notched ruler.

Ruling In grey, mainly neat, regular and consistent; edge-to-edge lines slightly erratic but mainly first, third and last lines so ruled.

Lines per page Q. 1: 37, QQ. 2–10: 36.

Page design
fols. 1–80v

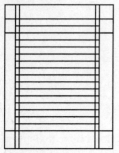

II SCRIBES

One scribe wrote the text throughout and some of the rubrics in a compressed, upright and regular English hand, *c.*1160–70, several scribes correcting his work. He used ampersand throughout and provided very marked serifs on tall ascenders (e.g. d, b, l). Hyphens are placed at the outer vertical line of the bounding columns. Paraphs and capitulum marks signal new chapters and some of these are elaborately flourished, perhaps by a slightly later hand (e.g. fols. 11v, 19v, 41v etc.). Correctors' hands supplied the rubrics on fols. 14, 14v, 53, 78, 78v.

The main corrector added punctus flexus punctuation marks throughout, particularly at the beginning of the text, erasing 'ticks' to insert the flex or adding the flex to points supplied by the scribe.

III DECORATION, RUBRICS AND ARTICULATION OF TEXT

Text initials The scribe wrote mainly rustic capitals, but Roman S which is usually thickened.

Minor initials 1) 1-line mixed capitals, alternately green and red, used for capitula at the beginning of each of the first three books (fols. 1, 14, 29). The scribe provided initials for the capitula on fols. 53v–54, but also left spaces as if for coloured capitals. These were filled with chapter numbers in red. 2) 1- or 2-line, green or red, plain initials, occasionally with very simple flourishes (e.g. fol. 42v: I), or with reserved scalloped lines within the stem (e.g. fol. 36v: A, fol. 54v: P), used to mark certain passages, often the beginning of the words of the interlocutors.

Major initials Good plain or slightly decorated initials at major divisions in the text, though none for book 2 which was provided with a 2-line green C, a mistake. The letter required was D(uas).

Fol. 1: **7-line green D**(ialogorum), with reserved scalloped lines, simple red fringed line decoration inside the letter and a red cross-hatched patch at the end of the horizontal ascender. Fol. 1: **3-line red Q**(uadam), plain. Fol. 14v: **3-line red V**(enerabilis), with reserved scalloped line. Fol. 14v: **8-line green F**(uit) in 3-line space, the vertical stroke extended in the margin, with reserved scalloped line and with tiny reserved triangles nestling in the curves, finely executed. Fol. 54: **9-line green P**(ostquam) in 3-line space, the vertical stroke extended in the margin, with reserved scalloped line, and elegant coiled tail, finely executed. Fol. 79: **6-line green E**(xigui), letter filled with red scrolls and foliage inside the letter, a different pattern in each segment. Fol. 79v: **4-line red D**(ominico) with reserved scalloped line, otherwise undecorated.

Historiated initials None.

Display script Fol. 1: (D)**ialogorum Gregorii** in 1-line red mixed capitals followed by red rustic letters; elsewhere, first word or two after a coloured initial in brown rustic letters by the scribe.

Title page None.

Titles etc. No running titles; incipits and explicits to capitula and texts written in a variety of hands in red ink or brown ink with red shading, using minuscule or small rustic capitals; names of interlocutors in red rustic capitals.

IV CONTENTS

Table of contents No original table survives, but capitula were supplied for each of the 4 books. List of contents on paper flyleaf in a later hand, s.xvii.

Main text Gregory, *Dialogues*.

1. Fol. 1: 'Dialogor*um* gregorii p*a*pe urbis Rome libri numero iiii. De miraculis patru*m* italicor*um*. Incipiunt capitula de libro i⁰. Dc honorato abbate monasterii fundensis'. Capitula unnumbered; last ends fol. 1: 'De severo p*re*bendo. Expliciunt cap*itula*. Incipit liber primus beati Gregorii Diagolorum. Quadam die nimiis quor*um*dam s*ae*cularium tumultib*us*'. Ends fol. 79: 'si ante mortem deo hostia ipsi fuerimus. Explicit Dialogus beati Gregorii pape urbis Rome de vita et virtutibus virorum sanctorum in italia commanentium.' *PL* LXXVII, 127.

2. Fol. 79: 'Ep*isto*la fr*atru*m Remensis cenobii ad fratres monasterii in Monte Cassino constituti. Exigui ac per modici regularis vite sectatores fratres qui sunt remis constituti in monasterio beati *et* gloriosi confessoris *christ*i, remigii archiepiscopi'. Ends fol. 79v: 'atq*ue* in modu*m* pitatioli hec verba beato conscripsit Remigio.'

3. Fol. 79v: 'Ep*isto*la beati Benedicti ad beatum Remigium. Dominico sacerdoti remigio fr*ater et* conservus...S*anct*issimo tuo congratulans p*ro*fectui sacerdos regis'. Ends fol. 80: 'et om*ne*s qui audier[ant] dederunt glo*ri*am deo.' Explicit erased. *PL* LXVI, 935. At foot of page: 'Pascasius'.

Fols. 80v–81: originally blank, now with scribbles. Fol. 80v: 'Douse plesant, basstart' and other scribbles, and a half-page drawing of a bishop, s.xiv–xv. Fol. 81: on inner half of leaf unprotected by chemise pocket: 'Bmasmary Grenwa Grimelwa Coogth fuit ho[?c] Henr[?icus] Vim [?]' (James interprets this as 'Henr. Vm pin vanif'); 'pine Vanif pinarex Wynghamfe [?] mr Tomas greneway' and an ex libris (see below) in various hands.

V ORIGIN AND PROVENANCE

Ex libris 1) Fol. 1, in upper margin: 'Liber s*anct*e marie de Byldewas' in red ink by the undulating ex libris hand known from other books (B.1.3, B.1.31, B.1.34, B.14.5). **2**) Fol. 80, in brown ink in a hand s. xv: 'Liber S*anct*e marie de Byldewas'.

Secundo folio de venerabiliu*m*

The origin of the book is not beyond doubt but it is very likely that it was made at Buildwas. If not made there, the punctuation was certainly adapted for Cistercian use, and the simple decoration is also of Cistercian character. The fact that the book was used for reading aloud is attested by stress marks added throughout the text. The text was among those listed in the *Registrum*, but the Buildwas copy was not recorded.

The name Tomas Greneway (fol. 81) appears in other Buildwas books, e.g. Lambeth 477, in which there are also passages in code – a likely explanation of some of the words listed here – and in B.3.15 where it is written in conjunction with the name Upton. Since in B.3.15 the name Upton is written with that of Gnowsal (Gnossal) the name of the Abbot of Buildwas between 1428 and 1443, and in view of the different modern provenance of Lambeth 477 and the Trinity volumes, it would seem likely a) that Greneway and Upton were also names connected with Buildwas, and b) that the s.xv ex libris also on this page indicates the then contemporary and not the former home of the book.

The book was acquired by Archbishop Whitgift s.xvi ex and given by him to Trinity College.

VI NOTES

VII BIBLIOGRAPHY AND PLATES
James, *Trinity MSS*, I, 4–5; Ker, *MLGB*, 15.

6. CAMBRIDGE, TRINITY COLLEGE MS B.3.8
1. Jerome, De Assumptione Beate Marie Virginis; 2. Vita Sancti Martini; 3. Vita Sancti Nicholai. **Date** *c.*1160–1170
Leaves [ii paper] 75, [ii paper]
Foliation 1–75 (parchment leaves only)
Origin Buildwas

I PHYSICAL DESCRIPTION
Binding Rebound s.xvi–xvii; covering and sewing supports cracked along the length of the spine at the front joint; opens well.
Endleaves
 Front *Pastedown* Parchment leaf in place, fol. 1 of a bifolium, fol. 2 excised completely; the leaf has been turned so that the cut spinefold edge has become the fore-edge with a fragment of the conjoint leaf at the lower corner, the leaf sewn in along its former fore-edge, producing an adjacent stub (see below, Flyleaves); the surviving elements of the spinefold bear clear thread impressions and some sewing holes which are consistent with other evidence. Folio count, old and new shelfmarks (ink), Trinity College book-plate, remains of laid paper fore-edge label, otherwise blank.
 Flyleaves Laid paper bifolium, sewn with double thread into parchment spinefold (stub and pastedown, see above); watermark: a four-petalled motif between letters D and G, surmounted by a crown. All blank except second leaf recto: title written twice in ink, s.xvii.
 Back *Flyleaves* Laid paper bifolium, sewn into parchment bifolium (stub and pastedown, see below), present endband tied down into spinefold; no watermarks, all leaves blank.
 Pastedown Parchment leaf in place; second leaf of a bifolium, the first excised to a stub; pen trials and stylus scribbles, otherwise blank.
Sewing stations Now 6; impressions and marks, eg. on front pastedown and fol. 1, indicate earlier, probably originally, 3: (tail) I 45 K 45*85*83*47 K 25 I mm (head), approximately. The detectable marks are not consistent at all points.
Sewing Now all-along with discoloured S-twist thread; impressions on the front

pastedown (see above) indicate former, probably original, all-along sewing with Z-twist thread.

Sewing supports Now 6 rolled, white tawed skin supports, 4mm wide, broken at the front joints and breaking at the back, tie marks across back of spine. Creased indentations in spinefolds, especially at beginning and end of book, suggest formerly, probably originally, 3 sewing supports, c.85mm apart. 2 very faint impressions on back pastedown, 8–10mm wide, appear to coincide with the upper and lower of these indentations.

Lacing path Now over outer edges of boards, through tunnel to inner face of boards and fixed close to the spine edge. No firm earlier evidence, though impressions on back pastedown suggest earlier lacing paths were parallel.

Endbands Present at head and tail, thin rolled skin core, sewn with discoloured blue and pink threads; not now and perhaps never laced into boards; tied down in 4 spinefolds.

Tabs None present; no other evidence.

Spine lining None present; no other evidence.

Boards White pasteboard, 342 x 220 x 5mm, projecting beyond the leaves c.5mm at all edges.

Primary covering Dark tanned leather, surface crackled as if glazed; triple fillets parallel and close to all four edges, front and back, the centre fillet gilt; small, impressed gilt Whitgift arms, front and back. Faint impression of turn-ins roughly trimmed at an angle on turned front pastedown, at what were formerly the spine corners.

Fastenings Ends of 2 rolled fabric ties now cut flush with outer surface of covers, set into covers front and back, c.45mm from fore-edges.

Chemise None present; outer three-quarters of back pastedown cleaner than inner quarter and with none of the ink and stylus marks that are evident on the inner quarter; probably once protected by a deep chemise pocket.

Bosses None present; no other evidence.

Chain attachments None present; no other evidence.

Labels Remains of laid paper fore-edge label on front pastedown; three printed paper labels on spine each bearing elements of the present shelfmark.

Notes Edges of leaves now stained yellowish-green. The stubs of extra leaves (singletons) after fols. 38 and 71 and stubs of excised leaves after fol. 14 clearly show pairs of rough holes (20–25mm apart) near upper and lower edges; the two after fol. 71 have, in addition, a pair of similar holes in the centre, fols. 14 and 38 have three holes near the lower edge. These holes may have been left by tackets used to hold leaves and bifolia together during copying (see below, Collation).

Structure of Book

Parchment Fair to poor quality, with many hard patches and large holes (eg. fol. 70), and some flaymark damage (eg. fols. 7, 14); hair side very yellow.

Collation 1^8, 2^8 (7 and 8 excised, probably blank), $3-5^8$, $6^8 + 1$, $7-9^8$, 10^4 + two after 4; hair side outside except q. 7, where flesh side outside, presumably to match the facing flesh side of the extra leaf after q. 6; last leaf verso of q. 7 is blank.

Quire nos. None.

Catchwords None.

25

Page Layout
Dimensions
Page 333 x 220mm, roughly trimmed at all margins (evidence of lost inscriptions and notes, and a folded corner on fol. 29).
Space ruled for writing 247 x 145–152mm (item 1, scribes 1 and 2); 255 x 147–265 x 145 (items 2 and 3, scribe 3).

Columns 2.

Pricking QQ. 1–6: leaves folded, outer margin only, 1→8; q. 7: single inner bounding line, double outer; singleton after q. 6 pricked with q. 7.

Ruling In grey sometimes appearing brown, clear, but erratic as to respect for vertical bounding lines. 2, 3 or no lines at the top and/or bottom are ruled edge-to-edge, erratic rather than designed; scribe 3's ruling often practically invisible; q. 9: only one bounding line ruled, though two pricked, the left-hand marks used on versos and the right on rectos. These inconsistencies are reflected in this scribe's copying (see below).

Lines per page QQ. 1–2, 3–5: 26; qq. 6–8 (to last leaf recto fol. 70): 31; fol. 70v: 32; qq. 9–10: variable.

Page design
fols. 1–75

II SCRIBES
Item 1 Fols. 1–14 (qq. 1–2) were written by two scribes *c*.1160–1170. **Scribe 1** wrote fols. 1–1v (col. a) in a large, upright, compressed and clear English hand, with a pronounced, unclosed lower loop to g, using ampersand and placing the point at mid-letter. **Scribe 2** took over at the second word four lines from the bottom in the first column and completed this text (fols. 1v–14v). His hand is similar to that of scribe 1 though beginning smaller; he also used ampersand, but the point is on the line. This scribe placed text capitals in the vertical margins in an ungainly manner, separating this letter from the remainder of the word. Corrections are noted in several hands, in ink and stylus, in the margin. The corrections were usually made and the marginal note often erased (e.g. fol. 6), though on fol. 5 a passage has been erased in the text and the correction noted in the margin, but not transferred to the text. Flex marks were added by another hand to points throughout the whole of this text.

Items 2 and 3 **Scribe 3** wrote the remaining items (fols. 15–75; qq. 3–10) in a large, regular, contemporary hand. There are triangular clubs to minims, letter g is made like a figure of 8, ampersand is neat and streamlined in the continental manner, and the point is at mid-letter. The hand becomes considerably smaller and more compressed in the course of the copying; guide letters for the initial maker were systematically made. This scribe seems sometimes to have used the punctus flexus punctuation mark, but a corrector has also added flex to points throughout this item. Corrections were made throughout directly into the text over erasures by several hands; longer omissions (eye-skip errors) were added in margins on fols. 29v and 31v by a backward sloping hand which also made other corrections, e.g. fol. 47 (an interlinear correction). Other emendations were noted in the margin by many other hands (e.g. fols. 54v, 58v, 62, 65 etc.). Many of these are obviously readers' notes, in hands dating from s.xii to s.xiii med.

Trial punctus flexus and other punctuation marks, together with a few trial letters, appear in the lower margins on fols. 27, 56v, 57.

III DECORATION, RUBRICS AND ARTICULATION OF TEXT

The articulation of the text is characterised by a very haphazard approach to the rubrication. This appears to have been done at a late stage in the production of the book, at least after the initial on fol. 1 was made, and by many scribes who themselves made mistakes which were corrected by others (see below, Titles etc.). Compare St. John's D.2, and Trinity B.2.30, made a little later.

Text initials One-line capitals alternately red and green for capitula on fols. 16v–17 and fol. 45v; alternately red and blue for capitula on fol. 45. Other text capitals in brown ink by text scribes.

Minor initials *Item 1* None. *Items 2 and 3* A series of 2-line initials, mainly red or green but sometimes blue (e.g. fols. 23v, 25v, 26–29, 35–38 etc.). The initials which mark new chapters are plain or have reserved lines and/or are minimally decorated with one of the other colours. These initials (fols. 16–75) are sometimes characterised by decoration consisting of dotted lines alongside elements of the initial.

Major initials The initials at the opening of texts or major sections of texts are not always clearly major in stature or design. Fol. 1: **6-line ochre C**(ogitis), with thin and sparse, asymmetrical scroll flourishes in red, green and ochre; this scribe also executed the display script here, but his work does not reappear in this book. Fol. 15: **5-line green E**(go) with well executed scroll design in green and red in both compartments; this scribe also executed the rubrics on this leaf. Fol. 15v: **9-line green and red P**(lerique), with extended tail, the colours separated by a reserved wavy line, and symmetrical red and green scroll-like design like that on fol. 15, executed by the artist who also did the rubrics on this page. Fol. 17v: **8-line green and red I**(gitur) with extended tail, the colours separated by a reserved wavy line, also by the scribe of fol. 15. Fol. 56: **2-line green S**(icut) with minor decoration in red.

Historiated initials None

Display script Fol. 1: (C)**ogitis me o Paula** in 1-line mixed Roman and uncial capitals, first word red, second green, rest ochre, by the scribe who made the initial C (see above). Fol. 15: (E)**go quidem librum quem de vita sancti martini** in small rustic capitals in brown ink by the text scribe. Fol. 15v: (P)**lerique mortalium** in small rustic capitals in brown ink by the text scribe. Fol. 17v: (I)**gitur martinus sabarie pannoniarum**, the first two words in 1-line red mixed Roman and uncial capitals, the second two words in small rustic capitals in brown ink shaded with red. Elsewhere, the first line, few words or word following a coloured capital are executed in small rustic capitals written in brown ink by the text scribe, the extent of the 'display' script decreasing toward the end of the book.

Titles etc. No running titles except on fols. 2–4; incipits and explicits in red ink by various hands which are worth listing because the list sheds useful light on book production at Buildwas.

Item 1 Fol. 1: incipit in red (oxidised) probably by scribe 2, added after initial letter completed. Fol. 14v: explicit in red in a backward sloping, thin and rather wavery hand, not unlike that of the 'flyleaf scribe'.

Item 2 Fol. 15: incipit in the hand that made the initial, probably scribe 3. Fol. 15v: explicit and incipit in same hand (scribe 3) but explicit crossed out and corrected by the backward-sloping 'flyleaf-like hand'. Fol. 16v: explicit (to the preface) and incipit (capitula) in red by a small hand with very tall ascender to l. Fol. 17v: explicit and incipit in red by scribe 3. Fol. 33: explicit and incipit in red by scribe 3, partly crossed out in brown ink and corrected by an unknown hand. Fol. 35: explicit and incipit in pale red by another unknown hand in mixed capitals. Fol. 37: explicit in red by the 'capitula hand' (see. fol. 16v), partly erased and corrected in brown ink by a hand which made other text corrections. Fol. 38: explicit and sub-headings by the 'capitula hand' crossed out in ink and the passage marked 'vacat'. Fols. 45, 45v: explicit and incipit by the 'flyleaf-like hand' of fol. 15v. Fol. 53v: explicit and marginal sub-headings by the 'flyleaf-like hand' of fol. 15v. Fol. 54v: 2 marginal sub-headings added by the 'flyleaf like hand'.

Item 3 Fol. 56: Incipit by the 'flyleaf-like hand'. Fol. 56v: explicit and incipit in red by text scribe 3, partly crossed out, and corrected by the 'flyleaf-like hand'. Fol. 75: explicit by the 'flyleaf-like hand'.

The 'capitula hand' provided numbers for the lists of capitula, but in the text provided them only for the first few chapters.

Title page None.

IV CONTENTS

Table of contents None

Main texts Jerome, *De assumptione beate marie virginis. Vitae sanctorum.*

1. Fol. 1: 'Sermo s*ancti* ieronomi p*res*byt*er*i ad paula*m et* eustochium...de assumptione beate marie virginis. Cogitis me o Paula *et* eustochium immo caritas *christi* me compellit'. Ends fol. 14v: 'c*um* ipso *et* vos appareatis in et*er*na glor*ia* sine fine amen. Explicit sermo s*ancti* ieronomi p*res*bit*er*i de assu*m*ptione beate marie virginis.' Rest of fol. 14v blank.

2. Fol. 15: 'Incipit ep*istol*a severi ad desid*er*ium de vita s*ancti* martini. Ego quid*em* libru*m* quem de vita s*ancti* martini scripseram'. Ends fol. 15v: 'loquat*ur* materia*m* n*on* loquat*ur* autore*m*. Explicit ep*istol*a.' Fol. 15v: 'Incipit p*re*fatio Pleriq*ue* mortaliu*m* studio *et* glor*ie* seculari'. Ends fol. 16v: 'tacere quam falsa dicere malvissem. Explicit p*re*fatio.' Fol. 16v 'Incipiu*n*t Capitula i De s*an*cta conversatione adolescentie'. Ends fol. 17v: 'xxiii...nu*m*quam ab oratione laxaverit. Expliciunt cap*itul*a. Incipit vita s*ancti* martini. Igitur Martinus sabarie pa*n*noniarum oppido oriundus fuit'. Ends fol. 33: 'n*on* quicu*m*que legerit sed quicu*m*que crediderit.' ('Explicit liber' lined through). Fol. 33: 'Incipit ep*istol*a severi ad eusebium ep*iscopu*m presbiterum. Esterna die cu*m* ad me pleriq*ue* monachi venissent'. Ends fol. 35: 't*em*ptatu*m* quidem illo martinus p*er*iculo sed probatu*m*. Explicit epistola severi ad eusebium presbitum.' Fol. 35: 'Incipit epistola severi ad aurelianum diaconem. Postea quam a me mane digressus es'. Ends fol. 37: 'ex q*ua*da*m* n*ost*ri co*n*fabulatione p*re*staret carta solantiu*m*. Explicit ep*istol*a severi ad aurelianum diacone*m*.' Fol. 37: 'Ep*istol*a Sulpicii Severi Basule parenti venerabili de tr*a*nsitu beati martini. Sulpicius severus

basuli...Si parentes vocari'. Ends fol. 38: 'que m*i*hi sunt comp*e*rta participe*m*. Explici*t* ep*istol*a. Q*u*al*i*te*r* migr*a*vit beatus martinu*s* ab hoc mu*n*do ad *christum* [marked vacat]. Martinus igit*ur* obitu*m* suu*m* longe ante prescivit'. Ends fol. 45: 'Ita parit*er* accepta galli sonsione surreximus. Explicit liber *tertius*. Incipiunt cap*itul*a libri quarti. i. Lucescit a galle surgendum est'. Ends fol. 45v (capitulum 21)*:* 'et pie visitari sepulturam *proponi*.' Fol. 45v: 'Incipit liber *quartus* dialogi severi in vita sancti martini archiepiscopi. Lucescit a galle surgendum est'. Ends fol. 53v: 'sed n*on* minore ex n*os*tris fletib*us* dolore discessu*s* est. Explicit liber quartus dialogi severi in vita s*ancti* martini archie*piscop*i.'

This text is followed by (fol. 53v): 'Narratio Gregorii turonensis ep*iscop*i de transitu s*ancti* martini. Archadii vero et honorii sec*un*do imp*er*ii anno'. Ends fol. 54v: 'anni q*u*adrigenti duodec*im* computant*ur*.' Fol. 54v: 'Visio beati severini coloniensis ep*iscop*i de obitu s*ancti* martini. Beatus aut*em* severinus coloniensis'. Ends fol. 54v: 'q*uo* s*anctus* severin*us* audivit psallentiu*m* choru*m*.' Fol. 54v: 'Visio s*ancti* ambrosii de transitu s*ancti* martini achie*piscop*i. Eo tempore beatus ambrosius cui*us* hodie flores'. Ends fol. 55: 'et sp*irit*u s*anct*u vivit *et* regnat d*eus* per om*n*ia sec*u*la sec*u*lorum amen.' Rest of fol. 55 and fol. 55v blank.

3. Fol. 56: 'Incipit p*ro*logus de vita sancti nicholai. Sicut om*n*is materies si ab imp*er*ito'. Ends fol. 56v: '*et* ab inimicis tutos fore letemur. Explicit p*ro*log*us*. Incipit vita s*ancti* nicholai. Beatus nicholaus ex illustri p*ro*sapia ortus civis fuit patere urbis'. Ends fol. 68: 'ut tuis patrocinus p*ro*tecti s*em*per adiuvemur apud *christum* qui cum deo patre...sec*u*lorum sec*u*la am*en*.' Fol. 68: 'Incipiunt miracula s*ancti* nicholai. Quoddam t*em*pore advenit queda*m* mulier de vico'. Ends fol. 75: '*christo* sanctoque nicholao fidelis p*er*mansit. Explicit s*ancti* nicholai'.

Fol. 75 blank except for scribbles s.xii, s.xiii.

V ORIGIN AND PROVENANCE

Ex libris fol. 1 in upper margin, in red ink: 'Liber monachor*um* s*ancti* marie de Buldewas', s.xii ex.

Secundo folio [sanctis]simu*m* corp*us*

None of the scribes or decorators in this book are known from other surviving Buildwas books unless the backward sloping rubricating hand, which bears a resemblance to the hand of the 'flyleaf scribe', is in fact a slightly later manifestation of this scribe's work (known from Trinity B.1.3 and Harley 3038). However the book is very likely to have been made there during the early book-producing campaign. It is comparable to BL Add 11881 which is also a collection of lives of saints, and the piecemeal addition of rubrics is echoed in other Buildwas books. The addition of the flex to points throughout is also characteristic and the initial letters are Cistercian in their relative plainness.

The book was among those acquired by Archbishop Whitgift s.xvi ex and was given by him to Trinity College.

VI NOTES

1. The three items are numbered i, ii and iii consistently throughout over the right column on the recto of each leaf.
2. On fol. 65 is a note possibly in the hand of the Buildwas indexer (see Trinity B.14.5).
3. The last endleaf and pastedown are covered with a variety of scribbles and inscriptions, some partially erased: fol. 75v: 2 partially erased inscriptions, largely

illegible: 'karissimo amico suo Wilel[mo]'. Similar inscriptions occur in Trinity O.7.9 and Lambeth 477. On the inner quarter of the pastedown, other scribbles in ink and stylus in various hands s.xii–xiii.

4. On fol. 35 is a silverpoint sketch of an architectural decorative motif in the outer margin.

VII BIBLIOGRAPHY AND PLATES
James, *Trinity MSS*, I, 108–9; Ker, *MLGB*, 14.

7. LONDON, BRITISH LIBRARY ADDITIONAL MS 11881

Vitae sanctorum   **Date** *c*.1170
Leaves [iii parchment], i, 108, i, [iii parchment]
Foliation 1–108
Origin Probably Buildwas

The book has been much mutilated, and many of its coloured initial letters have been cut out.

I PHYSICAL DESCRIPTION
Binding Rebound s.xix and at least once previously; breaking at joints.
Endleaves
    Front *Pastedown* **1**) Single leaf of heavy black paper in place; **2**) detached leaf, possibly used as a pastedown at some stage (see below, Flyleaves 3).
    Flyleaves **1**) Heavy single composite leaf, black paper (recto) pasted to a white parchment leaf (verso); blank except for various shelfmarks in pencil; **2**) parchment bifolium (not original), blank; **3**) single leaf, a part of the original endleaves; recto: an offset, lower edge, upside down (see below, Scribes), 2 holes at fore-edge, impressions of two different covering turn-ins, and 1 clear and 1 faint impression of earlier sewing support channel (see below); verso: pencil title, British Library shelfmark etc. including 'Sale Cat. 493'.
    Back *Flyleaves* **1**) Medieval flyleaf, fol ii of bifolium (fol. i carries end of text), probably formerly a pastedown, with slight paste remains coinciding with impressions of former covering turn-in (not coloured), otherwise blank except for folio count in pencil (recto); **2**) parchment bifolium, not original, blank; **3**) parchment leaf not original, blank, with black paper leaf pasted to verso.
    Pastedown **1**) Single leaf of heavy, black paper, in place.
Sewing stations Now 5; evidence of earlier sewing stations obscured (but see below, Sewing).
Sewing Now resewn with S-twist thread. On fol. 45 at spinefold and elsewhere in the same quire, impressions of another sewing thread are visible, but are difficult to interpret.
Sewing supports Now 5 cords. Impressions on the original front pastedown indicate an earlier binding on an unknown number of supports, 8–10mm wide: one, 83mm from lower edge, 18mm from spine edge and 34mm long; another 110mm from upper edge, 27mm from spine edge and 25mm long. There are few distinct marks or impressions on the surviving original back endleaf.
Lacing path Present lacing unclear, possibly through thickness of boards to inner face, fixed under the pastedown. Impressions on detached pastedowns indicate earlier parallel lacing paths at least 52mm long.

Endbands Present at head and tail, double cores of rolled tawed skin, sewn with blue and brown threads; never laced into the present boards. No other evidence.

Tabs None present; no other evidence.

Spine lining None present; no other evidence.

Boards Pasteboard, 367 x 255 x 4mm, now warped; projecting beyond edges of leaves.

Primary covering Now tanned leather with blind stamped, frame-shaped decoration to front, back and inner projecting edges and across the spine; gold stamp front and back, with bishop's mitre encircled by a belt inscribed 'Bibliotheca Butleriana'. Single gold fillet along all edges (thickness) of both covers. Leaves which earlier served as pastedowns (see above) both carry impressions of turn-ins of 2 covers: a deep turn-in with irregular edges consistent with an early covering, and a narrow turn-in stained brown, consistent with a later covering of tanned leather.

Fastenings None present; two greenish holes at the fore-edge of the original front pastedown indicate the former presence of a fore-edge strap; correspondingly, repaired holes, rusted and green, 65 and 70mm from centre fore-edge of fols. 108 and 109 respectively (last 2 leaves), probably mark the position of a former central pin.

Chemise None present; no other evidence.

Bosses None present; no other evidence.

Chain attachments None present; no other evidence.

Labels 3 red leather British Museum labels on spine with number and title in gold; 2 printed paper labels also on spine: '470' and 'F.6'.

Structure of Book

Parchment Fairly good quality, much follicle marking, some traces of blood remaining in veins (e.g. fol. 62). Some contemporary repairs (fols. 64, 68, 75, 81, 88, 89), but also extensive modern repairs, particularly large patches, many in the first quire, where initial letters have been excised (e.g. fol. 47); laid paper appears to have been used for some repairs (e.g. fol. 60).

Collation 1–4 missing; 5 (1 leaf and 1 stub only remain), 6^8 (1 and 8 missing), 7–8^8, 9^8 (1 excised), 10^8 (1 excised), 11–12^8; 13–15 missing; 16–18^8, 19^8 (1 leaf missing), 20^8, 21^8 (3 excised), 22^8, 23 (2 leaves).

Quire nos. QQ. 7–20 in brown ink small lower case Roman numerals, lower margin verso of last leaf, some partially trimmed.

Catchwords None.

Page Layout

Dimensions

Page Variable: 348–351 x 245mm, trimmed at all edges.

Space ruled for writing Variable: 237–249 x 163–165mm.

Columns 2.

Pricking QQ. 1–5: mutilated, no evidence; qq. 6–23: much evidence trimmed: remains suggest quires were pricked with leaves folded, outer margins only, 1→8 except qq. 10 and 17, where upper and lower margins are pricked 8→1. The 'mirror-image' patterns of the prick marks suggest that a template was used for pricking upper margins and turned over for pricking lower margins.

Ruling Blind ruling; lines 1 and 3, and the last and third from last lines ruled edge-to-edge in outer margin, but first 3 and last 3 in inner margin.

Lines per page Variously 31 and 32.

Page design

fols. 1–108

II SCRIBES

One scribe wrote and rubricated the text throughout in a large open hand (*c.*1170), having the character of the work of the 'master scribe' of Christ Church 88 (q.v.). Corrections were made mainly by the scribe over erasures (e.g. fols. 24, 61, 78v, 79v, 81, 88 etc.) but a few were executed by another hand (s.xiii) over erasures (e.g. fol. 28). Corrector's and rubricator's notes (the latter presumably the scribe's own) survive in lower margins (e.g. fols. 78v, 79v, 81). The scribe used punctus flexus on the present fol. 1 (and presumably in the early missing quires), but not thereafter. Offsets of the text of this book appear in upper and lower margins of some leaves and on the recto of the original front pastedown; the scribe seems to have placed completed leaves in a pile before the ink was completely dry.

III DECORATION, RUBRICS AND ARTICULATION OF TEXT

Text initials Fols. 74–74v: small 1-line capitals for capitula, alternately red and purple; elsewhere 1-line brown ink capitals.

Minor initials Plain but elegantly executed 3-line initials indicate major divisions within any text, and 2-line initials for minor divisions, alternately red and purple, except fols. 3, 8v–9, 17, 24v–25, 38, 54, 55, 62, 70, 78, 94, where green is used instead of purple. Letter A often has an elaborate first ascender or cross stroke.

Major initials Many quires and leaves are missing, and initials on most surviving leaves have been excised, perhaps indicating that they were of good quality: fol. 1v: I; fol. 4v: P; fol. 5v: B; fol. 6v: G; fol. 47v: P. On fol. 74 the initial and the first two capituli are entirely excised. The two surviving initials are plain. Fol. 39v: **11-line red I**(n) with broad central section of letter reserved, and extended, elegant, bifurcated and scrolled tail also red; fol. 98: **8-line red E**(rat), plain.

Historiated initials None extant, probably none originally.

Display script Fol. 1v: [I]**nclitus rex** in 1-line brown, mixed square and uncial capitals; fol. 4v: [P]**rima** in 1-line brown mixed capitals; fol. 5v: [Be]**atissimo** in 1-line brown Roman capitals; fol. 6v: [G]**regorius** in 1-line brown ink Roman capitals; fol. 39v: (I)**n illis tem**/poribus in 1-line brown ink mixed capitals; fol. 47v: [P]**resentie** in 1-line brown ink mixed capitals; fol. 74: initial and display script excised; fol. 98: (E)**rat** in 1-line brown ink Roman capitals.

Title page None, but early leaves lost.

Titles etc. No running titles or chapter headings. Incipits and explicits in red ink by the text scribe; no final explicit.

IV CONTENTS

Table of contents None, but early leaves lost.

Main texts *Vitae Sanctorum*.

1. Fol. 1: Life of St. John begins imperfectly: 'eum *et* dixit illi ancilla dei Quo vadis serve dei?' Ends fol. 1v: 'Ceci ibidem illuminant*ur* demonia effugant*ur* lep*ro*si mundant*ur et* fiunt ibi divina beneficia usq*ue* in presente*m* diem. Prestante d*omi*no n*os*tro ieh*s*u *christo* qui vivit...sec*u*la sec*u*lorum Amen. Explicit vita sanc*ti* joh*ann*is abba*tis*.'

2. Fol. 1v: 'Incipit passio s*ancti* eaduuardi regis *et* martiris xv kale*nd*s aprilis: [I]nclitus Rex Eaduuardus alto et nobilis'. Ends fol 4v: 'Elevatus *est* itaq*ue* sacratissimu*m* corp*us* eius anno vicesimo primo ex quo illic tumulatum fuerat qui erat annus ab incarnatione d*omi*ni millesimus p*ri*mus regnante eodem d*omi*no n*os*tro...*per* sec*u*la sec*u*lorum Amen. Explicit passio s*ancti* ead[uua]rdi regis et martiris.'

2a. Fol. 4v: '[Inci]piunt miracula [e]iusdem. [P]rima [ ] edwardum [ ] de quib*us* pauca [mirac]ulo inserere'. Ends fol 5v: 'in celesti ier*usa*lem p*er*frui mereamur. prestante d*omi*no n*os*tro...*per* immortalia [secu]lor*um* Amen. Explic*iu*nt [mi]rac*u*la s*ancti* eaduuar[di re]gis *et* mart*i*ris.'

3. Fol. 5v: 'In[cipit] p*ro*logus in vita [G]regorii pape. [Be]atissimo [et] felicissimo d*omi*no iohanni s*ancti* catholice'. Ends fol. 6v: '[ ]diter liberari per [Explicit] prefatio. Incipit [vi]ta s*ancti* Gregorii...[Gre]gorius [g]enere romanus arte philo[soph]ani [sic] viri clarissimi'. Ends fol. 39v: 'saltem verba que vale minime denegasse cognoscar. Explicit vita s*ancti* gregorii romane urb*is* ap*os*tolici.'

4. Fol. 39v: 'Incipit passio sancti theodosie virg*in*is et m*a*rtiris iiii non*as* aprilis. In illis temporibus dioclitiano quater imperante'. Ends fol. 47v: 'quod magnum e*st* anime ve*st*re. Explicit passio s*anct*e theodosie virginis et martiris.'

5. Fol. 47v: 'Incipit vita [san]cti nicetu ep*iscop*i [i]iii^{to} nonas aprilis. [P]resentie divine bonum [ ]q*ue* regno suo p*ro*videat [ ]cicat'. Ends incomplete fol. 53v: 'Credo quia potens e*st* de*us* egregia operari'.

6. Fol. 54: Life of St. Augustine begins imperfectly: 'memoret q*uam* p*ro*fectuosus extiterit suscepta *christ*ianitate'. Ends incomplete fol. 74: 'De his q*uoque* septe*m* primis anglice ecc*lesi*e columnis tarpeia derune' (final words excised with initial etc. of next text).

7. Fol. 74: Life of St. Marculfus begins imperfectly at capitulum 3: 'Tertius est gratui [ ]. Quartus ad e*st* iust*us*'. Text begins fol. 74v: 'De innumeris v*er*o signis que in hoc requietionis sue dormitorio'. Ends fol. 98: 'referens manipulos suos cum exultatione ad d*omi*num n*os*trum *ihesum christum* qui ab initio nunc *et* semper vivit *et* regnat Amen. Explicit vita s*ancti* marculfu [sic] conf*essoris*.'

8. Fol. 98: 'Incipit p*assio* s*ancti christ*ofori martiris: Erat quidam *christ*ianus nomine *christ*oforus vir sanctus *et* valde clarus'. Ends imperfectly fol. 107v: 'Quare n*on* vis credere? Ecce rursu*m* hoc ipsu*m* dico hoc ipsum repeto deos'.

9. Fol. 108: Passion of St. Barbara begins imperfectly: 'tue gra*tia*m ut siquis memoraverit nomen tuum etiam nomen famule tue.' Ends.fol. 108: 'Martyrizata est virgo beatissima barbara sub maximiano imp*er*atore pridie nonas decembris regnante d*omi*no n*os*tro...in secula seculor*um* Amen.'

V ORIGIN AND PROVENANCE

Ex libris None survives.

Secundo folio (now) pro palari

There is no conclusive evidence that this book originated in a Buildwas scriptorium; Watson (*MLGB Supplement*, 5 n. 1) directs the reader to Sir Thomas Phillipps's catalogue of Samuel Butler's MSS (see below). Phillipps wrote of this book that it was 'said to be Ex abbatia Buildwas', though no evidence is cited. Watson is of the view that this MS was made in the scriptorium which produced Christ Church 88 (q.v.), perhaps by the same scribe. The scribes are not, in fact, the same, though the hand of the 11881 scribe is similar to that of the 'master scribe' in the Christ Church book. The 11881 scribe uses the punctus flexus on the first surviving leaf (though not thereafter), and the contents complement those of Trinity B.3.8, also a collection of lives of saints. There are no recognisable marks of known Buildwas readers on the surviving leaves.

The book was purchased by the British Museum from the Rt. Rev. Dr. Samuel Butler, Lord Bishop of Lichfield, in 1841.

VI NOTES

Phillipps's list of the contents of the book coincides with the present contents, except that 'S. Cantuar' appears between St. Christopher and St. Barbara.

VII BIBLIOGRAPHY AND PLATES

Catalogue of Additions to the Manuscripts in the British Museum in the years MDCCCXLI–MDCCCXLV (London, 1850), 15; Sir Thomas Phillipps, *Catalogus Manuscriptorum Magnae Britanniae* (1850), 5 (no. 66); Watson, *MLGB Supplement*, 5 and n. 1.

8. CAMBRIDGE, UNIVERSITY LIBRARY MS Ii.2.3.

1. William of Malmesbury, De Gestis Regum Anglorum. (2. Henry of Huntingdon, Historia Anglorum)   **Date** *c.*1170

Leaves [ii (s.xvi)], 203, i. Fols. 139–146 are s.xvi replacements.

Foliation 1–206; also paginated in red crayon s.xvi on rectos only, 1–409. Foliation used here.

Origin Item 1 (fols. 1–138v): probably Buildwas; item 2: unknown.   **Figs.** 10, 13

The two texts were almost certainly first bound together as one in the sixteenth century by Matthew Parker, whose secretary paginated the double volume and began to construct an index. There is no evidence that booklet 2 ever belonged to the Buildwas library.

I PHYSICAL DESCRIPTION

Binding Rebound at least twice, s.xvi and xviii; current binding s.xix–xx; spine recovered more recently. Book opens fairly well.

Endleaves

Front *Pastedown* Fol. 1 of replacement bifolium in place, with worm holes, 3 rust marks at the corners from former metal fittings, probably bosses (a fourth probably obscured by old spine title, see below), titles of both texts (s.xvii) and provision for an alphabetical index (letter headings, 3 to a page), some entries added in a s.xvii hand (see below, Notes). Shelfmarks: 'Ii.2.3.' and '252', University Library book-plate and the spine label from an earlier covering

(?s.xviii) now also attached.

Flyleaves **1)** Fol. 2 of bifolium (a discarded ?legal document, see below) conjoint with pastedown, with worm holes and 4 rust marks from former metal fittings matching those on pastedown; recto: continuation of index provision with some entries in one hand s.xvii; white parchment label 27 x 74mm, formerly fixed to cover by 6 nails (evidence of holes in parchment), inscribed (s.xvi in): 'W Malmesbery de regibus Historia h. huntedonensis'; verso: ?legal text in English (s.xvi) now appearing vertically and obscured by a leaf of laid paper pasted over the written side; index continues on the paper leaf; **2)** later parchment leaf pasted in (stub now under pastedown); recto: Malmesbury's dedication text supplied s.xvi with illuminated initial (see below); verso: blank.

Back *Flyleaves* Fol. 1 of separate bifolium with many wormholes and 4 rust marks probably from earlier metal fittings, probably bosses (cf. front endleaves); index provision continued from the front with some entries recto and verso, otherwise blank. The character of this leaf and the conjoint pastedown is the same as that carrying the Huntingdon text and the bifolium is probably contemporary with it (s.xiii in). It bears wormholes which match those on the final leaves of the text, but otherwise, the only marks now visible on it are the s.xvii index notes.

Pastedown Fol. 2 of bifolium in place, conjoint with flyleaf, much damaged and discoloured with marks from metal fittings; index provision concludes on the recto of this leaf.

Sewing stations Now 4: (tail) I 22 K 56*63*68*58*31 K 24 I mm (head) Earlier, probably originally, item 1 was marked-up for sewing on 3 supports with prick marks about 5mm from spinefold, 8→1, including kettle stitch station (see e.g. fol. 67 where sewing thread impressions are also visible): (tail) I 22 K*47* 85*85*43 K* 40 I mm (head). Item 2 is marked-up only for sewing on 4 supports and these marks coincide with the present sewing. Item 1 shows no such marking-up.

Sewing Now with white Z-twist thread. Sewing thread impressions here and there, e.g. at the tail of fols. 62v–63 and at fols. 66v–67, suggest that the book was earlier also sewn with Z-twist thread.

Sewing supports Now 4 narrow white split tawed skin supports, broken front and back; item 1, originally 3 supports (evidence of marking-up and sewing thread impressions).

Lacing path Present evidence unclear; probably over the outer edges, through to the inner face of boards and fixed under the pastedown. No earlier evidence.

Endbands None present. Impressions of tying-down thread at head and tail indicates former presence of endbands, and a fragment of yellow S-twist thread survives at fols. 200–201, probably from the s.xvi sewing.

Tabs None present; no other evidence.

Spine lining None present; no other evidence.

Boards Pasteboard, 329 x 238 x 3mm, now bowing inwards towards the text leaves. Wormholes on first and last leaves indicate that earlier boards were of wood.

Primary covering Boards covered with faded purple laid paper. Spine recently recovered with brown leather (calf). Stains and impressions at all outer edges of front and back pastedowns and flyleaves indicate the former, but not original, presence of a stained primary covering, irregularly trimmed.

Fastenings None present; no other evidence.

Chemise None present; no other evidence.

Bosses None extant. Green marks on upper and lower spine edge corners of fol. 1 and perhaps a third and fourth in the fore-edge corners were probably left by boss nails on the original binding of item 1; there are none on the back endleaves of the book as now bound. Rust marks probably from 4 corner boss nails are evident on present front and back endleaves, evidence of metal furniture on a later binding (s.xvi).

Chain attachments Rust marks at lower fore-edge corner of front pastedown and similar marks on first flyleaf suggest probable former presence of chain staple.

Labels Parchment label s.xvi now pasted to front flyleaf (see above, Front flyleaves 1).

Notes 1) Page markers (remains and evidence in the form of sewing holes) found as follows in item 1: fol. 33: holes and impression of a marker marking the succession of Saxon Kings in Book 2; fol. 76v: remains of thread and needle holes at beginning of the preface to book 3; fol. 93: similar evidence marking the beginning of the chapter on Berengar of Tours and on fol. 104 marking a chapter headed 'Quomodo ordo cisterciensis sumpsit inicium'. Thread at the lower edge of fol. 147 marks beginning of item 2. **2**) On the fore-edges of the leaves is written: 'Wilhelmi Malmesb. de Regibus et 24 historia Henrici Huntingdon' probably in the hand of the reader who began to make entries in the index (evidence of the similarity of some letter forms).

Structure of Book

Parchment *Booklet 1*: Fairly good quality, supple parchment, with a good nap and of even colour; some holes, and a number of patch repairs (e.g. fols. 14, 42, 45 etc.). The last quire (q. 18), supplied s.xvi, is very much whiter and thicker. *Booklet 2*: thinner parchment and much smoother than that used for item 1.

Collation *Booklet 1*: i²(+ a singleton s.xvi, first leaf is pastedown), 1–17⁸, 18⁸ (s.xvi replacement); hair side outermost. *Booklet 2*: 1–6¹⁰; hair side outermost.

Quire nos. *Booklet 1*: none; *Booklet 2*: qq. 1, 4 in brown ink Roman numerals, lower margin of last leaf verso. Others probably trimmed.

Catchwords *Booklet 1*: none; *Booklet 2*: fragment of catchword survives at the end of q. 4.

Page Layout

Dimensions

Page 322 x 231mm, trimmed at all three outer edges (evidence of trimmed notes, initials etc.).

Space ruled for writing Booklet 1: 267 x 157mm; *Booklet 2*: 235 x 160mm.

Columns 2 (both items).

Pricking *Booklet 1*: Leaves folded, both margins, 1→8 except qq. 11 (both margins) and qq. 6, 12 and 16 (inner margins only), 8→1. *Booklet 2*: leaves folded, both sides (though outer pricking trimmed away), 1→10.

Ruling *Booklet 1*: in grey sometimes appearing brown, neat and consistent and according to pricking; running title lines pricked as well as ruled. *Booklet 2*: in brown.

Lines per page *Booklet 1*: 40 throughout, written above top line. *Booklet 2*: 52,

written below top line.
Page design
fols. 3–146 (booklet 1)   fols. 147–205 (booklet 2)

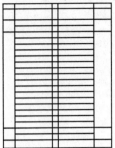 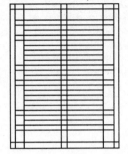

II SCRIBES
Booklet 1: One scribe wrote the entire text except for a few passages on fols. 3–3v and rubricated his own work except perhaps on fol. 3. The hand is upright, neat and compact and well above the ruled line until q. 5 (fol. 35). It becomes even more compact and also changes aspect with changes of pen and ink (e.g. fol. 99). This scribe used the punctus flexus punctuation mark. There are very few corrections, mainly by the scribe himself over erasures (e.g. fols. 18, 74, 118, 127), and there are additions to the punctuation on fol. 93.
Fols. 137–144 were supplied by Archbishop Parker's scribe who also supplied the dedication inscription on the second flyleaf.
Booklet 2: Written by more than one scribe, s.xiii in.

III DECORATION, RUBRICS AND ARTICULATION OF TEXT (Booklet 1 only)
The decoration of this book was executed by one scribe in a strikingly personal style. He produced a series of very beautiful penwork initials, particularly elaborate in the early part of the book, characterised by elliptical, curved, wave-like flourishes of the sort revived by Art Nouveau, frequent use of a starburst motif, of a reserved element which projects like a tube into the adjacent space, and ochre for filling-in and shading initials. Curiously, however, except for the first, the major initials were not decorated, although minor initials were frequently extended and elaborated more than their function in the text required, and paraphs were also often decorated (e.g. on fols. 6, 41v). Some of the reds (e.g. on fols. 1, 8v) are beginning to oxidise to black; others (e.g. on fol. 21v) are still remarkably brilliant and glossy.
Text initials Rustic letters in brown ink supplied by the text scribe shaded with ochre. This was done consistently throughout the text to the very end.
Minor initials 2-line and 3-line initials throughout, alternately red and green, and also blue from fol. 70 onwards The vertical elements of letters are very often considerably extended in the margin, especially letters I of which there are many. Many of these initials are unadorned, or have simple, self-colour motifs or flourishes and/or ochre shading. Others are fully decorated, taking on the status of a major initial. For example: fol. 8v: **17-line red I**(nterim) with extended tail and with a central line reserved against the parchment and shaded with yellow; fols. 18: **15-line I**(ta), very similar to that on fol. 8v but in blue, with ochre

shading; fol. 21v: **6-line red A**(nno) with extended first stroke, the red still very glossy (compare a similar blue and grey initial I on fol. 18;) fol. 79v: **10-line red I**(lle) with extended tail, flourished, shaded with ochre; compare this with 3 large letters I on fols. 81v–82, and others on fols. 88, 94, 95, 117v, 118, 121v etc.

Major initials Fol. 3 (preface): **11-line red R**(es), against parchment ground, the upright with inset cable design and both sections of the letter filled with symmetrical scroll and leaf design; fol. 3v (book 1): **10-line blue A**(nno), a swirling asymmetrical, very beautiful design which trails in the margin towards the bottom of the page, embellished with elliptical flourishes; the blue is a particularly striking sky-blue though slightly rubbed; a very similar design is used for the 2-line blue A(nno) with an extended tail on fol. 33; fol. 28v (book 2): **8-line blue S**(uperiori), very sparsely decorated, possibly unfinished; fol. 77: (book 3): **6-line red R**(obertus), very similar to that on fol. 3; fol. 98v (book 4): **6-line red V**(villilmus), terminals flourished but otherwise undecorated; faint drawing inside letter possibly for a design not executed; fol. 128 (prologue book 5): **5-line red O**(rdine) filled with symmetrical red motifs and shaded with ochre; fol. 128v (book 5): **11-line green H**(enricus) extending into the margin from its 4-line space, with green elliptical flourishes, inset reserved cable design within each vertical element of the initial, and touches of ochre shading.

All subsequent initials are undecorated.

Historiated initials None in text. Later dedication page (fol. 1; s.xvi): Initial **D**(omino) in gold enclosing Parker's arms in silver and gold, red and blue.

Display script Fol. 3: (R)**es A**(nglorum) in 1-line brown capitals by text scribe; fol. 28v: (S)**uperiori** in 1-line brown capitals by text scribe; elsewhere the first word or the first few letters following a coloured initial of any grade is executed in small rustic letters or, more usually, minuscule, written by the text scribe and shaded with ochre or occasionally another colour.

Titles etc. Running book numbers in brown ink sometimes shaded with ochre; incipits and explicits in red by the text scribe; also occasional sub-headings or chapter headings in the margin in red.

IV CONTENTS

Table of contents None, but possibly lost.

Main texts William of Malmesbury, *De Gestis Regum Anglorum.*

1. Fol. 2 (s.xvi): 'Wilhelmus Malmesbury de gestis Regum Anglorum. Domino venerabili et famoso Commiti filio Regis Roberto Wilhelmus Malmesburie monachus'. Fol. 3: 'Incipit prologus willelmi monachi malmesbirie in libro primo de gestis regum anglorum. Res Anglorum gestas Beda vir maxime'. Ends fol. 3v: 'industrie testimonium. Explicit prologus.' Fol. 3v: 'Incipit liber primus. Anno ab incarnatione domini cccc^{mo} xl° ix^{no} venere angli *et* saxones britannia'. Ends fol. 146: 'arbitrio qui non errandi eligendi iudicio. Laus deo. Expliciunt gesta Wilhelmi digne memorie monachi malmesberii cenobii de Regibus Anglorum.' Fol. 146v blank.

Printed in W. Stubbs, ed., *William of Malmesbury, Gesta Regum Anglorum,* 2 vols, (London, 1887–9).

2. Fols. 147–205: Henry of Huntingdon, *Historia Anglorum*, printed in Thomas Forester, transl. and ed., *The Chronicle of Henry of Huntingdon* (London, 1853). Facsimile reprint, Felinfach, 1991, and in *Historia Anglorum: the History of the English People,* ed. and transl. by D.E. Greenway, (Oxford, 1996). Fols. 205v–206 originally blank, now with provision for index.

V ORIGIN AND PROVENANCE

Ex libris Fol. 3, upper margin, largely erased: 'Liber Sancte Marie de B[uildwas?M]' s.xii, in blue rustic and uncial capitals.

Secundo folio q*ue* p*e*regrinationis

Booklet 1 was probably made as a self-contained volume at Buildwas, though the scribes who copied and decorated it have not so far been identified in other Buildwas books. There is no evidence at all that the Henry of Huntingdon text was bound with it before the early sixteenth century, when a parchment label once fixed to the cover of the book was written, nor that this text was at Buildwas, although it is also annotated by various hands s.xiii and later which are similar to the annotating hand of item 1.

The hand of the dedication page and of the last quire is identified in the University Library Catalogue (see below) as that of Archbishop Parker's scribe, so the book must have been in Parker's collection in the mid-sixteenth century. The amalgamation of the two texts was almost certainly carried out by Parker himself. The Malmesbury text must by this time have been in a poor state, possibly having lost its first leaves (endleaves and dedication text), and its last quire certainly lost or very badly damaged, indicating that the binding had degraded by then, the covers probably having been detached or lost.

It had been acquired by Cambridge University Library by 1883 when it was described in that Library's catalogue of manuscripts.

VI NOTES

1. Parts of the text of item 1 were annotated by several readers including the late thirteenth-century reader/librarian who constructed the index in Trinity B.14.5 (q.v.), whose interest appears to have been principally the contents of Book 2. He signposted passages of interest to him by adding a name or a word in the margin (e.g. fol. 29v), added little marginal tables demonstrating the family trees of kings of England, and used sigla to tie marginal comments to a precise point in the text (e.g. fol. 34).
2. Chapter numbers in Arabic numerals were added in Book 2 only beside each coloured initial in a yellowish-brown ink. The ink is not unlike that used by the Buildwas indexer, but the match is not exact, and it may have been done at his instigation by one of the other annotators.
3. The later, seventeenth-century indexer provided, in addition to his subject heading, a page and a column number reference. He sometimes also provided a line number. The system is almost identical to that used in Trinity B.14.5 by the Buildwas indexer, though the latter did not provide column numbers, but only notae occasionally in the margin to direct the reader to the indexed text.
4. On fol. 169v–170 is the rusted impression of a key, 80mm long, with a roughly oval ring at the top.

VII BIBLIOGRAPHY AND PLATES

A Catalogue of the MSS Preserved in the Library of the University of Cambridge (Cambridge, 1883), 372; Watson, *MLGB Supplement*, 5.

9. LONDON, BRITISH LIBRARY MS HARLEY 3038

Leviticus and John, glossed

Leaves [ii paper, ii paper], i, 89, [i paper, ii paper]   **Dated** 1176

Foliation 1–91 (parchment flyleaf is fol. 2)

Origin Buildwas   **Fig**. 4

As far as is known at present, this is the only glossed book to have been made at Buildwas. The very particular choice of prefatory texts, which were all copied at one time by one scribe, merit further attention since, together with the dated ex libris inscription, they suggest a special commission.

I PHYSICAL DESCRIPTION

Binding Rebound at least twice, present binding with hollow back, 1948 (note on last flyleaf).

Endleaves

Front *Pastedown* **1**) Single brown paper leaf in place, blank; **2**) single parchment leaf, s.xii, detached, once the pastedown (see below, Flyleaves 3).

    Flyleaves **1**) Buff wove paper bifolium, first leaf affixed to a second single brown paper leaf; blank except for British Library note of printed texts and notices; **2**) 2 laid paper leaves, probably a bifolium, fol. 1 stained at edges by covering turn-in (not the present one); watermark: horn within a crest, with letters LVG; the second leaf has a single leaf of the same paper affixed to it; both leaves blank except for stamped MS number and a few pencil notes; **3**) parchment leaf once part of a bifolium, written on both sides by hand s.xii (*c*.1160–65) with grainy paste remains recto, marks made by earlier sewing supports at former spine edge but now at fore-edge though there are no sewing support lacing paths or covering turn-in impressions. Rectangular parchment label pasted to recto, with partially erased ownership inscription: 'Sum Liber Rolandi ffau[ ] ex dono Edwardi [ ]' etc.; **4**) rectangle of white tawed skin 170 x 67mm now visible between the laid paper bifolium and the parchment flyleaf, written on flesh side in hand s.xv, verses in English and Latin.

    Back *Flyleaves* **1**) Laid paper bifolium the leaves now adhering to form a single leaf stained at edges by a former tanned leather primary covering turn-in; no visible watermark, blank except for folio count dated November 1881 in pencil, recto; **2**) paper bifolium, fol. 2 stiffened with brown paper; blank.

    Pastedown Brown paper leaf in place, blank.

Sewing stations Now 5. Marks on flyleaf suggest that in an earlier, probably the original, binding there were 3 sewing stations: (tail) I 20 K 40*90*90*62 I mm. (head); no evidence relating to upper kettle stitch, no marking-up visible.

Sewing Now all-along with white, S-twist thread. Thread impressions partially visible fol. 36 indicate that a former sewing was also all-along.

Sewing supports Now sewn on 5 cords. Marks on former spinefold of flyleaf (see above) indicate that the book was once, probably first, sewn on 3 supports *c*.10mm wide.

Lacing path Now over the outer edges of the board; other evidence obscured.

Endbands Present at head and tail; double core sewn with dark blue and white threads. No other evidence.

Tabs None present; no other evidence.

Spine lining None present; no other evidence.

Boards Heavy pasteboard, 319 x 220 x 4mm.

Primary covering Blue leather covering, impressed, gilt Harleian crest front and back inscribed 'virtute et fide'. Title and book number on spine, gilt.

Fastenings None on present binding. On front detached parchment pastedown, 2 greenish holes formerly on fore-edge but now at the spinefold, 14mm apart, suggest that an earlier binding had a central fastening device of some sort, probably a strap and pin.

Chemise None present; the rectangle of white tawed skin now among the front flyleaves is probably part of a former chemise from this book. It is very clean and the flesh side, on which there is writing s.xv, bears no sign whatever of paste.

Bosses None present; no other evidence.

Chain attachments None present; no other evidence.

Labels Former ownership label s.xvi, inscription partially erased, pasted to front detached parchment flyleaf.

Structure of Book

Parchment Quite good quality, evenly coloured and with good nap on both sides; some follicle marks; some sewn repairs e.g. fols. 30, 66 (repaired tear from flay mark).

Collation $1-11^8$, 12 (one leaf only remains).

Quire nos. QQ. 2, 4–5: lower margin of verso of last leaf in tiny 'lower case' Roman numbers; q. 4 partly trimmed. Other numbers probably also trimmed away.

Catchwords QQ. 9, 11: at the bottom of the verso of the last leaf, near spinefold.

Page Layout

Dimensions

Page 310 x 215mm.

Space ruled for writing 228–232 x 170–175mm.

Columns Fols. 3–8: 2; fols. 8v–91: mainly one central text column with gloss column on either side, all 3 columns varying greatly in width from page to page and within a single page; text or gloss sometimes written across 2 columns or the entire ruled space.

Pricking Leaves folded, both margins 1→8 (except q. 1: upper and lower margins 8→1) for gloss lines. Idiosyncratic patterns of prick marks repeated from quire to quire clearly indicate that a template was used, the same one throughout the book. After q. 1 only the outer vertical bounding lines pricked.

Ruling In brown, neatly done; text lines ruled at every 3rd gloss line, the line above it also ruled, perhaps to control the height of the minims of the text hand. Text and gloss lines ruled continuously and at one time. Fols. 3–8: lines 1 and 3 and the last line ruled edge-to-edge; fols. 8v–91: first and last lines only ruled edge-to-edge. Fols. 3–57v: the ruling seldom crosses the vertical bounding lines; fols. 59–91: this practice is less carefully adhered to. Inner vertical bounding lines ruled ad hoc after fol. 8.

Lines per page 59 gloss lines. Text written below top line, gloss above top line.

Page design

fols. 3–8   fols. 8v–57   fols. 58–58v

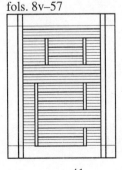
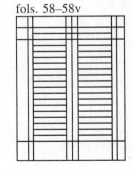

fols. 59–91

II SCRIBES
One scribe wrote text and gloss throughout, though his hand changed quite markedly. First the letters increase in height and width and the pen strokes thicken (e.g. fol. 24); then the hand develops a backward slope (e.g. fol. 40) and at the same time the letters decrease somewhat in height. At the end of item 2 (fol. 57v) the hand is smaller, even more angular and backward-sloping, and is identical at the beginning of item 4 (fol. 59). It is subsequently more consistent. The scribe's gloss hand (also used for the text on fols. 58–58v) is less variable, but also develops a backward slope and the letters become very small by the end of item 2. At the outset the scribe made a series of elaborate paraph marks (fols. 13–22) but soon abandoned this practice. There are very few, if any, corrections.

A second scribe wrote 5 text lines on fol. 36v and the associated interlinear gloss, though the main scribe wrote the marginal gloss. This scribe's hand is much rounder and more upright than that of the main scribe, and he used lighter ink.

III DECORATION, RUBRICS AND ARTICULATION OF TEXT
Text initials Brown ink initials written by text scribe.
Minor initials In item 1, small 2-line initials alternately red (oxidised) and green, sometimes with reserved lines, flourished occasionally with the same or a contrasting colour; fol. 7v: **4-line red E**(sichus) the red oxidised, with 'curled leaf and horn' motifs in each half of the letter in blue.
Major initials Fol. 8: **4-line blue V**(ocavit) with extended red (oxidised) 'curled leaf and horn' motifs inside letter and other extended flourishes in red; fol. 59: **9-line green H**(ic) with scalloped line reserved against the parchment in both vertical strokes; fol. 59v: **18-line red I**(n) with reserved undulating line, an elaborate serif at the top of the letter and an extended tail with a curled leaf, both in red.
Historiated initials None.
Display script Fol. 59: (H)**ic** in 1-line brown ink capitals; fol. 59: (I)**n principio** in 1-line brown ink rustic capitals.
Title page None.
Titles etc. Abbreviated running titles added in upper margin of rectos probably by a later hand s.xiii. Incipit and explicit to Leviticus only, in red (oxidised) by scribe.

IV CONTENTS
Table of contents None.

Main texts Leviticus and John, glossed.

1. Fols. 3–7: a series of notes, many (fols. 4v–6v) illustrated with freehand diagrams of the family tree type. Begins fol 3: 'Recte orthografie que hic annotatur, sic ubi prevaricatur". Fol. 3: 'Trini dei trinam ymagine [sic] et autoritas testatur'. Fol. 3v: 'De scientiarum atque virtutum inicus. Ut plenariam in suo genere scientiam et virtutem haberet hoc'. Fol. 3v: 'De scienciis. Est autem scientia comprehensibilius agnito' (diagram). Fol. 4: 'Virtutem describit philosophus habitum mentis optimus' (diagram fol. 4v). Fol. 4v: 'De fide. Fidem assignat apostolis esse'. 'Divisio fidei'. Fol. 5v: 'De fide et spe et karitate. De his tribus queritur ad quas virtutes'. Fol. 5v: 'De distancia meritorum et virtutum'. 'De gracia'. Fol. 6: 'De libero arbitrio'. Fol. 6v: 'Malum nichil aliud est ut ait augustinus quam absencia boni' (diagram). Ends fol. 7v: 'incidere in manum dei.'

2. Fol. 7v gloss begins: 'Esichius pre omnibus necesse est interpretationem legis ad anagogen trahi'. Text begins fol. 8: 'Vocatus autem'. Ends fol 57: 'in monte synai. Explicit Leviticus.' Gloss ends fol. 57v: 'dormivit moyses in christo post quam decantavit audite celi.'

3. Fol. 58: 'Septem gradus descensionis habet humilitas'. Ends fol. 58v: 'exercere in virtute nutrire in infirmitate'.

4. Fol. 59 preface: 'Hic est iohannes evangelista unus ex discipulis dei'. Gloss: 'Iohannis interpretatur gratia'. Preface ends fol 59v: 'et querentibus fructus laboris et deo magisterii doctrina servetur amen.' Gloss ends fol 59v: 'nosci aparvulas.' Text begins fol 59v: 'In principio erat verbum'. Gloss begins: 'In principio id est in patre qui est principium'. Text ends imperfectly fol. 91v: 'Cucurrit ergo et venit ad symonem petrum' (ch.20 v. 2). Gloss ends: fol. 91v: 'Cucurrit nuntiare discipulis ut aut secum dolerent'.

V ORIGIN AND PROVENANCE

Ex libris Fol. 7v in hand of the scribe in red: 'Liber sancte marie de bildewas. Scriptus anno ab incarnatione domini millesimo centisimo septuagesimo sexta'.

Secundo folio Virtutem

The book was written at Buildwas, though the scribe has not so far been recognised in any other Buildwas book. The scribe used the punctus flexus punctuation mark occasionally, and the ex libris and date inscription follows exactly the wording of the slightly earlier ex libris and date of Oxford, Christ Church 88 (q.v.). The 'curled leaf and horn' motif which is widely used in the later twelfth-century book decoration at Buildwas may have been introduced to the scriptorium by this scribe. More important is the fact that the hand which wrote the text on the flyleaf is that of a known Buildwas scribe. Another discarded sheet from the same text (Gregory, *Moralia in Job*) forms the flyleaf to Trinity B.1.3 (q.v.), the two flyleaves having come from the same quire. Both texts were evidently bound at Buildwas. (See also Lambeth 109.)

The ownership inscription on fol. 2 is interpreted by C.E. Wright, *Fontes Harleiani: a Study of the Sources of the Harleian Collection of Manuscripts* (London, 1972), 87, as 'Sum liber rolandi Faune' or Vaughan. Wright maintains that the inscription records the gift of the book to Roland Vaughan by Edward Pount, armiger.

Robert Harley, the first Earl of Oxford, or his son Edward, acquired the book in the late seventeenth or early eighteenth century. It was sold by the Harley estate to Parliament in 1753, not long after Edward's death.

VI NOTES

1. The front parchment flyleaf was originally part of a bifolium which was intact in 1881, the date of the present foliation, when the surviving half was numbered 2. It was presumably only in the most recent rebinding that one leaf, possibly already partly detached, was removed and discarded, and the surviving leaf reversed so that the edge formerly at the spinefold was then at the fore-edge. This reused endleaf bifolium was itself once a single leaf of a very large format book, the leaves from it perhaps discarded at the outset because it was likely to prove uneconomical, and perhaps rewritten (see Lambeth 109). The present dimensions of the surviving half leaf suggest that the projected size of the original book was in excess of 420 x 300 mm, a not unusual size for twelfth-century copies of Gregory's *Moralia*. The leaf is ruled in grey, pricked on both sides of each page.

2. The text of the verses written on the chemise fragment at the front of this book is transcribed in the *Catalogue of the Harleian MSS* (727, see below) as follows: 'Do mon for the selffe wyl thou art olyve / ffor he that dose after thi dethe god let him never thryve. / Da tua dum tua sunt post mortem tunc tua non sunt./ Wyse mon if thou art of thi gods [goods] take part or thou heuse wynde / ffor if thou leve thi part in thi secataris ward thi part non part at last end./ too Secataris and an Overseer make three theves.' The text might well indicate that the book had already fallen into secular hands by this date (the fifteenth century).

VII BIBLIOGRAPHY AND PLATES

A Catalogue of the Harleian Manuscripts in the British Museum, 4 vols (London, 1808), I, 727; E.A. Bond and E.M. Thompson, eds., *The Palaeographical Society Facsimiles of Manuscripts and Inscriptions* (London, 1873–83), III, pl. 37; S.H. Thomson, *Latin Bookhands of the Later Middle Ages, 1100–1500* (Cambridge, 1969), pl. 86; E. Maunde-Thompson, *Introduction to Greek And Latin Palaeography* (1912), pl. 179; A.G. Watson, *Catalogue of Dated and Datable Manuscripts c.700–1600 in the Department of Manuscripts, the British Library*, 2 vols. (London, 1979), I, 131; II, pl. 104; Marc Drogin, *Medieval Calligraphy* (London, 1980). pl. 108; C.F.R. de Hamel, *Glossed Books*, 25, 36 n. 52; Sheppard 1990, 199; Sheppard 1995, 183–4.

10. CAMBRIDGE, UNIVERSITY LIBRARY MS ADD. 4079

Missal, fragment   **Date** *c.*1175–80
Leaves [i], 62, [i]
Foliation   Two sequences, in grey: **i)** estimated original foliation: 1–206; **ii)** existing leaves: 1–63 (including front flyleaf, excluding back flyleaf). The latter foliation used here.
Origin   Probably Buildwas   **Fig**. 14

I PHYSICAL DESCRIPTION

Binding   Resewn s.xiv/xv, old boards reused and re-covered; spine since re-covered ?s.xviii/xix, now cracking; boxed.

Endleaves

Front *Pastedown* Fol. 1 of parchment bifolium in place (?contemporary with spine re-covering); *verso*: two printed bookplates: one records Samuel Sandars's bequest in 1894, the other is that of the University Library Cambridge. Otherwise blank.

Flyleaves Fol. 2 of parchment bifolium, conjoint with pastedown; recto: 'Saml. Sandars, 7 DeVere Gardens, London 1890', in ink, and a reference in another hand, also in ink to Rev. Dr. Mostyn's opinion of the rarity of the book, two printed catalogue entries (Quaritch) s.xix ex, and some further notes in pencil about the provenance of the book and its contents in Sandars's hand and initialled by him. Verso: blank.

Back *Flyleaves* Fol. 1 of parchment bifolium in place, conjoint with pastedown (?contemporary with spine re-covering); blank except for note of leaf count and dimensions in pencil.

Pastedown Fol. 2 of parchment bifolium; recto: pasted-on fragment of an earlier pastedown (almost certainly the original) on which the tanned leather turn-ins of present covering material have left once-matching marks, and possibly also an earlier white tawed skin covering (at lower edge), as have three sewing support channels (corresponding to those visible under present pastedown) and the pin of an earlier fastening device. Two holes at the upper edge of this fragment at spine and fore-edges could not have been made by any attachment on the present cover, and were probably made by former boss nails. On recto of fragment, verses in hand s.xiv: 'Gaude flore virginali honore que speciali' etc. on the 7 Joys of the Virgin, pen trials and an incomplete ownership inscription (s.xvi in): 'Rychard Wossold of Wycke in the county of'.

Sewing stations Now 4: (tail) | 20 K 43*54*57*58 K 20 | mm (head). Earlier possibly 3 (evidence of position of lacing channels; see below, Boards): (tail) approx. | 82*75*75*77 | mm (head); no evidence for kettle stitches.

Sewing Now all-along, with thin white S-twist thread. Earlier sewing all-along to 3 supports with thicker Z-twist thread (evidence of impressions in spine-fold, e.g. fols. 34v–35).

Sewing supports . Now 4 twisted cords laced into boards, all now broken. Earlier probably 3 supports *c.*11mm wide.

Lacing path Lacing paths of present (4) sewing supports not visible; the earlier (3) supports laced into boards through tunnels from spine edge, to channels on outer then inner surfaces, lacing paths parallel (evidence of supports in channels visible under pastedowns), *c.*85–100mm.

Endbands None extant; impressions and wormholes on pastedown fragment (see above) suggest that a head endband *c.*10mm wide may once have been laced into the boards at a very acute angle to the spine, though the evidence is confused by the impression of the covering turn-in.

Tabs None present; no other evidence.

Spine lining None present; pastedown fragment shows no clear evidence of former presence of a spine lining.

Boards Wood, 309 x 210 x 12mm; all corners square, all outer edges bevelled and flush with leaves. Impressions under primary covering (visible under raking light) of 3 channels on both surfaces of back board and the inner surface of the front board, together with their bevelled edges suggest the boards are original, reused in the medieval re-binding.

Primary covering Brown, shiny tanned leather with asymmetrical, erratic patterns on each cover of irregular stamps (3 designs) and fillets. Spine replaced s.xviii/xix with thin tanned leather and decorated with stamps of similar design but much smaller and all identical.

Fastenings
Front: remains of white strap, 15mm wide, fixed into slot in top board with oblong-headed brass nail which has left a green mark on fore-edge of fol. 3 (fore-edges of fols. 1–2 have been trimmed). Back: corresponding hole with remains of pin in board, 108mm from fore-edge; marks of pin also on pastedown fragment (see above).
Chemise None present; no other evidence.
Bosses None present; two holes in pastedown fragment (see above) suggest that in a previous binding the book may have been provided with bosses.
Chain staple None present; no other evidence.
Labels None.

Structure of Book
Parchment Discoloured, showing signs of much handling but probably once of good quality; scar tissue holes (e.g. fol. 11), parchment maker's repairs (e.g. fols. 28, 30), flay marks (e.g. fol. 45); a patch across a bifolium (fols. 3–4) roughly sewn on with shiny, parchment-coloured S-twist thread; the same thread used to repair a cut in the parchment fol. 48. Other slits in parchment repaired with rough stitching in coloured thread (e.g. fols. 37, 38, 39). Lower margin excised fols. 55–58, 61.
Collation (Surviving quires numbered in present fragmentary order): $1^4 // 2^8$, 3^8 (2 excised), 4^8 (6 excised), 5^8 (outer 2 bifolia missing, 4 excised) $// 6^8$, 7^8 (2 excised), 8^8, 9^8 (7 excised) $// 10$ (three leaves). Judging by the estimated foliation (1–206), 81 leaves are missing between qq. 1 and 2, 8 between qq. 5 and 6, 34 between qq. 9 and 10 and an unknown number after q. 10. Hair side outside in quires which are complete.
Quire nos. None.
Catchwords QQ. 6, 8 and 9 in lower margin of last leaf near spine; q. 6 in red, q. 8 partly trimmed.

Page Layout
Dimensions
  Page 308 x 210mm; many leaves trimmed to text.
  Space ruled for writing 221–226 x 141–145mm.
Columns 2.
Pricking Leaves folded, 1→8 in both margins; double pricks indicate edge-to-edge ruling in all qq. except q. 2.
Ruling Fols. 1–27v: neatly executed in brown (scribe 1); fols. 28–63: less careful, in darker brown with more edge-to-edge lines (scribe 2). On the last 3 leaves, pricking was done for 5 sets of triple edge-to-edge lines, but these sets of lines were only erratically ruled.
Lines per page Fols. 1–27v: 30 (except fol. 3, 29); fols. 28–63: 29.

Page design

fols. 1–27v   fols. 28–60v   fols. 61–63v

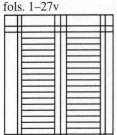 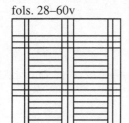 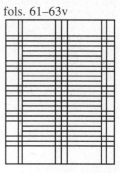

II SCRIBES

The surviving text was written by two main scribes *c.*1175–80. **Scribe 1** wrote fols. 1–27v (the Temporale) in a large, upright, compact hand, feet of letters flat (no serifs), tops of minims usually angular or clubbed. Versicles etc. are written in smaller version of same hand. **Scribe 2** wrote fols. 28–63 (the surviving leaves carrying the Canon, Sanctorale and Votive Masses) in an equally large but rounder hand with few angular strokes, very fine and regular; becoming slightly smaller and inclined to slope backwards towards the end of the extant text. Scribe 2 used the punctus flexus punctuation mark. A third scribe wrote lines 19–27 of col. b on fol. 35, and from line 11 on fol. 35v to line 10 on fol. 36, writing below the top line in a compressed hand with many strokes at 45° to the line and a finishing stroke to t which joins the cross-stroke. This scribe also used the punctus flexus. A fourth scribe wrote fol. 63 col. b, lines 1–10. There are numerous corrections, mostly over erasures (e.g. fols. 30, 32, 42v, 50, 52v). Omissions are supplied in the margins and keyed to the text with sigla (e.g. fols. 30v, 36), or are simply supplied in the text with omission marks (e.g. fols. 2v, 53, 63v).

III DECORATION, RUBRICS AND ARTICULATION OF TEXT

Text initials Thickened brown ink capitals written by the scribe.

Minor initials Each section of the text is opened by a coloured capital letter, varying in size between 1 and 3 lines depending on its importance but often extended in the margin (especially I, F, P etc.); each of the main scribes appears to have been responsible for the initials on the pages he wrote: fols. 1–27 recto: elegantly plain initials, alternately red and green (except blue I on fol. 7v), occasionally with reserved line decoration (e.g. fol. 8) or simple flourishes in the alternate colour (e.g. fol. 21). Fol. 27v (last page of Scribe 1's work): initials made by the same scribe are flourished in the manner of initials on succeeding leaves. Fols. 28–63: initials less well proportioned, alternately red and green with several blue initials randomly interspersed (e.g. fols. 36v, 37v, 45), the green slightly darker than on earlier leaves; frequently decorated with reserved lines in a variety of patterns, and virtually all flourished in the contrasting colour (red or green and sometimes blue) in a repetitive and sometimes clumsy manner, very much like the initials in other books made at Buildwas at this period. Guide letters in this section are supplied in red. Fol. 58v: 2-line brown ink M supplied over an erased red initial, a correction.

Major initials Fol. 28v: **13-line green, red and yellow P**(er), extending in the central and lower margins from an 8-line space, drawn in brown ink with intertwining scrolls with folded leaf terminals in bowl of letter and at the tail, uncoloured; intervening spaces coloured red, green and yellow. The stem is divided into panels and coloured with red and green in a zig-zag design, interlace motif at top. Bowl of letter only set against a pale yellow square field.

Historiated initials None.

Display script Fol. 28: (P)**er omnia secula seculorum amen** in 1-line capitals, the words alternately brown and red, enhanced with reserved lines. Elsewhere coloured initials are followed by a single thickened capital or by minuscule.

Titles No running titles; headings in text supplied by the current scribe in red minuscule.

Title page None extant.

IV CONTENTS

Table of contents None.

Main texts Cistercian Missal, fragmentary. Many leaves and therefore much text is missing throughout (see above, Collation).

Calendar lost. **Temporale** begins imperfectly fol. 1 in the gospel for Advent III: 'regum sunt. S*ed* q*ui*d existis videre?' (Matthew 11.8); ends fol. 27v: 'vitiosum est ipsius medicationis dono curetur p*er* d*omi*nu*m*.' Rest of page blank. **Canon** begins imperfectly fol. 28: 'Gloria in excelsis deo'. Ends fol. 30: '*et* om*n*iu*m* sanc*t*or*um* suor*um* misereatur no*st*ri omnipotens d*omi*nu*s* am*e*n.' **Sanctorale** begins imperfectly fol. 31, the Conversion of St. Paul: '[reli]quimus omnia *et* secuti sumus te'. Ends fol. 60v: (St. Luke) 'op*er*ari autem pauci. Rogate *ergo* d*omi*nu*m*'. **Votive masses** begin imperfectly fol. 61: 'Missa p*ro* peccatis. Omnia que fecisti nob*i*s'. Ends incomplete fol. 63v: 'Collecta. D*eu*s in quo vivimus movemur *et* sum*us*'.

Several variants and additions made by several hands in margins as follows:

Fol. 6v lower margin, in red: 'pref*atio et* com*mune* t*antu*m in die dicant*ur*', in a hand very like that of text scribe; in another hand also s.xii ex: '*et* in octavo die'.

Fol. 34 lower margin: 'Milb*er*ge v*irgini*s q*ue*re om*n*ia in die s*an*c*t*i mar*i*e magdal*e*ne', s.xii ex.

Fol. 36v lower margin in red: 'S*an*c*t*i cuthb*er*ti ep*iscop*i. Om*n*ia sic*ut* in die s*an*c*t*i Cedde ep*iscop*i' in hands s.xii/s.xiii (St. Chad's name added later over erasure).

Fol. 39 lower margin in red: 'De s*an*c*t*o Georgio q*ue*re i*n* fine libri' (s.xii ex.)

Fol. 39v lower margin in red: 'festivitas s*an*c*t*i marci ev*an*g*el*iste...v v*el* vi f*er*ie pasche, dicetur G q*ue*re i*n* die s*an*c*t*i lucem ev*an*g*el*iste Alle*l*ui*a* primus ad syon' (s.xii ex).

Fol. 41v in same hand as on fol. 39: 'De s*an*c*t*o barnaba q*ue*re i*n* fine libri'. Also, in same hand as on fol. 6: 'Wenefrede V*irginis* Dilexisti i*u*sticia*m* etc*etera* Om*n*ia sic*ut* i*n* die lucie v*irginis*'.

Fol. 43v lower margin in red, in same hand as on fol. 39: 'S*an*c*t*or*um* iohann*i*s *et* pauli q*ue*re i*n* fine libri'.

Fol. 47v outer margin in red, in same hand as on fol. 39: 'Margarete v*irginis* q*ue*re i*n* fine libri'.

Fol. 47v added over the name of Mary Magdalene, twice: 'mi*l*berge v*irginis*' (s. xii).

Fol. 49v lower margin in red in small hand s.xiii: 'Off*icium*. os iusti m*e*ditabitur. D*omi*nici *con*fessoris etc*etera*. omnia sic*ut* die s*an*c*t*o Ieronimo'.

Fol. 51v in outer margin in red and brown: 'Pref*atio* Et te in assu*mpt*i*one respi*ce ad dexte*r*am'.
Fol. 52v in outer margin in red next to correction: 'Quere in fine libri'.
Fol. 56v outer margin in red: 'De s*anct*o lambe*r*to in fine libri quere' (s.xii ex).
Fol. 60v outer margin in red: 'De s*anct*o edwardo fiat sicut de s*anct*o ieronimo' (s.xii ex).

V ORIGIN AND PROVENANCE

Ex libris None (but all prefatory leaves missing).
Secundo folio egrediatur
Although there is no early ownership inscription, several factors make it certain that this is a Buildwas Missal. It was made for a Cistercian house (evidence of the liturgy itself); commemorations for local saints are included in the Sanctorale (St. Chad, with Sts. Winifred, and Milburga added); the scribes who copied it used the punctus flexus and the second-rate flourisher of initials who worked on fols. 28–62v also worked in Bodley 730, St. John's D.2 and other books. The emendation of the collect for St. Bernard (fol. 159v) suggests that the book was made after 1174 when St. Bernard was canonised, and 1202 when this mass was replaced (Cambridge University Library, unpublished description. See also below, Bibliography: Chadd). On the evidence of the script, the date of copying was very soon after the terminus post quem, though additions and alterations to the text continued into the next century. The style of the decorated initial on fol. 28v is rather old-fashioned for the date, but the flourishes added to the other initials may well be a little later than the date of copying.
On fol. 29v the name Edwardus Burnel is added in the margin of the Memento of the Dead in the canon of the Mass in a hand s.xiv, and under it, the inscription '*pro animabus domini* Ricard*i* comitis et uxoris eius' in a later hand s.xiv ex. Edward Lord Burnell owned lands in Shropshire and died in 1315; Richard Fitzalan, Earl of Arundel, was either his uncle who died in 1302, or most likely his grandson who died in 1375 (Cambridge University Library, unpublished description).
On Fol. 40v is written vertically in the margin: 'Rychard Wossold on*e*th this bocke he that stelleyth this bocke is to blame' in a hand s.xvi in, and on the fragmentary endleaf now pasted to the replacement pastedown, the same hand has written: 'Rychard Wossold of Wycke in the conty of', and on fol. 61v: 'Aster day is the secon day of Aprill'. There are nine places now called Wick throughout the British Isles, one called Wyck and three called Wyke. One of the latter is in Shropshire, a mile or two from Buildwas. It is therefore just possible that Richard Wossold or his forbears acquired the Missal directly from Buildwas Abbey itself.
Other scribbles in some of the margins are associated with two names in the same hand, s.xvii–xviii: fol. 6: 'Thom' and letters L and G; fol. 14: 'George' and letters L, G and S together with some interlace flourishes and 'George' partially erased; fol. 16: scribbles and 'George' (twice), with other words now illegible; fol. 36: 'Thomas (?)Ge' and interlace flourishes. There is nothing at present to suggest the significance of these names. Two sketches in the same yellowish-brown ink, both executed across the text in a series of short diagonal lines; fol. 15v: profile head in a helmet; fol. 16: bearded head in three-quarters profile.
On the front flyleaf, Samuel Sandars recorded that Quaritch, from whom he bought the book on October 31 1891, acquired it from 'a Manchester bookseller who failed'. Sandars gave the book to the University Library in 1894.

VI NOTES

1. The binding history of the book is complex. It seems to have been first sewn on three sewing supports as were its contemporaries (Bodley 730 and St. John's D.2). It was subsequently resewn on 4 cords which were laced into the old boards, and a new cover of brown leather decorated randomly with blind stamps supplied. This may have been as late as the early sixteenth century, since Richard Wossold's ownership inscription is very slightly trimmed, as if to correct the projection of leaves from the reused boards or to make them more even. Probably at the same time, the rough patch was sewn to fols. 3–4. All the remains of page markers (see below) are also now flush with the edges of the leaves. Later still, the spine of the book was re-covered, probably towards the end of the nineteenth century when new endleaves were supplied front and back, and Quaritch catalogue labels were pasted to the front flyleaf by Samuel Sandars, who also wrote notes on it.

2. *Page markers* survive as follows: fol. 11v: thick, discoloured white cord sewn to fore-edge with thin Z-twist thread (first Sunday after Whitsun); fol. 28: discoloured white skin marker sewn to lower margin with shiny S-twist red thread (Canon); fol. 29: white skin marker crudely sewn to lower edge with white Z twist thread over the remains of an elaborate inverted T-shaped marker made of yellow and red S-twist thread and sewn on with shiny green thread of indeterminate twist; sewing holes in centre of lower edge are probably evidence of an earlier marker (?Edward Burnel memorial); fol. 30: i) sewing holes in lower margin, ii) strip of parchment partly cut from lower edge of this leaf and threaded through slits in the same leaf (?end of Canon); fol. 32: outer margin, strip of parchment cut from leaf and threaded through slits in the same leaf (St. Agatha); fol. 35: lower margin, 2 sets of sewing marks (St. Chad); fol. 37v: fragment of blue and discoloured white cord sewn crudely to fore-edge with shiny red S-twist thread (Annunciation to Virgin); fols. 38, 44, 52: sewing marks at lower outer corner (St. Ambrose, Vigil Saints Peter and Paul, St. Bernard respectively); fol. 43: strip of parchment partly cut from lower edge and threaded through slits in same leaf (St. John); fol. 59: lower corner, two sets of sewing marks, one with stains from blue thread (St. Michael); fol. 62: multicoloured marker of different S-twist threads: red, pink and white, with a fragment of discoloured blue thread and discoloured white cord, crudely sewn with pinkish-brown thread to lower edge (?Missa pro peccatis). All page markers now flush with leaf edges, probably due to trimming during the course of one of the repairs.

VII BIBLIOGRAPHY AND PLATES

D.F.L. Chadd, 'Liturgy and liturgical music: the limits of uniformity' in *Cistercian Art and Architecture in the British Isles*, ed. by C. Norton and D. Park (Cambridge, 1986), 299–314, especially 307–8 and pl. 190; Sheppard 1990, 194.

11. OXFORD, BALLIOL COLLEGE MS 229

Jerome, Augustine, St. Ignatius, John Chrysostom: various texts   Date *c.*1180
Leaves [i paper], i, 170, [i parchment, i paper]
Foliation i, 1–171 (exluding front endleaf).
Origin Buildwas   **Fig**. 15

I PHYSICAL DESCRIPTION

Binding Resewn and recovered at least twice: ?s.xv and s.xviii/xix. Boxed.

Endleaves

Front *Pastedown* Laid paper leaf in place, once conjoint with paper flyleaf, no watermark; Balliol College bookplate; inscribed 'Arch D.8.' and 'MS 229' in pencil.

Flyleaves **1)** 1 leaf, probably fol. 2 of a bifolium of which fol. 1 may have been the original pastedown. Recto: upper margin, pledging note dated 1421; verso: list of contents and partly erased ex libris s. xii; **2)** laid paper leaf, once conjoint with paper pastedown, no watermark, blank.

Back *Flyleaves* **1)** Earlier probably fol. 1 of bifolium and conjoint with detached pastedown, now excised, stub visible at lower spinefold; **2)** laid paper leaf, no watermark, blank.

Pastedown **1)** Detached pastedown, originally fol. 2 of a bifolium (fol. 1 excised to stub), a discarded leaf, with text recto and verso (a dialogue between Paulus and Eutropius on the Roman wars) in a humanist hand s.xv, and with marks that are evidence of an earlier, probably the late medieval rebinding ?s.xv; **2)** laid paper leaf in place, no watermark; blank except for R.A.B. Mynors's folio count dated 12.11.38.

Sewing stations **1)** Now 5 situated at old sewing stations. **2)** Earlier 5 (evidence of sewing support impressions on back detached pastedown: tail I 65* 55*58*58*54*53 I mm (approx.) head (no evidence about kettle stitch). Fols. 53v–54: one earlier sewing hole is easily visible in the lower spinefold, coinciding with the sewing support impressions closest to the tail (see below); **3)** fol. 57v: holes pricked 8→1 *c*.5mm from spine edge and separate from pricking done for ruling: tail I 51*54*125*72*38 I mm head; this may well indicate the position of two original sewing stations with upper and lower kettle stitches.

Sewing **1)** Now all-along with heavy brown S-twist thread; **2)** fols.57v–58 (and elsewhere), short fragments of thick white S-twist thread remain, detached, probably surviving from an earlier sewing.

Sewing supports Now on 5 double cords; impressions on the back detached pastedown indicate that an earlier binding was on 5 supports, 13–15mm wide.

Lacing path Over outer edges of boards, to inner face where fixed under pastedown, lacing path *c*.15mm. Earlier supports laced into the boards in part through short (*c*.25mm), parallel channels on the inner face of the board, 10–15mm from spine edge (total length 35–40mm).

Endbands Endbands present at head and tail, rolled white tawed skin core (the tail endband core apparently also wrapped in printed paper) and sewn with blue and brown S-twist threads, tied down at 5 points at head and tail; these endbands were never laced into the present boards.

Tabs None present; no other evidence.

Spine lining None present; no other evidence.

Boards Pasteboard replacements, 344 x 237 x 4mm (back board 348 x 240 x 4mm).

Primary covering Now rough calf with blind-stamped, decorative frame front and back; impression on back detached pastedown of turn-ins of an earlier covering, possibly brown with mitred corners, and turn-in edges slit; this may be evidence of the ?s.xv rebinding.

Fastenings Green-edged holes on the fore-edge of the detached back pastedown, 74mm from lower, 84mm from upper edges, suggest former position of fastenings.

Chemise None present; no other evidence.

Bosses Green-edged holes near all corners of back detached pastedown and at the centre possibly suggest the former presence and position of bosses, at least on the back board.

Chain attachments Faint impressions and a rusted hole in lower fore-edge of back detached pastedown suggest former position of a chain attachment post-dating the ?s.xv rebinding.

Labels On spine, remains of paper label with title in ink ; printed paper label with present shelfmark.

Structure of Book

Parchment Fair quality, much evidence of scraping; many neat sewn repairs throughout (probably by the parchment maker), contemporary corner repair (fols. 108–9) and patch (fol. 31); hair and flesh sides not markedly different in colour until q. 13, after which colour is more variable.

Collation $1-6^8$, 7^{10}, 8^6, $9-16^8$ // $17-18^8$ // $19-20^8$, 21^{10}. Hair side outside in each quire.

Quire nos. QQ. 1, 2, 3 (in red), 7, 17, 19, 20: lower margin of verso of last leaf; qq. 17 and 19 numbered I, q. 20 numbered II; other numbers may have been trimmed.

Catchwords QQ. 4, 5, 6, 7, 15, 16, 17, 19, 20: lower margin of verso of last leaf, in centre (qq. 4, 5, 6, 17) or near the spine (qq. 7, 15, 16, 19, 20).

Page Layout
Dimensions
Page 340 x 234mm (all margins trimmed; see especially fol. 50v).
Space ruled for writing 253–258 x 180mm.

Columns 2.

Pricking Leaves folded, both margins, 1→8 (except possibly inner margins qq. 20–21: 8→1); double pricks at lines 20 and 39 to indicate edge-to-edge ruling.

Ruling In brown, mostly neatly executed; until fol. 147, after which it is less careful and consistent; qq. 1–17 (fol. 1): lines 1–2, 20–21, 39–40 are ruled edge-to-edge; qq. 17 (fol. 1v)–21: lines 1–3, 20–22, 38–40 are ruled edge-to-edge; lines ruled ad hoc for running titles fols. 1–147.

Lines per page 40.

Page design

fols. 1–31, 52v–129   fol. 31v–52   fols. 132–170v

(Fols. 129v–131v. and 143–144: variable.)

II SCRIBES

Several scribes contributed to the writing of the text. **Scribe 1** wrote fols. 1–117v (col. a line 24), items 1–4, in a compressed, upright and fairly angular hand, with clubbed minims, thickened, sometimes slightly bifurcated and backward-sloping ascenders, and usually fairly flat feet to minims; this scribe used ampersand and crossed Tironian 'et', and executed his own rubrics to fol. 103. **Scribe 2** wrote fols. 117v (col. a line 25)–130v (col. b line 14), items 5–6, taking over from scribe 1 at the beginning of a new text, in a similar but more angular hand and using a much darker ink; this scribe used the punctus flexus, and took over the rubrication from fol. 103. **Scribe 3** wrote fols. 130v (col. b line 15)–142 (col. b line 7), end of item 6, in a less even hand than the previous two, which became smaller; he executed his own rubric (explicit) at the end of his stint.

Four scribes wrote item 7. **Scribe 2** wrote $9^{1}/_{2}$ lines at the beginning of the new text on fol. 142 (col. b lines 10–19), after which a succession of hands wrote small sections of text. **Scribe 4** wrote fol. 142 (col. b line 19)–fol. 144 (col. a line 16). **Scribe 5** wrote fol. 144 (col. a line 17)–144v (col. b line 17). **Scribe 6** wrote fol. 144v (col. b lines 18–36, the end of a text). Hands 5 and 6 are very different from the other text hands, later (?s.xiii), and these scribes used a much paler ink; they may have completed the text that was left unfinished in the original campaign.

Scribe 7 (or perhaps scribe 3) wrote fols. 145–170v (qq. 19–21), items 8–10, in a slightly smaller hand than on fols. 130–142v, less tall, even more compressed and also making errors. This scribe executed his own rubrics. Another scribe, the scribe of Edinburgh 6121, wrote the list of contents on fol. i verso.

There are not very many corrections, but an extensive one over an erasure on fol. 134 (scribe 3). Others on fols. 48, 140 (omission supplied in lower margin), 154, 155, 157v (scribe 7 or 3).

III DECORATION, RUBRICS AND ARTICULATION OF TEXT

Text initials Capitula (fol. 1v): alternate titles begin with a 1-line green capital, the alternate initials not supplied at the time of writing and put in by a later hand in brown; fol. 96: 1-line capitals alternately red and blue to mark significant sections in Augustine's text, also in some sections of Jerome.

Minor initials Fols. 57, 93 and elsewhere as the texts demand: 2-line initials alternately blue and red, sketchily flourished in the other colour, probably by scribe 2. Letters I and A etc. which are extended in the margin are more elaborately flourished, also by scribe 2. The final texts (fols. 129–170v) have alternate 1- or 2-line plain initials, alternately green and red, the green often more aqua than the usual darker green.

Major initials Each text begins with a large 4–8-line initial in several colours, probably executed by 2 initial scribes in 3 main styles, though some initials (e.g. on fols. 31, 35) are not decorated at all. The initial scribes are not identifiable with the text scribes. **Initial scribe 1** made the opening initial on fol. 1, a 21-line red and blue I(n), the red now silvered and the colours separated by a reserved curved, scalloped and angled line, with an extended tail and neatly and regularly executed flourishes along the entire length of the latter in red, blue and yellow. Other initials by this scribe are made in a similar style, often using green instead of blue, round letters filled with firmly and neatly drawn, interlocking and striated leaf forms or a 'curled leaf and horn' design. The curled leaves are delicately shaded with very fine lines, usually in ochre. This scribe also executed initials on fols. 6v, 7, 13, 20, 27v, 28, 129v, 130, 145, 160. He made initials which are very similar to those in Pembroke 154 (e.g. on fols. 6, 12v), differing mainly in being more finely executed in the Balliol MS. The work in Balliol 229 may be slightly later and more practised. **Initial scribe 2** made initials in two styles. He also made initials in both styles in Edinburgh 6121. In the first (e.g. fol. 38v, 5-line red P(ius)), the letter is generally of one colour (red or green), with reserved straight or stepped lines, the letter filled and flourished with dense, profuse but repetitive red and green or blue leaf, stalk and circle motifs and this initial alone with a square field also composed of the same flourishes. The character of this decoration is rather sparse and thin compared with the lushness of similar initials by initial scribe 1. The initial by this hand on fol. 31v (4-line green V(oce)) is finer; compare E on fol. 60 in Edinburgh 6121, to which it is virtually identical. Other initials in the same style are on fols. 51, 103. The second style (e.g. on fol. 45, 5-line blue B(eatissimo)) comprises initials of a single colour, alternately red and blue, often but not always with a simple reserved line, filled usually with one or two centrally designed, crudely executed decorative motifs in red, blue and sometimes ochre against uncoloured parchment, on a squared background, red letters on ochre, blue letters on red. A recurring motif in these initials is a sunburst of radiating lines in red or blue, which may be derived from the type of elegant shading in penwork initials such as those in Balliol 35A. Initials in this style on fols. 42, 51v, 52, 57v, 117v are virtually identical to those in Edinburgh 6121.

Historiated initials None.

Display script Fol.57: (V)**enerantissi/** in small brown-ink mixed capitals touched with red; /**mis urbium et mo**(nast*eriorum*) in brown minuscule touched with red; fol. 57v: (C)**um** in small brown mixed capitals, touched with red; fol. 68: (C)**um** in small brown ink capitals; fol. 79v: (S)**ermonum quem** in 1-line brown mixed capitals; fol. 91: (M)**isericordiam** in 1-line brown mixed capitals; fol. 117v: (Q)**uis** in 1-line brown mixed capitals; fol. 129v: (Q)**ui** in 1-line red capitals; **in principiis** in red minuscule. Elsewhere, first letters are occasionally emphasised in the form of small rustic capitals (e.g. fols. 1, 117v) by the text scribe, or not emphasised at all.

Titles etc. Running titles across the opening as far as fol. 147, possibly trimmed from this point, the upper margins now having become increasingly narrow; incipits and explicits throughout in red by the text scribes.

Title page None.

IV CONTENTS

Table of contents Fol. i verso: 'In hoc volumine continentur ista' with list of titles s.xii ex.

Main texts Various patristic works.

1. Jerome, *Epistole*. Mynors, *Balliol MSS*, 237–240, provides a detailed list and identifies each letter. The first begins fol. 1: 'Ieronimu*s* ad fabiolam de mansionib*us* filior*um* isr*ael* p*er* heremum. In septuagesimo vii° psalmo'. Ends fol 57 (the last letter is headed 'Ieronimu*s* de psalme centesimo x° vii°'): '*n*ec credentes *christo iehsu in* filios abraha*m* in filios d*e*i om*n*ipotentis adoptati sumus p*er* ips*um* d*omi*nu*m* cui est gl*or*ia in s*e*cu*l*a sec*u*lorum amen.'

2. Augustine, *De Mirabilibus*. Begins fol. 57: 'Incipit p*r*ologus beati augustini ep*iscop*i de mirabilibus novi *et* veteris testamenti. Venerantissimis urbiu*m* ...salutem. Beatissime dum adhuc vivere'. Ends fol 57v: 'occasione aliq*u*id n*o*n fastidiant. Explici*t* p*r*olog*us*. Incipiunt cap*itu*la' (i–xxxiii). 'Incipit liber primus...Cum omnipotentis d*e*i auxilio de mirabilib*us*'. Ends fol. 67v: 'Explicit

liber primus. Incipiunt cap*itu*la libri secundi' (i–xxxi). Fol.68: 'Incipit liber secundus...Cum moyse egrediente'. Ends fol. 73. 'Incipit liber tercius... Octoviani augusti cesaris'. Ends fol. 79v: 'et cet*eri* exemplo hui*us* castigarentur.' *PL* XXXV, 2149–2200.

3. Augustine, *De Sermone Domini in Monte Habito.* Begins fol. 79v: 'Incipit liber aurelii augustini de sermone domini in monte habito. Sermonem que*m* locutus *est* d*ominu*s'. Fol. 91: 'Liber secundus. Misericordiam usq*ue*'. Ends fol. 102v: 'si volumus edificare sup*er* petram. Explicit liber s*ecundus*...in monte habito *et* de misericordia.' *PL* XXXIV, 1229–1308.

4. St. Ignatius of Antioch, *Epistole.* Begins fol. 103: 'Ep*istole* beati ignatii discip*u*li s*anc*ti ioh*anni*s ev*an*g*e*liste ad mariam'. 12 letters, the first: 'Ignatius qui et theoforus...salutem. Optima q*uidem* figuratio litt*er*e'. Two short texts follow; ends fol. 117v: 'Incolumes estote in d*omi*no *iehsu christo* in gra*ti*a cum omnib*us* v*es*tris amen. Explicit ep*isto*la sancti policarpi m*a*rt*ir*is Smyrneoru*m* ep*iscop*i discipuli s*anc*ti iohannis evangeliste.' Mynors records that Archbishop Ussher published this text (Oxford, 1644) using Balliol 229 as his source.

5. St. John Chrysostom, *De Reparatione Lapsi.* Begins fol.117v 'Sermo beati iohannis crisostomi de reparatione lapsi ad theodor*um* monachum. Quis dabito [sic] capito meo'. Ends fol. 129: 'q*uod* si hoc libenter legas alia ultra medicamenta non queras.'

6. Jerome, *De Hebraicis Quaestionibus in Genesi.* Begins fol. 129v: 'Incipit prefatio sancti Ieronimi presbiteri de hebraicis questionib*us* in Genesi. Qui in principiis librorum debebam secuturi'. Ends fol. 142v: 'qui servientes altari vivant de altari. Explicit liber beati ieronimi pr*esbiter*i de hebraicis questionib*us* in genesi.' *PL* XXIII, 935–1010.

7. Jerome, *De Membris Domini.* Begins fol.142v: 'Ieronimus de membris d*omi*ni. [O]m*ni*potens d*omi*nus pat*er* et filius...Unus in natura tr*inus* in p*er*sonis'. Ends fol. 144v: 'manifestum demonstrare.' *PL* XLII, 1199–1206. Mynors points out that this is spurious.

8. Jerome, *De Hebraicis Quaestionibus in Samuel.* Begins fol.145: 'Incipit lib*er* s*anc*ti ieronimi de hebraicis questionib*us* in samuel. Fuit vir unus...Ramathan int*er*p*re*tatur excelsa domino'. Ends fol. 153: 'aream v*er*o sexcentis aureis emisse. Explicit liber sancti ieronimi de hebriacis questionibus in samuel.' *PL* XXIII, 1330–1361.

9. Jerome, *De Hebraicis Quaestionibus in Paralipomenon.* Begins fol. 153: 'Incipit liber eiusdem de hebraicis questionib*us* in paralipomenon. In diebus eius divisa *est* terra'. Ends fol 160: 'cyrus ut ruinas templi restauret. Explicit lib*er* s*anc*ti ieronimi pr*esbiter*i de hebraicis questionib*us* in paralipomenon.' *PL* XXIII, 1366–1402.

10. Jerome, *De Locis.* Begins fol.160: 'Incipit p*re*facio s*anc*ti ieronimi in librum de locis. Eusebius qui a beato pamphilo'. Ends fol. 160v: 'me posse credo. Explicit p*re*facio. Incipit lib*er* s*anc*ti ieronimi de locis. De genesi. Ararat armenia siq*ui*dem in montib*us*'. Ends fol. 170v: 'In presens vicus ostend*itur* u*bi* absc*on*ditus *est* d*avi*d. Explicit liber s*anc*ti ieronimi pr*esbiter*i de situ sive distantiis vel nominib*us* locorum.' *PL* XXIII, 859–928. Rest of page blank.

V ORIGIN AND PROVENANCE

Ex libris 1) Fol. i verso, after table of contents: Liber monachorum s*anc*te marie de Bildwas in red, partly erased; **2**) fol. 1, lower margin: Liber dom*us* de Balliolo in Oxon. ex dono Will*elmi* Gray Eliens*is* Ep*iscop*i.

Secundo folio s*anc*tam

The contents of this book have the same character as those of Edinburgh 6121 and Pembroke 154: all are miscellanies mainly of patristic texts. The main scribe of Edinburgh 6121 wrote the contents list in this volume, and since these two books also share initial makers, and because one of the scribes of this volume used the punctus flexus, it seems certain that this book was made at Buildwas. Though not companion volumes in the physical sense, the Edinburgh, Pembroke and Balliol volumes were probably intended as complementary texts. The monastery's ex libris is an early one. The indexer or another reader supplied running text numbers in a manner similar to that used in the Edinburgh volume in the later thirteenth century, demonstrating that the book was probably still in use at Buildwas then.

John Chrysostom's *De Reparatione Lapsi* and Augustine's *De Sermone Domini in Monte,* and *De Mirabilibus,* Jerome's various *De Questionibus Hebraicis,* are all texts which are listed in the *Registrum,* though none is recorded as having been found at Buildwas (cf. the Edinburgh and Pembroke texts). Jerome's letters were found at Buildwas, but since the compilers missed several texts in Balliol 229 and Pembroke 154 which were on their list, it is possible that the copy the compilers saw may have constituted a separate volume with a larger, perhaps a complete, collection (cf. also Lambeth 457). The pledge note (see below) dated 1421 indicates that the book had left Buildwas by that date.

The book was among those acquired by William Gray during the fifteenth century, and given by him to Balliol College. If the first rebinding was carried out during the fifteenth century, it may have been done for Gray.

VI NOTES

1. The texts were given running numbers on the top rectos of each leaf in Arabic numbers, including 1.
2. On the front parchment flyleaf recto: 'Caucio m*agister* Joh*anne*s posita in cysta Langto*n* p*ro* xxvi s viii d in vig*ilia* cathedre s*an*cti pet*ri* a*n*no d*o*m*i*ni mcccxxi'.

VII BIBLIOGRAPHY AND PLATES

Mynors, *Balliol MSS,* 237–240; Ker, *MLGB,* 15; Sheppard 1990, 196; Rouse & Rouse, 316–317.

12. EDINBURGH, NATIONAL LIBRARY OF SCOTLAND MS 6121

Jerome, Augustine and others, Theological treatises   Date *c.*1180
Leaves 146
Foliation 1–146 (see also VI below for medieval foliation)
Origin Buildwas   **Figs.** 16, 33

I PHYSICAL DESCRIPTION

Binding   Original, s.xii ex; sewing thread breaking on spine, primary covering mostly missing at spine, chemise in two pieces. Not repaired; opens well. Boxed.
Endleaves
  Front *Pastedown*   Parchment leaf in place, once fol. 1 of a quaternion, blank except for a few pen trials.
     Flyleaves   None extant, originally probably fols. 2–4 of quaternion, fols. 2–3 now excised to stubs 6mm wide. Fol. 4 (now 50mm stub), was pricked, and ruled on verso, possibly for a list of contents; a cut along the pastedown

corresponding to the edge of the stub suggests that this may have been removed after the other flyleaves, possibly when the book changed hands.

Back *Flyleaves* None extant, probably once comprising at least a bifolium, now excised to two stubs (5mm).

Pastedown Parchment leaf in place though torn and partly detached; possibly once part of a bifolium (or quaternion as at the front); torn section reveals grainy paste on verso. Inscription s.xvii at upper edge: 'Mr. John Hughs', and a few pen trials.

Sewing stations 3, these and lower kettle stitch marked with pricks 8→1, 5–10mm from spinefold, upper kettle stitch not marked, but is level with top line of text: (tail) I 29 K 50*78*81*45 K 28 I mm (head).

Sewing All-along with whitish Z-twist thread; herringbone pattern on spine.

Sewing supports 3 white tawed skin supports, split, varying width: 12mm (lower), 15mm (middle), 11mm (upper).

Lacing path Laced into boards through tunnels from spine edges, channels on outer then inner surfaces; lacing paths parallel; ends secured with wooden wedges.

Endbands Present at head and tail, white tawed skin, split, 10mm (tail) and 12mm (head) wide, laced into boards at slightly less than 45° from spine edges through tunnels from the corners, channels on outer then inner surfaces, ends anchored with wooden wedges. Sewn through the split with a chain pattern along ridge and through the tab to the centre of each quire with discoloured white Z-twist thread.

Tabs Semi-circular tabs present at head and tail, made of 2mm-thick white tawed skin, each extending to nearest primary sewing support; sewn at edges with discoloured white Z-twist thread, with chain-stitch pattern along the perimeter and at the base of the sewing on either side of the tab. Fragment of the primary covering still attached by the sewing to the upper tab.

Spine lining An extra piece of thick white tawed skin the width of the spine survives between the lower and middle sewing supports, filling that space. It is held in place by a wide strip of white tawed skin and extends from head to tail of the spine. This is the same thickness as the primary covering. It once lined the entire spine under the primary covering but is now partly lost. The spine strip is slit to accommodate the sewing supports as they enter the tunnels in the boards, and the outer edges of the strip are pasted to the inner surface of the boards parallel to the spine under the pastedown, the corners mitred to fit with the primary covering turn-in. No piece of skin has survived between the middle and upper sewing supports.

Boards Wood, 311 x 218 x 15mm, both back (i.e. spine) corners rounded, edges (including spine edge) bevelled, and flush with leaves. Sewing support channels are cut exactly to fit the varying width of the supports, but are very roughly executed.

Primary covering White tawed skin now discloured to yellow, torn, partly detached, and mostly missing at spine; mitred at both outer and inner corners. Where covering detached, remains of both white and grainy paste evident.

Fastenings Central fore-edge strap of thick, discoloured white tawed skin, 23mm wide x 2mm, fixed (probably nailed but evidence not visible) into groove on fore-edge of front board, under chemise and probably also under primary covering; whole strap scored across width (perhaps for flexibility); end broken off 120mm from fore-edge; 4 small holes at end of strap probably indicate former position of protective metal fitting incorporating a hole for the pin. Hole on back board 85mm from fore-edge and equidistant from upper and lower edges visible in chemise; remains of pin visible in same position on inner surface of back board. Strap now broken off at fore-edge of board but preserved with the book.

Chemise Thick brown leather in 2 pieces once joined by sewing along centre of spine, sewing executed through thickness of the leather and invisible on outside (fragment of chemise still sewn together survives separately; a split in the chemise over front board also repaired thus, sewing intact). Attached to boards by white tawed skin pockets 150mm wide (front) 145–160mm (back), sewn to chemise along outer edges of board; protective flaps survive intact along upper edge (45mm wide) and fore-edge of back cover (c.35mm wide); these edged with a folded strip of tawed skin sewn to the inner surface of chemise through its thickness with brown hairy S-twist thread (5 strands each Z-twist).

Bosses 4 on front board, brass; star-shaped (8 points), 25mm diameter, 8mm high; each apparently attached with a single nail (rusted), visible on inner surface of board, 20–24mm diagonally from each corner. No evidence of bosses on back board.

Chain attachments 1) Front board, lower edge, 2 pairs of iron rust marks in a line 58mm long, 25mm from lower edge (only 3 visible on inner suface) and also on fols. 1–3, one iron pin still projecting. 2) Back board, lower edge near spine, remains of 4 nails visible on inner surface in slightly trapezoid formation (20 x 30 x 18 x 30mm), corresponding holes in primary cover and chemise.

Labels 1) An impression on chemise on back board, 80 x 80mm, with 8 nail holes at edges (also penetrating primary cover and board) indicate former presence of a label. 2) Diamond-shaped piece of paper 12mm across pasted onto remains of primary cover at lower spine inscribed in ink: '556 b'.

Structure of Book

Parchment Mixed quality, fair to good; hair and flesh sides clearly distinct especially from q. 16 onwards, where hair sides are very yellow with much follicle marking. A good nap on both sides qq. 1–15; less apparent qq. 16–19. Some repairs, e.g. a patch fol. 106 and a tear, roughly sewn probably by the parchment-maker and cut out before writing (e.g. fols. 119–121).

Collation $1-2^8$, 3^{10}, $4-18^8$. Hair side outermost in each quire except q. 3 which begins with a flesh side.

Quire numbers None, but fol. 8v of qq. 7–15 marked '+' in lower margin in pale ink. The scribe of fols. 18–26 supplied tiny letters in red to the lower margin between the central vertical lines: fols. 18v and 19: a; fols. 19v and 20: b; fols. 20v and 21: c. Fols. 21v–22 comprise the central bifolium of the quire.

Catchwords QQ.1–15, lower margin near spine.

Page Layout
Dimensions
Page 310 x 219mm.
Space ruled for writing 223–226 x 149–151mm.
Columns 2.
Pricking Leaves folded, both margins. QQ. 3, 5, 7–9, 11: 1→8; qq. 1, 4, 10, 12–18: 8→1; qq. 2, 6: inner and outer margins pricked in different directions. Evidence for q. 16 is partly trimmed. Outer margins only double pricked for edge-to-edge ruling 3 lines from the bottom except qq. 8, 9, 14, where both margins are so pricked. Q. 11 pricked twice in all 4 margins, for 38 lines, in the wrong place on the page. A template used for pricking.

Ruling In brown, regular and neat, writing lines kept within vertical margins except those ruled edge-to-edge.

Lines per page 37.

Page design

fols. 1–17v, 27–146   fols. 18–26v

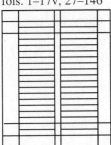 

II SCRIBES

2 main scribes wrote the text. **Scribe 1** wrote fols. 1–17v, fols. 27–146 and the running titles in an upright, compact hand *c.*1180; c and e are angular and ascenders tend to be flat-topped. This hand also wrote the list of contents in Balliol 229, fol. i verso. Scribe 1 corrected his own work, e.g. over an erasure fol. 115, and supplied omissions on lines in margins which he ruled for the purpose: fol. 51 with red signe de renvoi, fols. 80v and 132 also framed in red with signes de renvoi. **Scribe 2** wrote fols. 18–26 in an upright, equally compact, regular and fluent hand, similar to that of Scribe 1 but with less angular letter forms. Scribe 2 provided letters in red in the lower margin (see above: Quire numbers). A third hand wrote fol. 59 col. a lines 20–37, and a fourth wrote fol. 59 col. b lines 1–10, both hands taking over in mid-sentence. Scribes 1 and 2 both used punctus flexus, and each supplied his own headings.

III DECORATION, RUBRICS AND ARTICULATION OF TEXT

Text initials Fols. 1–25 (items 1–3): 2–5-line plain Roman capitals, alternately green and red (q. 1) and blue and red (qq. 2–3). Fols. 25v–46v (items 4–6): small brown ink capitals by text scribe. Fols. 46v–48 (item 7): 2–3-line capitals alternately blue; and red. Fols. 48–52 (item 8): small brown ink capitals by text scribe. Fols. 52–60 (item 9): brown ink capitals by text scribe, sometimes emphasised by red paraphs. Fols. 60–68 (item 10): 1-line capitals, alternately red and green. Fols. 68–146 (item 11–17): brown ink capitals by text scribe.

Minor initials None.

Major initials Fol. 1: **9-line blue O**(mnis) with reserved scalloped undulating line, filled with red and blue flourishes and partial 'sunburst' motifs in green; set against a square, plain red background. Fol. 1v: **18-line red I**(nicium) with reserved scalloped undulating line, and extended tail with light flourishes. Fol. 12v: **6-line red and blue E**(rat), the colours divided by a reserved line, each half of the letter filled with interlocking 'curled leaf and horn' motifs in blue with red circles and striations; compare initial E on Balliol 229 fol. 7. Fol. 18: **6-line blue and red C**(ontinuare), similar to that on fol. 12v, but filled with symmetrical blue 'folded leaf'motifs, and flourishes and tiny red circles. Fol. 25v: **7-line red and blue P**(ropter), the two colours separated by a reserved line, the stem extending the whole length of the page; the tail flourishes terminating with a dragon's head extending across the entire lower margin; the bowl of the letter filled with a 'curled leaf and horn' motif in blue and red. Fol. 39: **18-line red P**(restabit) decorated with reserved scalloped lines, the lightly flourished stem and tail extending into the lower margin; the bowl of the letter filled with radiating pairs of facing curled leaves in blue with blue flourishes, coloured with ochre and red and interspersed with partial 'sunburst' motifs in green; the whole set against a square field of green; compare initials D and Q in Balliol 229 fols. 45 and 117v respectively. Fol. 45v: **18-line red P**(assionem) decorated with reserved wavy and scalloped lines, the extended stem and tail lightly flourished in blue and red; the bowl of the letter filled with a symmetrical pattern of leaves and flourishes in blue with red 'sunburst' motifs and circles, set against a square blue field edged with green. Fol. 46v: **4-line red N**(on) the left stroke decorated with a reserved line and flourished in blue; letter filled with design of striations and flourishes (similar to that on fol. 45v) along an S-curve in blue. Fol. 48: **6-line blue S**(unt) with reserved line, against a square ochre field; each half of the letter filled with a design mainly of striations and dots in blue and red. Fol. 52: **7-line red C**(orona) with reserved scalloped line and set against a square blue field; letter filled with 2 semi-circular scrolls with leaf terminals each divided in 2 by a motif shaped like an arrow-fin in red, further decorated with red flourishes and green and blue partial 'sunburst' motifs. Fol. 60: **7-line green E**(xtorsisti) with reserved stepped line, each half of the letter completely filled with fine line red flourishes and tiny circles in red, some of the lines touched with green; the outer rim of the letter also flourished in red; both the initial and the decoration obscure the rubrics; this initial is exactly like initial V in Balliol 229 fol. 31v. Fol. 68: **5-line blue S**(anctis) with reserved line against a squared green field; each half of the letter filled with one large folded leaf design with red edges and green striations. Fol. 78v: **6-line red L**(ibrum) in a 2-line space, and extending into upper margin, undecorated. Fol. 95: **9-line red L**(ectis) with reserved lines and red flourishes. Fol. 107v: **5-line red D**(omino) with reserved scalloped lines, otherwise undecorated. Fol. 110: **4-line red D**(omino), undecorated. Fol. 112: **4-line red D**(ixisse) filled with red flourishes. Fol. 125v: **7-line red I**(am) with clumsily flourished tail. Fol. 143v: **6-line red I**(n) with clumsily flourished tail.

Historiated initials None.

Display script Fol. 1: (O)**mnis scriba**, 1-line mixed Roman and uncial capitals alternately red and brown. Fol. 1v: (I)**nicium evangelii** (sic) **iehsu xpi filii** (sic) **dei**, the first word in 1-line mixed Roman and uncial capitals alternately red and black, the rest in black minuscule. Fol. 12v: (E)**rat autem pascha azi**(morum) in mixed rustic and minuscule letters, the words alternately red and brown. Fol. 48: (S)**unt qui putant** in 1-line mixed Roman and uncial capitals, the words alternately red and black. Fol. 52: (C)**orona** in 1-line red Roman capitals. Fol. 60: (E)**xtorsisti michi** in red minuscule. Elsewhere the first letter, or all or part of the first word of a new text is written in brown rustic capitals by the scribe, or these are written in minuscule with no emphasis.

Titles etc. Running titles in red (a line ruled only on fol. 67v); incipits, explicits and the names of the speakers in the disputation (item 9) in red throughout, by the scribe of the text; red tadpole-shaped paraphs used to signify words belonging to line above.

Title page None, but prefatory leaves lost.

IV CONTENTS
Table of contents None extant, but the stub of fol. iv verso is ruled, perhaps for a list of contents.
Main texts
1. Fols. 1v–17v: Pseudo-Jerome, a commentary on St. Mark's Gospel with Prologue. Prologue begins: 'Omnis scriba doctus in regno celorum.' Text begins: 'Inicium evangelii iehsu christi filii domini sicut scriptum est in Ysaia propheta'. *PL* XXX, 589–644.
Fol. 17v originally partly blank; notes added in English s.xvii.
2. Fols. 18–25: *Continuatio Veteris et Novi Testamenti.* Rhymed version of Hegesippus, *De Bello Iudaico.* Text begins: 'Continuare volumus quedam que dicit iosephus'. Ker (*MMBL,* ii, 527) refers to F. Römer (*Die handschriftliche Uberlieferung des Werke des Heiligen Augustinus,* II (Vienna, 1972), 116), who observes that these two texts are also found together in Cambridge, Emmanuel College MS 56, s.xv.
3. Fols. 25v–39: Augustine, *De Gratia et Libero Arbitrio ad Valentinum Monachum. PL* XLIV, 881–912.
4. Fols. 39–45v: Augustine, *Sermo de Proverbiis Salomonis. PL* XXXVIII, 221–235.
5. Fols. 45v–46v: Augustine, *Sermo de Resurrectione Domini. PL* XXXIX, 2059–2061.
6. Fols. 46v–48: Augustine, *De Decem Preceptis Legis et de Decem Plagis Egiptiorum. PL* XXXIX, 1783–6.
7. Fols. 48–52: Augustine, *De Fide Rerum Invisibilium. PL* XL, 171–80.
8. Fols. 52–60: Augustine, *De Agone Christiano. PL* XL, 289–310.
9. Fols. 60–68: ?Augustine, *Disputatio contra Felicianum Hereticum. PL* XLII, 1157–72.
10. Fols. 68–78: Augustine, *De Perfectione Iusticiae Hominum. PL* XLIV, 291–318.
11. Fols. 78–95: Augustine, *De Natura et Gratia. PL* XLIV, 247–90.
12. Fols. 95–107v: Augustine, *De Correptione et Gratia. PL* XLIV, 915–46.
13. Fols. 107v–110 Letter of St. Prosper of Aquitaine to St. Augustine. Text begins: 'Domino beatissimo pape ineffabiliter mirabili incomparabiliter honorando'. *PL* XLIV, 947–53.
14. Fols. 110–112 Letter of Hilary Bishop of Arles to St.Augustine. Text begins: 'Domino beatissimo ac toto affectu desiderando'. *PL* XLIV, 954–9.
15. Fols. 112–125v Augustine, *De Predestinatione Sanctorum. PL* 44, 959–92.
16. Fols. 125v–143v: Augustine, *De Bono Perseverantia. PL* XLIV, 993–1034.
17. Fols. 143v–146: *Omelia Beati Iohannis Episcopi super Mattheum xxi 1–2.* Preface begins: 'In illo temporum: Cum appropinquasset'. Text begins: 'Lectio evangelica que vobis recitata est'.
Fol. 146v: blank.

V ORIGIN AND PROVENANCE
Ex libris None extant.
Secundo folio congruenter
The facts that the main scribe of this text wrote the list of contents for Balliol 229 (q.v., a certain Buildwas book), that both text scribes use the punctus flexus, and that many of the decorated initials in this book and those in Balliol 229 were made by the same scribe (see notes above in description of initial letters), indicate that this book was also made at Buildwas. There is also a striking

familial resemblance among some of the initials in Edinburgh 6121 and those in Pembroke 154 (e.g. Edinburgh 6121, fol. 12v), but it cannot be said with certainty that the Pembroke initial scribe is the same as any working in Edinburgh 6121. The texts in the Edinburgh book and those of Balliol 229 and Pembroke 154 are of a similar character.

Seven of the texts (items 1, 3, 5, 6, 8, 15, 16) were recorded in the *Registrum* as having been held at Buildwas, though four (items 9–12), listed in the *Registrum,* are not recorded as being held there.

Ker (*MMBL* 124), notes that the s.xv pressmark in the upper margin of fol. 1 (?'Mlu^m') is that of the London Carmelites, indicating that the book was no longer at Buildwas at that date. A lengthy note in a blank column and a half on fol. 17v, in a hand s.xvii (post 1664) notes that the book had been found in Herriot Kirk 'where it is probable it has long remained'. The writer goes on to say that since 'it does contain some important truths', it is a fit place to record 'sundry particulars anent this parish as to civil matters'. He then describes certain agreements regarding the property (lands) of Lord Borthwick of Crookston. In the lower margin in a slightly different hand, is the testimony of George Viscount Tarbat that 'what is above written' is true. It is dated Edinburgh 17 April 1688 and signed 'Tarbat'. The book appears to have remained in the Borthwick family into the 19th century; the printed bookplate of John Borthwick of Crookston is pasted to the chemise pocket inside the front cover. The book was purchased by the National Library of Scotland in 1946.

VI NOTES

1. *Medieval leaf and text numbers* **i)** In addition to the modern pencil foliation, the book is foliated at the top right corner of each recto in Arabic numbers in a s.xiii hand in pale, greyish ink which is not unlike that used by an annotator (s. xiii) who made occasional notes throughout (compare notes and numbers on fols. 108 and 131). This early hand omitted the number 77 and so from his leaf 78 onwards, his numbers are incorrect. **ii)** Above the right hand column on each recto, another s.xiii hand wrote the number of the current text in Arabic numbers using a dark ink. This continues throughout the book. **iii)** Each item has been provided with its own sequence of leaf numbers by a s.xiii hand. These are entered at the very bottom of the verso of each leaf of each item near the spinefold, beginning always on leaf 2. The numbers are tiny, and Arabic except for ten which is written in Roman. Eleven is written in Arabic except in item 3, where it is written in Roman. When an item covers fewer than 3 leaves, no text leaf numbers are provided. These early numbers suggest that an index of the kind found in Trinity B.14.5 (q.v.) may have been intended for this volume.

2. *Later leaf numbers* The leaves on which the first item is written (fols. 1–17) were foliated by a later hand, almost certainly the same as the hand s.xvii which so copiously annotated much of the book (evidence of similarity of number forms between notes and foliation, and ink colour). This writer's numbers are modern Arabic in form, and are found at the top right corner of the rectos of fols. 3–9, 13–17 (end of item 1). They either clarify the numbers of the medieval foliator, or are written alongside them. It is clear that he did so because he was not at first familiar with the earlier forms of the numbers 3–9 (even the 9 in the hand of the medieval foliator is written in an unusual way), and he simply replaced those he found difficult to read. He did not find it necessary to do so on subsequent leaves.

3. *Annotations* A s.xiii hand added notes with sigla neatly in upper and lower margins and may also have added foliation (see above). There is also copious annotation in another hand (s.xvii), which provided cross-references to chapters, to other texts, and comments. This hand almost certainly also added foliation to fols. 3–17.

4. *Scribal practices qq. 1–3* Scribe 1 appears to have pricked qq. 1–2, using a different system for each quire. He ruled a page at a time (evidence: in q. 2, fol. 9, lines 1 and 3 are ruled edge-to-edge, but on fol. 16v, the conjoint leaf, lines 1, 2 and 3 are so ruled, and the edge-to-edge lines stop just short of the spinefold; both leaves of the central bifolium may have been ruled at once). Having reached the end of q. 2 he found he needed one more leaf to finish the first text. He seems either to have selected a bifolium and pricked it separately 8→1, or to have taken it from another pile (the prick marks are equally strong on each leaf). He ruled 1 leaf only, a page at a time (the second leaf of the bifolium, fol. 10 of q. 3, has double bounding lines ruled by scribe 2) and completed his text. Scribe 2 had possibly already begun his text at the top recto of a quire of 8 leaves, which he had pricked using the same template as scribe 1, 1→8. He also ruled a page at a time (evidence: discrepancies in edge-to-edge ruling on a single bifolium) and, reaching the end of his quire, was told to continue writing on the blank leaf of scribe 1's extra bifolium. This he did, ruling it in his way with double margins, though on the recto, perhaps influenced by the ruling of scribe 1 on the opposite verso, he ruled lines 1 and 3 and 35 and 37 edge-to-edge, and not 1 and 2, 36 and 37 as he usually did. On the verso he ruled the first 2 and the last 3 lines edge-to-edge. Scribe 2 was able to complete his text on this leaf. Scribe 1 began the 3rd text at the beginning of q. 4, pricking 8→1 and ruling in his preferred way, with single margins and lines 1 and 3, 35 and 37 ruled edge-to-edge.

VII BIBLIOGRAPHY AND PLATES
National Library of Scotland. Catalogue of Manuscripts Acquired since 1925 (Edinburgh, 1982), IV, 103–4; Watson, *MLGB Supplement*, 5; Ker, *MMBL*, II, 527; Sheppard 1995, 190, and figs. 2, 7.

13. CAMBRIDGE, PEMBROKE COLLEGE MS 154
Cyprian, Letters; Peter of Blois; Anselm etc. **Date** *c.*1180
Leaves 191
Foliation 1–190 (leaf after 182 omitted)
Origin England, probably Buildwas **Fig**. 22

The pricking and ruling of the first quire of this book, and the fact that this quire alone has the flesh side outermost suggest that the book was originally intended to contain Cyprian's tracts and letters only, two bifolia being pricked 1→8, hair side outermost, to serve as front pastedown and flyleaf and to carry the list of contents (a common Buildwas practice). Before the work had progressed very far, however, (though after the writing of a list of contents), it was decided to add Peter of Blois's text (item 1), and another bifolium was inserted and pricked in the outer margin only, 8→1 and ruled slightly differently from the rest of the book, becoming the pastedown and fol. 5. Similarly, at fol. 149 (the beginning of q. 19, where the colour of the parchment changes), the authorship of the texts copied becomes miscellaneous (see items 17–21 below). The (original) list of contents on fol. 4v contains Cyprian's texts, but not the *Passio Cypriani* on fol. 5. The list of contents made (subsequently) on fol. 1 contains a summary of the titles of all the texts.

I PHYSICAL DESCRIPTION

Binding s.xii ex, repaired at least twice, most recently 1976 (by D. Cockerell: note inside back board); boxed.

Endleaves

Front *Pastedown* Fol. 1 of first quire in place, blank except for pressmark s.xvii: $C^{st}\cdot\underline{nT}$ $\overline{f}$ and '154' in red.

Flyleaves Fol. 2 of first quire blank, list of contents on recto.

Back *Flyleaves* Fol. 9 of last quire, now excised, probably once served as flyleaf; text ends on recto of previous leaf (fol. 190).

Pastedown Fol. 10 of last quire, blank.

Sewing stations 3, these and lower kettle stitch marked with pricks 8→1, c.10mm from spinefold; upper kettle stitch not marked, but is level with top line of text: (tail) I 40 K 53*93*97*55 K 35 I mm (head).

Sewing Most quires resewn with soft, white 'woven' thread; originally sewn all-along with thick, white Z-twist thread, left in place when resewn and visible in many quires, e.g. at fols. 25v–26, 105v–106, 113v–114.

Sewing supports 3 white tawed skin supports, all broken but repaired (see D. Cockerell's report: 'cords sewn across spine on each side of the 3 bands'), c.13mm wide.

Lacing path Laced into boards through tunnels from spine edges, channels on outer then inner surfaces, lacing paths parallel, 85–95mm long (front board), c.82–91mm (back board); ends now secured with wedges made of a loosely woven material.

Endbands Of white tawed skin c.10 mm wide, split, once laced into boards at 45° through tunnels, channels on outer then inner surfaces of boards; sewn through the split with Z-twist thread discoloured to brown, through the tab and tied down in every quire and with a herringbone pattern along the ridge. All endbands now broken.

Tabs Semi-circular tabs of discoloured white tawed skin present at head and tail; sewn to primary covering with discoloured white Z-twist thread with a herringbone pattern around the perimeter and at the base of the sewing on each side of the tab. Thread now missing on upper tab, still present on lower. Replaced covering pasted to outer surfaces of both tabs.

Spine lining No evidence now visible, repairs having obscured inner surfaces of boards.

Boards Wood, 377 x 263 x 12mm; corners damaged, edges slightly and unevenly bevelled, once flush with edges of leaves but leaves now projecting slightly along fore-edge.

Primary covering White tawed skin, badly discoloured to yellow, lower half missing on back board and replaced at spine; corners obscured, probably mitred (evidence of worm holes on pastedown); hole in original skin over front board near top right boss repaired with an extra piece of skin inserted under it; evidence of equal discoloration of patch and covering suggests that this repair' may be early, if not original.

Fastenings 2 fore-edge straps, almost certainly replacements of two earlier straps, of brown leather, 27 and 26 mm wide, 105mm from upper and lower edges of board (measured to centre of strap); inserted into slots in front board (primary covering slit to facilitate this) and fixed by brass pins with rectangular heads (one partially visible); slits in covering re-sewn. Straps now cut off flush with fore-edge. Remains of several pins on back board coincide only roughly with straps, *c.*92mm from upper edge, 105–115mm from lower edge of back board.

Chemise Not extant, but circles of thick brown skin of former chemise survive under extant bosses on front board.

Bosses Once 5 (evidence of holes on cover): one at each corner and one in the middle; 3 extant on front board, brass, hemispherical, *c.*26mm diameter with flattened tops; UL: plain; UR: with radial grooves and petal design; LL: concentric grooves. No evidence of bosses on back board. (D. Cockerell's report refers to 4 brass bosses on front board and 1 fore-edge boss missing.)

Chain attachments 4 nails at lower edge of back board in slightly trapezoid formation: 16 x 18 x 17 x 17mm, show former position of chain attachments.

Labels Paper printed label on pastedown, ex libris of Pembroke Hall.

Notes 2 strips of white tawed skin, *c.*129 x 3mm, now loose (at fols. 92v–93 and 148v–149) probably once served as bookmarks.

Structure of Book

Parchment Mostly uniformly yellowish, hair sides of qq. 19–23 very yellow; considerable nap on both hair and flesh sides. Some sewn repairs, probably by parchment maker, often cut out before writing if within text space, e.g. fols. 11–12, 97, 187–188. Much evidence of scraping.

Collation i^6 (first leaf is pastedown), 1–21^8, 22^{10}, 23^{10} (9 excised, probably blank; 10 is pastedown); hair side outermost in all quires except q. i.

Quire nos QQ. 1–21: lower margin of verso of last leaf (at various points), in various styles of Roman numerals, i–xxi; q. 21: in red, qq. 22–23: no numbers.

Catchwords None.

Page Layout
Dimensions
Page 371 x 265mm.

Space ruled for writing 248–262 x 182–186mm.

Columns 2.

Pricking Leaves folded, both margins, qq. i, 4, 10–15, 17, 20, 22–23: 1→8; qq. 1–3, 5–9, 16, 18–19: 8→1. Q. 21: unclear, probably 8→1. Q. 20: last leaf repricked 8→1. Double pricks indicate lines to be ruled edge-to-edge.

Ruling In brown except q. 23 (grey); mostly neatly executed.

Lines per page Fols. 1–149: 39; fol. 149v: 40; fols. 150–191: 41.

Page design

fols. 1–4	fols. 4v–13v	fols. 14–157v

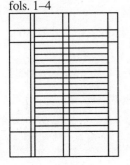 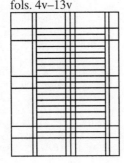 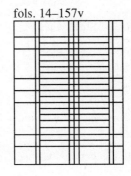

fols. 158–189v

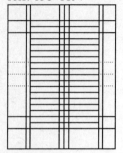

II SCRIBES

The text is unevenly copied. Few pages exhibit clear changes of hand and it is difficult therefore to say with certainty how many scribes cooperated in the copying of this text. There could be as many as three (the variation in the execution and positioning of quire numbers is consistent with a cooperative effort in copying) or it may have been the work of a single scribe whose hand and methods were variable. Letter forms and punctuation marks, however, are virtually identical throughout, and duct variations are only perceptible when two pages from different parts of the book are compared. Sometimes differences seem to reside only in the execution of the feet and shoulders of minims. A change of hand is arguably detectable on fol. 7 (col. a line 18), the 'new' scribe having possibly already written 5 lines on fol. 6v (col. b lines 21–25). Col. b on fol. 21 also appears to exhibit changes of hand, emphasised by different ink colour, but a part of these apparent changes is due to the intervention of a correcting hand, which is very compact and upright with sharply rising serifs to the feet of minims, especially of n and m, which touch the following stroke. The list of contents on fol. 4v was also written in this hand. Another scribe, who wrote the added texts on fols. 1–5, also seems to have contributed to the copying of the later parts of the main texts.

III DECORATION, RUBRICS AND ARTICULATION OF TEXT

Colour notes (fols. 6–167) in the form of the letters r (rubeus), a (azurus) and v (viridis), made with a stylus, appear in the margins. These instructions are followed to fol. 155, except for the occasional substitution of ochre for blue (e.g. on fol. 66v). At fol. 155, though the colour instructions continue to dictate the green blue red sequence, use of blue is discontinued to the end of this series of letters.

Text initials Small, alternately red and green capitals are used for capitula on fols. 4v, 60, 67–67v and for the first line of the Paschal Hymn on fol. 149. Red capitals only are used for the capitula on fol. 174v.

Minor initials None.

Major initials These may be the early work of one of 'initial scribe 1' who made certain initials in Balliol 229 (q.v). Fol. 1v: **5-line red R**(everendo), with reserved lines in all 3 strokes and coarse blue flourishes; fol. 5: **8-line red T**(usco), with scalloped reserved lines, red symmetrical 'folded leaf' decoration with nodules and the 'horn' motif with green striations; fol. 6: **16-line red and blue B**(ene), the colours' separated by a reserved stepped line, filled with a symmetrical 'folded leaf design outlined in red and with red nodules, and striated with parallel pen strokes in green and ochre. Outer edges of letter flourished with red and brown ink, the designs also striated. Fols. 8v–149, 149v, 168, 174, 175v: a repetitive series of 79 4–7-line initials, red, blue or green, often with reserved line decoration, most with either an unvarying 'folded leaf' or 'leaf and horn' motifs with striations in either or both of the other two colours or in brown ink and sometimes with ochre, or interlocking patterns of folded leaves. Letters with extended stems are often flourished. One variation, a symmetrical spray of folded leaves on long stalks interspersed with trefoil-shaped flowers also on long stalks which flank a central elongated stylised leaf (e.g. on fols. 102, 113v, 126), is similar to a design found in other Buildwas books. Fols. 47v–80 (items 2j–2l): a series of 2–7-line initials often with reserved lines and extended tails, in colour sequence green, blue and red. Fols. 149v–167v (item 4): a series of 2–7-line plain initials in colour sequence red, green and blue and sometimes ochre. Fols. 174v–181 (item 8): a series of 2-line red undecorated initials were made for the final text.

Historiated initials None.

Display script Fol. 6: (B)ene admones donate karissime in green and red 1-line capitals, underlined with ochre. Elsewhere in the book, the first few words, the first line or the first two lines of a text which is introduced by a coloured initial are written in brown ink Roman and rustic capitals, sometimes shaded with red (e.g. fol. 1v: (R)everendo; fol. 19 (C)um moneat do(minus)). The first four lines of Cyprian's *De disciplina*. (fol. 8v), the *Pater Noster* (fol. 25), and the opening lines of Cyprian's letters on fols. 122v, 126 are written alternately in red and brown minuscule.

Titles etc. No running titles. Incipits and explicits in red, by the text scribes.

Title page None.

IV CONTENTS

Table of contents Fol. 1 in red: 'In hoc volumine continentur ista', followed by a list of contents. Fol. 4v, in red: 'In hoc volumine continentur epistole beati Cypriani', followed by a list of tracts and letters written by Cyprian: 'Epistola ad donatum. una...De laude cypriani ep*isto*la. una.'

Main texts A very detailed account of the contents is given in James, *Pembroke MSS*, 148–52.

1. Fols. 2–4: Peter of Blois. *De Transfiguratione Domini. PL* CVII, 777.
2. Fols. 5 –5v: Passion of St. Cyprian.'Incipit Passio beati cipriani ep*isco*pi. Tusco et Basso consulib*us* cartagine in secretario pate*r*nus p*ro*consul cyp*r*iano episcopo dixit'. Ends fol. 5v: 'c*um* voto *et* t*r*iumpho magno in laudem d*omi*ni no*st*ri *ihesu christi* cui est...sec*u*la sec*u*lor*um* am*en*. Explicit passio s*anc*ti cyp*r*iani cartaginiensis ep*isco*pi *et* m*artiris*.'
Fol. 5v: i) 'Ieronimus de s*anc*to cypriano. Cyp*r*ian*us* afer p*r*imum glo*r*iose'. Ends: 's*ed n*on eode*m* anno.' ii) 'Cassiodorus de s*anc*to cypriano. Impossibile *est* omnino complecti'. Ends: 'venustate conscripsit.' iii) 'Beat*us* etiam augustin*us* in libris suis'. Ends: 'multa com*m*endat.'
2a. Fols. 6–8v: Cyprian, *Ad Donatum. CCSL* IIIA, 1.
2b. Fols. 8v–12v: Cyprian, *De Disciplina et Habitu Virginum. PL* IV, 439.
2c. Fols. 12v –19: Cyprian, *De Lapsis. CCSL* III, 217.
2d. Fols. 19–24: Cyprian, *De Ecclesiae Catholicae Unitate. CCSL* III, 243.
2e. Fols. 24–30: Cyprian, *De Dominica Oratione. CCSL* IIIA, 87.
2f. Fols. 30–34: Cyprian, *De Mortalitate. CCSL* IIIA, 15.
2g. Fols. 34v–39: Cyprian, *De Opere et Eleemosynis. CCSL* IIIA, 53.

67

2h. Fols. 39–43: Cyprian, *Ad Demetrianum. CCSL* IIIA, 33.
2i. Fols. 43v–47v: Cyprian, *De Bono Patientiae. CCSL* IIIA, 115.
2j. Fols. 47v–50: Cyprian, *De Zelo et Livore. CCSL* IIIA, 73.
2k. Fols. 50–56v: Cyprian, *Ad Fortunatum. CCSL* III, 181.
2l. Fols. 56v–80: Cyprian, *Ad Quirinum, Testimonium Libri Tres. CCSL* III, 1.
2m. Fols. 80–147v: Cyprian, *Epistole. PL* IV, 193.
2n. Fol. 147v: 'De laude Cypriani. Inter varios et multiplices frater dolores nobis constitutis'. Ends fol. 148v: '*sed* humilitas atq*ue* subiectio.'
Fol. 148v: 'Hoc est q*uo*d penetenciam p*ro*bat'. Ends 'potuit a *christo* in communicatione retineri. Bene vale f*rater* in *christo.*'
3. Fol. 149: *Ymnus de Pascha.* Begins: 'Est locus ex omni medius q*uem* credim*us* orbe'. Ends: 'Hoc lignum vite cunctis credentib*us*. Amen.'
4. Fols. 149v–166v: Anselm, *Meditationes. PL* CLVII, 709.
5. Fol. 166v: *Oratio ad Sanctum Angelum Dei.* Begins: 'S*an*cte ac beate a*n*gele d*e*i cui me divina bonitas'. Ends fol. 167v: '*et* cum omnib*us* s*an*ctis visionis ei*us* p*er*petua *et* sola beatitudine p*er*frui merear ip*so* p*ote*state qui cum patre et sp*iritu* s*an*cto una est divinitas equalis gl*ori*a coet*er*na maiestas amen.' A note kept with the MS provides the following reference: Dom A. Wilmart O.S.B., *Auteurs spirituels et textes dévots du moyen âge latin* (Paris, 1932), 537: 'Prières a l'Ange Gardien' no. iv (544): 'Oratio ad Proprium Cuiusque Angelum'. Pembroke 154 is noted as one of the 2 chief sources of this text.
6. Fols. 168–169v: Peter of Blois, *De Conversione Sancti Pauli. PL* CCVII, 791.
7. Fol. 169:–173: Roger of Byland, *Lac Parvulorum.* Begins: 'Scribens dilecto meo nec spumeum verborum ambitum'. Ends fol. 173: 'Mariam super omnia dilige. Amen.' A transcription of this text and a translation by Father Lawrence C. Braceland (St. Paul's College, Winnipeg, 1977–8) is kept with the MS. In notes to the translation, Father Braceland refers to C.H. Talbot's edition (see below) and the fact that Talbot believes the author of the text to be Roger, Abbot of Byland Abbey 1142–1193 and the recipient, Gilbert of Hoyland. Braceland describes the letter as 'an invitation to follow the Cistercian vocation.' Roger had been one of twelve monks who set out from the Savigniac abbey of Furness in 1134 to establish a house at Calder (eventually Cistercian). See C.H. Talbot, 'A Letter of Roger, Abbot of Byland', *Analecta Sacri Ordinis Cisterciensis*, 7 (1951), 218–231.
8. Fols. 174–190: Peter of Celles, Letter to Henry of Troyes, prefaces to John of Salisbury and others, and *De Claustrali Disciplina. PL* CCII, 1097.

V ORIGIN AND PROVENANCE
Ex libris   Fol. 4v, partially erased: 'Liber:sancte:Marie:semp*er*:virginis:de Bildewas', in red.
Secundo folio vi*r*ga conve*r*sa
The book was made at Buildwas in the early part of the second phase of activity, together with Edinburgh 6121 and Balliol 229 (q.v.) to which this book is linked by common scribes and/or by the character of its contents. Some of the initials were executed and flourished by the artist(s) of Balliol 229 (cf. initials in Balliol 229 fols. 38v and 129v, for example and those in Pembroke 154 fols. 1v, 30, 34v, 108, 113v, 117v. The ubiquitous 'curled leaf and horn' motif is also occasionally found in Edinburgh 6121 though not certainly executed by the same artist.
Items 1, 2, 4, 6, and 8 are recorded in the *Registrum* as having been held at Buildwas, but while most of the shorter Cyprian texts are also listed in the

Registrum, they are not recorded as being held at Buildwas.
The acquisition of the book by Pembroke College is unrecorded.

VI NOTES

1. *Medieval leaf and text numbers* The leaves carrying Cyprian's letters were given a reference system in the lower margins near the spinefold in ink in Arabic numbers by a thirteenth-century hand. The number of Cyprian's current letter was added to the lower right corner of the verso of each leaf for the first 3 letters, after which another hand took over this task, adding running Arabic numbers in brown in the centre of the lower margins of the rectos of each leaf. The thirteenth-century hand also wrote the letter number in the top right corner of the rectos (now mostly obscured by the later leaf numbers), and the number of the leaf within each letter on the lower left corner of the rectos. This hand used Arabic and not the Roman numeral for 10, but the Arabic numerator in brown sometimes used Roman x, xi, xii etc, and sometimes Arabic 10, 11, 12 etc. Sometimes the numbering of the leaves begins with 1 on leaf 1, but more often with leaf 2. Letter 14 has no numbers at all. Letters 18, 21, 26, 28, 30, 49, 56, 57, 59, 60, 63, 67, 68, 69 and 71 are additionally numbered in a small hand in the upper margin. The chapters of Peter of Celles's text on fols. 175v-190 are numbered in Arabic numerals from 2–25, using x for ten, but Arabic for 11, 12 etc. The three last chapters each entitled *De Meditatione Mortis* are each numbered 24.
2. *Later numbering* A seventeenth-century hand added numbers to the list of Cyprian's Letters on fol. 4v, including the titles (and numbers) of three which were omitted from the original list, and supplied these numbers in the upper margins over the column where the text of each new letter begins. This hand also added leaf numbers to the top right corners of the rectos throughout the book over the letter numbers provided by the s.xiii hand, and to the list of contents on fol. 4v. This hand supplied the occasional cross-reference in the margins, e.g. on fols. 116, 117.
3. The Buildwas indexer, who may have been responsible for some of the Arabic numbers, inscribed his nota mark in a flourished form on fols. 153, 153v, and he may have written a partially erased note on fol. 190v: 'epi*sto*lam...ad deme*tria*num', one of the headings omitted from the list of letters on fol. 4v which the seventeenth-century hand later supplied.

VII BIBLIOGRAPHY AND PLATES

James, *Pembroke MSS*, 147–152; Ker, *MLGB*, 14; Cheney 1953, 377 (1974, 332); Chibnall, *VCH*, 56; Andreas Petzold, 'Colour Notes in English Romanesque Manuscripts', *The British Library Journal*, 16 (Spring 1990), 16–25 and fig.2; Rouse & Rouse, 316–317; Sheppard 1995, 191–192.

14. OXFORD, BODLEIAN LIBRARY MS BODLEY 395
Isidore, Etymologiae (incomplete)   **Date** s.xii ex.
Leaves iii, 168
Foliation i–iii, 1–169 (partly detached back pastedown included)
Origin Buildwas   **Figs**. 21, 34

I PHYSICAL DESCRIPTION
Binding s.xii ex, spine flat; boxed.

Endleaves

Front *Pastedown* First leaf of a quire of 3 bifolia, now detached, conjugate leaf excised; blind ruled, written on both sides in 2 columns in a large hand, s.xii med., 30 lines to the page; text (now inverted) is part of the Mass from: 'num et iustum est. Nos tibi semper et ubique gracias agere...acceptabilem que facere'. Small coloured initials supplied to (current) verso but not rubrics, for which an 11-line space left between 'et iustum est' and 'Nos tibi semper', and no initials supplied to (current) recto. An alphabet written vertically in central column s.xii/xiii; shelfmarks: Th and I 1 13.

> *Flyleaves* 2 leaves (leaves 2 and 5 of original quire of 3 bifolia, fols, 3, 4, and 6 excised), of better quality parchment than pastedown. Both remaining leaves pricked and ruled in grey, 40 lines per page. Fol. ii: written in hands s.xii ex: i) '(M)elius est de commun bono gratulari quam de privato gloriari...quia ad hoc agendum incitavit nos oculus caritatis.' ii) A Greek alphabet with Latin word equivalents. iii) '(L)icet mores pre omnibus curandi sint et vite sanctitas amplectenda...tam in metro quam in sono pro una littera accipi debent.' iv) The Lord's Prayer in Greek (first line also in Latin). v) A versified version of the same prayer: 'O pater alme. tuum nomen sit sanctificatum...Si tutela malo tua nos de fondat abomini.' vi) An Hebrew alphabet, written in inaccurate order, some letters poorly written, some making no sense and others missing. In upper margin, 'Isadorus Ethymologia' s.xv; lower margin, shelfmarks: 'NE.D.5.7' and '(2215) Bodl.395'. Fol. ii v: list of contents s.xv. Fol. iii: blank; fol. iii v: list of chapter headings and numbers s.xii ex.

Back *Flyleaves* Once possibly one or more leaves of q. 22, now excised.

> *Pastedown* Fol. 8 of q. 22, partly detached, blank; bears impressions of primary covering turn-ins, and grainy paste remains on verso. Once pasted over a chemise pocket attachment which left traces of white tawed skin (extant), on verso of the lifted pastedown and board when subsequently removed.

Sewing stations 3, not marked: (tail) I 34 K 42*79*79*42 K 36 I mm (head).

Sewing Sewn all-along with white thread, Z-twist.

Sewing supports 3 white tawed skin supports, split, c.12mm wide. All supports now broken.

Lacing path Laced into boards through tunnels from spine edges and channels on outer then inner faces; lacing paths parallel, 62–70mm (front board), 75–78mm (back board); ends secured with wooden wedges.

Endbands White tawed skin split endbands present, c.8mm wide; laced into the boards at approx. 45° through tunnels from spine edges, channels on outer then inner faces, ends secured with wooden wedges. Sewn with pale blue and white Z-twist threads, through the tab and tied down in the centre of each quire; chain stitch pattern along ridge. Head endband broken front and back.

Tabs Semi-circular tabs present at head and tail, made of thick, white tawed skin, which extend beyond the kettle stitch. Sewn to matching extension of primary covering at perimeter with pale blue and white Z-twist threads, with herringbone and chain stitch patterns.

Spine lining The spine is lined along its length by three irregularly sized pieces of white tawed skin which are pasted to the inner surface of both boards but not to the backs of quires. Sections are cut away where necessary to accommodate the sewing supports. The lining passes between tabs and primary covering, and at head and tail it is pasted over the primary covering turn-ins.

Boards Wood, 311 x 222 x 12mm, all corners square and edges sharply bevelled;

once flush with edges of leaves, though leaves now project slightly at fore-edge. Remains of brown grainy paste, and of a chemise pocket once pasted under pastedowns and now torn away.

Primary covering White tawed skin, discoloured to yellow, cracking along inner spine edges of boards and split entirely at back; outer corners mitred, inner corners square and turn-ins slit.

Fastenings 1) Slot (25 x 20mm) for central fore-edge strap cut into front board, now empty, with marks of 3 nails which once fixed a strap in place; corresponding hole with remains of pin in centre of back board, 98mm from fore-edge; this probably the earliest fastening; 2) two pairs of green-rimmed holes each with remains of two nails near fore-edge of front board, 70 and 80mm from upper and lower edges, may indicate the position of later catchplates, primary covering slit to accommodate replacements; two corresponding sets of remains of three brass nails within triangular impressions at fore-edge of back board.

Chemise Not extant, but clear traces of paste and traces of white tawed skin which comprised the pasted-down pocket attachment remain on inner faces of front and back boards and on adjacent sides of detached pastedowns. Grainy paste remains on pastedowns are under the chemise remains, suggesting that the pastedowns were lifted to accommodate the chemise, pasted down and then lifted again when chemise was removed.

Bosses 5 holes, 1 at each corner and 1 in centre of front cover indicate former presence of bosses; faint impressions on covering suggest that the bottom right and central bosses may have been hexagonal, the top left, square. 4 holes on back cover, 1 in each corner, indicate former presence of bosses also on this cover.

Chain attachments Considerable evidence of a succession of chain attachments: 1) Front cover under the pastedown, 2 rusted nail marks set vertically c.18 and 43mm from lower edge with the rusted marks skewed and the covering damaged as if by a metal strip which had become loose; 2) front cover, 2 nail holes at right angles to upper fore-edge, with corresponding greenish impression of a pointed metal strip on the pastedown; 3) back cover very near spine and lower edge, 4 rusted holes in covering and board, in roughly trapezoid formation (17 x 23 x 13 x 22mm).

Labels None.

Notes Several book and page markers; 3 tawed skin thongs knotted together above upper edges of leaves and knotted at lower ends (now at fols. 9, 61, 128), that at fol. 128 is pale pink; several parchment strips cut from the page and threaded through slits to mark the position in the book of diagrams and tables (e.g. fols. 25, 60).

Structure of Book

Parchment Quite thick with nap on both hair and flesh sides; many blemishes usually in margins, some rough, parchment maker's sewn repairs cut out to neaten edge (e.g. fols. 93, 106).

Collation 1^{10} (1 excised), 2^8 (3 entirely excised, conjugate leaf loose), 3^8, 4^6, 5–21^8, 22^8 (3–7 excised). Hair side outside in all quires.

Quire nos. QQ. 8–20 numbered I–XIII, lower margin of verso of last leaf.

Catchwords QQ. 1, 2, 4 and 6: lower margin of verso of last leaf, near spine. The catchword at the end of q. 4 is not for q. 5 but for q. 6. The book, however, is not misbound.

Page Layout
Dimensions
Page 309 x 220mm.
Space ruled for writing (QQ. 1–7): 228–230 x 160–164mm; qq. 8–21: 225 x 160mm; q. 22: 228 x 165mm.
Columns 2.
Pricking QQ. 1–7: variable, leaves folded, qq. 1–3: both margins; qq. 4–7: outer margin only, 1→8 except inner margin q. 3, 8→1; outer margin q. 5 pricked twice, pricking trimmed qq. 6–7. QQ. 8–21 (scribe 7): leaves folded, both margins, direction of pricking variable: q. 8: all margins 1→8, but both outer margins pricked twice; qq. 9–11: inner upper and lower margins 1→8, outer margins 8→1; qq. 12–13: all margins 1→8 (but inner margins also pricked 8→1, not used) except lower margin q. 12: 8→1; qq. 14–22: all margins 1→8 except outer margin q. 21: 8→1. This scribe (scribe 7) double pricked lines 19–21.
Ruling Uneven and erratic in quality, in grey and in brown, fols. 1–28v (scribes 1–3) very faint indeed. Fols. 55–166, the first, last and middle three lines are ruled edge-to-edge.
Lines per page Fols. 1–54v: variable from scribe to scribe, 46–50; fols. 55–168: 40.
Page design

| fols. 1–24v (scribe 1) | fols. 25–38v (scribes 2–5) | fols. 39–54v (scribe 6) |

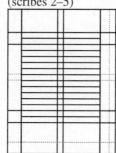
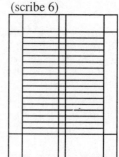

fols. 55–168
(scribes 7–8)

II SCRIBES

Six scribes contributed to the writing of qq. 1–7 and a seventh wrote the remainder, s.xii ex. **Scribe 1** wrote fols. 1–24v in a small, compact hand with very little elaboration of minims. This scribe did his own rubrication except on fols. 1–2 where it was done by scribe 4. **Scribe 2** took over at the beginning of q. 4 and wrote fols. 25–27v (to capitula book VI)) in a larger, clear fluent hand. He ruled fewer lines than scribe 1 had pricked (47); scribe 4 did the rubrication. **Scribe 3** began after the capitula to book VI and wrote fols. 27v–28 in an irregular hand using lighter brown ink. Scribe 4 did the rubrication. **Scribe 4** wrote fols. 29–32v taking over in mid-line and mid-sentence, in a bold, upright round hand using a dark brown ink; he used the punctus flexus and did his own rubrication. **Scribe 5** wrote fols. 32v (col. a line 24)–38 (end of q. 5) in a square, slightly backward-sloping hand with flat feet and serifs, and did his own rubrication. His punctuation was corrected by another hand. **Scribe 6** began at q. 6 and wrote fols. 39–54v (end q. 7) in a regular, very compressed hand; rubrication by scribe 4. **Scribe 7** wrote fols. 55–161 in an upright, uneven hand with a very square form of ampersand. This scribe repricked previously pricked quires for 41 and then 40 lines per page and adopted a different page layout (see above). He also numbered his quires, beginning with I at his own first quire, and did his own rubrication.

An eighth hand s.xii ex/xiii in wrote an additional text on the remaining leaves of q. 21 and added a further quire to complete it (now mostly excised, text incomplete; fols. 161–168v). The notes on fol. ii are by yet another contemporary hand.

III DECORATION, RUBRICS AND ARTICULATION OF TEXT

There is a very large number of small, brightly coloured initials in a variety of styles, mostly nicely executed, making this a very attractive book to read.

Text initials 1-line initials in alternate colours, e.g. red and green or red and blue for capitula etc.

Minor initials Fols. 1–24 (scribe 1): 3–line initials in pink, green, blue and sometimes red, colours rotating but in no particular sequence, with pen flourishes in a contrasting colour or foliate decoration. Fols. 25–27v (scribe 2): 4-line spaces left by scribe, same initial maker as before. Fols. 27v–38 (scribes 3, 4, 5): 2- or 3-line plain initials alternately red and green. Fols. 39–54 (scribe 6): 3- or 4-line initials, alternately green and red with self colour or contrasting colour (sometimes pale blue) flourishes and other decoration. Fols. 55–161 (scribe 7): 3-, 4-, or 5-line initials, alternately red and green with reserved lines, characterised by elegant trailing elements such as extended tails with curled leaf terminals, and vertical tendrils. Fol. 161: **5-line red P**(hilosophi), plain.

Major initials Fol. 1: **9-line green D**(omino) with scalloped reserved line and green bordering line; ascender elaborated into a folded leaf and thick tendril, with cross-hatched shading. Fol. 2: **7-line green D**(isciplina) with curved reserved line. Fol. 10: **7-line red R**(hetorica) with reserved line in each stroke and flourished decoration in red. Fol. 16v: **7-line green M**(usica) with fine curved and scalloped reserved lines, extended tail to first vertical stroke. Fol. 20: **6-line red M**(edicina) with reserved line. Fol. 22: **7-line green M**(oyses), very like that on fol. 16v. Fol. 24v: **6-line green C**(ronica) with scalloped reserved line; some flourishes within letter sketched in grey. Fol. 27v: **4-line green V**(etus), plain. Fol. 32v: **10-line red A** with scalloped and straight reserved lines, an extended and split tail with foliate terminal; some slight flourishes also in red;

the scribe (4) left a sloping space for this initial which the artist exploited. Fol. 35v: **12-line green B**(eatissimus) with elegant scalloped reserved line. Fol. 44: **8-line red E**(cclesia) with scalloped and straight reserved lines. Fol. 51: **9-line green L**(inguarum) for which no space left by scribe 6; red barley-sugar pattern overlaid on green, with red flourishes. Fol. 61v: **5-line green O**(rigo) with red pen flourishes inside initial. Fol. 70: **5-line green N**(atura) with extended tail to first stroke and scalloped reserved line in diagonal stroke; both vertical strokes have horizontal line and dot embellishment. Fol. 79: **5-line red O**(mnibus) with scalloped reserved line; fol. 92: **4-line green M**(undus) with scalloped and straight reserved lines. Fol. 99: **6-line red T**(erra) with reserved strip in vertical stroke with red lines producing the effect of interlocking rectangular shapes. Fol. 107v: **4-line green D**(e) with curved reserved lines and tiny leaf terminals. Fol. 116: **6-line red P**(ulvis) with reserved lines. Fol. 127: **6-line red R**(erum) with reserved lines. Fol. 138: **10-line red P**(rimus) with undulating reserved lines, extended tail with elaborate leaf terminal. Fol. 145: **4-line red A**(rtium) with reserved line, extended tail with curled leaf terminals and vertical tendrils. Fol. 154v: **7-line green P**(rimus) with scalloped reserved lines and extended tail with curled leaf terminal and vertical tendril.

Historiated initials None.

Display script. Fols. 1–24 (scribe 1): often coloured capitals are followed simply by minuscule, except: fol. 10: (R)**hetorica est** in 1-line brown mixed capitals (followed by small rustic capitals); fol. 16v; (M)**usica est pericia** in 1-line brown mixed capitals; fol. 20: (M)**edicina** in 1-line brown mixed capitals; fol. 22: (M)**oyses gentis** in 1-line brown mixed capitals; fol. 24v: (C)**ronica** in 1-line brown mixed capitals. Fols. 25–161: the first letter or two after a coloured initial are capitals, usually rustic, or unemphasised.

Titles etc. Running book numbers, fols. 1–142: fols. 1–87 in red, fols. 87v–100 green; fols. 100v–107v: brown; fols. 108–118: green; fols. 118v–142: sometimes green, sometimes red. Book and chapter titles in pinkish-red not unlike that used in Bodley 371; fol. ii: 'Isadorus ethimologia' s.xv.

Title page None (but some prefatory leaves are lost).

IV CONTENTS

Table of contents fol. ii v, 'In hoc volumine continen*tur* libri subscripti' with list of contents s.xv; after 'Primo ysadorus ethimologu*s* continentes xx lib*ros*' are listed: 'Item tractatus gramatice, Item multa notabilia cronicis, Item liber methodii Ep*iscop*i', the last two items usefully indicating which texts were on the leaves now excised from q. 22. Fol. iii v: 'Ut val*e*as que requiris cito in hoc corpore invenire, hec tibi lector pagina monstrat, de quibus reb*us* in libris singulis conditor hui*us* codicis disputavit' with list of chapter headings and numbers (but not leaf or page numbers), s.xii ex.

Main texts Isidore, *Etymologiae*.

Fol. ii, added texts s.xii ex (see above, front flyleaves).

1. Fol. 1: 5 letters from Isidore to Braulio, the first: 'Ep*isto*la s*anc*ti ysidori ad braulionem episcopu*m*. D*omin*o et dei servo braulioni episcopo ysidorus om*n*i desiderio...ora p*ro* nobis beatissime d*omin*e *et* frater. Ep*isto*la braulionis ad Ysid*ori*. D*omin*o meo *et* vere d*omin*o...Solet repleri leticia homo i*n*teriori*um*'. Fol. 2: 'Incipit lib*er* ethymolgiarum beati ysidore hispalensis archiep*iscop*i. Disciplina'. Ends fol. 161: 'ut vis morbi ignis ardore siccetur. Explicit liber ethimologiarum beati isidori hispalensis archiep*iscop*i.'

2. Fol. 161: A grammatial treatise in 10 books. Begins with list of books: 'Primus liber de voce, littera silliba dictione oratione...Decimus de adverbio, interiectione coniunctione'. Text begins: 'Philosophi diffiniunt vocem esse aerem tenuissimum ictum. Vel suum sensibile aurium'. Fol. 168v ends incomplete: 'Unus dii et diis cum pro monosillabis ponuntur; per sineresin proferuntur in i longam'.

V ORIGIN AND PROVENANCE
Ex libris Fol. iii verso partially erased, 'Liber sancte marie de buildwas', the words alternately green and red.
Secundo folio suggesimus
Scribe 4, who wrote parts of the first section of the book in a distinctive round hand, and who executed the rubrication on fols. 25–55, worked in three other Buildwas books: Bodley 730, St. John's D.2 and Trinity B.2.30. This group of books has other scribes in common, which makes it certain that they were all made at Buildwas.
The book was given to the Bodleian Library by the Dean and Canons of Windsor in 1612.

VI NOTES

VII BIBLIOGRAPHY AND PLATES
Madan *et al Summary Catalogue,* II, 1, 262–3; Ker, *MLGB*, 15; Sheppard 1995, 186–7, figs. 1, 4, 5, 6.

15. CAMBRIDGE, ST. JOHN'S COLLEGE MS D.2
1. Aelred of Rievaulx, Speculum Caritatis 2. Rabanus Maurus, Cena Cypriani
Leaves [i paper], 91, i, [I]   **Date** s.xii ex
Foliation Not continuously foliated; first leaf in each quire numbered as if in a continuous sequence; actual fol. 90 wrongly numbered 92, two stubs of the replacement endleaves now sewn in behind the last quire after fol. 89, apparently having been counted as two excised leaves.   **Fig**. 18
Origin Buildwas

I PHYSICAL DESCRIPTION
Binding Original, s.xii ex, repaired quite early as well as more recently; spine now rigid, primary covering cracking along inner spine edges of boards; repaired in 1971 (J.P. Grey, pencil note on last endleaf).
Endleaves
Front *Pastedown* A single parchment leaf in place, probably a replacement, slightly too large for the board; now with no conjugate leaf, pasted down over a more recent white parchment board lining. Two printed labels: 1) 'E libris Guiliemi Crashaw A.M. Hujus Collegii Olim Socii Codices manuscriptos CLXVII Coemptos DD vir Honorabilis Thomas Comes Southamptoniensis AD 1635'. 2) St. John's College bookplate.
    Flyleaves A single paper leaf pasted in (watermark: hammer and anvil), to which a small piece of very thick white tawed skin (*c.*184 x 125mm) is affixed by means of a parchment hinge (see below, Chemise). The fragment bears several inscriptions s.xvii: '40S Aelredus'; 'Tho.C.S.'; 'in Bibliothecam patrum

Coloniensi scribiter Aëlredii abbas Rievallensis'; titles of the contents in several hands s.xvi; shelfmark 'A 315' and shelfmark of St. John's College: 'D.2'.

Back *Flyleaves* **1**) First 3 leaves of a quaternion (fol. 2 now excised to stub, fol. 4 originally the pastedown) to which an additional text added; **2**) a parchment leaf (a replacement), now cut to half its width and sewn in behind the last quaternion (see below, Pastedown 1); blank.

 Pastedown **1**) A parchment leaf (replacement) in place, blank, now sewn in behind last quaternion (see above) together with the half-leaf which is adjacent to it (the stubs are visible before q. 11 (last quire)). This pastedown is itself now pasted over a more recent white parchment board lining. Worm holes are evident on the present pastedown along the lines of the present primary covering turn-in and lacing paths which are not visible on the former pastedown (see 2 below). However the present pastedown does not bear rust marks from metal attachments which are present on the original pastedown (see 2 below) and which have also left marks on present cover. This seems to indicate a repair at a fairly early date. **2**) A former pastedown, almost certainly the original one, is now the second flyleaf (once fol. 4 of a quaternion, a common endleaf structure in Buildwas books); it bears remains of grainy paste and impressions of covering turn-ins, three sewing support channels and chain attachments which match those elements or their remains which are still present on the back board (see below). It also bears impressions of the edges of a spine lining, and the outer three-quarters are markedly paler than the inner quarter, probably once protected by a chemise envelope. Inscription on the unprotected strip near spine: 'Noli accipere malam de arbore male' written in a small hand, s.xii, now partly erased (conjoint leaf bears part of text item 2).

Sewing stations 3, not marked: (tail) I 26 K 32*61*59*33 K 26 I mm (head).

Sewing Sewn all-along with white S-twist thread. Replacement endleaves (back) also sewn with white S-twist thread; this must be a re-sewing and not the original.

Sewing supports 3, white tawed skin split supports *c.*10mm wide. Those primary sewing supports visible at front joint are intact.

Lacing path Through tunnels from spine edges, channels on outer then inner faces, lacing paths parallel, 57–65mm (front board), 50–60mm (back board); ends secured with wooden wedges.

Endbands Rolled white skin cores, laced into boards at approx. 45° through tunnels from corners, channels on outer then inner faces, ends obscured. wrapped around with thick white S-twist thread and sewn through the tab and tied down in the centre of each quire. Additional, roughly executed sewing, certainly part of a repair, consists of 4–5 long stitches running across the entire width of the spine between endband and leaf edge, passing through the tab and primary covering. The endbands are very thin compared to the width of the channels cut for them, and they are likely to be replacements. The remains of wider endbands can be seen in place through the holes made by the upper left boss nail (front) and upper right chain attachment nail (back).

Tabs Semi-circular tabs present at head and tail, made of thick white tawed skin and extending along the spine approximately half-way to the nearest primary sewing support. Sewn to matching extension of primary covering at perimeter with white thread, with herringbone pattern along ridge and at the base of the sewing on either side of the tab. The tab, primary covering and endbands are also roughly sewn together (see above, Endbands), part of a repair.

Spine lining The spine is lined along its length with a single piece of white tawed skin (visible at front joint), which is pasted to the inner surface of both boards. Sections are cut away to accommodate the sewing supports. At head and tail the corners pasted to the boards are cut at an angle, to fit with the corners of the turn-in of the primary covering. Impressions of the edges of the spine lining are visible on the now detached back pastedown.

Boards Wood, 237 x 170 x 12mm, all corners square, all edges bevelled; once flush with leaves though leaves now project slightly at fore-edge.

Primary covering White tawed skin discoloured to yellow, cracking along inner spine edges of boards; corners not visible, but impressions on back pastedown suggest corners are mitred. Impressions of sewing across front and back covering (see below, Chemise).

Fastenings Central fore-edge strap of white tawed skin, 13mm wide, fixed into a groove in the front board by 2 black nails with rectangular heads; now cut off at fore-edge of board. Corresponding rusted hole on back board, 68mm from fore-edge, suggests position of original pin; fragment of pin survives in the hole.

Chemise Not extant, but a fragment of the former chemise, with inscriptions, is now attached to front paper flyleaf. Impressions of sewing on primary cover on front and back board may have been left by thread holding together pieces of skin which comprised the chemise; impressions of sewing extending three-quarters of the width of each board at lower edge, and the comparative whiteness of outer three-quarters of original pastedown, indicate that the pocket attachment of the chemise to the boards was very deep, c.130mm.

Bosses Holes close to each corner of the front board suggest the former position of bosses; no such remains on bottom board.

Chain attachments Back board, lower edge, near spine, four large rusted holes in a roughly trapezoid formation (25 x 30 x 23 x 33mm), suggest the earlier presence of a chain attachment. No corresponding marks are found on the present pastedown, but one rust stain in a position corresponding to the lower right hole is clearly evident on the leaf which formerly served as a pastedown. Top right hole coincides with empty endband tunnel running between inner and outer surfaces of board.

Labels On the spine, 2 small printed paper labels pasted to spine with shelfmark D and 2.

Structure of Book

Parchment Fair quality, hair side mostly very yellow and clearly distinct from flesh side, qq. 8–11 whiter, finer and more evenly coloured, especially q. 10. A few holes: flaymarks (e.g. fol. 61), scar tissue (e.g. fol. 27) and holes repaired by parchment maker (e.g. fol. 6).

Collation $1-10^8$, 11^8 + 1 leaf after 8, (2 stubs of replacement endleaves), a quaternion (fol. 2 excised to stub; fol. 4 was pastedown) + 1 leaf after last text leaf (replacement flyleaf). Hair side outside in each quire.

Quire nos. QQ. 1–11: lower margin of last leaf of each quire, in small Roman numerals.

Catchwords QQ. 2–4, only, lower margin fol. 8v.

Page Layout
Dimensions
Page 237 x 170mm.

Space ruled for writing 172–174 x 107–110mm.

Columns Item 1: long lines; item 2: 4 columns.

Pricking Leaves folded, 1→8, template used; qq. 1–2: outer margin only, qq. 3–11: both margins; qq. 1–4 only: double pricked for edge-to-edge lines. Pricked for 31 lines throughout.

Ruling In brown, usually page by page (evidence of variations in ruling on conjoint leaves).

Lines per page Mostly 31, but fols. 12v–16: 26–23; fols. 17–24: 25; fols. 25–32: 24–28; (these quires written by scribe 2 who also used catchwords).

Page design

fols. 1–12v   fols. 12v–32   fols. 33–89

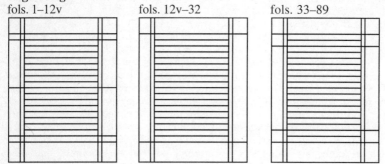

II SCRIBES

The writing was a cooperative effort by 8 scribes, several of whose hands (s.xii ex) are recognisable in other Buildwas books. All used punctus flexus. **Scribe 1** wrote fols. 1–12v in a small, uneven hand which has the appearance of having been rapidly executed; no angularity but very sharp serifs and triangular clubs to minims, high curved finishing stroke to terminal t and e; crossed Tironian 'et' as well as a round ampersand. **Scribe 2** wrote fols. 12v–32 in a more angular hand, quite neat but with ungainly capitals and ampersand with very long ascending stroke; the hand is small at first but rapidly enlarges, with fewer lines per page; the scribe ignored the pricking and ruled a variety of lines per page. **Scribe 3** wrote fol. 33 only in a very large upright hand, flat serifs and flat feet to minims. This scribe mistook punctus flexus in his exemplar for 'etiam' which he wrote in abbreviated form, and then had to erase it to insert the correct punctuation. The same scribe wrote two pages in Bodley 730 (q.v.), where he made the same mistake. **Scribe 4** wrote fols. 33v–36v in a neat, compressed hand which tends slightly to slope backwards; this scribe was responsible also for the rubrics on fols. 1–31. **Scribe 5** took over from scribe 4 at line 8 and completed this page only (fol. 36v) in a small neat hand. **Scribe 6** completed this text (fols. 37–89v) in a small hand with a distinctive backward trailing lower loop to g and S. This scribe also wrote a short text at the end of Bodley 730 (q.v.). **Scribe 7** wrote the second text (fols. 89v–91v) slightly later than the main text, in a small, neat and regular hand. **Scribe 8** was responsible for the rubrics from fol. 33v–89v. His hand is distinctively round with long ascenders, and he used reversed c as an abbreviation for con. This scribe worked in other Buildwas books, notably Bodley 395 and 730 and Trinity B.2.30 (q.v.). Corrections were usually made over erasures by the current scribe (e.g. fol. 6) or in the margin (e.g. fols. 4v, 5, 17).

III DECORATION, RUBRICS AND ARTICULATION OF TEXT

Colour notes were supplied for major initials, probably throughout, though several now erased or trimmed off; r (rubeus) and a (azurus) alternate, but the letters marked *a* are executed throughout in a yellowish-green. On fols. 41 and 65 the colour note *r* is made in red ink.

Text initials Fols. 2v–4v: capitals for capitula in red minuscule; otherwise small brown ink capitals are made by each scribe.

Minor initials None.

Major initials 2–5-line initials open each new section of text, alternately red and yellowish-green, sometimes with a straight or delicately undulating reserved line (e.g. fols. 40v, 69v); each initial is lightly flourished in the contrasting colour (i.e. red or green) in a repetitive manner, by a flourisher who also worked in Bodley 730, Trinity B.2.30 and CUL Add. 4079 (q.v.)

Historiated initials None.

Display script Scribes occasionally wrote the first letter or two after a coloured capital in small rustic capitals in brown ink. Otherwise none.

Titles etc. No running titles; incipits, explicits and chapter headings written in red minuscule by several scribes. Chapter 11 of book 3 (fol. 67) was omitted by the text scribe (perhaps eyeskip due to similarity of chapter headings), but the headings continued to be supplied in the expected sequence. A contemporary hand noted: 'hoc capitulum deest' and proceeded to cross out the incorrect headings and substitute the appropriate ones in the margin. On fols. 80 (recto and verso) and 84, the correct headings are noted in a small hand (s.xii ex) vertically in the margins. The hand which corrected the headings may also have written the final explicit.

Title page None, but prefatory pages may have been lost.

IV CONTENTS

Table of contents None extant; titles added to flyleaf by later hands, s.xvii.

Main texts Aelred of Rievaulx, *Speculum Caritatis*; Rabanus Maurus, *Cena Cypriani*.

1. Fol. 1 prefaces: i) 'Ep*i*st*o*la be*a*ti bernardi abb*a*tis Clarevall*i*s ad ailred*um* abb*a*tem. Est quidem s*anctorum* v*i*rt*us* p*er* maxima humilitas [sic]'. Ends fol. 1v: 'm*i*hi q*u*i *i*nvit*um* coeg*er*im imputetur.' ii) 'Incipit prefacio abbatis ailredi in libr*um* qui inscribi*tur* de speculo caritatis. Vere s*anctorum* vera *et* discreta humilitas'. Ends fol. 2v: 'negligend*um* decernite.' 'Incipiunt cap*itu*la p*ri*mi libri. i. Quod nich*i*l digni*us* qu*am* ut creator a sua amet*ur* creatu*r*a'–xxxiiii; fol. 3v: 'cap*itu*la libri ii' i–xxv; fol. 4: 'cap*itu*la libri iii' i–xlv. Ends fol. 4v: 'Quom*odo* in vic*em* frui debeam*us*.'
Fol. 4v: 'Incipit liber qui insc*ri*bit*ur* de speculo caritatis. Quod nichil dign*us*... Extendisti d*omi*ne sic*ut* pelle*m* celum tuu*m* pon*ens*'. Ends fol. 89v: 'aput iustum *et* mis*eri*cor*dem* iudicem interecedat. Expli*ci*t liber aelredi abb*a*ti*s* Riewallis de speculo karitatis.' *CCCM* I, 1–161; *PL* CXCV, 501. An omitted chapter (11 in Book 3) is supplied on a slip of parchment sewn to the outer margin of fol. 67 in a hand s.xiii ex, possibly that of a librarian.

2. Fol. 89v: '[D]*omi*no excellentissimo atq*ue* serenissimo regi Lothario ultim*us* ves*t*re sollempnitatis alumpn*us* maurus. Cupienti mihi...et brevitas animum legentis attolleret.' Fol. 90: '[Q]uidam vir magnus *et* pr*a*epotens rex habitans in partib*us* orientis nom*i*ne Abbathieos'. Ends fol. 91v: 'Et sic omn*es* congratulantes ad domum p*ro*pri*am* sunt reversi.' Rest of page blank. James records (*St.*

John's MSS, 103) that this revision of Cyprian's *Cena* by Rabanus Maurus was printed (from a damaged MS at Berne) by Hermann Hagen, 'Eine Nachamung von Cyprian's Gastmahl durch Hrabanus Maurus,' *Zeitschrift für Wissenschaft Theologie*, XXVII (1883), 164–187. The copy in the St. John's MS is complete.

V ORIGIN AND PROVENANCE
Ex Libris Fol. 89v: 'Liber sancte marie de Bildeuuas' in a very large minuscule at end of first text, s.xii ex.

Secundo folio Neque

The book has scribes and initials makers in common with several other books from Buildwas (Bodley 395 and 730, Trinity B.2.30 and CUL Add. 4079), which makes it certain that it was a product of the later twelfth-century scriptorium at the monastery. Aelred's *Speculum* is listed in the *Registrum* but Buildwas is not listed as owning a copy.

It was acquired first by William Crashaw (a member of St. John's College) and subsequently by Henry, Earl of Southampton, who bought it with others from Crashaw's library for St. John's. His son made good this intention, giving 167 books to St. John's College in 1634. At the top of fol. 1 is an inscription: R. Benet, s. xvi, possibly the name of an intermediate owner or book seller. The name appears in several of St. John's MSS (see James, 103).

VI NOTES
Medieval book and chapter numbers. The chapters in the *Speculum* are numbered throughout in the upper margin in Arabic numbers (except x for 10 only). The chapter number is written over the column in which it begins, and if the chapter continues over more than one opening, in the top right corner of the rectos. From fol. 38v (Book 2) the abbreviated sign *Pars* •• is added to the top right corner of each recto together with the chapter number, and similarly after fol. 60 (Book 3), the sign *Pars* •••.

VII BIBLIOGRAPHY AND PLATES
James, *St. John's MSS*, 103; Ker, *MLGB*, 14; CW.P.O., 'The Southampton Manuscripts', *The Eagle* (June 1918), 207–213; Cheney 1953, 377 (1973, 332); Chibnall, *VCH*, 56; Sheppard 1995, 189–190.

16. OXFORD, BODLEIAN LIBRARY MS BODLEY 730
John Cassianus, Regula, Decem Collationes   **Date** s.xii ex.
Leaves ii, 146, i
Foliation i–ii,1–147 (including detached pastedown)
Origin Buildwas   **Figs**. 17, 19

I PHYSICAL DESCRIPTION
Binding s.xii ex, repaired, spine flat; boxed.
Endleaves
Front *Pastedown* Fol. 1 of a quaternion, detached, with impressions of present sewing support channels, primary covering turn-ins and former spine lining, and marks from bosses and chain attachments. No sign of usual paste remains, but residue of brown paste. Recto: various shelfmarks in various hands: '(2709) Bod. 730' s.xix; 'MS Bodley 730' s.xix–xx; 'This out of C II 10' in ink, and 'MS Med 110'.

Flyleaves Fol. 4 of quaternion (fols. 2–3 excised); recto blank; list of contents and partially erased ex libris on verso in black and green ink.

Back *Flyleaves* None remaining; fols. 1–5 of last quire excised to stubs.

Pastedown Fol. 6 of last quire, detached, blank; verso, impressions of present primary covering turn-ins and sewing support channels and the irregular edge of a former spine lining pasted under turn-ins; residue of paste and splashes of glue.

Sewing stations 2, station for lower kettle stitch apparently pricked 8→1 (e.g. fol. 24) but no evidence that other stations marked: (tail) I 47 K 56*100*62 K 44 I mm (head). The single marking-up prick might have been associated with tacketing.

Sewing supports 2 white tawed skin supports, split, 11mm wide.

Sewing Sewn all-along with white Z-twist thread.

Lacing path Supports laced into boards through tunnels at spine edge, channels on outer then inner faces, lacing paths parallel, 70mm (front board), 80mm (back board); ends not visible (front board); repaired (back board) with replacement supports of brown leather probably sewn to original supports, and these now laced into back board through existing path and fixed with new wedges.

Endbands Narrow white tawed skin supports, split, 8mm wide, probably entering boards through tunnels at the corners of boards (corners obscured), to channels on outer then inner surfaces, lacing paths at 45° to board edges, ends secured with wooden wedges. Tail endband (back) missing from channels; endbands sewn with white thread, S-twist at head and Z-twist at tail, with herringbone pattern of stitches along edge of each band.

Tabs Present at head, cut off at tail; white tawed skin with matching extension of primary covering, sewn together with blue and white threads with herringbone pattern of stitches at perimeter and at base of sewing on both sides of tab.

Spine lining None extant, but on each detached pastedown are impressions of the irregular edge, parallel with the spine, of a spine lining. Not clear from impressions whether this lining was made of one or of several pieces of skin, but those on back pastedown indicate that the spine lining was pasted under the covering turn-ins.

Boards Wood, 309 x 207 x 11mm, all corners square, all edges bevelled and flush with edges of leaves.

Primary covering Discoloured white tawed skin, very marked and scuffed and with areas of impressions of loose woven material like hessian; corners mitred. All corners repaired with white tawed skin pasted to boards underneath primary covering, inside and outside (visible through holes and tears). Shelfmarks written on covering over spine: *730* (head), *Med 110* (tail).

Fastenings One fore-edge strap (showing slight pink pigment) in place, 20mm wide, fixed to the board under the primary covering, now cut off flush with fore-edge of board. Corresponding hole in centre of back cover, 100mm from fore-edge.

Chemise None present, but impression of line of sewing on front covering parallel with spine may have resulted from a join in a former chemise.

Bosses Holes in each corner and one in the centre of front cover show former position of brass bosses (nails have left green-edged holes on detached pastedown); faint impressions surrounding holes indicate that the bosses may have been hexagonal. No indications of bosses on back cover.

Chain attachments **1**) Upper fore-edge of front cover, two holes parallel with upper edge (17 and 40mm from fore-edge) within the impression of a pointed strip on inner and outer surfaces indicate former position of a chain attachment; **2**) centre of lower edge front cover, 3 rusted holes on outer surface and 2 on inner surface indicate former position of chain attachment(s) (holes have burned through to fol. 3). **3**) lower edge of back cover near spine, 4 rusted holes in trapezoid formation (10 x 26 x 9 x 28mm) (no matching holes on inner surface).

Labels Upper half back cover near spine, a cleaner rectangular patch (420 x 800mm) with 6 small nail holes at the edges indicate former position of a label.

Structure of Book

Parchment Mostly evenly white, with nap on both sides, but with very many holes, mostly at edges of leaves; parchment maker's repairs have been neatly cut out (e.g. fol. 22) or left (fol. 77); flaymarks fols. 7, 13.

Collation i^4 (2, 3 excised), $1-13^8$, 14^{10}, $15-18^8$, 19^6 (1–5 excised); qq. 1–2: flesh side outermost; qq. 3–19: hair side outermost.

Quire nos. QQ. 9–13 numbered I–V, lower margin of verso of last leaf.

Catchwords QQ. 1–5, 7, 14–15, 17, lower margin of verso of last leaf, near spine. Fol. 131: catchword provided recto (within a quire) for next scribe.

Page Layout
Dimensions
Page 307 x 209mm.
Space ruled for writing 224 x 135mm.

Columns 2.

Pricking Leaves folded, both margins, 1→8; qq. 1–8: 3rd line from bottom is consistently pricked twice to signal edge-to-edge ruling. QQ. 9–19: the double pricks are erratic (e.g. qq. 9–10: no double pricks; q. 11: every 8th hole double pricked; q. 12: no double pricks, etc.). QQ. 1–2 have multiple pricks in upper and lower margin. Template used for each margin in turn; the double pricks evidently not part of the template.

Ruling In brown, fairly neatly executed, but edge-to-edge ruling not consistent.

Lines per page 36 throughout.

Page design

fols. 1–64, 65–80   fols. 80v–130   fols. 131–146

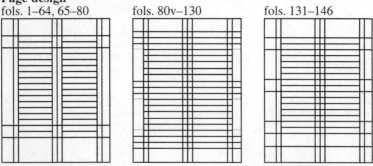

II SCRIBES

At least 5 scribes contributed to the writing of the text. **Scribe 1** wrote fols. 1–64v in a compact, slightly backward-sloping hand, using punctus flexus. He used very dark ink, and mostly supplied his own rubrics, but omitted them on fols. 22v–32, 53–56. These are supplied by two other hands. He ruled consistently in brown. Scribe 1 also added a text on fols. 145v–146. **Scribe 2** took over at the beginning of a new quire and text, and wrote fols. 65–130v in an upright, angular hand with diamond-shaped clubbed tops and flat feet to minims, using punctus flexus. This scribe mostly provided his own rubrics either in the spaces he occasionally left in the text but more often in the margins, except fols. 73, 73v, 75, 76, 81, 88v–130v. **Scribe 3** wrote only column b of fol. 130v in a very large hand, with similarly formed minims. This scribe once wrote 'eti*am*' instead of supplying a punctus flexus and erased and corrected his own mistake (cf. St. John's D.2, scribe 3). **Scribe 4** wrote only fol. 131 (q. 17 fol. 1) in a neat, angular and upright hand, similar to that of scribe 3 but more compressed and using different ruling; this scribe put a catchword at the bottom of his page for the next scribe. **Scribe 5** wrote the remainder of the main text on fols. 131v–144 in a smaller, irregular hand, less angular than the previous three hands. He used the punctus flexus, and very pale ink.

A seventh scribe s.xii ex added a glossary on fols. 144–145 and another glossary on fols. 146–146v.

Corrections over erasures and in margins.

Where not provided by scribe 2, rubrics were mostly supplied by another scribe using a distinctive round hand. He worked in other Buildwas books (Bodley 395, St. John's D.2, Trinity B.2.30). Fol. 93v: marginal note: 'rubrica De euno*corum* tepore*m*' (sic). There is no rubrication after fol. 143.

III DECORATION, RUBRICS AND ARTICULATION OF TEXT

Text initials Not emphasised in any way.

Minor initials Fols. 1–64v (scribe 1): 2–line plain, well executed initials, alternately red and green, all extended into the margins well beyond their 2-line space; elegantly designed, with occasional reserved lines (e.g. fol. 58) or elaborated terminals (e.g. fols. 14v, 60). These and the major initials are executed by the same scribe/artist (see also below fols. 145v–146). Fols. 65–131 (scribes 2–4): 2- or 3-line initials, alternately red and green, and flourished in a repetitive manner in the contrasting colour; the work seems to be that of the maker of the major initials in this section of the text. Fols. 131v–144 (scribe 5): initials as on immediately previous leaves but the green is now a distinctive yellowish-green. Fols. 145v–146: scribe 1 supplied his own 2-line black initials to the text which he added (evidence of ink colour), elegantly made and flourished. The M on fol. 146 is especially elegant and supports the probability that scribe 1 made all the red and green initials on fols. 1–64.

Major initials Fols. 1–64 (scribe 1): fol. 1: initial excised. Fol. 2: **5-line red and green D**(e institutis), the colours separated by angular and curved reserved lines, with symmetrical patterns of serrated-edged curled leaves inside letter and slight red flourishes to left of letter. Thereafter the beginning of each book is introduced by an elegant 4-line red or green letter, undecorated (except fol. 32: S(ecundum) which has red flourishes filled with ochre, probably by another hand). Fols. 65–144 (scribes 2–5): fol. 65: **6-line red D**(ebitum), with scalloped reserved lines, the letter filled with two clumsy green striated circular motifs with serrated edges and some slight flourishes. Fol. 65v: **5-line green C**(um) with reserved line, letter filled with two green circular serrated-edged motifs with plant-like formation of lines and dots (like tadpoles) in each; the design is

83

clumsy and heavy, unlike the letter itself. Fol. 74: **6-line red D**(e) with curved reserved line, filled with two heavy green symmetrical striated leaf motifs, very like that on fol. 65. Fol. 82: **11-line red I**(n) with double curved reserved lines, extended tail with simple leaf and tendril terminal, and flourishes in green. Fol. 89v: **4-line red I**(inter) (extended tail to lower edge of page) with reserved scalloped line and flourishes in green, the whole initial very like that on fol. 82. Fol. 95: **9-line red I**(n) with undulating reserved line and green flourishes. Fol. 103: **11-line red I**(n) with curved and scalloped reserved line and extended tail and simple leaf and tendril terminal and green flourishes, very like that on fol. 82. Fol. 110: **5-line green S**(umme) with undulating and scalloped reserved line, each half of the letter filled with clumsy design of red circles and lines ('tadpole' motifs) in serrated-edged folded leaf shape. Fol. 119v: **4-line red C**(onsummatis) with scalloped reserved line and clumsy green serrated edge design like those described above. Fol. 127: **5-line red D**(e) with extended vertical ascender, scalloped reserved lines and filled with a dotted horizontal bar and serrated-edged curled leaf motifs in each half with 'tadpole' motifs, flourished with green. Fol. 137v: **11-line red I**(nter) with scalloped reserved line, and extended tail with simple leaf and tendril terminal, and striated yellowish-green flourishes along its length, the flourishing line also having a simple curled leaf and tendril terminal.

Historiated initials None.

Display script Fols. 1–64v: first word or first few letters following a coloured initial in small brown rustic capitals. Fol. 65: (D)**ebitum** in 1-line mixed capitals in brown ink, probably by the scribe; elsewhere first word or first few letters following a coloured initial in rustic capitals, or not emphasised.

Titles etc. Running titles supplied spasmodically to fol. 13v only in upper margin; text and chapter headings, incipits and explicits in red in various hands, usually by the current scribe (see above, Scribes). Final explicit by last text scribe in brown ink (fol. 144).

Title page None.

IV CONTENTS

Table of contents Fol. ii verso: 'In hoc volumine continentur ista' in green, followed by the two titles, in black with green capitals.

Main texts Johannes Cassianus, *Regula; Decem Collationes.*

1. Fol. 1 (initial and some text excised): 'Incipit prologus regule sancti iohannis [ ] castorio pape in [ ] scripsit. [ ]eris instrument[ ] narrat his'. Ends fol. 2: 'eadem observantie perfectio etiam in impari facultate. Explicit prologus. Incipit liber primus de habitu monachi. De cingulo monachi. Capitulum primum. De institutis ac regulis monasteriorum dicturi'. 12 books. Ends fol. 64: 'eius esse muneris in veritate credamus. Explicit de superbia liber duodecimus.' Rest of page blank. *PL* XLIX.

2. Fol. 64v: 'Gennadius massiliensis episcopus in libro quem de illustribus scriptoribus fecit de iohanne cassiano qui has collationes edidit talem sententiam tulit dicens. Cassianus natione scita constantinopolim a iohanne magno episcopo diaconus ordinatus'. Ends: 'et in his scribendi apud massiliam et vivendi finem fecit theodosio et valentiniano regnantibus. Amen.'

Fol. 65: 'Incipit prefatio iohannis heremite in decem collationibus missa ad papam leoncium et helladium fratrem karissimum. Debitum quod beatissimo pape castorio'. Ends fol. 65v: 'Sed nec iam ad collationes eorum et instituta properemus. Explicit prefacio. Deinde prosequitur narratio libri eiusdem de

habitatione schitie *et* proposito abba*t*is moysi. Cum in he*r*emo scithie ubi monachor*um'*. Ends fol 66: '*nost*ris ita exorsus est.' Fol. 66 (added in upper margin): 'Incipit collatio abba*t*is moysi de monachi destinatione *v*el fine. Om*n*es inq*uit* artes *v*el discipline'. Ends fol. 144: 'ad deum ver*s*iculi hui*us* meditatione servaverint. Finit coll*atio* s*ecun*da abbatis ysaac de or*at*ionis perfectione.' *PL* L.
3. Fol. 144 a glossary: 'Hic scribo plane ventrem caudamq*ue* Dian e Politicus di*citur* custos civitatis'. Ends fol. 145: 'un*us* in orbe potens unus u*bique* pius.'
4. Fol. 145v verses in praise of the Virgin: 'Hodierne lux diei celebris in ma*t*ris dei agit*ur* memoria'. Ends fol. 146: 'Ubi salus u*bi* vita ubi quies perpessita ubi lux est in finita ubi deus omnia. Amen.' Madan *et al, Summary Catalogue* II, 1, 507, state that two verses in this MS are not known elsewhere. See G.M. Dreves, ed., *Analecta Hymnica Medii Aevi,* 58 vols (Leipzig, 1886–1922), LIV, 346–349 (no. 219).
5. Fol. 146 a Latin–Old English glossary. Begins: 'Menbrum an lim. Caput heapod', and continues for 10 lines, written continuously. Begins again fol. 146v: '[M]enbrum an lime Capud heapod' written now as a list in three columns, one word and its equivalent to a line in each column making it much easier to use. Ends, possibly incomplete, fol. 146v: 'Altor vel nut*r*itor foster feder Altrix vel nitt*r*ix foster moder'.

V ORIGIN AND PROVENANCE
Ex libris 1) Fol. ii v, partly erased: 'Liber sancte marie', the words alternately in green and black, s.xii. 2) Fol. 1 upper margin: 'I66[iii] Conven*t*us carmeli*tarum* london*ie* ex ass*ignacione f*ratri*s Tho*me* Walden' s.xv.
Secundo folio /lia non solum.
Several of the scribes (scribes 2, 3 and the round-handed rubricator) and the maker of yellowish-green initials and repetitive flourishes are all known in other Buildwas books (St. John's D.2, Bodley 395, Trinity B.2.30, CUL Add. 4079) and this book is therefore certainly, like these, a product of the late twelfth-century scriptorium at Buildwas itself. Running book numbers of the kind added to several Buildwas books during the thirteenth century (see below, Notes) suggest that the book may still have been at Buildwas then. The *Registrum* lists both the *Regula* and the *Decem collationes* but does not register a copy found at Buildwas. While absence from the *Registrum* by no means proves that the book was not in the Buildwas library in the early fourteenth century, it is worth noting that the inscription on fol. 1 indicates that by the fifteenth century the book was in the possession of the Carmelites in London, having already come into the possession of one Thomas Walden. Madan *et al*, 507, state that the MS 'must have come into the [Bodleian] library in 1603 or 1604.'

VI NOTES
Medieval numbering. At the lower edge of the recto of each leaf between the central vertical lines are minute Arabic numbers which are running book numbers. Fols. 3–63 (item 1) are numbered 1–12 (x for ten, 11 for eleven); fols. 65–143 (item 2) are numbered I–X.

VII BIBLIOGRAPHY AND PLATES
Madan *et al, Summary Catalogue* II, 1, 507; Ker, *MLGB*, 15; Sheppard 1995, 187–189.

17. CAMBRIDGE, TRINITY COLLEGE MS B.2.30

Palladius: Vitae Sanctorum Patrum (Lausiac History) **Date** s.xii ex
Leaves i, 61, i, [i paper]
Foliation 1–62 (all parchment leaves)
Origin Buildwas **Fig**. 20

This book is here newly attributed to Buildwas. Ker, *MLGB*, 39, rejected it as a Canterbury book.

I PHYSICAL DESCRIPTION

Binding Rebound at least once; present binding s.xvi; spine now glued and rigid.

Endleaves

Front *Pastedown* Single laid paper leaf, once second leaf of a bifolium, the first excised to stub now pasted under current pastedown; sewing thread is trapped in the spinefold. No evident watermark, blank except for old and current shelfmarks and folio count; remains of paper fore-edge label.

Flyleaves Fol. 1 of former quaternion, flesh side outermost, only one leaf extant (three stubs visible after first leaf); parchment of remarkably different quality from that of text leaves, thick, stiff and with very yellow hair side. Recto: dirty and splashed with materials including a dark ?glue; faint impressions of three parallel sewing supports, former primary covering turn-in (probably uncoloured) and green-rimmed holes at each corner, probably from metal furniture, e.g. boss attachments. Verso: note in hand s.xvii: 'Haec est Palladii Historia Lausiaca quam Gentianus Hervetus iterum vertit et editit Parisys 1555'; Trinity College bookplate.

Back *Flyleaves* **1**) Parchment leaf, possibly once fol. 2 of a separate bifolium, of stiffer parchment than that of text leaves (as at the front), a stub of similar quality visible in front of it but not necessarily conjoint (hair side of stub seems to face flesh side of extant leaf), with impressions of two spine lining strips (see below) between faint impressions of three former sewing supports. Impressions also of former primary covering turn-in (see below). Flesh side only very roughly scraped, some flesh still adhering; **2**) Laid paper leaf, once part of a ?quaternion (see below, Pastedown), at least one leaf excised; no watermark, blank.

Pastedown Laid paper leaf in place, once fol. 2 of a ?quaternion, now pasted over the wide stub of a conjoint leaf (sewing thread trapped in spinefold); no evident watermark, blank.

Sewing stations Now 3. Faint impressions on surviving parchment endleaves suggest 3 sewing stations in an earlier, possibly the original, binding: (tail) I 65* 65*75*68 I mm (head). Measurements are approximate; no evidence about kettle stitch.

Sewing Surviving sewing at endleaves suggests sewing throughout is all-along with white S-twist thread. Spinefolds inaccessible for evidence of earlier sewing.

Sewing supports Now sewn on 3 narrow, white tawed skin supports, although there are three very prominent, raised double supports across the spine. Faint impressions on both surviving parchment endleaves indicate that an earlier binding was sewn on 3 supports *c*.10mm wide.

Lacing path Now over the outer spine edge of the boards, and through them to the inner face where the ends are fixed on the surface. Impressions on surviving parchment endleaves indicate earlier, parallel lacing channels were between 35 and 60mm long.

Endbands In place at head and tail, rolled skin core, sewn with blue and white discoloured S-twist threads, tied down in three spinefolds, near the front and back and in the centre; not now laced into boards.

Tabs None present; no other evidence.

Spine lining None present. Impressions especially on the surviving back parchment endleaf indicate former presence of at least two lining strips on the inner face of the boards, between three sewing support channels (cf. Shrewsbury XII).

Boards Pasteboard, 282 x 190 x 5mm.

Primary covering Dark brown leather, with overlapped corners (fore-edge turn-in over upper and lower turn-ins, its edges parallel with upper and lower edges); triple fillets close to and parallel with all four board edges, the central fillet gilt, front and back, four stylised five-petalled flowers impressed on the spine between the sewing supports, once gilt; small impressed, gilt arms of Archbishop Whitgift on front and back. Unstained impressions of turn-ins on parchment endleaves were left by an earlier covering; evidence about the corners is unclear.

Fastenings Ends of two rolled textile ties, 13mm from fore-edge, present front and back, the ends trapped under the pastedown; now cut off flush with outer face of boards. No other evidence.

Chemise None present; no other evidence.

Bosses Four green-rimmed holes, one in each corner of the front flyleaf, suggest former presence of 4 corner bosses on front board. No such holes in back flyleaf.

Chain attachments None present; no other evidence.

Labels Remains of paper fore-edge label on front paper flyleaf and on fol. 61; printed paper labels on spine with shelfmark.

Notes Fol. 43: page marker of parchment cut from the leaf and folded through slits may have been intended to mark any of the four chapters on fols. 43–43v headed: 'De sancta paula', 'De sabiniana et asella virgine Christi', 'De juliano monacho', 'De Adolio monacho'. Another on fol. 51 might have been intended to mark any of three chapters (fols. 51–51v): 'De Olimpiade femina', 'De Candida femina', or 'De Salomone monacho'. It is worth noting that the first chapters on both marked pages are about female saints, and that there is a concentration here of added stress marks. Some punctuation marks and possibly added hyphen marks on these pages (but also elsewhere), indicate that the book was used for reading aloud, possibly in the refectory. The evidence of former bosses (see above) supports this.

Structure of Book

Parchment Good quality white parchment, supple; many holes, most once roughly sewn (probably by parchment maker), some trimmed so as to remove sewing marks (e.g. fols. 29, 51; cf. Bodley 730 and other books in this group).

Collation 1–7⁸, 8⁴.

Quire nos. QQ. 1–7 in centre of lower margin of verso of last leaf (except q. 3 which also has a number in the same position on the recto of the first leaf), i–vii in brown ink; text scribe numbered qq. 2, 3, 4, another scribe numbered qq. 1, 5, 6, 7, the latter possibly the same hand as that which noted corrections in the

margins on fols. 39, 57v etc..
Catchwords None.

Page Layout
Dimensions
Page 275 x 186mm; leaves trimmed at outer margins (lost annotations), and upper and lower margins (evidence of former boss holes and trimmed rubrics and initials, e.g. fols. 37, 47v etc.).
Space ruled for writing 205–209 x 137mm.
Columns 2.
Pricking Much outer pricking trimmed, surviving evidence suggests leaves folded, both margins, 1→8; qq. 5–8, double pricks in inner margin at lines 16 and 31 (lines which are ruled edge-to- edge).
Ruling Neatly executed in grey sometimes appearing brown, to a mainly constant pattern; lines 1 and 3, 16 and 18, 31 and 33 ruled edge-to-edge. There is some variation in the central edge-to-edge ruling in first quires until q. 5 onwards, when line 16 is double pricked.
Lines per page 33.
Page design
fols. 2–61v

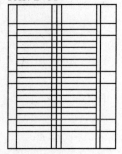

II SCRIBES
One scribe wrote the text throughout in an upright, heavy hand, clear but ungainly, with flat bottoms to minims and using a very dark ink. He did not use punctus flexus, but a corrector has changed several elevatus marks (ticks) to flex. This scribe is scribe 2 of Bodley 730. A second scribe who did use punctus flexus interpolated almost 16 lines on fol. 2v (col. b lines 1–17) in a somewhat similar but clearly different hand. Additions (or supplied omissions) added in the margins e.g. on fols. 16, 39 and 45v (where the supplied passage is written on lines ruled for the purpose). On fol. 56 two further corrections are noted in the margin and the incorrect word crossed through, but the correction was not made in the text; also on fol. 26v. The text scribe made corrections over erasures e.g. on fols. 6, 15 and 56, where he rewrote an extensive passage in col. b. This passage itself contains an error, noted in the margin, but the correction was not carried out. On fols. 1–1v, a corrector added several punctus flexus punctuation marks, sometimes as a correction over an erasure; this may be the same hand as that which supplied two missing letters also on fol. 1 (am*ato*re), and may in fact be the same as the interpolating hand of fol. 2v.
The rubrication was done by 2 different scribes, one certainly known from other

Buildwas books. Rubricating scribe 1 (who worked mainly on fols. 1–5) is the interpolating text hand of fol. 2v (see above). This hand also provided the rubrics on fols. 10v, 13 and 20v, and possibly the explicit on fol. 58v in brown ink. The second rubricating hand (fols. 6–61) is the 'round hand' of Bodley 730 and 395, and St. John's D.2 (q.v.). On fols. 58v–61 this 'round hand' scribe wrote the long rubrics for the additional passages (see below, Texts). The rubrication seems as careless here as in the other books, though the text scribe frequently left insufficient space for the rubrics. The rubric on fol. 6 was first crossed out then erased, though not corrected. A missing rubric on fol. 32 was supplied in brown ink by another hand. On fol. 57, a correction noted in the margin was supplied over an erasure in red probably by the 'round hand' scribe.

III DECORATION, RUBRICS AND ARTICULATION OF TEXT

On fol. 44, the 'round hand' scribe began to make a chapter heading in green ink but finished it in his usual red. The green and red he used appear to be the same as that of the many, rather carelessly made and flourished initials, so it may be that the uninventive flourisher of this group of books is the same as the 'round hand' rubricator who also worked in these books. However a doodled penwork flourish in brown in the margin on fol. 16 is also similar in character to the flourishes on the coloured initials.

Text initials 1-line brown ink capitals in the hand of the text scribe. A reader shaded those on fols. 19v–25 in silver point, often turning them into fat paraphs such as those in red on fols. 42, 42v.

Minor initials None as such; the initials described below under 'major initials' are minor in size and quality, but the function they serve is that of major initials.

Major initials A series of 97 2- or 3-line initials, often extended in the margins (especially letters P and I), one at the beginning of each text division: fols. 1–29: red; fol. 29 onwards: alternately red and green, with a variety of reserved line patterns and simply decorated tails, and mostly flourished with the complementary colour. The initials are quite nicely executed but the flourishing is often incompetent. A few red initials, e.g. on fols. 5v, 22, 25, 26v, 27, 28, 41v, 42, 49v etc. are executed in a duller, paler red than others, though all are flourished by the same flourisher. On fol. 25 the 'round hand' rubrication overlaps the initial which was clearly executed first.

Historiated initials None

Display script Fol. 2v: (M)**ulti quidem multos** in 1-line brown ink mixed capitals by the interpolating scribe who wrote the next $15^3/_4$ lines. Subsequently the first letters or word after a coloured initial often, but not always, executed in small brown ink rustic letters by the text scribe.

Titles etc. No running titles; chapter headings, incipits and explicits in red minuscule (fol. 58v: brown) by a variety of hands.

Title page None, but first leaves lost.

IV CONTENTS

Table of contents None, but first leaves lost.

Main texts Palladius, *Vitae Sanctorum Patrum.*

1. Fol. 2: 'Incipit prefatio heradidis episcopi de vita sanctorum patrum ad lausium prepositum palatii. In hoc libro quem de vita sanctorum patrum scripturi sumus'. Ends fol. 2v: 'ad recuperationem vite nobilioris reversos. Explicit prefatio.

Incipit prologus. Multi quidem multos variosque libros diversis temporibus'. Ends fol. 5: 'et praedicabiles mores. Explicit prologus. Incipit liber de vita sanctorum patrum qui appellatur paradysus.' Fol. 5v: 'Cum primum alexandrinam attigi civitatem in secundo senioris imperatoris theodosii consolatu.' Ends fol. 58v 'Pax legentibus et audientibus in Christo Amen. Explicit liber qui dicitur paradisus.' PL LXXIV, 243. Dom Cuthbert Butler, The Lausiac History of Palladius, 2 vols (Cambridge, 1898, 1904), I, 59–60 lists this copy (no. iv) as an example of 'the first Latin version' in which there are lacunae.

2. Fols. 59–61v: 13 chapters, the first 11 numbered 33–43. The first begins: 'Sicut namque immensa gloria'. The last ends fol. 62v: 'et hoc ipsum quod intellige remeruimus eius esse muneris in veritate credamus.' These passages are preceded by a long rubric written by the 'round hand' scribe (who also provided the chapter numbers and an omitted contraction mark on fol. 61v in red) in the lower margin of the previous page (fol. 58v): 'Quod sicut magna remuneratio monacho debetur secundum institutiones primum laboranti, ita et pena similiter tribuatur negligenti, et ideo non debeat facile quis admittet in monasterio.'

Fol. 61v: a hand s.xiv ex–xv in has scribbled: 'Confitemini domino quoniam bonus quoniam in seculum misericordia eius. Laudate dominum omnes gentes laudate omnes populi', the opening verses from Psalms 117 and 116, or 135. James (Trinity MSS, I, 91) further deciphered: 'Scripsit hoc Jhones Glave. Os facies mentum dens guttur lingua palatum'.

V ORIGIN AND PROVENANCE

Ex libris None. On fol. 2: 'Extat Graecae Manuscripte in Bibliotecham Sionianam Londini' s.?xvii.

Secundo folio viderit

The book was made at Buildwas in the second phase of book production by scribes and rubricators known from other books of certain Buildwas origin (e.g. Bodley 395, 730, St. John's D.2). The text is not listed in the Registrum. The inscription on fol. 2 indicates that the book was once in the library of the Sion congregation, whence Archbishop Whitgift may have obtained it. He gave it to Trinity College s.xvi ex.

VI NOTES

1. The book is remarkable for its ugly, carelessly executed appearance, its extensive correction but lack of evidence of readers' annotations. This is consistent with other evidence that the book was used for reading aloud rather than for private study.

2. James (Trinity MSS, I, 90) notes that this MS is no. 141 in the Catalogus Manuscriptorum Angliae (1697), and observes that it is 'very likely the copy in Edwards, p. 151.'

3. Fol. 37: in the lower margin in the right vertical column, '37' is written in tiny Arabic numbers in brown ink. It is like other numbers found in Buildwas books, but is the only one evident in this book.

VII BIBLIOGRAPHY AND PLATES

James, Trinity MSS, I, 90–91.

18. LONDON, LAMBETH PALACE LIBRARY MS 107

Hugh of Fouilloy, De Claustro   **Date** s.xii ex

Leaves [ii paper], ii, 94, [i paper]

Foliation   Not foliated throughout; first leaf of each quire numbered as if numbering were continuous.

Origin Probably Buildwas   **Fig**. 29

I PHYSICAL DESCRIPTION

Binding Rebound at least once, most recently s.xvii, refurbished 10. 6. 58 (note on back pastedown); spine now recovered, corners and joints repaired.

Endleaves

Front *Pastedown* **1**) Single leaf laid paper in place, blank; **2**) original pastedown now detached (see below, Flyleaves 2).

  Flyleaves **1**) 2 laid paper leaves, possibly once a bifolium, both watermarked: large crest with fleur-de-lis, surmounted by crown and with WR monogram below; **2**) parchment bifolium, first leaf originally pastedown. Fol. 1: paste remains, faint impressions of 3 sewing support channels and edges of earlier covering, 5 holes made by former bosses; many contemporary sewn repairs, otherwise blank; fol. 1v: blank, outer $^5/_6$ lighter than remainder, probably once protected by a deep chemise pocket (cf. back detached pastedown). Fol. 2: ex libris inscription and pen trials, and framed list of contents s.xii; fol. 2v: 2 faint stylus inscriptions, one below the other, partly obliterated: 'Rogerus mon[ ] monacus de Buldewas an*i*ma eius, Ricadus de [rdellou?] mon[acus] de buldewas' in hand s.xiv/xv.

Back *Flyleaves* **1**) Last leaf of last quire, originally the pastedown now detached. Recto: blank except for pen trails near spine, a strip *c*.18mm wide adjacent to spine markedly darker than remainder which is unmarked and clean, probably once protected by a deep chemise pocket. Verso: grainy paste remains, impressions of (uncoloured) primary covering turn-ins, sewing support and endband channels and holes made by bosses. Original flyleaves, fols. 6–7 of last quire, now excised. **2**) Laid paper leaf, probably once conjoint with paper pastedown, watermark: monogram TCV; blank.

  Pastedown **1**) Single leaf of laid paper in place, blank except for refurbishment note in pencil; **2**) original pastedown, now detached (see above, Flyleaves 1).

Sewing stations Now 6; originally 3 (evidence of impressions on front detached pastedown): (tail) I 60*85*95*78 I mm (head), upper and lower leaf edges trimmed; no evidence about kettle stitch; no pricking or other marking-up visible.

Sewing Spinefolds inaccessible.

Sewing supports Now 6 cords; impressions on detached pastedowns suggest originally 3 supports, *c*.10–12mm wide.

Lacing path Now over outer edges of boards and through to inner surfaces, fixed under pastedown. Impressions on detached pastedowns indicate that three supports were laced into earlier boards through parallel channels, those on the inner face of the board *c*.40mm from spine and *c*.23–25mm long.

Endbands Thin endbands present at head and tail, replacements, sewn with brown and white threads; not laced into present boards. Impressions of channels and associated wormholes on detached back pastedown (and faintly on front) show the earlier (probably original) binding to have had endbands *c*.8mm wide, laced into the boards at an angle of rather more than 45° from the upper and lower board edges, through channels with a total length of $c.50$–55mm.

Tabs None present; no other evidence.

Spine lining No clear evidence.

Boards Pasteboard, 337 x 226 x 5mm.

Primary covering Now brown calf with deeply impressed double fillets parallel with all four edges of both covers, and a single gold fillet along the three outer edges (thickness) of both covers. Bishop's arms with mitre and pallium stamped in gold, front and back, with author's name and the shelfmark in gold on spine.

Fastenings None present; no other evidence.

Chemise None present. Evidence of clean sections on detached back and front pastedowns and position of pen trials suggest that the book was still protected by a chemise with very deep pocket in the late thirteenth century, and possibly later.

Bosses None present; greenish holes on detached pastedowns show that there were at one time 5 bosses on each cover, one at each corner and one at the centre.

Chain attachments None present; two rust marks on back detached pastedown, 17 and 67mm from spine and 65 and 68mm (respectively) from the lower edge may have been made by a chain attachment – a characteristic chain attachment point for Buildwas books.

Labels None.

Structure of Book

Parchment Uniformly yellowish, but hair sides more so than flesh; much dark follicle marking, many small holes mostly where parchment maker's repairs were cut out, e.g. fols. 34, 51, 54, 65, or where skin has been damaged, e.g. throughout q. 5; many other parchment maker's repairs survive, e.g. fols. 24, 67, 68, 72.

Collation $1–11^8$, 12^8 (6 and 7 excised, probably blank, 8 was pastedown).

Quire nos. QQ. 1–3: I–III; qq. 4–8 and 10–11: iiii–viii, x–xi; q. 9: Arabic 9 in paler ink, in a later hand, probably associated with re-binding.

Catchwords QQ. 5–6: lower margin near spine; q. 9: lower margin near spine, in different ink, the same as that used for the Arabic quire number (see above).

Page Layout
Dimensions

Page 318 x 221mm (trimmed at all margins).

Space ruled for writing 229 x 155mm.

Columns 2.

Pricking Leaves folded, both margins, 1→8 except fol. 57 (q. 8 fol. 1): 8→1. Two templates used, one for qq. 1–6, another for qq. 7–12. QQ. 1–6: no double pricking for edge-to-edge lines; qq. 7, 11, 12: penultimate line double pricked, qq. 8–10: last line double pricked. In q. 12 there are 2 rows of pricking in the outer margin (inner not visible). The reason for this is quite plain. The last quire was pricked as usual with the current template beginning near the upper edge of the leaves leaving a wide lower margin. Fol. 1 of this quire was to receive a full-page drawing but it was discovered that this leaf had a hole which would have spoiled it. The scribe turned the quire top to bottom, making the holed leaf the last one, and repricked the quire 1→8 using the current template.

Ruling In brown, mostly regular and neat, but sometimes careless (e.g. fol. 16v).

Lines per page QQ. 1–6: 36; qq. 7–12: 38.

Page design
fols. 1–93v

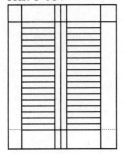

II SCRIBES

The text was written mainly by one scribe who used a very dark ink. His letter forms are characterised by straight backs to e and c, and a rather angular loop to a. Otherwise the hand is still fairly rounded, with ungainly, flat serifs at the tops of the letters. The hand changes throughout the text; by the second quire it is a little more compact and regular. In the last quire the flat serifs give way to clubbed serifs and the hand is even more angular. The scribe used punctus flexus throughout.

Interspersed are the hands of other scribes as follows: fol. 5 col. b: the last 5 lines written in a very upright, compressed, rather ungainly hand. Fols. 5v (col. b line 14)–6v: written in a very compressed, black hand which tends to slope backwards, and with short, thick ascenders; this scribe also used the punctus flexus punctuation mark. Fols. 18v (col.b)–19: written in a very compact, upright hand using a laborious, ugly form of g. Another scribe added the list of contents on fol. ii in an upright compact hand not unlike the interjecting hands but not identical to any. On fol. 90, an apparent change of hand is probably simply the result of a change of pen.

There are a few corrections, e.g. fol. 8v (mis-spelling); fol. 31 by another scribe over an erasure; fol. 38v by another scribe in the margin; fol. 76 a rubric corrected over an erasure, etc.

III DECORATION, RUBRICS AND ARTICULATION OF TEXT

Text initials Where necessary, 1-line plain capitals alternately red and green, e.g. fols. 56v–57 for capitula.

Minor initials The divisions of each text marked throughout by 2-line, plain initials, alternately green and red; letter I always executed in the margin, no space having been left for it by the scribe.

Major initials Fol. 1: **6-line green R**(oberti) with red folded-leaf-shaped flourishes, some coloured in with ochre. Fol. 1v: **15-line red I**(ncipientibus) in the margin, with an extended serif (top) and an elegant, bifurcated tail. Fol. 17v: **4-line red Q**(uoniam) with bifurcated tail extending across the column of text and into the nearby lower margin, the bifurcation decorated with green foliate flourishes touched with ochre; the letter filled with symmetrical 'curled leaf' motif very similar to that in the flourishes, in green touched with ochre. Fol. 34v: **5-line green N**(osti [sic]) with reserved line in diagonal stroke and extended tail which is elegantly flourished along its length in red with yellow shading and with a tri-partite 'curled petal' terminal decorated with red and yellow; within the letter 2 different 'curled leaf' motifs in red shaded with ochre. Fol. 34v: **5-line red and green A**(nime), the colours separated by reserved lines, with extended tail very like that of the N on the same page and with a simple 'curled petal' terminal in red touched with yellow; within the letter a double 'curled petal' motif in green and red with ochre shading. Fol. 56v: **12-line green and red R**(ogas), the colours separated by a reserved stepped line; the letter filled with repeated 'folded leaf' motifs (like that on fol. 1) in red with green and ochre touches and yellow shading. Fol. 57: **6-line green C**(ivitatis) filled with single flower motif with elongated curled petals in red; green 'ladder' motifs along central length of petals, with ochre and green shading. Fol. 83v: **4-line red S**(icut) with simple 'folded leaf' motif in green in each half of the letter, shaded with ochre and brown. Fol. 88v: **3-line red P**(ost), undecorated.

Historiated initials None.

Display script The first word or letters after major initials sometimes executed in small rustic capitals, but usually there is no display script proper.

Titles etc. Incipits and explicits in red by the text scribe.

Title page None, but there is an elaborated contents list (see below).

IV CONTENTS

Table of contents Fol. ii: 'In hoc volumine continentur libri q*uinque*' followed by 5 titles, written in a hand that is different from any of those of the text scribes. The list is framed by a double red line. Underneath this a hand, s.xvii, possibly that of Archbishop Sancroft or his secretary, has written: 'Auctor, Hugo de Folleio, vel Folietanus, Monachus Corbiensis'.

Main texts Hugh of Fouilloy, *De Claustro*.

1. Fol. 1: *De Eo Quid Noceat Claustralibus*. Prologue begins: 'Rogasti nos f*r*ater amantissime quatinus aliqua remedia temptationum'. Text begins fol. 1v: 'Incipientibus edificare querendus est locus fundamenti'. Ends fol. 17: 'deo autem vindicta commitentes finem ponamus.'

2. Fol.17: *De Ordinatione Claustro Materiali et de Abusionibus Eius*. Prologue begins: 'Locuturus karissime de his'. Text begins fol. 17v: 'Quoniam de ordinatione claustri materialis'. Ends fol. 34: 'pendet summa tocius religionis.'

3. Fol. 34v: *De Claustro Anime*. Prologue begins: 'Nosti [sic] karissime quod ea que de ordinatione claustri materialis'. Text begins fol. 34v: 'Anime claustrum contemplatio dicitur'. Ends fol. 56: 'non manufactum quod est in celis per venire.'

4. Fol. 56v: *De Claustro Non Manufacto Quod Non Est in Celis*. Prologue begins: 'Rogas, karissime, rogas et obnoxius de precaris'. Fol. 57: Capitula. Text begins: 'Civitatis magne ierusalem quedam pars'. Ends fol. 83v: 'fortitudinem immortalitatis benedictus deus. Amen.' *PL* CLXXVI, 1017–1182.

5. Fol. 83: *Liber de Duabus Rotis*. 'Incipit prologus de rota p*r*elationis. Sicut comperi non est tibi frater onerosum diu fuisse discipulum'. Ends fol. 84: 'rotam p*r*elationis in capite p*r*esentis opusculi pinga*m*. Explicit prologus.' Capitula. Fol. 84v: full page ink drawing: 'Hec rota est religionis vita'. Fol. 85: 'De his que sunt in rota. Vita veri religiosi sic*ut* rota volvitur.' Ends fol. 88v: 'peccat si culmen p*r*elationis ascendere contradicat.' Fol. 88v: 'Incipit prologus de rota simulationis. Post rotam vere religionis locuturi sumus de rota simulationis.' Ends fol. 88v 'a legente facilius intelligi possint. Explicit prologus.' Capitula. Fol. 89: full-page drawing: 'Hic rota est hypocritice vita'. Fol. 89v: 'De his que continentur in rota. Statura rote similtundine*m* designat hypocrite.' Ends fol.

93v: 'donec de his aliquis potiora dicat. Explicit liber duab*us* rotis.'
The two full page drawings are very finely executed in brown ink with ochre
shading, and inscribed in red, green and black ink probably by the text scribe.
They are each enclosed in a plain frame composed of green, ochre and brown
ink lines. There is nothing of comparable quality in other Buildwas-produced
books of this period.

V ORIGIN AND PROVENANCE

Ex libris Fol. 2 in pale brown ink, in a hand s.xii ex: 'Liber S*anc*te Marie de
Bildewas'. The ink is the same colour as that used to colour the drawings.
Secundo folio quidum fiat
There is no indisputable evidence that this book was made at Buildwas, though
its scribes' use of the punctus flexus is indicative of a Cistercian origin, and it
was certainly in the library very soon after it was written (evidence of the ex
libris). It seems likely that the book was copied at Buildwas during a period at
the end of the twelfth century, when books were still actively being produced.
As part of this campaign, in the early thirteenth century, the artist of Balliol 150
copied the figure of the good abbot from the drawing on fol. 84v. The fact that
the book obviously once had bosses suggests that it was used on a lectern.
The activities of the chapter and leaf numerator (see below) and the stylus
inscriptions of Roger and Richard, monks of Buildwas, on the front endleaf (see
above) demonstrate that the book remained at Buildwas at least throughout the
thirteenth century, and possibly well into the fourteenth and even fifteenth
centuries.
Like other books now in Lambeth Palace Library, this volume was among those
acquired in the early seventeenth century by Archbishop Sancroft.

VI NOTES

Book and chapter numbering. The book contains evidence of several efforts to
number books and/or chapters within books and/or leaves within chapters.
More than one hand was probably involved, and it seems as if the approach was
experimental rather than systematic. The main efforts are summarised below:

Item 1: 'Liber 1' (Arabic) or '*Liber*•' in upper margins near corners; running
leaf numbers in tiny Arabic numbers in lower margin near spine, which seem to
stop at 6, but later numbers may have been trimmed off; tiny running chapter
numbers (Arabic) top right recto and in upper margin over column where
chapter begins, and in tiny Roman numbers over the title of the chapter itself.
Other numbers here and there in the outer margins, seem to number items or
points in Hugo's text.

Item 2: 'Liber 2' (Arabic) over the Prologue column (fol. 17), '*Liber*••' on fol.
17v, then this numbering ceases. It is replaced by a tiny Arabic number 2 in the
upper margin, centre, throughout. Arabic chapter numbers top right recto except
where the chapters are short and there are several per opening, when these
numbers are placed over the relevant column. Tiny Roman numerals over
incipits to each chapter; at chapter 7 ('De duodecimi abusionibus'), the Roman
numerals begin again at i while the Arabic numbers continue the original
sequence. Running leaf numbers within chapters in lower margin in the centre
cease (or have been trimmed off) after 3–4 leaves.

Item 3: 'Liber 3' over left column fol. 34v, then '*Liber*•••', then this numbering
ceases. Tiny Arabic 3 the upper margin (left central column) begins on leaf 2 of
Book 3 and continues throughout. Chapter numbers in Arabic over relevant

column or in top right corner of rectos if the chapter is continuing; tiny Roman numerals over each incipit as in previous books. From fol. 46 (the second leaf of the very long chapter 11), the leaves within this chapter are numbered in tiny Arabic numbers in the lower margin in the left of the two central columns.

Item 4: '*Liber*••••' at the beginning of this book in top left margin fol. 56v; subsequently tiny Arabic 4 in upper margin in the left central column beginning on fol. 2 of Book 4. Chapter numbers over the incipits are now in Arabic numbers, but this numerator uses x for 10 (but Arabic 20). Chapter numbers in the upper margins appear spasmodically.

Item 5: The first part of item 5 has rough chapter numbers in brown over the columns where new sections begin, and a running book number in the upper margin, now in Roman numerals. Tiny Arabic numbers over most of the incipits. The second part of item 5 has no numbers at all.

All the tiny numbers, whether Arabic or Roman, seem to be by the same hand, and were presumably done at the same time. The form of Arabic 8 with a small tail is found in other Buildwas books.

VII BIBLIOGRAPHY AND PLATES
James, *Lambeth MSS*, 182–183; Ker, *MLGB*, 14; Sheppard 1990, 202, pl. 21; Cheney 1953, 377 (1973, 332); Chibnall, *VCH*, 56.

19. OXFORD, BODLEIAN LIBRARY MS BODLEY 371
Peter Cantor, Commentary on Kings and Chronicles (incomplete)
Leaves i, 98   **Date** s.xii ex
Foliation 1–98
Origin ?France   **Fig**. 35

I PHYSICAL DESCRIPTION
Binding s.xii ex, with chemise; spine flat; repaired; boxed.
Endleaves
   Front *Pastedown* Parchment leaf in place, under chemise pocket, fol. 1 of a separate bifolium wrapped round q. 1, the folded edge visible after fol. 8; blank except for part of torn paper label with shelfmark 'MS Bodl. 371' in pencil.
     Flyleaves Fol. 2 of a separate bifolium wrapped round q. 1 (see above, Pastedown); recto: various shelfmarks: '(2717)', 'Bod. 671' (crossed out in pencil), written on a parchment strip *c*.56mm deep pasted along the top of the leaf; 'MS Med 118' in brown ink circled in pencil, and note: 'this booke taken from C.1.6' in a hand s.xvi/xvii; verso: ex libris and shelfmark 'C I' in brown ink s.xv ex.
   Back *Flyleaves* Fol. 1 of separate bifolium wrapped round q. 12 (see below: Pastedown); excised to stub.
     Pastedown Parchment leaf in place, fol. 2 of a separate bifolium wrapped round q. 12 (folded edge visible before first leaf of q. 12); blank.
Sewing stations 4; (tail) l 22*99*103*100*18 l mm (head). No kettle stitch.
Sewing Sewn with white S-twist thread, a separate thread (and therefore a separate needle used) for each support, so that the two loops of the stitch are visible in the spinefold but there is no thread at the back of the spine, an unusual type of sewing.
Sewing supports 4 split supports of white tawed skin, 13mm wide.

Lacing path Laced through tunnels from spine edges, channels on outer then inner faces, lacing paths parallel; ends secured with pegs. Lacing paths $c.83$–89mm (front board), 90–92mm (back board).

Endbands None (primary supports are within 20mm of head and tail of spine).

Tabs Semi-circular tabs present at head and tail, of thick white tawed skin, probably continuous with the spine lining (see below); sewn to matching extension of primary covering with blue and white Z-twist threads in a chevron pattern.

Spine lining Under the pastedowns (front and back), the edges of a strip (or strips) of tawed skin which is pasted to the inner faces of both boards, are clearly visible along almost the entire length of the spine. The strip is visible where the pastedown is damaged in the lower corner of the front board. Here the strip is cut to accommodate the sewing support, and is pasted to the board under the primary covering turn-in. Also visible here is a fragment of white skin which is clearly part of the tab. It appears to have been once integral with the spine lining, a possibility supported by the evident overlapping of both inner board edges by the other tab. The lining/turn-in relationship is confirmed by impressions on the back pastedown. It is not clear whether the lining strip is made of a single piece or of several pieces of skin.

Boards Wood, 345 x 236 x $c.11$mm; all corners square, all edges slightly bevelled and flush with edges of leaves.

Primary covering White tawed skin, visible only where not covered by chemise (e.g. at board edges; turn-in corners near spine are parallel with the spine edge of the board, and are pasted over the spine lining.

Fastenings 2 fore-edge straps of pink skin, 15mm wide, nailed into slots in front board $c.90$mm from upper and lower edges; straps emerge through a gap in the sewing of the chemise pocket to the primary covering, but are now cut off at the fore-edge of the board. Two sets of holes in chemise on back board, 108 and 118mm from fore-edge (upper); 106 and 110mm from fore-edge (lower) suggest former position of pins, the projecting remains of which are visible on the inner face of the board inside the chemise pocket attachment. The existence of 2 holes at each position, indicates that fastenings were replaced at some point; the pink straps also are almost certainly not original.

Chemise Present, made of thick tawed skin, now very discoloured and scuffed, with clean white skin showing through holes (that on lower back cover probably a repair; see below, Chain attachments) and two sewn patches of white skin on back cover and spine. Patch on spine of very soft thin skin now torn, revealing fragmentary writing (minuscule) along primary covering of spine, possibly a title. This suggests that the chemise was not a part of the original binding. Attachment pocket on front cover torn, on back cover made of two pieces of skin, both attachments pasted to cover over pastedowns. An extension flap of brown skin sewn to edges of back cover, now mostly trimmed off very close to sewing; fragment of discoloured edging of skin still sewn to chemise at lower spine edge. All this sewing with white S-twist thread. Number '371' on chemise at head of spine; 'Med 118' at tail. Titles written on back 'Exp*ositi*o pet*ri* Cantoris 2º f*olio*' (rest erased); below this: '2º f*olio* v*el* falsum', s. xiii ex; below: 'Exp*ositi*o mag*ist*ri Petri Cantoris sup*er* iiii^{or} libros Reg*um* sup*er* ii° libros paralipomenon' in a larger hand s.xiv/xv, and between these some letters, erased, possibly ending 'C I' (cf. front flyleaf).

Bosses Holes at each corner and one in the centre on chemise over front cover

show former position of bosses; impressions indicate that the bosses were
c.25mm across and roughly hexagonal in shape, secured with one central nail.
No such indications on back cover.

Chain attachments 1) 2 holes, vertically disposed at lower edge of front cover
indicate earlier presence of a chain staple; iron nails caused rust burn to
pastedown (which has torn) and board (here exposed). No evidence of this
chain attachment survives on chemise, so these marks pre-date the chemise (see
above, Chemise). **2)** 4 holes in chemise over back board at lower edge near the
spine in trapezoid formation (21 x 35 x 17 x 35mm) are typical of chain
attachment marks on other Buildwas books; holes now repaired with white skin
pasted to chemise between chemise and board.

Labels Half of a torn paper label pasted to front chemise pocket inscribed 'MS
Bodl. 371' (s.xix).

Notes '371' in ink on lower edges of leaves.

Structure of Book

Parchment Well prepared, thick, uniformly white, with nap; many holes, probably
parchment-maker's repairs cut out before writing (e.g. fols. 68–9), mostly at
edges of leaves. Pasted parchment patch corner repair fol. 53. White hair of
animal still attached around holes (flaymarks) fols. 40, 66.

Collation 1–10^8, 11^{10}, 12^{10} (9 and 10 excised). Hair and flesh sides not clearly
distinct.

Quire nos. QQ. 1–11, lower margin of verso of last leaf (partly trimmed at qq. 5, 8,
9; not visible at all q. 10).

Catchwords QQ. 1, 3, 5: lower margin of verso of last leaf, near spine.

Page Layout
Dimensions
Page 345 x 236mm.

Space ruled for writing 233 x 148mm.

Columns 2.

Pricking Leaves folded, 1→8, both margins; double pricks for the penultimate
line.

Ruling In grey sometimes appearing brown, very neat and regular, the first and
last two lines ruled edge-to-edge; lines ruled for running titles and marginal
notes (e.g. fol. 97).

Lines per page Fols. 1–25 (qq. 1–3): 40; fols. 26–98: 39.

Page design
fols. 2–98.

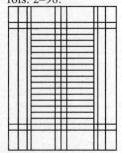

II SCRIBES
One scribe wrote the whole text including rubrics and marginal notes in a compressed, upright and regular hand s.xii ex, with slight angularity in some letters (e.g. h, e) and flat tops or slight bifurcation to ascenders. This scribe also wrote the running titles.

III DECORATION, RUBRICS AND ARTICULATION OF TEXT
The articulation and decoration appear uniform, probably all by one scribe, as is the copying of the text. A frequently used pinkish-red seems to be the same for text underlining, rubrics and some initials and flourishing.
Text initials 1-line capitals, written by the scribe either alternately red and green, or in brown ink with red shading.
Minor initials None.
Major initials Fol. 1: **6-line red** S(urgens) (oxidised) filled with pattern of repeated green 'folded leaves' and flourishes. Fol. 2: **13-line green** F(uit) with extended stem, filled with symmetrical pattern of red 'folded leaves' and flourished with red. Fol. 15v: **12-line red** F(actum) filled with green 'folded leaf' flourishes. Fol. 31v: **7-line green** E(t) with rows of 'folded leaves' in red (cf. fol. 1). Fol. 51v: **18-line red** P(revaricatus) with extended stem, no flourishes but a reserved motif (like a jigsaw piece) at the top of the stem. Fol. 70: **6-line red** L(iber), undecorated. Fol. 70v: **5-line green** E(usebius), each half of letter filled with a different formation of red 'folded leaves'. Fol. 71: **6-line red** A(dam) with extended tail and reserved scalloped, vertical and parallel reserved lines with dots between them; green 'folded leaf' and trailing flourishes in red. Fol. 88: **6-line green** C(onfortatus) filled with repeated red 'folded leaf' flourishes.
Historiated initials None.
Display script Fol. 1: (S)**urgens Dominus,** 1-line red mixed Roman and uncial capitals (oxidised). Fol. 2: (F)**uit,** 1-line Roman capitals, brown ink. Fol. 15v: (F)**actum,** 1-line mixed Roman and uncial capitals, brown ink. Fol. 31v: (E)**t Rex David,** 1-line mixed Roman and uncial capitals, brown ink. Fol. 51v: (P)**revaricatus,** 1-line mixed Roman and uncial capitals, brown ink. Fol. 70: (L)**iber iste,** 1-line mixed Roman and uncial capitals, brown ink touched with red. Fol. 70v: (E)**us**(ebius), rustic capitals, brown ink. Fol. 71: (A)**dam,** rustic capitals, brown ink. Fol. 88: (C)**on**(fortatus), rustic capitals, brown ink.
Title page None.
Titles etc. Running titles in rustic capitals in brown ink across openings on pricked and ruled lines throughout, and incipits and explicits in red, all executed by text scribe; for commentary on Chronicles, sub-headings and chapter numbers in the margin throughout in red; biblical text underlined in red throughout, with loop to accommodate descenders.

IV CONTENTS
Table of contents None (but titles written on chemise).
Main texts Peter Cantor, Commentaries on Kings and Chronicles.
1. Fol. 1 preface: 'Incipit expositio magistri petri cantoris parisiacensis super prefationem beati ieronimi prebendi in libros regum. Surgens dominus a cena'. Ends fol 2: 'Canes. detractores meos rabido insane. Explicit expositio. Fol. 2: 'Incipit expositio eiusdem super librum regum primum. *Fuit:* Diversi reges cronica sua *et* diversa scripsere'. Ends fol. 15v: 'plangentes saul *et* filios eius. Exlicit liber primus.' Fol.15v: 'Incipit ii^us. Factum. Mortuo saul prosequitur esdras hystoriam de david'. Ends fol. 31v: 'ei pro precio vendidit. Explicit

expositio'. Fol. 31v: 'Incipit expositio ei*us*dem sup*er* libru*m* regu*m* terciu*m*. Et rex david. Duo p*re*cedentes libri samuel nuncupant*ur*'. Ends fol. 51v: '*q*u*i*a excelsa non abstulit. Expliciunt glose magistri petri cantoris'. Fol. 51v: 'Incipiunt glose ei*us*dem super librum regum quartum. Prevaricatus. Repetit de ochozia ut ostendat'. Ends fol. 68v: 'qui precessit nabugodonosor. Explicit expositio ma*gi*stri petri cantoris.'

2. Fol. 69v: 'Incipit expositio ei*us*dem super libru*m* qui dicit*ur* paralipomenon p*rimum* capitulu*m* p*rimum*. Expositores hui*us* libri sunt ieronimus et beda. Liber iste censetur paralipomenon grece'. Ends fol. 70v: 'conclamare *et* applaudere nob*is* surde sunt. Explicit p*rima* prefatio. Incipit alia. Eusebi*us* ieronim*us* et*cetera*. Alium p*ro*logu*m* permittit huic op*eri*'. Ends fol. 71: 'no*n* legitur in hebraicis voluminibus.' Fol. 71: 'Incipit expositio ma*gi*stri petri cantoris parisiensis sup*er* paralipomenon. Adam. suple genuit seth *vel* seth suple *est* filius adam'. Ends fol. 88: 'et in puncto ad inferna descendunt. Explicit liber i*us*.' Fol. 88: 'Incipit ii*us*. Confortatus *christus* sed *quando* in morte triumphavit'. Ends imperfectly fol. 98v (II, 20): 'in ei*us* ess*et* natura *quo*d tremere pos'.

V ORIGIN AND PROVENANCE

Ex libris Fol. 1v in a very tall (25mm), very compressed backward sloping hand in red rustic capitals, s.xii ex/xiii in: 'Liber monachor*um* s*an*cte marie de bildewas'.

Secundo folio *vel* falsum

There is no direct evidence to connect this book with a scriptorium at Buildwas; the scribe and initial maker do not appear elsewhere in Buildwas books, though the general appearance of the page has much in common with those being made at Buildwas at the end of the century. However the way in which the endleaves are attached, the unusual sewing, the chevron endband sewing and the continuity of tab and spine lining are all uncharacteristic of surviving Buildwas books and it seems likely that it was bound, and therefore probably written, elsewhere, possibly in France. It had made its way to Buildwas, however, very early in its life. The only text by Peter Cantor which is listed in the *Registrum* as having been held at Buildwas is *Super Vetus Testamentum*, which is probably this text.

It was acquired by the Dean and Canons of Windsor who gave it to the Bodleian Library in 1612.

VI NOTES

Medieval chapter numbers A hand (s.xiii?) added chapter numbers to fols. 1–9v (chapters 1–16), in the upper margin above the start of each chapter and in the ruled margin adjacent to the start of each chapter with a paraph mark; this hand also added the number of the current chapter to the top right recto of the first 9 leaves. There are several nota signs throughout the text in the margins, though none are recognisable as those of the Buildwas indexer (see Trinity B.14.5).

VII BIBLIOGRAPHY AND PLATES

Madan *et al.*, *Summary Catalogue*, 510–511; Ker, *MLGB*, 15; Cheney 1953, 377 (1973, 332); Rouse & Rouse, 317; Sheppard 1995, 186, 192–3; C. Clarkson, 'A Hitherto-unrecorded English Romanesque Book-sewing Technique', in *The Compleat Binder: Studies in Book-making and Conservation, in Honour of Roger Powell,* ed. by J.L. Sharpe (Turnhout, 1996), 215–239.

20. OXFORD, BALLIOL COLLEGE MS 39

Alexander Nequam, Commentary on Song of Songs, books 1–3
Leaves [i paper, ii parchment], 131, [i paper]   **Date** s.xii ex/xiii in
Foliation 1–133 (including parchment replacement flyleaves)
Origin Unknown   **Figs**. 24, 36

I PHYSICAL DESCRIPTION

Binding Resewn, rebound and repaired, present binding s.xvii; boxed.

Endleaves

Front *Pastedown* Single printed paper leaf (e iii) from a disbound law book s.xvi, in place, headed '[Des] Justices 7 Droitz dicelles' and 'Le seigneur hault iusticier iiii fo.xxxv', text in Latin, bounding lines hand drawn.

Flyleaves **1)** Single leaf of laid paper, watermark: pot surmounted by crown and crescent moon, letters EDH on body of pot; inscribed 'Vol 1 346', and bearing offset of shelfmark inscribed on facing parchment flyleaf (s.xvii). **2)** A bifolium of thick parchment, pricked for sewing to replacement sewing supports (q.v.); first leaf recto (flesh side) with impressions of earlier turn-ins, stain of present covering turn-ins, brown corroded marks in a line *c*.30–40mm from spinefold and greenish mark of former chain attachment. Inscribed '346' and (s.xvii) 'Arch E.8.2'. and with Balliol College bookplate. Title and ex dono inscription on second leaf verso (s.xv). Rest of leaf blank.

Back *Flyleaves* **1)** Formerly last leaf of last quire, now trimmed to stub, probably blank. **2)** Single leaf of laid paper, watermark as for front flyleaf, blank.

Pastedown Single printed paper leaf (e ii) from a disbound law book (see above), in place, headed 'Des Justices. etc.' and 'Le droit de indire iiii fo.xiiii'.

Sewing stations Now 5, not pricked except on replacement flyleaves; impressions visible in some spinefolds suggest that earlier there were 5 sewing stations, approximately as follows, with no kettle stitch: (tail) I 7*93*89*89*83*17 I mm (head), but leaves are all trimmed (see below, Sewing supports).

Sewing Resewn all-along with thin, brownish S-twist thread. Impressions, e.g. at the head and tail of fols. 46v–47, show that book was earlier, perhaps originally, sewn with thick Z-twist thread. Throughout, but especially in qq. 8–10 (e.g. on fols. 67, 75), impressions at head and tail and in some spinefolds (where these are visible, e.g. fols. 46v–47) are impressions of sewing done with one needle per support so that there is no thread in the spinefold (cf. Bodley 371).

Sewing supports Now 5, of rolled tawed skin. Evidence of former sewing impressions indicate that earlier, probably originally, there were 5 split sewing supports.

Lacing path Over the outer edges of boards, through to inner surface, ends fixed under pastedowns.

Endbands Present at head and tail, rolled brown leather core sewn with blue and with white thread, both cut off at each end, probably never laced in to present boards.

Tabs None present; no other evidence.

Spine lining None present; no other evidence.

Boards Pasteboard, 387 x 288 x 5mm.

Primary covering Now tanned calf with 3 dark fillets parallel with edges and across spine.

Fastenings Remains of 2 cords near fore-edge of front and back boards, now cut off flush with surface of boards. Green dent at fore-edge of fols. 3–10, 9 x 2mm, may have been made by a former clasp fitting at one end of a strap which became trapped between the cover and the first leaves.

Chemise None present; no other evidence.

Bosses None present; no other evidence.

Chain attachments Impression of chain attachment with pointed end on lower fore-edge of front cover and first parchment flyleaf, matching green marks on laid paper endleaf.

Labels On spine: 1) Remains of paper label with shelfmark and title; 2) modern printed label with shelfmark

Notes Edges of leaves now speckled red.

Structure of Book

Parchment Fair quality, hair and flesh sides not very distinct; widespread evidence of abrading; surfaces have considerable nap. A large number of patch repairs, within leaves and at corners, most of them clearly contemporary (e.g. on fols. 12, 17, 22, 25, 40, 42 etc.).

Collation $1-16^8$, 17^4 (4 excised, probably blank). Hair side outside in each quire.

Quire nos. None (but leaves trimmed).

Catchwords None (but leaves trimmed).

Page Layout
Dimensions
Page 378 x 287mm, trimmed at all margins.
Space ruled for writing 290 x 207mm.

Columns 2.

Pricking Leaves folded, both margins, $1\rightarrow8$.

Ruling Mostly regular and neat, in fine lines which sometimes appear brown, sometimes grey. In later quires the added ruled bounding lines at the extreme outer edges are very narrowly spaced, and in the last 2 quires are sometimes absent altogether.

Lines per page 38, written above top line.

Page design

fols. 3–30v	fols. 31–90v	fols. 91–131

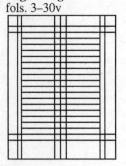 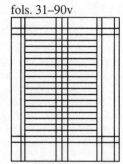 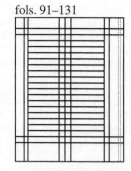

II SCRIBES

One scribe wrote the entire text in a tall, very compressed, slightly backward-sloping, fairly angular hand, s.xii ex/xiii in. Some letters (e.g. a, p, n, r, and ampersand) are often formed with unjoined strokes, which give the hand a distinctive, not altogether pleasant appearance. The scribe used brown and black ink. He also used the punctus flexus, and did his own corrections, of which there are very many, over erasures and in the margins (e.g. fols. 28, 116v, 125). The scribe also wrote the textual marginalia in a smaller hand and enclosed each in a red frame. There is an extensive marginal interpolation in a contemporary hand on fol. 89v. Another hand made one correction to a rubric on fol. 95.

III DECORATION, RUBRICS AND ARTICULATION OF TEXT

Text initials 1-line capitals alternately red and blue or bright green.

Minor initials At all major text divisions, 3- or 4-line plain capitals alternately red and blue or bright green (letters with tails, e.g. I and P, sometimes extending to 17 lines in all). At first (to fol. 10) these initials flourished with blue or red, thereafter no flourishing except red I (fol. 96) and C (fol. 98) with blue .

Major initials Fol. 3: **10-line green, red and yellow** [**H**]umilitas; the letter itself excised), with page-length stem of interlocking scrolls (derived from tapering flourishes used elsewhere in the book) coloured green and ochre, tapering to a very thin red patterned tail and curving upwards to an 8-petalled, symmetrical terminal in ochre, red and green. Fol. 6: **19-line green, red yellow and blue I**(n) drawn with brown ink with thin extended tail patterned like that on fol. 3 but in blue, terminating in 2 dragons, outlined in brown ink and coloured green and ochre, now severely trimmed at lower edge; the body of the letter filled with geometrically patterned panels and decorated with red flourishes. Fol. 66v: **8-line red and blue O**(sculetur), the colours separated by a scalloped reserved line and filled with a design of simple stylised leaf sprays in red and ochre; set against a square field bounded by double brown lines and coloured ochre, the corners filled with a sketchy leaf design surrounded by green. Fol. 98: **6-line red and blue G**(loriosa), the colours separated by a scalloped reserved line, the letter filled with simple stylised leaf sprays outlined in red and reserved against the parchment, decorated with blue circles and with ochre background; no square field.

Historiated initials None.

Display script Fol. 3: [H]**umilitas ve**[**ra**], trimmed when initial excised, in 1-line brown capitals. Fol. 6 (I)**n principio** in 1-line in brown capitals. Fol. 66v: (O)**sculetur** in 1-line red capitals. Elsewhere sometimes the first word or the first letter(s) after an initial in brown rustic capitals. Most opening words not distinguished in any way.

Titles etc. Fol. 2v: 'Primum volumen Alex*andri* Nekk*imus* super Cantica' in a later hand, s.xv; no running titles; incipits and explicits in red by scribe.

Title page None (but opening leaves lost).

IV CONTENTS

Table of contents None (but opening leaves lost).

Main texts Alexander Nequam, *Super Cantica Canticorum*, books 1–3.

Fol. 3: 'Incipit prohemium operis. [H]umilitas vera dignitatis feliciter adauget'. Ends fol. 5v: 'benedictus in secula amen.' Another preface: 'Ortus delitiar*um* paradisi celestis scripture'. Ends fol. 6: 'fulcite me floribus. Explicit prologus. Incipiunt cap*itu*la libri p*r*imi. Cap*itulum* i. Ut lectioni sacre sc*r*ipture diligens impendat*ur* op*er*a' (–xvi). Fol. 6: 'Explic*iunt* cap*itu*la. Ut lectione sacre...In principio creavit d*eus* celum *et* terram. Domine puteus sacre sc*r*ipture altus est'. Ends fol. 66: 'oscul*et*ur me osc*u*lo oris sui. Explicit liber p*r*imis. Incipiunt cap*itu*la sec*un*di libri. i. De misterio incarnationis d*omi*ni' (–xxiiii).

Fol. 66v: 'Incipit expositio super cantica canticorum in laudem gloriose ac perpetue virginis marie. De misterio...Osculetur me osculo oris sui. Audite celi que loquor'. Ends fol. 98: 'qui est benedicta in secula amen. Exlicit liber secundus. Incipiunt capitula libri tercii. Capitulum i. Commendatio gloriose virginis' (–xxiiii). 'Expliciunt capitula'.
Fol. 98: 'Incipit liber tercius. Commendatio...Gloriosa dei genetrix est'. Ends fol. 133: 'Quod nobis praestare dignetur qui est benedictus in secula amen. Explicit liber [quartus crossed out and corrected in margin] magistri alexandri nequam super cantica canticorum.' Fol. 133v blank.

V ORIGIN AND PROVENANCE
Ex libris Fol. ii verso: 'Liber domus de Balliolo in Oxon. de dono reverendi in Christo patris et domini domini Willelmi Gray Eliensis Episcopi.' (s.xv).
Secundo folio umbra [mutilated] comparis. 'Umbra' is written again above the damage, as is the mutilated word on the verso, ?s.xv.
The place of origin of the book is not clear. It has been ascribed to Buildwas because it is the first volume of a 2-volume set, of which Balliol MS 40 (q.v.) is the second volume, and is itself linked to known Buildwas library books with the monastery's ex libris. This volume's text scribe's use of the punctus flexus suggests Cistercian manufacture, the minor initials on fol. 10 were flourished by the rather poor flourisher of initials of Balliol 40 and the initials on fols. 66 and 98 were executed by another, rather better scribe who also made the initials in Balliol 40, and this might support Buildwas as the place of origin. But other Buildwas library books certainly made elsewhere can be shown to have had initials added, probably at Buildwas (e.g. Trinity B.1.6). If the initials were added at Buildwas, however, the Abbey must have been a very early owner, if not the first owner, of the book. The evidence of an unusual former sewing structure which was identical to that in Bodley 371 (q.v.), might support a Buildwas origin if it is supposed that the monks were curious to imitate it, or it might be held to count against a Buildwas origin since no other surviving book known to have been made there was sewn in this manner (the origin of Bodley 371 is also not certain). Nequam's text is recorded in the *Registrum* as having been held at Buildwas.
Bishop William Gray who died in 1478, acquired the book and gave it to Balliol in the fifteenth century. By then, or very shortly afterwards, the book was resewn and provided with new parchment endleaves.

VI NOTES
The difference in appearance between Balliol 39 and its apparent companion volume Balliol 40 is remarked by Mynors (*Balliol MSS*, 28) although Mynors claimed that the books were of comparable size. In fact MS 39 is considerably trimmed at all margins, the curtailed dragons on fol. 6 making it certain that at least 10mm, and possibly up to 20mm, have been lost from the lower margin alone. The coloured frames round the marginalia are trimmed throughout, and the upper margin is now disproportionately narrow, and must also have been trimmed more than a little, though there is no concrete evidence to support this. If the book was once sewn like Bodley 371, with no kettle stitch, the upper and lower sewing supports were probably not very far from the upper and lower edges of the leaves. The trimming may have been carried out precisely to make MSS 39 and 40 more uniform in appearance.
On fol. 3, the number 38 is written at the top of each column in different hands,

and the mark N.9 also appears in the upper margin.

VII BIBLIOGRAPHY AND PLATES
Mynors, *Balliol MSS*, 28; Ker, *MLGB*, 15; R.W. Hunt, *The Schools and the Cloister. The Life and Writings of Alexander Nequam (1157–1217)*, ed. and revised by M. Gibson, (Oxford, 1984), 66 n. 42, 137; Sheppard 1990, 196, pl. 3; Rouse & Rouse, 317; Sheppard 1995, 193.

21. OXFORD, BALLIOL COLLEGE MS 40
Alexander Nequam, Commentary on Song of Songs, books 4–6   **Date** s.xiii in
Leaves [i paper], 118, [i paper]
Foliation 1–118
Origin Probably Buildwas   Fig. 25

I PHYSICAL DESCRIPTION
Binding Resewn and recovered; present binding s.xviii/xix; boxed.
Endleaves
    Front *Pastedown* Fol. 1 of laid paper bifolium in place, inscribed 'Arch.E 83 MS 40' in pencil; Balliol College bookplate.
    Flyleaves Fol. 2 of laid paper bifolium, no watermark, inscribed recto 'Vol. 2 3 Lib'; otherwise blank.
    Back *Flyleaves* Fol. 1 of laid paper bifolium, no watermark, blank.
    Pastedown Fol. 1 of laid paper bifolium in place, blank except for R.A.B. Mynors's folio count dated May 1932.
Sewing stations Now 5. No evidence now visible of earlier sewing stations (spinefolds largely inaccessible).
Sewing Resewn all-along with brown S-twist thread. No evidence visible of earlier sewing.
Sewing supports Now 5 cords. No evidence visible of earlier sewing supports.
Endbands Present at head and tail, rolled white tawed skin core sewn with blue and faded red threads, S-twist; cut off and not laced into boards.
Lacing path Over outer edges of board to inner face and fixed under pastedown *c*.15mm from spine edge.
Tabs None present; no other evidence.
Spine lining Paper lining present; no other evidence.
Boards Pasteboard, 370 x 255 x 4mm.
Primary covering Now brown leather with suede surface and blind-stamped frame-shaped panel of foliate designs front and back. No evidence remains of earlier cover.
Fastenings None present; no other evidence.
Chemise None present; no other evidence.
Bosses None present; no other evidence.
Chain attachments None present; no other evidence.
Labels Old paper label with title on spine; modern paper label inscribed '40'.
Notes 1) Fol. 1: shelfmarks '38, N 10, 346' in various hands. 2) Fol. 68 lower fore-edge: remains of white S-twist thread, possibly once a page marker (the penultimate leaf of book 4).

Structure of Book
Parchment Fair quality, hair and flesh sides often difficult to distinguish; central

bifolia in qq. 10 and 11 (fols. 78–9, 86–7) are of a very different skin, possibly goatskin (see also below, Collation). Very large, contemporary, pasted corner patches, e.g. on fols. 62–3, 73, 85, 87–8.

Collation 1 missing, 2–3⁸, 4¹⁰, 5–14⁸, 15¹⁰ + 2 added after 10. Some quires (e.g. qq. 2 and 4) appear to have hair side outside; others (e.g. qq. 3, 7, 8 etc.) appear to have flesh side outside. Within quires, the leaves are not always regularly arranged, i.e. hair side facing hair side etc., and in q. 10, the central ?goatskin bifolium is the 'wrong' way round, presumably to keep the two very yellow hair sides facing each other. In q. 11, the central ?goatskin bifolium is the 'right' way round, perhaps because the disparity between the two hair sides in this quire is not nearly so great.

Quire nos. QQ. 2–4: centre of lower margin of last verso, II, III and iiii, in red ink. Other numbers may have been trimmed in rebinding.

Catchwords QQ. 3, 4, 5, 6, 7 and 11: lower margin of last verso of quire, near spine.

Page Layout
Dimensions
Page 365 x 250mm, trimmed certainly at lower and fore-edges (see. fols. 19, 30, 34) and probably also at upper edge.
Space ruled for writing 270 x 172–175mm.

Columns 2 text columns, flanked by a wide outer and a narrower inner column ruled for notes which are a part of the text.

Pricking Much pricking has been trimmed. The remaining evidence suggests leaves folded, both margins 1→8; marks are double at lines 19 and 39 to indicate lines to be ruled edge-to-edge.

Ruling In grey sometimes appearing brown; the number of vertical text bounding lines varies between fols. 17 and 61, sometimes single, sometimes double, thereafter single; vertical lines at extreme inner edges also sometimes single, sometimes double; lines 1–3, 19–21, 39–41 and the upper and lower framing lines are ruled edge-to-edge (in q. 15, lines 1–3, 21–23, 45–47).

Lines per page 41 ruled lines; q. 15 (fols. 107–118): 47 ruled lines. Text written below top line.

Page design
fols. 1–60v

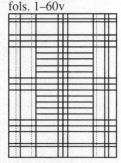

fols. 61–118

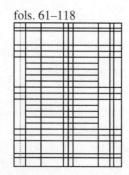

II SCRIBES
One good scribe wrote the text throughout (below top line) in a neat hand with a square aspect, with clubbed minims and forked ascenders. He used punctus flexus, crossed x, and both ampersand and crossed Tironian 'et'. The hand is

more compact from the middle of the text onwards. The scribe executed his own rubrics and marginal notes mostly in red (green on fols. 56, 114). He also made many corrections, sometimes extensive, over erasures and in margins (e.g. on fols. 8, 15, 18v, 21, 22, 23, 27, 28v, 32 etc.). Column a of fol. 50 is erased, the page re-ruled with 48 lines and column a entirely rewritten (book 5, chapter 8).

III DECORATION, RUBRICS AND ARTICULATION OF TEXT

Text initials Small 1-line (sometimes 2-line) capitals in red or blue, frequently flourished in the contrasting colour. Otherwise, brown ink capitals written by the text scribe, embellished with swellings or a series of short cross strokes applied to various elements of the letters.

Minor initials A series of 58 initials, mostly 4- or 5-line, in combinations of red, blue, green, ochre, brown ink and brown wash. They are by one initial maker, often crudely executed, and they have the same character as the major initials. The flourishing, where it occurs, is more competent though repetitive and is almost certainly by a different hand. Typically the minor initials are red and blue, the colours separated by scalloped and/or angular reserved lines, filled with stylised leaf sprays, the whole letter set against a square background usually orange with a green edge and brown and red dotted diaper pattern, e.g. fol. 7: E, fol. 9: Q, fol. 13: C, fol. 14v: S etc.; or they are identically constructed letter forms filled with crudely executed red or blue flourishes touched with ochre and flourished in the margins with the alternate colour (e.g. fol. 1v: E, fol. 4: F, fol. 11v: L etc.). Other variations, usually in colour rather than in design, are sometimes attempted, perhaps for the sake of variety, but these are frequently ungainly and unsuccessful (e.g. fol. 21v: V, fol. 40: S).

Major initials Fol. 38: (book 5) **9-line blue and red** S(urge), an inset red slash separated from the rest of the blue letter by reserved lines; filled with brown ink sprays of coiled leaves or tendrils against a brown and ochre background; the whole letter set against a square field of orange with red dotted diaper pattern and framed with a green border edged in brown. Fol. 66: **8-line red and blue** P(ulchra) with extended stem, the colours divided with a reserved line describing almost geometric angles and curves; the bowl of the letter filled with 2 brown sprays of curled leaves or tendrils surrounded by reserved spaces, and each in a rough circle, one with a brown, one with a green background, and set against a square orange field with red dotted diaper pattern. The stem is fluently flourished, possibly slightly later, and probably by another hand, in brown touched with ochre and red. Fol. 79: (book 6) **8-line red and blue** Q(uid), the colours separated by a scalloped reserved line, the letter filled exactly as is the P on Fol. 66, set against a square orange field with a dotted diaper pattern of brown lines and red dots, and a thick green frame, also very like that on fols. 38, 66. Fol. 117: **23-line red and blue** P(rolixitas), almost identical to the P on fol. 66 except that the central leaf sprays are both set against a green background, and the stem of the initial is flourished in brown and red.

Historiated initials None.

Display script The first letter or two after a large initial occasionally in brown rustic capitals rather than minuscule. Otherwise opening words not distinguished in any way.

Titles etc. Fol. 1 upper margin: 'Secundum volumen Alexandri Neckam super Cantica' ?s.xvii. No running titles; chapter headings in red by the scribe (in blue-green on fol. 114); marginal notes which are a part of the text written in red (fol. 56 in green) by the scribe and given green and ochre frames, quite elaborate in design on fols. 1-2.

Title page None, but first quire is missing.

IV CONTENTS

Table of contents None, but first quire is missing.

Main texts Alexander Nequam, *Super Cantica Canticorum*, books 4–6.

Fol. 1: Text begins imperfectly (book 4, chapter 4): 'istius de igne tribulationum et persecutionum'. Ends fol. 38: 'dilectus n*oste*r *iehsus christus* qui e*st* benedic*tus* in secula am*en*. Explicit liber quartus. Incipiunt capitula libri quinti i. De mist*er*io incarna*t*ionis (–xvii). Explici*un*t ca*pitula*'.

Fol. 38: 'Incipit lib*er* q*ui*ntus. De mist*er*io...Surge aquilo veni auster'. Ends fol. 69v: 'in aliis complexi desid*er*amus in nob*is* c*om*pleat *iehsus christus* d*omin*us n*oste*r cui honor in s*ec*ul*or*um secula amen. Explicit liber quintus. Incipiunt capitula lib*ri* sexti.' Fol. 70: 'i. De assumt*ion*e gl*ori*ose v*ir*ginis (–xxv). Explici*un*t capitula lib*ri* sexti.'

Fol. 70: 'De assumpt*ion*e...Quid videbis in sunamite'. Ends fol. 118: 'cui laus *et* honor et imp*er*ium infinita s*ec*ula s*ec*ul*or*um amen.' Rest of fol. 118 blank. Fol. 118v: pledging notes (see below, Notes).

V ORIGIN AND PROVENANCE

Ex Libris None.

Secundo folio (Now) Et ecce

The book was almost certainly made at Buildwas. It is the companion volume to Balliol 39 although it does not match it and was probably copied slightly later. However it does share peculiarities of the parchment and extensive corner patches with Balliol 150 (q.v., a certain Buildwas book), and the scribes of 40 and 150 are also one and the same. The initial maker of Balliol 39 also worked in 40 (and 150). Balliol 39 may have been acquired from elsewhere, undecorated, but it seems certain that the monks of Buildwas made their own second volume. Nequam's text is recorded in the *Registrum* as having been held at Buildwas.

Mynors (*Balliol MSS*, 29) notes that Langbaine recorded that this book was a gift to Balliol of William Gray (s.xv); the pledging notes are dated 1424 and 1425 and so the book must have left Buildwas at a fairly early date, presumably together with Balliol 39.

VI NOTES

1. On fol. 118v, 2 pledging notes: 'Cauc*io* m*a*gist*ri* Thome Chace posita in cista T*ur*bewyle in oct*avis* s*anct*i Laur*en*cii p*ro* ?viis ?viiid Anno d*omi*ni m*i*ll*esi*mo CCCC^mo vicesimo quarto', and 'Cauc*io* m*a*gist*ri* Thome Chace expos*ita* in cista t*ur*bevyle in f*esto* s*anct*i Joh*an*nis ant*e* portam latin*am* Anno d*omi*ni mill*esi*mo cccc° xxv^to Et h*abe*t supple*mentum* un*am* peci*am* argent*eam* pond*eris* 1 ?unc. et ?di. in cui*us* fundo sc*ri*bit*ur* rota s*anct*e Katerine et iac*et* p*ro* xxvl s viii d'. For Dr. Thomas Chace, see Mynors, *Balliol MSS*, xvi–xvii.

2. The chapters in each book (including chapter 1) are numbered in the top right corner of the rectos in Arabic numbers. The form of 8 with a tail is like that found in other books and may be by the same hand.

VII BIBLIOGRAPHY AND PLATES
Mynors, *Balliol MSS*, 28–9; Ker, *MLGB*, 15; Sheppard 1990, 196, pl. 1; Rouse & Rouse, 317; Sheppard 1995, 193.

22. OXFORD, BALLIOL COLLEGE MS 150

St. Bernard of Clairvaux, Sermons   **Date** s.xiii in
Leaves [i paper], 175, [i paper]
Foliation 1–175
Origin Buildwas   **Figs.** 23, 26, 27

I PHYSICAL DESCRIPTION
Binding Resewn, recovered s.xviii/xix, spinefolds obscured with glue; boxed.
Endleaves
> **Front** *Pastedown* Fol. 1 of laid paper bifolium in place; inscribed 'Arch. E.6.4.' s.xviii, 'MS 150' (pencil); Balliol College bookplate. Otherwise blank.
> *Flyleaves* Fol. 2 of laid paper bifolium, now detached from conjoint leaf; no watermark, chain lines horizontal, blank.
> **Back** *Flyleaves* Fol. 1 of laid paper bifolium; no watermark, chain lines horizontal, blank.
> *Pastedown* Fol. 2 of laid paper bifolium in place; blank except for R.A.B. Mynors's folio count dated 30 May 1939.

Sewing stations Now 5; no other clear evidence.
Sewing Now all-along with brown S-twist thread; sewing thread impressions indicate that an earlier sewing was also all-along.
Sewing supports Now 5 double cords; no other evidence.
Lacing path Over the edges of the boards, to the inner face and fixed under the pastedown, lacing path *c*.15mm. long. No other evidence.
Endbands Present at head, fragments only at tail; rolled white leather core sewn with blue and white S-twist threads; cut off at each end, probably never laced into boards.
Tabs None present; no other evidence.
Spine lining Edges of paper lining visible under pastedowns; no other evidence.
Boards Pasteboard, 401 x 296 x 4mm.
Primary covering Brown leather, suede side outermost, with blind-stamped, frame-shaped design, front and back.
Fastenings None present; no other evidence.
Chemise None present; no other evidence.
Bosses None present; no other evidence.
Chain attachments None present; slight rust mark lower fore-edge fols. 1–2 may indicate position of earlier chain attachment.
Labels On spine, old paper label inscribed with title; printed paper label with present shelfmark. Fol. 1, centre of lower edge: marks of sewing thread, evidently once a page marker.

Structure of Book
Parchment Very variable quality, fair to poor, with many natural and some man-made holes and many very neat parchment maker's repairs. Also a considerable number of contemporary patches, both within the leaf (e.g. fols. 32, 46, 56, 58v, 63) and at the corners (e.g. fols. 42, 44, 48, 150, 151, 164, 166, 167, 168, 174).

Possibly mixed skins: goatskin and sheepskin. Compare for example qq. 9–10 with 13–14.

Collation 17^{10}, 8^{10} + 1 leaf before 1, 9^{12}, 10^{14} + 1 leaf after 14; 11^{10}+1 leaf before 1, 12–15^{10}, 16^{10} (fols. 1 and 10 are single leaves) + 1 leaf after 10, a bifolium (2nd leaf excised), 17^4 (fols. 1 and 4 are single leaves). Flesh sides outside in most quires except qq. 9–10; uncertain in qq. 13, 16, 17; sequence of hair and flesh sides is often irregular, e.g. in qq. 14 and 15.

The stubs of all single leaves were once pasted onto neighbouring leaves. The flourishes to initial A on fol. 160 (q. 16 fol. 1) were executed on a stub which is still partly pasted in place. Some stubs are pricked and ruled.

Quire nos. Q.1 only: I, lower margin of fol. 10, in two concentric circles coloured yellow.

Catchwords QQ. 12, 15, lower margin of last leaf of quire, near spine.

Page Layout
Dimensions
Page 391 x 300mm.
Space ruled for writing Slightly but frequently variable: 291–301 x 207–215mm.
Columns Two.
Pricking Some pricking trimmed, but surviving evidence suggests leaves folded, 1→10 in all margins. Evidence here and there also suggests that templates were used to prick first one side and then the other of some quires (e.g. fols. 53, 116), but the variability of lines per page probably means that several such templates were in use in the making of this book, or that templates were used carelessly. Double pricks indicate the first of the middle and lower group of lines to be ruled edge-to-edge, starting from the top of the page.
Ruling In grey, sometimes appearing brown; the first middle and last 3 lines ruled edge-to-edge. Framing lines ruled consistently at the extreme edges of each leaf.
Lines per page Very variable, written below top line: qq. 1–8: 44 lines written (45 ruled); Q.9: 45–6 (46–7); q. 10: 42 (43); q. 11: 40 (41); q. 12: 44 (45); q. 13: 44 (45) except last leaf, fol. 139v, 43 (44); q. 14: 43 (44); q. 15: 46 (47); q. 16: 48 (49); q. 17: 49 (50).

Page design
fols. 1–175

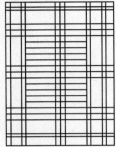

II SCRIBES
One scribe wrote throughout in a neat, slightly angular hand with a square aspect s.xiii in, with clubbed minims and bifurcated ascenders. The same scribe wrote

Balliol 40. The hand becomes more compressed in the later part of the book, and the upright d at the beginning of the text changes to sloping d in the process, suggesting that this book was copied first. The scribe used ampersand and punctus flexus, made his own corrections over erasures (e.g. fols. 26v, 78) and supplied frequent omissions in the margins which he framed, providing signes de renvoi. He also provided running sermon numbers in the upper margins in brown ink framed by brown concentric circles (to fol. 144, thereafter enclosed within red paraphs); rubrics, marginal notae enclosed in rectangular or elliptical oval frames coloured ochre, and marginal sub-headings in red (fols. 27v–28).

III DECORATION, RUBRICS AND ARTICULATION OF TEXT

Text initials Mainly 1-line brown ink capitals written by the scribe, embellished with swellings and short cross-strokes; sometimes (e.g. fols. 88–9) when the text is subdivided, and for capitula (e.g. fol. 2–2v), alternate red and blue 1-line capitals are used.

Minor initials A long series of multicoloured initials, one at the beginning of each sermon. They are mainly 5- to 6-line in height, but here and there, 7- or 8-line spaces were left by the scribe for no obvious reason. The colours used include red, blue, grey-blue (fol. 67v), brilliant yellow, ochre, green, white, opaque chocolate-brown (fol. 76v), aqua (fol. 165), pinkish-brown, biscuit, and transparent brown and ochre washes.

Typically the initials are of red and blue, the colours separated by a scalloped or an alternately angled and curved reserved line. Most are set against coloured square fields, sometimes framed with another colour or brown ink, sometimes decorated with diapers, dots, or circles, and sometimes entirely plain. Letters I and A are never given coloured squares, and in the second half of the book, the squares are often omitted altogether. Many initials, especially those with stems and I and A are expertly flourished in red and/or blue, in the midst of which often nestle grotesque profiles along the length of the stem (e.g. fols. 32v, 59, 157).

The infill decoration of the letters is usually one of 4 main types: **1)** a spray of leaves (e.g. fols. 75, 75v, 81v); **2)** repeated square panels with a roughly symmetrical foliate or floral central motif arranged around crossed diagonal lines (which Mynors aptly compared to floor tiles); these are usually yellow/ochre/brown (e.g. fols. 32v, 59, 157); **3)** crudely executed flourishes forming simple foliate designs (e.g. fols. 4v, 68, 106; cf. Balliol 229 fol. 37); **4)** clumsy imitations of the complex flower forms of early to mid-12th-century decoration (e.g. fol. 21).

An extraordinary exception is the 5-line P on fol. 28, which consists of the letter itself with a very extended stem roughly drawn in ink over a mustard yellow squared P-shaped background. Another exception is on fol. 77, a brown 5-line C against a square field of yellow which is filled with a large 8-petalled stylised flower, green ochre and reserved parchment, which is like the flower terminal on fol. 3 of Balliol 39.

It is difficult to say if all the initials are made by one person, though they have little to recommend them by way of inventiveness or execution. Initials by the same hand or hands are found in Balliol 39 (compare fols. 66v, 98), and 40 (compare passim). The flourisher, however, was very competent and imaginative, though he was probably not the same as the flourisher who worked in the other

111

Buildwas books at Balliol.

Major initials There are 3 major initials each introducing a set of sermons (though some of the initials at lesser text divisions appear to have the same weight as those described here). Fol. 2v: **12-line historiated H** (see below). Fol. 81v: **8-line red and blue E**(ternam), the colours separated by a reserved scalloped line, each half of the letter filled with brown ink and ochre sprays of leavews against a green (top) and yellow (bottom) background, the letter set against a yellow square decorated with two types of diaper pattern, with a green frame. Fol. 110: **9- or 10-line V**(icit), now excised.

Historiated initials Fol. 2v: **12-line red and blue H**(odie), the red as triangles set into the blue initial, the blue decorated with white dots, the top of the ascender decorated vertically and laterally in the upper margin with red and blue flourishes, and the extended thin blue tail of the letter decorated with vertical, 'jawbone' motifs in red, green and yellow and with an insignificant terminal; the letter filled with a figure of St. Bernard (copied from Lambeth 107, fol. 84v) in white habit and with a tonsure, holding a crook (left), the right hand raised in a gesture of blessing, against a pinkish-brown background decorated with white circles and dots. Fol. 24: **6-line red and blue M**(agna), the colours separated by a scalloped reserved line; a vertical green-scaled fish in each half of the letter against a brown background; the whole letter set against a yellow square field with brown ink frame. Fol. 63: **5-line red and blue N**(ossumus), the colours separated by a scalloped reserved line, a vertical green-scaled fish like those on fol. 24 against green inside the letter, and the letter against a pale brown square field with brown ink frame.

Display script Fol. 2v: (H)**odie Fr**a**tre**s **celebram**us in 1-line brown ink mixed capitals touched with red. Fol. 4v: (A)**udivimus** in 1-line brown ink mixed capitals touched with red. Fol. 5: (I)**n adventu Domini** in 1-line brown ink mixed capitals. Fol. 6v (I)**n celebracione** in 1-line brown ink mixed capitals touched with red. Fol. 23: (T)**ria rerum** in 1-line brown ink mixed capitals; fol. 26v (I)**n circumcisione** in 1-line brown ink capitals. Fol. 110 (V)**icit leo dei Tribu** in 1-line brown ink capitals. Elsewhere the first word or letters are occasionally made in small brown ink capitals, e.g. on fols. 99, 139, but for the most part opening words are not distinguished.

Title page None, but prefatory leaves lost.

IV CONTENTS

Table of contents Fols. 1–1v: list of initia for parts 1 and 2; fols. 1v–2v: summaries of contents of each sermon with indications of the points in the liturgical calendar at which they should be read; fol. 109, list of initia for part 3.

Main texts St. Bernard of Clairvaux, *Sermons*.

Fol. 1: 'Incipiunt cap*itu*la sermonum libri sequentis' followed by initia of sermons grouped, distinctio fashion, for use during different liturgical periods of the year: 'In adve*n*tu d*om*ini–dominica in palmis' (i–lxxvii). Fol. 1 col.b: 'Finit prima pars. In cena d*om*ini. Hic sequu*n*t*ur* q*ui*dam serm*o*nes gen*er*ales' (lxxviii–cviii). ciii and cviii are marked 'vacat'; cviii ('Rex dives et pr*ae*potens') not copied out. Fol. 1v: 'Incipi*un*t cap*itu*la s*er*mon*um* b*e*a*ti* b*er*nar*di* abb*at*is' followed by a contents list for the above 108 sermons, also grouped as above, written in a smaller version of the hand: 'In adventu domini. i. De ratione nominis adventus'. Ends fol. 2v: 'cviii De filio prodigo s*er*mo p*ar*abolic*us* ad conventu*m* de clarevalle ab urbe roma.' Fol. 2v: 'Incipit liber s*er*monum b*e*a*ti* b*er*nardi

112

abbatis. Sermo in adventu dominica prima. Hodie fratres celebramus adventus initium'. Ends fol. 81: 'et tam multipharie necessariam esse sentimus. Explicit prima pars sermonum beati bernardi abbatis primi clarevallis.' Mynors, *Balliol MSS*, 136, found 66 of these printed as *Sermones de Tempore* in *PL* CLXXXIII, and 2 (xxxiii, lxx) among the *Sermones de Diversis* (*PL* CLXXXIII).

Fol. 81: 'Hic secuntur quidam sermones generales'. Fol. 81v: 'Sermo beati bernardi abbatis exhortatorius ad conversionem lxxviii. Eternam celestis patrie'. Ends fol. 107: 'utique super omnia deus benedictus et laudabilis et gloriosus in secula amen.' Rest of page ruled, but blank; fol 108v blank. Mynors found 27 of the 30 printed as *Sermones de Diversis* (*PL* CLXXXIII).

On fol. 26v, a marginal note records the two sermons that are missing: 'In natali innocentium. Tolle puerum et ma xxi' (this seems to be an error); 'Tolle puerum xxii quere in primo folio libri'.

Fol. 109: 'Incipiunt capitula sermonum libri sequentis' followed by capitula grouped in distinctio style as above: 'De sancto pascha – In dedicatione ecclesi.' Fol. 109v: blank. Fol. 110: 'Sermo beati bernardi abbatis de clarevalle de resurrectione domini. Vicit leo dei tribu iuda'. Ends fol. 175v: 'ut ad eum perveniatis ad quem ipse pervenit qui est benedictus in secula.' Mynors found some printed in *Sermones de Tempore* (*PL* CLXXXIII), some among *Sermones de Diversis* (*PL* CLXXXIII) and others in *PL* CXCIV. See Mynors, 136, for observations about the authenticity of some of the sermons.

V ORIGIN AND PROVENANCE

Ex libris Fol. 2v, in red, mostly erased: 'Liber sancte marie monachorum de Buldewas'.

Secundo folio De verbis

The book was written and decorated at Buildwas. The text scribe wrote Balliol 40, and the ex libris and list of contents in Trinity B.1.29, q.v. The artist of the initial on fol. 2v copied the figure of St. Bernard from the figure of the good abbot in Lambeth 107 fol. 84v, a book which also has the Buildwas ex libris. On fol. 153v, the Buildwas indexer's distinctive nota mark appears in both margins, in both ink and stylus, confirming that the book was still at Buildwas in the late thirteenth century, and its presence at Buildwas was recorded in the *Registrum* in the early fourteenth century.

By the mid fifteenth century it was owned by Robert Thwaites, Master of Balliol, who died in 1458; see Mynors, *Balliol MSS*, 136; on fol. 2v is the note of his legacy: 'Liber domus de Balliolo in Oxon. ex legat magister Roberti Thwaites quondam magistri eiusdem Domus ac decanus de Aukland.' For Thwaites, see Mynors, xxxviii.

VI NOTES

1. The materials and workmanship are less good than those of the twelfth century, but the facts that corrections were extensively done and that such a very large number of initials were supplied using such a variety of pigments show that the monastery was maintaining in the early thirteenth century the text-acquiring momentum established in the previous century.

2. Fol. 35 (at sermon 32), marginal note in red: 'Sermo iste non legatur'.

VII BIBLIOGRAPHY AND PLATES

Mynors, *Balliol MSS*, 135–6; Chibnall, *VCH*, 56; Ker, *MLGB*, 15; Cheney 1953, 377 (1973, 332); Sheppard 1990, 196–7, 202, pls 2, 20; Rouse & Rouse, 317.

23. LONDON, LAMBETH PALACE LIBRARY MS 73
1. William of Newburgh, Historia Rerum Anglicarum; Sermons. 2. Pastor Hermae Date s.xiii in

Leaves [i paper], ii, 152, ii, [i paper]

Foliation 1–148 (including last 2 parchment endleaves); nos. 91–96 used twice (as 91a–96a after 96); medieval foliation erratic.

Origin Possibly Buildwas

I PHYSICAL DESCRIPTION
Binding Rebound at least twice, most recently s.xix/xx; refurbishment note (27.2.59) on last endleaf.

Endleaves

Front *Pastedown* 1) Laid paper leaf in place; watermark: large fleur-de-lis surmounted by crown; 2) an earlier pastedown, now detached (see below, Flyleaves 2).

Flyleaves 1) Laid paper leaf, probably once conjoint with pastedown, now repaired at joint; blank except for 73 printed (recto) and in pencil (verso); 2) parchment bifolium, discarded leaves from a book of Homilies on the Gospels in French belonging to the Common of Saints (James, *Lambeth MSS*, 117–18); carelessly ruled in brown, written in 2 columns in a neat hand s.xii ex/xiii in. The first leaf has been used as a pastedown, but little can be conclusively deduced from it. There are clear marks left by brown leather covering turn-ins with overlapped corners, and 2 sets of holes parallel with the spine (a set of 4 holes and another of 6 slits; see below, Sewing stations), presumably evidence of earlier sewings. An inscription on the first leaf recto, upside down, is a scribbled and partially obscured note in a hand s.xvi/xvii of which only 'From' and 'the' are clearly legible; first leaf verso, also upside down, Henrici Savelli liber (s.xvii). Given the unclear evidence of these endleaves (see below), the inscriptions may not relate to the history of the present book.

Back *Flyleaves* 1) Parchment bifolium ruled in brown and written in long lines in French (s.xii ex/xiii in), a commentary on the Psalter, the Psalter text in red and with small blue initials flourished in red and one larger initial, 9-line red and pink I(udicame domine; Psalm 25) with blue flourishes. The second leaf was once a pastedown, with marks left by a brown leather covering with an overlapped corner (top), the lower corner possibly mitred. The first leaf, like the front flyleaf, shows six pairs of slits plus one near head and tail, slightly to the right of a clear former spinefold 10mm from the inner margin of the text, and was clearly associated with the front bifolium in the same binding (see below, Sewing stations); 2) laid paper leaf, probably once conjoint with the present pastedown, now repaired at joint; no watermark, blank.

Pastedown 1) Laid paper leaf in place, blank except for refurbishment note; 2) an earlier parchment pastedown, detached (see above, Flyleaves 1).

Sewing stations 1) Now probably 5; spinefolds inaccessible. 2) There is no clear evidence about previous sewings unless the set of 4 holes visible on the front parchment flyleaf (see above) date from the re-use of this bifolium as endleaves for the present book: (tail) I 25 K 37*70*70*70*40 K 22 I mm (head). This set of holes is c.35–40mm from the inner text margin on a leaf c.235mm wide, but only 14mm from the inner text margin of the conjoint leaf. Similar holes are not, however, visible on the back flyleaf. 3) Another set of holes is visible on the second front parchment flyleaf and on the first back parchment flyleaf. This set consists of 6 pairs of vertically arranged slits 5mm apart, each pair between 40 and 50mm (variable) apart, plus one slit near head and tail, presumably for a kettle stitch. This set, however is very slightly to the left of former spine folds and only 8mm from the nearest text margin, so if either endleaf had been at one time bound in a book, these marks are unlikely to have been associated with those bindings. The set of 6 pairs of holes on both front and back endleaves do suggest that they were associated in an earlier binding as endleaves, but they cannot certainly be associated with an earlier binding of Lambeth 73.

Sewing Present sewing practically invisible. No evidence, beyond that described above, about earlier sewings.

Sewing supports There are now 5 raised supports visible on spine. No other evidence.

Lacing path Now over the outer edges of the boards. No other evidence.

Endbands Flat endbands with a skin core present at head and tail, sewn with red, blue and yellow threads, tied down in several quires but not laced into boards.

Tabs None present; no other evidence.

Spine lining No evidence.

Boards Pasteboard, 359 x 246 x 5mm, slightly warped, curving towards textblock.

Primary covering Now blue leather (morocco) with gilt fillets in rectangular frame formation, and crest inscribed 'Bibliotheca Lambethiana', front and back; letters in gilt on spine (title, library and shelfmark). Brown stain on endleaves made by an earlier, brown leather covering may not relate to this volume (see above, Endleaves).

Fastenings None present; no other evidence.

Chemise None present; no other evidence.

Bosses None present; no other evidence.

Chain attachments None present; no other evidence.

Labels None.

Structure of Book

Parchment Good quality with considerable nap, evenly coloured, yellowish, with few if any defects (a few flaymarks, e.g. fols. 85, 90).

Collation ii, 1–19^8, hair side outside in each quire.

Quire nos. QQ. 1–2: i on last verso and ii on first recto of these quires, centre of lower margin, both trimmed. None thereafter.

Catchwords None.

Page Layout
Dimensions
Page 335 x ?237mm (tight rebinding makes width measurement difficult); leaves trimmed at all edges (evidence of trimmed marginalia).
Space ruled for writing 251 x 161mm.

Columns 2.

Pricking Leaves folded, both margins 1→8; insufficient evidence to say whether or not a template was used; the lines of pricks are very straight and regular; edge-to-edge lines double pricked.

Ruling Very neat, in grey sometimes appearing brown; an elaborate layout, changing after Q.2.

Lines per page QQ. 1–2: 40; qq. 3–19: 41; text written above top line.

Page design

fols. 1–16v fols. 17–146

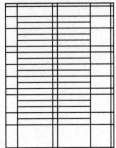

II SCRIBES

The text was mainly written by one scribe in a small, fairly angular hand, s.xiii in. The ascender of d is exaggerated and very often virtually horizontal, projecting into the left margin (though this is sometimes more prominent than at others), giving the hand a characteristic aspect. Tironian 'et', which is made with minimal lifting of the pen and having a squat appearance, is also distinctive, and the ampersand has a continental form, the upper loop lying along the rising stroke. The scribe used punctus flexus occasionally in the body of the text and very frequently at the end of rubrics and capitula, and as the last punctuation mark of a paragraph or chapter. There are only a few corrections: by the scribe himself over an erasure (e.g. fol. 43), or another scribe over an erasure (e.g. fol. 48) or in the margin (e.g. fol. 5).

III DECORATION, RUBRICS AND ARTICULATION OF TEXT

All the decoration displays a similarity of style and was probably done by one scribe, though the A on fol. 63v is of a better quality than most, and the H on fol. 1v clumsier than most.

Text initials Fols. 1v, 19v, 41v: 1-line plain capitals alternately red and green for capitula.

Minor initials **1**) The first capitulum in each list is often given a 2- or 3-line coloured initial (fol. 62v has a 5-line initial), decorated and flourished in a similar way to the major initials. **2**) Fol. 104: **3-line red C**(um), plain, with green 'hairpin' flourishes, and filled with 'lion's paw' terminals branching from a simple coiled scroll, introduces the first of the sermons. **3**) All text divisions are introduced by 2-, 3- or 4-line initials, alternately red and green, decorated with 'hairpin' and 'bird's head' flourishes and sometimes filled with 'folded leaf' flourishes, at each sub-division of a chapter. A and I frequently extend lavishly into adjacent margins, as do the tails of other letters like Q, P, M etc. Occasionally a series of initials within a section of text is executed only in red, e.g. fols. 52v–53, 56v–60, so that the alternate colours series is interrupted, possibly deliberately for emphasis.

Major initials Fol. 1: **7-line green R**(everendo) with reserved scalloped and angled lines, decorated with 'hairpin' flourishes in red and green, filled with rather awkward, overlapping red coils terminating in circular swellings in which quite often are 'tadpole' motifs in green; the whole design also decorated here and there with green dots. Fol. 1v: **8-line red H**(ystoriam) with scalloped reserved line in the single vertical stroke, very rubbed; decorated with 'hairpin' flourishes in green with red, the letter filled with clumsy, stiff coils formed by green or red outline with multiple 'lion's paw' terminals, each with a single 'tadpole' motif superimposed; the upper half red against a green background, the lower half green against red. Fol. 19v: **7-line red A**(nno), decorated on the left with 'hairpin' flourishes and filled with a pattern of 'folded leaf' motifs, all in red. Fol. 41v **10-line red and green A**(nno), the colours separated by a jagged and scalloped reserved line; decorated on the left with red 'hairpin' flourishes; filled with stiff scroll formed by green outline against uncoloured parchment, with 'trefoil' and 'lion's paw' terminals each with a red 'tadpole' motif superimposed; dots in threes are also scattered in the spaces between scrolls. Fol. 63v: **9-line red and brown A**(nno), the left and horizontal strokes combined into an extended E-shaped curve in brown and red, the colours separated by a reserved line; the right-hand vertical stroke brown with a central red strip decorated with reserved motifs: X, one above the other; the whole initial decorated with 'hairpin' and 'lion's paw' flourishes, in red (left) and brown (right); the letter filled with a complex mosaic of elegant scrolls with myriad 'lion's paw' and 'folded leaf' terminals each decorated with a 'tadpole' motif; the spaces between all these are cross-hatched, all in brown ink. The whole initial is more elegant and of better quality than the others. Fol. 89: **10-line red R**(ex) with reserved scalloped and angled line in the vertical stroke, and slight 'hairpin' and 'bird's head' flourishes in green (with red) on the left; the letter is filled with stiff green outlined scroll with several 'lion's paw' terminals in each half, the spaces interspersed with red circles (top), incomplete (bottom); it is very like the initial on fol. 41. There are no major initials after fol. 89.

Historiated initials None.

Display script Occasionally the letters following a coloured capital are executed as small capitals by the text scribe (e.g. fol. 19v: (A)nno), but mostly no emphasis is given to opening letters or words.

Title page None (but original endleaves probably missing).

Titles etc. None; incipits and explicits are in the hand of the scribe in red; in the upper margin of fol. 104, another hand wrote: 'sermo in Asumpcionis vigilia sancte Marie, de evangelica lectione'.

IV CONTENTS

Table of contents None.

Main texts William of Newburgh, *Historia Rerum Anglicarum*. James, *Lambeth MSS*, 120, provides a very full account of each item.

1.Fol. 1: dedicatory letter to Ernald, Abbot of Rievaulx: 'Reverendo patri *et* domino ernaldo abbati riewallensis suus willelmus...Litteras sanctitatis vestre suscepi'. Ends fol 1: 'ad rem pertinent ante historie ingressum prelibans. Explicit epistola. Incipiunt capitula primi libri. i. Proemium sequentis historie–xxix (fol. 1v) *et* mortis regis stephani. Expliciunt capitulam [sic]. Incipit liber i Proemium sequentis. Hystoriam gentis nostre idest anglorum venerabilis presbyter *et* monachus Beda conscripsit'. 5 books each preceded by chapter list. Ends fol. 103: 'ut etiam si angelis de celo id omittendum suaderet. anathema illi esset.' Printed in R. Howlett, ed., *Chronicles of the Reigns of Stephen, Henry II and Richard I*, 4 vols (London, Rolls Series 82, 1884–5), I–II. See also Preface (vol. I), xi–xii and xxxix. Also in T. Hearne, ed., *Historia Rerum Anglicarum,* 3 vols (Oxford, 1719), I–II.

Fol. 103b: a note in another hand about a dispute between the Abbots of

Buildwas and Savigny about the custody of St. Mary's of Dublin, a daughter house of Buildwas: '[A]nno d*o*mini Millesimo Trecentesimo Primo. Contentione mota i*n* capit*u*lo gen*e*rali ap*u*d Cisterciu*m* int*er* Abbates de Savig*niaco* et de Bildewas de pat*er*nitate dom*us* sanc*te* Marie iuxta Dublinia*m*: idem capit*u*lum cognita veritate tande*m* diffinivit sic. Filiatione*m* abbatie beate marie iuxta Dublinia*m* auditis rationib*us* utriusq*ue* partis *et* diligentius examinatis Abbati de Bildewas adiudicat capit*ul*um generale.' Rest of fols. 103 and 103v, blank.

2. Sermons, 'most likely by William of Newburgh' (James, *Lambeth MSS*, 119). Begins fol. 104: 'Cum loqueretur Ihesus ad turbas'. Fol. 110: 'Sermo de Trinitate'; Fol. 115v: 'Sermo de S. Albane'. Ends fol. 121. Printed in Hearne, *Historia,* III, 819–902.

3. Fols. 121–145, *Pastor Hermae*. Printed in O. de Gebhardt, A. Harnack, T. Zahn, eds., *Patrum Apostolicorum Opera,* 3 vols (Leipzig, 1875–77), III, 184, though the printed text differs from the text in Lambeth 73. James, echoing Gebhard on p. xv, observes that the Lambeth text is the only copy which is 'free from a manifest interpolation common to the others' and that it is in need of editing.

Fol. 146 blank. Fol. 146v, in pale ink: ειμι βιβλιον Ταλβωτον και φιλοτεισ.

V ORIGIN AND PROVENANCE

Ex libris None.

Secundo folio (ce)saris imp*er*ium

There is no indisputable evidence about where this book was made, though it has every appearance of being Cistercian in origin (decoration and punctuation). Newburgh completed his texts in about 1198 and James (120) observes that Lambeth 73 was copied from Stowe MS 62 (s.xii ex, incomplete) which belonged to Newburgh Abbey. The facts that Newburgh wrote the *Historia* and the sermons at the request of Ernald, Abbot of Rievaulx, together with the relatively close proximity of Newburgh Abbey and Buildwas, make it seem quite possible that the Buildwas copy was made by a Buildwas scribe, though it may have been made for Buildwas at Newburgh. The use of a continental form of ampersand and the French texts on the endleaves are unusual in a Buildwas context, judging from the surviving evidence.

The addition of the note about the dispute about St. Mary's, Dublin (which was settled in 1301 at the Cistercian General Chapter) to a blank column of an historical text is appropriate and attests to Buildwas ownership of this copy at least by this date. Chibnall, *VCH*, 56, surmises that this note was made by William of Ashbourne, a Buildwas monk and proctor to the Abbot of Buildwas on the occasion of this particular general Cistercian chapter. She observes that William 'dabbled in history' and was later Abbot of St. Mary's, Dublin. On fol. 89v, a late medieval hand has written 'No*ta* cisterciens*is*' against a reference to Cistercians in Book 5 chapter 1 of William of Newburgh's *Historia*.

The presence of the two sets of endleaves written in French in late twelfth- or early thirteenth-century hands is confusing, and complicated by the presence of former sewing holes. Only the bifolium with uncompleted decoration seems to bear the marks of an earlier independent sewing; but both bifolia show identical sewing marks which it is not possible conclusively to associate with MS 73. It is likely that the endleaves were added to MS 73 only in a much later rebinding and that Henry Saville's ownership inscription on the front endleaf refers to a quite different book.

James, 120, surmises that the inscription in Greek (at the end of the copy of the translated Greek text *Pastor Hermae)* is that of Robert Talbot, antiquary and canon of Norwich in 1547. By the mid sixteenth century the book may have been his. It was acquired, much later, by Archbishop Sancroft for Lambeth.

VI NOTES

1. *Medieval foliation* The book was foliated in a medieval hand in arabic numerals, though carelessly, as follows: fols. 1–5: i–v; fol. 6 omitted; fols. 7–55: vi–liiii; fol. 56 omitted; fols. 57–63: lv–lxi; fol. 64 omitted; fols. 65–67: lxii–lxiiii; fols. 68–77: lv (for lxv?)–lxiiii; fols. 78–89: lxiiii–lxxv; fol. 90 omitted; fol. 91: lxxvi; fol. 92: lvvvii (for lxxvii?); fols. 93–96: lxxxviii–lxxxxi; fol. 91a omitted; fols. 92a–96a and 97: ii–vii; fol. 98 omitted, fols. 99–100: viii–ix; fol. 101 omitted; fols. 102–103: x–xi (end of first text); fol. 104: xii. Medieval foliation abandoned at fol. 105.

2. *Other numbering*

Fol. 1, Book I: Capitula numbered by a later hand with Roman numerals i–xxix; the same hand (evidence of colour of ink and pressure on pen nib) may have added 'Ca*pitulu*m 1' in the margin alongside the beginning of chapter 1 and similarly for successive chapters, and also running Book numbers ('Liber prim*us*') in various forms and variously disposed in the upper margins to qq. 1–2, after which they had been supplied by the text scribe. Here and there this numerator also added a running capitulum number to the top right recto (e.g. fols. 2–10, 16–18, fol. 88; others perhaps trimmed), and seems also to have been responsible for one style of marginal pointing hand with a distinct finger nail.

Fol. 19, Book 2: The scribe continued to provide running book numbers in the upper margin ('*Liber*' on versos, '.II.' on rectos, fols. 24–26 in red); the capitula table is numbered in red Roman numerals by the scribe. The later numerator continued to add capitulum numbers only in the margins.

Fol. 41, Book 3: Capitula are numbered in red, and the numbers are added to the margins as for book 2.

Fol. 62v, Book 4: Capitula table not numbered; but the chapters are numbered in the margin as before, but with large numbers in graphite here visible alongside the inked numbers. The graphite numerator wrote VIII twice and so is one behind the ink numerator from this point to the end of the book.

Fols. 88v–89: Capitula numbered by scribe and numbers only added in the margin as before.

VII BIBLIOGRAPHY AND PLATES

James, *Lambeth MSS*, 117–120; Ker, *MLGB*, 14; C. Bunsen, *Christianity and Mankind,* 7 vols (London, 1854), I, 184–5; Cheney 1953, 377 (1973, 332); Chibnall, *VCH*, 56.

24. CAMBRIDGE, TRINITY COLLEGE MS B.1.29

1. Jerome on Cantica Canticorum; 2. Epistles of Paul, glossed (incomplete); 3. Andrew of St. Victor, Commentary on Kings and Chronicles; other historical notes; 4. Notes on Martianus Capella's De Nuptiis; 5. Legal tracts.

Leaves ii, 218   **Date** s.xii in–xiii in
Foliation 1–220
Origin Uncertain; booklets 1–3: ?Northern France   **Fig.** 28

The book as it now exists is a Buildwas compilation of the early thirteenth century, although the booklets themselves have various dates and places of origin. It is possible that some of the texts now contained in it, especially items 1–3, were part of Master Robert's library (see Introduction).

The binding of the book as it now exists will be described first and then each booklet independently. The Provenance, Notes and Bibliography for the whole book will be given at the end.

I PHYSICAL DESCRIPTION

Binding Rebound s.xvi ex–xvii in, repaired and rebacked since. Spine rounded but fairly flexible; guards sewn in between each quire.

Endleaves

Front Pastedown None in place; fol. 1 of a separate bifolium of thicker parchment than the rest of the book, sewn in but now detached; parchment has white ?crease marks on hair side, associated with erratic groups of holes as if made by a needle over the central section of the bifolium; remains of a grainy paste on recto with marks suggesting it may have been spread with a comb, and impressions of earlier sewing support channels; otherwise blank.

Flyleaves Fol. 2 of bifolium; recto: ex libris and contents list, s.xiii in brown ink; *verso*: identical ex libris and list of contents s.xiii in, elegantly written on specially ruled lines, alternate lines red and green with initials of the other colour. This in turn annotated by a hand s.xvii: 'Notae in Martianus Capellam de Nuptiis *etc.* sunt autem vel Alexandri Neckami, vel non valde dissimiles iis quas in Martianum scripsit'; the same note in the same hand is written in the margin fol. 144. A further list of contents in reverse order added s.xvi–xvii, and Trinity College bookplate.

Back *Flyleaves* None.

Pastedown None.

Sewing stations Now 5; formerly, possibly originally, 2 (evidence of marks of sewing support channels on front detached pastedown); fols. 51v–52 (booklet 2): multiple old sewing holes visible, 1 set with faint sewing thread impressions coincides with the sewing support impressions on the detached front pastedown: approx. (tail) I 24 K 27*94*27 K 45 I mm (head), leaves now trimmed, more at tail than at head.

Sewing Now all-along with very thin white, Z-twist thread; little evidence of earlier sewing (see above), faint thread impressions visible fols. 7–8.

Sewing supports Now 5 cords. Impressions on front pastedown suggest that an earlier sewing of all or part of the present book may have been on 2 supports (max. 11mm wide).

Lacing path Now laced into the thickness of the pasteboard and fixed into short inner channels at an angle (front) and straight (back); impressions on detached pastedown suggest earlier sewing supports laced through channels on the inner face of the boards, 25mm and 30mm long.

Endbands None present. Impressions on front detached pastedown near the head show the path of former endband lacing, certainly contemporary with the other lacing impressions.

Tabs None present; no other evidence.

Spine lining None present; no other evidence.

Boards Pasteboard, 227 x 154 x 5 mm. A brown stain (inner face front board) and a purple stain (inner face back board), apparently brushed or wiped on. No obvious paste remains to suggest earlier presence of pastedown in this replacement binding.

Fastenings None. 3 greenish holes at centre of fore-edge of pastedown suggest a former central fastening device.

Primary covering Dark brown leather with both mitred and overlapped corners, fillets parallel with all edges of both covers, inner as well as outer surfaces. Coat of arms impressed on both covers and coloured red, white and yellow (those of Thomas Nevile, Dean of Canterbury who was Master of Trinity 1593–1615).

Chemise None present; no other evidence.

Bosses None present; no other evidence.

Chain attachment 3 rusted holes on last leaves at inner corner of lower margin suggest possible position of earlier chain staple or staples, similar to the 4-hole patterns found in other Buildwas books.

Labels Printed paper label on spine each bearing elements of present shelfmark.

Notes All leaf edges now clumsily stained red.

BOOKLET 1: fols. 1–47

Structure of Booklet

Parchment Of variable colour and thickness, hair sides mostly very yellow, surface smooth.

Collation 1^{10}, 2^8 (5 a replacement, pasted onto stub), $3-5^8$, 6^2 (2 is now pasted onto a stub), plus 1 leaf after q. 6. The last word on the last leaf is squeezed onto the page as if it were the last word of a sentence or section. James, *Trinity MSS* 1, 33, observes that the text is incomplete. QQ. 1–6: hair side outside, though the two central bifolia of q. 1 are both arranged flesh side outermost.

Quire nos. None.

Catchwords None.

Page Layout

Dimensions

Page 215 x 145mm (all margins roughly trimmed).

Space ruled for writing 205 x 110mm.

Columns 2.

Pricking Inconsistent; leaves folded, outer margins only, q. 1 unclear, qq. 2, 4, 5, 1→8, q. 3: 8→1 but first leaves re-pricked 1→8; q. 6: 1→8. A template was used for qq. 2–6.

Ruling Blind, on hair side, neatly and carefully executed within the vertical bounding lines.

Lines per page Q. 1: 33; qq. 2, 4: 37; qq. 3, 5, 6: 38.

Page design

fols. 1–45

1/II SCRIBES

One scribe wrote the text throughout in a small, neat and scholarly continental hand s.xii in. Correction in a different hand fol. 17v; change of pen and ink fol. 18.

1/III DECORATION, RUBRICS AND ARTICULATION OF TEXT

Text initials Small capitals, mainly rustic in character, written by scribe.
Minor initials None.
Major initials Fol. 3: **5-line red I**(ntentio) inserted in the margin since only a 1-line space left by scribe, thick central reserved line; severely trimmed at top.
Historiated initials None.
Display script None.
Title page None.
Titles etc. Fol. 3 in tiny brown ink capitals: 'Incipiunt Cantica Cantico*rum*'. Upper margin severely trimmed, thus no evidence of running titles.

1/IV CONTENTS

Table of contents None for this booklet, but see below, 130.
Main texts Jerome, *Commentary on Cantica Canticorum.*
1. Fol. 1: preface: 'Intentio Salomonis e*st* in hoc libro *p*ersuadere unicui*que* fideli anime ad oscul*atum et* dilectione*m* sponsi id est *christi p*ervenire'. Ends fol. 1: 'osculandu*m et* diligendu*m* e*ss*e dicens.' James, *Trinity MSS*, I, 33, suggests comparison with Honorius of Autun, *PL* CLXXII, 250A.
Fol. 3: 'Incipiunt Cantica Canticorum quasi dicat. Si Cantica frequentissim*um* alioru*m* canticoru*m id est* si cantilene in choreis v*el* in aliquando alio'. Ends fol. 47v 'id est sublimes et excelsi in virtutibus.'

1/V ORIGIN AND PROVENANCE

Ex libris Not for this booklet, but see below, 130.
Secundo folio illa quae
The scribal hand suggests a Northern France origin.

BOOKLET 2: fols. 48–103

Structure of Booklet
Parchment Fairly uniformly thin and evenly coloured, creamy-white. Some holes resulting from flaying; a slight nap
Collation 1–7[8]; hair side outside in all quires.
Quire nos. Q. 5 numbered .v. lower margin last leaf of this quire.
Catchwords None.

Page Layout
Dimensions
Page 218 x 145mm (all margins trimmed).
Space ruled for writing Slightly variable: 190–196 x 120–125mm.
Columns 2.
Pricking QQ. 1, 5: outer margins only from central bifolium to outer bifolium; qq. 2–4, 6–7: leaves folded, outer margins only, qq. 2–4, 6: 1→8, q. 7, outer bifolium 8→1, inner bifolia 1→8 .
Ruling Blind ruling on hair side, now very faint; written above top line.
Lines per page 54 (except q. 4: 52–53).

Page design
fols. 46–103

2/II SCRIBES
One scribe wrote virtually the whole text in a tiny, round, neat scholarly continental hand s.xii med. From fol. 70v he ceased to underline the Epistle text, making the booklet difficult to use. On fols. 75 col. b (whole column) and 76 col. b (lines 25–45) a slightly less even, more compressed hand with a distinctive form of g intervened, using darker ink. A correction over an erasure by text scribe, fol. 48.

2/III DECORATION, RUBRICS AND ARTICULATION OF TEXT
Text initials Brown ink capitals of rustic type written by text scribe, thickened in the earlier pages to make them prominent, but this practice ceases.
Minor initials None.
Major initials Fol. 48: **4-line green** U(idetur), plain. Fol. 69v: **9-line green** P(aulus), in 4-line space, plain with stem extended in the margin. Fol. 85: **10-line green** P(aulus), plain, extended as on fol. 69v. Fol. 94: **2-line blue** G(alathia), plain. Fol. 99: **3-line purple** E(phesus), plain.
Historiated initials None.
Display script Fol. 48: (U)**idetur** in 1-line thickened brown ink capitals; elsewhere, the first word after a coloured initial written in tiny rustic capitals by scribe.
Title page None.
Titles etc. Fol. 48: 'Ep*istol*a Pauli Glos*ate*' in a hand s.xvii. Slight marks at very top of trimmed leaves suggest possibly once running titles; title at the head of text on fol. 48 in 1-line rustic capitals written in brown ink by scribe; incipits on fols. 48, 69v, 85, 94, 99 in rustic capitals written by scribe in brown ink.

2/IV CONTENTS
Table of contents None for this booklet, but see below, 130.
Main texts Epistles of Paul, glossed, in continuous layout.
1.Text begins fol. 48: 'Ad Romanos. Videtur sup*er*flua q*uod* doct*r*ina epistola*rum* quia facte sunt p*ost* e*v*angelium...Paul*us* eb*r*aicum *sed* grati*am* in*ter*pretatione*m* q*u*iet*us* d*i*citu*r*'. Ends fol. 69v: '*et con*firmare vos *et*cete*r*a q*ue* secuntu*r*.' Fol. 69v: 'Incipit ad Corinthios I. Paulus ipse ide*m* p*r*aedicaverat chorinthiis ad fide*m* converterat'. Ends fol. 85: '*et* h*o*c sit in *christo* i*hesu* id es*t* p*r*opte*r* amore *christ*i i*hesu*. Amen id est ita fiat.' Fol. 85: 'II ad Corinthios. Paulus ite*ru*m ha*n*c epistola*m* sc*r*ibit ad corinthios q*uorum* alios sufficien*ter* correxerant'. Ends fol.

94: '*id est* spiritus *com*munica*ns* vob*is* grati*a*s suas sit c*um* o*m*nib*us* vob*is* amen.' Fol. 94: 'Ep*isto*la ad Galathas. Galathia lo*cus* q*ui*dda*m est* in gr*e*cia'. Ends fol. 99v: 'G*rati*a d*om*ini n*ostri* in *christi* sit c*um* spiritu v*estro* amen.' Fol. 99v: 'Ad Ephesios. Ephesus civitas *est* in asia. N*on* h*ec est* asia'. Ends incomplete fol. 103v: 'ita mulieres subdite s*ed* viris *in* o*m*nib*us* qu*ae* opportet. Mulieres'. Rest of page blank.

Beryl Smalley, *The Study of the Bible in the Middle Ages* (Indiana, 1964), 99 n. 2, says of this commentary that it 'uses the *Gloss* and derives from the school of Laon, perhaps from Ralph of Laon himself.' See also A.M. Landgraf, *Introduction a l'histoire de la littérature théologique de la scolastique naissante* (Montreal, 1973), 66–67.

2/V ORIGIN AND PROVENANCE
Ex libris None for this booklet, but see below, 130.
Secundo folio in*peri*ciar vobis
There is no clear evidence about where this booklet was copied, but the scribal hand and the possible origin of the text suggest Northern France.

BOOKLET 3: fols. 104–143
Structure of Booklet 3
Parchment Rather poor quality, very many holes; fols. 121–126 much shorter than the other leaves, hair side very yellow.
Collation 1–5^8, hair side outside in each quire.
Quire nos. None.
Catchwords None.

Page Layout
Dimensions
Page Variable: 215 (fol. 121: 195) x 140–145mm (all margins trimmed).
Space ruled for writing Very variable: 197 x 120mm, but, e.g., fol. 104: 193 x 117.
Columns 2, but fol. 133: long lines recto and verso.
Pricking Leaves folded, outer margin only, 1→8.
Ruling In grey, erratic edge-to-edge ruling, most commonly first 2 and last 1 or 2, outer vertical bounding line sometimes double.
Lines per page QQ. 1–3: 46; qq. 4–5 (to fol. 140): 45; q. 5 (fols. 140v–143v): 38 or 39.
Page design
fols. 104–143

3/II SCRIBES

One scribe wrote all the texts in a very small, neat and scholarly hand, probably continental c.1160, with occasional use of elongated descenders for the last line on some pages (e.g. fols. 1, 8v), an open loop to g and a long upward-sweeping stroke at the end of words, especially at the end of a line. He did his own corrections, often supplying omissions vertically in the margin (e.g. fols. 105v–106).

3/III DECORATION, RUBRICS AND ARTICULATION OF TEXT

Text initials Unemphasised brown ink capitals throughout, written by the text scribe.

Minor initials None.

Major initials Fol. 104: **7-line red F**(uit) in 2-line space, with bifurcated tail extended in margin. Fol. 122: 4-line space left for I(n), not supplied.

Historiated initials None.

Display script None.

Title page None.

Titles etc. No contemporary titles, but general heading: 'Quaedam notulae in Libros Regum' added in later hand s. xvii. Lines were left, possibly for titles, on fols. 104, 122, 126, 132.

3/IV CONTENTS

Table of contents None for this booklet, but see below, 130.

Main texts See James, *Trinity MSS* I, 34–36, for a full exposition of the contents.

1. Fol. 104: Andrew of St. Victor, *Commentary on Kings and Chronicles* (written in the form of a continuous gloss). Text begins: 'Fuit vir unus...Ad commendationem sancti Samuel prophete utriusque parentis illius et generis dignitas et vite religiositas...Vir. hoc nomen in sacra scriptura non solum ad sexus distinctionem sed frequentissime ad corporis vel animi probitatem notationem ponisolet'. Ends fol. 122: '*Trullas*. Instrumenta illa quibus mundantur et raduntur pavimenta'. Beryl Smalley, *The Study of the Bible*, 176, observes that this is the earliest English copy of this text. See also p. 154. Both Smalley and James mention other copies: Cambridge, Corpus Christi College MSS 30.2.and 315.5.

2. Fols. 122–126, A Commentary on Chronicles. Text begins: '[I]n hac ultima huius operis particula que sint reliqua verborum uniuscuiusque regum iuda'. Ends fol. 126: 'Quis ex vobis est ex omni populo eius sit dominus deus eius est eo et ascendat'. After a 1 line gap: 'viii.iii regni annum haberet ioachim filius iosie.' Ends fol. 127: 'darius vero in mediam ducens urbem secundum danielem prophetam remeavit.'

3. Fol. 127: A Chronicle of the Reigns of the Kings of Judah and Israel. Text begins: 'Roboam filius Salamonis de naama ammanitude matre natus'. Ends fol. 128: 'Achaz que finitum est regnum filii romelie usque ad xii annum regni eiusdem achaz viii sed annos regnum israel sine rege fuit.'

4. Fol. 128: A Chronicle of Maccabees and Herod. Text begins: 'Principatum israelitice gentis post mortem moysi et successoris ihesu'. Ends fol. 132: 'claudii filius agrippine uxoris sue ei in regnum successit.'

5. Fol. 132: An Historical Chronicle from Adam to the Desertion of Britain by Rome (see James, 34–5 for a full analysis of text). Text begins: 'Adam annorum

cxxx genuit seth cui supervixit annos dccc. Seth annorum cv genuit enos cui
supervixit annos dcccvii'. Ends fol. 134v: 'britones minus sufficienter stipendia
darent.'

6. Fols. 135–136: A Chronicle of the Ptolemies 'in the form of a commentary on
Daniel chs.x–xi and excerpts from Justin's Histories.' (see James, 35–6, for a full
description of the text). Text begins: 'In egipto ii primus regnavit phtolomeus
laigi filius id est ad meridien. In macedonia philippus qui zarideus frater
alexandri id est ad occidentem'. Ends incomplete fol. 143: 'cum suis relictus
ptolomeus cum regem se non'.

3/V ORIGIN AND PROVENANCE

Ex libris None for this booklet, but see below, 130.

Secundo folio None agente

There is no evidence about where this booklet was compiled and copied, but a
Northern France origin is likely in view of the script and the nature of the texts,
especially item 1.

BOOKLET 4: fols. 144–179v

Structure of Booklet

Parchment Fair quality, thin, flesh side very white.

Collation 1–3^8, 4^4, 5^8 (8 excised except for upper strip). Hair side outside in all
quires.

Quire nos. Q. 1, trimmed mark lower verso of last leaf, probably a quire number.

Catchwords None.

Page Layout
Dimensions

Page 216 x 146mm (all margins trimmed).

Space ruled for writing Variable: 184 x 124mm, (fol. 167: 197 x 130).

Columns 2; fols. 178–9: long lines (s.xiii).

Pricking Much evidence lost, surviving evidence suggests: qq. 1–3: leaves
folded, outer margins only, 1→8; qq. 4–5: leaves folded, both margins, q. 4:
4→1, q. 5: 1→8. In q. 4, where new scribe takes over, leaves are repricked to
make both columns of equal width.

Ruling QQ. 1–2: in grey; qq. 3–4: in grey, outer column up to 10mm wider than
inner; q. 5: in grey sometimes appearing brown. Patterns of edge–to–edge ruling
vary with scribes, as does the ruling in general. The change from scribe 1 to
scribe 2 occurs on fol. 1 of q. 2, so scribe 1 probably pricked and ruled both
quires. The change from scribe 2 to scribe 3 occurs on fol. 1v of q. 3, so it was
probably scribe 2 who pricked and ruled this quire very unevenly. Scribe 3
perpetuated the unevenness of column width. The change from scribe 3 to
scribe 4 occurs on fol. 2v of q. 4 which had been ruled by scribe 3 up to the end
of his stint. Scribe 4 re-ruled his quires, making the columns and margins more
even.

Lines per page Q. 1: 60; q. 2: 57; q. 3: 57–60; q. 4: 51–55; q. 5: 55. Text written
on top line.

Page design
fols. 144–159v fols. 160–169v fols. 170–177v

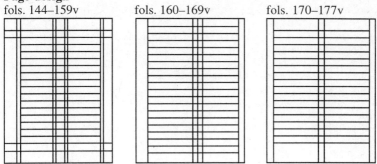

4/II SCRIBES
Four scribes s.xii ex shared in the copying of the text: **Scribe 1** (fols. 144–152 col. a) wrote in a very small neat upright hand with continental characteristics. **Scribe 2** (fols. 152 col. a–160v) took over in mid-line 4 lines from the bottom of the page in a similar but slightly more pointed hand. **Scribe 3** (fols. 160v col. b–169v col. b) took over 7 lines from the bottom of the page with a less regular, untidier hand; this scribe made his own corrections vertically in the margins. **Scribe 4** (fols. 169v col. b–177) took over at line 16 using a lighter ink and writing in a small, fine neat hand with continental characteristics. On fol. 170v an extensive addition, evidently an omitted passage, was made by a later hand, s.xiii. Fols. 177v–179: various hands s.xiii added notes.

4/III DECORATION, RUBRICS AND ARTICULATION OF TEXT
Text initials None.
Minor initials None. 1-line space left on fol. 160 for V(enit), and on fol. 166, a 1-line space left for S(ed), neither supplied.
Major initials None. Space not left on fol. 144 for an initial I(n), and initial not afterwards supplied.
Historiated initials None.
Display script Not as such, but first words of books 1 and 2 written in small rustic capitals.
Title page None.
Titles etc. No original running titles are visible, upper margins severely trimmed. A s.xvii hand added the title in the lower margin fol. 144, the same hand and the same title as on the flyleaf. This hand also wrote 'Finis libri primi de Nuptiis etc.' on fol. 166, and 'Explicit liber secundus' vertically in the central margin fol. 77.

4/IV CONTENTS
Table of contents None for this booklet but see below.
Main texts Commentary on Martianus Capella's *De Nuptiis*.
1. Fol. 144: Text begins: '(I)n h*uius* libri martiani p*r*incipio quattuor h*ec* p*er* consid*er*anda constituim*us*.' Ends fol. 177v: 'appolinea lira [sic] p*er* h*anc* intellige sap*ienti*am. Explicit. Ammo*do* instabit s*er*mo de *v*era artiu*m* sap*ienti*a.'
2. Fols. 177v–179, in various hands s.xiii, legal notes added to what were originally blank leaves, headed 'De exceptione rei Judicate libri xliiii, lxc, xi'. Fol. 179v (remaining strip) blank except for heading 'Glo*ssa* sup*er* Martianu*m*'.

4/V ORIGIN AND PROVENANCE
Ex libris None for this booklet, but see below, 130.
Secundo folio ab altioribus
There is no evidence about the origin of this booklet though some of the scribes may have been continental.

BOOKLET 5: fols. 180–221
Structure of Booklet
Parchment Variable thickness, hair and flesh sides distinct, hair sides very strongly follicle marked.
Collation 1^8 (7 excised), 2^8, 3^{10}, 4–5^8. Hair side outside in each quire.
Quire nos. None.
Catchwords None.

Page Layout
Dimensions
Page 216 x 149mm (all margins trimmed).
Space ruled for writing Variable, even within quires: e.g. fol. 182: 170 x 86mm; fol. 188: 185 x 89mm; fol. 220: 185 x 110mm.
Columns Long lines.
Pricking Some evidence lost, surviving marks suggest: qq. 1–3: leaves folded, both margins, 1→8; qq. 4–5: leaves folded, outer margin only, 1→8.
Ruling In grey sometimes appearing brown, neatly executed; first 2 and last 2 lines usually ruled edge-to-edge but this not consistent, and edge-to-edge lines in mid-page are erratically placed but always above the middle of the page.
Lines per page Q. 1: 36; q. 2: 39; q. 3: 40; q. 4: 40 increasing to 46; q. 5: 47 increasing to 49.
Page design
fols. 180–220

5/II SCRIBES
2 scribes wrote this densely written text. **Scribe 1** (fols. 180–198, item 1) wrote in a very small hand s.xii ex with tall, bifurcated ascenders and using skeletal capital letters, especially S; he did his own corrections. **Scribe 2** (fols. 198v–221, items 2–15) wrote in a slightly larger hand with clubbed but not bifurcated ascenders, becoming increasingly compressed.

5/III DECORATION, RUBRICS AND ARTICULATION OF TEXT
Text initials Enlarged capitals in brown ink written by scribes mark new paragraphs.

Minor initials None. *Item 1*: sub-divisions of the text marked with paraphs and enlarged initial letters, often skeletal. *Item 2*: spaces left for minor initials which were not supplied.
Major initials None. Spaces left (e.g. on fols. 198v, 207v) for initials which were not supplied. Fol. 207v has small prompt initial f in margin. On fol. 180, no space was left for an initial U(t) and it was not supplied.
Historiated initials None.
Display script None, but the first two lines on fol. 180 were left free, probably for a title and or incipit.
Title page None.
Titles etc. None (upper margins trimmed).

5/IV CONTENTS
Table of contents None for this booklet but see below.
Main texts Legal texts. See James, *Trinity MSS*, I, 36 for a detailed account of the texts in this booklet. In the Trinity College copy of James, a type-written addendum provides a more detailed list of contents and identifications of the texts or extracts for fols. 198v–220v. It is based on a review article published by H. Kantorowicz in *Zeitschrift der Savigny-Stiftung für Rechtsgeschichte, Romanische Abteilung*, 52 (1932), 438–441. The typed list provides folio numbers only for the beginning of each text. An attempt has been made below to add line numbers to the folio reference, but not all initia have been located.
1. Fols. 180–198: *De Dilatoriis*: '[U]t insurgentum in innocentes indebite improbe accionis re retenetur audacia'. Ends fol. 198: 'Unde dilationem habebit etiam invito iudice.' Rest of page blank.
2. Fols. 198v–205v: *Anonymi Ordo Iudiciorum*: '[Q]uia iudiciorum sunt preparatoria et multa prevenit iudicia tanquam preludia.'
3. Fols. 205v (6th line from bottom of page)–207: Pileus Bambergensis, *Tractatus de Violento Possessore*: '[C]um multiplices varie que sint acciones constitutiones.'
4. Fols. 207–210v: *Anonymi Doctoris Nostri Collectio 55 Quaestionum in Schola*: 'Bononie anno 1188 disputatarum'.
5. Fols. 210v–211v: Johannes Bassianus, *Tractatus de Accusationibus*: 'Quoniam omnium legumlatorum'.
6. Fols. 211v (line 22)–212: Johannes Bassianus, *Consilium*: '[I]nter omnes legum doctores'.
7. Fol. 212 (line 33): Johannes Bassianus, *Distinctio*: '[Q]uandoque lex presumit ex qualitate'.
8. Fol. 212 (line 37): Johannes Bassianus, *Distinctio:* '[E]st quaedam possedio que'.
9. Fols. 212 (line 41)–212v: ?Johannes Bassianus, *Distinctio*: '[C]um quis petit restitutionem'.
10. Fols. 212v (line 4)–213: Pileus Bambergensis, *Tractatus de Conceptione Libelli*: '[C]um essem mutine'.
11. Fols. 213 (line 29)–214: Johannes Bassianus, *Tractatus de conceptione libelli*: '[Q]uicumque vult actionem'.
12. Fol. 214 (line 5): Johannes Bassianus, *Consilium*: '[F]irmissime dico'.
13. Fols. 214 (last line)–217v: Johannis Bassiani, *Tractatus de iudiciis*: '[P]ropositum presentis operis est'.
14. Fol. 217 (line 18): Pileus Bambergensis, *Tractatus de testibus*: '(Q)uoniam in iudiciis frequentissime'.

15. Fols. 217v (4th line from bottom)–220v: Pileus Bambergensis, *Tractatus de reorum exceptionibus*: '(P)recib*us et* instantia congruenti'.

5/V ORIGIN AND PROVENANCE
Ex libris None for this booklet, but see below.
There is no evidence about the origin of this booklet.

V PROVENANCE OF TRINITY B.1.29
Ex libris Fol. 2v: 'Liber monachor*um* s*an*ct*e* marie de Bildewas' in red with green initial L, in a hand s.xiii in. Also on fol. 2 in a hand s.xiii, in the same form.
Table of contents Fol. 2v, the items written in booklets 1–4 are listed by the hand s.xiii in which wrote the ex libris as 5 titles (items 3 and 4 in the list are both in booklet 3). On fol. 2 the contents are listed in the same form exactly by the scribe (s.xiii) who wrote the ex libris on this page. The facts that the contents of booklet 5 (legal texts) are not included in either contents list, that they do not fit comfortably with the subjects of the first 4 booklets and that the last leaves of booklet 4 were originally blank and therefore possibly intended to serve – and in fact may have served – as endleaves suggest that the legal texts were not originally a part of the Buildwas book. Indeed they may not even have been a part of any Buildwas book, but added in a subsequent rebinding elsewhere.
The earlier ex libris scribe wrote Balliol 40 and 150 (q.v.). The texts listed were therefore apparently gathered together at Buildwas and bound there in the early thirteenth century, when the front endleaves were added. Booklets 1 and 2 at least seem, from evidence of earlier sewing, to have been bound together quite early.
The fact that some of the hands are early and continental raises the possibility that the texts may have come from Savigny with the founding monks. However, it is more likely that they were a gift to the monks, perhaps from several donors, among whom may have been Master Robert. The first three booklets especially, given their date and the schools origin of two of them, may have been his, though there is no evidence of his ownership of any of the texts.
The book was given to Trinity College by Thomas Nevile s.xvi ex/xvii in.

VI NOTES

VII BIBLIOGRAPHY AND PLATES
James, *Trinity MSS*, I, 33–36; Ker, *MLGB*, 14; Chibnall, *VCH*, 56; Cheney 1953, 377 (1973, 333); Sheppard 1990, 202, pl 19 (though this is printed back to front).

25. CAMBRIDGE, TRINITY COLLEGE MS O.7.9
1. Peter Comestor, Sermons (1–77); 2. Alexander Nequam, De Utensilibus; Phale Tolum; Formulae Epistolarum; 3. De Proprietatibus Ignis; 4. Boethius, De Sophisticis Elenchis; 5. Various sermons etc.
Leaves [i paper], iii, 182, [i paper]   **Date**. s.xii med, s.xii ex, s. xiii
Foliation 1–182 (parchment leaves only)
Origin Various: booklets 1 and 2, possibly Northern France; item 5, possibly Buildwas.
The book as it now exists is a Buildwas compilation of the early thirteenth

century although the booklets themselves have various dates and places of origin.
The binding of the book as it now exists will be described first and then each booklet independently. The Provenance, Notes and Bibliography for the whole book will be given at the end.

I PHYSICAL DESCRIPTION

Binding A composite volume first assembled s.xiii, rebound, most recently ?s.xix, spine solidly glued, barely opens at all.

Endleaves

    Front *Pastedown* **1)** Laid paper leaf in place, first leaf of a bifolium, broken at joint, no watermark, blank. **2)** A single parchment leaf after a paper flyleaf (see below), formerly a pastedown now detached, first leaf of a quaternion, conjoint with its last leaf; very considerable grainy paste remains on recto (hair side), much worn and damaged, impressions of former primary covering turn-ins and evidence of former fore-edge clasps but no other conclusive evidence of earlier binding(s).

      Flyleaves **1)** Laid paper leaf, second leaf of bifolium once conjoint with pastedown, broken at joint, no watermark, blank; **2)** 3 parchment leaves formerly part of a quaternion: the first formerly a pastedown (see above); the second now a single leaf (stub of former conjoint leaf just visible at tail). First leaf recto: shelfmarks in ink, 'D5, 223'. Verso: Buildwas ex libris, an abbreviated list of contents s.xiii, Trinity College bookplate. The other remaining leaf conjoint with former parchment pastedown (see above), with numbered list of initia of Comestor's sermons in order of the liturgical year s.xii ex/xiii in.

    Back *Flyleaves* Laid paper leaf, first leaf of a bifolium, broken at joint, no watermark, blank.

      Pastedown Laid paper leaf in place over another leaf, second leaf of a bifolium, no watermark, blank.

Sewing stations Now 5; no recoverable evidence about original stations which may have been different in each section of the composite book.

Sewing Now all-along with white S-twist thread; no recoverable evidence about earlier sewing(s).

Sewing supports Now to 5 cords; no recoverable evidence about original supports.

Lacing path Now laced in over the outer edges of the board, pulled through to the inner face very close to the spine edge and fixed under the pastedown.

Endbands None present; no other evidence.

Tabs None present; no other evidence.

Spine lining None present; no other evidence.

Boards Thin pasteboard, 180 x 120 x 3mm. Wormholes on front endleaves indicate that earlier boards were of wood.

Primary covering Faded purple laid paper, neatly trimmed, overlapped corners with very deep fore-edge turn-in. Spine covered with parchment to which the backs of all spines have been glued.

Fastenings Greenish holes on fore-edges of former parchment pastedown and first flyleaf indicate earlier presence of fore-edge fastening device.

Bosses None present; no other evidence.

Chain attachments None present; no other evidence.

Labels Printed paper labels on spine with modern shelfmark.

BOOKLET 1: fols. 1–121

Structure of Booklet

Parchment Quite good quality, hair and flesh sides increasingly distinct towards end and quality more variable; large contemporary pasted patches fols. 47, 104; remains of animal hair at lower corner fol. 77.

Collation $1-2^8$, 3^8 (4 and 5 seem to be singletons), $4-6^8$, 7^6+ 1 after 3, $8-9^8$, 10^{10} (10 excised), 11^8, 12^4, 13^{12} (9 and 10 excised), 14^8, 15^2, 16^{10} (10 excised). Hair side outside in each quire.

Quire nos. QQ. 1–6, lower margin of verso of last leaf, .i.–.vi., very faintly, perhaps partially erased.

Catchwords None.

Page Layout

Dimensions

Page Variable: *c*.173 x 115mm, all margins very roughly trimmed.

Space ruled for writing Variable: 129–135 x 75–87mm.

Columns Long lines.

Pricking Almost all pricking has been trimmed off; q. 1: leaves folded, both margins 1→8. QQ. 2-16: most inner margins are inaccessible (but see below, Ruling); q. 10: 8→1.

Ruling In grey, apparently a page at a time (lines per page are not necessarily the same on conjoint leaves); edge-to-edge ruling is haphazard, fol. 61 (see below) bears what was probably the intended page layout pattern.

Lines per page Variable, e.g. fol. 1: 34; fol. 21: 38; fol. 65: 37; fol. 97: 40; fol. 117: 37.

Page design

fols. 1–121 (basic)   fol. 61

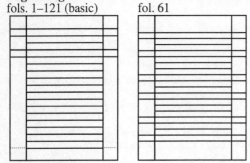

1/II SCRIBES

One main scribe wrote text throughout in a very small, neat scholarly hand mainly without serifs, s.xii ex. Fol. 5v was written by another scribe with a similar hand. A third scribe wrote the list of sermons arranged in order of the liturgical year on fols. i–i verso in a contemporary or very slightly later hand.

The main text scribe wrote most of the sermon titles in red, but a larger contemporary hand supplied omitted titles on fols. 60–65; this hand may belong to the scribe who supplied the red initials (same colour of ink); it is similar to that of the 'round hand' rubricator known from other late twelfth-century books.

The text scribe made his own corrections and inserted omissions in the margins. Sermon 70 was written on a single bifolium (fols. 111–112v; q. 15) by the text scribe though in a slightly larger hand, using a different ink and perhaps a different pen. It seems that it had been inadvertently omitted.

1/III DECORATION, RUBRICS AND ARTICULATION OF TEXT

Text initials No special emphasis applied to text initials, though in Sermon 26 (fols. 42–44), sub-divisions in the text are marked by brown ink paraphs and 1-line red initials.

Minor initials Small 2-line red capitals often squeezed into 1-line spaces at the beginning of each sermon, usually plain but occasionally with some slight decoration (e.g. fol. 105v: 2-line A, fol. 106: 2-line I); on fols. 35, 83, capitals are green with red shading. Spaces were left in the list of sermons (fol. i–i verso) for small capitals but these were never supplied.

Major initials None.

Historiated initials None.

Display script None.

Titles etc. No running titles, but sermons numbered in red at the top of each page (except sermons 1–14 which are numbered in greenish blue); sermon titles in the text and sermon numbers in the margins written in red.

Title page None.

1/IV CONTENTS

Table of contents Fol. i–i verso: initia of sermons listed according to subject arranged first in the order of the liturgical year and subsequently under general headings, giving the number of the sermon and its initia. This list was sporadically annotated by a reader (shown in brackets { } below), though the purpose of the annotations is not clear.

Begins: [I]n adventu   xxxv [I]n igne   {Et rex david sene*ctutus*}

                      xliii [A]spiciebam   {Erat ier*usa*lemus}

                      lx [C]onverti   {ex egypto}

Ends: [I]n dedic*atio*ne

        ec*cle*sie   vi [A]postol*us*   {no note}

                    vii [V]erei   {no note}

Main texts Peter Comestor, *Sermons*.

Text begins fol. 1: 'In epiphan[iam]. C*um* nat*us* *e*sset *iehsus* *in* betlee*m* iude *in* dieb*us* H*er*odis regis'. Ends imperfectly fol. 121v (sermon 77): 'Una eade*m*que *est* dom*us*.' *PL* CLXXXXVIII.

Fol. 34v is blank except for the last line of sermon 22.

In the lower margin of fol. 121v a hand s.xvii wrote the title of the next item: 'sequitur Alexander Neckam de utensilibus. v. exemplar aliuto [sic] in Col*legium Sancti* Petri Cantab.'

1/V ORIGIN AND PROVENANCE

Ex libris Not for this booklet, but see below, 140.

Secundo folio voluit.

Since this copy of the Sermons must have been made quite soon after they were written, it may have originated in Northern France.

BOOKLET 2: fols. 122–151

Structure of Booklet

Parchment Variable: q. 1: good quality, supple, evenly coloured and with good nap; qq. 2–3: thinner, smoother, hair and flesh sides more distinct; q. 4: similar to qq. 2–3 but clearly cut economically from offcuts of skin, the lower corners substantially trimmed from the central bifolium.

Collation 1^{10}, $2-3^8$, 4^4. Hair sides outside in each quire except q. 4 where hair sides face flesh side throughout.
Quire nos. None.
Catchwords None.

Page Layout
Dimensions
Page Variable; fols. 122–151v: 173 x 115mm (all margins very roughly trimmed).
Space ruled for writing Variable; fols. 122–151v: 130 x 70mm; fols. 142v–151v: *c.*142 x 100mm, but varies from page to page, written almost to the edges of each page.
Columns Fols. 122–142: wide central text column with narrow gloss columns on either side or on fore-edge side only. Vertical gloss columns rarely ruled. Fols. 142v–151v: long lines.
Pricking: Fols. 122–142: leaves folded, 1→8 in outer margins only; q. 1 (fols. 122–131) pricked for gloss; fols. 132–142 (qq. 2–3), text lines only. Double marks from fol. 132 at lines 1 and 3 for edge-to-edge lines but not used until fol. 133v and thereafter erratically. Fols. 142v–147v (q. 3): repricked, leaves folded, 1→8 in outer margins only. Fols. 148–152v (q. 4): no pricking evidence, probably none executed.
Ruling Barely visible, mostly in grey, often obscured by text, not very carefully done if at all, evidently a page at a time; edge-to-edge ruling spasmodic. Fols. 138v–139 are ruled in a more complex way than other pages (see below). Q. 4: no evidence.
Lines per page Q. 1: 17 text lines; qq. 2–3 (to fol. 142): 20 text lines; q. 3 (fol. 142–147v) and q. 4: varies from page to page, 27 increasing to 42 (fol. 151v).
Page design
fols. 122–142   fol. 138v.   fols. 142v–151v

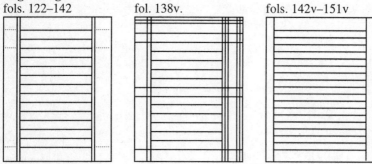

2/II SCRIBES
Fols. 122–142: 2 scribes wrote text s.xiii in. **Scribe 1** wrote fols. 122–131 (except lines 4–12) in a slightly backward-sloping hand with some continental characteristics, the strokes separated. **Scribe 2** took over from scribe 1 at the beginning of a new sentence mid-line and wrote $7^1/_2$ lines (fol. 131, lines 4–12) in a neat and regular hand, and from fol. 131v to the end of this section of the text (fol.142). The glosses were added by a number of scribes including both text scribes, apparently on an ad hoc basis.
Fols. 142v–151v: a third scribe wrote this text in a neat and variable hand, but rather cramped in the effort to squeeze much text into a small space.

2/III DECORATION, RUBRICS AND ARTICULATION OF TEXT
Fols. 122–142: all the articulation was done by a single hand, the red a distinctive pinkish shade.
Text initials No special emphasis; two initials on fols. 122, 122v, shaded with red for emphasis.
Minor initials Some 2-line red initials fols. 122v–126, some with fine but sparse flourishes; space left on fol. 137v for initial, not supplied.
Major initials Fol. 122: **3-line red Q**(uibum) decorated with fine, slight pen flourishes in the same colour, now rubbed.
Historiated initials None.
Display script None as such, but words following small red initials fols. 122–122v crossed through in red.
Titles etc. No running titles; fol. 135, an elaborate explicit by Scribe 2 in mixed rustic and minuscule letters in brown ink.
Title page None.
Fols. 142v–151v: No articulation of any sort. Space was left for an initial and rubrics on fol. 142v; the rubric was supplied in brown minuscule in pale ink by a different hand, but not the initial.

2/IV CONTENTS
Table of contents Not for this booklet, but see below, 140.
Main texts Various.
1. Alexander Nequam, *De Utensilibus*. Text begins fol. 122: 'Qui b*ene* vult dispon*ere* familie sue *et* reb*us* suis v*el* domo sue'. Ends fol. 135: 'de ostario de hospiciario de portitore re de ranitore [sic] dico q*uia* p*er*sone sint. Explicit lib*er* mag*is*tri Alexand*ri* Nequ*am*.' The interlinear glosses are in Latin, not in French (cf. James, *Trinity MSS*, III, 352).
2. Fol. 135: 'Phale tolum cillentib*us* radus p*er*spicuu*m* cum iam p*ro*spicerem'. Ends fol. 141v: 's*ed* ill*ud* inutile e*ss*e a me sepe accepisti.' Fol. 141v: '(I)nstrumenta ecc*lesi*e sunt h*oc* lavacrum'. Ends fol. 142: 'Sed div*er*sis causis forciunt*ur* vocab*ula*ri*a* diversa etc*etera*.'
3. Fol. 142v Letter formulae. '(E)pistola e*st* or*atio* prosayta favores petitiuuva [sic]'. Fol. 143: 'et fallerata v*er*bor*um* festivitas imp*en*dat*ur*.' Last formula begins: '(E)quitate*m* redolet radice*m* ram*un*dinc*u*lo fonte*m*'. Ends fol. 151v: 'esse p*ar*ticips v*est*re co*n*v*er*sationis etcetera. Finito libro reddatur cena mag*is*tro.'
4. Fol. 151v Passages on privileges. 'Quida*m* ep*iscopus* imp*et*ra*v*it p*ri*vilegiu*m* dom*in*i'. Ends fol. 151v.

2/V ORIGIN AND PROVENANCE
Ex libris Not for this booklet, but see below, 140.
Secundo folio Cuius
There is no clear evidence about the origin of this booklet.

BOOKLET 3: fols. 152–159
Structure of Booklet
Parchment Very thick, quality and colour variable.
Collation 1^8, no regular sequence of hair and flesh sides.
Quire nos. Not applicable.

Catchwords Not applicable.

Page Layout
Dimensions
   Page Variable, shape and sizes of bifolia very ragged, probably ends and scraps: 158 x 109mm (approx.).
   Space ruled for writing Very variable, different on each page.
Columns Long lines
Pricking None is visible; possibly none executed (see below, Ruling).
Ruling Mixed, grey and brown, all except central bifolium apparently ruled separately.
Lines per page Varies from page to page, though openings usually have roughly the same number of lines per page: 38; 36–36; 37–39; 29–28; 26–26; 23–26; 26–26; 24–24; 26.
Page design None evident.

3/II SCRIBES
One scribe probably wrote the entire text in a very variable hand, s.xiii in, beginning in a small neat bookhand on fol. 1, becoming first more vigorous and informal with large loop to g and very many more abbreviations, and then smaller towards the end of the text. A few marginal corrections by the text scribe; longer marginal passages added fols. 152, 153 etc. in another hand.

3/III DECORATION, RUBRICS AND ARTICULATION OF TEXT
Text initials Skeletal initials written by text scribe, sometimes shaded with red. After fol. 152, emphasis provided by brown ink paraphs.
Minor initials None.
Major initials None; space was left on fol. 152 for a 2-line I(gnis), but this was not supplied.
Historiated initials None.
Display script None.
Titles etc. Fol. 152: incipit written as if a heading in upper margin possibly by the text scribe. Marginal sub-headings added by text scribe fols. 153v, 155v. Various headings added in another hand in upper margin: fols. 152v–5: 'Dyonisius *super* Ierarchiam'; fols. 156v–8: 'De Ierarchio'. Fol. 152: 'Textum adaptatio' written vertically by text scribe in outer margin.
Title page None.

3/IV CONTENTS
Table of contents Not for this booklet, but see below, 140.
Main texts *De Proprietatibus Ignis.*
1. Fol. 152: 'Incipiunt *propr*ietates ignis. (I)gnis sensibilis q*ui*dem sic dicendum in om*n*ib*us et p*er omn*ia.' Ends fol. 159v: 'Ignorantia*m* aut*em* dico q*u*am minores h*ab*ent n*un*c ista sufficiant'.

3/V ORIGIN AND PROVENANCE
Ex libris Not for this booklet, but see below, 140.
Secundo folio [minorati]onem
There is no clear evidence about the origin of this booklet. It was perhaps made by a reader for his own use.

BOOKLET 4: fols. 160–175

Structure of Booklet
Parchment Fair quality, hair and flesh sides markedly distinct.
Collation 1–2^8; hair side outside in each quire.
Quire nos. None.
Catchwords None.

Page Layout
Dimensions
Page Uneven and variable, *c.*171 x 115mm.
Space ruled for writing 126 x 76–81mm.
Columns Long lines.
Pricking Q. 1: leaves folded, 1→8 outer margin only; q. 2: no pricking visible.
Ruling In brown, fairly regular though untidy towards end, disregarding pricking; number and pattern of edge-to-edge lines varies from page to page.
Lines per page Variable, 26–29.
Page design
fols. 160–175

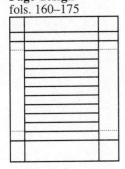

4/II SCRIBES
One scribe wrote the texts throughout in a neat, upright hand (*c.*1170) which becomes smaller and rather more cramped towards the end. There are many corrections mainly supplied by another hand, but the scribe supplied an omission in the margin fol. 163v.

4/III DECORATION, RUBRICS AND ARTICULATION OF TEXT
Text initials Small neat capitals by scribe sometimes thickened for emphasis e.g. fols. 163v–164.
Minor initials None. Text divisions marked by paraphs made by the text scribe.
Major initials None, though spaces were left for a 5-line initial on fol. 160, and 2- or 3-line initials throughout, not supplied except on fol. 160 where a later hand ?s.xiii wrote a clumsy 2-line D(e).
Historiated initials None
Display script Fol. 160: (D)e **Sophisticis** in 1-line mixed capitals by scribe. Fol. 168: (D)e **Responsione** in 1-line rustic letters by the scribe.
Titles etc. None.
Title page None.

4/IV CONTENTS
Table of contents None for this booklet, but see below, 140.

Main texts Boethius, *De Sophisticis Elenchis.*

1. Fols. 16: 'De Sophisticis autem elenchis et de his qui vid*e*ntur elenchi'. Ends fol. 168: 'in agonsticis ex*c*ercitat*i*onib*us* distum est.'

2. Fol. 168: 'De Responsione aut*em et* q*u*om*o*do oport*et* solvere'. Ends fol. 175v: 'artis induct*i*one*m* inventis [?a'] multas h*a*b*e*re grates.' *Cod. Boethiani*, 82–3, no. 52.

Fol. 175v over erased passage by text scribe, notes by several hands s.xiii including: 'Acta in cr*a*stina post octave s*a*n*c*ti kenelmo c*o*m*par*uit coram nob*is* Rog*e*rus de S[?]gham', and another note written in the same hand. Further comparisons may reveal other links with the later Lambeth books in which there are similar notes. A hand known from Lambeth 456 (scribe 7, q.v., the 'lecture notes hand') made a note on this leaf and at the top of fol. 175.

The text is among those that were classed as 'nova logica' within the Trivium.

4/V ORIGIN AND PROVENANCE

Ex libris Not for this booklet, but see below, 140.

Secundo folio Duplex

There is no clear evidence about the origin of this booklet.

BOOKLET 5: fols. 176–182

Structure of Booklet

Parchment Fair quality, hair and flesh sides distinct.

Collation 1^8 (8 excised, probably blank); hair side outside.

Quire nos. Not applicable.

Catchwords Not applicable.

Page Layout

Dimensions

Page Irregular, *c.*169 x 105mm (leaf edges very roughly trimmed).

Space ruled for writing 135 x 80mm.

Columns Long lines.

Pricking Leaves folded, 1→8 in outer margin only.

Ruling Blind ruled on hair side, edge-to-edge lines irregular.

Lines per page 31–32.

Page design

fols. 176–182

5/II SCRIBES

One main scribe wrote most of the texts in an upright English hand, *c.*1160–1170, very like known Buildwas hands of this period, though smaller. Another hand

wrote the last four lines on fol. 181v but this item is incomplete. The final item is written by the main scribe alternating with a third whose hand is like that of the main scribe.
A fourth hand corrected over an erasure on fol. 177.

5/III DECORATION, RUBRICS AND ARTICULATION OF TEXT
Display script and titles in small brown and red rustic capitals all provided by the same scribe.
Text initials Brown ink rustic capitals written by text scribe. Fol. 182: capitula, the text capitals are shaded in red.
Minor initials None.
Major initials Fol. 176: **2-line plain red S**(acramenta). Plain 2-, 3- or 4-line red capitals also on fols. 176v (T), 177v (I), 178 (V). Spaces left for initials on fols. 178v, 179, 182, but initials not supplied.
Historiated initials None.
Display script Fol. 176: (S)**acramenta panis** in small brown ink rustic capitals. Fol. 176v: (T)**anta** in small brown rustic letters. Fol. 177v: (I)**ndicatum est** in small brown rustic letters shaded in red. Fol. 178: (V)**eritas ait** in small brown rustic letters. Fol. 178v: (O)**portet sacerdotes** in small brown rustic letters. Fol. 179: (I)**n fine igitur** in small brown rustic capitals. Fol. 182: (Q)**ue** in brown rustic letters shaded with red.
Titles etc. Titles in small red rustic capitals on fols. 178, 181; incipit in red minuscule fol. 182 and chapter numbers in red or in brown or black ink touched with red. Spaces left for titles or headings on fols. 176v, 179, 181v, not supplied.
Title page None.

5/IV CONTENTS
Table of contents Not for this booklet, but see below, 140.
Main texts
1. Fol. 176: 'Sacramenta panis *et* vini c*um* aqua qu*ae* in missar*um* sollemnis [sic] *domin*o *d*eo offerunt*ur*'. Ends fol. 176v: 'agn*us* tamen q*ui* sacrificat*us* *est* integer p*er*severat *et* vivus.'
2. Fol. 176v: 'Tanta dignitas human*ae* conditionis e*ss*e cognoscit*ur*.' Ends fol. 177v: 'in *pr*imo ada*m* *c*ondidit mirabili*us* in secu*nd*o reformavit. Amen.'
3. Fol. 177v: 'Dictum domini Lanfranci anglor*um* archipresul*is*. Indicatum est m*ihi* q*ui*a de cui*us* es monasterio recedere'. Ends fol. 178: 'et si bone vite fuerit, ut stabilitate*m* suam firmet suadere.' (Epistle 60; *PL* CL, 549.)
4. Fol. 178: 'Sermo beati Augustini utr*um* sub figura an sub veritate hoc mystici calicis fiat sacramentum. Veritas ait. Caro mea vere est cib*us*'. Ends fol. 178v: 'In hoc ergo verbo creatur illud corpus.'
5. Fol. 178v: '[O]pportet sacerdotes ad quor*um* *d*omi*n*i pop*ulus* curam com*m*issus est.' Ends fol. 179: '*et* sacrificiu*m* *no*n accipia*m* de manib*us* *v*estris q*ui*a polluti estis.'
6. Fol. 179: '[I]n fine igitur mundi credentes hebrei *c*onveniant'. Ends fol. 181: 'in mutabili *pr*eparatu*m* est voluntate t*un*c erit.'
7. Fol. 181: 'Gregorius. Comp*r*ehendit sapientes *d*ominus in astutia eor*um*'. Ends fol. 181v: 'q*ui* hanc subiecto cordis humero nolens portare.'
8. Fol. 181v: '[E]t prudentia eius percussit superbum'. Ends incomplete fol. 181v: '*pr*o absolvendis hom*in*ibus inveniri. Neq*ue*'. Last 4 lines of page blank.
9. Fol. 182: 'Capi*t*ula Calixti pape se*c*undi in concilio Remensi. i. [Q]ue s*a*nctor*um* patru*m* sanctionib*us*'. Ends fol. 182: 'vi....com*m*unione careant

*christ*iana.' P. Jaffé, ed., *Regesta Pontificum Romanorum*, 2 vols (Leipzig 1885, 1888), I, 780–821; II, 755.

Fol. 182v: blank.

5/V ORIGIN AND PROVENANCE

Ex libris Not for this booklet, but see below.

Secundo folio movens

The scribe may well be a Buildwas scribe, and several of the texts (by patristic and other authorities) are like those that the monks were evidently acquiring during the third quarter of the 12th century.

V ORIGIN AND PROVENANCE OF MS O.7.9 AS CURRENTLY BOUND

Ex libris Fol. ii verso: 'Liber s*ancte* marie de buldewas' in an untidy hand using black ink, s.xiii. The same hand wrote a list of contents: 'Sermones pet*ri* manducatoris. Qui b*ene* vult dispon*ere*. Liber elenco*rum et* qu*ae*dam alia.'

Item 5 may have been written at Buildwas on the evidence of the character of the scribal hands and the contents, though the Comestor Sermons may have originated in Paris since they must have been copied not long after the author's death. But there is no firm evidence of the origin of any of the items. The texts, predominantly sermons, were probably collected and bound together at Buildwas in the thirteenth century at a time when, on the evidence of some of the Buildwas books now at Lambeth Palace, there was considerable scholarly activity at Buildwas, particularly in connection with preaching (but see also below, Notes). The book is very small and it would therefore have been easily portable.

There is no evidence about this book's later history.

VI NOTES

Boethius's *De Sophisticis Elenchis* (booklet 4) was among the texts comprising the 'nova logica' of the Trivium. 'Nova Logica' is one of the headings in the list of contents in Lambeth 488, though no 'nova logica' texts seem to have survived in the group of Lambeth texts (now Lambeth 488, 457 and 456) that were once bound into a single volume at Buildwas. The presence of the Lambeth 456 'lecture notes hand' in booklet 4 of Trinity O.7.9 reinforces the supposition that some Buildwas monks were studying formally in the thirteenth century. See below, Note on Lambeth 488, 457, 456.

VII BIBLIOGRAPHY AND PLATES

James, *Trinity MSS*, III, 351–353; Ker, *MLGB*, 14; A.M. Landgraf, *Introduction à l'histoire de la littérature théologique de la scolastique naissante* (Montreal, 1973), 141–142.

NOTE ON LAMBETH 488, 457 AND 456

These three manuscripts are now essentially seventeenth-century books. Each comprises miscellaneous texts written on parchment and paper by hands dating from the twelfth to the sixteenth centuries. Each has a list of contents written on one of the front paper flyleaves by or for William Sancroft (Archbishop of Canterbury 1677–1689), whose compilations these were (James, *Lambeth MSS*, 632, 635, 676).[1] Each has quire signatures and a seventeenth-century binding.

Other evidence permits some of the texts now dispersed among these three volumes to be linked and attributed to Buildwas.[2] First, Lambeth 488 retains medieval endleaves on one of which is written an ex libris and a record of the use of the book as witness to an indenture between John Gnossal (Abbot of Buildwas in the second quarter of the fifteenth century) and Henry, a monk of Savigny, written in the fifteenth century, and on the other, a list of contents in a s.xiv/xv hand. Second, throughout the three volumes are dispersed quires which had once been numbered in stylus in uniform large (lower case) Roman numerals, i–xxvi (xxii is used twice).

The medieval contents list is not now complete since it has been trimmed at the top and at least one title has certainly been lost. One entry (the second from last) has been erased beyond recall and another (the last) is the summary title: 'vetus logica et nova'.[3] It has been scored through as have the Seneca and Priscian entries (presumably when these texts were removed), but is easily legible. The two text titles to survive unobliterated are among those now bound with Lambeth 488, but the leaf on which the list was written is now, and probably always was, part of a separate endleaf bifolium.

It is not possible to date the quire numbers. The numbered quires carry the texts which are listed in the medieval list of contents, but the order of texts reflected by the numbers is not that of the contents list. The stylus numbers must therefore reflect a re-ordering of these quires at some point between the making of the contents list and Sancroft's final re-ordering of these and other texts, though this may have been a plan that was not actually carried out. The current bindings do not permit the recovery of evidence about earlier sewings.

Whatever its first form, the original book was always a compilation of various texts written at different times by different scribes, as the codicological and scribal evidence demonstrates. It seems always to have been a study book; Lambeth 456 contains some of the texts required by students of logic and rhetoric. However it is likely that the original compilation was made in the early thirteenth century, shortly after the latest text in the group had been copied, and when other such compilations were being made at Buildwas (e.g. Trinity O.7.9). The evidence for this is that the scribe with a distinctive hand responsible for copying most of the text in Lambeth 488 added marginal notes to the Seneca excerpts in the same volume and also added a paragraph to the end of a text now in another volume (Lambeth 457 fol. 230v). Similarly this scribe seems to have added the words 'fluvius egrediabatur', using a stylus, to fols. 12 and 54 of Lambeth 456, the first two words of a sermon copied by him in Lambeth 488 (fol. 99). If this is so, then this scribe was a reader as well as a copyist, and it is likely that the composite book was largely written as well as bound at Buildwas. The 'lecture notes hand' (Lambeth 456) also annotated the other texts in this group and made a brief note in Trinity O.7.9, fols.175, 175v.

---

[1] See N.R. Ker, 'Archbishop Sancroft's Rearrangement of the Manuscripts of Lambeth Palace Library', in E.G.W. Bill, *A Catalague of Manuscripts in Lambeth Palace Library, 1222–1860* (Oxford, 1972), 1–51.

[2] Ker, *MLGB*, 15 listed the folios concerned; Watson, *MLGB Supplement*, 5 amended an error in Ker's original.

[3] For 'vetus logica' and 'nova logica' and their place in the Trivium, see *Cod. Boethiani*, 2–7. No 'nova logica' texts survive in this group of books, though Boethius's *De Sophisticis Elenchis* is bound with other texts in Trinity O.7.9 (booklet 4).

Summary of the evidence relating to the order of texts in successive bindings.

MS.	present quire*	stylus quire no.	text	place in s.xv contents list	scribe
488	flyleaf		Contents list		
	1	xxv	Sermons.	? (?trimmed entry)	488/1
	2	xxvi	↑De Mul. Chanan.	1	488/1
	3	3 leaves only	↑Aelred De. Onere	2	488/1
	4	xxiiii	Comm. on Psalms.	? (?erased entry)	488/2
457	1	i	Jerome (s.xv: headed 'Seneca ad Lucilius')	?3	457/1
	2	ii	Jerome	?3	457/1
	3	iii	Jerome	?3	457/1
	4	iiii	Seneca	3	457/1 & 488/1
	5	v	Seneca	3	457/1
	6	vi	Seneca	3	457/1
	7	vii	Seneca	3	457/1
	8	?viii (last fols. missing**)	Gilbert	? (?erased entry)	457/1 & 2
456	1	xii	Priscian	4	456/3
	2	xiii	Priscian	4	456/3
	3	xiiii	Priscian	4	456/4
	4	xv	Priscian	4	456/3?
	5	xvi	Porphyrius	6 (vetus logica)	456/5
	6	xvii	Porph./Aristotle	6	456/5–6
	7	xviii	↑Aristotle Predic.	6	↑456/6
	8	xix	Arist.Peri Ermenias	6	456/6
	9	xx	Peri Erm./ 'Gilbert'	6	456/6
	10	xxi	'Gilbert'/Boethius	6	456/6
	11	xxii	Boeth. (Divisione)	6	456/6
	12	xxii (repeat)	↑Boeth. (Topicis)	6	456/6
	13	xxiii	Boeth. (Topicis)	6	456/6
	14	ix	Lecture notes	6	456/7
	15	x	Lecture notes	6	456/7
	16	xi	Lecture notes	6	456/7

*quire order in present volumes refers only to the texts formerly part of the Buildwas book.

**since the stylus sequence of quire numbers continues in MS 456 with ix, the Gilbert excerpts probably never occupied more than one quire.

↑indicates that text or scribal stint begins in previous quire.

26. LONDON, LAMBETH PALACE LIBRARY MS 488 fols. 89–126
Sermons; William of Lafford, De Muliere Chananeae; Aelred, De Onere Babilonis; Commentary on the Psalms (fragment) Date s.xiii
Leaves [iv paper, 88 paper], 37, [69 paper, ii paper]
Foliation 1–198, of which fols. 89–126 only were once part of a Buildwas book.
Origin Various; fols. 89–126 probably Buildwas **Fig.** 12

See note above about this and other Buildwas fragments at Lambeth Palace.

I PHYSICAL DESCRIPTION
Binding A composite volume, rebound several times, now opens very poorly. Present volume bound together in s.xvii in present order; rebacked since then. Superficially refurbished 14.1.59.
Endleaves
Front *Pastedown* **1)** Single laid paper leaf, in place, probably once conjoint with a flyleaf (joint repaired), blank; **2)** fol. 89, a discarded parchment leaf from a Service book with musical notation on 4-line staves, s.?xv; recto: stave drawn in red but overlaid with brown, square notes with stem on right, and text; verso: red lines, text, no notes. This leaf bears faint impressions of an uncoloured skin primary covering turn-in and worm holes, and was probably the original pastedown for the late medieval volume; recto now also inscribed at the head: '# N.Q 15 qu*art*o Vol 29' s.xvii; ex libris inscription verso s.xv in.
  Flyleaves **1)** 5 leaves of laid paper, the first two pasted together to form one leaf, one of these possibly once conjoint with pastedown, blank except for shelfmark (first leaf recto), and Archbishop Sancroft's list of contents (fourth leaf verso); **2)** medieval parchment leaf, now fol. 90, thinner, smaller and whiter than other leaves in the book; recto: a symmetrical square diagram of the type used by Boethius (cf. those reproduced in *PL* LXIV, 322, 471), roughly executed, inscribed 'contrarie, sub contrarie, contra dictorie' etc., possibly by the scribe who wrote the ex libris inscription fol. 89v; verso: a list of contents in an untidy hand s.xv, trimmed at upper edge, one entry is erased and others are crossed out.
Back *Flyleaves* 2 laid paper leaves, the first leaf has crest and plume watermark, blank; one leaf probably once conjoint with pastedown (joint repaired).
  Pastedown Single laid paper leaf in place, probably once conjoint with a flyleaf (joint repaired), blank except for refurbishment note.
Sewing stations Spinefolds not visible; see below, Sewing supports.
Sewing Spinefolds not visible.
Sewing supports 4 raised cords on the spine.
Lacing path Now over outer edges of boards; no other evidence.
Endbands Present at head and tail: sewing at head obscured by dirt and earlier covering remains; tail endband wound with blue and with white thread and tied down here and there.
Tabs None present; no other evidence.
Spine lining None present; no other evidence.
Boards Pasteboard, 230 x 151 x 4mm.
Primary covering Brown calf, with double fillets parallel with outer edges of covers and the spine; remains of gilding in fillets along thickness of fore-edges and tail edges. Spine covering renewed.
Fastenings None present; no other evidence
Chemise None present; no other evidence.

Bosses None present; no other evidence.

Chain attachments None present; no other evidence.

Labels None; contents, present library name and shelfmark tooled in gilt on spine.

Structure of Booklet (fols. 89–126) (See James, *Lambeth MSS*, 676–678, for fols. 1–88, 127–198).

Parchment Variable; qq. 1–3: hair sides very yellow and with extensive follicle marks; q. 4: thinner parchment. Careful repairs: an oval patch fol. 89; outer strip of fol. 115 (q. 2) completely replaced (original repair).

Collation $1-2^{12}$, 3 (three leaves), 4^{12} (1–3 ?missing); hair side outermost in each quire.

Quire nos. Q. 1: xxv, q. 2: xxvi, q. 3 not numbered (last leaves lost), q. 4: xxiiii, all in large lower case numerals in stylus in lower margin, qq. 1 and 4 on last leaf verso of the quire, q. 2 on penultimate leaf.

Catchwords None.

Page Layout
Dimensions

Page 188 x *c.*140–145mm (leaves are roughly trimmed, and tight rebinding makes an accurate measurement impossible).

Space ruled for writing Very variable, from 140–150 x 104–114mm.

Columns Long lines.

Pricking Fols. 91–117v: none survives; fols. 118–125: leaves folded, outer margin only $1\rightarrow12$.

Ruling Fols. 91–117v: very faint, in brown, edge-to-edge lines inconsistent; fols. 118–125: in grey, neatly executed.

Lines per page QQ. 1–3: very variable from page to page, about 41, written above top line. Q. 4: 61, written below top line (60 lines of text). Fols. 125v–126: not ruled.

Page design

fols. 91–117v   fols. 118–125

II SCRIBES

Two scribes wrote the texts. **Scribe 1** wrote fols. 91–117v (items 1–3), including marginal subheadings, in brown, the rubricated headings on fols. 102–106 (item 2), and an incipit in red, fol. 106v (item 3). His hand is small, neat and semi-cursive with at first, elaborate loops to g which he eventually relinquished to some extent as pressure on vertical space increased. This scribe used the punctus flexus. He also interpolated a paragraph in Lambeth Palace MS 457 fol.

230v, and annotated texts in the same volume, especially Seneca. **Scribe 2** wrote fols. 118–124v (item 4) in a minute hand, very upright and compressed, tending to angularity.

III DECORATION, RUBRICS AND ARTICULATION OF TEXT

Text initials *Items 1–3* (fols. 91–117v): Brown ink capitals often in skeletal form; fols. 114v–117v: many text capitals touched with red. No special treatment given to text initials in item 4.

Minor initials Fol. 95v: **2-line red R**(eddidit) with simple pale blue flourishes. Fol. 97: **4-line blue L**(egimus) with slight red flourishes; executed in margin since no space was left by scribe. Fol. 99: **7-line red F**(luvius) with extended tail and slight, red flourishes; executed in the margin since no space was left by scribe. Fol. 112v: **5-line red I**(n), undecorated; executed mainly in margin since 1-line space only left by scribe. Most sections of item 2 (fols. 101–106) are introduced by 1- or 2-line coloured initials, red or pale blue and some of these have flourishes in the other colour. Not all are supplied, e.g. on fol. 102v. None for items 3 and 4.

Major initials Fol. 91: **8-line pale blue I**(n) with extended tail with very simple red flourishes; reserved line separates top left corner of the letter from the rest. Fol. 106v: **2-line green Q**(uoniam) with extended tail, filled with simple red flourishes. Fol. 116v: **2-line red P**(er) with extended stem, clumsily executed and clumsily flourished in red. None for item 4.

Historiated initials None.

Display script The first letter after a coloured initial is often slightly enlarged and given a skeletal form for emphasis.

Titles etc. No running titles; some incipits and explicits and sub-headings for item 2 were executed by the text scribe in red, but not all are supplied. There are no titles in items 3–4.

Title page None.

IV CONTENTS

Table of contents Fol. 90v is the contents page (s.xv in) for an early or the original compilation of texts of which those in Lambeth 488 are only a part. 'Expo*sitio* cui*usd*am de muliere cananea; Q*uidam* t*r*actat*us* dompni aldredi abb*atis* de on*ere* babilonis; Sen*ec*a ad lucillum' (crossed out); 'Priscian*us* de *c*onstructi*one*' (crossed out); erased entry; 'Vetus logica et nova' (crossed out). Archbishop Sancroft's list of contents for the present volume is on the first paper flyleaf, fol. 1. The deleted items refer to texts not now present in the seventeenth-century book.

Main texts Sermons.

1a. Fols. 91–93: 'In illa die er*it* dic*it* zacharias q*uo*d sup*er* frenu*m* [ ] s*a*nctu*m* d*om*ino'.

1b. Fols. 93–95v: 'Carduus libani misit ad cedr*um* qu*ae* *est* in libano dicens'.

1c. Fols. 95v–97: 'Reddidit deus malu*m* quod fecit Abimelech'.

1d. Fols. 97–99: 'Legi*mus* in t*er*cio Regu*m* qu*o*d Rex Salomon fec*it* duos cherubin'.

1e. Fols. 99–101: 'Fluvi*us* eg*r*ediebatur de loco voluptatis ad irrigandu*m* pa*r*adisum'.

2a. Fol. 101: William of Lafford, *De Muliere Chananaea*. 'Reverendo patri in christo...Lic*et* a p*r*imo die quo *m*ihi *v*estre dulcedi*n*is honestas...Valeat ap*u*d deu*m* et homi*n*es pat*er*nitatis *v*estre begnignissi*m*a s*a*nctitas. Explicit ep*isto*la.

145

Incipit exposicio. Egressus *ihesus* secessit in partes tyri et sidones...Qui vim ve*r*bi egrediendi sive n*o*mi*n*is ve*r*balis q*u*od est eg*r*essio p*r*udente*r* intelligit'. The text, a commentary on Matthew 15, 21–28, is articulated by sub-headings. Ends fol. 106: 'In hac vita egenit p*e*nite*n*t*i*am veram et plenam co*n*sequitur indulgentiam...p*er* infinita se*c*ula se*c*ulo*rum* Amen. Explicit omelia Will*hel*mi de Lafford de Muliere chananaea. Gratul*at*io auctoris...de consu*m*pnatione op*er*is sui amen.'

2b. Fol. 106: immediately after the previous explicit and in the same hand: '(I)am tandem aliqu*a*ndo p*r*opte*r* s*a*nct*e*'. Ends: 'p*er* bona temporalia ut non amittam*us* eternam Amen.'

3. Fol. 106v: Aelred, *De Onere Babilonis*: 'Incipit t*r*actat*us* do*m*pni eylredi abb*at*is de on*er*e babilonis. Quod enim multis parit idem se*r*mo lect*i*o'. Ends fol. 117v: 'quia no*n* est qui fumili*us* pessimi agmen afugiat.' *PL* CXCV, 196ff. The text in Lambeth 488 appears to be an extract, beginning part way through sermon 2 (*PL*, CXCV, 394) and ends before the end of the printed text.

4. Fols. 118–124: a commentary on the Psalms, fragment. Begins imperfectly (just before Ps.34, 2): '*Et tunc* revelabit te*r*ra s*a*ngui*n*em suum'. Ends imperfectly at Ps. 44, 2.

Fols. 124v–125: ruled, not written; fols. 125–126: blank.

V ORIGIN AND PROVENANCE

Ex Libris Fol. ii verso: 'Hec [sic] liber est de monasterio de buldewas p*er* d*o*minum Joh*a*nne*m* Gnowsal abb*at*em p*r*aedicti loci in custodia ff*r*at*r*is henrici de valle monachi de Savigniaco posit*us* ut p*er* una*m* indentura*m* int*er* ip*s*os factam plenius apparet etc etc'. John Gnossal was the Abbot of Buildwas between 1428 and 1443 (Chibnall, *VCH*, 59).

Secundo folio (Text on parchment): p*r*ofundum

There is no firm evidence about where the texts were copied. However the fact that Scribe 1 also added a paragraph to and annotated Lambeth 457 (q.v.) suggests that Buildwas may have been the place of origin. The explicit of the text *De Muliere Chananaea* containing the author's name was not noted by James, and William of Lafford has not so far been identified. The character of the rubric, unique in the surviving Buildwas books, suggests that the author may have been a Buildwas monk and perhaps that this copy was in his own hand (the scribe used the characteristic punctus flexus). If this were the case, William's participation as scribe 1 in Lambeth 488 and his interpolation and annotation in Lambeth 457 would constitute evidence of a named Buildwas writer and scholar. An early thirteenth-century Abbot of Buildwas was called William, as was another just after the middle of the thirteenth century (Chibnall, *VCH*, 58). However such rubrics were often simply reproduced unthinkingly by subsequent copyists and this may account for the note here. When the list of contents was made, the identity of the author seems to have been unknown ('Expositio cuiusdam').

VI NOTES

VII BIBLIOGRAPHY AND PLATES

James, *Lambeth MSS,* 676–678; Ker, *MLGB,* 15.

27. LONDON, LAMBETH PALACE LIBRARY MS 457 fols. 193–254
Excerpts from Jerome's Letters; Excerpts from Seneca's letters; Excerpts from 'Abbot Gilbert'   **Date** s.xiii in
Leaves [ii paper, 132 paper], 122, [ii paper]
Foliation 1–254, of which fols. 193–254 only carry texts from Buildwas
Origin Various; fols. 193–254: ?Buildwas

See note above about this and other Buildwas fragments at Lambeth Palace.

I PHYSICAL DESCRIPTION
Binding A composite volume, rebound several times, now opens poorly; present volume bound together s.xvii in present order; rebacked since then. The present composite volume has quire letters on first leaf of each quire: A–Z, a–d. These must refer to the s.xvii rebinding. A note (fol. 133, the first parchment leaf) is marked in a s.xvii hand: 'Bundle 3 5 C'.

Endleaves
Front *Pastedown* Single laid paper leaf in place, blank; possibly once conjoint with a flyleaf (see below).
    Flyleaves 2 laid paper leaves, one probably once conjoint with the pastedown; joint now repaired; 2nd leaf has watermark: a jester's head in profile, partially trimmed. All blank except for shelfmark and list of present contents (fol. ii verso) in Archbishop Sancroft's hand (see James, *Lambeth MSS*, 635).
Back *Flyleaves* 2 laid paper leaves, one leaf probably once conjoint with present pastedown; the first has partial watermark: three balls arranged in a triangle joined by a stem; blank.
    Pastedown Single laid paper leaf in place, probably once conjoint with a flyleaf; joint now repaired; blank.
Sewing stations Now 4 (but see below, Sewing); most spinefolds now inaccessible, therefore no available evidence about earlier sewings.
Sewing Now sewn all-along with thick S-twist thread (see fols. 181–182, 189–190), usually not on all 4 sewing supports in every quire.
Sewing supports Now 4 raised cords. No earlier evidence.
Lacing path Now over outer edges of board and laced through the pasteboard boards. No earlier evidence.
Endbands Present at head and partially at tail; sewn with discoloured blue and white threads in a herringbone pattern; tied down in the centre of 5 quires (evidence of thread impressions). Remains of skin, possibly part of an earlier primary covering, still apparently attached to the head endband.
Tabs None present; no other evidence.
Spine lining No evidence visible.
Boards Pasteboard, 204 x 144 x 4mm.
Primary covering Brown calf with double fillets parallel with outer edges of boards and spine; remains of gilt in fillets along the lower and fore-edges of the boards.
Fastenings None present; no other clear evidence.
Chemise None present; no other evidence.
Bosses None present; no other evidence.
Chain attachments None present; no other evidence.
Labels None. Title, present library name and shelfmark tooled onto spine in gold.

Structure of Booklet (fols. 193–254) See James, *Lambeth MSS*, 635–8 for fols. 1–132 and 133–192.

Parchment Fairly good quality, uniformly yellowish; few holes except fol. 250; fol. 199: corner now torn away; some scraping and judder marks.

Collation 1–3⁸, 4⁶, 5–8⁸. Hair sides outermost except q. 6.

Quire nos. QQ. 1–8 are numbered 20–27 in pencil, in lower margin of last leaf in each quire and I–VIII in stylus; they are also marked in centre of lower margin of first leaf: V–Z, a–d in ink (see above). The stylus marks seem to indicate the order of these 8 quires in an earlier, though not the original, book, which also comprised quires now bound in other books.

Catchwords None.

Page Layout
Dimensions
Page 195 x *c.*130mm (variable).
Space ruled for writing 140 x 87mm for all texts.
Columns Long lines.
Pricking Leaves folded, 1→8, outer margin only; template used.
Ruling In grey, rather carelessly; edge-to-edge lines inconsistent, notably in q. 1.
Lines per page 32, written above top line.
Page design

fols. 193–200ᵛ   fols. 210–216ᵛ   fols. 217–254

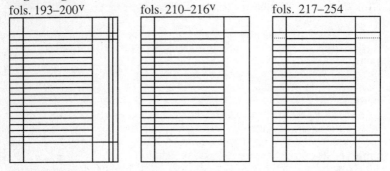

II SCRIBES
One scribe wrote all except the last leaf verso in a very small, neat and fluent hand s.xiii in, characterised by trailing tails to x, s, q and g. This scribe also wrote some of the notes in the margin and executed the rubrication. A second scribe with a similar hand wrote the last leaf verso (fol. 254v). A third added a paragraph to the end of the first text, fol. 230v, and added many marginal notes to the second text. This scribe also wrote items 1–3 in Lambeth 488 (q.v.).

III DECORATION, RUBRICS AND ARTICULATION OF TEXT
Text initials Written in brown ink by the text scribes.
Minor initials 1- or 2-line plain initials, alternately red and green, introduce most of Jerome's letters. Fol. 199: the **2-line green N**(ec) is given extended ascender and tail and is flourished in red with touches of ochre. Fol. 208: the **2-line brown A**(udi) is flourished in brown. Fol. 216: **2-line green I**(sto) is provided with a brown paraph which has an extended tail with green flourishes. Fols. 231–254 (item 2): similar 1- or 2-line initials, alternately red and green, introduce

each of Seneca's letters, probably by the same scribe, though this series of initials tends more towards extensions in the margin often 3 or 4 lines high. Fol. 248v: **1-line red Q**(uereris) has a tail, flourished with brown, which extends to the bottom of the page.

Major initials None.

Historiated initials None.

Title page None.

Display script None; the first word following a coloured initial is sometimes underlined in red (e.g. fols. 219, 219v).

Titles etc. Headings and rubrics in red in the hand of the text scribe. Fol. 193 was headed 'Seneca ad Lucillum' (s.xiv/xv), but this now crossed out and 'S. Hieron.' added in a s.xvii hand which also provided other headings and is probably that of Archbishop Sancroft. In q. 1 only, the extracts from Jerome seem to be given a letter as well as an abbreviated source identification by the scribe. Here and there throughout, one or more hands, s.xiii, added headings in the margin (e.g. fols. 199, 252). The same hand(s) may also have added the numbers in the lower margin.

IV CONTENTS

Table of contents 1) see Lambeth 488; 2) the contents of the entire volume as presently bound were provided by Archbishop Sancroft on the second flyleaf, s.xvii.

Main texts

1. Jerome, excerpts from the letters. The first begins fol. 193: 'Damasus ad Jeronimum. Ab offerente libenter accipio'. The last begins fol. 230: 'Ad pammachium de morte pauline. Sanate'. Ends fol. 230v: 'et de radice pervenis ad cacumen.' The complete letters are printed in *PL* XXII, 525ff.

Fol. 230v, an added paragraph in another hand (see Scribes above) beginning 'Quidam que cum amicis conmittenda sunt'.

2. Fols. 231–254: Seneca, excerpts from the letters. The first begins fol. 231: 'Ita fac mihi Lucili. Quaedam tempora eripiuntur nobis quedam subducuntur'. The last begins (fol. 254): 'Quocunque. quocunque me verti argumenta senectutis mee video'. Ends fol. 254: 'quae senex vivere incipiens. Non adicere et cetera.' The letters to Lucillus are printed in *PL Suppl.* I, 674–678.

3. Extracts from Abbot Gilbert; Begins fol. 254v: 'Ex dictis domni Gileberti abbatis. Bonus tactus ihesu sed attrectatus melior. Bonum opus vel querere ihesum vel tenere. Bene collocaris in lectulo'. All sentences begin with 'bonus'. Ends imperfectly fol. 254v: 'Bonum est foveri et inflammari in amplexu'. These extracts seem not to be from the writings of Gilbert Crispin as James suggests. See A.S. Abulafia and G.R. Evans, eds., *The Works of Gilbert Crispin Abbot of Westminster*, The British Academy: Auctores Britannici Medii Aevi, VIII (London, 1986).

V ORIGIN AND PROVENANCE

Ex libris Not for this booklet, but see Lambeth 488.

Secundo folio At one time (i.e. according to the stylus quire numbers): tis nec gratia

There is no clear evidence about the origin of this booklet, but the presence of the work of the main scribe of Lambeth 488 at the end of item 1 and his annotations in Lambeth 457 suggest that at least some of the copying was done at Buildwas by a Buildwas scribe/reader.

VI NOTES

1. *Numbering systems.* On the recto of most leaves in the lower margin near the vertical ruled line are small, mainly Arabic numbers (probably s.xiii) which record the cumulative total of the extracts from Jerome which are included in this compilation. A similar series was added to the leaves bearing extracts from Seneca. But for the latter text alone, Arabic leaf numbers were also added to the inner margin of the rectos, many now almost illegible. Each extract itself is numbered, probably with reference to the numbering in the collection from which the extracts were made, mainly in Arabic but some in Roman. The use of Arabic and Roman is erratic. Thus in the Seneca text, the numbers run: i...xix, xx, 21, 22, 23...39, xl, xli, 42...49, li. lii etc. On fols. 229–230, c is used for 100, and c6 for 106.

2. The reader who did the numbering in mixed Arabic and Roman numbers (see above), also made other notes (e.g. on fols. 235, 235v), an extended note on fol. 253v, and the actual (i.e. 'original') letter numbers and sometimes the sub-headings for the letters (e.g. fol. 235). This annotator's hand is small and very cramped, and he used a pale brown ink. He may have been among those who annotated some of the texts in Lambeth 456 (q.v.), e.g. the Porphyrius.

3. *Cross references or index* On fol. 254, at the end of the Seneca extracts, two short lists of words are written with an Arabic number beside each as follows: '27 inquiro; 28 desidarum; 30 cedum; 43 epistolam; 24, 83 anime; 22 quae maximus 32; 39 librorum'. The purpose of the list is not clear; it may have constituted preparatory notes for some sort of reference apparatus or index. Other numbers in the same hand are added to marginal notes on the same page. Both the 'index' and the numbers are comparable with similar interpolations in other Buildwas books (cf. Lambeth 477, Trinity B.14.5).

VII BIBLIOGRAPHY AND PLATES
James, *Lambeth MSS*, 635–638; Cheney 1953, 377 (1973, 332); Ker, *MLGB*, 15; Chibnall, *VCH*, 56.

28. LONDON, LAMBETH PALACE LIBRARY MS 456 fols. 1–126
Priscian Minor, De Constructionibus; Porphyry, Isagoge; Aristotle, Predicamenta, Peri Ermenias; 'Gilbert', De Sex Principiis; Boethius, De Divisione, De Topicis; Notes Date s.xiii
Leaves [ii paper], 127, [20 parchment and paper, 74 paper, ii paper]
Foliation 1–220 (excluding all endleaves, the number 48 used twice), of which fols. i, 1–126 only are from Buildwas.
Origin Various; fols. 1–126: probably Buildwas

See note above about this and other Buildwas fragments at Lambeth Palace.

I PHYSICAL DESCRIPTION
Binding. A composite volume, rebound several times and rebacked. Quire marks A–Q in a s.xvii hand on fol. 1 of each quire. Here and there, e.g. fols. 68, 69, 70, there are groups of lines in blue (\\ \\\ \\\\) which seem to be binder's marks, though it is not clear with which binding of the book they are associated. Superficially refurbished in 1956.
Endleaves
Front *Pastedown* Single laid paper leaf in place, probably once conjoint with a flyleaf, joint repaired; blank.

Flyleaves **1)** 2 laid paper leaves, 1 probably once conjoint with pastedown (joint repaired); first leaf has half of an elaborate watermark, shield-shaped, flanked by creatures rampant, elaborately decorated; blank except for stamped shelfmark 456; second leaf recto: blank; verso: Sancroft's contents list; **2)** parchment leaf, fol. 1 of first quire of book as now composed, poor quality and much dirtier than following leaves; recto: notes in cramped hand s.xiii, almost illegible; verso: Latin verse written as prose s.xiii (see James, *Lambeth MSS,* 632).

Back *Flyleaves* 2 laid paper leaves, 1 possibly conjoint with pastedown, joint repaired; first leaf, blank; second leaf has upper half of an elaborate crest watermark surmounted by a crown with ball and cross; blank.

Pastedown Single laid paper leaf, possibly once conjoint with an endleaf, joint repaired; blank except for refurbishment note.

Sewing stations Unclear, spinefolds largely inaccessible; at fols. 86v–87, only two stations used plus kettle stitches. But see below, Sewing supports.

Sewing Spinefolds inaccessible except at fols. 86v–87 where S-twist thread is just visible. No evidence about earlier sewings.

Sewing supports 4 raised cords on spine. No evidence about earlier sewing supports.

Lacing path 4 slips visible under pastedowns at front and back, laced through the pasteboard boards. No evidence about earlier lacing paths.

Endbands Present at tail only, cord core sewn with blue and white threads, tied down in 5 quires only.

Tabs None present; no other evidence.

Spine lining None present; no other evidence.

Boards Pasteboard, 204 x 153 x 4mm.

Primary covering Brown calf with double fillets parallel with outer edges of both covers and the spine and a single fillet along the edges (thickness); remains of gilding in fillets along the lower edge and fore-edge of covers.

Fastenings None present; no other evidence.

Chemise None present; no other evidence.

Bosses None present; no other evidence.

Chain attachments None present; no other evidence.

Labels None. Contents, library name and shelfmark tooled in gold on the spine.

Structure of Booklet (fols. 1–127) (See James, *Lambeth MSS,* 631–635 for fols. 128–220).

Parchment Variable quality, q. 1 very poor and discoloured; hair sides very yellow; all poorly prepared (tears, judder marks); quite thin, and with many holes.

Collation 1^8, 2^{10}, 3^{10} (9 lost), 4–5^8, 6^{10}, 7^8 (6 lost), 8–13^8, 14^6, 15^8, 16^8 (7 and 8 excised to stubs). Arrangement of hair and flesh sides erratic: qq. 1, 6, 7, 14, 5: hair side outside, but q. 6 with irregular placement of central bifolium; qq. 2, 3, 4, 5, 8, 9, 10, 11, 12, flesh side outside, but qq. 9 and 10 having irregular arrangement of bifolia within the quire.

Quire nos. QQ. 1–13 numbered in large, lower case Roman numerals xii–xxiii (xxii used twice), and qq. 14–16 similarly numbered ix–xi, in stylus in lower margin of the last leaf of each quire. QQ. 1–16 also given letters A–Q in lower margin of first leaf in each quire, in ink s.xvii. The stylus numbers indicate an earlier, but not the original, order of the texts once at Buildwas.

Catchwords None.

Page Layout
Dimensions
Page Trimmed at all margins and variable. QQ. 1–4: 190 x *c.*149mm; q. 5: 191 x 144mm; qq. 6–13: 191 x 150mm; qq. 14–16: 186 x 150mm.
Space ruled for writing Very variable indeed: qq. 1–4: 107–112 x 83–87mm; qq. 5–12: 106–110 x 63–66mm plus 2 gloss columns totalling 46mm; q. 13: 124 x 70 plus 48mm (to accommodate end of text within this quire); qq. 14–16: 150 x 110mm.
Columns Variable: fol. i: 2; qq. 1–4: long lines; qq. 5–13: long lines and 2 gloss columns; qq. 14–16: 2.
Pricking Outer margins much trimmed, inner margin largely inaccessible. Available evidence suggests leaves folded, outer margins only, 1→8 except q. 13: 8→1.
Ruling Mostly carelessly done in grey and in brown.
Lines per page Very variable; qq. 1–4: 28, then 27–30 towards end of text; written above top line. QQ. 5–6: 27 decreasing to 23, written below top line. QQ. 6–13: 23–26 increasing to 33 in last quire, written below top line. QQ. 14, 15, 16: 46, 53, 59 respectively, written below top line.
Page design Variable, even within a single text. Basic layouts only given below.

fols. 1–34v (qq. 1–4)   fols. 35–51v (qq. 5–6)   fols. 52–98 (qq. 7–12)

fols. 99–106 (q. 13)   fols. 107–126v (qq. 14–16)

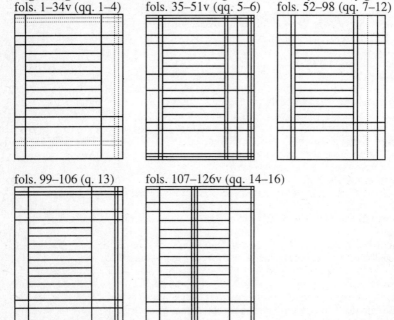

II SCRIBES
Many scribes (up to 7) contributed to the copying of the texts in this group. Usually each is responsible for at least one complete text. Texts do not always begin at the beginning of a quire, however (though changes in hands and ruling usually do), and so some degree of co-operation is demonstrated. It is a study book, with annotating hands possibly common to more than one text and one

text hand found among the annotators (scribe 7). **Scribe 1** wrote a half column of notes on the first leaf (endleaf) recto in a minute, ugly, very much abbreviated hand, s.xiii. **Scribe 2** wrote some lines of verse in prose form in an extremely tiny hand s.xiii, which tends to slope backwards; loop of g is large and parallel with the written line. **Scribe 3** wrote fols. 1–17v (qq. 1–2) and probably also fols. 27–34v (q. 4) in a very small, neat and clear hand, s.xiii. He may also have written the glosses to this text in an even smaller and more abbreviated hand in a separate stint. **Scribe 4** wrote fols. 18–26 (q. 3) in a hand of similar aspect to that of scribe 3 and using ink of identical colour, but the minim strokes, e.g. in m, n, u, i, v, are not linked but are made by separated pen strokes. **Scribe 5** wrote fols. 35–42v (q. 5) in a very compressed, upright (tending to slope backwards) book hand s.xiii in, with very short ascenders and descenders, virtually serif-less and the letter forms almost rectangular. The text written by this scribe is glossed by several hands; it is not clear whether any is the hand of the text scribe. **Scribe 6** wrote by far the largest proportion of these texts, fols. 43–106v (qq. 6–13) in a semi-cursive hand, beginning rather roughly and unevenly but achieving a more even aspect by the beginning of the second text. It is characterised by a loop to g which is parallel with the written line, a continental form of ampersand as well as crossed Tironian 'et', and the abbreviation for 'est' comprising an upper dot, wavy line and a comma-shaped stroke below. The loop to g is lost towards the end of this scribe's stint as the size of the letters decreases and the number of lines per page and words per line increases in an effort to complete the texts within q. 13. On fol. 76v the hand suddenly becomes smaller, perhaps owing to a new pen. **Scribe 7** wrote fols. 107–126v (qq. 14–16) in a spiky, cramped hand s.xiii, the text ('probably lecture notes,' James, 633), is very much abbreviated. This hand also annotated the other texts in this group, passim, and also made some brief notes in Trinity O.7.9 fols. 175, 175v.

III DECORATION, RUBRICS AND ARTICULATION OF TEXT

The decoration was almost certainly executed by one scribe all at the same time, after some of the marginal annotation had been added. It is undistinguished in quality.

Text initials Brown ink capitals written by each text scribe; no special emphasis.

Minor initials Item 1 (fols. 1–34v): 3-line plain initials alternately red and blue, sometimes with stems or tails extended in the margin making them more prominent. The first, P(rimum), on fol. 1 was executed after the marginal annotations were made and the initial is adapted to accommodate it. Item 2 (fols. 35–45): 3-line initials, alternately red and blue, sometimes extended in the margin; plain except red V(idetur) fol. 35 which is ineptly scribbled over (an attempt to flourish?) in brown. Items 3–4 (fols. 45v–70v): 3-line initials as for previous text, but also with many red and blue paraphs which have their own alternating sequence. Item 5 (fols. 71–80): fol. 71, **2-line red S**(ub) flourished with blue; thereafter all initials are blue, some flourished with red (e.g. fol. 75: U(bi)); paraphs as in the previous text, alternately red and blue. Item 6 (fols. 80v–92): no minor initials, but paraphs alternately red and blue as in previous texts. Item 7 (fols. 92–106v): fol. 92v: **2-line blue P**(ropos) with extended stem; alternately red and blue paraphs; no initials or paraphs after fol. 96.

Major initials Fol. 1 (item 1a): **5-line blue Q**(uoniam) with vertical trailing tail, flourished with red; executed after the addition of marginal annotation which the tail accommodates. Fol. 27 (item 1b): **5/6-line blue I**(n) with vertically trailing tail, flourished in red. Fol. 35 (item 2): **9-line red and blue C**(um), the colours separated by an angular reserved line; serifs joined to close letter and extended to coils; letter filled with clumsy red flourishes and tiny blue circles, the exterior of letter likewise flourished with red and blue. fol. 45v (item 3): **4-line blue E**(quivoca) filled and otherwise decorated with undistinguished red flourishes. Fol. 61 (item 4): **5-line blue P**(rimum) the stem extending to half the depth of the written space; filled and otherwise decorated with undistinguished red flourishes. Fol. 71 (item 5): **5-line blue F**(orma) with stem extending two-thirds the depth of the written space, filled and otherwise decorated with undistinguished red flourishes. Fol. 80v (item 6): **3-line blue Q**(uam), the tail extended to entire depth of page to the lower margin; filled and flourished with red penwork flourishes; across the width of the text in the upper margin but distinct from (though just touching) the initial Q, a horizontal decoration consisting of repeated 'comb' or 'jawbone' motifs in red and blue. Fol. 92 (item 7): **3-line blue O**(mnis) filled with red flourishes which also extend towards the upper and lower margins.

Historiated initials None.

Display script There is, unsurprisingly, no systematic approach to emphasising opening words. Fol. 35: (C)**um sit** is written in compressed, 4-line mixed Roman and uncial capitals alternately red and blue with minimal fine line flourishes in the other colour. Fols. 26, 99v: **Explicit liber primus** is written in chancery capitals possibly by the same scribe. Otherwise no emphasis is provided for opening words, but alternately red and blue paraphs are used (see notes under Minor initials above).

Title page None.

Titles etc. A hand s.xv has added abbreviated titles from q. 5 onwards; possibly the same hand supplied similar titles in Lambeth 457.

IV CONTENTS

Table of contents 1) See Lambeth 488. 2) the contents of the entire volume as presently bound were provided by or for Archbishop Sancroft on the second endleaf verso s.xvii.

Main texts

First endleaf recto: Notes on logic (James, 632).

First endleaf verso: A poem written as prose: 'Samson dux fortissime Victor potentissime'. Printed in full in James, 632.

1. Priscian, *De Constructionibus*, 2 Books. Begins fol. 1: 'Quoniam in an*te* expositis libr*is* de p*er*abu*s* orat*io*nis in plerisq*ue* appelo in auctoritat*em* simi*us* [sic] secuti'. Ends fol. 26. Fol. 26v blank. Book 2 begins fol. 27: 'In sup*er*iori libro de articlor*um* et p*r*onominiu*m* constructioni*bus*'. Ends imperfectly fol. 34v: 'hegio meum'. See H. Keil, ed., *Scriptores Latini, Grammatici Latini*, 7 vols (Leipzig, 1855–80), II–III.

2. Porphyry, *Isagoge*. Begins fol. 35: 'Cum sit nec*essariu*m grissarorii [sic] *et* ad eam que *est* apud ari*stotele*m predicamentorum doctrinam'. Ends fol. 45: 'com*m*unitatis *et* tradititionem.' Across the bottom of fol. 45, a drawing of the Porphyrian Tree.

3. Aristotle, *Predicamenta*. Begins fol. 45v: 'Equivoca dicu*n*tur quor*um* nomen solu*m* com*m*une est'. Ends fol. 60v: 's*ed* qui dici consueveru*n*t pene om*n*es enum*er*ate sunt.' I. Bekker, *Aristoteles Opera*, 5 vols (Berlin, 1831–70).

4. Aristotle, *Peri Ermenias*. Begins fol. 61: 'Primum op*p*ortet constituere quid sit nom*en* et quid v*er*bum'. Ends fol. 70v: 'non conti*n*git inesse co*n*traria.'

5. 'Gilbert', *De Sex Principiis.* Begins fol. 71: 'Forma *et* composi*ti*oni contingens simplex'. Ends fol. 80: '*secundum* nat*u*ram move*r*i ut ignis. Explicit.' See Albanus Heysse, ed., *Liber de Sex Principiis Gilberto Porretano Ascriptus* (Monasterii Westfalorum: Opuscula et Textus Series Scholastica, 1953). The text is now not attributed to Gilbert Porretanus (*Cod. Boethiani,* 6).

6. Boethius, *De Divisione.* Begins fol. 80v: 'Quam magnos studiosis afferat fructus scientia divid*e*ndi'. Ends fol. 92: 'brevitas pariebat*u*r dilig*e*nt*e*r ex-pressim*u*s. Explicit.' *PL* LXIV, 875–892.

7. Boethius, *De Topicis.* Begins fol. 92: 'Omnis rat*i*o disserendi q*u*am logicen. *p*eripatetici veteres appellaver*unt*'. Fol. 99v: 'Explicit liber primus.' Ends imperfectly fol. 106v: '*si*m*i*lis *enim* est navis civitati'. *PL* LXIV, 1173–1216; *Cod. Boethiani,* 164–165, no. 148.

8. Fols. 107–126: probably lecture notes on philosophy (James, 633). G. Lacombe, *Aristoteles Latinus,* 2 vols (Rome, 1939), I, 374, lists item 8 as 'Annotationes in Logicam. Philosophia dupliciter dicitur, secundum nomen et secundum rem.'

V ORIGIN AND PROVENANCE
Ex libris Not for this booklet, but see Lambeth 488.
Secundo folio heremus
There is no clear evidence about the origin of this booklet. However, the fact that the 'lecture notes hand' made a note in Trinity O.7.9 increases the likelihood that this scribe/reader was a Buildwas monk and that this booklet was made at Buildwas.

VI NOTES
The texts are all among those studied in the Trivium ('vetus logica' and rhetoric).

VII BIBLIOGRAPHY AND PLATES
James, *Lambeth MSS,* 631–635; G. Lacombe, *Aristoteles Latinus,* 2 vols (Rome, 1939), I, 374, no. 289; Ker, *MLGB,* 15; Chibnall, *VCH,* 56;

29. LONDON, LAMBETH PALACE LIBRARY MS 477
Pictor in Carmine; Themes for Sermons; Concordances etc.
Leaves [i paper], ii, 288, [ii paper]   **Date** s.xiii med.–ex.
Foliation 1–290 in pencil; medieval foliation: leaves 3–250 numbered 1–250 in centre of upper margin verso of leaves in Arabic numbers (some numbers missing or omitted, see below, Notes). Pencil foliation used here.
Origin Possibly Buildwas

This small book is a compilation, in some ways like others from Buildwas such as Trinity B.1.29 and O.7.9. All the material gathered in this book, however, relates to sermons: themes, sources, instruction, examples. It is essentially a medieval preacher's handbook. It is not beautifully made; quite clearly it was the contents that were of primary importance. It was evidently much used.

I PHYSICAL DESCRIPTION
Binding Rebound s.xvii, repaired and rebacked since; spine rigid, book opens extremely poorly.
Endleaves
Front *Pastedown* Single leaf of laid paper, blank.

Flyleaves **1**) Single leaf of laid paper in place, once conjoint with pastedown, partial watermark visible near spine comprising an elaborately decorated shield surmounted by a small cross with a circle at each extremity; blank except for stamped numbers 477; **2**) parchment bifolium, fol. ii once completely excised and then sewn back to its stub. Fol. i: notes on 'Qui vidit mulierem ad concupiscendum'; fol. i verso: a herbal remedy: 'Ista valent ad cancerosa capita. Sparge fenicts radix parelle et co[tid]ie donec radix tenera sit et vespere lavare capitam et mane cum liquore tepido istarum herbarum'. List of contents written by or for Archbishop Sancroft s.xvii (James, *Lambeth MSS*, 657) and other notes and pen scribbles; the name 'grenewey' s.xv. Fol. ii: scribbles, the names 'Tomas', 'grenewey' and 'uptun'; fol. ii verso: some verses: 'Fallitur eva dolo cibus ada gaudia finis' and 'Cum fuerint anni Completa mille ducenti'; an antethema in various hands and other scribbles, including 'greneway' some partially erased, s.xv.

Back *Flyleaves* Two single leaves of laid paper, partial watermark visible on second: bearded profile of man in a ?jester's cap; one leaf possibly once conjoint with pastedown.

Pastedown Single laid paper leaf, blank except for refurbishment note 12.6.58.

Sewing stations Now probably 4; no other evidence accessible.

Sewing Not accessible.

Sewing supports Now 4 raised cords on spine; no other evidence accessible.

Lacing path Now over outer edges of boards; no other evidence.

Endbands Present at head and tail, sewn with blue and with white thread.

Tabs None present; no other evidence.

Spine lining No evidence.

Boards Pasteboard, 176 x 124 x 4mm.

Primary covering Brown leather (calf), double fillets parallel with outer edges and spine; a gilt fillet along each edge of both covers.

Fastenings None present. 2 rusted holes at centre fore-edge of front endleaves and visible on several subsequent leaves may indicate an earlier fastening device. No clear evidence at back, but a mark in the centre of the last leaf might have been made by a central fastening pin.

Chemise None present; no other evidence.

Bosses None present; no other evidence.

Chain attachments None present; no other evidence.

Labels None.

Structure of Book

Parchment Thin, hair side yellow with prominent follicle marks, though these characteristics are less evident after q. 1. Contemporary pasted repair fols. 20, 25; sewn repair, possibly contemporary, fol. 256.

Collation Because of tight rebinding, the collation, which is irregular, is almost impossible to check; the following is taken mostly from James, *Lambeth MSS*, 657, but two front parchment endleaves are not here treated as q. 1: 1^{12}, 2^{12} (wants 1 leaf), 3^{12}, 4^{10}, 5^{10}, 6^{14}, 7^{12} (5 and 12 are singletons), 8^{12} (3 is stub), 9^{12} (5 is stub), 10^{14}, 11^{12} (3 and 9 are stubs), 12^{14} (3 is stub; including 4 after 7, quite different, very stiff parchment), 13^{12}, 14^{16}, 15^{12} (5 and 6 are singletons), 16^{14} (1 is missing), 17^{14} (14 is stub), 18^{16}, 19^{12}, 20^{12}; 21–25^{8}.

In the first section (qq. 1–20), the arrangement of the hair and flesh sides of the leaves is not consistent. Most quires have a flesh side outermost and subsequently follow a fairly regular order of hair and flesh sides facing. But several quires (e.g. 3, 4, 8, 18) have hair sides outermost, and some (e.g. 3, 4) have a markedly erratic sequence of hair and flesh sides.

Quire nos. None, but leaves are trimmed. Each quire is lettered in lower margin of fol. 1; this relates to a later, almost certainly the present, rebinding.

Catchwords None, but leaves are trimmed.

Page Layout
Dimensions
Page Variable, leaves are trimmed at all margins: *c.*166 x 120mm.

Space ruled for writing Very variable, depending on the text; trimming is close to the edges of the ruled space in most texts.

Columns Variable, depending on the text (see below, Page design).

Pricking Inner margins not visible; outer margins much trimmed leaving very little evidence.

Ruling Very variable, even within a single text, in grey and/or brown, often very carelessly done. Edge-to-edge ruling also very erratic, both as to whether any lines are so ruled and as to which lines, especially in mid-page (see, for example, fols. 64–72). Writing is above top line.

Lines per page Variable from text to text, much of it ad hoc and changing with the ruling pattern (see below): q. 1 (items 1–2): 35; qq. 2–3 (to the 6th leaf verso; item 3): 39–43; qq. 3 (7th leaf recto)–4 (items 4–5a): 40; qq. 5–19 (items 5b–11): 34–40; q. 20 (1st leaf to 10th recto; item 12): 42; q. 20 (10th leaf verso to 12th; items 13–14): 35; qq. 21–25 (item 15): 38.

Page design
fols. 3–14 (q. 1)   fols. 15–31v (qq. 2–3)   fols. 32–47 (qq. 3–4)

fols. 48–238 (qq. 5–19)   fols. 239–248 (q. 20)   fols. 251–290
and fols. 248v–250v   (qq. 21–25)

157

II SCRIBES
Very many scribes participated in the compilation of these texts, especially the major Concordance on fols. 58–216v, which was ruled and headed before any text was written. The other, shorter texts are each generally written by a single scribe, all in very small, cramped hands s.xiii med. It is difficult to say if any text scribe reappears except in the long concordance. Of greater interest are some of the annotators. See below, Notes.

III DECORATION, RUBRICS AND ARTICULATION OF TEXT
Text initials No special effort to distinguish capitals in the texts.
Minor initials None.
Major initials None
Historiated initials None.
Title page None.
Display script None.
Titles etc. Running title and heading in several hands, mainly in red ink.

IV CONTENTS
Table of contents No original table survives. On first front parchment flyleaf verso, a list of contents provided by Archbishop Sancroft, s.xvii.
Main texts (See James, 658–660 for a very full account of the contents of this book.)
1. Fols. 3–10v: *Pictor in Carmine*, incomplete, ends at item 129 (9 items are missing). Printed in an article by M.R. James published posthumously in *Archaeologia*, 94 (1951), 141–166. The Lambeth MS is the 13th of 13 copies listed by James (144).
2. Fols. 11–14: *Tematha in Assumptione*; themes for sermons on the Feast of the Assumption and on other Feast days, the last (fol. 14): *Thema ad Clerichos*. Fol. 14v blank.
3. Fols. 15–31v: *Concordancie de Biblia Secundum Alphabetum Composite*. Begins: 'Abire in solitudinem Deut 6; Abire in via chynn. Jude c. Deut*eronomo* xix b'. Ends fol. 31v: 'Zelare Jud*ices* ix b S*apientia* i f.' 'Zorababel Zacheria*s* iii' added later. This is a verbal concordance to the Vulgate, based on or derived from that invented by Hugh of St. Cher (at the Dominican house of St. Jacques in Paris) in the 1230s but containing very few Biblical references for each word.
4. Fols. 32–47: Texts and extracts relating to the seven deadly sins, and sermons: Begins: *De Superbia*. 'Daniel v Quoniam elevatu*m* est cor nabug*odnosor*'. Fol. 47v blank.
5a. Fol. 48: *De Duplici Adventu*.
5b. Fols. 48–49v: 'In die apostolorum petri et pauli'.
5c. Fols. 49v–50v: 'Leo fortissim*a* bestia ad nulli*us* pavebit occurs*um*'.
6. Fols. 50v–57v *Ars Predicandi*. 'Quoniam emulatores estis spirituum'. A note by J.A. Russell attached to the Lambeth Palace copy of James states that this text is by Richard of Thetford.
7. Fols. 58–216v: *Concordancie de Biblia Secundum Alphabetum Composite et Primo de hac Littere a Amor...Zelus*. This appears to be a version of the *Concordanciae Anglicanae*, a fuller concordance based on St. Hugh's work (see item 3 above) but elaborated by English Dominicans, also at St. Jacques, some decades later. Here, lengthy passages under each subject heading are entered, with Biblical or patristic references in the margin. It appears to be more a thematic reference work than a concordance proper. In several blank spaces in

this text, Buildwas tituli (see below, Origin and provenance), the names 'greneway' and 'upton' and passages in code are added by later hands, s.xiii, xv.

8. Fols. 216v–217: *Sermo in Festivitate Omnium Sanctorum*. 'Ecce ergo sternam per ordinem lapides tuos'.

9. Fols. 217v–225v: *Capitula Operis Sequentis*; notes and biblical texts for sermons on 65 topics from 'Contra acceptores personarum' to 'De susuratione'. Fol. 226: *Sermo de Sancto Johanne Baptista*.

10. Fols. 227–236 Notes on virtues: 'Compilationes quedam de virtutibus. De patiencia'.

11. Fols. 236–238: Sermon: *In Nativitate Sancti Iohannis Baptiste*. Fol. 238, a half leaf: verso blank except for scribbles (Greneway, Upton) erased.

12. Fols. 239–248: *Libellus de Species Specierum;* notes in tabular form on the seven deadly sins.

13. Fols. 248v–249v: Extracts from the epistles of Jerome. Begins: 'Ad eliodorum exhortativa epistola 32. Licet parvulus pendat ex colla nepos'.

14. Fols. 250–250v: *Sermo Beati Bernardi Abbatis de Proprietate Dencium*. Begins: 'Dentes tui sicut grex tonsarum'.

15. Fols. 251–290: *Interpretationes Hebraeorum Nominum Secundum Remisium* [sic] *per hanc Litteram a et post Sequitur*. Begins: 'Aaz apprehendens vel apprensio vel testimonium'. Ends: 'Zusum Consiliantes eos vel consiliatores eorum.'. The sequence of words is ordered alphabetically to the second letter.

Fol. 290–290v: various notes. 'De figuris algorismi. Novem sunt figure', 'De irregularibus', and various scribbles, e.g. 'greneway'. Fol. 290v: the same antethema as on fol. ii verso, and other notes.

V ORIGIN AND PROVENANCE

Ex libris None, but Buildwas tituli s.xiii/xiv on fols. 94v, 129v and 132v indicate that the book was at Buildwas then: 'Titulus monasterii beate Marie de Buldewas ordinis Cisterciensis...'.

Secundo folio Nascitur

It is not possible to say for certain where this book was made, but its character as a preacher's handbook and the indications that the book was at Buildwas at least by the late thirteenth or fourteenth century (see above) make it quite possible that it was made, or at the very least, compiled there. If the notes with cross-references to Gregory's *Moralia in Job* (see below, Notes 2) are in the hand of the Buildwas indexer, this would also confirm the book's presence at Buildwas

The names Grenewey and Upton, which appear here and there throughout this book, appear also in other Buildwas books: Trinity B.1.4, B.1.14, B.3.15. The name Upton is associated in other books with that of John Gnossal, Abbot of Buildwas *c*. 1428–1443, and this would seem to link the book to Buildwas in the fifteenth century. On fol. 178v the names are written with the addition: 'karissime ffrater monasterie Benderellus' together with the beginning of the Lord's prayer. So far, Benderell is unidentified. The same hand wrote part of another prayer on fol. 210. The hand which completed the titulus on fol. 129v also seems to have written 'Thomas' in the upper margin using a very similar greyish ink. The name Thomas is associated with Greneway in other Buildwas books.

The book was among those acquired for Lambeth Palace Library by Archbishop Sancroft s.xvii.

VI NOTES

1. The medieval foliation in the centre of the upper margins of each verso is now inaccurate and may always have been so. Numbers 83, 98, 122, 128, 134, 186 are missing (cf. Lambeth 73). Fol. 238 is a half-leaf and was not numbered by the foliator. The foliator added notes and cross-references here and there throughout the concordance (evidence of colour of ink and Arabic number formation). On fol. 183v (his fol. 182), this hand wrote: 'de xii *proprietatis* palme q*ue*re post i*n* 184 fol'; on the page facing his fol. 184 (actually fol. 186), the twelve properties are listed in his hand. On his fol. 180 under the sub-heading: 'pax', he wrote: 'de pace quere post 183 fol.', and on the page facing his fol. 183, a long passage on pax is written in his hand. At the top of this leaf he also added a cross-reference:'plus sup*er* 180 fol.' The same hand made other lists elsewhere, e.g. fols. 102, 157v, 185, 188v.

2. Throughout the long Concordance a late thirteenth-century hand, possibly that of the Buildwas indexer (see Trinity B.14.5) added references to appropriate chapters in the first 5 books of Gregory's *Moralia in Job*, a copy of which was held at Buildwas. Fragments of books 6–10 survive as Lambeth 109, and its surviving leaves are numbered throughout and within each chapter. In Lambeth 477, the variation in the ink colour and the character of the annotating hand itself (e.g. fol. 153), indicate that the notes were added at different times.

3. On fol. 120v there is an inscription: 'No*ve*rint uni*ve*rsi per praesentes quod ego Walter*us* dedi *con*cessi *et* hac'. It is followed by 2 passages in cypher (printed in James, *Lambeth MSS*, 659). Another cypher was written by the same hand on fol. 142v.

VII BIBLIOGRAPHY AND PLATES
James, *Lambeth MSS*, 657–660; Ker, *MLGB*, 15.

30. OXFORD, BALLIOL COLLEGE MS 35A
Peter Lombard, Magna Glossatura on the Psalms (imperfect)   **Date** s.xii ex
Leaves [i paper], i, [ii], i, 255
Foliation 1–259 (includes all parchment leaves)
Origin ?Northern France   **Fig.** 11

This book is one of only three illuminated books that have survived from Buildwas. The others are Balliol 173B, to which 35A is related, and Trinity B.4.3. All appear to have been gifts to the monastery. This book seems in particular to have been highly prized since it has a unique ex libris/ex dono inscription which includes an anathema against anyone who might be tempted to steal it. The inscription was written by the indexer of Trinity B.14.5.

I PHYSICAL DESCRIPTION
Binding Resewn at least twice, present binding s.xviii; boxed.
Endleaves
  Front*Pastedown* 1) Laid paper leaf in place, first leaf of a bifolium, inscribed verso 'Arch.E.5.4'. (s.xviii), 'MS 35a' (pencil) and with Balliol College book-plate. 2) Earlier parchment pastedown now detached and trimmed by *c.*70mm along fore-edge (see below, flyleaves 2).
    Flyleaves 1) Second leaf of laid paper bifolium, no watermark, blank. 2) Detached pastedown, once the first leaf of a bifolium, conjoint leaf now excised

to stub; recto: remains of brownish paste and white paste near spine (in a strip *c*.60mm wide); impressions of 5 sewing support insertions (see below), rusted holes possibly left by boss nails on an earlier cover and, at upper and lower edges, impressions of 2 different brown leather covering turn-ins. Verso: Balliol College ex libris/ex dono inscription, and title s.xv (this repeated in lower margin fol. 4). **3)** A misplaced parchment bifolium, the first leaf excised to wide stub (*c*.40mm) with marks of an earlier binding recto and strip of laid paper pasted to verso. Recto of the second leaf blank, verso with titles (Jerome), Balliol ex libris/ex donor inscription and impressions of a full-page red initial letter P. This bifolium is from another book (MS 155; Mynors, *Balliol MSS*, 25), the leaves probably misplaced during the eighteenth-century rebinding. **4)** Second leaf of a bifolium, the first excised to narrow stub; recto: an inscription recording donation of the book to Buildwas in 1277; verso: section of gloss (an omission) with marginal notes, contemporary with text.

Back *Flyleaves* None present, no other evidence.

Pastedown Single leaf of laid paper in place, blank except for Mynors's folio count May 1932.

Sewing stations Now 6. Impressions in some spinefolds and on detached pastedown indicate that earlier there were 5: (tail) I 20 K 41*64*68*71*61*45 K 25 I mm (head).

Sewing Now all-along with brown S-twist thread. Impressions in some spinefolds (e.g. fols. 63–4) indicate an earlier sewing, all-along.

Sewing supports Now 6 thin, double cords. Marks on detached pastedown show that in an earlier binding (but probably not originally) the book was sewn on 5 supports *c*.10mm wide.

Lacing path Over the outer edges of boards, through to inner surface and fixed under pastedown. Impressions on detached pastedown indicate that earlier supports were laced into the boards through channels which included parallel channels on the inner faces of the boards, 45–50mm long, beginning *c*.10mm from spine edge.

Endbands Present at head and tail, thin white skin cores, sewn with blue and brown S-twist threads; fragmentary at head, still tied down twice with blue thread at tail; no evidence that these were laced into present boards.

Tabs None present; no other evidence.

Spine lining None present; a strip of white paste remains, *c*.55–65mm wide, covering all sewing support insertion impressions on front detached pastedown, may have been left by an earlier spine lining.

Boards Pasteboard, 403 x 297 x 4mm.

Primary covering Now rough calf, with stamped decorative frame design on front and back covers; stains on the detached pastedown indicate an earlier (but probably not original) cover also brown, with narrow turn-ins.

Fastenings None present; no other evidence.

Chemise None present; no other evidence.

Bosses Holes at top and bottom of detached pastedown at head and tail of inner margin indicate the earlier presence of bosses at least on front board (fore-edge trimmed); fol. 3 and following leaves show clear marks at each corner of the former position of bosses, each once attached by 4 nails irregularly disposed.

Chain attachments A vertical pair of small, rusted holes in the centre of both upper and lower margins of detached pastedown may indicate the position of earlier chain attachments.

Labels On spine, fragment of old (?s.xviii) paper title label, handwritten; modern printed paper label: '35'.

Structure of Book
Parchment Fair quality, fairly evenly coloured but now badly cockled throughout, with widespread signs of water damage. Several later repairs to cuts in fore-edge with pink, ?silk S-twist thread (e.g. fols. 9, 36, 37).
Collation $1-32^8$; hair side outside in each quire.
Quire nos. QQ. 1–32 in Roman numerals, lower margin of verso of last leaf, some partly trimmed: q. 1 in blue, q. 2 in red, elaborately flourished in red and green; qq. 3–32 in small brown ink numerals, qq. 10–11 in different style and ink.
Catchwords QQ. 17, 19–20, 23–26, 28–29, 31–32: lower margin of verso of last leaf; others may have been trimmed.

Page Layout
Dimensions
Page 400 x 295mm.
Space ruled for writing (primary text): slightly variable: qq. 1–2: 237–240 x 160; qq. 3–32: 250 x 161mm.
Columns 2 columns for text and gloss which are written successively; a narrow column ruled at inner margin and 2 at the outer margin for further notes. These fluctuate slightly in width.
Pricking Pricked for the gloss, leaves folded, 1→8 in both margins except q. 2: 8→1. Q. 2: double pricking for last and 6th from last lines. Several groups of quires show repeated irregularities indicating use of a template, but different templates were evidently used for qq. 1–2, qq. 3–5; qq. 6–32 (see below: Lines per page).
Ruling Q. 1–middle q. 3 (fol. 23v): heavy grey lines, lines 1 and 6, 6th from last and last ruled from edge-to-edge and across the central vertical lines; thereafter the ruling is fainter in brown, all lines ruled across the central vertical lines, and lines 1 and 2, 5 and 6, the 6th and 5th from last and last 2 lines are ruled edge-to-edge. The annotator, who added copiously to each page, ruled his own very narrow lines in all margins ad hoc, and these have often obscured the scribe's ruling.
Lines per page Ruled for the gloss, the text written on alternate lines; text and gloss written below top line. qq. 1–2: 51 ruled (50 written); qq. 3–5: 53 ruled (52 written); qq. 6–21: 52 ruled (51 written).
Page design
fols. 4–23v

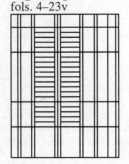

fols. 24–259v

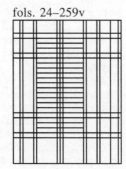

II SCRIBES

The text was written by 2 main scribes. **Scribe 1** wrote text and gloss on fols. 4–23v (col. a). His text hand is a large, upright, fairly compressed hand s.xii ex, more angular at the tops of the letters than at the bottom, with clubbed minims with deliberately applied feet and thickened ascenders, especially to d. He used ampersand. His gloss hand is less angular. At least 3 scribes shared the writing of text and gloss in the next two columns (fols. 23v col. b–24v col. a). **Scribe 2** wrote the remainder of the text and gloss on fols. 24v (col.b)–259v in a similar hand to that of scribe 1, but slightly more angular and with flat feet to minims. This scribe also used ampersand, and many more abbreviations than scribe 1. A third hand wrote a passage on fol. 3v which had apparently been omitted from the gloss.

Contemporary additions to the marginal notes were made by one or two readers (e.g. fols. 23v, 33v).

III DECORATION, RUBRICS AND ARTICULATION OF TEXT

Text initials 1) The opening of each passage of each psalm is marked by a 2-line red or blue initial, each finely flourished in the other colour. New sentences within the same passage begin with similar but slightly smaller initials, similarly flourished. **2)** Each gloss passage begins with a 1-line initial in red or blue, with flourishes in the other colour as for the Psalm initials.

The alternation of colours is continuous throughout text and gloss and all must have been made at the same time. They were executed by the artist of the minor penwork initials who may also have been the painted initial artist (compare initials on fols. 73 and 137).

Minor initials Those psalms which do not stand at major divisions of the Psalter open with beautifully executed penwork initials, which show considerable invention. Typically they are 7- or 8-line in height (some are slightly smaller), with no coloured field, the letter formed in red, blue or red and blue, the colour(s) split or divided by reserved lines in various configurations and/or by panels filled with patterns. They are filled with interlocking foliate and flower motifs in brownish-pink (often used as a background within the letter), blue, red, green, yellow, sometimes all 5 together, the colours often separated by elegant lines reserved against the parchment. No two initials are exactly alike; many, especially A and I, have carefully flourished extended stems or tails, often edged with green. They are neat and elegant, working very effectively with the painted initials in signalling psalms not at major divisions.

Major initials A series of fully painted initials with gold at each of the major divisions of the Psalter, that for Psalm 1 now excised. Each is set on a square field of colour, mostly blue, but sometimes grey; one is red and one gold. The fields of colour are framed with green and red, or green and white lines, and are decorated with delicate white dots arranged in threes and around a circle in flower formation. Exceptions are the gold field (fol. 122), which has no other decoration, and the red on fol. 73.

1) Historiated initials Fol. 46v: **12-line shaded red D**(ominus; Ps. 26), with gold inset crescents and with terminal comprising a coiled dragon biting a channel-style 'white lion'; inside letter, against a gold background, bearded figure of Samuel (right) in long red and purple robes, holding a blue flask and anointing the eyes or forehead of David (left) who wears a short blue tunic and who holds a club; blue field. Fol. 177v: **13-line shaded-blue C**(antate; Ps. 97) with inset gold crescent and red dragon's-head terminals; inside letter, against a gold

163

background; David (left), bare-legged in a short red tunic and with dishevelled hair defends himself with a large green shield against a large, erect brown lion. David's right hand is clenched, as if he were holding a sword, but no sword is shown; grey field.

2) **Decorated initials** Fol. 4: **12-line gold C**(um), inside letter against a red background with abraded gold dots, a blue coiled dragon (with leaf terminal to tail) biting a channel-style 'white lion'; grey field. Fol. 5: **20-line B**(eatus, Ps. 1), excised. Fol. 73: **12-line blue D**(ixi, Ps. 38) with inset gold crescents, the letter filled with a single, very elaborate stylised flower in red, green, blue, grey, ochre and brown, exquisitely executed, with a smaller flower in the coiled terminal to the ascender (cf. Balliol 173B, fol. 139v); red field. Fol. 95v: **13-line shaded red Q**(uid; Ps. 51) with inset gold crescents; inside letter against a gold background, a bald, shaded blue scroll with 2 stylised flower terminals and 6 intertwined channel-style 'white lions'; tail of letter is formed by a dragon hanging by its tail, confronting a cowering blue lion, the whole extension heavily outlined in green (compare with terminal to P, Balliol 173B, fol. 152); pale blue field. Fol. 96v: **9-line gold D**(ixit; Ps. 52) with inset panels of red with delicate overlaid lines and scrolls in white (compare P, Balliol 173B, fols. 112, 152); inside letter against a red background with delicate white flourishes, 2 bald, shaded blue scrolls with tri-lobed 'folded leaf' terminals; grey field. Fol. 122: **12-line shaded blue and pink S**(alvum; Ps. 68) the letter formed by two interlocking scrolls with soft-edged white lines and dots along their lengths, terminating in biting heads and in stylised flowers; 4 contorted 'white lions' are intertwined in the scrolls; the background to the letter is continuous with its rectangular colour field, which is gold. Fol. 152: **12-line red and gold E**(xultate; Ps. 80) with inset gold crescent; inside each half of the letter against a gold background, delicately incised with elegant scrolls, a blue naked man seated on the back of and struggling with a 2-headed pink channel-style lion-like monster with a bushy tail; blue field. Fol. 181: **13-line gold D**(omine; Ps. 101); inside letter against a red background, 4 bald blue and green, shaded scrolls with small flower and dragon's-head terminals interlock, and entwined among them are 2 channel-style 'white lions'; the ascender is formed by a dragon with a foliate tail and red biting head, enclosed by a thick green line continuous with the initial outline; blue field. Fol. 202: **12-line shaded blue D**(ixit; Ps. 109) with inset gold panels; inside the letter against a gold background are 4 bald pink, blue and green scrolls with very simple leaf and 'snake's-head' terminals, each with a figure inside the scroll: a blue bear-like creature playing a harp, a greyish ?monkey with a crutch, a blue naked man and a greyish creature with a pale human head playing a stringed instrument with a bow; the upper stroke of letter is formed by a thin scroll with an elaborate flower terminal; purple square field patterned with lines and circles in blue and pink and with white, green and yellow border.

Display script 1) Inconsistently provided at the beginning of psalms: fol. 4: (C)**um omnes** in 3-line compressed capitals, alternately red and blue, decorated with hairline flourishes in the other colour. Fol. 5: (Ps. 1): completely excised. Fol. 46v (Ps. 26): (D)**ominus** in 3-line compressed capitals, alternately red and blue. Fol. 122 (Ps. 68): (S)**alvum** ('a' originally omitted) in 3-line compressed capitals alternately red and blue. Fol. 15 (Ps. 80): (E)**xultate** in 3-line compressed capitals alternately red and blue. Fol. 202v (Ps. 109): (D)**ixit dominus** in 2-line mixed capitals alternately red and blue, flourished in the other colour.

2) In q. 2 only by a less good scribe: fol. 6: (Q)**uare** in 2-line mixed capitals alternately red and blue. Fol. 7v: (D)*omine* in 2-line mixed capitals alternately red and blue, final e flourished in red. Fol. 8v: (C)**um** in 1-line mixed capitals alternately red and green, final m flourished in red. Fol. 10v: (V)**erba** in 2-line mixed capitals alternately blue and red. Fol. 12v: (D)*omine* in 1-line mixed capitals alternately blue and red. Fol. 14v: (D)**omine** in 1-line mixed capitals, alternately red and green. Fol. 17: (D)**omine** in 1-line mixed capitals in red. Fol. 18v: (C)**onfitebor** in 1-line mixed red capitals.

Titles No running titles; Psalms are numbered in red throughout in small Roman numerals in the margin by scribe 2. The texts of the tituli are noted vertically in the margin for each psalm, but these are seldom supplied by the rubricator. Fol. 1v: 'Glos*a* sup*er* psalter*ium*' in hand s.xv.

Title page None.

IV CONTENTS

Table of contents None.

Main texts Peter Lombard, *Magna Glossatura* (on the Psalms).

Fol. 3v: an omitted gloss passage: 'Greg*orius*. Job ait. Non salvat *im*pios *et* paup*eribus* iudicium t*ri*buit'. Ends: 'iudiciarie potestatis ost*en*ditur.'

Fol. 4: 'Cum omnes p*rophe*tas sp*iritu*s s*an*cti'. Fol. 5 text begins: 'Beatus vir'. Gloss begins: 'Beatus cui om*n*ia optata succedere'. Ends imperfectly at Psalm 146, 9: Text: 'Qui dat iumentis escam ipsorum et pullis corvorum invocantibus eum'. Gloss ends: '*pullis corvorum* id est filius paga[norum]'. *PL* CXCI, 55–1277.

V ORIGIN AND PROVENANCE

Ex Libris Fol. 1v: 'Liber domus de Balliolo in Oxon. de legat m*agister* Roberti Thwaites quond*am* mag*ist*ri eiusd*em* domus ac Decan*us* de Aukland', s.xv.

Fol. 3: 'Liber s*an*cte Marie de Buldewas q*uem* mag*iste*r Walt*eru*s de Brug' d*ictu*s le Paumi*er* legavit eid*em* domui Anno do*mini* m° cc° lxx° vii° temp*ore* frat*ris* Will*elm*i Tyrry tu*n*c Abbatis loci eiusd*em* q*u*i com*m*uni assens*u* convent*us* sui int*er*veniente s*en*t*en*tiam excom*m*unicationis in om*n*es ip*s*ius alienatores vel eius alienationis fautores sollempnit*er* fulminavit.' The hand is that of the Indexer (see Trinity B.14.5).

Secundo folio titulus

The book was made probably on the continent in the very late twelfth century, possibly together with Balliol 173B (q.v.), a related text, which may have been decorated by the same painter, or at least in the same workshop. Chibnall, *VCH*, 55, surmises that Walter the Palmer of Bridgnorth, who gave the book to Buildwas in 1277, may have been related to Master Alan the Palmer of Bridgnorth who made William, Abbot of Buildwas, an executor of his will *c*.1296. Since the book was bequeathed to Buildwas only in 1277, it is unlikely that Walter himself was the original owner.

By the mid-fifteenth century it was in the possession of Robert Thwaites (for a time Master of Balliol and Chancellor of the University, who died in 1458; see Mynors, *Balliol MSS*, xx). Thwaites, who may well have bought the book in Oxford, bequeathed it to Balliol College.

VI NOTES

VII BIBLIOGRAPHY AND PLATES

Mynors, *Balliol MSS*, 25; Ker, *MLGB*,15; Chibnall, *VCH*, 55–6; Wittekind, *Kommentar*, 257.

31. OXFORD, BALLIOL COLLEGE MS 173B
Peter Lombard, Pauline Epistles, glossed (imperfect)   **Date** s.xii ex
Leaves i, 204, ii
Foliation 1–207 (including fol. 3, largely excised)
Origin ?Northern France

This book is one of only three illuminated books that have survived from Buildwas. The others are Balliol 35A, to which 173B is related, and Trinity B.4.3. All appear to have been gifts to the monastery.

I PHYSICAL DESCRIPTION
Binding Resewn probably twice, most recently s.xvii; boxed.
Endleaves
> **Front** *Pastedown* None present. Possibly originally fol. 1 of a separate bifolium of which now only a stub remains.
> *Flyleaves* Fol. 2 of a separate bifolium, conjoint with stub (see above); recto blank; list of capitula for Romans, verso.
> **Back** *Flyleaves* **1)** Fol. 1 of a bifolium; lower half recto inscribed (inverted) with book title and Balliol ex dono and ex libris inscription s.xv. **2)** Detached pastedown (see below), conjoint with other flyleaf; blank except for impressions and marks.
> *Pastedown* None present. A detached pastedown, fol. 2 of a separate bifolium, bears glue or paste remains, impressions of sewing support channels and present covering turn-ins. On upper edge verso, a different, colourless impression of another turn-in, probably contemporary with sewing support impressions. Otherwise blank.

Sewing stations Now 4; earlier 4 different stations: at fols. 117v–118, impressions of another sewing thread and sewing holes (approx): (tail) I 17 K 34*80*86* 81*76 I mm (head); no evidence about upper kettle stitch. Evidence of sewing support impressions on detached pastedown (approx.): (tail) I 71*79*85*73*64 I mm (head), approximately the same (though inverted; see above, Back Flyleaves) as those indicated at fols. 117v–118; no evidence for kettle stitch.
Sewing Now all-along with thin, beige S-twist thread. Fragments of thick, white S-twist thread surviving in some spinefolds may have been part of a previous sewing; such thread could have made the Z-twist impressions visible in the lower spinefolds of the centre quires.
Sewing supports Now 4 double, brown leather supports. Earlier, 4 supports, 7–9mm wide (evidence of impressions on detached pastedown).
Lacing Pattern Over the outer edges and through to inner face of boards *c.*37mm from the spine edge; slips run parallel on the inner face for *c.*25mm and are then pulled into the thickness of the board to secure them.
Endbands Present at head and tail; rolled white tawed skin core, sewn with natural coloured S-twist thread, tied down in several quires, the endbands never laced into present boards. Earlier endbands sewn with thick S-twist thread (evidence of thread impressions in spinefolds).
Tabs None present; no other evidence.
Spine lining None present; no other evidence.
Boards White pulpboard, 390 x 278 x 7mm; a few printed letters and fragments of cord visible in pulp of board. Inside top board, Balliol book-plate inscribed '345' (ink), 'Arch E.10.6' (ink) and 'MS 173B' (pencil).

Primary covering Now brown leather (calf) with dark triple fillets at all 4 extreme edges of both covers and double fillets on board edges and across spine. The turn-in of an earlier, probably uncoloured, covering left an impression on the detached pastedown (see above).

Fastenings 2 holes at fore-edge of detached pastedown (back), 90mm from upper and 83mm from lower edges, may indicate the position of earlier catches or fore-edge strap attachments.

Chemise None present; no other evidence.

Bosses Holes on both back endleaves at upper and lower edges near spine and at upper edge near fore-edge may indicate the position of earlier corner bosses. It is unclear how another green-rimmed hole on the detached pastedown came about. It is too far off-centre to have been made by a regularly placed central boss, even taking leaf trimming into account.

Chain attachments None present. A former chain attachment left a rectangular impression with holes at lower fore-edge of front cover. The marks are on the present primary covering and are thus clearly contemporaneous with or postdate the present binding.

Labels On spine, remains of paper label with handwritten title and shelfmark s.xvii and xviii; modern printed label with present shelfmark.

Notes The endleaf bifolium now at the back of the book must once have been at the front since the inscription is at present upside down. This leaf would originally have been the second leaf of a front endleaf bifolium, the s.xv inscription then written on the verso. This exactly reflects the front endleaf structure of Balliol 35A, a companion volume. It does not, however, fit with the extant stub and flyleaf structure now at the front. The now misplaced endleaf bifolium must have been added in a medieval rebinding, predating, or contemporary with, the Balliol inscription (s.xv ex) and moved to the back during the seventeenth-century rebinding.

Structure of Book

Parchment Good quality, well prepared, evenly coloured; now badly cockled at spinefold.

Collation Several quires are missing: 1 (2 excised), 2–5⁸ // 8⁸ // 12–15⁸ // 18–24⁸ // 26–28⁸, 29⁸ (wants 3–6), 30–34⁸. Hair side outside in all quires except q. 12.

Quire nos. QQ. 1–34, lower margin of verso of last leaf in large Roman numerals in the scribe's brown ink, those for qq. 1–3, 5 with flourishes; qq. 22–34 in different style of large lower-case numerals in brown ink.

Catchwords None.

Page Layout
Dimensions

Page 378 x 278mm. Unevenly trimmed at all margins, probably in the seventeenth century. A folded-over corner at upper inner corner of second back endleaf shows that at least 10mm was trimmed from the upper edge for the present covers. This degree of loss is borne out by lost notes etc. at the edge of all margins, especially the upper margin.

Space ruled for writing Very difficult to measure because of cockling; c.280–286 x 194–207mm.

Columns 2 columns for text and gloss which are written continuously; further columns at outer edges ruled for subheadings.

Pricking Much pricking in all outer margins trimmed, and very difficult to see in many inner margins, but available evidence indicates outer (including upper and lower) margins are pricked 1→8, and inner margins 8→1. This is a sensible practice since it ensures that at least two sets of holes are clearly available on all double leaves to guide the horizontal ruling.

Ruling In grey sometimes appearing brown, neatly done, though edge-to-edge lines are inconsistently ruled, sometimes not at all. Generally, the first and last three lines are so ruled. Ruled for the gloss.

Lines per page 44; text written on alternate lines below the top line; gloss written above top line.

Page design

fols. 2–207

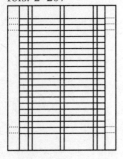

II SCRIBES

One scribe wrote text and gloss throughout in a clear, very upright and fairly angular hand, s.xii ex. The same scribe provided sub-headings in the margins and the names of authorities in red. The text and gloss are extensively corrected throughout, the corrections often executed by the scribe over an erasure (e.g. fols. 66v, 69, 80) or omissions supplied interlinearly. Two correctors seem to have been co-operatively at work in the margins. It appears that one corrector wrote out the precise passage in need of correction and another, possibly an assistant but possibly the scribe himself, supplied in a smaller hand the text which must be erased in order to provide room for the correction to be incorporated (e.g. fols. 84v, 86v, 89v, 120v). Sometimes the smaller hand wrote out the whole of the passage to be corrected, including text needing to be erased (e.g. fol. 102v). It perhaps suggests that the exemplum against which the text was being corrected was available for a very short time, and was not to hand when the corrections were actually being made.

III DECORATION, RUBRICS AND ARTICULATION OF TEXT

The text initials and minor initials were executed by the same scribe.

Text initials Text passages open with 2-line initials alternately red and blue, undecorated except on fols. 8v–9; gloss passages, and divisions in the gloss passages and the topic headings preceding each epistle, open with 1-line undecorated capitals, alternately red and blue.

Minor initials Prefaces open with 4-line initials, red or blue, those for the first 3 epistles decorated with simple flourished motifs in the alternate colour; lists of topics which precede each epistle open with a 3-line initial, red or blue, those for the first 3 epistles decorated with the other colour in a similar style: fols. 90–

90v; 111v–112; 127–127v; 139–139v; 146–146v; 151–151v; 163; 166; 169v; 171.

Major initials A series of double, fully painted initials with gold to text and gloss, several lost with missing quires or excised from extant leaves. The stems of each pair of letters are abutted, the larger opening the epistle and the smaller the gloss. The bowl of each letter, large or small, is set against a square field of colour, often with tiny white dots in triangle or flower formations, and usually this field is framed with a thin (usually white) and a thick (usually green) line. This outer line sometimes outlines the entire double initial. This formula is repeated throughout the book. The initials on fol. 147 are covered with a piece of silk.

Fol. 2: **10-line P**(rincipia), excised. Fol. 3: **P**(aulus) leaf excised]. Fol. 91: **P**(aulus) initial excised. Fol. 112 (text): **8-line blue P**(aulus) with foliate tail, the letter constructed of framed panels of gold and pink/beige; filled with blue shaded scrolls with grey, blue, pink and ochre foliate terminals, against a pink/beige field. Fol. 112 (gloss): **5-line gold P**(aulus) with extended foliate tail complementing that of the larger initial; filled with a one-headed, double-bodied ochre 'lion' on a blue background, against a red square field framed with white and green lines. Fol. 127v (text): **8-line blue P**(aulus) with extended stem and simple foliate terminal; filled with blue and pink intertwining scrolls with flower terminals on a pink and gold background, against a red field with darker red penwork scrolls delicately touched with white. Fol. 127v (gloss): **4-line gold P**(aulus) with extended stem and simple foliate terminal complementing that of the larger initial; filled with a green, ochre and white 'centaur' (human-headed animal) with a horn against his mouth, on a dull blue background, against a blue field. Fol. 139v (text): **9-line red P**(aulus), the letter constructed of pink panels decorated with red diapers and framed with blue, divided horizontally with gold bands and with extended stem with foliate terminals; filled with 4 simple shaded scrolls, two blue, two green, each with a channel-style beige lion within, and small leaf and biting 'snake's-head' terminals on a pink background, against a blue field framed with red and green lines. Fol. 139v (gloss): **5-line blue P**(aulus) decorated with white lines, dots and circles along the length of both vertical elements; filled with a single elaborate stylised flower in blue, green and red (silvered) on a gold background, against a grey field framed with red and green lines. Fol. 147 (text): **7-line gold P**(aulus) constructed of panels of red decorated with white wavy lines; filled with shaded blue and green interlocking scrolls with simple foliate terminals on a pink background, against a grey field. Fol. 147 (gloss): **5-line gold P**(aulus) with inset pink panels decorated with wavy lines; filled with a winged dragon with coiled, shaded blue scroll tail and stylised flower terminal, on a red background, against a blue field. Fol. 152 (text): **7-line gold P**(aulus) with inset pink panels decorated with white wavy lines and with extended stem and dragon terminal; filled with 2 shaded pink and green scrolls with flower terminals on an undecorated blue background, against a red field. Fol. 152 (gloss): **5-line gold P**(aulus) with leaf terminal to stem, with two grotesque animals, one blue with an ochre head, the other pink and blue, sitting on blue mounds playing the same harp, on a pink background, against a blue field framed with black and green lines. Fol. 163: **P**(aulus) excised. Fol. 166 (text): **7-line gold P**(aulus) inset with panels of pink decorated with white wavy lines; filled with blue and green interlocking foliate scrolls with stylised flower terminals on a pink background, against a blue field. Fol. 166 (gloss): **5-line gold P**(aulus) with grotesque blue creature with ochre head blowing horn held by its left front leg and carrying a crutch with the right, on a red background, against a grey field. Fol. 169v (text): **7-line red P**(aulus) now oxidised, with inset gold panels and with foliate tail; filled with interlocking, shaded blue and green foliate scrolls with 2 stylised flower terminals on a pink background, against a blue field. Fol. 169v (gloss): **5-line gold P**(aulus) with a foliate tail complementing that of the larger initials; filled with the figure of a small man in a short blue tunic and green stockings who holds a sword in his right hand and grasps the jaw of a winged bird or dragon in his left, on a red background, against a grey field. Fol. 171v: **M**(ultipharie) excised.

Historiated initials None.

Display script Fol. 2: (P)**rincipia rerum** in 2-line, very compressed mixed capitals, alternately red and blue, each decorated with fine vertical lines in the other colour. Fol. 91: (P)**aulus a**postolus in 1-line mixed capitals, alternately red and blue. Fol. 112: (P)**aulus** in 1-line square capitals alternately blue and red. Fol. 127: (P)**aulus** in 1-line mixed capitals alternately blue and red. Fol. 139v: (P)**aulus** in 1-line mixed capitals alternately red and blue. Fol. 147: (P)**aulus** in 1-line square capitals alternately blue and red. Fol. 152: (P)**aulus** in 1-line square capitals alternately blue and red. Fol. 163: (P)**aulus** in 1-line square capitals alternately blue and red. Fol. 166: (P)**aulus** in 1-line square capitals alternately red and blue. Fol. 169v: (P)**aulus** in 1-line square capitals alternately red and blue. Fol. 171v: (M)**ultipharie** in 1-line compressed mixed capitals alternately red and blue.

Titles etc. Running titles visible to fol. 36, increasingly near the upper edge of the page; thereafter possibly trimmed, though the presence of some running titles added in stylus in a later hand may indicate that the running titles were not completed during the original making of the book. No other titles or incipits or explicits; standard author references in red in outer margins, keyed to text by sigla and frequently including the title of the work cited. In gloss passages, biblical text underlined in red. No chapter numbers originally copied, though some have been supplied here and there by a later hand in Arabic numbers (e.g. fols. 15v, 35, 39). Fol. 4, upper margin, 'Rabanus' (crossed through) and 'Anonymus' [sic] written in the same hand ?s.xvii. Also '157' twice.

Title page None, but prefatory leaves lost. Fol. 206 (probably formerly a front flyleaf): 'Communis Glosa super Epistola pauli' s.xv.

IV CONTENTS

Table of contents None, but prefatory leaves lost.

Main texts Peter Lombard, The Pauline Epistles, glossed.

1. Fol. 1v: capitula for Romans, not numbered. Begins: 'De nativitate domini secundum carnem. Paulus servus christi'. Ends fol. 1v: 'De misterio domini ante passionem...vero ipsius revelatio. Ei autem'. Fol. 2 (opening excised): '[P]rincipia rerum requirenda sunt prius'. Ends fol. 205v: Text: 'Rogo autem... Gratia cum omnibus vobis amen.' Gloss ends: 'id est purgatorium peccatorum et alia dei munera sit cum omnibus vobis amen.'

V ORIGIN AND PROVENANCE

Ex libris No extant Buildwas ex libris. Fol. 206, now upside down: 'Liber domus de Balliolo in Oxon. de dono Reverendi in Christo patris et dominum Dominum Willelmi Gray Eliensis Episcopi'. Mynors, *Balliol MSS*, 178, observes that Langbaine says of this book: 'Donum Willelmi Gray, sed (quod ex initio constat)

fuit olim 'Liber sanctae Mariae de Bildewas'. Prae vetustate fatiscit et operimenti parte dimidia, posteriori scilicet mulctatus est.'
Secundo folio Principia
The book was not made at Buildwas, but the Buildwas indexer added a note in the lower margin of fol. 92v, confirming that the book was at Buildwas at least by the later thirteenth century, a fact supported by Langbaine's note. Its text is a companion to that in Balliol 35A (Lombard's gloss on the Psalms) and the decoration is very similar, coming from the same artistic milieu. Walter the Palmer of Bridgnorth, recorded as the donor of Balliol 35A to Buildwas in 1277, may, therefore, have acquired both books and given both to Buildwas, and the inscription Langbaine seems to have seen may have been the same as that which survives in Balliol 35A. It is curious that though both once at Buildwas, and now both at Balliol College, 173B was given to Balliol s.xv by William Gray, and the other bequeathed s.xv by Robert Thwaites. It perhaps suggests that both were on the market in Oxford in the very early fifteenth century, where the two men acquired their respective volumes.

VI NOTES

VII BIBLIOGRAPHY AND PLATES
Mynors, *Balliol MSS*, 178; Ker, *MLGB*, 15.

32. CAMBRIDGE, TRINITY COLLEGE MS B.2.6
Exodus, glossed   **Date** s.xii med
Leaves [ii paper], i (parchment stub), 134, [ii paper]
Foliation 1–134
Origin Probably England, not Buildwas

I PHYSICAL DESCRIPTION
Binding Rebound at least twice, s.xvi and xviii (evidence of endleaves and stub); since rebacked, spine now glued and rigid.
Endleaves
Front *Pastedown* 1) Laid paper leaf in place, probably once first leaf of a bifolium, blank except for two old shelfmarks; 2) parchment stub c.40mm wide, once part of a bifolium, now no conjoint leaf but very narrow stub just visible between this wide stub and fol. 1; probably once a pastedown, impressions of earlier, probably original, sewing supports laced through channels, and post-medieval primary covering turn-ins. Recto: inscription, beginning of a deed s.xv, a smudged offprint of this note on fol. 1; rubbed red mark from initial H on fol. 1 now near lower edge. Verso: pasted to a strip of laid paper which was applied after the detached parchment pastedown was trimmed (evidence of a slit in the parchment stub covered by uncut paper). These elements indicate that the stub was once the other way up and has been inverted during a rebinding. Laid paper is just visible pasted to the conjoint stub.
Flyleaves 2 laid paper leaves, possibly once part of endleaf bifolia (including pastedown and a folded stub); watermark: framed letters PMAVDVIT above a pattern comprising scrolled lines in a pendent formation, with a Maltese cross above and an inverted fleur-de-lis below; all leaves blank except first free leaf recto: text title s.xvii.

Back *Flyleaves* 2 laid paper leaves, possibly part of endleaf bifolia (including folded stub and a second stub now trapped under present pastedown); watermark as for front flyleaves, blank.

      Pastedown Laid paper leaf, separate and different from other endleaves and with chain lines running in a different direction; watermark: one-handled pot surmounted by a crown, letters P [?] on body of pot; blank except for 4 rust-rimmed holes, at upper and lower spine corners and at upper and lower edges *c*.50mm from fore-edge, possibly evidence of metal furniture on earlier boards.

Sewing stations Now 6; evidence of impressions on front parchment stub indicate **1**) an earlier sewing also at 6 sewing stations, roughly coinciding with the present stations but the marks not made by the present sewing supports: (tail) | 45*45*35*45*40*45*36 | mm (head); and **2**) a previous sewing to 3 supports: (tail) | 62*89*85*56 | mm (head). No evidence about kettle stitches.

Sewing Resewn at least twice; now all-along with thin, white S-twist thread; evidence of other sewings has been obliterated by the glue on the spine.

Sewing supports 6 brown leather supports, all broken at the joints front and back; impressions on front parchment stub indicate 2 earlier sets of supports: **1**) 6 double (?split) supports and **2**) 3 earlier supports of various widths, *c*.10mm.

Lacing path All present sewing supports broken at the joints; boards now attached by means of spine covering glued to the backs of the quires and board edges. An earlier group of 6 supports appear to have been laced in over the outer edges of the boards to short channels on the inner face; the group of 3 supports were laced though tunnels to short parallel channels on the inner face, emerging from tunnels *c*.20mm from spine edge and extending beyond the edge of the parchment stub which bears this evidence.

Endbands Present at head and tail, core not visible, sewn with blue and white S-twist threads, tied down in several quires. Impressions on front stub show evidence of earlier, probably original, head and tail endbands *c*.9mm wide laced through channels on the inner face of original boards at an angle of 45°.

Tabs None present; no other evidence.

Spine lining None present; no other evidence.

Boards Pasteboard, 298 x 210 x 5mm. Very considerable worm damage to first and last leaves, especially at the back, penetrating deeply into the book at both ends, indicates at least one earlier set of wooden boards, one of which may have been in a very fragile state when replaced. A wormhole on the front parchment stub is not matched by a hole on fol. 1, even allowing for the inversion of the stub, and may have been caused by infestation in replacement boards.

Primary covering Speckled leather (calf) with frame composed of triple fillets with stylised plant motif at each corner, front and back, and double fillets parallel with all 4 board edges, also front and back; double scalloped lines, gilt, along outer edges, a similar design across the raised cords on the replaced spine. Stain on upper and lower edges of front parchment stub and on the last leaf suggests that an earlier, but post-medieval, covering was of brown leather with overlapping corners.

Fastenings None present; no other evidence.

Chemise None present; no other evidence.

Bosses None present; stains on back paper pastedown (see above) may have been made by bosses on an earlier, but not the original, cover.

Chain attachments None present; no other evidence.

Labels Printed paper labels on spine each with element of present shelfmark.

Notes Edges of the leaves now stained yellowish-green. The number 24 written on fore-edges.

Structure of Book
Parchment Thick, white parchment, evenly coloured, good nap on both sides; many parchment-maker's repairs, some sewn repairs (e.g. fols. 24, 31 in brownish-red ?silk thread, probably not original, but early); a large number of original patch repairs in the last quire.

Collation 1–16⁸, 17⁸ (wants 7 and 8, probably blank); hair side outside in all quires.

Quire nos. QQ. 1–11, 13–16, lower margin of verso of last leaf in small brown ink Roman numerals. Number for q. 12 probably trimmed off.

Catchwords None.

Page Layout
Dimensions
Page 290 x 205mm (fore-edge margins cropped, evidence of lost marginal notes; other edges probably also trimmed).

Space ruled for writing Variable: 210–215 x 170, but fols. 84–90v: 178mm.

Columns Central text column with gloss column on either side, columns varying only very slightly in width from page to page. Gloss columns often sub-divided.

Pricking Leaves folded, 1→8 (qq. 11–12: 8→1), outer margin (inner margin not accessible), using template; text lines only are pricked. In qq. 11–12, the scribe inverted pricked quires so that largest margin is at the top, so opening at q. 10 (fol. 8v)–q. 11 (fol. 1) has unmatched top and bottom text lines.

Ruling In brown, text lines ruled separately, gloss lines ad hoc, roughly 3 gloss lines to a text line. Interlinear gloss lines also frequently ruled.

Lines per page Usually 17 text lines, but scribe often spaced text more widely than this.

Page design
fols. 1–134v

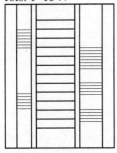

II SCRIBES
One scribe wrote text throughout in a clear, upright English hand s.xii med, with clubbed minims, and very short ascenders and descenders. He corrected his own work, e.g. over an erasure fol. 49. The text and gloss were clearly written in separate campaigns. The gloss was written by one main scribe whose hand appears much less even than that of the main scribe, though they may be one and the same. The gloss on fols. 80–80v has a different aspect but this may have

been caused by a different or recut pen. A correction in the gloss on fol. 86v was possibly made by the text scribe using a smaller version of his text hand.

The text was copied so that gaps consisting of partial text lines or one or more text lines were left to accommodate the gloss, either because the scribe was copying from a glossed exemplar, line for line, or because he was anticipating the space likely to be needed for a gloss of very variable density. In qq. 11–12 (fols. 84–93), the text scribe erased the last lines he had written and rewrote them at the top of the next page. This may have been necessitated by the fact that he had inverted these two quires, and realised his mistake only when a large section of the text had been copied, and recognised that it might cause problems for the gloss scribe, whether himself or someone else. The reason for his continuing to erase and rewrite from fols. 91–93, where the gloss is much less dense, appears to have been aesthetic, to ensure that facing pages matched (though he left fols. 80v–81 uneven). His writing in these two quires is very variable, as if he had lost his concentration.

The gloss in this copy of Exodus is erratically dispersed throughout the text, and there are several pages (e.g. fols. 31, 32, 123–4) on which there is no marginal gloss at all, only interlinear glosses. It is easy to see how this particular text caused layout problems for the scribes, but it is worth noting that no attempt was made to use the whole page for text when gloss passages were absent. Glosses may have been intended but not supplied. On fol. 4, the text scribe left three text lines blank, presumably to allow for an intruding marginal gloss. The lines were not used, and the gloss scribe or a reader filled them with scribbled lines.

III DECORATION, RUBRICS AND ARTICULATION OF TEXT

Text initials 1-line capitals in brown ink written by the text scribe. Red paraphs mark the beginning of each gloss passage; abbreviated names or initials identify the authorities cited in the gloss, and the small red capital used for the first word of each gloss, were mainly executed by the gloss scribe, though here and there they seem to have been supplied by another hand, perhaps that of the initial maker, using a differently shaped paraph mark and a different coloured red ink to fill in the gaps. From fols. 47v–50 (15.1–21: the *Canticum Moysis*, and the verses immediately following it), the text capitals are shaded with red (fols. 47v–48v) or coloured, alternately red and green (fols. 48v–50). The colours of red ink and the style of the paraphs are variable and indicate distinct rubricating hands. The use of green on some leaves and the use of ochre for all additions on fols. 64v–65 (see below) suggest that the initial maker also supervised and corrected the rubrication.

Minor initials Fols. 34v–80v (11.3–25): a series of 27 1- or 2-text-line initials (often extended in the margins) alternately red and greyish-green, some with white lines reserved against the parchment and/or with lightly flourished decoration in the complementary colour. They mark text divisions. On fol. 64v, the initial is in ochre as are the paraphs on fols. 64v–65.

Major initials Fol. 1: **3-text-line red H**(ec), unflourished, with reserved scalloped line and tiny triangles in vertical elements of letter. Fol. 33v: **5-text-line green F**(uitque) extended in the margin, with reserved wavy line, and decorated with red and green dots and flourishes.

Historiated initials None.

Display script Fol. 33: (F)**uitque mo**(yses) in 1-line mixed brown capitals written by the text scribe. Fol. 73v: (E)**cce ego mittam angelum** in 1-gloss-line mixed capitals in brown ink written by the text scribe. The first letter(s) or word(s) following a coloured initial occasionally written in rustic letters.

Titles etc. Fol. 1: 'Liber exodus' and 'Capitulum primum' in hand s.xv, possibly the same hand that supplied summary titles in Buildwas books now at Lambeth Palace. No incipit or running titles; fol. 134: explict in red written by scribe. Chapters numbered by later hands in Roman and Arabic numbers.

Title page None (but prefatory leaves lost).

IV CONTENTS

Table of contents None.

Main texts Exodus, glossed.

Fol. 1 Text begins: 'Hec sunt nomina'. Gloss begins: 'Rabanus. In pentatheuco excellit exodus in quo pene omnia sacramenta'. Text ends fol. 134: 'per cunctas mansiones suas. Explicit liber exodi.' Gloss ends: 'Dum spirat spiritus est. Dum sentit sensus est.'

Fol. 134, beginning of a deed in hand s.xv ex, incomplete: 'Omnibus christi fidelibus et maxime personis omnibus cisterciensis ordinis ad quoque noticiam nostre [l r e] pervenerint / iohannes abbas monasterii beati marie de Buldewas ordinis cisterciensis ligfeldensis diocesis salutem / in amplexibus salvatoris nostre universitate notificamus quod dilectum nobis in christo fratrem Ricardum Kirkeby nostrum monacum virum vitie ho'. The same hand may have added to the end of the right gloss on fol. 134 (et flamma per noctem): 'diem panem nostrum cotidianum da es nobis.'

Chibnall, *VCH*, 58–9, notes that Abbots of Buildwas were named John in 1318, 1402–7; 1428–1443 (John Gnossal, whose name appears in other Buildwas books), and 1471–9.

V ORIGIN AND PROVENANCE

Ex libris None, but see added text on fol. 134.

Secundo folio (Text) nostris expugnatisque; (gloss) Isidorus.

The book seems to have been written in England. It was owned by Master Robert, who annotated the text and gloss. In view of the fact that the Buildwas glossed books now at Trinity College remained together since then, the deed copied on fol. 134 very usefully confirms that they remained at Buildwas, presumably as a complete set, until at least the late fifteenth century. This is supported by similar evidence in other Buildwas books.

There is no evidence of Archbishop Whitgift's ownership of this book, though impressions of a post-medieval binding are consistent with its having been rebound in the same style as other Buildwas books that he owned. It must have been given with them to Trinity College Library by Whitgift s.xvi ex.

VI NOTES

1. On fol. 25v, a drawing in grey of an ornate architectural detail, ?s.xv.
2. On the stub at the front of the book is written in a hand of ?s.xv: 'In Reverendo patri in christo domino Willelmo dei gratia episcopo Conve[ntriensis]'.
3. Two or more hands supplied chapter numbers in the margins. One series in neat Roman numerals and another in larger, untidy Arabic numbers accompanied by the abbreviated capitulum sign. A third series was made by the hand s.xv (perhaps a Buildwas librarian) who wrote 'Liber Exodus Capitulum primum' on fol. 1 and 'Capitulum iiij' on fol. 10.

VII BIBLIOGRAPHY AND PLATES
James, *Trinity MSS* I, 63–4; Ker, *MLGB*, 14; Sheppard 1988, 287 n.1; Thomson 1995, passim.

33. CAMBRIDGE, TRINITY COLLEGE MS B.1.31
Leviticus, glossed   Date s.xii med.
Leaves [ii paper], i, 154, [ii paper]
Foliation 1–154
Origin ?Northern France

I PHYSICAL DESCRIPTION
Binding Resewn and rebound at least twice: ?s.xiii and ?s.xvi; present binding ?s.xix, spine very tight and book opens only moderately well.
Endleaves
> **Front** *Pastedown* Laid paper leaf in place, probably once fol. 1 of a bifolium, joint now repaired; blank.
> *Flyleaves* **1)** 2 laid paper leaves, probably once (with pastedown) part of 2 endleaf bifolia, 1 leaf completely excised; no watermark, blank; **2)** parchment leaf, first leaf of a quaternion (fols. 2v–4v carry prefaces); bears impressions of an earlier binding (see below). Recto: title (s.xvi) and shelf-marks, parchment patch over damage centre fore-edge. Verso: Trinity College bookplate; fragment of printed paper attached to verso of parchment patch (see above, Recto). Fol. 2 recto of this quaternion is blank except for Buildwas ex libris inscription.
> **Back** *Flyleaves* **1)** Fol. 6 of last quire (of 6 leaves); recto: originally blank, now with notes s.xii ex; verso: blank; **2)** 2 laid paper leaves, once part of a quaternion, fol. 3 completely excised, fol. 4 is pastedown; blank.
> *Pastedown* Laid paper leaf in place, once part of a quaternion; blank.

Sewing stations Now 5 (sewing supports palpable on spine, spinefolds inaccessible); evidence of marking-up (pricked), visible here and there especially at the lower kettle stitch (usually *c*.10mm from spinefold) indicates that earlier, there were 3 sewing stations: (tail) I 10 K 36*60*60*40 K 9 I mm (head). This disposition is reflected in the impressions of sewing support channels on front parchment flyleaf.
Sewing Too tightly rebound to permit examination of spinefolds.
Sewing supports Now sewn to 5 supports of unknown material. Impressions on first flyleaf show that an earlier binding was to 3 supports of varying width: 9, 7 and 10mm.
Lacing path Now laced over spine edges of boards and pulled through to inner face *c*.10mm from spine edge. Impressions on flyleaves indicate earlier supports were laced through parallel channels on the outer face to *c*.25mm from spine edge, then to parallel channels on the inner face *c*.25mm long and wedged.
Endbands In place at head and tail, rolled skin core, sewn with red and natural-coloured S-twist threads and tied down in 3 quires; not laced into the boards.
Tabs None present; no other evidence.
Spine lining None present. Strip-shaped impressions, parallel with and adjacent to the spine on last leaves, may have been made by an earlier spine lining.
Boards Pasteboard replacements, 228 x 156 x 3mm. Wormholes in first and last leaves indicate that earlier boards were of wood.
Primary covering Light brown calf, streaked and mottled, undecorated except

for impressed zig-zag and dot decoration along board edges. Impressions on first and last leaves indicate that an earlier cover had roughly trimmed turn-ins and overlapped corners.

Fastenings None present. Damage now repaired by a patch on centre fore-edge of first flyleaf was probably made by a former fastening device.

Chemise None present; no other evidence.

Bosses None present; no other evidence.

Chain attachments None present; no other evidence.

Labels Printed paper labels on spine each with elements of the present shelfmark. Red gilt title label possibly from an earlier binding.

Notes Leaf edges stained yellowish-green. Fingerprints, almost certainly recent, on verso of last parchment leaf.

Structure of Book
Parchment Quite good though variable quality, evenly coloured; large original patch fol. 102.

Collation iv, 1–18⁸, 19⁶; hair side outermost in each quire, though in q. 5, 3rd bifolium is out of sequence.

Quire nos. QQ. 1–18 lower margin of verso of last leaf in large 'lower case' Roman numerals.

Catchwords None.

Page Layout
Dimensions
Page 218 x 151mm, trimmed at all margins (evidence of lost marginal annotation and impressions of former binding).

Space ruled for writing Variable: q. 1: 144 x 116mm, increasing irregularly to q. 19: 150 x 124mm.

Columns Text in central column with gloss on either side, all varying in width sometimes from page to page.

Pricking All pricking in outer margins trimmed. Spinefolds too tight to examine. Ruling (see below) suggests text lines only pricked.

Ruling In brown, text and gloss lines ruled separately.

Lines per page Variable: q. 1: 11 text lines, increasing to 15 in q. 19, though not regularly; q. 1: 3–4 gloss lines per text line; q. 19: 2–3 gloss lines per text line; written above top line.

Page design
fols. 5–153v

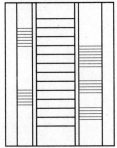

II SCRIBES

One scribe wrote text and gloss throughout in a neat, upright, compact hand with continental characteristics. He used Tironion 'et' in the gloss, but usually wrote 'et' in full in the text. This scribe also wrote the text in Trinity B.1.14 (q.v.), a glossed copy of Deuteronomy.

III DECORATION, RUBRICS AND ARTICULATION OF TEXT

Text initials Small capitals in brown ink written by the text scribe.

Minor initials None, though the first 3 prefaces are marked by elaborate paraphs in the scribe's hand.

Major initials Fol. 5: **4 text-line blue V**(ocavit) with 'curled leaf' decoration and flourishes in red with green and ochre outlines.

Historiated initials None.

Title page None.

Display script Fol. 5 (V)**ocavit** in 1-line Roman capitals alternately blue and red, with green shading.

Titles etc. No early text or running titles or incipits, but text scribe wrote the names of the authors over the prefaces (fols. 2v–4v) and the explicit (fol. 153v) in brown ink rustic capitals. Chapter numbers added by a later hand (s.xiii) in Arabic numbers. Title added to fol. 1 by later hand, s.xvii, and another, slightly earlier fol. 2v: 'Hesychius Hierosolymitanus Episcop*us*'.

IV CONTENTS

Table of contents None.

Main texts Leviticus, glossed.

1. Fol. 2v: a series of prefaces, the first: 'Esitius, Pre o*mn*ibus nece*s*se *est* inter*pr*etat*i*onem legis ad sanagogam [sic] trahi'. Fol. 2v: 'Esitus. Querendum est q*ua*re liber iste dicatur leviticus'. Fol. 3: 'Origene*s*. Si secundum quosdam'. Fol. 3: 'Esitus. Si quis querat quare'. The remaining 7 passages are for the most part glosses on 'Vocavit autem Moysen'. They are attributed to Esitus, Rabanus and Isidore. The last begins (fol. 4): 'Isidorus. Omnis hostiarum diversitas'. Ends fol. 4v: 'sinceritatis epulamur.' Rest of fol. 4v blank except for an addition to the penultimate passage by Master Robert.
Fol. 5: Text begins: 'Vocavit autem'. Gloss begins: 'Rabanus: Ieronim*us* singula sac*r*ificia immo'. Text ends fol. 153v: 'ad filios Isr*ae*l in monte sinay Explicit leviticus.' Gloss ends 'q*ui*a intencione*m* divina*m* celeste*m*q*ue* gerunt.'
2. Fol. 154: Notes on Leviticus in a slightly later hand s.xii ex: 'Sicut n*ec* prima*m* n*ec* secu*n*dam sed t*er*tiam tribu*m* cultui *et* sacrificiis tabe*r*naculi do*min*u*s* deputavit'. Ends fol. 154: 'ad ultimu*m* q*uo*mo*d*o se habe*re* debet qui se ip*sum* novit d*omi*no ostendit.' This is followed by a summary list of laws in the same hand.
Fol. 154v is blank.

V ORIGIN AND PROVENANCE

Ex Libris Fol. 2: 'LiBer s*an*c*te* maRie de bydewas' [sic] in red, written by the undulating ex libris hand found in other books (B.1.3, B.1.4, B.1.34, B.14.5).

Secundo folio Esitius. Querendum

The book was written by the scribe who wrote Trinity B.1.14, probably in northern France. Its initial was also made by the scribe who made the B.1.14 initial, and text scribe and initials maker may have been the same man. The book was owned s.xii med. by Master Robert, whose copious annotation and interventions can be seen on every page. In the prefaces alone, he corrected two passages over erasures (fols. 2v, 3) and added a section at the end (fols. 4–4v) in addition to making marginal annotations. The variation in the shade of brown ink and in the hand itself indicates that this text was one which he repeatedly read and annotated.

The book was at Buildwas by s.xii ex when the ex libris was inscribed by the hand that made similarly undulating inscriptions in other glossed books. James (*Trinity MSS*, 1, 43) cautiously suggests that the book came to Trinity College Library from Archbishop Whitgift s.xvi ex. In fact it must have come from that source, the glossed books at Trinity having remained together since the twelfth century.

VI NOTES

1. The evidence for the early, probably the earliest, binding in boards of this MS is of interest. The marking-up, which includes the kettle stitch station, and the endleaf structure (the first and last leaves of the quires at the front and back of the book that otherwise carry primary text) would suggest, on present evidence, that the book may not have been bound at Buildwas but that it was already bound when the monks received it (cf. Trinity B.1.14, written by the same scribe; also Bodley 371, see also Sheppard 1995, 181–198). In these respects, and bearing in mind the possibility that, quite early, the book had a spine lining composed of strips of material, probably skin, it appears that the earliest binding in boards of B.1.35 may have been like the surviving binding on Shrewsbury XII, another of Master Robert's glossed books. The earliest binding in boards may not, however, have been the original binding of the book. The possibility is quite high that, for practical reasons of portability, Master Robert may have used the book originally in a limp cover of some kind. However the present binding of the MS is such that it is not possible to ascertain whether any evidence of a limp binding has survived. Other glossed books with pricked marking-up are B.1.11, B.1.12, B.1.13, B.1.14 and Shrewsbury XII.
2. Harley 3038 (q.v.) also contains a glossed Leviticus, and among Master Robert's glossed books is a fragment of Leviticus, also glossed (Trinity B.1.39, booklet 3).

VII BIBLIOGRAPHY AND PLATES

M.R. James, *Trinity MSS*, I, 43; Ker, *MLGB*, 15; Sheppard 1988, 287, n. 1; Sheppard 1990, 197 and pl. 9; Thomson 1995, 238–243.

34. CAMBRIDGE, TRINITY COLLEGE MS B.1.35

Numbers, glossed   **Date** *c*.1160
Leaves [iii paper], 127, [iii paper]
Foliation 1–127 (parchment leaves only)
Origin ?Northern France

I PHYSICAL DESCRIPTION

Binding Rebound at least twice: s.xvii and ?s.xix, since rebacked; opens poorly.
Endleaves
    Front *Pastedown* Laid paper leaf in place (chain lines horizontal), probably once first leaf of a bifolium, repaired at joint; no watermark, blank.
        Flyleaves 3 laid paper leaves (chain lines horizontal), no watermark, blank.

Back *Flyleaves* 3 laid paper leaves as above: all blank.

Pastedown Laid paper leaf in place, last leaf of a bifolium (see above) repaired at joint, no watermark, blank.

Sewing stations Now 5; no clear evidence about earlier sewing stations.

Sewing Now all-along with ?S-twist thread. No clear evidence about earlier sewing.

Sewing supports Now sewn to 5 cords. No clear evidence about earlier supports.

Lacing path Supports laced over the outer spine edge, pulled through to inner surface very near the spine edge and fixed to surface of board under pastedown.

Endbands Present at head and tail, rolled tanned leather core sewn with discoloured red and white S-twist threads; not now and probably never laced into boards. Tied down in four spinefolds; tail endband broken, some repair sewing. Thread impression at fols. 124v–125 indicates earlier presence of an endband.

Tabs None present; no other evidence.

Spine lining None present; no other evidence.

Boards Pasteboard, 233 x 162 x 3mm, bowing inwards towards leaves. Wormholes on first and last leaves indicate that earlier boards were of wood.

Primary covering Now speckled and streaked leather (calf); impressed zigzag line with dots along the very thin edge of both covers. Stains on first and last parchment leaves suggest an earlier post-medieval cover was of tanned leather with overlapping corners.

Fastenings None present; no other evidence.

Chemise None present; no other evidence

Bosses None present; no other evidence

Chain attachments None present; no other evidence.

Labels Modern printed paper labels on spine, each with element of present shelfmark; red leather label with title in gilt probably from an earlier covering pasted to rebacked spine. Trinity College bookplate fol. 1.

Notes Edges of leaves stained greenish-yellow.

Structure of Book

Parchment Fair quality, even colour with good nap but with very many holes and sewn repairs (e.g. fols. 28, 50, 85), and many neat, original pasted patch repairs (e.g. fols. 50, 51, 59, 60, 121–127).

Collation 1–15^8, 16^8 (wants 8). Hair side outside in all quires.

Quire nos. QQ. 1–15, lower margin of verso of last leaf, Roman numerals in brown ink.

Catchwords None.

Page Layout

Dimensions

Page 226 x 160mm, fore-edges and upper edges trimmed (evidence of partial loss of annotations and ex libris inscription).

Space ruled for writing 168 x 132mm.

Columns Central text column with gloss columns on either side, but all 3 columns of very variable width from page to page and within pages according to demands of the texts, e.g. fols. 27–29: text in one wide column with no gloss column; fol. 87v: 6 lines of text, gloss written so as to surround them completely. There is less variation in scribe 2's stint (see below).

Pricking Most of the pricking has been trimmed, but remaining evidence suggests: leaves folded, 1→8, outer margin only, pricked for gloss lines.

Ruling Neatly done, in grey sometimes appearing brown, across all columns at one time. Top 2 lines ruled edge-to-edge.

Lines per page 36 gloss lines, gloss written above top line; text lines very variable, up to 18 when written on every other gloss line beginning below top line, but varies according to the needs of the texts, e.g. on fols. 88v–89: 8 and 6 text lines respectively.

Page design Very variable indeed, very few facing or successive pages alike. For example:

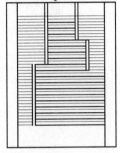

II SCRIBES

Two scribes wrote text and gloss *c*.1160. **Scribe 1** wrote fols. 1–118v in a large, compressed angular hand, with very short ascenders and descenders. He managed an extremely complex page layout with astonishing skill. **Scribe 2** took over on fol. 119 (mid q. 15) and completed text and gloss in a round hand with clubbed minims and ascenders and thin serifs on descenders. The layout of text and gloss pages in this section is more conventional and regular. Each scribe wrote his own gloss, scribe 2 wrote the final explicit.

III DECORATION, RUBRICS AND ARTICULATION OF TEXT

Text initials Ordinary capitals written by text scribes, no special emphasis.

Minor initials None.

Major initials Fol. 2: **6-line red L**(oquutusque), undecorated.

Historiated initials None.

Display script None.

Titles etc. Fol. 1: 'Liber numeri glosatus' s.xiii, and 'Liber Numerorum cum Glossa' s.xvii. No running titles or incipit. Fol. 127v: explicit in hand of scribe 2.

IV CONTENTS

Table of contents None.

Main texts Numbers, glossed

Fol. 1v: Prefaces. i. 'Ori*genes*. Divinis num*eris* non om*nes* digni sunt'. ii. 'Idem. Illud q*uod* consid*er*emus'. iii. 'Ratio q*uod* t*ri*buum distinctio ordinum'. Text begins fol. 2: 'Loquutusq*ue* est dominus'. Gloss begins fol 2: 'Rab*anus*. Iuxta fine*m* exodi sc*ri*ptum *est*'. Text ends fol. 127v: 'supra iordane*m* contra iericho. Explicit liber numeri.' Gloss ends fol. 127v: 'ambulans de virtute in virtutem.'

V ORIGIN AND PROVENANCE

Ex libris Fol. 1v: 'LiBeR S*ancte* MaRie de Bildwas' in brown ink s.xii ex,

slightly trimmed at upper edge.
Secundo folio me*r*ita
Written probably in France, and owned by Master Robert who copiously annotated and corrected text and gloss. It came to Buildwas by s.xii ex with the other glossed books in this collection.
James suggests that this book may have been given to Trinity by Whitgift. In fact it must have been given by him s.xvi ex, with the rest of the glossed books in this set.

VI NOTES
1. This is one of only a few of Master Robert's glossed books which were pricked for the gloss. C. de Hamel, *Glossed Books,* 24–27, has shown that this was a development in Northern French glossed books of the 1160s. See also Trinity B.1.1, B.1.32, B.1.33 and B.1.36. Robert evidently acquired glossed books over a quite long period.
2. Chapter numbers in large Arabic and small Roman numbers in the margin adjacent to the start of each chapter, with a chapter mark also against the first word of the new chapter
3. On fol. 34v a marginal KL, incomplete.

VII BIBLIOGRAPHY AND PLATES
James, *Trinity MSS* I, 45; Ker, *MLGB*, 14; Sheppard 1988, 287 n. 1; Thomson 1995, 238–243

35. CAMBRIDGE, TRINITY COLLEGE MS B.1.14
Deuteronomy, glossed   **Date** s. xii med
Leaves [i paper], 98
Foliation 1–98
Origin ?Northern France

I PHYSICAL DESCRIPTION
Binding Resewn and rebound s. xvi–xvii, uniform with B.1.13; spine rounded and rigid.
Endleaves
  Front*Pastedown* Laid paper leaf in place; watermark: one-handled pot surmounted by crown and orb. Trinity College bookplate and shelfmarks (in ink) . A parchment stub under pastedown.
  Flyleaves Laid paper leaf, conjoint with pastedown, blank.
  Back *Flyleaves* **1)** Fol. 10 of last quire, formerly a pastedown now detached; blank but with impressions of earlier binding, slight remains of grainy paste (near spine) and white paste (at fore-edge); **2)** stub of original front flyleaf now under present paper pastedown which is partially torn, revealing a fragmentary Buildwas ex libris inscription in red; **3)** laid paper leaf conjoint with pastedown, watermark as on the front pastedown with letters ?IFL; blank.
  Pastedown **1)** Parchment leaf detached, formerly a pastedown, see above 1); **2)** laid paper leaf in place, pasted over parchment stub but partially torn (see above, 2), blank.
Sewing stations Now 5; marking-up (pricks) for 3 earlier, probably original, sewing supports, very near spine 8→1: (tail) I 10 K 37*68*71*36 K 16 I mm (head).

182

Sewing Now all-along with brownish S-twist thread. Thread impressions indicate that an earlier sewing was also all-along, twist not discernible.

Sewing supports Now sewn to 5 double, white tawed skin supports. Impressions on last leaf (fol. 98v) indicate earlier presence of 3 narrow sewing supports which coincide almost exactly with sewing station marks (see above).

Lacing path Now over the outer edges of the boards, to channels on the inner face, then pulled to outer face and trimmed flush with outer face. Impressions on back detached pastedown indicate 3 earlier supports laced in parallel but unevenly. Lacing paths *c*.55–60mm long.

Endbands 1) Fragments present at head and tail of very narrow endbands, sewn but tied down only here and there; not now laced into boards; **2**) Impressions on back detached pastedown indicate earlier presence of head endband once laced into former board diagonally.

Tabs None present; no other evidence.

Spine lining None present; no other evidence.

Boards Wood, bevelled on inner edges, 255 x 175 x 6mm. Projecting square corresponds to width of bevel. Clear indentations visible of 2 slots, possibly for former fore-edge straps, now at spine edge of back board; no other evidence of board reuse, so these slots may have been cut in error.

Primary covering Dark brown leather with both overlapping and mitred corners; small gilt Whitgift arms impressed on front and back; triple fillets parallel with and adjacent to all edges and along inner bevelled edges. Gilt tassel motifs impressed between raised cords across spine; vertical impressions on covering over these raised supports to suggest sewing thread passing round them. Impressions on detached former back pastedown of earlier uncoloured primary covering turn-ins.

Fastenings 2 tanned leather strap ends under primary covering but not in slots, each fixed to fore-edge of front board with single daisy-headed pins; 2 corresponding brass catchplates each tapering to a point and fixed by 2 rivets on back board. 2 green-rimmed holes in centre of last leaf (fol. 98v) 60mm from fore-edge indicate position of earlier pin(s).

Chemise None present; no other evidence.

Bosses None present; no other evidence.

Chain staple None present; no other evidence.

Labels Remains of laid paper fore-edge label on back paper flyleaf. Printed paper labels on spine, each with an element of present shelfmark.

Notes Edges of leaves stained yellowish-green.

Structure of Book

Parchment Fine and well prepared, mostly evenly coloured (white) with few follicle marks; slight nap. Outer leaves (fols. 1, and 97–99) more discoloured, suggesting that the book may have been used for a time unbound.

Collation 1–11^8, 12^{10} (10 blank). Hair side outermost in each quire.

Quire nos. QQ. 1–11, lower margin of verso of last leaf in small Roman numerals.

Catchwords None.

Page Layout
Dimensions

Page 237 x 165mm (trimmed at all margins; see e.g. fol. 7 where folded corner indicates extent of trimming).

Space ruled for writing Variable: 154–169 x 128–132mm.

Columns Text in central column with gloss on either side, all 3 varying in width from page to page but never on the same page.

Pricking Much evidence trimmed; surviving evidence suggests leaves folded, 1→8, both sides, text lines only.

Ruling Grey changing to brown at fol. 83 (q. 11 fol. 3), neat, a page at a time without reference to pricking in upper and lower margins; text lines only; 2–3 gloss lines per text line, ruled ad hoc.

Lines per page Varies widely between 13 to 21 text lines, variations even on facing pages.

Page design
fols. 1–97

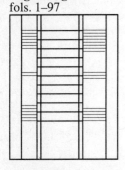

II SCRIBES
One scribe wrote text and gloss throughout, except fol. 84, in a neat, upright, compact hand s.xii med. Ascenders and minims are slightly clubbed, descenders have delicate serifs, and the scribe used Tironian 'et' throughout. Ink is very dark, and letters gradually increase in size for text and gloss, perhaps due to a thicker pen (cf. fols. 1 and 85). A second scribe wrote text and gloss on fol. 84 (q. 10 fol. 4) in a similar but slightly rounder hand using ampersand only in the text; elaborate paraphs in gloss. Main scribe corrected on fol. 13 in the margin and over an erasure.

III DECORATION, RUBRICS AND ARTICULATION OF TEXT
Text initials Plain rustic or Roman capitals written by text scribe.
Minor initials None.
Major initials Fol. 1: **6-line red H**(ec) with a white reserved line through each stroke of the letter. Decorated with simple folded and curled leaves in blue, green and ochre; vertical elements of letter very simply flourished.
Historiated initials None.
Display script Fol. 1: (H)ec in blue 1-line capitals flourished with green and ochre.
Titles etc. No running or text titles, but 'Incipit liber Deuteronomii' (s.xv) and 'Comment. in Deuteronomiam' (?s.xviii) both added on fol. 1. Explicit in hand of text scribe fol. 97v. Roman chapter numbers in pale brown ink added in outer margin, and Arabic numbers in grey in inner margin, probably s.xiii.
Title page None.

IV CONTENTS
Table of contents None.
Main texts Deuteronomy, glossed.

1. No prefatory material. Fol. 1: text begins: 'Hec sunt verba'. Gloss begins: 'Inter pharam *et* t*ophel et* l*aban et* as*seroth* auctus tophel insulsitas laban'. Text ends fol. 97: 'que fecit moyses coram universo israel. Explicit.' Gloss ends fol. 97v: 'pharam auc*tus* tophel insulsitas laban dealbatio aseroch atria.'
2. Fol 97: 2 passages from Ambrose, *De Fuga Seculi,* copied by Master Robert. Fol. 97: 1) 'Ambrosi*us* i*n* libro d*e* fuga sec*u*li congrue'. Ends fol. 97: 'p*er*cussus levitico gladio moria*tur* se*n*sus carnis ut vivat a*n*ima n*os*tra.' 2) Fol. 97: 'I*tem* A*m*brosius i*n* eode*m*. Sex autem civita*tes* refugia s*unt* v*er*o p*r*ima sit civitatu*m* refugias'. Ends fol. 97v: '*v*el instaurator*um* obsequi*o* v*el* i*n*t*er*dictor*um* decli*n*a*tione* veneremur.' Rest of page: notes and scribbles. Fol. 98 blank.

V ORIGIN AND PROVENANCE

Ex libris On stub under back paper pastedown (probably formerly at the front of the book): '[ ]R S*ancte* MAR[ ]' in red ink.

Secundo folio ad nos (text); moysen (gloss)

The book was probably written in Northern France and owned by Master Robert who annotated it heavily. The book was at Buildwas by s.xii ex when the ex libris was added to a front flyleaf.

On fols. 83v in the lower margin in stylus in elaborate gothic letters is the name Greneway, a name also found in Trinity B.1.4. and Lambeth 477. The same hand wrote other words in a similar style in the lower margins of fols. 78v, 81 (where he copied words from the last line of text) and on fol. 82. The name is associated elsewhere with the name Upton and (by extension) with the name of the fifteenth-century Abbot John Gnossal (see Trinity B.3.15 and Lambeth 488). Since Master Robert's set is still largely together, the glossed books must have remained at Buildwas until at least the mid fifteenth century (see also the evidence of a deed, s.xv ex, copied at the end of Trinity B.2.6). Some notes written on fol. 97v in the space left at the end of Master Robert's additional passages may have been added by the hand which wrote notes and coded passages in Lambeth 477.

Given to Trinity College by Archbishop Whitgift s.xvi ex.

VI NOTES

1. The text scribe also wrote Trinity B.1.31 (Leviticus, glossed, q.v). James thought the book probably came from Buildwas, but it was rejected by Ker.
2. This book, like B.1.31 (q.v.) and others (B.1.11, B.1.12, B.1.13 and Shrewsbury XII), has pricked marking-up. All include both kettle stitches.

VII BIBLIOGRAPHY AND PLATES

James, *Trinity MSS,* 1, 15–16; Ker, *MLBG*, 15; Sheppard 1988, 287 n. 3; Sheppard 1990, 197 n. 9; Thomson 1995, 238–243.

36. CAMBRIDGE, TRINITY COLLEGE MS B.3.16

Joshua, Judges, Ruth, glossed   Date *c.*1150–60

Leaves [i paper, i paper], 66, [ii paper , i paper]
Foliation 1–66 (parchment leaves only)
Origin ?Northern France

I PHYSICAL DESCRIPTION

Binding Rebound more than once, probably s.xvi and s.xviii; since repaired and rebacked, spine rounded, glued and rigid.

Endleaves

Front *Pastedown* Modern wove paper leaf in place, fol. 1 of bifolium; shelfmark, Trinity College book-plate, otherwise blank.

Flyleaves **1**) Modern wove paper leaf, fol. 2 of a bifolium (fol. 1 is pastedown); blank. **2**) Single laid paper leaf, no watermark; rust mark lower corner near spine matched by smaller mark fol. 1. Verso: title s.xvii, otherwise blank.

Back *Flyleaves* **1**) 2 laid paper leaves, probably a bifolium; watermark: large design of coiled lines forming a pendant-like design surmounted by a Maltese cross and framed letters PMAVDVIT. Second leaf stained by present covering turn-ins; **2**) a medieval parchment stub now at back of book once formed part of a flyleaf at the front; it bears an offset of the initial P on fol. 1 and matching wormholes. It was probably reused as a pastedown at the back during an earlier rebinding; the stub bears impressions and remains of an earlier binding on 6 supports (as now but not identical); heavy paste remains survive between faint impressions of lacing channels and are superimposed on the red offset (see above); a dark stain from an earlier primary covering turn-in present at upper and lower edges (not coinciding with the present turn-ins which are, in any case, light brown); **3**) Modern wove paper leaf, fol. 1 of bifolium (fol. 2 is pastedown), blank.

Pastedown Modern wove paper leaf in place, fol. 2 of a bifolium, blank.

Sewing stations Unclear; up to 6 (see below); spinefolds inaccessible.

Sewing Unknown, spinefolds inaccessible.

Sewing supports Unclear; 6 raised cords across the spine; faint impressions on former front pastedown stub suggest an earlier binding was on 6 supports *c.*10mm wide.

Lacing path No clear evidence. An earlier set of 6 supports appear to have been laced through short parallel channels on the inner face of the board.

Endbands Present at head and tail, white rolled skin core, sewn with blue and white threads now discoloured; not laced into boards. No earlier evidence visible.

Tabs None present; no other evidence.

Spine lining None present; no other evidence.

Boards Pasteboard, 321 x 231 x 6 mm. Considerable worm damage to first and last leaves indicate that earlier boards were of wood.

Primary covering Light brown leather (calf) speckled with black, with narrow turn-ins and overlapped corners; triple fillets forming a central rectangular frame with stylised plant design diagonally at each corner front and back; double fillets close to and parallel with outer edges front and back; gilded impressed double scalloped line along edges (thickness), spine recovered. Stains on parchment stub indicate an earlier covering was of dark brown leather.

Fastenings None present; no other evidence.

Chemise None present; no other evidence.

Bosses None present; no other evidence.

Chain attachments None present; no other evidence. The rust stain on the earlier front paper flyleaf and first parchment leaf may possibly have been made by a metal fitting but may equally have been accidental.

Labels 3 printed paper labels on spine with shelfmark; title in gilt on red leather on spine.

Notes Edges of leaves now stained yellowish-green.

Structure of Book

Parchment Well prepared, with few follicle marks; hair and flesh sides evenly coloured; 4 spots of paste-like material on fol. 8v, glue on fol. 45v.

Collation 1–7^8, 8^{10}. Hair side outside in all quires.

Quire nos. QQ. 1–3: lower margin of verso of last leaf .i.–.iii.; q. 4: lower margin trimmed; qq. 5–7: lower margin of verso of last leaf .i.–.iii.; last quire not numbered (qq. 1–4 carry Joshua; qq. 5–7 carry Judges and Ruth).

Catchwords None.

Page Layout
Dimensions

Page 316 x 225mm, fore-edge margin certainly trimmed (evidence of lost marginal notes), others probably trimmed.

Space ruled for writing Very variable indeed, almost every page different from the last and openings asymmetrical: e.g. fol. 5: 240 x 149mm; fol. 12: 229 x 173mm; fol. 62v: 247 x 170–184mm : fol. 66v: 256 x 170mm.

Columns Layout varies greatly from page to page. Underlying plan is a central column with gloss columns on either side, but text or gloss columns were expanded and contracted freely to accommodate the requirements of each text. Gloss columns themselves sometimes subdivided.

Pricking Virtually all pricking in outer margins has been trimmed, and book is too tightly rebound to permit examination of spinefold. Evidence in q. 1 only shows it to have been pricked 3 times, leaves folded 1→8; this may have been intended as separate pricking each for the preface, text and gloss, but is more likely to have been inadvertent or a mistake. The flexibility of the column widths suggests that pricking in upper and lower margins, if any, must have consisted of rows of marks like those in Trinity B.1.36.

Ruling In brown, mostly neatly done, though in q. 1 the elaborate pricking is not strictly adhered to. Text and gloss lines ruled separately, about 2 gloss lines to each text line, but all gloss lines on each page were ruled at one time regardless of particular requirements. Text and gloss written above top line. Divisions within gloss columns are ruled with double vertical lines.

Lines per page Varies from page to page between 24 and 33 text lines; 26–28 most common.

Page design

fol. 6   fol. 20   fol. 39

II SCRIBES

One scribe wrote text and gloss throughout in a large, upright, compact hand with continental characteristics. He began neatly, minims *c*.2.5mm high, and using ampersand only. Within a few pages his hand began to enlarge, possibly due to a different pen which he retained, the minims increasing in height to 4mm and the letters proportionately wider. Characteristic are a very small lower loop to g which barely descends below the line, and o which is formed with its first stroke sloping backwards. The scribe mostly abandoned ampersand in favour of Tironian 'et' after the first quire. The gloss hand increases in size in proportion to the text hand but remains at about 2 lines to each text line. The very complex layout is beautifully controlled, perhaps because the scribe was copying a glossed exemplar line for line.

III DECORATION, RUBRICS AND ARTICULATION OF TEXT
Text initials Fol. 1: 1-gloss-line capitals alternately red and blue for capitula. Fols. 1v–2v: 1-gloss-line initials alternately red and blue for each new gloss passage (fols. 1v–2: preface glosses, fols. 2–2v: text glosses), but abandoned almost at once in favour of brown ink capitals written by the scribe, all with brown ink paraphs.
Minor initials Fol. 1v: **1-preface-line blue I**(esus, second preface), plain; fols. 1–7: 1-line capitals, alternately red and blue to mark text divisions (possibly early chapters), but subsequently abandoned; fol. 66v: untidy 1-line red capitals (oxidised) for the generations of Phares (Ruth 4.18–22).
Major initials Fol. 1 (capitula): **9-gloss-line red P**(romisit) with reserved scalloped white line in vertical stroke, and blue flourishes. Fol. 1 (preface): **7-preface-line blue T**(andem) with red flourishes. Fol 1v: **4-gloss-line blue A**(damanthus), plain. Fol. 2: **4-text-line red E**(t) with stiff red and blue flourishes. Fol. 29v: space left for **E**(voluto, Joshua 23), not supplied. Fol. 33: **16-text-line red P**(ost) with two elegant reserved wavy lines, and a lower coiled leaf terminal, the upper part of the letter drawn with compasses. Fol. 62v: **11-text-line red I**(n) with reserved wavy line and leaf terminal.
Historiated initials None.
Display script Fol. 1–1v: first words following coloured initials in 1-line mixed capitals in brown ink by the scribe. Fol. 2: (E)**t factum est** in 1-line uncial and Roman capitals, alternately red and blue. Fol. 33: (P)**ost mortem** in untidy, thick red 1-line mixed capitals. This added later; a note for the rubricator was made by Master Robert at the top of this page. Fol. 62v: (I)**n diebus unius** in red minuscule.
Titles etc. No running titles; incipits and explicits and number of verses added in red (now oxidised) as follows: the text scribe executed the rubrics on fol. 1 and also flourished the initial T (identical ink); he therefore probably executed all the initials and display script on fols. 1–2. All subsequent rubrics including the minuscule 'display script' were executed by a later scribe, s.xii ex.
Some chapter numbers inserted by later, untidy hand ?s.xv, in Roman numerals, sometimes with the first word of the designated chapter to identify it. Chapter numbers also supplied in the margin in small Roman numerals by a neat hand, probably much earlier, seen in other Buildwas glossed books.
Title page None (but prefatory pages lost).

IV CONTENTS
Table of contents None.
Main texts Joshua, Judges, Ruth, glossed.
1. Fol. 1: Capitula (not numbered): 'Promisit d*ominu*s iosue dicens'. Last: 'Item

congregatis cum pacto atestationis alloquitur eos iosue.' 2 prefaces: i) 'Incipit prefacio ieronimi in iosue. Tandem finito pentateucho'. Ends fol. 1v: 'surda debeamus aure transire.' ii) 'Item alia. Iesus filius nave in typum domini'. Ends fol 1v: 'spiritalia regna describit.' Fol. 1v: a large number of glosses follow the prefaces. The first begins: 'Adamanthus. Donavit deus nomen quod est super omne'. The last ends fol 2: 'promissionis celestem hereditatem accipies per iesum christum dominum nostrum.' Text begins fol. 2: 'Et factum est'. Gloss begins: 'Adamantius. Moyses famulus nostris defunctus est.' Text ends fol. 32: 'in monte effraim. Explicit liber iosue bennun habens versus m. septingentos l.' Gloss ends: 'quod non illis imputetur.' Lower third of page excised, probably blank. Fol. 32v blank.

2. Fol. 33: Text begins: 'Incipit sopthim id est iudicum. Post mortem iosue'. Gloss begins: '[A]ugustinus. In fine libri iehsu nave breviter narrator'. Text ends fol. 62v: 'videbatur hoc faciebat. Explicit liber iudicum. Habens versus m.septingentos l.' Gloss ends fol. 60v: 'sed contra se rigida bonis vero omnibus sit submissa.'

3. Fol. 62v: Text begins: 'Incipit liber ruth. In diebus unius iudicis'. Gloss begins: '[A]biit homo etcetera. quem quidam ad decalogum legem interpretantur'. Text ends fol. 66v: 'Ysai genuit david regem. Explicit liber ruth.' Gloss ends: 'patriarcharum oraculum pertinet ad dispensationem domini nostri iehsu christi.'

V ORIGIN AND PROVENANCE
Ex libris None.
Secundo folio ierichontium
The book was probably written in Northern France, though it was evidently without most of its rubrics when owned by Master Robert (he provided a rubrication note on fol. 33), whose annotations indicate his early ownership. The book must have remained at Buildwas with the others in the set until at least the fifteenth century (evidence of the deed copied into Trinity B.2.6, q.v., and other datable inscriptions). It was acquired by Archbishop Whitgift who gave it to Trinity College s.xvi ex.

VI NOTES
1. The rubrication may very well have been supplied by a Buildwas scribe (cf. other possible Buildwas additions to unfinished books, e.g. the initials in Trinity B.1.6).
2. James thought that this book probably came from Buildwas, but Ker rejected it.

VII BIBLIOGRAPHY AND PLATES
James, *Trinity MSS*, I, 116–117; Ker, *MLGB*, 15; Sheppard 1988, 287 n. 3; Thomson 1995, 238–243.

37. CAMBRIDGE, TRINITY COLLEGE MS. B.3.15
Kings I–IV, glossed Date c.1150–60; s.xiii
Leaves [i paper], iii, 100
Foliation 1–103
Origin ?England (not Buildwas)

I PHYSICAL DESCRIPTION
Binding Rebound more than once and repaired, present binding ?s.xvi ex,

recently rebacked; very tight glued spine. There is now no recoverable evidence about the original sewing. Front endleaves stained by ?water.

Endleaves

Front *Pastedown* **1**) Laid paper leaf in place, fol. 3 of a quaternion now pasted over first two leaves; blank except for shelfmarks and Trinity College bookplate; **2**) Original pastedown probably once fol. 1 of quaternion, now trimmed to a stub and pasted down under the paper pastedown.

    Flyleaves **1**) Laid paper leaf, fol. 4 of a quaternion; watermark: one-handled pot, letters illegible; blank; **2**) fols. 2–4 of parchment quaternion: fol. 2, used as a pastedown in a rebinding, bears impressions (recto) of 3 sewing supports, and present covering turn-ins; otherwise blank except for title in ink, s.xvii–xviii; fol. 2v–3: capitula; fol. 4: preface.

Back *Flyleaves* None now free, see below, back pastedown.

    Pastedown Last 2 leaves of a quaternion excised to wide stub; all leaves and stubs now pasted onto board; blank.

Sewing stations Now 6; formerly 3 (evidence of impressions on former front parchment flyleaf subsequently used as a pastedown; see above, Flyleaves 2).

Sewing Resewn with thick S-twist thread. No evidence recoverable about earlier or original sewing.

Sewing supports Now sewn on 6 single tawed skin supports; marks on boards visible through paper pastedowns and impressions on first parchment leaf suggest that there were once 3 sewing supports.

Lacing path Now laced in over the spine edges of the boards; impressions on first parchment leaf suggest 3 earlier sewing supports laced in through parallel paths *c.*50–60mm long.

Endbands Present at head and tail: thin rolled tanned leather cores sewn with natural thread which was stained when edges of the leaves stained. Impression of thread at tail of front endleaves suggests earlier presence of a tied-down endband.

Tabs None present; no other evidence.

Spine lining None present; no other evidence.

Boards Wood, 335 x 238 x 10mm, inner edges bevelled and projecting beyond the edges of the leaves by the depth of the bevel (9–10mm). Boards apparently reused during post-medieval rebinding, the boards possibly swapped (front to back) when book resewn on 6 supports.

Primary covering Dark brown leather, corners overlapped; large impressed and gilt arms of Whitgift on both covers, now upside-down; dark triple fillets parallel with all edges and along inner bevel.

Fastenings 2 tanned leather straps on front board each fixed in place under primary covering by 2 daisy-headed nails; no slots to accommodate them in boards; 2 brass catchplates at fore-edge of back board each held in place by two rivets over primary covering, although slots in the board are visible under the primary covering. Rust marks slightly above centre of fore-edge of first 4 leaves suggest an earlier central fore-edge strap fastening, and square rust marks on fols. 17–23 appear to have been made by the metal end of a former fore-edge strap which was left unfastened and became trapped for some time between two leaves.

Chemise None present; no other evidence.

Bosses None present; no other evidence.

Chain staple None present; no other evidence.

Labels Remains of paper fore-edge label on last leaf. Printed paper labels on

spine, each with an element of present shelfmark.
Notes Edges of leaves stained yellowish-green.

Structure of Book
Parchment Thick, fairly good quality, even colour with a good nap on both sides; a number of holes, very many patch repairs, e.g. fols. 40, 41, 70, 74, 76, 78 etc. Remaining leaves of the first quaternion much thinner than the rest; q. 12 is also much thinner but is a later addition.
Collation 1–10^8, 11^4 (wants 4, probably blank; 3v is blank with scribbles); 12^{16}+1 leaf after 16 (q. 12 is an addition s. xiii). Hair side outside in all quires.
Quire nos QQ. 1, 3–4, 8, 10: lower margin of verso of last leaf in small Roman numerals; q. 8 numbered ix, q. 10 numbered xi (no quires are missing).
Quire signatures Q. 12, Lower right corner fols. 2–8 signed aa–aaaaaaaa.
Catchwords None.

Page Layout
Dimensions
Page 320 x 230mm, all margins trimmed.
Space ruled for writing 238–248 x 200–208mm.
Columns QQ. 1–11: central text column with gloss columns on either side, all 3 variable in width from page to page, gloss column sometimes subdivided, but text and gloss are always confined within their respective columns. Q. 12: 4 equal columns.
Pricking Most pricking trimmed, evidence remaining (qq. 1 and 10) suggests: leaves folded, 1→8 in outer margins only for text lines. Q. 12 is pricked in both margins, 1→8.
Ruling In grey and brown; q. 12 in grey sometimes appearing brown. Gloss lines ruled ad hoc.
Lines per page Variable: q. 1: 28–36 text lines; qq. 2–11: 30–34 text lines. Q. 12: 77–84.
Page design
fols. 1–86   fols. 87–103

II SCRIBES
The text was written throughout by one scribe in a fine, distinctive, even and fairly compact hand, possibly English, *c*.1150–60. This scribe made his own corrections (e.g. fols. 6v, 7, 35v), but his work was also corrected (fol. 53) by the preface and gloss hand. The preface and the gloss were written by a second scribe in an equally compact but less fluent hand. A third scribe, contemporary

with the other two, supplied the capitula and prefaces on fols. 1v–2v. Q. 12 is a later addition, and is written in a very small, neat hand, s.xiii.

III DECORATION, RUBRICS AND ARTICULATION OF TEXT

Text initials Rustic capitals written by the text scribe in brown ink. Fols. 1v–2v, 1-line capitals for each capitulum, alternately red and blue. 1-line red capitals and paraphs throughout at beginning of each gloss passage.

Minor initials Fol. 1v (first capitulum): **2-line red D**(ue) with simple blue flourishes inside letter. Fols. 87–103: 3-line capitals for headings for alphabetical list of Hebrew names, alternately blue and red embellished with a vertical line in the other colour (s.xiii; see also below, Notes).

Major initials The red and green terminal flourishes on several of these initials are very like those on the initials in Trinity B.2.6. Fol. 3: **8-line blue and red V**(iginti), the blue showing signs of erasure and alteration, with reserved lines, some of these filled with red dots; red and green flourishes to left upper terminal, and the letter filled with an elaborate flower and leaf motif in red and green, somewhat like those found in painted initials s.xii (cf. Trinity B.4.3, Balliol 35A and 173B). Fol. 4: **9-text-line red and green F**(uit), the colours separated by 2 opposed reserved zigzag lines, with red and green flourishes to the tail, the space between the two horizontal strokes of the letter filled with a floral design similar to that on fol. 3 but slightly less elaborate and less attractive, in red, green and brown ink. Fol. 24v: **8-line red F**(actum) with reserved wavy line, no other decoration. Fol. 43v: **2-text-line red E**(t), plain. Fol. 64v: **8-line blue P**(revaricatus) with single reserved line in vertical stroke and simple striated flourishes in red.

Historiated initials None.

Title page None.

Display script Fol. 3: (V)**iginti** in brown ink 1-line capitals. Fol. 4: (F)**uit vir unus de Ramathaim Sophim** in 1-line capitals, alternately red and green followed by one line of small rustic letters written by the text scribe.

Titles etc. Running titles for books I and II (fols. 4–43) added in stylus; incipits and explicits in hand of text scribe in red; chapter numbers in Roman numerals supplied in later hand s.xiii; names of patristic authors occasionally supplied in red capitals.

IV CONTENTS

Table of contents None.

Main texts Kings, books I–IV, glossed.

1. Fol. 1v: Capitula for first 2 books numbered consecutively i–xcviii: Begins: 'i Duo filii heli ophni et phinees'. Ends fol. 2v: 'xcviii Indignat*us* d*eus* cont*ra* isr*ael*...testimoni*um* n*on* offerendum holocausta gr*a*tivita n*i*si pr*o*to labore.' Fols. 3–3v: 5 short prefaces written as if glosses on the preface (see below): i) 'Isid*orus*. Helchana possessio d*e*i int*er*p*re*tatur'. ii) 'Ramatha sive armatha quod in aliis codicibus habetur'. iii) 'Hic habuit duas uxores quaru*m* nobilior, *id est* anna, sterilis erat'. iv) 'Primum librum regum scripsit samuel usque ad mortem suam'. v) 'Prim*us* historice p*ro*phe*te* g[e]n*er*atio dicenda'. Fol. 3: 'Incipit prefatio sancti ieronomi in libro Regum. Viginti duas esse litteras'. Ends fol. 3v: 'Ommutui *et* humiliatus sum *et* silui de bonis. Explicit prefatio.' Rest of page blank.
   Text (book 1) begins fol. 4: 'Fuit vir unus'. Gloss begins: 'Arimathia

192

interpretatur excelsa domino'. Text ends fol. 24: 'et ieiunaverunt septem diebus. Explicit samuhel id est regum liber primus habet versus dua milia trecentos'. Gloss ends fol. 24: 'philistinorum obprobrio eripiamur.'

Fol. 24: 'Incipit regum liber secundus.' Text begins fol. 24: 'Factum est autem'. Gloss begins: 'Cecidit super faciem. A parte totus. Non enim homo cadit'. Text ends fol. 43: 'et cohibita est plaga ab israel. Explicit samuhel liber secundus habet versus duo milia ducentos.' Gloss ends fol. 43: 'quem assumens obtulit pro filio.'

Fol. 43: 'Incipit malachim id est regum liber tercius.' Text begins fol 43v: 'Et rex David senuerat'. Gloss begins: 'Nonne tibi videtur si occidentem sequeris litteram'. Text ends fol 64v: 'que fecerat pater eius. Explicit malachim id est regum liber tercius habet versus tria milia.' Gloss ends fol 64: 'iudicio omnipotentes obtemperat.'

Fol. 64v: 'Incipit liber quartus.' Text begins fol. 64v: 'Prevaricatus est'. Gloss begins: 'Domus ochozie est sinagoga'. Text ends fol 86: 'omnibus diebus vite sue. Explicit malachim id est regum.' Gloss ends fol 86: 'conditoris nostri per secula contemplari.'

2. Fol. 87: 'Hic incipiunt interpretationes nominum hebreorum incipiencium per a litteram. Aaz apprehendens vel apprehensio'. Ends fol. 103: 'Zumin consiliantes eos vel consiliatores eorum.'

V ORIGIN AND PROVENANCE

Ex libris Fol 2v: 'Liber sancte Marie de Bildewas' in red in upper margin, now partly trimmed.

Secundo folio Fuit (text); [vir]is iabin (gloss).

The main text was possibly written in England, and was owned by Master Robert who annotated text and gloss. On fols. 27v (in fairly small letters) and 54 (in very large letters) s.xv, the name 'Gnowsale' is written with a stylus. On fol. 38v, the name 'upton' is written in stylus in the lower margin, and on fol. 87, 'Gnowsal', 'Upton' and 'Kphl' are written in very large Gothic letters, each stroke made with a double line, with a stylus. They were made by the same hand at the same time. Drawings of decorative motifs were made over these stylus additions. The name 'Upton' appears in an inscription Lambeth 477. John Gnossal was the Abbot of Buildwas from 1428 to 1443, and the name in this book and in others confirms that they all remained at Buildwas at least to the mid-fifteenth century.

The book was given to Trinity College by Archbishop Whitgift s.xvi ex.

VI NOTES

1. The list of Hebrew names is subdivided and headed indicating alphabetical arrangement of the names to the 2nd and sometimes the 3rd letter: e.g.: 'A post a sequitur c: Achab...B post b et a sequitur l: Bala Balaa Balaam'.

2. There are a number of marginal sketches throughout this book: fol. 6: a motif rather like a frilled ribbon disposed in a rectangular design in inner margin; fol. 17 upper margin, and passim: sketched letter O with the fol. 6 design inside; fol. 24v, under gloss in lower right margin: some roughly written musical notes; fol. 59v: rough sketch of the fol. 6 design in grey; fol. 80 lower margin: a rough diagrammatic sketch of a square within a circle and other angular lines (cf. the diagram in Lambeth 488), trimmed at lower edge; fol. 86v: several pen and ink sketches of a) the fol. 6 design, b) a symmetrical foliate design, c) a different

symmetrical design, possibly zoomorphic, and d) a large flower motif in brown ink, composed of curled petals and coloured with pen and ink in red and green; this is executed over the s.xv stylus-inscribed names (see above, Origin and Provenance); fol. 100v lower margin: a decorated O executed with a stylus.

VII BIBLIOGRAPHY AND PLATES
James, *Trinity MSS*, I, 115–116; Ker, *MLGB*, 14; Sheppard 1988, 287 n. 1; Thomson 1995, 238–243.

38. CAMBRIDGE, TRINITY COLLEGE MS B.1.13
Proverbs and Ecclesiastes, glossed   **Date** s.xii med
Leaves [i paper], 77, [i paper]
Foliation 1–77
Origin Northern France   **Fig.** 31

I PHYSICAL DESCRIPTION
Binding Resewn and rebound s.xvi–xvii, since repaired, rounded spine now very stiff and cracking.
Endleaves
Front *Pastedown* 1) A parchment leaf in place, now almost completely obscured by a paper pastedown; 2) fol. 1 of laid paper bifolium sewn in through a double (W-shaped) fold, the first leaf then pasted down over the parchment leaf and the extra fold of the paper bifolium; blank except for Trinity College bookplate and shelfmark in ink (s.xvii).
    Flyleaves Laid paper leaf, conjoint with pastedown; watermark: one-handled pot surmounted by crown and orb, initials PDB or PDR on the body of the pot; blank.
Back *Flyleaves* 1) Fol. 3 of last quire of 4, originally blank but with many scribbles in various hands s.xiii–xv; 2) laid paper leaf, with same watermark and probably conjoint with pastedown in a similar construction to that of front endleaves; blank.
    Pastedown 1) Once probably fol. 4 of last quire, now excised; 2) laid paper leaf in place, probably conjoint with flyleaf in a similar construction to that of front endleaves; blank.
Sewing stations Now 5; once, probably originally 2 (sewing stations were marked-up by pricks close to the spinefold): (tail) I 8 K 45*125*46 K 14 I mm (head). On the present boards there is clear evidence of earlier lacing paths of 3 sewing supports and laced-in endbands, though it is not certain that this evidence relates to MS B.1.13; the boards may have been originally used on another book: (tail) *c*.I 50*70*65*48 I mm (head).
Sewing Now sewn allalong with S-twist thread. No clear evidence of earlier sewing.
Sewing supports Now sewn to 5 white tawed skin supports; once sewn to 2 and then perhaps to 3 supports (see above Sewing stations).
Lacing path Now over the outer edges of the boards to a short channel on the inner face. Earlier 3 supports were laced into these boards in parallel paths of slightly unequal lengths, through tunnels, then channels in outer then inner faces of the boards where they were wedged. These lacing paths were *c*.55–60mm long. However this evidence may not relate to MS B.1.13.

Endbands Fragmentary endbands present at head and tail, not now laced in and not evidently tied down; obscured by covering fragments adhering to them. There is evidence on the boards of earlier endbands which were laced in at an angle of 45°, though this evidence may not relate to MS B.1.13.

Tabs None present; no other evidence.

Spine lining None present; no other evidence.

Boards Reused wooden boards, 246 x 168 x 6mm, inner edges slightly bevelled; projecting square, 6–7mm at upper and lower edges, 2mm at fore-edge.

Fastenings 2 tanned leather straps present under covering of top board but not set into slots, each held in place by a daisy-headed pin; 2 corresponding brass catchplates on back board attached over covering, roughly rectangular but tapering to a point away from the fore-edge.

Primary covering Dark brown leather, triple fillets parallel with and adjacent to all edges front and back, small impressed gilt Whitgift arms front and back. On the spine, raised bands with tie marks (also at kettle stitch); stamped gilt tassel motif in the spaces between them.

Chemise None present; no other evidence.

Bosses None present; no other evidence.

Chain attachments None present; no other evidence.

Labels Remains of laid paper fore-edge labels on front pastedown and back flyleaf. Printed labels on spine, each with elements of present shelfmark.

Notes Edges of leaves stained yellowish-green.

Structure of Book

Parchment Thin, heavily follicle marked and mottled, with holes, scar tissue etc. and marks of uneven scraping (e.g. fols. 30–31). Hair side yellow and very distinct from flesh side throughout; nap on flesh sides, less on hair sides. Last 2 quires different, even thinner than the rest (added slightly later).

Collation 1–7⁸, 8¹⁰, 9⁸, 10⁴ (4 excised, probably blank, possibly once used as a pastedown). Hair side outermost in each quire.

Quire nos. None.

Catchwords None.

Page Layout
Dimensions

Page 232 x 165mm, trimmed certainly at upper margin and fore-edge.

Space ruled for writing Slightly variable, $c.188$ x 135mm.

Columns Central text column with gloss columns on either side, all 3 columns varying considerably in width from page to page and within a page. Sometimes inner gloss column dispensed with, e.g. in the last 2 quires (added slightly later).

Pricking For text only, leaves folded, 1→8, though q. 4 appears to have been pricked when open at the centre; qq. 1 and 8: one side only, qq. 2–7 both sides; template used to prick qq. 1–7. Evidence lost, or non-existent, for qq. 9–10.

Ruling QQ. 1, 9–10 in brown; qq. 2–8 in grey. Text and gloss lines ruled separately as needed, about 3 gloss lines to 1 text line. QQ. 1, 9–10: no edge-to-edge lines; qq. 2–8: first and last lines ruled for the most part, edge to edge. QQ. 9–10: ruling practices inconsistent. Fol. 76v ruled in long lines in brown as if for an additional text, notes in brown written without reference to these lines.

Lines per page 17 text lines (fols. 68–69: 18 text lines).

Page design
fols. 1–66v (qq. 1–8)   fols. 67–76 (qq. 9–10)

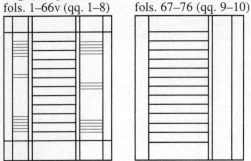

II SCRIBES
3 main scribes wrote both text and gloss.xii med. **Scribe 1** (q. 1) pricked leaves on one side only and ruled in brown. He wrote in a round hand with continental letter forms (note & and g), and wrote the text across ruled gloss columns if necessary (e.g. fols. 7v–8). **Scribe 2** (qq. 2–8) pricked leaves on both sides and ruled in grey. His hand is upright and compact, beginning small but becoming larger, with less markedly continental letter forms in the text hand, though more pronounced in the gloss. **Scribe 3** (qq. 9–10) was Master Robert himself, who wrote the text and most of the gloss in his neat, scholarly hand. Two assistants, one with a hand similar to Robert's own (e.g. fol. 67v) and another with a more irregular, untidy hand (fol. 69 and elsewhere), wrote parts of the gloss.

III DECORATION, RUBRICS AND ARTICULATION OF TEXT
Text initials Scribes 1 and 3 wrote mainly rustic capitals; scribe 2 wrote Roman and rustic capitals.

Minor initials Fol. 58: **1-line red M**(ulierem).

Major initials Fol. 1: **6-line red P**(arabole), plain, now rubbed. Fol. 60v: **3-line red M**(emi[ni]), plain. Fol. 61v: **2-line red V**(erba) with a reserved line, otherwise plain.

Historiated initials None.

Display script The first word or two following a coloured initial written by the text scribes in rustic capitals.

Title page None.

Titles etc. No running titles. Title supplied fol. 1 in late hand (s.xvii); fol. 60v, explicit (to Proverbs) and incipit (to preface to Ecclesiastes) supplied by later hand; Fol. 76, explicit (to Ecclesiastes) supplied by the scribe (Master Robert); another hand later added 'liber divine doctrine'.

IV CONTENTS
Table of contents None.

Main texts Proverbs and Ecclesiastes, glossed.

1. Fol. 1: 2 prefaces: i) 'Parabole salomonis secundum hebraicam veritatem translate'. ii) 'Ieronimus. Iungat epistola quos iungit sacerdotium'. Ends fol. 1: 'suum saporem servaverint. Explicit.' Text begins fol. 1: 'Parabole Salomonis'. Gloss begins (in text column): 'Parabole grece latine similitudines'. Gloss (in right column): 'Proverbiorum liber non ut simplices arbitrantur.' Text ends fol. 60v 'et laudent eam in portis opera eius. Explicit liber proverbiorum habens

ve*r*sus mille dcc*^{tos}* xl*^{ta}*.' Gloss ends fol. 60: '*proba*nte ac remun*e*rante d*e*o.'

2. Fol. 60v: Preface: 'Incipit p*r*olog*u*s beati iero*n*imi p*r*esb*it*e*r*i in libro ecclesiastes' (in a hand s.xiii). 'Memi[ni me] hoc ferme quinquen*n*io cu*m* adhuc rome essem'. Gloss begins: 'T*r*ib*u*s no*m*i*n*ibus vocatum fuisse salomone*m* sc*r*ipt*u*re'. Preface ends fol. 61v: 'forte v*e*ritatis omisso opinionu*m* rivulos consectarer.' Gloss ends fol 60: 'tene*n*tur int*e*reant.' Text begins fol. 61v: 'Verba ecclesiastes'. Gloss begins: 'Ieron[i]mus. V*e*rba ecclesiastes fi*li*i d*a*vid regis i*e*rusalem. Tribus no*m*i*n*ibus vocat*u*s est'. Text ends fol. 76: 'sive bonu*m* sive malum sit. Explicit'. Another hand has added: 'Liber divine doctrine.' Gloss ends fol. 76: 'cum vid*e*ratur i*n* m*u*ltis ad voluptates hortari.'

Fol. 76v: Notes, illegible, written in brown on page ruled with long lines.

Fol. 77: 'Hec acta s*u*nt in ec*c*lesi*a* s*a*ncti pet*r*i *et* pauli ap*u*d Londoni*um* anno domi*n*i millesima cc*^{a}* liii'. Other notes in brown possibly in the hand which wrote the notes on fol. 76v.

Fol. 77v: Further notes in brown, probably in the same hand. Also sentences and practice letters in ink s.xiv-xv: e.g. 'Bonu*m* vinu*m* *et* suave bibit abbas' and also 'Ego sum bon*u*s puer quem D*o*minu*s* amat.' This sentence also written in another hand s.xv. In another hand s.xv: 'Raulf'.

V ORIGIN AND PROVENANCE

Ex libris None.

Secundo folio principium

The book was probably written in Northern France and was owned at an early date by Master Robert who annotated the text and gloss and supplied the last 2 quires. Robert also annotated the glosses copied by himself and by the other scribes. He may have acquired the book second–hand and damaged, or he may have been associated with the scriptorium or workshop where it was produced. The inscription on fol. 77 (s.xiii) dated 1253 referring to the Church of Saints Peter and Paul in London seems to be a heading for a document not then copied out. Ths book must have remained at Buildwas with the others in this set until at least the mid-fifteenth century (see the evidence of a later document copied into Trinity B.2.6, datable names into B.3.15 etc.).

It was acquired by Archbishop Whitgift and given by him to Trinity College s.xvi ex.

VI NOTES

1. This book was thought by James to be from Buildwas, but rejected by Ker.
2. The sewing stations for this book are marked-up with pricks; cf. Trinity B.1.11, B.1.12, B.1.14, B.1.31 and Shrewsbury XII.

VII BIBLIOGRAPHY AND PLATES

James, *Trinity MSS*, I, 15; Ker, *MLGB*, 15; Sheppard 1988, 285 and pl. 4; Thomson 1995, 238–243.

39. CAMBRIDGE, TRINITY COLLEGE MS B.1.39

1. Ecclesiastes, glossed; 2. Song of Songs, glossed; 3. Leviticus (part), glossed; 4. Tobit (text only, unglossed); 5. Miscellaneous medical texts; 5a. Commentary on the Pauline Epistles, the 'Commentarius Cantabrigiensis'

Leaves [ii paper], ii, 183, [ii paper]   **Date** *c*.1140–50

Foliation 1–183

Origin ?Northern France

The book consists of 5 discrete items: 3 glossed books of the Bible and one unglossed, and a miscellany including an extended commentary on the Pauline epistles. The 4 Biblical texts are all contemporary and linked by their main scribe; the fifth cannot be securely linked with the others before the late thirteenth century, though it may have been linked with them as soon as they were copied.

The binding of the book as it now exists will be described first and then each booklet independently. The Provenance, Notes and Bibliography for the whole book will be given at the end.

I PHYSICAL DESCRIPTION

Binding Rebound s.xvii, possibly not for the first time; spine rebacked since then, and a guard sewn into the centre spinefold of many quires; opens well, but remains of glue (much now removed) and repairs obscure many centre spinefolds.

Endleaves

Front *Pastedown* Single laid paper leaf pasted over another paper leaf (probably a fairly recent repair), each possibly once conjoint with paper flyleaves (see below); joint now broken; blank except for pencil shelfmark.

Flyleaves **1)** 2 laid paper leaves pasted along spine edge to first parchment leaf; each possibly once conjoint with leaves now pasted down; no watermark; blank. **2)** separate parchment bifolium: fol. i recto: ex libris s.xiii ex, 2 lists of contents (s.xiii ex and s.xvii), early Trinity pressmark: R.11.10, modern Trinity College bookplate, shelfmark and stamp; inscription s.xii ex: 'michael fil*ius* Ric*ardi* Wa[ ] de aj[ ]*tem*'; fols. i verso–ii: prefaces for item 1.

Back *Flyleaves* Laid paper bifolium pasted along spine edge to last parchment leaf; blank.

Pastedown Laid paper leaf pasted over paper strip (joint repair); no watermark; blank.

Sewing stations Now 5; (tail) I 24 K 20*20*26*27*27*36 K 22 I mm head; at fols. 6v–7, slits across spinefold indicate sewing holes for a former sewing (not the original). In some spinefolds (where not obscured by glue, e.g. fols. 24v–25), other holes are visible mainly near the tail which may indicate that tackets once held the texts in a limp or other temporary binding. There is no clear evidence of another medieval binding, though the texts were clearly together by the end of the 13th century (evidence of the contents list).

Sewing Now resewn, all-along with very fine white Z-twist thread. No other evidence.

Sewing supports Now sewn on 5 thin cords. No clear evidence about original supports.

Lacing path Now over the outer edges of the board and fixed under pastedown. No other evidence.

Endbands None present; in some spinefolds (e.g. fols. 24v–25), impressions survive at head and tail indicating that a former endband was tied down. Evidence elsewhere is obscured.

Tabs None present; no other evidence.

Spine lining None present; no other evidence.

Boards Pasteboard, 195 x 133 x 4mm.

Primary covering Brown leather (calf), undecorated. Spine re-covered with a lighter coloured leather.

Fastenings None present; no other evidence.

Chemise None present; no other evidence.
Bosses None present; no other evidence.
Chain attachments None present; no other evidence.
Labels Printed paper labels on spine, each with an element of present shelfmark.
Notes Edges of leaves now stained yellowish-green.

BOOKLET 1: fols. i–ii, 1–29

Structure of Booklet
Parchment Variable thickness, a number of holes; hair side very yellow, flesh side very white.
Collation 1^8, 2^{10} (wants 10, probably blank), 3^{10}; hair side outside in each quire.
Quire nos. None.
Catchwords None.

Page Layout
Dimensions
Page Slightly irregular: $c.185$ x 130mm (trimmed at all margins).
Space ruled for writing 143 x 113mm.
Columns Fol. i verso–ii verso: 2; fols. 1–29: 3 Text in central column with gloss on either side, column widths constant.
Pricking QQ. 1–2: pricking visible only in upper margin; q. 3: leaves folded, $1 \rightarrow 8$, outer margin, text lines only.
Ruling In brown, untidily done; text lines ruled first, gloss lines ruled as needed. No edge-to-edge lines.
Lines per page 18–19 text lines (fol. 3: 16 text lines). Written above top line.
Page design
fols. 1–29

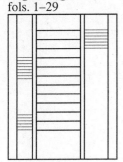

1/II SCRIBES
One scribe wrote prefaces, text and gloss in a hand $c.1140$–50, possibly continental, with somewhat open letter forms and sharply angled feet. He began text and gloss in a cramped manner, text and gloss hands not sufficiently different in size to make pages easily legible. By the beginning of q. 3 he had developed a smaller gloss hand. The scribe made some additions to the gloss in earlier parts of this booklet (e.g. fol. 3) in the even more distinct version of the gloss hand developed in booklet 2 (see below). The text seems to have been wholly written out before the gloss; different inks noticeable especially in q. 3.

1/III DECORATION, RUBRICS AND ARTICULATION OF TEXT
Text initials No special initials.

Minor initials None.
Major initials Fol. 1v: **2-line red M**(emini), plain with simple coiled terminal at the top the first stroke. Fol. 1v: **3-line red V**(erba), plain, now oxidised. Fol. 2: **4-text-line red V**(anitas), plain.
Historiated initials None.
Display script Fol. 1v: (V)**erba ecclesiastes** in brown ink rustic capitals.
Title page None.
Titles etc. Few supplied, though the scribe wrote a note for a rubricator in the lower margin of fol. i: 'Explic*it* p*ro*log*us*. I*n*cip*it* exp*ositi*o'. Fol. 29v: 'Explicit' written by scribe, the E touched with red and a red line drawn through the word for emphasis.

1/IV CONTENTS
Table of contents Not for this booklet, but see below, 207.
Main texts Ecclesiastes, glossed.
1. Fol. 1v prefaces: i) 'Memini me hoc ferme quinquennio cum adhuc rome'. Ends: 'rivulos *con*sectarer'. ii) 'Verba ecclesiastes filii D*a*vid regi*us* iud*a* ['iuda' marked for erasure] ierusalem. Tribus nominib*us*'. Ends fol. 2v: 'cui res est physicas enumerare liber.' Rest of page blank.
Text begins fol. 3: 'Vanitas vanitatu*m*'. Gloss begins: 'Om*n*ia que a bono creata sunt'. Text ends fol. 29v: 'sive bonu*m* sive malu*m* sit. Explicit.' Gloss ends fol. 29v: 'de ocioso verbo ex ignorantia p*ro*lato.'

1/V ORIGIN AND PROVENANCE
Ex libris Not for this booklet, but see below, 207.
Secundo folio hoc q*ui*d (gloss); Iam *enim* (text).
Probably written in Northern France and probably acquired by Master Robert as part of his set of glossed books (the scribe who copied this text copied others demonstrably in Robert's possession, including others bound with this booklet), although there is no clear evidence of his annotation of this text. For subsequent history, see below, 207.

BOOKLET 2: fols. 30–61
Structure of Booklet
Parchment Very like that of booklet 1, hair side markedly yellow and flesh side white.
Collation 1–3⁸, 4⁶, 5², hair side outside in all quires.
Quire nos. None.
Catchwords None.

Page Layout
Dimensions
Page Irregular, *c.*185 x 134mm (trimmed at all margins).
Space ruled for writing 133 x 115mm including gloss.
Columns Central text column with gloss on either side, all columns varying only very slightly in width from quire to quire and sometimes from page to page. Fols. 60–61: 2 columns for preface added to space at end of glossed text.
Pricking Much pricking now trimmed away; remaining evidence suggests leaves folded, 1→8, text lines only, in outer margin only. Q. 5 is not pricked.
Ruling In grey sometimes appearing brown, text lines ruled first, gloss lines as needed, 4–5 lines per text line.

Lines per page 10 widely spaced text lines. Written above top line.
Page design
fols. 30–60 (top 4 lines)   fols. 60–61

2/II SCRIBES

Two scribes contributed to the copying. Scribe 1 wrote the text in qq. 1, 2 and 4 in a large, round, neat hand using very few abbreviations. Scribe 2 wrote the text in qq. 3 and 5 (the latter comprises 3 words only) and the gloss throughout in a more angular hand. He also added the preface in the remaining space on the last bifolium. Scribe 2 is the same as the scribe of booklet 1; there are several identical letter forms, e.g. a complex g and distinctive 'orum' abbreviation and abbreviation mark, though the aspect here is slightly different, perhaps the result of an attempt to match the size of the text hand of his co-scribe.

2/III DECORATION, RUBRICS AND ARTICULATION OF TEXT

Text initials 1-line brown ink capitals written by scribes.
Minor initials None. The scribe left space on fol. 60 for L(iber) but this was not
  supplied.
Major initials Fol. 30: **3-text-line red O**(sculetur) with scalloped reserved line.
Historiated initials None.
Display script Fol. 6: (L)**iber** by scribe 2 in brown, mixed rustic capitals and
  minuscule.
Title page None.
Titles etc. A space was left above the first text line on fol. 30 presumably for an
  incipit which was not supplied. Fol. 60: 'Explicit Liber *Cantica* Canticor*um*'
  (scribe 2) in brown mixed rustic capitals and minuscule letters. Fol. 61: 'Explicit
  Liber C. Canticorum' in a hand s.xvii.

2/IV CONTENTS

Table of contents Not for this booklet, but see below, 207.
Main texts Song of Songs, glossed.
1. Text begins fol. 30: 'Osculetur me'. Gloss begins: 'Sinagoga *congregatio*'. Text
  ends fol. 60: 'super montes aromat*um*. Explicit liber c. canticor*um*.' Gloss ends:
  'dignare delabi ad valles.'
Preface added in remaining space. Begins fol. 60: '(L)iber iste cantica vocatur
  ca*n*ticor*um* *est* pluralit*er* vocatur [sic] *pr*opter multa*m* excellentia*m* divinitatis'.
  Ends fol. 61: 'In canticis canticor*um* ieronimus est expositor origenis
  expositionem sequens.' Fol. 61v: blank except for '*Pa*rs levitici' added s.xiii.

2/V ORIGIN AND PROVENANCE

Ex libris Not for this booklet, but see below, 207.

Secundo folio In pressuris (gloss); Nigra sum (text)
This booklet seems to have been written in the same place as booklet 1 since one scribe is common to both, and this scribe added marginal notes to the gloss on the text in booklet 1. The text was acquired s.xii med by Master Robert, who annotated and corrected the text and gloss and added punctuation. For later history, see below, 207.

BOOKLET 3: fols. 62–67
Structure of Booklet
Parchment Even quality, undamaged, hair and flesh sides distinct in colour.
Collation 1^6, hair side outside.
Quire nos. None.
Catchwords None.

Page Layout
Dimensions
 Page 184 x 135mm, probably trimmed at all margins, certainly at lower margin.
 Space ruled for writing Variable: 137 x 106–110mm.
Columns Central text column with gloss on either side, mainly of unvarying widths, but text column is slightly wider towards the end of the text.
Pricking All pricking trimmed except in upper margin: this suggests leaves folded, $1\rightarrow8$, outer margin only.
Ruling In grey and brown, faint, text lines only ruled first, gloss lines added as needed.
Lines per page 15 text lines, written above top line.
Page design
fols. 62–67

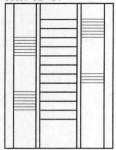

3/II SCRIBES
One scribe wrote text and gloss. The same scribe wrote booklet 1 and part of booklet 2 (see above). Two other scribes copied short texts on fol. 67v (col. b lines 8–22).

3/III DECORATION, RUBRICS AND ARTICULATION OF TEXT
Text initials Small 1-line capitals in brown ink, of rustic character written by text scribe.
Minor intitials None.
Major intials Fol. 62: **4-gloss-line red L**(ocutus), plain.
Historiated initials None.
Display script None.

Title page None.
Titles None. A later hand (s.xvii) added 'leviticus Cap.11' in upper margin, fol.
62.

3/IV CONTENTS
Table of contents Not for this booklet, but see below, 207.
Main texts Leviticus (11. 1–45 only), glossed.
1. Text begins fol. 62: 'Locutus est dominus ad moysen'. Gloss begins: 'Isidorus.
Quicquid a domino sanctum est ipsa institucionis auctoritate mundum est'. Text
ends fol. 67v: 'Sancti eritis quia ego sanctus sum.' Gloss ends 'et sciatis quid
comedere et quid respuere debeatis.'
2. Fol. 67v: a sequence of short prefaces and notes to the books of Solomon. i)
'Salomon id est pacificus quia in regno eius pax'. ii) 'Si vis ascendere ad
canticum canticorum'. iii) 'Notandum quod sponsa semper in domo vel in
lectul'. iv) 'Quatuor mihi in hoc opere videor invenisse personas'. v) 'Omnis
anime mocione'. vi) 'Materia sponsus et sponsa id est caput et ecclesia.' vii)
'Modus est quali desiderio'. viii) 'Finis est dilectio dei'.

3/V ORIGIN AND PROVENANCE
Ex libris Not for this booklet, but see below, 207.
Secundo folio pinnulas (text) Isidorus. In piscibus (gloss).
The text was evidently copied in the same place as booklets 1 and 2, and further
linked with them by the subjects of the prefaces copied on the verso of the last
leaf of this quire. It is not possible to say whether the extract was always
intended as such; the new chapter beginning at the top of fol. 62 might easily
have been preceded by other chapters, though clearly chapter 45 was left
unfinished with space still unused in the quire. This section of the text (on
which animals may be eaten and which not) is complete in itself, and may have
been considered by the book's owner as particularly significant. The text was
probably among those owned by Master Robert s.xii med (though there is no
clear evidence of his annotations), and given by him to Buildwas with the rest
of his glossed books s. xii ex. For later history, see below, 207.

BOOKLET 4: fols. 68–93.

Structure of Booklet
Parchment Q. 1: fair quality; qq. 2–3: many more holes, some of these due to
careless manufacture. Hair side very yellow.
Collation 1–2^8, 3^{10}, hair side outside in each quire.
Quire nos. None.
Catchwords None.

Page Layout
Dimensions
Page Irregular, c.185 x 133mm (probably trimmed at some or all margins).
Space ruled for writing c.143 x 111mm (but width irregular).
Columns Central text column with column for gloss on either side (not used), all
columns varying quite substantially in width. The text column sometimes
expands to almost the entire width of the page but never extrudes into adjacent
columns.
Pricking Leaves folded, 1→8 in outer margins only.
Ruling In faint grey, text lines only, carelessly ruled; gloss was not added.

Lines per page 15 text lines. Written above top line.
Page design Irregular, for example:
fol. 78   fol. 90

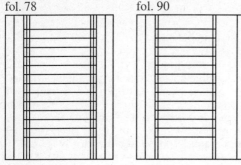

4/II SCRIBES
The text was copied by one scribe who was also the main scribe of booklets 1–3
above. He began by using a tall hand but gradually reverted to his more natural,
smaller letters. On fol. 90 he attempted again to achieve a large text hand, and
again was unable to maintain it.

4/III DECORATION, RUBRICS AND ARTICULATION OF TEXT
Text initials 1-line brown capitals written by the scribe, rustic in character.
Minor initials Fol. 72v: $1^1/_2$-**text-line red T**(extrinum), undecorated. A space
was left as if for an initial, though it is a mistake, since 'textrinum' is not the first
word in a sentence, and the initial T was, in any case, already written.
Major initials Fol. 68: **3-text-line red T**(obias), a central line reserved against
the parchment and with minor decoration in vertical stroke. Fol. 89v: **2-text-line
red M**(agnus), reserved lines in first diagonal and second vertical stroke, first
vertical stroke extending into margin.
Historiated initials None.
Display script. None.
Titles etc. Fol. 89v: 'Canticum Tobie senioris' by the text scribe in brown mixed
rustic capitals and minuscule letters fol. 93; explicit in hand of text scribe.
Chapter numbers were added in the margin in a later hand s.xiii with paraph in
text to mark the beginning of each chapter. On fol. 68, another later hand s.xvii,
probably that of Thomas Griffith (see below) added 'Tobie Liber'.

4/IV CONTENTS
Table of contents Not for this booklet, but see below, 207.
Main texts *Tobit*, intended for glossing but gloss not provided.
1. Fol. 68: Text begins: 'Tobias ex tribu et civitate nepthalim'. Ends fol. 93: '*et*
cunctis habitant*ibus* terre. Explicit Liber tobin clcccc. Illi qui p*ro*dunt culpas
d*omin*or*um* suor*um* v*el* parentu*m* suor*um* sentent*ia* cahm [sic] filii nbhe [sic]
dampnantur.'
Fol. 93v blank

4/V ORIGIN AND PROVENANCE
Ex libris Not for this booklet, but see below, 207.
Secundo folio *et* genuit

This text must have been produced in the same scriptorium as the glossed texts now bound with it since they have a common scribe. It has no annotations, and so it is probable rather than certain that it was part of Master Robert's set. If so, it is curious (in view of his completion of both text and gloss in Trinity B.1.13) that he did not either copy the gloss himself or have it copied. It was perhaps of less interest to him than other Biblical texts. For later history, see below, 207.

BOOKLET 5: fols. 94–103v, 104–183.

Booklet 5 appears to comprise two separate booklets, one containing medical and related texts (item 5), the other a commentary on the Pauline Epistles (item 5a). They are treated here as a single, two-part booklet because at the time that they were bound together, whether at Buildwas in the volume that is now Trinity B.1.39 or earlier and elsewhere, the quires were numbered continuously (see below). Where elements of the booklets seem to require it, however, they are described separately.

Structure of Booklet
Parchment Mainly fairly thin, thinner than other parchment in the same booklet, though q. 2 is markedly thicker and greasier. Many holes; hair and flesh sides clearly distinct.
Collation Item 5: 1^8 (7 excised), 2^4 (4 excised). Item 5a: 3^8 (3 and 6 are single leaves), 4^8, $5–7^{10}$, 8^8, 9^8 plus a single leaf folded to form half-size bifolium (fols. 162–3), 10^8, 11^6 (+ 1 leaf after 6); Hair side outside in each quire (but q. 3 fol. 6 is reversed).
Quire nos. QQ. 1, 3, 8–11, lower margin of verso of last leaf, in stylus numerals, i, iii, viii–xi; others possibly trimmed.
Catchwords None.

Page Layout
Dimensions
Page Variable: 183 x 130mm (all margins trimmed).
Space ruled for writing Very variable, e.g. in item 5, fols. 94–96: 153 x 110mm; fol. 96v: 161 x 110mm; fol. 101: 168 x 115mm; fol. 103v: 172 x 120mm. In item 5a, fol. 104 (q. 3): 160 x 115mm; fol. 182v: 168 x 118mm.
Columns 2, except for fols. 101v–103 (lists of herbs): 3 pairs of columns.
Pricking Probably in outer margins only but all pricking has been trimmed off.
Ruling QQ. 1–2, item 5: in grey sometimes appearing brown, very faint, fols. 94–96v possibly on hair side only. QQ. 3–11, item 5a: mixed ruling, blind or in grey (probably a stylus which did not mark regularly), very faint but neatly executed.
Lines per page Very variable: item 5, q. 1: 42–58; q. 2 (e.g. fol. 101): 64. Item 5a, qq. 3–11: as few as 49 (fol. 104) and as many as 67 (fol. 182v).
Page design Too variable to reproduce.

5/II SCRIBES
Item 5: one scribe wrote most of the text in a tiny, forward-sloping scholarly hand *c.*1150 or a little later, with continental characteristics. On fols. 171–172 several hands wrote short passages before the main scribe resumed. Fols. 96v–103 are written in different ink in a hand which is very similar to that of the main scribe, but the leaves present a distinctly different appearance. There are more lines per page in a wider ruled space, and the text on these leaves is provided with red

capitals unlike the remainder. This scribe uses a form of punctus elevatus in which the elevatus stroke is in fact horizontal.

Item 5a: one scribe wrote the whole text in a very neat, probably continental, scholarly hand s.xii med.

5/III DECORATION, RUBRICS AND ARTICULATION OF TEXT

Text initials No special emphasis.

Minor initials Fols. 96v–101v: initials at major text divisions are red.

Major initials None. On fols. 94, 96 and 104, space was left for capitals, but these were not provided.

Historiated initials None.

Display script The first word following a coloured initial or the space left for an initial usually written in small rustic capitals. On fols. 96v–101 (item 5), these letters shaded in red.

Title page None.

Titles etc. Fol. 94: 'Medicinalia quaedam' in later hand, s.xvii; fol. 101: 'De Urinis' in red rustic capitals, s.xii.

5/IV CONTENTS

Main texts item 5

1. Fol. 94: Hugh of St. Victor: '[V]elle scire ver*um* bon*um* est anime ut sic sequ*ens* de creatore t*ra*ctat*us* facilior'. Ends fol. 96v: 'i*n*telligibilior comparetur.' (Neil Ker's attribution of this text to Hugh is recorded in a note in the Trinity College copy of James, *Trinity MSS*, I).

2. Fol. 96v: a text on physiognomy: 'Magne aures stultice *vel* i*n*pudentie parve aures malignitatis su*n*t i*n*dices'. Ends fol. 97v: 'Que *enim* palemon dixit *et* co*n*sentanea su*n*t reliq*ui*s auctorib*us* prope mod*um* p*r*osecuti sumus.' The remainder of fol. 97v blank.

3. Fol. 98: 'Ex trib*us* auctorib*us* quos prae manu h*a*bui loxo medico A*ri*stot*e*le philosopho palemone declamatore qui de phisiagnomia [sic] sc*ri*pser*un*t'. Ends fol. 100: 'ex co*n*sulatione singular*um* partium q*uam* ex uni*ve*rsitate quam freq*uente* nominavimus.'

4. Fol. 100: 'Bonum aliq*ui*d divitiar*um* *et* vite nostre oportunu*m* est febru*m* diffe*ra*ns [sic] signa *et* curationes'. Ends fol. 101: 'His signis unis p*er*tinet non dubitabis.'

5. Fol. 101: *De Urinis*. 'Quoniam inf*er*ior*um* m*em*bror*um* certio non subiacet n*o*stris sensibus'. Ends fol. 101v: 'post ea facias inde pan*n*iculos *et* sepeius tepida suppone.'

6. Fol. 101: *Nomina Herbarum*. '[A]lleluia i*d* *est* panis aiculi. Antifarmacum i*d* *est* vincetoxic*um*'. Ends fol. 103: 'Talo i*d* *est* asin*us*. Talmus i*d* *est* oculus.' Remainder of fol. 103 recto blank.

7. Fol. 103v: '(R)osa sem*en* eius viola. Floribus et foliis utimur'. Ends fol. 103v: 'Selinuor i*d est* apivia.'

Main texts item 5a

8. Fol. 104: *A Commentary on the Pauline Epistles*. Prologue: '[S]icut universa sive celum sive te*r*ra sive cetera q*ui* in mu*n*do su*n*t'. Ends fol. 104: '*vel* ecclesie que magistra *est* omniu*m* ecclesiar*um* directa *est*.' Text: 'Paul*us* e*t*cetera. More scribentiu*m* epistolas salutatione*m* permittit.' Ends incomplete fol. 193: 'p*ro*meret*ur* deus i*d* *est* mo*n*strat*ur* quia ips*um* deum p*ro*meremu*r* hoc *est* ei placem*us*. Alledite *etc*.'. Rest of fol. 193 and fol. 193v blank.

This text has been identified as a work compiled by a pupil of Peter Abelard. Its author is unknown and this copy is unique. It has been called the *Commentarius Cantabrigiensis*. See A. Landgraf, ed., *Publications in Medieval Studies*, 4 vols (Indiana, Notre Dame, 1937–1945), and D. Luscome, *The School of Peter Abelard* (Cambridge, 1969), 145–153. The author is most grateful to Dr. Rodney Thomson for providing this information.

5/V ORIGIN AND PROVENANCE
Ex libris Not for this booklet, but see below.
Secundo folio simus primus
It is not clear where these texts were copied (though a continental origin seems very likely), or whether they were associated with the glossed texts and Buildwas before the early thirteenth century (when the table of contents for the present volume was first written). As is the case with all Buildwas texts of this kind, two possibilities need to be borne in mind. They may have come from Savigny (the founding house of Buildwas) or, and perhaps this is more likely, they may once have belonged to Master Robert. For later history, see below.

V ORIGIN AND PROVENANCE OF TRINITY B.1.39
Ex libris Fol. 1: 'Liber monachorum s*ancte* marie de byldewas' in brown ink, in an untidy uneven hand, s.xiii in.
Table of contents Fol. 1 in brown ink, s.xiii ex over erasure: 'Ecclesiastes Cantica cantico*rum* p*ars* levitici liber thobie No*mina* h*er*barum et qued*am* alia'. A later hand s.xvii has added: 'Hieronymi Expositio in Ecclesiasten. Cantic[a] Canticorum Etc.' Yet another hand s. xvii has added 'Levit: Cap: 11 ad ver: 45'.
The glossed texts are all linked by a common scribe, who also wrote the glossed texts in Shrewsbury XII (q.v.). These are undoubtedly books owned by Master Robert, though his hand is not discernible in all of them. They were not necessarily bound, or bound together, when they arrived at Buildwas, presumably when the other glossed texts did at the end of the twelfth century. At some point, certainly by the end of the thirteenth century, it was decided to bind the glossed texts with the medical notes and the Pauline commentary, perhaps because all needed binding and were about the same size, or possibly because they were already part of a single volume. It is curious, however, that the Pauline commentary is not named in either of the lists of contents, being subsumed under *quaedam alia* in the thirteenth century, and omitted altogether in the seventeenth. All the pages are now very severely trimmed, but this may have been done only when the book was rebound and the leaf edges stained in the seventeenth century.
The entire book, including the Pauline commentary, must have remained at Buildwas with the other glossed books until the late fifteenth century. It was among those given to Trinity College s.xvi ex by Archbishop Whitgift.

VI NOTES
Fol. 61: a hand s.xvii wrote 'A Dun a digon, Thomas Griffith' in a cursive hand, and a careful explicit in a hand that perhaps aimed to imitate the text hand.

VII BIBLIOGRAPHY AND PLATES
James, *Trinity MSS,* I, 50–52; Ker, *MLGB*, 14; Sheppard 1988, 287 n. 1; Thomson, 1995, 238–243, especially 242–3.

40. CAMBRIDGE, TRINITY COLLEGE MS B.1.32

Wisdom, glossed (fragment)   **Date** *c.*1160
Leaves [iii paper], 27, [i paper]
Foliation 1–27
Origin Northern France

I PHYSICAL DESCRIPTION

Binding Rebound at least twice (evidence of paper endleaves), present binding
s.xix, rebacked, spine now very tight so book opens poorly and much binding
evidence, present and past, is obscured.

Endleaves

    Front *Pastedown* Laid paper leaf in place, identical to flyleaves, probably once
conjoint with one of them and part of a quaternion; broken at joint, no
watermark, blank.

        Flyleaves **1**) 2 laid paper leaves, together with pastedown probably once
a quaternion, no watermark, blank; **2**) single laid paper leaf, different from
flyleaves 1) above; watermark: one-handled pot surmounted by a crown, letter
D on the body of the pot. Recto: old and current shelfmarks s.xvii; verso: titles
s.xvi, xvii, old shelfmark and Trinity College bookplate, otherwise blank.

    Back *Flyleaves* Laid paper leaf in place, identical to front flyleaves 1) above,
possibly once conjoint with pastedown, no watermark; fragment of last
parchment leaf now pasted to it, otherwise blank.

        Pastedown Laid paper leaf, probably once conjoint with flyleaf, no
watermark, blank.

Sewing stations Evidence obscured, probably 5.

Sewing Now all-along with natural (beige) S-twist thread (visible at back joint).

Sewing supports Evidence obscured, none visible or palpable.

Lacing path No clear evidence about board attachment which is now effected
by the spine covering.

Endbands Present at head and tail, rolled brown leather core, sewn with red and
white S-twist threads, tied down, e.g. at fols. 4v–5 and 21v–22 where clean
thread fragments visible. Not laced into boards.

Tabs None present; no other evidence.

Spine lining None present; no other evidence.

Boards Pasteboard, 227 x 161 x 2mm; worm holes in last leaves confirm earlier
boards were of wood.

Primary covering Now light brown leather (calf) with streaked ?acid marks,
otherwise undecorated except for impressed zigzag pattern interspersed with
dots along very thin board edges; replaced at spine.

Fastenings None present; no other evidence.

Chemise None present; no other evidence.

Bosses None present; no other evidence.

Chain attachments None present; no other evidence.

Labels Gilt title on red leather label on spine, probably from an earlier binding.
Printed paper labels also on spine, each bearing elements of present shelfmark.

Notes Edges of leaves stained yellowish-green.

Structure of Book

Parchment Fair quality, few blemishes or repairs (except fols. 4v–5), hair side
clearly distinct from flesh by follicle marks and colour, surface relatively smooth.

Collation 1–3⁸, 4⁴ (1 excised before writing, 4 trimmed to a horizontal strip 55mm deep carrying the end of the text and explicit only). Hair side outside in qq. 1–3; q. 4: flesh side outside.

Quire nos. The first three quires (here, qq. 1–3) are numbered iii–v, lower margin of last leaf, 'v' possibly not by text scribe. Two quires (the original qq. 1–2) are missing.

Catchwords None.

Page Layout
Dimensions
Page 218 x 155mm (evidence of trimming at fore-edge only).
Space ruled for writing 146 x 116mm.

Columns Basic layout consists of central text column with gloss columns on either side, all of varying widths, but there are variations according to the requirements of text and gloss, sometimes within one page (e.g. fols. 10, 13v). In practice, most pages have a single wide column of text with an outer column of gloss.

Pricking Leaves folded, 1→8, outer margins only, using a template. 27 lines pricked, i.e. for the gloss lines, though last prick not used (but see below, Ruling). In upper margin (lower margin trimmed), pricks for inner vertical lines arranged in two groups: 3 nearer the spinefold, 6 nearer the fore-edge. This allowed for flexibility in ruling columns of varying widths within each quire and within each page if necessary (e.g. fols. 9v–10v). A template was also used for this pricking.

Ruling In brown, rather carelessly executed. Fols. 1–12: all 26 lines ruled across the page at one time. Fols. 12v–27v: lines in text column ruled separately, gloss lines also ruled separately, not ad hoc but in advance, 2–3 lines per written text line (pricking not closely followed). Edge-to-edge ruling is inconsistent: any combination of the first line or first two lines and the last line are so ruled. The text begins on the second line, the gloss on the top line.

Lines per page 13 text lines; fols. 1–12: 2 gloss lines per text line, subsequently 2–3 gloss lines per text line.

Page design
fols. 1–12   fols. 12v–27

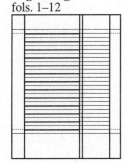 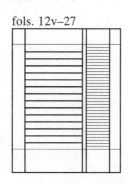

II SCRIBES
One scribe wrote text and gloss throughout in a regular, erect compact hand *c*.1160, with continental characteristics. The hand is characterised by a very pronounced straight, thin final stroke to the lower loop of g which usually does not close the loop but trails somewhat in the manner of a serif. The scribe used a

sloping ampersand and Tironian 'et' which descends well below the ruled line. A few corrections over erasures in the scribe's hand (e.g. fols. 4v, 9v, 12v, 26v). The scribe also provided many alternative readings in the margins.

III DECORATION, RUBRICS AND ARTICULATION OF TEXT

Text initials Capitals written by the scribe, many rustic in character, with no special emphasis provided.

Minor initials None.

Major initials None extant.

Historiated initials None.

Title page None extant.

Display script None extant.

Titles etc. No text or running titles. The scribe wrote the explicit on fol. 27; a later hand s.xv added 'Explicit liber sap*ient*ie' and other words, now trimmed and though offset onto facing page, illegible. Two series of text divisions added to the margins: one series in pale ink (many trimmed) seems to coincide with modern chapter divisions. Another series in darker ink and accompanied by sigla (which are also inserted into the text) divides the text into 46 sections.

IV CONTENTS

Table of contents None extant.

Main texts Wisdom, glossed (first chapters lost).

Fol. 1: Text begins imperfectly (7.23): 'capiat om*n*es sp*iritu*s intelligibile, mund*us* subtilis.' Gloss begins imperfectly fol. 1: 'Rab*anus*. Sp*iritu*s qui inplet omn*ia*'. Text ends fol. 27v: 'in om*n*i loco assistens eis. Explicit Liber Sapientie.' Gloss ends: 'M*u*lte *enim* t*r*ibula*ti*ones iusto*rum* s*ed* d o h l e d'; James, *Trinity MSS,* I, 43, expands this as follows: 'de omnibus hiis liberat eum dominus'.

Another hand s.xv added: 'Explicit liber Sap*ient*ie'. Remainder of the leaf cut away, but there are traces of more writing in the same hand underneath the explicit, now trimmed and illegible.

V ORIGIN AND PROVENANCE

Ex libris None extant (first leaves lost).

Secundo folio Now [ama]tor factus

The book was probably written in Northern France and was among the books owned by Master Robert. However there are only a few annotations certainly in his hand (e.g. fols. 9, 20v) though other very brief notes or marks are probably also his, including added punctuation. Another contemporary annotator made many more notes in the margins than Robert. This reader arranged his notes in the shape of an inverted triangle and roughly enclosed them between converging lines. Most of these notes are of an explanatory nature, usually beginning '*vel*' or '*id est*' and are keyed to the text by sigla. This reader may have been the same as the one who added the longer series of text division numbers (the size of numerals and colour of ink as well as the intensity of attention to the text suggest this).

There are extensive notes written with a stylus, now brown and partially erased and difficult to read, on fols. 23v, 24, 25, 26v, ?s.xiv, probably made by a Buildwas reader.

There is no direct evidence that the book was owned by Archbishop Whitgift (James cautiously suggests that it was), but in fact it must have remained at

Buildwas with the other books in this set, and come to Trinity College from the same donor.

VI NOTES
1. The scribe seems to have experimented with the later 'alternate line layout' (which de Hamel, *Glossed Books*, 24–27, shows to have been a development of the 1160s in Northern France), evidently without fully understanding it. His own practice seems to have been rooted in the earlier layout. His quires may have been pricked by someone else for the new layout, with which the scribe was unable or unwilling to persist. Trinity B.1.1, B.1.33 and B.1.35 are other glossed books from Master Robert's set that are pricked for the gloss.
2. Trinity B.1.32 was rejected by Ker as a Buildwas book.

VII BIBLIOGRAPHY AND PLATES
James, *Trinity MSS,* I, 43; Ker, *MLGB,* 15; Sheppard 1988, 287 n. 3; Sheppard 1990, 197 n. 9; Thomson 1995, 239–243.

41. CAMBRIDGE, TRINITY COLLEGE MS B.2.15
Isaiah, glossed   **Date** *c.*1160
Leaves [i paper], 130, [i paper]
Foliation 1–130 parchment leaves only
Origin England

I PHYSICAL DESCRIPTION
Binding Rebound s.xvi ex; spine rounded, rebacked since s.xvi.
Endleaves
Front *Pastedown* Single laid paper leaf in place, very marked and torn; pasted over paper repair leaf; no watermark visible; title s.xvii ex, old and new shelfmarks, Trinity College bookplate, otherwise blank.
　　Flyleaves Newer laid paper leaf, conjugate stub pasted under pastedown, broken at joint; watermark: large oval frame containing seated male figure holding a spear (left) and a cross or stylised leaf spray (right), a shield with cross beside him, the oval frame surmounted by crown with 2 Maltese crosses one above the other; blank.
Back *Flyleaves* Fol. 1 of laid paper bifolium, broken at joint; watermark: C.TAYLOR; blank.
　　Pastedown Fol. 2 of laid paper bifolium (see above), watermark as front flyleaf; blank.
Sewing stations Now 5; impressions at spinefolds, e.g. at fol. 59, indicate that earlier, probably originally, there were 3: (tail) l 18 K 35*77*77*38 K 26 l mm (head). Prick marks in a number of quires, 8→1, sometimes not penetrating to fol. 1, lower margin, *c.*10mm from spine edge and 17mm from edge of leaves; not part of a total marking-up system, though they coincide with the lower kettle stitch station; possibly a mark left by a tacket.
Sewing Now all-along with thin, white S-twist thread; thread impressions indicate earlier sewing was all-along.
Sewing supports Now 5 cords; earlier, probably originally, 3 (see above, Sewing stations). Indentations and remains observable under pastedowns are not clear, but seem to indicate perhaps 2 earlier sets of supports (see below, Boards).
Lacing path Now over the outer edge of the boards, through tunnels to

channels on inner face of boards. Indentations and remains visible under pastedowns, while not very clear, indicate earlier parallel channels on the inner faces of the boards.

Endbands None present; thread impressions in spinefolds indicate former presence of endbands tied down in every quire.

Tabs None present; no other evidence.

Spine lining None present; no other evidence.

Boards Wood, 292 x 192 x 6mm, inner edges bevelled. The boards seem to have been reused, but it is not clear whether from this book or another. On the back board there appear to be at least 2 sets of impressions of lacing paths: one is a group of 3 supports and another of 6 supports, none of which seems to coincide precisely with the expected lacing paths of the present 5 supports and so were probably not a part of the current binding structure. The set of three supports coincides only very roughly with the position of 3 earlier sewing stations (see above).

Primary covering Dark brown leather, edges roughly trimmed, with overlapped corners. Triple fillets parallel with all outer edges of boards and along covering over inner bevelled board edges, front and back. Gilt impressed Whitgift arms, front and back. No evidence of original covering.

Fastenings Two brass catchplates on fore-edge of front board, held in place with rectangular-headed brass pins; under the catchplates are the remains of 2 white tawed skin fore-edge straps set into slots in the fore-edge of the board, *c.*31mm (deep) x 19mm (wide). Ends of two fore-edge straps of tanned leather under the primary covering on back board, each held in place by 2 daisy-headed brass pins: upper strap 35mm wide, lower strap 30mm.

Bosses None present; no other evidence.

Chain attachments None present; no other evidence.

Labels Printed paper labels on spine, each bearing an element of the present shelfmark.

Notes Edges of leaves now stained yellowish-green.

Structure of Book

Parchment Quality only fair, some leaves with stained areas, e.g. fol. 3 (animal fluids?), 18–19, 38–39 (splashed material), very many holes (e.g. fols. 20, 22, 25–32, 34 etc., many the result of careless flaying), and patches, fols. 91, 102, 112. Hair and flesh sides fairly evenly coloured though now quite dirty and marked; hair side easily distinguishable by colour and nap.

Collation 1–16^8, 17^2; hair side outside in all quires.

Quire nos. QQ. 1–6, 8, 12: numbers trimmed away or absent; qq. 7, 9–11, 13–16, lower margin of verso of last leaf of each quire in small Roman numerals, some partly trimmed away.

Catchwords None.

Page Layout
Dimensions

Page 276 x 187mm, upper and fore-edge margins trimmed (evidence of lost marginal notes and folded upper corner fol. 6 showing earlier leaf edges).

Space ruled for writing Slightly variable: 206–210 x 156–163mm.

Columns Central text column with gloss columns on either side, text column gradually increasing in width through the book (47–75mm) at the expense of the outer gloss column which begins as the widest column and shrinks to the second widest; however there are two sudden changes in the text column width: at fol. 17v for 5 pages the text column is reduced to 30mm, and on fol. 65v it suddenly increases to 80mm; gloss columns sometimes sub-divided. Outer column wider than inner.

Pricking Much of the pricking in all margins has been trimmed away. Remaining marks suggest: leaves folded, 1→8, outer margin only, using a notched ruler or template. Only text lines pricked.

Ruling In grey sometimes appearing brown. Text lines ruled separately, interlinear gloss lines perhaps ruled at the same time, typically 2 lines above each text line. Marginal gloss lines ruled ad hoc, qq. 1–8: 4 gloss lines to a text line, qq. 9–17, 3 gloss lines to a text line. The first and last lines sometimes ruled edge-to-edge. On fol. 1 (preface page), 6 gloss lines to 5 preface lines.

Lines per page 17 text lines.

Page design

fol. 1(preface)   fols. 1v–64v (qq. 1–8)   fols. 65–130 (qq. 9–17)

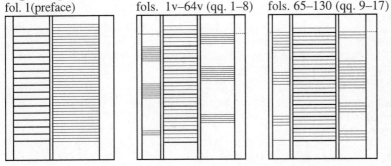

II SCRIBES

Two scribes were responsible for writing the bible text. **Scribe 1** wrote fols. 1–33v in a rather laboured round English hand *c*.1160, of which a characteristic is a long thin serif particularly on the descenders of p and q, and at the base of m and n. This scribe used ampersand and Tironian 'et'. **Scribe 2** (fols. 34v–130v) wrote in a more compressed hand, regular and fluent. He used ampersand exclusively. Scribe 1 was probably the scribe who wrote the gloss on fols. 1–64v (qq. 1–8). A second gloss scribe was responsible for the gloss on fols. 65–88v (qq. 9–11); a third on fols. 89–130v (qq. 12–17) but with the intervention of a fourth on fols. 91v–93. A fifth hand added a substantial passage on fol. 100v, but this is likely to have been the work of a slightly later reader (possibly a hand found in other Buildwas books). An omission was supplied by the second text scribe (fol. 22v).

III DECORATION, RUBRICS AND ARTICULATION OF TEXT

Text initials Unemphasised capitals, often rustic, written by the text scribe. On fols. 84v–85 only, 1-line red capitals for each new sentence (text begins: 'Ego dixi in dimidio dieru*m* meor*um*', interjected before Isaiah 38.10). The first gloss scribe provided each new gloss passage with an emphasised capital (except fols. 2-7v) in addition to brown ink paraphs. The second gloss scribe provided lightly flourished paraphs. The third gloss scribe provided unemphasised rustic capitals but heavy, emphatic paraphs at the beginning of each gloss passage.

Minor initials Fol. 1: **6-preface-line red N**(emo) with reserved scalloped and red and green flourishes. Fol. 84v: **3-text-line red and green E**(go), unflourished or

213

otherwise decorated, but the letter constructed from an outer circular form (in red) with reserved line, and 2 inner green loops which join to form the central stroke of the letter. The gloss precisely accommodates the shape of the initial which may indicate that the initial was made before the gloss was written.

On fol. 18 a space was left for an initial I(n anno quo mortuus est rex ozias; 6.1, the call of Isaiah) but it was not supplied. This chapter begins at the top of a new page, most of the previous page having been left blank.

Major initials Fol. 1v: **5-text-line red and green V**(isio), pen drawn, with brown outline, the colours separated into asymmetrical panels, and with upper terminals of 'folded leaf' design; coloured in with a pen by the display script scribe (colours identical) who also added the same colours to the foliate terminals of the letter.

Historiated initials None.

Display script Fol. 1v: (V)**isio Ysaie Filii Amos** in 1-gloss-line mixed capitals, alternately green and red. The interlinear gloss to these first 3 lines written in red.

Titles etc. None. Explicit on fol. 130v added by a later hand ?s.xii ex, possibly the same hand that added musical notation to this and other leaves (see below, Notes 2). Chapter divisions marked in small Roman numerals in brown ink, some also added in grey in Arabic numbers.

Title page None, but prefatory leaves lost.

IV CONTENTS

Table of contents None.

Main texts Isaiah, glossed.

Fol. 1 Preface: 'Nemo cum prophetas versibus viderit esse descriptos'. Ends fol. 1v: 'ecclesiis eius diutius insultarent.' 8 short gloss passages on fol. 1: i) 'Ieronimus. Sic ysaiam exponam ut non solum prophetam sed evangelistam'. ii) 'Ieronimus. Nemo putet me ysaiam'. iii) 'Ieronimus. Non sicut ait montanus'. iv) 'Ieronimus. Magni laboris est totum ysaiam'. v) 'Ieronimus. Puto lxx interpretes'. vi) 'Ieronimus. Sicut ubi pretermissis lxx de hebraico'. vii) 'Ysaias vir nobilis et urbane eloquentie'. viii) 'Quod in titulo sub ozia'.

Text begins fol. 1v: 'Visio ysaie filii amos'. Gloss begins at the top of fol. 1v, not adjacent to the beginning of the text: 'Visio ysaie. Tria genera sunt visionis primum corporale'. Text ends fol. 130v: 'ad satietatem visionis omni carni. Explicit ysaias propheta.' Gloss ends: 'visa et impiorum in effabili pena.'

V ORIGIN AND PROVENANCE

Ex libris Fol. 1: 'Liber monachorum sancte Marie de Buldewas', in red, in upper margin, s.xii ex/xiii in.

Secundo folio Audite (gloss); (ioa)than achaz (text).

The book was probably written in England. It was owned by Master Robert who annotated text and gloss. The book was at Buildwas by the late twelfth or early thirteenth century when an ex libris inscription was written on fol. 1. It must have remained there with the other glossed books in this group until the fifteenth century.

It was acquired by Archbishop Whitgift and given by him s.xvi ex to Trinity College.

VI NOTES

1. On fols. 8, 11v, 13, 16v, 21, 22v, 72v and 90 are drawings of heads in brown, grey and stylus, some cartoon-like (e.g. fol. 13), others more ambitious (e.g. fol.

11v, a three-quarter profile of a man's head). The drawing in brown on fol. 8 is of a full-length figure in a monk's habit.

2. On fols. 75v, on 5 unused gloss lines, are musical notes, including a clef centred on the 2nd line from the top; on fol. 130v a free-hand 5-line stave is drawn, with a clef centred on the second line from the top and notes of differing values in rising and falling sequences. The colour of the ink suggests that the hand responsible for the musical notes may have been that which supplied the explicit on fol. 130v, s.xii ex/xiii in.

VII BIBLIOGRAPHY AND PLATES
James, *Trinity MSS* 1, 70; Ker, *MLGB*, 14; Sheppard 1988, 287 n. 1; Thomson 1995, 238–243.

42. CAMBRIDGE, TRINITY COLLEGE MS B.1.1
Jeremiah and Lamentations, glossed   Date *c.*1160
Leaves [ii paper], 206, [ii paper]
Foliation 1–206
Origin ?Northern France

I PHYSICAL DESCRIPTION
Binding   Rebound at least once s.xvi (see below, Primary covering) and subsequently repaired or rebound; now also rebacked. Spine rounded and rigid, book opens very poorly, spinefolds and inner margins inaccessible.
Endleaves
Front *Pastedown*   None present; there must once have been a separate group of leaves which served as endleaves which were replaced in the ?first rebinding by a bifolium, stubs only now remaining (see below, Flyleaves 1). There is text on the present fol. 1 recto and on the penultimate leaf of the last quire (of 6 leaves), allowing no integral provision for pastedown and flyleaves.
    Flyleaves **1**) Earlier, but probably not originally, a bifolium comprising 2 parchment sheets, 175 and 190mm high respectively, which overlap to equal the full height of book. Now excised to stubs. **2**) Laid paper bifolium, watermark: pot surmounted by crown and orb, and with initials TB; blank except for inscription s.xvii (fol. ii), and titles.
Back *Flyleaves* **1**) Originally last leaf of last quire, lower half now excised, originally blank; now with added text s.xiii (see below, Contents). **2** First leaf of a bifolium, probably a replacement and conjoint with a pastedown, both leaves now excised to stubs. **3**) Laid paper bifolium with same watermark as front flyleaves, blank except for stain from primary covering turn-ins, very dirty and creased.
    Pastedown None present, stub of earlier bifolium only remaining (see above, Back flyleaves).
Sewing stations Now 4.
Sewing Spinefolds inaccessible.
Sewing supports Now 4 narrow white tawed skin supports. Ends of cord slips visible in addition to the skin ones, glued or pasted to the boards, a repair. Supports all broken.
Lacing path Supports now laced into boards over outer edges, through to their inner surfaces. The slips appear then to be laced again into the thickness of the boards to secure them. Visible lacing paths are 20–25mm long. A very faint

impression on the last stub (see above, Back Flyleaves 2) suggests former V-shaped lacing paths, though the marks converge close to the spinefold rather than at a distance from it.

Endbands Present at head and tail, roughly sewn with natural-coloured thread, but largely obscured by modern headcaps.

Tabs None present; no other evidence.

Spine lining None present; no other evidence.

Boards White pulpboard, curling slightly inwards; 281 x 205 x 7mm (front), 282 x 208 x 7–9mm (back).

Primary covering Brown leather (calf) with triple fillets close to and parallel with all edges of each cover, and further fillets along the edges (thicknesses) and on the inner face of the cover. Large gilt Whitgift arms (s.xvi) impressed on dark brown leather, possibly cut from another covering and pasted to present cover front and back, both upside down. Edges very roughly trimmed, corners overlapped. The lower corner of the first parchment endleaf stub is folded on itself. The folded stub and adjacent paper endleaf show a continuous stain from the present covering, but that part of the stub protected by the folded corner is clean. Unless this stub was only ever a stub, and folded from the outset (which is unlikely), it must earlier have been adjacent to a non-corrosive covering, or protected very thoroughly by other endleaves.

Fastenings None present; no other evidence.

Chemise None present; no other evidence.

Bosses None present; no other evidence.

Chain attachments None present; no other evidence.

Labels Trinity College bookplate fol. 1. Printed paper labels on spine, each with an element of the present shelfmark.

Notes A slip of thin parchment carrying the title of this book (s.xvii) is now loose among the endleaves. A hole near the lower edge in the parchment stub at the back is unexplained; it is too near to the spine to have been made by a boss nail.

Structure of Book

Parchment Well prepared and mostly uniformly white, with some blue-black follicle marks; considerable nap on both sides. Paper repair fol. 40.

Collation $1-25^8$, 26^6 (lower half of last leaf excised, probably blank). Hair side outside in each quire except last.

Quire nos. None.

Catchwords None.

Page Layout
Dimensions
Page 273 x c.197mm (trimmed at least at fore-edge; difficult to measure because of tightness of binding).
Space ruled for writing 182 x 133mm.

Columns Text in central column of variable width, gloss on either side, but 2 columns for prefaces on fols. 150v–151 and on fols. 176v–177, where there is an extensive gloss. A fourth column ruled in outer margin of each page, perhaps for notes.

Pricking Leaves folded, outer margins only, $1 \rightarrow 8$, gloss lines.

Ruling Grey, mostly regular and neat and coinciding with pricking, though pricks for vertical margins not always adhered to, edge-to-edge lines not always consistent. Gloss lines ruled, text written mainly on every other line, beginning on the second or the third ruled line; gloss written above top line.

Lines per page Fols. 1–9r: 39; fols. 9v–205v: 38.

Page design Constant throughout.

fols. 1–206

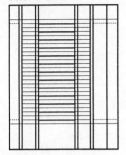

II SCRIBES

One scribe wrote both text and gloss in a clear, upright, regular hand *c.*1160, possibly continental. Characteristics are a trailing tail to x, a very straight-backed a, e, c and t, and unclosed loop to g.

III DECORATION, RUBRICS AND ARTICULATION OF TEXT

The decoration was all carried out by one scribe using alternately red and blue, the initials clearly and competently executed, and decorated for the most part with fine but simple flourishes in the contrasting colour.

Text initials Half-line mixed Roman and uncial capitals, alternately red and blue at each verse, frequently with a paraph of the contrasting colour.

Minor initials Fols. 150–151 (prefaces): 2-line capitals, stem sometimes extended into the margin, alternately red and blue, often flourished in the contrasting colour.

Major initials Fol. 1v: **10-line red and blue V**(erba), the colours separated by a reserved scalloped line, filled with a symmetrical design of fleshy scrolls and lobes mainly in blue. Terminals composed of similar motifs and whole letter decorated with simple and elegant flourishes. The letters 'erba' incorporated into the design. Fol. 151v: **9-line red and blue Q**(uomodo), the tail extending to the lower margin. Fol. 165: **7-line red and blue Q**(uomodo), the tail extending across the lower margin. Fol. 191: **6-line red and blue Q**(uomodo), with a reserved scalloped line and extended tail, flourished in red.

Historiated initials None.

Display script Fol. 1v: (V)**erba** in 2-line mixed capitals alternately red and blue, each flourished with the contrasting colour, arranged vertically between upper and lower serifs of the letter V. Fol. 151v: (Q)**uo**(modo) in 3-line capitals, elongated and laterally compressed, each flourished with the contrasting colour, written vertically and adjacent to the initial Q. Fol. 191: (Q)**uo**(modo), each letter compressed but of uneven size (3-lines and 1-line high respectively), both letters red, flourished with blue. Fol. 165: no display script. The names of the voices in Lamentations written in similar mixed, $1\frac{1}{2}$-line capitals, alternately red and blue, but less compressed than the display script elsewhere and without flourishes.

Title page None.

217

Titles etc. No running titles; explicit by scribe fol. 205v, another added by a later hand, s.xii–xiii on fol. 150. Names of authors of prefaces (fols. 150v–151) in red minuscule. Marginal chapter numbers in red ink, probably contemporary.

IV CONTENTS
Table of contents None.

Main texts Jeremiah and Lamentations, glossed.
1. Fol. 1: 2 prefaces: i) 'Origen Deus ad benefaciendum promptus est'. Ends fol. 1: 'possum eruere de captivitate qui tradidi.' ii) 'Hec eciam de nobis possumus intellegere'. Ends fol. 1: 'que locutus sum facere eis.' Text begins fol. 1v: 'Verba ieremie'. Gloss begins: 'Jeremiah ad Eusebium. Quia volumen longissimum et inplerisque hystoria manifesta'. Text ends fol. 150: 'ad diem mortis sue cunctis diebus vite sue.' Gloss ends fol. 150: 'ubi gemunt in perpetuum dampnati.'
2. Fol. 151: 7 prefaces: i) 'Pascasius: Sunt cantica canticorum sunt et lamentationes lamentorum'. ii) 'Pascasius: Constat multa esse genera fletuum multas differentias lacrimarum'. iii) 'Pascasius: Lamentatio est. Aut ex merore presentis vite'. iv) 'Tam terrene civitatis ruinam quam ecclesia dampna'. v) 'Pascasius: Quadruplici plangit alphabeto'. vi) 'Gislebertus: Lamentationes ieremie membro patet orationes maxime distingui'. vii) 'Gislebertus: Rethoricorum colorum splendorem et sententiarum gravitatem'. Text begins fol. 151v: 'Quomodo sedet sola civitas'. Gloss begins: 'Quomodo sedet sola civitas. Subversionem misere civitas et ruinam celestis'. Text ends fol. 205v: 'iratus es contra nos vehementer. Explicit.' Gloss ends fol. 205v: 'que de patrum fontibus hausi ego gillibertus altisiodorensis ecclesie diaconus.'
3. Fol. 206 originally blank. Text added s.xiii in: 'Inter trenos jeremie vere lugent syon vie quod non sit sollempni die qui sepulcrum visitet vel casum resuscitet huius prophetie'. Ends: 'Cum attendas ad quid tendo crucem tollas et vovendo dicas illi me commendo qui corpus et animam expendit in victimam pro te moriendo. Lignum crucis signum ducis sequitur excercitus.' etc. Printed in full in James, *Trinity MSS*, I, 1–3. James observes that this is a crusader hymn, the verses written as prose.
Fol. 206v: scribbles s.xv: 'Noverint universi per presentes nos Ricardum Alane... Noverint universi per presentes Amen quod Glowcestre Noverint universi per presentes nos Alanum Pountenay', and other phrases and pen trials.

V ORIGIN AND PROVENANCE
Ex libris Fol. 1: 'liber sancte Marie de Buldewas', in greenish-brown ink in a very large, upright hand s.xiv.
Secundo folio (us)que ad consummationem (text); qui ultimus (interlinear gloss).
The scribal hand and the decoration suggest that the book was made in France. The book is annotated and punctuated throughout by an annotator s.xiii in (e.g. fols. 104, 137, 158, 164v–165 etc.), whose notes are also found elsewhere in the glossed books once at Buildwas. There is little evidence of Master Robert's annotation, but notes on fols. 162v, 169v are certainly his. The book was still at Buildwas in the fourteenth century (evidence of the ex libris), and in fact must have remained there with the other glossed books in this set until at least the late fifteenth century.
It was acquired by Archbishop Whitgift who gave it to Trinity College s.xvi ex.

218

VI NOTES
1. The page layout in which the gloss lines are pricked and ruled and the text written on every second or third ruled line is a later glossed book development in Northern France, dated by C. de Hamel, *Glossed Books*, 24–27, to the 1160s.
2. The hand (s.xiii) which copied the Crusader Hymn also wrote 'ex libris jeremias' (fol. 150).

VII BIBLIOGRAPHY AND PLATES
James, *Trinity MSS,* I, 1–3; Ker, *MLGB,* 14; Thomson 1995, 238–243.

43. CAMBRIDGE, TRINITY COLLEGE MS B.4.3
Minor Prophets, glossed (imperfect)   **Date** *c.*1165
Leaves [i paper], 89, [i paper]
Foliation 1–89
Origin Probably England

This manuscript is unique among Master Robert's glossed books in having illuminated initials.

I PHYSICAL DESCRIPTION
Binding Rebound s.xvi, since repaired and provided with a hollow back; guards sewn into centre of each quire.
Endleaves
  Front *Pastedown* Single laid paper leaf in place, probably once part of a bifolium, conjoint leaf excised; watermark: one-handled pot surmounted by a crown, letters P ?D on body of pot; old and new shelfmarks, Trinity College bookplate, otherwise blank.
    Flyleaves Laid paper leaf, probably once part of a bifolium; stub of leaf visible under pastedown, broken at joint; watermark as for front pastedown, blank.
  Back *Flyleaves* Single laid paper leaf, probably once part of a bifolium; stub of leaf visible under pastedown; watermark as on front endleaves, blank.
    Pastedown Single laid paper leaf in place, probably once part of a bifolium, conjoint leaf excised; watermark as on front endleaves; blank.
Sewing stations Now 6; formerly, probably originally, 3 (evidence of visible thread impressions, e.g. at fol. 58: (tail) | 31 K 51*91*90*44 K 32 | mm (head). A prick mark in lower margin, *c.*34–38mm from lower edge and *c.*10mm from spine edge visible throughout, 8→1, seldom penetrating to first leaves in each quire, not apparently part of any primary sewing marking-up process, but just possibly connected with the tacketing of leaves together during copying. It coincides roughly with the lower kettle stitch station.
Sewing Now all-along with thin white S-twist thread; thread impressions indicate that earlier sewing was also all-along, twist of thread not decipherable.
Sewing supports Now sewn on 6 cords, some broken at joints. Earlier, probably originally, on 3 supports (see above, Sewing stations).
Lacing path Present cords laced over outer edges of boards and through tunnels to inner face, parallel channels on inner face *c.*45mm long. No evidence of earlier lacing path.
Endbands None present; earlier, probably originally, endbands tied down in each quire (evidence of sewing thread impressions).

Tabs None present; no other evidence.

Spine lining None present; no other evidence.

Boards Wood, 360 x 252 x 10mm, inner edges bevelled (width of bevel: 10–12mm).

Primary covering Dark brown leather, turn-ins unevenly trimmed, corners over-lapped. Triple fillets parallel with all outer edges, front and back, and along the three bevelled inner edges; large impressed gilt Whitgift arms front and back.

Fastenings Front: ends of two straps of brown leather each held in place under primary covering by two daisy-headed brass pins (one lost from lower strap). Back: two brass catchplates attached over primary covering.

Bosses None present; no other evidence.

Chain attachments None present; no other evidence.

Labels Printed paper labels on spine, each with an element of present shelfmark.

Notes Leaf edges now stained yellowish-green.

Structure of Book

Parchment Good quality, thick skin, hair side slightly yellow and often extensively follicle marked; several judder marks and flaymarks (e.g. fols. 5, 70); some parchment maker's repairs (e.g. fol. 68), and a patch fol. 4.

Collation $1–11^8$, 12 (one leaf remains, stub visible before fol. 81). Hair side outside in all quires.

Quire nos. Q. 3 numbered iiii, q. 6 numbered but trimmed, possibly vii, in lower margin of verso of last leaf; 1 quire is missing after q. 1. Other numbers may also have been lost in trimming.

Catchwords None.

Page Layout
Dimensions

Page 343 x 245mm, all margins trimmed (evidence of lost marginal notes, running titles and quire numbers).

Space ruled for writing Slightly variable: 248–250 x 197 increasing to 207mm at the end of the text.

Columns Central text column with gloss column on either side, mainly consistent in width, the inner the narrowest and the outer the widest. Gloss columns sometimes subdivided by ruling for parallel glosses. Prefaces and their glosses usually written across one of the vertical bounding lines to form two unequal columns, according to the requirements of the preface.

Pricking Text lines only; inner margins seldom visible, but on some leaves, e.g. fols. 58v–59, 88v–89, it is clear that the pricking was done with leaves folded, $1{\rightarrow}8$ in both margins. Where marks on fol. 8 are too faint, the page is repricked $8{\rightarrow}1$ (e.g. q. 10).

Ruling In grey sometimes appearing brown, not very carefully executed; text lines ruled first; gloss lines ruled ad hoc, 3–4 lines per text line; two lines ruled between each text line, ad hoc, for interlinear glosses. Preface lines ruled ad hoc slightly closer together than the text lines but further apart than gloss lines, and the preface page layout is adapted freely according to the requirement of each preface text and its glosses.

Lines per page 20 text lines, written above top line, but interlinear glosses written above top line of text where applicable.

Page design
fols. 1–89v

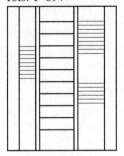

II SCRIBES

One scribe wrote the text in a large, regular, upright English hand, c.1165, lower loop to g often not quite closed. This scribe used ampersand. The gloss and prefaces were written throughout by a second scribe who also wrote the list of kings on fol. 1. This hand is compressed but very neat, with sharply angled serifs; this scribe used Tironian 'et'. He also provided short passages omitted from text in the margins of fols. 31, 36, 77. On fols. 41, 68, 89v, the gloss appears to have been written around the painted initial, suggesting that the text and initials were completed before the gloss, or that they were carried out to a certain extent simultaneously.

The text scribe wrote most of the incipits and explicits (e.g. for Hosea, fol. 2), at least for the texts; however because another scribe was to write the prefaces and glosses (for which the text scribe left large spaces) he usually did not write the rubrics for prefaces. Where he did, he often carelessly forgot to allow for the writing of the preface between the text explicit and the next text incipit which sometimes immediately follow one another (e.g. fols. 11v, 33), regardless of the space specifically left by him when copying the text for the insertion of prefaces. He seems to have provided the text rubrics (in red and/or green) before the initials were painted (evidence of overlapped descenders, e.g. fol. 20).

The preface and gloss scribe, however, also failed to provide the missing rubrics and, since rubrication notes are often provided in Master Robert's hand, it is clear that they were not in place or not complete when he acquired the book. The rubrics on fol. 62 (Sophonias) overlap the painted initial. Since the hands which provided the missing rubrics date to the latter part of s.xii, they may well have been provided by Buildwas scribes (cf. the illustrations to the Pauline Epistles, Trinity B.1.6).

Other hands, almost certainly those of readers, added lengthy passages to the gloss, e.g. on fols. 7, 7v and 8v (hand a); 42v, 59, 88 and 88v (hand b), among several others; hands a and b are English, hand a is that of the final text scribe in St. John's D.2, q.v. Master Robert also added passages, e.g. on fols. 11v, 16, 65.

III DECORATION, RUBRICS AND ARTICULATION OF TEXT

The book is characterised by a series, incomplete, of fully painted initials, one of which is historiated. On fol. 41, the painter executed only the inside of the letter, the form of the letter itself being provided by the display script scribe. The painter who made them executed most of the initials in a twelfth-century French

Bible in Oxford, Bodleian Library, MS Laud. Misc. 752 (see further below, Origin and Provenance). The initials painted by this artist are all (except that on fol. 41) formed by bands of shaded colour outlined in black, usually enclosing inset panels of another colour. The text scribe failed to leave space for painted initials on fols. 68, 72. It is evident that at least some of the initials were completed before the gloss was added (see especially fols. 41, 68, 89v).

Text initials 1-line brown ink capitals written by the scribe, often thickened for emphasis. Gloss passages begin usually with a rustic letter in red, and small red, mixed capitals are used for the name of the authority where cited.

Minor initials Prefaces throughout begin with 4- or 5-preface-line capitals alternately red and blue with flourishes in blue or red. The flourishes are usually slight but neatly done, characterised by a 'ladder' motif which frequently trails unattached at its lower end. These initials are on fols. 1v, 12, 19v, 33, 35v, 40v, 51, 56, 60 (for Habbakuk's prayer), 61v, 67v, 71v; initials on fol. 89 are by a different hand, perhaps provided at a different time.

Major initials Fol. 2: **5-text-line shaded green** V(erba) with inset panels of red in both ascenders and with a delicate foliate design superimposed in white (appearing pink), and simple leaf terminals; the letter filled with red against which are two blue scrolls with stylised flower terminals in green, ochre and red, the whole letter set against a stepped blue background with trios of fine white dots and framed with ochre, black and white lines. Fol. 12v: **4-text-line shaded ochre and white** V(erbum) with inset panels of green outlined in black; inside letter is an eagle painted in red, pink, black and white, its head turned to face backwards and one foot raised, against a blue background on which are trios of fine white dots; the whole letter against a red field with trios of fine white dots and a frame of white and black lines. Fol. 20: **4-text-line shaded red** V(erba); inside letter a shaded ochre scroll outlined in black with green tendril shoots against a red background, the whole set in a blue field with trios of fine white dots and framed with black and white lines. Fol. 33v: **historiated initial,** see below. Fol. 36: **4-text-line shaded green and white** E(t) with fine black lines inset, the letter filled with blue on which are trios of tiny white dots; in upper half of letter an ochre and white, channel-style stylised lion, in the lower half a red, pink, black and white long-necked bird (painted in a similar way to that on fol. 2) with head lowered and a worm in its mouth; the whole letter set on a plain, square, red background framed with white and black lines. Fol. 41: **4-text-line light brown** V(erbum) with thin green panels set into both ascenders, provided by the display script scribe; the letter filled with blue against which is a shaded ochre, black and white scroll and sparse stylised leaves of brown, purplish-pink and green terminating in a thin biting 'snake's-head' with an orange channel-style lion in its mouth; this initial has no field. Fol. 51v: **4-text-line shaded purplish-pink and white** O(nus), with a blue ass standing on a rocky outcrop against a green background (rubbed), playing a red harp; the whole letter set against a stepped field of blue with trios of fine white dots and framed by black and white lines. Fol. 56v: **4-text-line shaded purplish-pink and white** O(nus) with red inset panels roughly dotted with white; large central stylised flower in purplish-pink, ochre, green, blue and orange against a blue background; the whole letter set on a square green field (rubbed) framed with black and white lines. Fol. 62: **4-text-line purplish-pink** V(erbum) with inset green panels, a naked man wrestling with a black and grey bear against a red background; the whole letter set against a blue shaped field, with a frame of

222

white and black lines. Fol. 68v: **5-text line blue I**(n) with a fine wavy reserved line, extended tail and red flourishes; the gloss is written round this initial and must have been written after the initial had been made. Fol. 72: **5-text-line red I**(n) with a scalloped reserved line and blue flourishes. Fol. 89: **4-text-line shaded green and white O**(nus) with simple shaded purplish-pink scroll, 2 stylised leaves in ochre and both green leaf and biting 'snake's-head' terminals against a blue background; the whole letter set on a squared field of red with trios of fine white dots, and framed with white and black lines. The gloss is written so as to accommodate this initial which extends into the gloss column.

Historiated initial Fol. 33v: **4-text-line shaded ochre and white V**(isio) with green inset panels and simple leaf terminals; the letter filled with blue against which the prophet (Obadiah) stands wearing a green robe and a red cloak, modelled in a late, damp-fold style, holding an uninscribed scroll; the letter set against a stepped field of red with trios of fine white dots, framed with black and white lines.

Display script Fol. 1: (N)**on** in 1-preface-line brown ink capitals by the scribe. Fol. 2: (V)**erbum** in 2-gloss-line Roman capitals alternately red and blue. Fol. 12v: (V)**erbum** in 2-gloss-line blue Roman capitals with red abbreviation mark. Fol. 20: (V)**erba** in 2-gloss-line Roman capitals alternately red and blue. Fol. 33v: (V)**isio** in 2-gloss-line blue Roman capitals. Fol. 36: (E)**t factum** in 2-gloss-line blue Roman capitals with red abbreviation mark. Fol. 41: (V)**erbum** in 2-gloss-line capitals alternately green, red and light brown with red abbreviation mark. Fol. 51v: (O)**nus** in 2-gloss-line red Roman capitals. Fol. 56v: (O)**nus** in 2-gloss-line red Roman capitals. Fols. 62, 68, 72: no display script. Fol. 89: (O)**nus** in 2-gloss-line blue Roman capitals.

Titles etc. Running titles by a slightly later hand in red, all partly trimmed away, one of two hands which also provided a number of missing rubrics. Incipits and explicits in red or green mainly by the text scribe but another later hand (s.xii ex) provided those he had omitted on fol. 1v, and the running-titles-hand provided them elsewhere. The missing rubrics were evidently not all in place when Master Robert acquired the book since he provided notes for them.

Title page None, but prefatory leaves probably lost.

IV CONTENTS

Table of contents None.

Main texts The Minor Prophets, glossed (imperfect: Hosea is lacking 5.15–12.4; Malachi is incomplete after 1.6).

1. Fol. 1 in four columns: 'Nomina regum tribuum x; Nomina regum duarum tribuu*m*'. Each heading followed by lists of kings and the length of their reigns in years or months; the whole is repeated in the remaining columns but the length of reigns omitted.

2. Fol. 1v: General preface: 'Incipit pro*logus* beati ier*onomi* in duodecim pro*phe*tis. Non idem ordo est'. Ends: 'q*ui* ante eos h*abe*nt prophetaverunt.' Gloss: 'Ordo pro*phe*tarum sec*un*du*m* lxx'.

3. Fol. 1v: Hosea. '*Prologus* osee incipit. Temporibus ozie *et* ioathe achaz'. Ends fol. 1v: 'ac pu*ri*ficasse monstratur.' Gloss: 'Mat*eria* osee triplex *est*'. Fol. 1v: Incipit osee pro*phe*ta'. Text begins: Fol. 2: 'Verbum domini quod factum est'. Gloss begins: 'Osee. de tribu ysacar ortus in bethleemoth'. Text ends fol. 11v: 'prevaricatores vero corruent in eis. Explicit osee pro*phe*ta.' Gloss ends: 'ex postea fuerunt.' One quire missing carrying 5.15–12.4.

223

4. Fol. 11v: Johel. 'Incipit iohel propheta' (written in the wrong place by text scribe); 'Prologus ieronomi in Iohel prophetam'. Fol. 12: preface: 'Sanctus iohel apud hebreos post osee ponitur'. Preface ends: 'et ysias audite celi auribus percipe terra.' Gloss: 'Iohel fatuel filius describit terram'. Text begins fol. 12v: 'Verbum quod factum est'. Gloss begins: 'Ieromini. Fatuel propheta pater iohel propheta'. Text ends fol. 19: 'et dominus commorabitur in syon. Explicit iohel propheta.' Gloss ends: 'omnia sub peccato ut omnium misereretur.'

5. Fol. 19v: Amos. 2 prefaces: i) 'Prologus Ieronimi. Ozias rex cum dei religionem'. Ends: 'voluit demonstrare.' ii) 'Alius prologus. Amos propheta rusticus et ruborum'. Ends: 'qui evangelizas syon et exalta etcetera.' Gloss: 'Hic amos propheta non fuit pater ysaii prophete'. Text begins fol. 20: 'Incipit amos propheta. Verba amos'. Gloss begins: 'Amos non ad ierusalem sed ad israel in samara prophetat'. Text ends fol. 32v: 'dicit dominus deus tuus omnipotens. Explicit amos propheta.' Gloss ends: 'ad celestem paradisum pertingant.'

6. Fol. 33: Obadiah. Preface: 'Incipit abdias propheta' (written in the wrong place over space left free for preface): 'Iacob patriarcha fratrem habuit esau'. Ends: 'servuus [sic] domini in nostro sonat eloquio.' Gloss i): 'Abdias quanto brevior tanto est profundior'. ii) 'Secundum tropologiam factus est sermo'. Text begins fol. 33v: 'Visio abdie'. Gloss begins: 'Esau filius ysaac frater iacob'. Text ends fol. 35v: 'et erit domino regnum amen. Explicit abdias propheta.' Gloss ends: 'domino regnum parabunt.'

7. Fol. 35v: Jonah. Preface: 'Incipit prologus in Ionam prophetam. Secundum ionam hebrei affirmant filium fuisse mulieris'. Ends: 'Quo ibo a spiritu tuo et quo a. f. t. f.' 4 Glosses: i) 'Ionas columba et dolens'. ii) 'Sicut ait herodotus'. iii) 'Nullus tipi sui melior'. iv) 'Cum ionas secundum interpretationem'. Text begins fol. 36: 'Incipit ionas propheta. Et factum est'. Gloss begins: 'Et factum est. Ad ea que in mente prophete spiritu convolvebantur'. Text ends fol. 40: 'et sinistram suam et iumenta multa. Explicit ionas propheta.' Gloss ends: 'quid esset inter bonum et malum.' Lower part of this leaf cut out, probably blank.

8. Fol. 40v: Micah. Preface: 'Prologus ieronimi. Temporibus ioathe et achaz et ezechie regum iuda'. Ends: 'et interitum affuturum denunciavit.' 3 glosses: i) 'Sermo dei qui semper'. ii) 'Argumentum. Micheas de morasti'. iii) 'Micheas secundum hebraicam'. Text begins fol. 41: 'Incipit micheas propheta. Verbum domini'. Gloss begins: 'Humili et cho heredi christi sit revelatio'. Text ends fol. 50v: 'que iurasti patribus nostris a diebus antiquis. Explicit micheas propheta.' Gloss ends: 'qui extiterunt patres nostre fidei.'

9. Fol. 51: Nahum. Preface: 'Prologus ieromini [sic]. Naum prophetam ante adventum regis assiriorum'. Ends: 'adversum veros assirios futurus est dominus.' Gloss: 'Cum ionas et naum de eadem ninive'. Text begins fol. 51v: 'Incipit naum propheta. Onus ninive'. Gloss begins: 'Zelatur dominus in salutem eorum quos zelatur'. Text ends fol. 55v: 'non transiit malicia tua semper. Explicit naum propheta.' Gloss ends: 'que non est permanens sed transitoria.'

10. Fol. 56: Habakkuk. 4 Prefaces: i) 'Abacuc luctator fortis et rigidus'. Ends: 'abscondita est fortitudo eius.' ii) 'Abacuc amplexans'. Ends: 'et omnibus predicare.' iii) 'Commitatur ieronimus super osee'. Ends: 'ex superio tolosano episcopo.' iv) 'Quattuor prophete in xii prophetarum volumine sunt'. Ends: 'tribulationem et miseriam invenire desiderat.' No glosses. Text begins fol. 56v: 'Incipit abacuch propheta. Onus quod vidit'. Gloss begins: 'Massa apud hebreos ponitur'. Text ends fol. 61v: 'victor in psalmis canentam. amen. Explicit abacuch propheta.' Gloss ends: 'laudabo iniquitatem tuam.'

11. Fol. 61v: Zephaniah. Preface: 'Prologus ieronomi' (rubric added over wrong column). 'Sophonias speculator *et* archanorum dei cognitor'. Ends: 'qui involuti erant argento.' 2 glosses: i) 'Tradunt hebrei cuiuscu*mq*ue prophe*te*'. ii) 'In titulo generatio p*r*ophe*te*'. Text begins fol. 62: 'Incipit Sophonias p*r*ophe*ta*. Verbum domini'. Gloss begins: 'Ad sophoniam speculam *vel* archanum'. Text ends fol. 67: 'coram ocu*l*is *ves*tris dici*t* d*omi*nu*s*. Explicit sophonias p*r*ophe*ta*.' Gloss ends: 'consurg*ere* in confusione*m* ete*r*nam.'

12. Fol. 67v: Haggai. Preface: 'P*r*olog*us* ieronomi. Aggeus festivus *et* letus'. Ends: '*et* veniet desideratus cunctus gentibus.' 3 glosses: i) 'Cum cyrus rex pe*r*sarum'. ii) 'Ieremias p*r*ophe*t*am ob causam'. iii) 'Darius interp*r*etatur gen*er*ationes'. Text begins fol. 63: 'Incipit Aggeus prophe*t*a. In anno s*e*cundo'. Gloss begins: 'Aggeus sollennis in cui*us* manu sit sermo d*omi*ni'. Text ends fol. 71: 'q*ui*a te elegi dicit d*omi*nu*s* exercituu*m*.' Gloss ends: 'h*i*c qu*a*si anulo consignetur.'

13. Fol. 71v: Zachariah. Preface: 'P*r*olog*us* ieronimi. Zacha*t*ias [sic] memor d*omi*ni'. Ends: 'asine filium subiugalis.' 2 glosses: i) 'Secundo anno darii regis'. ii) 'Cirus rex pe*r*sarum'. Text begins fol. 72: 'Incipit zacharias p*r*ophe*t*a. In mense octavio'. Gloss begins: 'Novembri qui consumpto calore estatis inicium *est* hiemis'. Text ends fol. 88v: 'in domo d*omi*ni exercituum in die illo. Explicit zacharaias p*r*ophe*t*a.' Gloss ends: 'quia d*omi*nu*s* de eccle*si*a sua vendentes et em*m*entes eicit.'

14. Fol. 89: Malachi. Preface: 'Malachias etia*m* ap*er*te et infine omnium p*r*ophe*t*arum'. Ends: 'homini meo oblatio munda.' 3 glosses: i) 'Malachias latine int*er*p*r*etatur ang*e*lus'. ii) 'Malachi int*er*p*r*etatur ang*e*lus m*e*us'. iii) 'D*e*us per moysen p*op*ulo isra*e*li p*er*cep*er*at'. Text begins fol. 89v: 'Incipit Malachias p*r*ophe*t*a. Onus verbi domini'. Gloss begins: 'Isr*a*el vir *vel* sensus cernens d*e*um'. Text ends incomplete at 1.6: 'et servuus d*omi*nu*m* suu*m* timebit. Si ergo'. Gloss ends: 'Si pat*er* ves*t*er sum offerte'. Another hand s.xii ex has added: 'honore*m et* pietate*m*. Si d*omi*nu*s* ne *con*tempnatis s*ed* timere', evidently aiming to complete the sense of the gloss. The same hand supplied an omission in left marginal gloss on the same page.

V ORIGIN AND PROVENANCE

Ex libris Fol. 1v: 'Liber sancte Marie de Bildewas', s.xii ex, the words alternately green and red.

Secundo folio Osee. de tribu (gloss); Verbum (text).

It is not clear exactly where the book was written, though Thomson surmises that the scribal hand is a west-country one (Thomson 1995, 240). The other known work of the painter is in Oxford, Bodleian Library, MS Laud. Misc. 752, a French Romanesque one-volume historiated bible, which must have been executed while the book was still in France, though the channel style he practised was common in both England and France. Master Robert was manifestly teaching and collecting glossed books in France around the middle of the century, but must have come to England later on since his books were at Buildwas at least by the end of the century, and it seems that he may also have acquired one or two glossed books made in this country. On the basis of other artistic evidence in Laud Misc. 752, it is tempting to posit Savigny (the founding house of Buildwas and a great centre of learning which had, in its heyday, an enormous library) as the link between Laud Misc. 752 and Trinity B.4.3. However, so far there is no evidence for such a connection, and no evidence that the Laud Misc. Bible was ever at Buildwas, though it has certain Cistercian characteristics. An examination conducted in 1989 of the few books from Savigny so far identified revealed no links with the surviving Buildwas books or with Laud Misc. 752.

The evidence of three initials (on fols. 44, 68, 89v) suggests that the text and painted initials, including the penwork ones, were executed first, and the gloss and prefaces added after this, perhaps because the purchaser wished to select prefaces and/or control the way the gloss was written. On fol. 2, Master Robert added a punctuation mark which overlaps the border of the painted initial, supporting the premise that text and painted initials were finished before he acquired the book. This raises the possibility that Master Robert himself organised the copying of the gloss and prefaces. This would be quite consistent with his completion of Trinity B.1.13 (q.v.) and his habit of editing glosses generally. Many substantial passages of the gloss were added by other hands than that of the main gloss scribe. Among the annotators is an irregular hand with a vertically compressed g which is frequently found in the Buildwas glossed books, and the scribe who wrote part of St. John's D.2. Quire 2, now missing, was probably in place when the reader who provided marginal and running chapter numbers (probably s.xiii) worked on the book; the quire was perhaps lost as a result of a deteriorating binding, probably after its removal from Buildwas. The last quire, however, on the evidence of the hand which completed the last sentence of the gloss, may have been lost quite early on.

This book must have come to Buildwas with the others and, on the evidence of inscriptions and deeds in other books in this set, remained at Buildwas at least until the fifteenth century.

It was acquired by Archbishop Whitgift and given to Trinity College s.xvi ex.

VI NOTES

1. Chapter numbers were provided by two hands: small neat Roman numbers and larger, untidy capitulum signs with a series of Arabic numbers. The latter hand also added running chapter numbers in Arabic numbers on the right corner recto. On fol. 5v, in lower margin, within left-hand double bounding lines, Arabic numbers '1' and '20' in stylus.

2. The fact that the last quire may have been missing from an early date might be evidence of the book's having been used at first in a temporary, limp binding in which outer quires would have been especially vulnerable (cf. Trinity B.1.13).

VII BIBLIOGRAPHY AND PLATES

James, *Trinity MSS*, I, 141; Ker, *MLGB*, 14; O. Pächt and J.J.G. Alexander, *Illuminated Manuscripts in the Bodleian Library* (Oxford, 1973), III, no. 245, pl. 25; C.M. Kauffmann, *Romanesque Manuscripts 1066–1190* (London, 1975), 124; J.M. Sheppard, *The Giffard Bible* (New York, 1986), 62–69, pls. 38–60, 88–103, 107–111, 120–121, 131–137; Sheppard 1988, 287 n. 1; Thomson 1995, 238–243, especially 240–241.

44. CAMBRIDGE, TRINITY COLLEGE MS B.1.10

1. Matthew, glossed; 2. ?Anselm, Commentary on John

Leaves [i paper], 80, ii, 57, [i paper] **Date** *c.*1130–35; s. xii med

Foliation 1–139

Origin Northern France

This book contains two separate texts, only one of which, the glossed Matthew, was certainly owned by Master Robert. This is the earliest of all his glossed books. It is not clear when the two texts were first bound together. Trinity B.1.10, at least its first text, is here newly attributed to Buildwas.

The binding of the book as it now exists will be described first and then each booklet independently. The Provenance, Notes and Bibliography for the whole book will be given at the end.

I PHYSICAL DESCRIPTION

Binding   Resewn and rebound s.xvi and again since then, spine recently recovered; opens poorly. Virtually no evidence remains of earlier bindings.

Endleaves

Front *Pastedown*   Single blue laid paper leaf, now pasted down over stub which is conjoint with present flyleaf; blank.

Flyleaves   Blue laid paper leaf (chain lines horizontal) pasted to white laid paper leaf (chain lines vertical), conjoint with stub now under pastedown; blank.

Back *Flyleaves*   White laid paper leaf (chain lines vertical) pasted to blue laid paper leaf (chain lines horizontal); conjoint with stub now under pastedown; blank.

Pastedown   2 half leaves of thick blue laid paper pasted down over stub of flyleaf; blank.

Sewing stations   Now 4; faint thread impressions just visible on fol. 17 suggest that earlier, there were 2 sewing stations.

Sewing   Not visible.

Sewing supports   Now 4, material not known, probably cord.

Lacing path   Over outer edges of boards, slips fixed under pastedown. No other evidence.

Endbands   None present; no other evidence.

Tabs   None present; no other evidence.

Spine lining   None present; no other evidence.

Boards   Pasteboard, 260 x 170 x 6mm, with projecting square of c.3mm at all edges.

Primary covering   Dark brown leather, corners overlapped, spine re-covered; small gilt, impressed Whitgift arms on both covers; triple fillets frame each cover, remains of gold in centre fillets.

Fastenings   Remains of 2 thin rolled skin ties near fore-edge of both covers.

Chemise   None present; no other evidence.

Bosses   None present; no other evidence.

Chain attachments   None present; no other evidence.

Labels   Laid paper fore-edge label s.xvii inscribed 'Anselm[us super iohannem]', referring to the second text.

Notes   1) On fol. 80v at the outer lower corner of the leaf, there is an offset of, or some partially erased, undecipherable writing. If an offset, it was not made by anything now facing this leaf. 2) Edges of leaves now stained greenish-yellow.

BOOKLET 1: fols. 1–80

Structure of Booklet

Parchment Hair and flesh sides clearly distinguishable, hair side slightly greasy; very many areas of follicle marking and many holes; an original sewn repair on fol. 52 (the gloss is written around it).

Collation 1–10⁸. Hair side outermost in each quire.

Quire nos. QQ. 1–9, lower margin of verso of last leaf, in small Roman numerals.

Quire signatures QQ. 1–10, signed a–i in a minute minuscule, lower fore-edge of last verso of each quire.

Catchwords None.

Page Layout
Dimensions
Page 250 x 166mm.
Space ruled for writing Variable width, variations occurring mainly in outer gloss column: fol. 2v: 158 x 131mm; fol. 36: 158 x 146mm.
Columns 3; 1 central text column with 2 flanking gloss columns; text column is of constant width.
Pricking Outer margins only visible but much evidence trimmed away; remains suggest leaves folded, 1→8, using a template; only text lines pricked.
Ruling Text lines blind ruled on hair side; gloss lines, if ruled, also blind.
Lines per page 20 text lines, 2 or 3 gloss lines per text line, as needed.
Page design
fols. 1–80v

1/II SCRIBES
One scribe wrote the text in a small, round, upright minuscule *c.*1135–40 with slightly clubbed serifs. The gloss was written by the text scribe in a rather variable hand, some passages in paler ink as if not written continuously. Another hand wrote a short gloss on Omnia, fol. 1.

1/III DECORATION, RUBRICS AND ARTICULATION OF TEXT
Text initials Small rustic capitals written by scribe.
Minor initials None.
Major initials Space left fol. 1v for M, not supplied.
Historiated initials None.
Display script None.
Title page None.
Titles etc. No running titles. An annotating hand s.xii wrote a note for the incipit and explicit to the Argumentum on fols. 1v and 2 respectively, for a rubricator. The incipit to the Argumentum added in red above top line fol. 1v, now rubbed. A much later hand (s.xvi–xvii) added chapter numbers in top

margins fols. 5–13 (chapters 2–5). The same hand added notes on fols. 2v–8 and a small initial m in the space left on fol. 1v.

1/IV CONTENTS
Table of contents Fol. 1 in a later hand, s.xvii: 'Anselmus in Mattheum *et* Johannem. in fine adjicitur Sermo S*anc*ti Augustini'.
Main texts Matthew, glossed
1. Preface fol. 1v: '[M]atheus ex iudea sicut in ordine p*rimus* ponitur'. Ends fol. 2: 'querentib*us* non tacere.' 2 glosses fol. 1v: i) 'Cu*m* multi scripsisse evang*e*lia leg*untur* soli iiii*or*.' Ends: 'si n*on* reculationem [sic] c*om*passionem.' ii) 'Querit*ur* animo dic*atur* christi n*on* pecasse'. Ends fol. 2: 'hoc simil*iter* in christo.' Text begins fol. 2v: '[L]iber generationibus'. Gloss begins fol. 2v: 'Fidelissimi *generatio*nis auctores eligun*tur*'. Text ends fol. 80v: 'ad consu*m*mationem seculi amen.' Gloss ends fol. 80v: 'qui divina mansione sunt digni.'

1/V ORIGIN AND PROVENANCE
Ex libris None.
Secundo folio [testimo]niu*m* non
The hands of the text and gloss scribes are continental, and the booklet was almost certainly made in France, probably in the second quarter of the twelfth century. The page layout is that of the earliest glossed texts (de Hamel, *Glossed Books*, 14–15, cf. figs. 1–3). Annotations and additions to the gloss were made in a more carefully written version of Master Robert's hand (e.g. fols. 9v–10, 15v etc.) and he may have been its first owner.

BOOKLET 2: fols. 81–139
Structure of Booklet
Parchment Very thick and well prepared with good nap, hair and flesh sides nearly uniform in colour; almost no marks, holes or repairs.
Collation $1-6^8$, 7^6 (+ a slip inserted after 6), 8^2 (plus 1 after 2).
Quire nos. None.
Quire signatures QQ. 1–8 signed a–h in mixed capital, rustic and minuscule letters, centre of lower margin on fol. 1 recto of each quire in brown ink.
Catchwords None.

Page Layout
Dimensions
Page 250 x 166mm (trimmed at all edges).
Space ruled for writing Slightly variable: fol. 83: 221 x 130mm; fol. 92: 230 x 130mm; fol. 134: 225 x 135mm.
Columns 2.
Pricking None visible in inner margin, outer edges cropped. Probably in outer margin only.
Ruling Blind ruling on hair side now almost invisible. Neat and fairly regular, horizontal lines contained within inner lines of vertical columns.
Lines per page Variable; q. 1: 43; q. 8: 51, but not increasing regularly.
Page design Text and commentary written continuously, text written in larger letters and underlined in red, though some text passages missed.

fols. 82–139

2/II SCRIBES

One scribe s.xii med, probably wrote the whole text and commentary continuously, using a larger hand for the text passages which are mostly underlined in red. The hand is very variable, the variations caused in part by changes in pen and/or ink, e.g. on fols. 128, 131. In some places the changes in aspect are dramatic, and the possibility of the intervention of one or two other scribes cannot be ruled out. In general the hand is small, compact and upright but rather uneven, with slightly clubbed ascenders and serifed minims and descenders. The scribe supplied an omission on a slip after fol. 136 written in long lines, and corrected himself frequently in the margins.

2/III DECORATION, RUBRICS AND ARTICULATION OF TEXT

Text initials Text (as opposed to commentary) initials: written in thickened rustic or Roman letters in brown ink; commentary initials are generally not distinguished at all, though for the final text on fols. 138v–139 these small capitals are touched with red, including the first L(egimus).

Minor initials Fol. 82v: **1-line red O**(mnibus), undecorated.

Major initials Fol. 83: **13-line red I**(n principio), with a simple coiled extension of the tail in red and blue.

Historiated initials None.

Display script Fol. 83 (I)n principio in red 1-line capitals.

Title page None.

Titles etc. 'Anselm*us* sup*er* ioh*ann*em' added in the upper margin of fol. 83, in brown ink s.?xv: 'sermo *sancti* aug*ustini*' written in the upper margin fol. 138v in red, s.xii.

2/IV CONTENTS

Table of contents None (except that added s.xvii on fol. 1).

Main texts ?Anselm, Commentary on John.

1. Fol 81: blank, but ruled; 2 prefaces fol. 82: i) '[I]n principio erat v*er*bum. Verb*um* substantiale intelligit*ur* q*uo*d *in* ipso hom*inem* manet i*s*tus [sic]'. Ends fol. 82: 'O*mn*ipotentissima miseratione salvavit.' Rest of page blank. Fol. 82v: ii) 'Omnibus divine script*ure* paginis evangelium* excellit'. Ends fol. 82v: 'et sic humanis m*entibus et* sensibus intimare.' Rest of page blank. Fol. 83: Text begins: 'In principio erat verbum. Fili*us* v*er*bum vocat*ur* q*ui*a p*er* eu*m* pat*et*

mundo i*n*notuit.' Ends fol. 138: 'Qua*m*vis salva fide rer*um* pleru*s*que v*e*rbi videant*ur* exced*e*re fide*m* p*er* hiberbolen. Finit. amen.'

2. Fol. 138v: A sermon of Augustine on John's text, begins: 'Sermo s*a*nc*ti* Aug*u*sti*ni*. Et v*e*rbum caro s*a*nctum est. Legimus sec*un*du*m* moysen pop*u*lo d*ei* pr*a*ecepta dante*m*. Ubi dixit: Audi isr*a*el. D*omin*u*s* d*eu*s tuus d*eu*s unu*s* e*st*. Non pot*est* e*ss*e maior. N*on* potest e*ss*e minor.' Ends fol. 139: 'nec eni*m* alt*er* unigenit*us* sup*er* terr*a*m venit aut alia virgo unigenitu*m* genuit'. *PL* XXXIV, 2196 (appendix 245). Rest of fol. 139 and fol. 139v blank except for random lines in red ink.

2/V ORIGIN AND PROVENANCE
Ex libris None.
Secundo folio In principio
Written in a continental hand probably in Northern France.

V ORIGIN AND PROVENANCE OF B.1.10
Although the commentary on John is now bound with a book once owned by Master Robert, there is no indisputable evidence that the two texts were bound together before s.xvi ex. Equally, there is no firm evidence that they were not, although the rather different sequences of quire letters in each might suggest that they were each bound with another text before being bound together. Both fol. 1 of the book as presently bound (and much of q. 1) and the last leaves, especially fol. 139, are marked with single worm holes scattered over the leaves as if both were once adjacent to similar boards with similar paste generating similar worm damage patterns. The endleaves in the centre of the book as presently bound, however, show no such holes and no evidence of any other previous binding, which might suggest that booklet 2 was always bound with another text, and that this may well have been booklet 1. Evidence (holes and marks) in the spinefold at fol. 138v is very unclear; it does not seem to match that on fol. 17.

The two texts comprise an appropriate pair. There are no user's marks which are indisputably common to both texts, though the second text does have one or two marginal corrections which are made in one or more scholarly hands. Notes on fols. 83 and 103 just might be Master Robert's.

The whole book in its present form was bound or rebound for Archbishop Whitgift who gave it to Trinity College s.xvi ex.

VI NOTES

VII BIBLIOGRAPHY AND PLATES
James, *Trinity MSS,* I, 12–13;Thomson 1995, 238–243.

45. CAMBRIDGE, TRINITY COLLEGE MS B.1.11
1 Matthew, glossed; 2 Mark, glossed   **Date** c. 1150-60*;* s.xii med
Leaves [ii paper], i (stub), [i paper], 225, [i paper, ii paper]
Foliation 1–225
Origin Northern France   **Fig.** 30

This book contains two separate though related texts, both of which were owned by Master Robert; his ownership inscription survives on a front endleaf stub. It is not clear when the two texts were first bound together.

The binding of the book as it now exists will be described first and then each booklet independently. The Provenance, Notes and Bibliography for the whole book will be given at the end.

I PHYSICAL DESCRIPTION

Binding Resewn and rebound at least three times: first probably s.xii ex (not necessarily as one volume), then in s.xvi and again s.xviii/xix; since rebacked. Book opens fairly well.

Endleaves

Front *Pastedown* **1**) Single leaf of laid paper in place, watermark: letters [?IC]ONARD surmounted by a Maltese cross, a stylised lion's head and a large crown; blank. **2**) Stub of earlier parchment pastedown with impressions of 5 sewing supports and channels and former primary covering turn-in.

Flyleaves **1**) Laid paper quaternion, watermark: letters HG surmounted by fleur-de-lys and large crown; first two leaves cut to stubs and pasted together, blank. **2**) Laid paper bifolium, watermark: one-handled pot surmounted by small crown; first leaf cut to stub and pasted to recto of parchment pastedown stub.

Back *Flyleaves* **1**) Laid paper bifolium, watermark as flyleaves 2) above; second leaf cut to stub and pasted to parchment stub of former pastedown (see below); free leaf has worm holes from contact with an earlier wooden board, otherwise blank. **2**) Two leaves of a laid paper quaternion, watermark as flyleaves 1) above; third leaf cut to stub, fourth is pastedown; all blank, no wormholes.

Pastedown **1**) Fourth leaf of a laid paper quaternion in place, other leaves are flyleaves; blank; **2**) Single parchment stub of an earlier pastedown with impressions of 5 sewing supports and channels and former primary covering turn-in; pasted to fol. 2 of paper flyleaf bifolium.

Sewing stations 1) Now 5. **2**) Evidence on parchment stubs indicate a former, but not the original, binding had 5 sewing stations: (tail) I 39*41*41*38*47*39 I mm (head); no evidence about kettle stitch station; very similar to present disposition of sewing stations; **3**) Marking-up pricks *c*.6mm from spinefold indicate positions of even earlier, probably earliest sewing stations: e.g. at fol. 70v (item 1): (tail) I 11 K 36*71*74*30 K 19 I mm (head). This disposition is reflected by sewing thread impressions e.g. at fol. 112 (item 1). Marking-up in item 2, e.g. at fol. 135v, indicates 3 sewing stations as follows: (tail) I 7 K 36* 67*73*45 K 16 I mm (head). This disposition is reflected by sewing thread impressions, e.g. at fol. 130 (item 2). Except for a considerable disparity in distances between uppermost sewing stations and kettle stitch stations, these two sets of measurements are similar enough to suggest that their first binding in boards was as one volume, probably at Buildwas. It is not possible, however, to be certain of this.

Sewing Now all-along with very thin white S-twist thread. Thread impressions suggest that an earlier, probably the original, permanent sewing was also all-along with S-twist thread.

Sewing supports Now sewn to 5 very narrow white tawed skin supports. Impressions on pastedown stubs show that earlier, though not originally, the book was sewn to 5 split supports, approx. 9mm wide.

Lacing path Sewing supports now laced in over the edge of the boards and pulled through to the inner face, 10mm from spine edge. The pastedown stub impressions suggest that the 5 supports of an earlier sewing were laced in through short channels on the outer surface of the boards and then pulled through holes to the inner face *c.*10mm from spine edge and into channels of various lengths, 15–30mm.

Endbands Replacement endbands present at head and tail, core material unknown, probably very thin cord, not laced into boards; sewn in herringbone pattern with shaded brown S-twist thread, and tied down at 6 points.

Tabs None present; no other evidence

Spine lining None present; no other evidence.

Boards Pasteboard, 250 x 170 x 5mm.

Primary covering 1) Light brown, speckled leather (calf) covering with roughly trimmed turn-ins and overlapped corners; decorated front and back with a rectangular frame of triple fillets with stylised plant design at each corner and double fillets at each edge (perimeter); gilt scalloped design impressed along outer edges (thickness) of each cover. 2) Stained impressions and fragments of earlier (s.xvi?) primary covering with very erratically trimmed, or untrimmed, turn-ins and overlapping corners survive on the inner set of paper flyleaves front and back and these are probably associated with that binding.

Fastenings None present; no other evidence.

Chemise None present; no other evidence.

Bosses None present; no other evidence.

Chain attachments None present; no other evidence.

Labels Remains of laid paper fore-edge label fol. 127. Trinity College bookplate, fol. 1. Printed paper labels on spine, each with element of present shelfmark.

Notes Edges of leaves now stained yellowish-green; 'Com. in Matt.' written in ink across upper fore-edge fols. 1–126, comprising exactly the leaves on which Matthew is written.

BOOKLET 1: fols. 1–126

Structure of Booklet

Parchment Good quality, evenly coloured, little damage, very few marks or repairs; good nap.

Collation Very difficult to check: spinefolds not always accessible, quires have been inaccurately lettered (e.g. one omitted between d and e): James, *Trinity MSS*, I, 13, gives collation as follows: 1^6, 2^8, 3^{10}, 4^8, 5^8, $5a^8$, 6^6+1, $8–16^8$. Hair side outermost in each quire.

Quire nos. None.

Catchwords None.

Page Layout

Dimensions

Page 242 x 168mm (trimmed at all margins; evidence of lost marginal notes and impression of covering).

Space ruled for writing 153 x 118mm increasing to 155 x 124mm.

Columns Except for prefaces (2 columns: 1 text, 1 gloss), 1 central text column with 2 flanking gloss columns, all of variable width within the ruled space.

Pricking All the pricking at the fore-edge has been lost; remaining evidence suggests leaves folded, both margins,1→8, text lines only.

Ruling Text and gloss lines ruled independently in brown; only scribe 1 ruled the top line edge-to-edge. Lines for interlinear glosses sometimes, but not always, ruled continuously with the gloss lines in one of the outer columns. Vertical lines seldom coincide with pricking as column widths adjusted page by page.

Lines per page Variable: qq. 1–10: text lines increase from 11 (fols. 1–6) to 13 (fol. 6v onwards); qq. 11–16: text lines increase to 16. About 2–3 gloss lines per text line. Written above top line.

Page design

fols. 1v–3 (prefaces)   fols. 3v–125   fol. 126

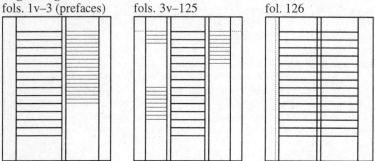

1/II SCRIBES

Two scribes contributed to the copying of the text. Each wrote both text and gloss and ruled his own quires. **Scribe 1** wrote fols. 1–55v (qq. 1–7) in a large, regular, compressed and upright continental hand using ampersand throughout. Descenders and the first foot of minims such as n, m, have a long, angled, usually separately written serif. The ink used by this scribe is very dark at the outset of his stint, but fades to a very pale golden brown towards the end. **Scribe 2** wrote fols. 56–127 (qq. 8–16), also in a continental hand but strikingly more angular than that of scribe 1. He used both ampersand and Tironian 'et'.

1/III DECORATION, RUBRICS AND ARTICULATION OF TEXT

Text initials Fols. 1–55v (scribe 1): brown ink rustic capitals written by the scribe. Fols. 56–126v (scribe 2): 1-line plain mixed capitals, alternately red and blue.

Minor initials Fol. 7v: **2-line red and blue C**(um) flourished with blue.

Major initials Fol. 1v: **6-line red and blue M**(atheus), the colours separated by a scalloped reserved line, with light flourishes also in red and blue. Fol. 3: **8-line red and blue L**(iber), similar in structure to the M on fol. 1v but with slightly more elaborate flourishes in red and blue.

Historiated initials None.

Title page None.

Display script Fol. 3: (L)**iber generacionis**, in 1-line mixed capitals, alternately red and blue.

Titles etc. No running titles, incipits or explicits; chapter numbers added in margins by a later hand. Titles of items 1 and 2 inscribed on fol. 1, s.xvii.

1/IV CONTENTS

Table of contents None.

Main texts Matthew, glossed.

1.Fol. 1v preface: 'Matheus ex iudea sicut in ordine primus ponitur'. Preface ends fol. 3v: 'diligen*ter esse* dispositionem querentib*us* non tacere.' 3 glosses: i) 'Cum multi scripsisse evangelia legantur'. ii) fol. 2: 'Tres tesseres cedecades in gen*eratione*'. iii) fol. 3: 'Matheus in hac vita'. Text begins fol. 3v: 'Liber

generacionis Iehsu christi'. Gloss begins: 'Matheus apostolus cum primum predicasset'. Text ends fol. 125v: 'usque ad consummationem saeculi.' Gloss ends fol. 125v: 'qui divina mansione sunt digni.'
Fol. 126: a series of short passages: 'Tria sunt quae principes beatos efficiunt.' Ends fol. 126v. Rest of page blank.

1/V ORIGIN AND PROVENANCE
Ex libris Not for this booklet, but see below, 236.
Secundo folio [prin]cipium
This text was copied in Northern France probably c.1155-60.

BOOKLET 2: fols. 127–225
Structure of Booklet
Parchment Good quality, evenly coloured, good nap.
Collation 1^8+1 leaf before 1, 2–12^8, 13^2. Hair side outermost in each quire.
Quire nos. QQ. 1–12, lower margin of verso of last leaf, with lower case Roman numerals.
Catchwords None.

Page Layout
Dimensions
Page 242 x 168mm (trimmed at all margins, evidence of trimmed notes).
Space ruled for writing 166 x 118mm.
Columns 3; 1 central text column, 2 flanking gloss columns, all of variable width within ruled space.
Pricking Leaves folded 1→8, text lines only, template used. QQ. 1–5: both margins; qq. 6–13: outer margin only.
Ruling In soft brown, text and gloss lines ruled independently.
Lines per page 16 text lines; written above top line.
Page design
fols. 128–225

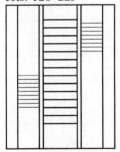

2/II SCRIBES
One scribe wrote text and gloss in a small, angular, backward-sloping continental hand s.xii med, with sharply angled serifs. The hand is not markedly compressed and the lower loop to g barely descends below the line. This scribe used ampersand and Tironian 'et', and the ascender of rounded d is horizontal. The aspect of the hand changes throughout the text.

2/III DECORATION, RUBRICS AND ARTICULATION OF TEXT
Text initials Small Roman capitals, alternately red and blue to fol. 130, then alternately pea-green and red.
Minor initials None.
Major initials Fol. 128: **6-line red M**(arcus), with a reserved scalloped line in the centre of the vertical elements; lightly flourished with blue. Fol. 129v: **10-line red and blue I**(nitium), the colours separated by a straight reserved line along the length of the letter, and with reserved, diagonal tube-shaped motif reserved against the parchment; extended tail with light red and blue flourishes.
Historiated initials None.
Display script Fol. 128: (M)**arcus evangelista dei** in mixed 1-line capitals, alternately blue and red. Fol. 129v: (I)**nitium evangelii Iehsu Christi filii dei**, written in mixed 1-line capitals on 4 lines, the lines alternately red and blue.
Titles etc. No running titles, incipits or explicits.
Title page None.

2/IV CONTENTS
Table of contents None.
Main texts Mark, glossed
Fol. 127 (flyleaf) in a different hand from text hand s.xii med: 'De decem apparitionibus christi post resurrectionem. i) Prima maria videt surgentis gaudia christi...x) Iam decimo cernunt celestia regna petentem.' Remainder of this page blank; verso: partially erased inscription along upper edge beginning 'Sa'; remainder not legible; at lower edge a partially cropped note, possibly a pen trial, ends 'primum bonum vinum'. Otherwise blank. A strip of laid paper over fore-edge (former fore-edge label) has received offsets from facing page.
1. Fol. 128: preface: 'Marcus evangelista Dei et petri in baptismate filius'. Ends fol. 129v: 'Qui autem incrementum praestat deus est.' Many glosses to the preface, the first fol. 128: 'Marcus excelsus mandato'. The last begins fol. 128v: 'Exempla ut hoc discite a me'. Ends fol. 128v: 'qui in lacrimis timoris.' Text begins fol. 129v: 'Initium evangelii iehsu christi'. Gloss (left): 'Matheus dicitur filii david. Marcus dicitur filii dei'; (right): 'Quattuor evangelia unum sunt et unum quattuor'. Text ends fol. 225: 'et sermonem confirmante sequentibus signis.' Gloss ends fol. 225: 'per totum orbem seminaverunt.' Fol. 225v blank.

2/V ORIGIN AND PROVENANCE
Ex libris Not for this booklet, but see below.
Secundo folio Denique
This text was also copied in northern France.

V ORIGIN AND PROVENANCE OF B.1.11
Ex libris Fol. 1v: 'Liber sancte Marie de Bildewas', in red rustic capitals in lower margin s.xii ex.
The two texts were produced by three different scribes who were nevertheless working in the same milieu. The texts were owned by Master Robert who wrote his name on the first flyleaf of the first booklet (now just a stub) which was later covered by a paper pastedown: 'Iste liber est magistri Roberti amiclas'. The texts are heavily annotated by Master Robert (but see below, Notes 2). The books had been acquired by the Buildwas monks by the later twelfth century, when the monastery's ex libris was written on fol. 1v. It seems likely, though the evidence is not absolutely conclusive, that the two texts were bound together

then for the first time. The books continued in use and were further annotated by several readers, sometimes at length, e.g. fols. 23, 96v–7, 166, 167–167v.

There is no direct evidence that the book was among Archbishop Whitgift's collection but it is unlikely to have been separated from Master Robert's other books. The later binding evidence supports this supposition. It was presumably Whitgift who preserved the original endleaf with Master Robert's ex libris, recognising its bibliographical significance. The book must have come with the others from Whitgift to Trinity College during the late sixteenth century.

VI NOTES

1. The first scribe of booklet 1 also wrote Trinity B.1.36. In B.1.11, he used the old glossed text layout, pricking for the text only and ruling these lines first, though his ad hoc gloss lines sometimes extended into the text column as lines for interlinear glosses. In B.1.36 (q.v.) he used the new layout.

2. It is interesting to observe that the fragmentary text of Matthew in Trinity B.1.33 (1.–7.27), which has more copious glosses than the same text in B.1.11, is vigorously annotated by Robert, but that the same section of text in B.1.11 is not annotated at all. However on fol. 37 in B.1.11, at precisely 7.27 where B.1.33 breaks off, there is a stylus mark #, and all the glosses except that duplicated on the last leaf of B.1.33 are marked with a bracketing line. There is a tiny marginal note on fol. 37, but annotation begins in earnest on fol. 40. It appears that Robert used these two copies of Matthew in conjunction.

2. B.1.33 may be a slightly later copy of Matthew than B.1.11 (evidence of the page layout). But the fact that the B.1.11 scribe also wrote a complete text, (B.1.36, owned by Master Robert), using the new layout (see 1 above) suggests that there may have been very little difference in the dates of B.1.11 and B.1.33. Robert probably was the first owner of the copy of Matthew in B.1.11.

3. During the ?eighteenth-century rebinding, some of the earlier paper endleaves were preserved, though others were trimmed to stubs and pasted together. Master Robert's inscription was pasted over, this time surviving evidently by accident. Another set of paper endleaves was also provided during this rebinding.

VII BIBLIOGRAPHY AND PLATES

James *Trinity MSS*, I, 13–14; Ker, *MLGB*, 14; Sheppard 1988, 281–288 pls 1–3; Sheppard 1990, 193–204; Thomson 1995, 238–243.

46. CAMBRIDGE, TRINITY COLLEGE MS B.1.33

Matthew, glossed (fragment)   Date *c.*1160
Leaves [ii paper, i paper], 57, [i paper]
Foliation 1.–57
Origin Northern France

I PHYSICAL DESCRIPTION

Binding Rebound at least twice; present binding s.xix, spine rigid, earlier binding evidence largely obscured, breaking at joints.

Endleaves

   Front*Pastedown* Laid paper leaf in place, conjoint with first flyleaf, probably once part of a quaternion; no watermark, blank.

Flyleaves **1)** 2 laid paper leaves, 1 conjoint with pastedown, probably once part of a quaternion, one leaf completely excised; no watermark, blank; **2)** laid paper leaf, quite different in quality from other flyleaves; watermark: one-handled pot surmounted by a crown, letters ?PDB on the body of the pot; impressions of earlier covering turn-in and worm holes. Recto: old and current shelfmarks; verso: Trinity College bookplate, otherwise blank.

Back *Flyleaves* Laid paper leaf, fol. 1 of a bifolium, no watermark, blank.

Pastedown Laid paper leaf in place, fol. 2 of a bifolium, blank.

Sewing stations Now 5. No earlier evidence visible.

Sewing All-along with S-twist thread, visible at the joints only. No other evidence visible.

Sewing supports Now sewn to 5 very thin cords; no earlier evidence visible.

Lacing path Cords laced in over edges of board; no other evidence.

Endbands Present at head and tail, rolled brown leather core, sewn with red and with white S-twist thread and tied down in 3 quires.

Tabs None present; no other evidence.

Spine lining None present; no other evidence.

Boards Pasteboard, 235 x 170 x 2mm. Worm holes on third front paper flyleaf indicate that earlier boards were of wood. These holes differ from those on the parchment leaves which probably came from the original boards.

Primary covering Now light brown leather (calf) with streaked ?acid marks, zigzag lines interspersed with dots along very thin board edges. Impressions on third front paper flyleaf and fol. 1 suggest that an earlier covering was of dark brown leather with overlapped corners.

Fastenings None present; no other evidence.

Chemise None present; no other evidence.

Bosses None present; no other evidence.

Chain attachments None present; no other evidence.

Labels Red leather label on spine with title in gilt letters, possibly from an earlier binding. Printed paper labels also on spine, each with an element of present shelfmark.

Notes Edges of leaves faintly coloured with yellowish-green stain.

Structure of Book

Parchment Good quality, evenly coloured with a marked nap.

Collation $1-7^8$ plus one leaf. Hair side outside in all quires, but second bifolium in q. 2 and centre bifolium in q. 3 are out of sequence.

Quire nos. None.

Catchwords None.

Page Layout

Dimensions

Page 226 x 172mm (probably trimmed at all margins, certainly at fore-edge).

Space ruled for writing 156 x 118mm.

Columns Central text column with gloss columns on either side. Column widths remain constant, though gloss often spreads into central column displacing text (e.g. fols. 6v–7; fols. 6, 29 have 6 lines of text only), and gloss columns themselves are sometimes subdivided (e.g. fol. 30v).

Pricking Leaves folded, 1→8, outer margins only; pricked for 33 gloss lines.

Ruling In brown, all lines ruled across the page. Random patterns of edge-to-edge ruling. On last leaf only lines 1–16 are ruled, and only 4 lines of text and 7 gloss lines (both below top line) actually written, as if the scribe intended to stop where he did.

Lines per page 33 or 34. Text written no closer than on alternate lines but is often displaced by gloss which spills from gloss columns interrupting the pattern. Top line used sometimes for gloss, sometimes for text. Text and gloss must have been written concurrently or copied line for line.

Page design
fols. 2–57

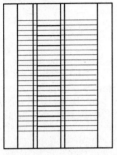

II SCRIBES
One scribe wrote text and gloss throughout in a regular, elegant, upright and compact hand with continental characteristics. He used ampersand mainly, but towards the end of the text also a large Tironian 'et', both strokes curved, and made paraphs in brown ink. The text-gloss layout is beautifully controlled. He made a few corrections himself over erasures, e.g. fol. 8v, and sometimes added omitted words or phrases in the margin, e.g. fol. 18.

III DECORATION, RUBRICS AND ARTICULATION OF TEXT
Text initials Fols. 1–6: 1–line brown ink capitals written by text scribe. Subsequently, 1-line coloured capitals as follows: fols. 6v–12: red; fols. 12v–16v: alternately red and blue; fols. 17–33: red; fols. 33v–36: yellowish-green and red; fols. 36v–41: green only, except red E fol. 40v; fols. 41v–57: no initials supplied.
Minor initials Fol. 7v: **2-line red C**(um). Fol. 9: **2-line red E**(cce) introducing passages about the Virgin. Fol. 13: **2-line red Q**(ui), all undecorated.
Major initials Fol. 1: **6-line blue M**(atheus) with meagre red pen flourishes in asymmetrical design. Fol. 2: **12-line red and blue L**(iber), colours separated by a scalloped reserved line, meagre flourishes in red on left side of letter.
Historiated initials None.
Title page None extant.
Display script Fol. 2: (L)**iber,** 2-line blue mixed capitals with some slight red flourishes. First 1 or 2 letters after a coloured initial usually written in rustic letters by scribe.
Titles etc. None. Scribe wrote explicit on fol. 1v for the prologue. Fol. 1: 'Matthaeus glossatus us*que* ad Cap.7.27' in hand s. xvii; same hand wrote 'Matt. Cap.7.27' at the end of the text.

IV CONTENTS
Table of contents None.
Main texts Matthew, glossed: 1.–7.27.

Fol. 1: prologue: 'Matheus ex iudea sicut in ordine primus ponitur'. Ends fol. 1v: 'querentibus non tacere Explicit prologus.' Glosses begin fol. 1v: i) 'Hec causa matheum scribere conpulit'. ii) 'Matheus cum primo predicasset evangelium in vincula' followed by 4 other very short passages. The last ends fol. 2: 'unus et idem auctor ostenditur.' Text begins fol. 2: 'Liber generationis'. Gloss begins: 'Jeronimus. Generationis singulariter quia unius christi'. Text ends fol. 57: 'et cecidit fuitque ruina eius magna.' Gloss ends fol. 57: 'qualibet temptatione peiores fiunt.' Rest of page blank.

V ORIGIN AND PROVENANCE
Ex libris None.
Secundo folio [re]cepta sunt
The book was written in France using the later 'alternate line' layout (de Hamel, *Glossed Books*, 24–25) but apparently abandoned, unfinished. It is annotated by several readers among whom was Master Robert. One annotator made notes (e.g. on fols. 5, 8, 13, 20, etc.) in a hand perhaps slightly later than Robert's, (probably a Buildwas reader's), found in other Buildwas books. It is characterised by a very squat form of g, an elegant paraph and the use of a dark ink. The notes are of a similar type to Robert's. Robert supplied a passage (perhaps a missing or an additional gloss) fol. 27v which he labeled 'g,' and labeled other passages passim with letters a–g.
The book was clearly among those owned by Master Robert and must have come to Buildwas with the others in Robert's set. James only tentatively suggests that the book was owned by Archbishop Whitgift, but it must have remained with the other glossed books from Buildwas and have come to Trinity College with them s.xvi ex.

VI NOTES
1. In view of Robert's completion of the text and gloss in Trinity B.1.13, he may well have intended to finish this abandoned text himself. This may have been made unnecessary by the acquisition of the (very slightly earlier) glossed copy of Matthew, now part of Trinity B.1.11 (q.v.), which is complete, though the glosses are not identical. It is interesting to observe that this partial text with its more copious glosses is vigorously annotated by Robert, but that the same section of text in B.1.11 is not annotated at all. It appears that he used these books in conjunction. See B.1.11, Notes.
2. B.1.12 was rejected by Ker as a Buildwas book.

VII BIBLIOGRAPHY AND PLATES
James, *Trinity MSS*, I, 44; Ker, *MLGB*, 15; Sheppard 1988, 287 n. 3; Sheppard 1990, 197 n .9; Thomson 1995, 238–243.

47. CAMBRIDGE, TRINITY COLLEGE MS B.1.12
Luke, glossed **Date** s.xii med
Leaves [iv paper], ii, 139, i [iv paper]
Foliation 1–143 (all parchment leaves)
Origin Northern France

I PHYSICAL DESCRIPTION
Binding Resewn and rebound at least twice; present binding s.xviii/xix, recently

repaired (hollow back and guards in all centre spinefolds). Opens well.

Endleaves

Front *Pastedown* **1)** Laid paper leaf in place, probably once conjoint with a flyleaf now excised, joint repaired; elaborate but indistinct watermark (shield surmounted by crown with letters below: PICONARD; blank except for Trinity College bookplate and shelfmarks; **2)** see below, flyleaves 2).

Flyleaves **1)** 2 wove paper bifolia, modern, blank; **2)** parchment bifolium: fol. 1 probably the original pastedown now detached, with marks and impressions of 2 earlier bindings, otherwise blank; fol. 2: prefaces written on recto and verso by one of the text scribes.

Back *Flyleaves* **1)** Once fol. 5 of last quire, now excised, probably blank; **2)** fol. 6 of last quire, originally pastedown, now detached, with marks of earlier bindings, chain attachments etc.; **3)** 2 wove paper bifolia, blank.

Pastedown **1)** Laid paper leaf in place, probably once conjoint with a flyleaf now completely excised, joint repaired, blank; **2)** original pastedown now detached, see flyleaves 2) above.

Sewing stations Now 5. At one time 3 (evidence of pricked marking-up including kettle stitch close to spinefolds, 8→1 and sewing support impressions on pastedowns): (tail) I 11 K 44*67*66*42 K 13 I mm (head).

Sewing Now resewn all-along with S-twist thread; thread impressions at fols. 11 and 139 suggest an earlier sewing also all-along with S-twist thread.

Sewing supports Now sewn to 5 cords. Impressions on extant original pastedowns show that an earlier, probably the original, binding was to 3 flat supports *c*.8–10mm wide. A set of 3 wedge impressions on front pastedown do not quite coincide with these impressions and might suggest another sewing using the original sewing stations but different boards.

Lacing path Now, supports laced over the edges of the board through a short channel on the inner face of the boards and pulled through to the outer face to be fixed in place. Impressions on pastedown indicate the earlier supports were laced through outer, then inner, channels and wedged, the lacing paths between 50 and 60mm long.

Endbands Very new endbands now present at head and tail, sewn with white S-twist thread (different from that now used in the primary sewing) and tied down in each quire. Earlier an endband had been laced into the boards (evidence of impressions on surviving pastedown).

Tabs None present; no other evidence.

Spine lining None present; a 19mm-wide impression along the spine edge of the detached back pastedown, over covering turn-in impression at the head and under it at the tail, may have been made by an earlier spine lining.

Boards Pasteboard, 252 x 164 x 4mm.

Primary covering Light brown leather (calf) with triple fillets forming a frame design with a stamped foliate motif diagonally at each corner, front and back. Some gilding survives in a scalloped design impressed on all edges (thicknesses) of covers. 2 earlier covering turn-ins have left marks (stains and impressions) on pastedowns.

Fastenings None present. 3 rusted holes, centre fore-edge of front pastedown and a hole with greenish edges in centre of back pastedown show that the book was at one time fastened with a single fore-edge strap and pin.

Chemise None present; no other evidence.

Bosses None present; no other evidence.

Chain attachments 4 rusted holes on back pastedown at the lower edge near the spine indicate former presence of chain staple. The marks show the characteristic asymmetrical disposition characteristic of marks left on other Buildwas books. Such marks were made while the book was still at Buildwas.

Labels Printed paper labels on spine each with an element of present shelfmark.

Notes The remains of a threaded parchment page marker at lower edge fol. 74 (11.33–40; on hiding one's light under a bushel). Edges of leaves now stained yellowish-green.

Structure of Book

Parchment Variable quality, thin and very smooth, with considerable markings and stains especially on the hair sides, making hair and flesh sides readily distinct.

Collation ii, 1–17^8, 18^6 (5 excised, probably blank; 6 is pastedown). Hair side outermost in each quire.

Quire nos. QQ. 1–17: lower margin of verso of last leaf in small Roman numerals; q. 1 in hand of first text scribe, qq. 2–17 by second text scribe.

Catchwords None.

Page Layout
Dimensions

Page 245 x 164mm, trimmed very roughly at lower edge.

Space ruled for writing Slightly variable: 159–166 x 126–132mm.

Columns Text in central column with gloss on either side, all 3 columns of slightly variable width. Prefaces (fol.2–2v): long lines.

Pricking Much pricking trimmed: surviving evidence suggests leaves folded, 1→8, in all margins, except q. 13, which seems to have been pricked 1→8 in inner margins but 8→1 in the outer margins. Pricked for text lines only.

Ruling QQ. 1–3: brown; qq. 4–18: grey sometimes appearing brown: text lines ruled separately; gloss ruled as needed, roughly 3 lines per text line.

Lines per page 16 text lines.

Page design

fols. 2–142v

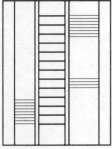

II SCRIBES

Two scribes wrote text and gloss, and pricked and ruled their own quires. **Scribe 1** wrote qq. 1–3 in a small rounded hand, s.xii med., probably continental, with a straight-backed a without a loop, clubbed minims and tagged e. **Scribe 2** wrote

242

qq. 4–18 in a taller and more compressed but contemporary hand, with continental characteristics such as a forward-sloping ampersand. He also wrote a cumbersome, 6-stroke g. The scribe seems to have changed pens at fol. 39 (mid q. 5) and the hand increases in size at this point. This scribe also wrote the preface on fols. 2–2v on completion of the text, and probably also supplied the first words after the initials on fol. 3v which were not supplied by the display script writer.

III DECORATION, RUBRICS AND ARTICULATION OF TEXT

Text initials Both scribes wrote text initials of a rustic type.

Minor initials Fol. 2: **3-line blue L**(ucas) with a few red flourishes.

Major initials Fol. 3: **5-line red Q**(uoniam) with reserved scalloped panels partially filled with blue; letter filled with split petal and simple scroll design in blue with some red. Fol. 3v: **5-line red and blue F**(uit), the colours separated by a reserved scalloped line, with very simple scroll decoration in red and blue and flourished with blue.

Historiated initials None.

Title page None.

Display script Fol. 3: (Q)**uoniam**, small plain Roman capitals, alternately blue and red. Space left by scribe 1 for display script fol. 3v but this supplied in minuscule probably by scribe 2.

Titles etc. Fol. 2: 'Comment. in Lucam' s.xvii; fol. 142v, 'explicit liber' in hand of scribe 2.

IV CONTENTS

Table of contents None.

Main texts Luke, glossed.

1. Fol. 1: blank. Fol. 2: preface: 'Lucas sirus natione et antiochensis arte medicus discipulus apostolor*um*'. Ends fol. 2v: 'qua*m* fastidientib*us* prodesse.' No gloss. Text begins fol. 3: 'Quoniam quidem'. Gloss begins fol. 3 (left): 'Vitulus sac*er*dotal*is* hostia'. (right): 'Lucas de om*n*ibus que fecit *iehsus et* docuit'. Text ends fol. 142v: 'laudentes *et* benedicentes d*eu*m. Explicit liber.'

V ORIGIN AND PROVENANCE

Ex libris None.

Secundo folio Quoniam (text) Titulus (gloss)

The scribal hands and style of the initials suggests that the book was written in northern France. Its first owner was probably Master Robert, who annotated the text and gloss. The book must have been acquired by the monks of Buildwas with Master Robert's other books towards the end of the twelfth century, where it must have remained with the others until at least the fifteenth century. It was given to Trinity College by Archbishop Whitgift s.xvi ex.

VI NOTES

Thought probably to be a Buildwas book by James, but rejected by Ker.

VII BIBLIOGRAPHY AND PLATES

James, *Trinity MSS*, I, 14; Ker, *MLGB*, 15; Sheppard 1988, 287 n. 3; Thomson 1995, 238–243.

48. CAMBRIDGE, TRINITY COLLEGE MS B.1.36

John, glossed   **Date** *c*.1160

Leaves [ii paper], 109, ii, [ii paper]

Foliation 1–111 (parchment leaves only)

Origin Northern France

I PHYSICAL DESCRIPTION

Binding Rebound at least twice (evidence of endleaves), s.xvi/xvii and xviii/xix; since rebacked; spine rigid, book opens poorly.

Endleaves

Front *Pastedown* Laid paper leaf in place, possibly once part of a quaternion, chain lines horizontal, broken at joint; blank except for Trinity College bookplate and present shelfmark.

   Flyleaves 2 laid paper leaves, probably once part of a quaternion with pastedown, one leaf completely excised; chain lines horizontal, no watermark, blank.

Back *Flyleaves* **1**) 2 parchment leaves, a bifolium (fols. 110–111). Fol. 1: notes (extracts from Augustine etc.) in Master Robert's hand, trimmed at top. Fol.2v: ruled in grey as for this book with three lines of text (duplicate of text on first 3 lines of fol. 5) now upside down, written by text scribe; impressions of earlier lacing channels (probably original) and primary covering turn-ins (probably post medieval); old shelfmark and old Trinity College bookplate also upside down; **2**) 2 laid paper leaves, possibly once part of a quaternion with pastedown, 1 leaf completely excised; chain lines horizontal, no watermark, blank.

   Pastedown Laid paper leaf, possibly once part of quaternion; chain lines horizontal; broken at joint, blank.

Sewing stations Now 7; impressions on back parchment flyleaf indicate earlier, probably originally, 2: (tail) | 56*107*55 | mm (head) (no evidence for kettle stitch).

Sewing Now all-along with natural S-twist thread. No evidence visible about earlier sewing.

Sewing supports Now 7 cords, all broken front and back. Impressions on first and last leaves suggest earlier, probably originally, sewn to 2 supports, *c*.10mm wide.

Lacing path Now no evidence, sewing supports broken and boards attached by means of glued replacement spine covering to backs of quires. Impressions on last parchment endleaf indicate earlier, probably originally, sewing supports laced into boards through parallel tunnels and channels, emerging onto inner face of boards *c*.33mm from spine edge and through channels *c*.30mm long and then wedged.

Endbands Present at head and tail, probably a rolled skin core not laced in, sewn with red and white S-twist threads, also repair sewing at tail; tied down in 3 quires. Impressions on last parchment flyleaf indicate earlier, probably originally, endbands *c*.9mm wide laced into boards at angle of 45° through lacing paths *c*.50mm long.

Tabs None present; no other evidence.

Spine lining None present; no other evidence.

Boards   Pasteboard, 228 x 160 x 3mm. Wormholes on first and last leaves indicate that earlier boards were of wood.

Primary covering   Now light brown leather (calf), undecorated except for impressed zigzag lines interspersed with dots along very thin edges. Spine re-covered; title in gilt letters on red leather possibly from an earlier binding, pasted onto re-covered spine. Impressions on first and last leaves suggest an earlier but post-medieval covering (dark brown) with overlapping corners.

Fastenings   Rust-stained hole on fol. 111 45mm from fore-edge may be evidence of an earlier pin from a strap and pin fastening, though the hole is now not quite central on the vertical axis of the board.

Chemise   None present; no other evidence.

Bosses   None present; no other evidence.

Chain attachments   None present; no other evidence.

Labels   Printed paper labels on spine each with an element of present shelfmark.

Notes   Edges of leaves now stained yellowish-green.

Structure of Book

Parchment   Fairly good quality, even colour, good nap; lower corners in first few quires indicate bifolia economically made, incorporating extreme edges of the skins.

Collation 1^2, $2–14^8$, 15^4 (4 excised).

Quire nos.   None.

Catchwords   None.

Page Layout

Dimensions

Page   221 x 154mm trimmed at all margins (evidence of lost marginal notes).

Space ruled for writing   Variable, according to the demands of the text and gloss: 138–143 x 97–105mm.

Columns   Central text column with gloss columns on either side, all 3 sometimes varying in width from page to page but not within a page; gloss columns sub-divided on fol. 3 only (beginning of gospel text). Text lines sometimes extending for a whole page into the inner gloss column.

Pricking   Most pricking has been trimmed, remaining marks suggest leaves folded, 1→8, outer margin only, for gloss lines. Upper and lower margins possibly supplied with groups of pricks to allow for the flexibility of central columns width; the reason for the discarding of the leaf now part of the back endleaves seems to have been that the text column had been made too narrow.

Ruling   In grey sometimes appearing brown; all lines ruled across the page, a page at a time (this supported by the discarded leaf now part of back endleaves). Edge-to-edge ruling of first line is more or less consistent; fols. 3–20: a further outer vertical line ruled for marginal comments, perhaps added by Master Robert, who certainly used this space on these leaves.

Lines per page   Very variable: 36–41 gloss lines. Fols. 3–10 (first full quire): 13 text lines, i.e. every third ruled line; from fol. 10v onwards: 16–18 text lines, i.e. alternate ruled lines. Text and gloss written above top line.

Page design

fols. 1–2v   fols. 3–10   fols. 10v–109v

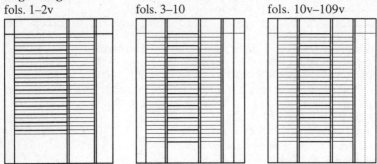

II SCRIBES

One scribe wrote text and gloss in a continental hand c.1160. The same scribe wrote Trinity B.1.11 fols. 1–55, though in that book he used the old style of page layout.

III DECORATION, RUBRICS AND ARTICULATION OF TEXT

Text initials Fols. 1–56: 1-line capitals written by scribe in brown ink. Fols. 57v–109v: 1- or 2-line mixed capitals, alternately red and blue, mark divisions in the text, though each passage comprises more than a modern verse.

Minor initials Fol. 13v: $1^1/_2$-line red C(rediderunt). Fol. 27v: 2-text-line blue P(ost) with slight red flourishes.

Major initials Fol. 1: **3-text-line red H**(ic), with scant but very regular blue flourishes. Fol. 3: **6-text-line red and blue I**(n principio), with flourished tail extending the letter to almost a full page length, the colours separated by a scalloped reserved line, with red and blue flourishes.

Historiated initials None.

Display script Fol. 1: (H)ic e*st* ioh*anne*s ewange(lista) in untidy 1-line mixed capitals in brown ink, almost certainly a correction over an erasure. Fol. 109v: **Deo gra*tia*s Explicit ewangelium Joh*anne*s** in mixed rustic and minuscule letters by text scribe. There is no display script after the major initial at the beginning of the Gospel text fol. 3, but the first 3 letters are written in rustic capitals.

Title page None.

Titles etc. No original titles; text divisions numbered in small Roman numerals by a contemporary hand; fol. 1: 'Glossa in Evangelium Joh*ann*is' in later hand ?s.xvii/xviii.

IV CONTENTS

Table of contents None.

Main texts John, glossed.

1. Fol. 1: preface: 'Hic e*st* Ioh*anne*s ewangelista unus ex discipulis dei'. 2 glosses: i) 'Ioh*anne*s interpretatur gr*aci*a sive in quo est gracia'. ii) 'Omnib*us* divine scripture paginis evang*e*lium excellit'. Preface ends fol. 2v: 'et deo magisterii doctrina servetur.' Gloss ii ends fol. 2v: 'cui et matrem virginem virgini comm*men*davit.' Text begins fol. 3: 'In principio'. Gloss begins fol. 2v: 'Contra

eos qui p*ropter* temp*or*alem nativitatem dicebant, non *christum* semp*er* fuisse. Incip*it* de ete*r*nitate verbi dicens in principio erat verbum'. Text ends fol. 109v: . 'qui scribendi s*unt* libros. Deo gra*tias*. Explicit ewangelium ioh*annis*.' Gloss ends: 'oportet ut sibi eligat otium.'

2. Fol. 110: several short extracts from Augustine on John in Master Robert's hand, trimmed at the top. i) 'Au*gustus* sup*er* ioh*anne*m. sic*ut* misit me vivens p*ater* et ego vivo p*ropter* p*at*rem'. ii) 'Au*gustus*. ego su*m* via ve*ritas* et vita'. iii) 'Item. aliud v*erbum* d*e*i est aliud h*oc* s*ed* v*erbum* caro s*anctu*m e*st*'. iv) 'Au*gustus* sup*er* ioh*ann*em. Venit *ergo* ad petru*m* qui*s* eni*m* nesciat p*rimum* ap*osto*loru*m*'. v) 'Au*gustus* super ioh*ann*em. Vado ad patrem q*uia* pat*er* maior me e*st*'. vi) 'Item. agnos cam*us* geminam'.

V ORIGIN AND PROVENANCE
Ex libris Fol. 2: 'Liber s*ancte* marie de Bildewas' in red ink, oxidised, in a neat hand which also wrote the ex libris in Trinity B.1.11.

Secundo folio incorruptibile (text); videt (gloss)

The book was written in Northern France by the same scribe who wrote the first part of booklet 1 in Trinity B.1.11, and was owned by Master Robert, who annotated the text and gloss and added notes at the end of the text. Another annotator whose hand is regularly found in these glossed books also made notes in this text (e.g. Trinity B.1.34). It was at Buildwas by s.xii ex, when the ex libris was written on fol. 2.

Although there is now no evidence of Archbishop Whitgift's ownership, this book must have remained with the others in this set, and was among those given by him to Trinity College s.xvi ex.

VI NOTES
1. This book and Trinity B.1.11 provide unusual and interesting evidence of a scribe who had to change the way he pricked, ruled and wrote a glossed text (cf. the scribe of B.1 32 who appears to have abandoned the new layout part way through his copying). Side by side and superficially, pages in the two books present a rather similar appearance, but the different pricking and ruling in B.1 36 is unmistakeable.

2. Fol. 58v: an offset of a 3-text-line red H itself offset onto the facing leaf, the vertical stroke divided by a reserved line, is not a part of this book.

VII BIBLIOGRAPHY AND PLATES
James, *Trinity MSS*, I, 45; Ker, *MLGB*, 14; Sheppard 1988, 281 and pl. 3; Sheppard 1990, pl. 5; Thomson 1995, 238–342.

49. CAMBRIDGE, TRINITY COLLEGE MS B.1.34
Acts of the Apostles, glossed   **Date** s.xii med.

Leaves [ii paper, ii paper], i, 109, i, [ii paper]
Foliation 1–111 (parchment leaves only)
Origin Northern France

I PHYSICAL DESCRIPTION
Binding Rebound at least twice (evidence of endleaves), present binding

s.xviii/xix with hollow back.

Endleaves

Front *Pastedown* Laid paper leaf in place, possibly once fol. 1 of a quaternion, broken at joint; no watermark, blank except for modern shelfmark.

      Flyleaves **1**) 2 laid paper leaves, possibly once part of a quaternion, one leaf completely excised, no watermark, blank. **2**) 2 laid paper leaves quite different from the adjacent leaves, probably a bifolium; watermark: one-handled pot surmounted by a crown, letters RDB on the body of the pot; blank except for old and current shelfmarks on first leaf. **3**) Parchment leaf, probably part of a bifolium, the other leaf now excised; recto: blank except for impressions of earlier primary covering turn-in; verso: Buildwas ex libris; title in hand s.xvi; Trinity College bookplate.

Back *Flyleaves* **1**) parchment leaf, possibly once part of a bifolium, fol. 1 excised; blank except for marks left by an earlier binding; **2**) 2 laid paper leaves, probably once part of a quaternion (pastedown is fol. 4), one leaf now excised, no watermark, blank.

      Pastedown Laid paper leaf in place, probably once part of a quarternion, broken at joint, no watermark, blank.

Sewing stations Now 6; thread impressions (e.g. at fols. 42v–43) indicate earlier, probably originally, there were 2: (tail) l 15 K 41*110*36 K 18 l mm (head).

Sewing Now all-along with white S-twist thread; earlier sewing (on 2 supports) also all-along.

Sewing supports Now sewn on 6 cords. Earlier, probably originally, 2 sewing supports (see above, Sewing stations).

Lacing path Evidence obscured; all supports broken at joint; no other visible evidence.

Endbands Present at head and tail, rolled dark leather core sewn with red and with white S-twist thread, tied down in a few spinefolds; not laced into present boards.

Tabs None present; no other evidence.

Spine lining Spine now hollow; no other evidence.

Boards Pasteboard, 230 x 153 x 3mm; wormholes in first and last leaves indicate that earlier boards were of wood.

Primary covering Brown leather. Impressions on first and last leaves suggest earlier presence of post-medieval cover (brown) with overlapped corners.

Fastenings Roughly central green-rimmed hole, 56mm from fore-edge of last leaf indicates earlier position of a central pin for a strap and pin fastening.

Chemise None present; no other evidence.

Bosses None present; no other evidence.

Chain staple None present; no other evidence.

Labels Red leather label on spine with title in gilt, possibly from an earlier binding. Printed paper labels on spine, each with an element of present shelfmark.

Notes Edges of the leaves now stained yellowish-green.

Structure of Book

Parchment Quite good quality, evenly coloured, good nap.

Collation 1–13⁸, 14⁶ (1 leaf excised).· Hair side outside in each quire.

Quire nos. None.

Catchwords None.

Page Layout
Dimensions
Page 219 x 147mm (probably trimmed at all margins, evidence of loss of marginal notes).
Space ruled for writing Slightly variable: 153–156 x 113–120mm; last quire, 156 x 126mm.
Columns Text in central column with gloss on either side, all 3 columns of variable width, generally text column becoming wider through the book, but no variation of any column widths within a single page.
Pricking Much of the pricking has been trimmed; surviving evidence suggests: leaves folded, 1→8, one side only for 15 text lines, using a template.
Ruling In grey sometimes appearing brown, not very carefully done. Text lines ruled first (e.g. fols. 101v–102), gloss lines ruled in gloss columns and interlinearly, ad hoc; no edge-to-edge ruling.
Lines per page 14 or 15 text lines (q. 14: 16 lines); interlinear gloss, 2 lines above each text line; marginal gloss, 3 lines to 1 text line;
Page design

fol. 2   fol. 2v   fols. 3–110v

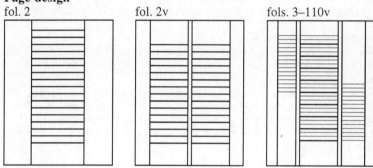

II SCRIBES
One scribe wrote text and gloss throughout in a very compressed hand with continental characteristics s.xii med. It is variable, even untidy in aspect, and tends to slope backwards. The scribe used ampersand and Tironian 'et'. He wrote additional glosses vertically near the edges of many pages, and the colour of the ink suggests that he copied the text first, and then the glosses.

III DECORATION, RUBRICS AND ARTICULATION OF TEXT
Text initials Some plain red 1-line capitals (e.g. fols. 2–2v), but most are brown ink rustic capitals with red shading, written by the scribe, in both text and gloss. Paraphs at the beginning of each gloss passage also shaded in red, though the shading is less consistently applied towards the end of the book.
Minor initials None.
Major initials Fol. 3: **full page red, blue, green, ochre and gold P**(rimum) in a north French style, neatly executed, with fleshy leaf scrolls and biting heads on a pale green field spattered with trios of red dots.
Historiated initials None.
Title page None.
Display script Fol. 1: i) **Incipit liber actu***m* **ap***osto***loru***m* in 1-line mixed capitals alternately red and green with some dotted decoration. ii) (P)**rimum quidem**,

first word in 2-line red capitals with green shading and red flourishes, 2nd word in 1-line capitals, alternately red and green with red flourishes.

Titles etc. No running titles. Later hand s.xvi in has written 'Glossa in Acta Apostolorum' on fol. 1v in brown ink. Chapter numbers sometimes added in margins in Roman and/or Arabic numbers.

IV CONTENTS
Table of contents None.

Main texts Acts of the Apostles, glossed

Fol. 2 prologues: i) 'Lucas medicus antiochiensis'. ii) 'Suspicant*ur* quidam quociens cum*que* paulus'. iii) 'Lucas natione syr*us*'. Fol. 2v: iv) 'Act*us* Ap*osto*lorum nuda*m* vident*ur*'. v) 'De loco q*uidem* in quo actus'. vi) 'Ite*m* de causis sc*r*ibendor*um*'. Text begins fol. 3: 'Primum quidem sermonem'. Gloss begins: 'B*eda*. Primu*m* sermone*m id est* evan*geli*um'. Text ends fol. 110v: 'cu*m* om*n*i fidutia sine p*r*ohibitione.' Gloss ends: 'martyrio coronatus est.'

Note: James, *Trinity MSS,* I, 44, notes that the first words of the gloss are (fol. 2): 'Rab*anus et* beda mag*istri* nece*ss*ar*i*i i*n* expo*sitione*m *et* glo*sa* magist*er* alb*er*icus'. This may be so, but they are written in the hand of Master Robert.

V ORIGIN AND PROVENANCE
Ex libris Fol. 1v: 'LiBer S*ancte* MaRie de Byldewas' in red ink s.xii ex., written in the 'undulating hand' also found in Trinity B.1.3, B.1 4, B.1.31 and B.14.5.

Secundo folio Incipit

The book was written and decorated in Northern France and was owned by Master Robert, who corrected and annotated text and gloss (e.g. fol. 14). There is no evidence that the book was in Archbishop Whitgift's possession, but it must have remained with the others in Master Robert's set of glossed books, and was given by Whitgift s.xvi ex to Trinity College.

VI NOTES

VII BIBLIOGRAPHY AND PLATES
James, *Trinity MSS,* I, 44; Ker, *MLGB,* 14; Sheppard 1988, 287 n. 3; Thomson 1995, 239–243.

50. CAMBRIDGE, TRINITY COLLEGE MS B.1.6
Epistles of Paul, glossed   Date *c.*1160
Leaves [i paper], 131
Foliation 1–131
Origin England   **Fig.** 32

This book is here newly attributed to Buildwas.

I PHYSICAL DESCRIPTION
Binding Tightly resewn and rebound s.xvi/xvii, spine rounded and breaking. Little clear evidence survives of earlier bindings.

Endleaves

Front *Pastedown* 1) laid paper leaf, in place over parchment stub; blank except for Trinity College bookplate and shelfmarks (ink). 2) Earlier, fol. 1 of parchment bifolium, now excised to wide stub.

Flyleaves **1**) Laid paper leaf, conjoint with paper pastedown; watermark: one-handled pot surmounted by a crown-like motif, and letter PB on the body of the pot; blank except for title (recto). **2**) Earlier, fol. 2 of parchment bifolium, now excised to wide stub.

Back *Flyleaves* **1**) Originally last leaf of last quire and fol. 1 of a bifolium, both excised to stub, probably blank; **2**) laid paper leaf, once fol. 1 of a bifolium, now pasted down over its conjoint leaf (see below) watermark as for front flyleaf.

Pastedown **1**) Originally fol. 2 bifolium, now excised to stub; **2**) laid paper leaf in place under its conjoint leaf, once a flyleaf.

Sewing stations Now 5; formerly 3 (evidence of indentations on boards made by former lacing paths, and old sewing holes just visible on fol. 33): (tail) I 15 K 32*73*75*33 K 27 I mm (head). Indistinct impressions (fols. 28–9) suggest an even earlier sewing on 2 supports: (tail) I 41 K 45*92*48 K 29 I mm (head), but it is also possible that some of these unclear impressions may have been made by tackets.

Sewing Now probably all-along; no clear earlier evidence.

Sewing supports Now 5 single supports of rolled tawed skin. Indentations visible on front board suggest 3 earlier flat supports, probably tawed skin; see also above, Sewing stations.

Lacing path Supports now laced in over edges of boards, then to an inner channel; total length *c.*25–33mm. Parallel indentations made by earlier lacing path (3 supports; see above) are *c.*40–50 mm long.

Endbands In place at head and tail, broken at back and front; tied down in 3 or 4 quires only. Not laced in; indentations of earlier endband lacing channels at 45° from back corners visible on boards.

Tabs None present; no other evidence.

Spine lining None present; no other evidence.

Boards Wood, possibly reused, 271 x 183 x 7mm, inner edges bevelled, leaf edges level with inner edge of bevel.

Primary covering Dark brown leather, overlapped corners; small gilt, impressed Whitgift arms on both front and back covers; triple fillets (black) parallel with and adjacent to all edges front and back and on inner bevelled edges, and across spine above and below each sewing support; double thread impressions across head and tail of spine.

Fastenings 2 straps fixed under primary covering on back board with brass daisy-headed pins; brass catch plates set into recesses on front board but over primary covering.

Chemise None present; no other evidence.

Bosses None present; no other evidence.

Chain attachments None present; no other evidence.

Labels Printed paper labels on spine each with an element of present shelfmark.

Notes Edges of leaves now coloured yellowish-green. On fol. 16, a page marker of neutral-coloured thread is knotted into the fore-edge of the leaf, 53mm from the lower edge.

Structure of Book

Parchment Hair sides very yellow, flesh sides white, considerable follicle marking remains; little if any nap; some sewn repairs, e.g. fols. 86, 127.

Collation 1–16⁸, 17⁴ (wants 4, probably blank). Hair side outermost in each quire.

Quire nos. Trimmed off except fol. 64v, where upper part of Roman VII survives (fol. 8v of q. 8, centre of lower margin).
Catchwords None.

Page Layout
Dimensions
Page 257 x 180mm, trimmed at all margins (evidence of trimmed quire numbers, tie-down impressions, reader's notes etc.).
Space ruled for writing 150–153 x 176–178mm.
Columns Text in central column with gloss on either side, all 3 columns of variable width.
Pricking Much evidence trimmed, surviving marks suggest leaves folded, outer margins only, 1→8, text lines only; template used for pricking vertical bounding lines.
Ruling In grey, the text lines separately from the gloss lines which are ruled as needed. Variation in column width often achieved by using only one of the pair of prick marks in the horizontal margins and inventing a second to the right or left.
Lines per page 18 text lines, gloss lines not in regular ratio to text lines, but roughly 3 to 1.
Page design
fols. 1–131

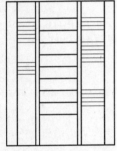

II SCRIBES
One scribe wrote text and gloss throughout in an English hand *c.*1160, upright and very compact with triangular clubs to minims.

III DECORATION, RUBRICS AND ARTICULATION OF TEXT
Text initials Rustic capitals written by text scribe.
Minor initials 3–6-line red capitals, plain, minimally flourished or with a line reserved against the parchment, for prefaces, e.g. fols. 55v, 70, 78, though initials for prefaces not always supplied.
Major initials A series of large initials supplied after Master Robert had added notes, several accommodating these notes, e.g. fol. 1. The letters themselves (except that on fol. 1), and especially their decoration, are clumsy; several seem to be attempts at 'channel-style' decoration (cf. Trinity B.4.3 and Balliol 35A and 173B), executed without skill.
Fol. 1: **16-line red P**(aulus) with extended tail, scalloped and curved lines reserved against parchment, well executed, no decoration. Fol. 30v: **14-line red P**(aulus) with extended tail and a rectangular terminal consisting of 'curled leaf

and horn' motifs, stepped lines reserved against parchment; 3 spotted, worm-like serpents within the letter, drawn freehand in brown ink against red and green background, stem flourished with green. Fol. 56: **15-line red and green P**(aulus) with slender tail, colours interlocking in large stepped pattern with intervening reserved line; 2 coiled serpents within letter in brown ink, green flourishes along stem. Fol. 70: **11-line red P**(aulus), with jagged reserved line, slender tail and large terminal (red); rough striated flourishes within letter, unfinished. Fol. 78: **7-line red P**(aulus), curved line reserved against parchment and unfinished symmetrical decoration of striated flourishes in brown ink inside letter. Fol. 85v: **11-line red P**(aulus) with roughly flourished tail and roughly scalloped reserved line; dense dotted and striated design in red and brown ink inside letter. Fol. 90v: **10-line red P**(aulus) with curved and scalloped reserved line, elaborate tail and striated wing-like decoration in bowl of letter. Fol. 95: **11-line red P**(aulus) with slender tail, scalloped reserved line, more competently flourished perhaps by a different hand in brown and red ink; dense symmetrical 'leaf and horn' design inside letter in pale and dark brown and red ink by the flourisher (cf. Edinburgh 6121). Fol. 99: **8-line red P**(aulus) with thin extended tail now trimmed at lower edge of page, scalloped and stepped reserved lines; curved design in bowl of letter faintly sketched in grey. Fol. 101v: **8-line red P**(aulus), separate curved and stepped reserved lines; no other decoration. Fol. 107: **15-line red P**(aulus), curved reserved line; no other decoration. Fol. 110: **10-line red P**(aulus), scalloped reserved line which is filled with a line in brown ink; no other decoration. Fol. 112: **13-line red P**(aulus), straight reserved line; no other decoration. Fol. 113: **11-line M**(ultifarie) with slender extended tail to first stroke ending in decorated terminal, scalloped reserved lines filled with red and brown lines in ink; no other decoration.

Historiated initials None.

Display script Fol. 1: (P)**aulus** in Roman capitals alternately green and red. Elsewhere the first word after an initial in small rustic letters in brown ink written by the scribe.

Title page None (but no flyleaves remain).

Titles etc. Running titles fols. 1v–2 in red in a contemporary hand; fols. 3v–30, in brown ink or with stylus, by later hand. Incipits and explicits in red, probably not by the text scribe, these rubrics often squeezed in since space was not left for them by the text scribe. Titles are often also written in stylus in the margin, suggesting the rubrics were not originally present; on fol. 107 the red initial overlaps the stylus title.

IV CONTENTS

Table of contents None.

Main text The Epistles of Paul, glossed.

1. Fol. 1 (short preface: 'Pro altercatione scribit romanis'. Ends: 'superbiam destruit.' Text begins fol. 1: 'Incipit epistola ad romanos prima. Paulus servus *ihesu christi*'. Gloss begins: 'Paulus hebraice quietus grece modicus latine'. Fol. 30: 'Explicit epistola ad romanos.'

2. Fol. 30: 'Incipit argumentum epistole I ad corinthos. Corinthii sunt achaici et hi similiter ab apostolis'. Fol. 30v: 'Explicit argumentum.' Text begins: 'Incipit epistola prima ad corinthios. Paulus vocatus apostolus'. Gloss begins: 'Cum omnibus id est omnibus scribit suffraganeis corinthi'. Fol. 55v: 'Explicit epistola prima ad corinthios.'

253

3. Fol. 55v: 'Incipit argumentum ii ad corinthios. Post peractam penitentiam'. Fol. 56: 'Explicit argumentum.' Text begins: 'Incipit epistola ii ad corinthios. Paulus apostolus'. Gloss begins: 'Benedictus. Primum perfectis loquitur de tribulatione'. Fol. 69v: 'Explicit epistola ad corinthios secunda.'

4. Fol. 69v: 'Incipit argumentum epistola ad galathas.' Fol. 70: 'Galathie sunt greci hi verbum veritatis...Explicit argumentum.' Text begins: 'Incipit epistola ad Galathas. Paulus apostolus non ab hominibus'. Gloss begins: 'Non ab hominibus ut quidam ab apostolis'. Fol. 78: 'Explicit epistola ad Galathas.'

5. Fol. 78: 'Incipit argumentum ad ephesios. Ephesi sunt asiani hi accepto verbo...Explicit argumentum.' Text begins: 'Incipit epistola ad ephesiosi. Paulus apostolus'. Gloss begins: 'In christo opere christi non meritis'. Fol. 85v: 'Explicit epistola ad ephesios.'

From item 6 onwards, the prefaces are written in the gloss columns as if they were glosses.

6. Fol. 85v: 'Incipit epistola ad philippenses.' (Preface: 'Philippenses sunt macedones'.) Text begins: 'Pauli et Timotheus'. Gloss begins: 'Servi dicit ut et ipsi pro domino ferant dura'. Fol. 90v: 'Explicit epistola ad philippenses.'

7. Fol. 90v: 'Incipit epistola ad colosenses.' (Preface: 'Colosenses sunt asiani'.) Text begins: 'Paulus apostolus'. Gloss begins: 'Ostendit bona [esse] que receperat'. Fol. 95: 'Explicit epistola ad colosenses.'

8. Fol. 95: 'Incipit epistola ad thessalo' [sic]. (Preface: 'Thessalonicenses sunt macedones'.) Text begins: 'Paulus et sylvanus'. Gloss begins: 'Spes existens.' Fol. 99: 'Explicit epistola prima ad thessalonicenses.'

9. Fol. 99: 'Incipit epistola ii ad thessalonicenses.' (Preface: 'Quia in prima epistola quibusdam dixit de adventu domini'.) Text begins: 'Paulus et sylvanus et timotheus'. Gloss begins: 'Orta graviori tribulatione item monet patientiam'. Fol. 101v: 'Explicit epistola ii ad thessalonicenses.'

10. Fol. 101v: 'Incipit epistola prima ad timotheum.' (Prefaces: i. 'Jeronimus. Timotheus iste fuit filius mulieris fidelis'. ii. 'Thimotheo [sic] in asia relicto episcopo'.) Text begins: 'Paulus apostolus'. Gloss begins: 'Misericordia quod in aliis epistolis gratia id est remissio peccatorum'. Fol. 107: 'Explicit epistola i ad thimotheum.'

11. Fol. 107: 'Incipit epistola ii ad thimotheum.' No preface. Text begins: 'Paulus apostolus'. Gloss begins: 'Gratias ago quod abeam memoriam tui'. Fol. 110: 'Explicit epistola ii ad thimotheum.'

12. Fol. 110: 'Incipit epistola ad tytum.' (Preface: 'Tito relicto crete episcopo'.) Text begins: 'Paulus servus dei'. Gloss begins: 'In spem vite eterne. Hec res hic fructus commendat officium'. Fol. 112: 'Explicit epistola ad titum.'

13. Fol. 112: 'Incipit epistola ad philomonem.' (Preface: 'Philomoni familiares litteras mittit pro onesimo servo eius'.) Text begins: 'Paulus vinctus'. Gloss begins: 'Paulus vinctus. non dicit apostolis nomen dignitatis'. Fol. 112v: 'Explicit epistola ad philomonem.'

14. Fol. 112v: 'Incipit argumentum epistole [sic] ad hebreos. In primis dicendum est cur apostolis paulus'. Fol. 113: 'Explicit argumentum.' Text begins: 'Incipit epistola ad hebreos. Multifarie multisque modis'. Gloss begins: 'Olim. non est novum deus'. Fol 131: 'Explicit epistola ad hebreos.'

Fol. 131: An ?omitted passage and gloss added by text scribe: 'Qui reddis iniquitatem primum filiis ac nepotibus in terciam et quartam progeniem. Gregorius. Cum scriptum sit quid est quod inter vos parabolam vertitis in proverbium istud'. Ends fol. 131v: 'ut non cum hoc mundo dampnemur.'

Fol. 131v: added in space below added passage in different hand s. xii: 'Siquis aut*em* edificat supra fundam*entum* hoc aur*um* argent*um*...Sepe p*er* aur*um* sapientia designat*ur*.' Ends fol. 131v: 'p*er* igne*m* mundantur ut digni fiant elector*um* num*er*o sociari.'

V ORIGIN AND PROVENANCE
Ex libris None.
Secundo folio fidem (text) Nulli (gloss)
Written in England *c.*1160 and acquired very soon after it was written by Master Robert, who heavily annotated text and gloss. While owned by him the book had no initials and probably no rubrication; the decorated initials at least were probably supplied at Buildwas which acquired the book later in the twelfth century with the other glossed books. The initials on fols. 56, 95, 112 are added around Master Robert's annotations, and on fol. 1 round those of another reader, s.xii, whose annotations are found in other Buildwas books, especially the glossed books. The book must have remained at Buildwas, together with the other glossed books, until at least the fifteenth century.
The books were acquired by Archbishop Whitgift and given to Trinity College s. xvi ex.

VI NOTES
1. On two lines at the bottom of fol. 131v, a list of texts is written in Master Robert's hand: 'epistolae pauli; Lucam; Ioha*nnem*; Ecclesiaste*n*; Cantica Cantico*rum*; Apocalipsi*n*; Epistol*ae* canonicas; Tobia*m*; Sacr*amenta* Iuonis; Libr*um* cintillar*um*; Teod*ulum* glosatu*s*; Exempla v*er*sifican*di*; t*ractatus* de scientia lune; Tabul*am* gerlan*di*; Tabul*am* Rimachie; Glosulas pet*ri* maiores *et* minores; Glosulas de Iuvenali.' These may be books that he himself owned; the list begins with the title of the book in which it is written. See Thomson 1995, 241–242, for a commentary on these texts.
2. The decoration in some of the added initials may have been intended to imitate later channel style decoration such as that in Master Robert's glossed Minor Prophets (Trinity B.4.3).
3. Chapter numbers were added to margins in dark brown ink, ?s.xiii.

VII BIBLIOGRAPHY AND PLATES
James, *Trinity MSS*, I, 6–7; Thomson 1995, 238–243.

51. SHREWSBURY SCHOOL, MS XII
Apocalypse and Canonical Epistles, glossed   **Date** s.xii med.
Leaves 128, i
Foliation 1–129
Origin Northern France

I PHYSICAL DESCRIPTION
Binding s.xii, spine flat, primary sewing supports breaking at entry into boards; covering over spine cracked along inner edges of boards, repaired with glue (1897), spine now rigid. Otherwise intact. Boxed.
Endleaves
   Front *Pastedown* Missing, probably once fol. 1 of bifolium, stub only remaining; considerable deposits of brown grainy paste on inner surface of top board.

     Flyleaves Missing, probably fol. 2 of separate bifolium, now excised to stub.

Back *Flyleaves* Missing, probably once fols. 1–3 of separate quaternion, probably blank, now excised to stubs.

     Pastedown Detached, fol. 4 of separate quaternion, with considerable deposits of grainy paste and impressions of binding elements which are still visible on inner surface of back board.

Sewing stations 2: these and both upper and lower kettle stitch marked with pricks 8→1, *c*.5 mm from spinefold: (tail) I 26 K 37*77*35 K 25 I mm (head).

Sewing All-along, with white Z-twist thread.

Sewing supports 2 white tawed skin supports, split, 9mm wide.

Lacing path Supports laced into boards through tunnels from spine edges, channels on outer then inner surfaces (lacing paths parallel, 60–65mm long); ends secured with wooden wedges.

Endbands White tawed skin supports, split, *c*.7–8mm wide, present at head and tail; laced into boards through a tunnel from the spine edge of board (i.e. not from the corner) and a channel on the outer surface at *c*.45° to spine edge; slips pulled through to inner face and secured with wooden wedges. Sewn with white Z-twist thread through the split with herringbone pattern along ridge, and through the tab to the centre of each quire. Endbands unbroken except at entry to front board at the tail.

Tabs Semi-circular tabs present at head and tail, made of thick white tawed skin which extends along spine as far as the primary sewing supports; sewn to matching extension of primary cover along the semi-circular edge with blue Z-twist thread, with herringbone pattern along the ridge and at the base of the stitches on either side of the tab.

Spine lining The spine is lined along its entire length with 4 irregularly shaped strips of white tawed skin, of similar thickness to the primary covering. 2 strips are placed (adjacently) between the two primary sewing supports, and one each between sewing support and head- and tail-endband, passing over the tab lining extensions. Each end of each strip is pasted to the inner face of front and back board, over the covering turn-ins. The spine lining is not pasted to the back of the spinefolds, but the primary cover is now glued to the spine lining. Impressions on back pastedown exactly reflect current state of inner face of back board. If, as seems to be the case, the pastedown is contemporary with the binding, the spine lining strips are original (cf. Edinburgh 6121, Bodley 370 and 395).

Boards Wood, 204 x 137 x 10mm; all corners square, edges (including spine edge) bevelled, and once flush with leaves, but leaves now project slightly at the fore-edge.

Primary covering Discoloured white tawed skin, corners mitred at fore-edges, parallel with spine at spine edges. Worn almost through along inner spine edges of boards, evidently at one time completely detached along spine-edge of front board. This repaired with translucent glue (traces visible on cover) in 1897, fixing cover at spine to spine linings. Old shelfmark 'Mus.III' written on upper turn-in over front board; book titles (now mostly erased) and secundo folio written on upper half of back covering.

Fastenings 1) Central fore-edge strap of white tawed skin (possibly two thicknesses), 19mm wide x 4mm thick inserted in a groove cut into the top board and fixed under primary cover which is cut to accommodate it (mode of fixing not visible), strap now cut off at fore-edge; corresponding pin hole on back board 63mm from fore-edge. **2**) Dark brown leather replacement straps fixed over top board and under primary cover, which has been slit to accommodate them, by a single brass rectangular-headed (2mm) pin through a tiny brass plate 8 x 8mm (upper), 8 x 6mm (lower). Straps now cut off flush with fore-edge of board; marks of catchplates now lost at corresponding points on back board, each with 2 holes (part of one brass pin still in place), and signs of wear on fore-edge of lower board. These straps were probably added after the book's acquisition by Shrewsbury School.

Chemise None present; no other evidence.

Bosses None present; no other evidence.

Chain attachments 1) 4 nails embedded in lower half of bottom board near spine in roughly trapezoid configuration (16 x 30 x 14 x 29mm) are evidence of a chain attachment, probably earlier than 2); **2**) Rust marks parallel with and 33mm from upper edge of front board, 50 x 10–15mm, with remains of 2 iron nails, are remains of a Shrewbury School chain attachment *c*.1650; similar attachments have survived on other Shrewsbury books (information very kindly provided by Shrewsbury School's Librarian, James Lawson).

Labels 1) 2-line inscription on upper part of primary cover back board, now mostly illegible but probably a summary of contents; **2**) 'Notae in Apocalypsin' in ink in hand, s.xvii, almost certainly that of Thomas Chaloner, Headmaster of Shrewsbury School 1636–64 ; **3**) 3 small paper labels on spine with Shrewsbury School shelfmark: Mus. III 50. 1788; the same mark written in ink on upper turn-in of front cover.

Structure of Book

Parchment QQ. 1–7, very poor quality, with much scar tissue and many flay-marks; discoloured; hair and flesh sides very distinct; qq. 8–17 slightly better, thicker parchment except towards the end of the book. Few repairs, fol. 74: roughly mended hole (probably by parchment maker). Fol. 52 apparently previously folded and pricked before use in this book, though conjoint leaf shows no such folds.

Collation 1–6⁸, 7⁶, 8–11⁸, 12⁶, 13⁸ (3 and 6 are single leaves), 14–15⁸, 16–17⁶, 18⁴ (1–3 excised, probably blank). Hair side outside in each quire.

Quire nos. QQ. 1–6: lower margin of verso of last leaf in small Roman numbers i–vi framed with dots; qq. 10–16: lower margin of verso of last leaf in small Roman numbers iii–ix.

Catchwords None.

Page Layout
Dimensions
Page Variable: 200–204 x 135–139mm.

Space ruled for writing Variable: 124–142 x 109–113mm.

Columns Central text column with gloss column on either side, all 3 varying only very slightly in width from page to page.

Pricking Leaves folded, outer margin only, 1→8 (text lines only). QQ. 13–17 show clear cross-shaped marks (+). Gloss lines not pricked.

Ruling In brown, fairly neatly done though vertical margin pricks often ignored; text and gloss lines ruled separately, gloss lines ad hoc, as needed.

Lines per page QQ. 1–7: 15 text lines; qq. 8–17: 12 text lines. 2 gloss lines to each text line.

Page design
fols. 1–2

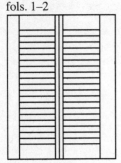

fols. 2v–128.

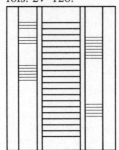

II SCRIBES

One scribe wrote text and gloss throughout in a clear, upright hand s.xii med with continental characteristics. It varies in size as the text proceeds (cf. this scribe's work in Trinity B.1.39). The scribe made his own corrections over erasures (e.g. fol. 114), and provided elaborate paraphs in brown ink in prefaces and gloss (e.g. fols. 1v, 49v, 51).

III DECORATION, RUBRICS AND ARTICULATION OF TEXT

Text initials Fols. 1–2: 2- or 3-preface-line red capitals, undecorated, oxidised; elsewhere, brown ink capitals written by the scribe.

Minor initials None

Major initials Fol. 2v: **3-text-line red A**(pochalipsis) with reserved lines in all 3 strokes and with simple extended leaf terminal, the red now oxidised; letter awkwardly placed in space left by scribe. Fol. 10: **4-text-line red P**(ost), undecorated, red oxidised. Fol. 15v: **3-text-line red P**(ost), undecorated, red oxidised. Fol. 16v: **3-text-line red P**(ost), undecorated, red oxidised. Fol. 51v: **1-text-line red C**(lama), undecorated, red oxidised. Fol. 55v: **2-preface-line red N**(on) with lines and swellings in vertical strokes and tendril terminal. Fol. 55v: **2-preface-line green Q**(uia) plain, with slight red flourishes. Fol. 56v: **6-text-line red I**(acobus) with scalloped reserved line, and coiled tendril tail. Fol. 60v: **3-text-line red F**(*ratres*) with delicate undulating reserved line in vertical stroke, red oxidised. Fol. 74v: **3-text-line red S**(imon) with curved reserved line, red oxidised. Fol. 75: **4-text-line red P**(etrus) with delicate undulating reserved line in both strokes, red oxidised. Fol. 89v: **3-text-line red K**(arissimi), undecorated, red oxidised. Fol. 92: **2-text-line red H**(umiliamini)) with delicate reserved line in both vertical strokes. Fol. 93: **2-text-line red S**(imon) with reserved line, red oxidised. Fol. 105: **3-text-line red Q**(uod), undecorated, with curved tail. Fol. 119v: **3-text-line red S**(enior) with reserved line, red oxidised. Fol. 121v: **3-text-line red S**(enior) with reserved line, red oxidised. Fol. 123v: **3.5-text-line red I**(udas) with undulating reserved line, oxidised.

Historiated initials None.

Display script Fol. 105: (Q)**uod fuit**, 1-text-line Roman capitals in brown ink. Elsewhere opening words or letter(s) are either in minuscule or in very small capitals hardly distinguishable from minuscule (e.g. fol. 60v).

Titles etc. No running titles originally, but these added by a roughly contemporary hand in the upper margin of the epistles only in brown; incipit on fol. 1 only (preface) in tiny rustic capitals, and explicits fol. 50 (Apocalypse) in a mixture of rustic capitals and minuscule letters, both by the text scribe; and an explicit on fol. 74v (Epistle of James) in minuscule in another hand. Chapter numbers (Arabic) added by a later hand s.xiii.

Title page None, but prefatory leaves lost.

IV CONTENTS

Table of contents None (but prefatory leaves lost).

Main texts Apocalypse and Canonical Epistles, glossed.

1. Apocalypse. Fols. 1–2v: a long series of prefaces beginning: i) 'Incipit prefatio ieronimi presbiteri in vero apocalipsis. Iohannes apostolus *et* evangelista'. ii) 'Asia minor asie pars'. iii) 'Apocalipsis h*aec*'. iv) 'Intentio ei*us est* exhortari'. v) 'Hec p*r*ima visio'. vi) (fol. 2): 'Hunc que sit ei*us* mate*r*ia'. vii) 'Intentio v*er*o nos invitare'. viii) 'Et est notand*um* quare'. ix) 'Prave nimis et p*r*ocul a sac*er*dotis [sic]'. Ends fol. 2: 'quolibet modo querere compendium.' Fol 2: 'In apocalipsi expositores sunt Beda Haimo Primasius Ambrosius Alb*er*icus' followed by a passage added by Master Robert: 'Nom*en etiam* auctoris queri*tur*'. Text begins fol. 3: 'Apochalipsis *Ihesu Christi*'. Gloss begins (left): 'Litt*er*a sic*ut* ac si dic*er*et ita comeneret'; (right): 'Preparat auditores benivolos et attentos'. Text ends fol. 50: 'G*r*at*i*a d*o*m*i*ni n*o*st*r*i *ihesu* cum omnibus vobis. Amen. Explicit.' Gloss ends fol. 50: 'conversio ad deum.'

2a. Fol. 50v: 'Iaspidis viridis virorum fidei inmarcessibilem significat'. Ends fol. 51: 'semp*er* regni memoria*m in* humiliu*m* ani*m*o.'

2b. Fol. 51: 'Grad*us* etat*is* sex s*unt*. Infantia Pueritia Adolescentia Iuvent*us* Gravit*as* Senect*us*'. Ends fol. 51v: 'q*uo*d sit t*er*minus vi etatis.'

2c. Fol. 51v: 'P*r*ima mu*n*di etas ab ada*m* usq*ue* ad noe continens annos iuxta hebraica*m* v*er*itatem m.dc.lv'. Ends fol. 51v: 'p*er*henniter regnab*unt* expectant.'

3. Fol. 51v: extract from Isaiah (58.1–59.5): 'Isaiah. Clama ne cesses q*uas*i tuba exalta'. Gloss: 'Clama *enim* d*omin*us ad p*r*ophetam *vel* apostolus'. Text ends fol. 54: 'erumpet in regulum.' Gloss ends fol. 54: 'p*er* aera volentes'. Fol. 54v blank.

4. Fol. 55, added in a later hand s.xii to page originally blank: 'Int*r*oitu*s* in ep*isto*las canonicas, [O]stendit m*i*hi d*omin*us dicit zacharias p*r*oph*et*a'. Ends: 'huic op*er*i in q*u*o ostendit se ordinasse et correxisse ep*isto*las canonicas.'

5. Fol. 55v: Epistle of James. 'P*r*ologus beati Ieronimi. Non ita ordo est apud grecos. Quia in circumcisione *ch*r*is*ti natus erat iacobus apostolus'. Ends fol. 56. Text begins fol 56: 'Iacobus dei et domini nostri. Gloss begins: 'A p*er*fectiorib*us* de extrinsecis temptationibus.' ('Iacob*us* iste ecc*l*esie ierosolimitane' is a later addition). Text ends fol. 74v: '*et* op*er*it multitudine*m* pecc*at*orum.' ('Explicit ep*isto*la s*an*c*t*i iacobi' in another hand). Gloss ends fol. 74v: 'gaudia vite celestis sibi co*n*quirit.'

6. Fol. 74v: Epistle of Peter I. Preface: 'Simon petrus filius iohannis provincie galilee'. Ends: 'In nova*m* vita*m* proficer*e*.' Text begins fol. 75: 'Petrus apostolus'. Gloss begins: 'Tempore quo cepit ecclesia quidam de gentilitate'. Text ends fol. 93: 'qui estis in *christo ihesu*. amen.' Gloss ends: 'p*er* orbem terra*rum* ecclesiis scribo.'

7. Fol. 93v: Epistle of Peter II. Text begins: 'Simon petrus servus et apostolus'. Gloss begins: 'Istam eiusdem q*uibus et* prima*m*'. Text ends fol. 104v: 'et in diem eternitatis amen.' Gloss ends: 'f*r*ena lax*antes et* alia multa.'

8. Fol. 104v: Epistle of John I. Preface: Ends fol. 105: 'q*uo*d odiu*m* sit int*er*fectionis occasio.' Text begins fol. 105: 'Quod fuit'. Gloss begins (left): 'In

principio epistole ad commendationem sermonis'; (right): 'Scripserat iohannes evangelium adversus dogmata hereticorum'. Text ends fol. 119v: 'custodite vos a simulacris.' Gloss ends: 'simulacrorum servitus.'

9. Fol. 119v: Epistle of John II. Text begins: 'Senior electe'. Gloss begins: 'Seniores dicuntur presbitero'. Text ends fol. 121v: 'Gracia tecum.' Gloss ends: 'ex persona electorum salutat.'

10. Fol 121v: Epistle of John III. Text begins: 'Senior Gaio karissimo'. Gloss begins: 'Videtur gaius fuisse corintius'. Text ends fol. 123v: 'Saluta amicos nominatim.' Gloss ends: 'salute monstret extraneos.'

11. Fol. 123v: Epistle of Jude. Text begins: 'Iudas ihesu christi servus'. Gloss begins: 'Iudas qui et thadeus contra eosdem'. Text ends fol. 128: 'in omnia seculorum secula amen.' Gloss ends: 'cui nichil resistit.'

Fol. 128: 'De investigatione v mariarum quas agiographa sepe commemorat'. Ends: 'cuius prosapia non inquiritur.' Fol. 128v blank except for ex libris (s.xvi) and scribbles. Fol 129 blank.

V ORIGIN AND PROVENANCE

Ex libris Fol. 128v at top of page: 'Liber de sancte marie de Buldwas' s. xvi.

Secundo folio [di]vino sufflamine

The book was probably written in Northern France. The main scribe is the same as that of the glossed texts of Ecclesiastes, Song of Songs, Leviticus (fragment) and Tobit (text only) in Trinity B.1.39 (q.v.). It was owned by Master Robert who annotated text and gloss. It came to Buildwas with the other glossed books in this set, s.xii ex, although the extant ex libris was not inscribed until s.xvi when it must already have left the Buildwas library. The writer, however, obviously knew where the book had come from. It is the only known glossed book in Master Robert's set which did not remain with the rest. Its survival makes it possible to hope that others which became separated once the books left Buildwas may surface. Master Robert's hand and his manner of annotation are distinctive.

The book was purchased by Shrewsbury School with school funds in 1617 at a time when the School was purchasing books from Richard Meighen, a bookseller in the city of London and brother of John Meighen, Headmaster at that time. John Meighen kept a record of the School's acquisitions of manuscripts, and MS. XII is described as follows: 'Bound in one volume in 4⁰ with board hillinge covered with white tawed skin and clasped with one clasp lapped over.' The title 'Notae in Apocalipsin' inscribed on the front cover is almost certainly in the hand of Thomas Chaloner, Headmaster from 1636 to 1664 (information very kindly provided by Shrewsbury School's Librarian, James Lawson).

The name 'Thomas' is inscribed in the upper margin fol. 36 (s.xvi) and 'Fardinando' is inscribed in the lower margin of fol. 72v and on fol. 128v (s.xvii).

VI NOTES

1. The apparently planned inclusion of multiple short passages in a glossed text is paralleled in Harley 3038 (written probably at Buildwas in 1176), and similarly, the inclusion of an excerpt from an Old Testament book (see fols. 51v–54) is paralleled in the group of glossed texts copied principally by the Shrewsbury

XII scribe in Trinity B.1.39 (see fols. 62–67: Leviticus11.1–45).

The hand of a second annotator, s.xii ex/xiii in, who made comments in other glossed books from Buildwas, is also found in this book, e.g. fol. 117, lower margin.

VII BIBLIOGRAPHY AND PLATES

Ker, *MLGB*, 15; Sheppard 1988, 285, 287; Sheppard 1990, pls. 6, 10; A. Piper and N. Ker, *Medieval Manuscripts in British Libraries,* 4 Vols (Oxford 1992), IV, 302–3; Sheppard 1995, 194 and fig. 8.

APPENDIX

Texts recorded as having been held at Buildwas in the
Registrum Anglie de Libris Doctorum et Auctorum Veteris

It has been recently shown that the *Registrum* was compiled in the early 14th century by Franciscans, probably in Oxford. It is a location list for copies of selected works of selected authors, mainly patristic. It survives in three manuscripts copies: Oxford, Bodleian Library MS Tanner 165, Cambridge, Peterhouse MS 169 and London, British Library MS Royal 3.D.1 (a late copy of Peterhouse 169). The text was established by R.A.B. Mynors and has been published with an exhaustive account of the original compilation, a record of surviving manuscripts etc., by Richard and Mary Rouse (see Rouse & Rouse, *Registrum*).

In the *Registrum*, Buildwas is denoted by the numeral xii. Two photographs of leaves in Oxford, Bodleian Libary MS Tanner 165, the fifteenth-century copy of the *Registrum*, are reproduced in *Manuscripts at Oxford: an Exhibition in Memory of Richard William Hunt (1908–1979)*, ed. by A.C. de la Mare and B.C. Barker-Benfield (Oxford, 1980). Figs. 34 and 35 show pages from the record of texts by Jerome. Buildwas (as xii) appears six times, recording Buildwas's ownership, among others, of Jerome's Letters ('Ep*istole* Jeronimi'), possibly those surviving in Balliol 229 and Lambeth 457.

It is clear from a comparison of surviving books known to have been at Buildwas with those recorded in the *Registrum* that the compilers missed a number of copies of the texts they were searching for. For example, the compilers recorded some texts contained in Edinburgh 6121, but omitted one that was on their list. The Edinburgh MS is in its original binding, so there cannot be any question of subsequent rebinding and the re-ordering of the contents. Some of these apparent inconsistencies might be thought to be explained by the fact that certain books had already left Buildwas by the time the Franciscans arrived. However, the evidence in a large number of Buildwas books indicates that the monks were still actively using them in the late thirteenth century. The conclusion must be that the Franciscans only selectively, or at least unsystematically, recorded texts bound in any one volume, and that certain books, disposed in a variety of places throughout the monastery, were not brought to their attention.

The texts and their attribution are noted below as they appear in the *Registrum*.
111 texts are listed, of which 18 survive.

Author	Text	Surviving
Augustine	De Agone Christiano	Edinburgh 6121
	De Genesi ad Litteram	
	De Fide et Operibus	
	De Gracia et Libero Arbitrio	Edinburgh 6121
	De Predestinatione Sanctorum	Edinburgh 6121
	De Bono Perseverantie	Edinburgh 6121
	Super Evangelium Iohannis Omelie 124	Christ Church 88
	Quam Sit Fructuosa Penitentia	
	Epistole Augustini 143	

262

De Institutione Vite
De 10 Preceptis et 10 Plagis
De Sacramento Altaris
Sermo de Eo Semper Gaudete
Sermo super Mulierem Fortem
Sermo de Resurrectione

Gregory   40 Omelie
Super Ezechielem   Trinity B.1.3

Ambrose   De Penitentia
Super Lucam
De Fuga Seculi   (excerpts added to
Trinity B.1.14)

Super Octonarium
De Patriarcha Ioseph
De XII Patriarchis
De Bono Mortis

Jerome   Maius Breviarum
Glose Septime Ebdomade
De Quinque Sensibus
Super Ecclesiasten   Trinity B.1.39
De Nativitate Beate Marie contra Elvidium
Vitas Patrum
Super Psalterium
Super Ieremiam
Super Ysayem
Super Danielem
Super Matheum
Super Marcum   Edinburgh 6121
Epistole Ieronimi   Balliol 229; Lambeth 457
De Illustribus Viris
Super Parabolas
Super Cantica Canticorum   Trinity B.1.29

Bede   Cronica
Super Marcum
Super Lucam
De Historia Anglorum

Isidore   Ethimologiarum   Bodley 395
Catologus Virorum Illustrium
Repetitio Nomimum Sanctorum Patrum
    quid Significent
Super Pentateuchum
Super Iosue
Super Iudicum
Super 4 Libros Regum
Orthographia

Origen	Super Vetus Testamentum Super Cantica Canticorum Epistole } *Buildwas the Lamentationes } *only repository	
Rabanus	Ethimolgiarum Super Matheum	
Cassiodorus	De Institutione Scriptuarum	
Cyprian	Epistole Omelie	Pembroke 154
Haimo	Super Epistolas Pauli	
Leo	Sermones	
Innocent	De Contemptu Mundi *Buildwas the only repository Tractatus de Missa	
Anselm	De Propria Voluntate Cur Deus Homo Meditationes	Pembroke 154
Bernard	Omelie Super Cantica Canticorum Sermones Epistole De Consideratione De Precepto et Dispensatione Super Missus Est De 12 Gradibus Humilitatis De Gratia et Libero Arbitrio De Diligendo Deo Ad Eugenium Meditationes De Visitatione Infirmorum	Balliol 150
Ralph of Flaix	Super Leviticum	
Alexander Nequam	Super Cantica Canticorum Super Ecclesiasten De Naturis Rerum Regule super Theologiam	Balliol 39–40
Peter of Blois	Epistole Super Iob Belligeronticon De Transfiguratione Christi Sermones }* De Conversione Sancti Pauli }* *Buildwas the only repository	Pembroke 154 Pembroke 154

264

Peter Cantor	Super Vetus Testamentum	Bodley 371

Gilbert   Sentencie
               Super Cantica Canticorum

Stephen   Super 12 Prophetas
  Langton   Super Regum
               Super Ysaiam

Hugh of St.   Super Illud Tota Pulcra Es
   Victor   De Archa Noe
               De Incorrupta Virginitate Matris Domini
               De Institutione Noviciorum
               De Arra Anime
               De Sacramentis
               De Operibus Trium Dierum
               Didascolicon
               De 12 Abusionibus Claustri

Richard of St. De Templo Ezechielis ad Litteram
   Victor   Super Quid Est Tibi Mare
               Super Ego Nabugodonosor
               Super Omne Caput Languidum
               Super Psalmos
               De Benjamin et Fratribus eius

INDEX OF SURVIVING TEXTS

Author and Text/Initia	Manuscript
Aelred of Rievaulx	
Speculum Caritatis	St. John's D.2
De Onere Babilonis	Lambeth 488
Alexander Nequam	
Super Cantica Canticorum	Balliol 39–40
De Utensilibus	Trinity O.7.9
Ambrose	
De Fuga Seculi (2 excerpts copied by Master Robert)	Trinity B.1.14
Andrew of St. Victor	
Commentary on Kings and Chronicles	Trinity B.1.29
Anselm	
Commentary on John	Trinity B.1.10
Meditationes	Pembroke 154
Aristotle	
Predicamenta	Lambeth 456
Peri Ermenias	Lambeth 456
Augustine	
De Agone Christiano	Edinburgh 6121
De Bono Perseverantia	Edinburgh 6121
De Correptione et Gratia	Edinburgh 6121
De Decem Preceptis Legis et de Decem Plagis	Edinburgh 6121
De Fide Rerum Invisibilium	Edinburgh 6121
De Gratia et Libero Arbitrio	Edinburgh 6121
De Mirabilibus Novi et Veteris Testamenti	Balliol 229
De Natura et Gratia	Edinburgh 6121
De Perfectione Iusticiae Hominum	Edinburgh 6121
De Predestinatione Sanctorum	Edinburgh 6121
De Proverbiis Salomonis	Edinburgh 6121
De Sermone Domini in Monte Habito	Balliol 229
De Resurrectione Domini	Edinburgh 6121
?Disputatio Contra Felicianum Hereticum	Edinburgh 6121
Omelie in Evangelium Secundum Iohannem	Christ Church 88
Sermo: Et Verbum Caro Sanctum Est	Trinity B.1.10
Sermo sub Figura an sub Veritate hoc Mystici Calicis	Trinity O.7.9
Pseudo-Augustine	
Sermo de Suscitatione Lazari	Christ Church 88
Benedict	
Epistola ad Beatum Remigium	Trinity B.1.4

Hugh of Fouilly
De Claustro   Lambeth 107
Liber de Duabus Rotis   Lambeth 107

(Hugh of St. Cher)
Concordanciae de Biblia   }derived from   Lambeth 477
Concordanciae Anglicanae   }Hugh of St. Cher   Lambeth 477

Hugh of St. Victor
Velle scire verum bonum   Trinity B.1.39

Ignatius of Antioch
Epistole ad Mariam   Balliol 229

Isidore
Ethymologiae   Bodley 395

Jerome
Sermo de Assumptione Beate Marie Virginis   Trinity B.3.8
De Hebraicis Questionibus in Genesi   Balliol 229
De Hebraicis Questionibus in Paralipomenon   Balliol 229
De Hebraicis Questionibus in Samuele   Balliol 229
De Locis   Balliol 229
De Sancto Cypriano   Pembroke 154
Epistole (selected)   Balliol 229
Epistole (excerpts)   Lambeth 477
Epistole (excerpts)   Lambeth 457
De Membris Domini   Balliol 229
Super Cantica Canticorum   Trinity B.1.29

Pseudo-Jerome
Commentary on Mark   Edinburgh 6121

John Bassianus
Legal Tracts   Trinity B.1.29

John Cassian
Regula   Bodley 730
Decem Collationes   Bodley 730

John Chrisostom
De Reparatione Lapsi ad Theodorum   Balliol 229

Lanfranc
Indicatum est mihi quia de cuius es monasterio   Trinity O.7.9

(Martianus Capella)
De Nuptiis (a commentary on)   Trinity B.1.29

Palladius
Vitae Sanctorum Patrum (Lausiac History)   Trinity B.2.30

Omelia Beati Iohannis Episcopi Super Mattheum xxi	Edinburgh 6121
Opportet sacerdotes	Trinity O.7.9
Oratio ad Sanctum Angelum Dei	Pembroke 154
Passio Beati Cypriani	Pembroke 154
Pastor Hermae	Lambeth 73
Pictor in Carmine	Lambeth 477
Phale tolum	Trinity O.7.9
Philosophi diffiniunt vocem esse aerem tenuissimum	Bodley 395
Quadratum quippe lapidem in quamcunque partem	Trinity B.1.3
Quidam episcopus impetravit privilegium domini	Trinity O.7.9
Recte orthografie que hic annotatur	Harley 3038
Reddidit deus malum quod fecit Abimelech	Lambeth 488
Rosa semen eius viola	Trinity B.1.39
Sacramenta panis	Trinity O.7.9
Samson dux fortissime victor potentissime	Lambeth 456
Septem gradus descensionis habet humilitas	Harley 3038
Sermo in Festivitate Omnium Sanctorum	Lambeth 477
Siquis autem edificat supra fundamentum hoc aureum	Shrewsbury XII
Tanta dignitas humanae conditionis	Trinity O.7.9
Temata in Assumptione	Lambeth 477
Texts for sermons	Lambeth 477
Thema ad Clericos	Lambeth 477
Tria sunt quae principes beatos efficiunt	Trinity B.1.11
Trini dei trinam ymagine	Harley 3038
Virtutem describit philosophus habitum mentis	Harley 3038
Vitae Sanctorum (Martin and Nicholas)	Trinity B.3.8
Vitae Sanctorum (Edward, king and martyr, Gregory, Theodosia, Nicetus, Augustine, Marculsi, Christopher, Barbara)	BL Add.11881
Ymnus de Pascha	Pembroke 154
Missal (fragmentary)	CUL Add.4079

THE BIBLE

1. Glossed Books (ex Master Robert)

Exodus	Trinity B.2.6
Leviticus	Trinity B.1.31
Leviticus (ch.11 only)	Trinity B.1.39
Numbers	Trinity B.1.35
Deuteronomy	Trinity B.1.14
Joshua	Trinity B.3.16
Judges	Trinity B.3.16
Ruth	Trinity B.3.16
Kings I-IV	Trinity B.3.15
Tobit (not glossed)	Trinity B.1.39
Proverbs	Trinity B.1.13
Ecclesiastes	Trinity B.1.13
Ecclesiastes	Trinity B.1.39

Song of Songs	Trinity B.1.39
Wisdom (fragment)	Trinity B.1.32
Isaiah	Trinity B.2.15
Jeremiah & Lamentations	Trinity B.1.1
Minor Prophets	Trinity B.4.3
Matthew	Trinity B.1.10
Matthew (fragment)	Trinity B.1.33
Matthew	Trinity B.1.11
Mark	Trinity B.1.11
Luke	Trinity B.1.12
John	Trinity B.1.36
Acts	Trinity B.1.34
Pauline Epistles	Trinity B.1.6
Canonical Epistles	Shrewsbury XII
Apocalypse	Shrewsbury XII

2. Other Glossed Books

Leviticus	Harley 3038
John	Harley 3038
Psalms (Peter Lombard)	Balliol 35A
Pauline Epistles (Peter Lombard)	Balliol 173B

3. Commentaries (unattributed)

On Psalms (fragment)	Lambeth 488
On Chronicles	Trinity B.1.29
On Pauline Epistles (?Ralph of Laon)	Trinity B.1.29
On Pauline Epistles (Commentarius Cantabrigiensis)	Trinity B.1.39

INDEX OF BUILDWAS MANUSCRIPTS

Location and catalogue numbers (in brackets) of extant Buildwas manuscripts

CAMBRIDGE

Pembroke College 154 (13)

St. John's College D.2 (15)

Trinity College B.1.1 (42)
B.1.3 (4)
B.1.4 (5)
B.1.6 (50)
B.1.10 (44)
B.1.11 (45)
B.1.12 (47)
B.1.13 (38)
B.1.14 (35)
B.1.29 (24)
B.1.31 (33)
B.1.32 (40)
B.1.33 (46)
B.1.34 (49)
B.1.35 (34)
B.1.36 (48)
B.1.39 (39)
B.2.6 (32)
B.2.15 (41)
B.2.30 (17)
B.3.8 (6)
B.3.15 (37)
B.3.16 (36)
B.4.3 (43)
B.14.5 (3)
O.7.9 (25)

University Library Add. 4079 (10)
Ii.2.3 (8)

EDINBURGH

National Library
of Scotland 6121 (12)

LONDON

British Library Add.11881 (7)
Harley 3038 (9)

Lambeth Palace
Library 73 (23)
107 (18)
109 (2)
456} part (28)
457} part (27)
488} part (26)
477 (29)

OXFORD

Balliol College 35A (30)
39 (20)
40 (21)
150 22)
173B (31)
229 (11)

Bodleian Library Bodley 371 (19)
Bodley 395 (14)
Bodley 730 (16)

Christ Church 88 (1)

SHREWSBURY

Shrewsbury School XII (51)

See Cat. 2, Notes, for Cambridge, Pembroke College MSS 177, 178, 179, here rejected as Buildwas books.

INDEX OF PERSONS

OXFORD BIBLIOGRAPHICAL SOCIETY PUBLICATIONS

Orders for the Society's publications should be addressed to The Honorary Treasurer, Oxford Bibliographical Society, Bodleian Library, Oxford OX1 3BG.

New Series 1948–1992

Several volumes are out of print. Limited stocks of the titles listed below are available to non-members at the following prices (postage extra); members' prices are given in parentheses.

NS 15   D.F. McKenzie & J.C. Ross (eds.), A Ledger of Charles Ackers, Printer of *The London Magazine* (1968) £10 (£6.75)

NS 16   N.R. Ker, Records of All Souls College Library, 1473–1600 (1971) £10 (£6.75)

NS 17   D.F. McKenzie (ed.), Stationers' Company Apprentices, 1641–1700 (1974) £10 (£6.75)

Professor McKenzie's volume covering the period 1605–1640 (Charlottesville, 1961) may be had from the Society at the same price. The three-volume set of Stationers' Company Apprentices is available at £25 (£20).

NS 18   Studies in the Book Trade in Honour of Graham Pollard (1975) £25 (£17.50)

NS 19   D.F. McKenzie (ed.), Stationers' Company Apprentices, 1701–1800 (1978) £17.50 (£12.50).

NS 20   Nicolas Contat *dit* Le Brun, Anecdotes typographiques, ed. by G. Barber (1980) £20 (£15)

NS 21   The Bodleian Library Account Book, 1613–1646, ed. by G. Hampshire, intro. by I.G. Philip (1983) £20 (£15)

NS 22   N.K. Kiessling, The Library of Robert Burton (1988) £25 (£17.50)

NS 23   D.W. Nichol (ed.), Pope's Literary Legacy: The Book-Trade Correspondence of William Warburton and John Knapton (1992) £25 (£17.50)

Occasional Publications (Wrappered) 1967-1995

Prices are the same for members and non-members (postage extra).

OP 2   J.D. Fleeman, A Preliminary Handlist of Documents & Manuscripts of Samuel Johnson (1967) £4.50

OP 3   E.J. Devereux, A Checklist of English Translations of Erasmus to 1700 (1968) £4.50

OP 4   A.B. Emden, Donors of Books to S. Augustine's Abbey, Canterbury (1968) £4.50

OP 5   G. Barber, French Letterpress Printing: A List of French Printing Manuals and Other Texts in French Bearing on the Technique of Letterpress Printing, 1567–1900 (1969) £4.50

OP 6   E.A. Read, A Checklist of Books, Catalogues and Periodical Articles Relating to the Cathedral Libraries of England (1970) £4.50

OP 7   Hodson's Booksellers, Publishers and Stationers Directory 1855 (A Facsimile of the Copy in the Bodleian Library, Oxford), intro. by. G. Pollard (1972) £4.50

OP 8   K.I.D. Maslen, The Boyer Ornament Stock (1973) £4.50

OP 9   J.R. Tye, Periodicals in the Nineties (1974) £4.50

OP 10   C.L. Oastler, John Day, the Elizabethan Printer (1975) £4.50

OP 11   J. McLaverty, Pope's Printer, John Wright: A Preliminary Study (1976) £4.50

OP 12   R. Ford, Dramatisations of Scott's Novels: A Catalogue (1979) £7.50

OP 13   R.A. Sayce, Compositorial Practices and the Localization of Printed Books, 1530–1800 (1979) £4.50

OP 14   J. Mosley, British Type Specimens before 1831: A Handlist (1984) £7.50

OP 15   H. Forster, Supplements to Dodsley's Collection of Poems (1980) £7.50

OP 16   J.P. Feather, The English Provincial Book Trade before 1850: A Checklist of Secondary Sources (1981) £7.50

OP 17   J.D. Fleeman, A Preliminary Handlist of Copies of Books Associated with Dr Samuel Johnson (1984) £7.50

OP 18   G. Pollard (continued by E. Potter), Early Bookbinding Manuals: An Annotated List of Technical Accounts of Bookbinding to 1840 (1984) £7.50

OP 19   D. Pearson, Durham Bookbinders and Booksellers, 1660–1760 (1986) £7.50

OP 20   The 'Missing' Term Catalogue: A Facsimile of the Term Catalogue for Michaelmas Term 1695, with a List of Identified Books (1987) £7.50

OP 21   J.C. Ross, Charles Ackers' Ornament Usage (1990) £7.50

OP 22   P.S. Morrish, Bibliotheca Higgsiana: A Catalogue of the Books of Dr Griffin Higgs, 1589–1659 (1990) £7.50

OP 23   J.P. Feather, An Index to Selected Bibliographical Journals, 1971–1985 (1991) £7.50

OP 24   J.K. Moore, Primary Materials Relating to Copy and Print in English Books of the Sixteenth and Seventeenth Centuries (1992) £12.50

OP 25   J.H. Bowman, Greek Printing Types in Britain in the Nineteenth Century: A
Catalogue (1992, issued 1993) £7.50

OP 26   G. Barber, Arks for Learning: A Short History of Oxford Library Buildings
(1995) £15

Third Series 1996–

TS 1   D.G. Selwyn, The Library of Thomas Cranmer (1996) £37.50 (£28)